OPERATION HEAL AMERICA

The Time Has Come for Spiritual Healing and Revival from Our House to the White House

James Spence

Trilogy Christian Publishers
A Wholly Owned Subsidiary of Trinity Broadcasting Network
2442 Michelle Drive
Tustin, CA 92780

For information, address Trilogy Christian Publishing
Rights Department, 2442 Michelle Drive, Tustin, Ca 92780.
Trilogy Christian Publishing/ TBN and colophon are trademarks of Trinity Broadcasting Network.

For information about special discounts for bulk purchases, please contact Trilogy Christian Publishing.

Manufactured in the United States of America

10 9 8 7 6 5 4 3 2 1

Library of Congress Cataloging-in-Publication Data is available.

ISBN 978-1-64773-362-9 (Print Book)
ISBN 978-1-64773-363-6 (ebook)

CONTENTS

◆◆◆◆◆

CONTENTS

ACKNOWLEDGMENTS

◆◆◆◆◆

To my Lord and Savior, Jesus Christ:

No words can express how grateful I am for what you, through the power of the Holy Spirit, have revealed to me in the pages of this book. Your timing, as always, is perfect! Thanks to you, we now have everything we need in the middle of the greatest spiritual crisis this nation has ever faced to usher in the greatest spiritual healing and revival for your glory! Thank you for allowing the burden I've carried to now be a blessing to your people and this nation!

I came to you when I was weary and, as promised, found rest. You invited me to take your yoke upon my shoulders and learn from you (Matthew 11:28–29), and now I find myself deeper in love with you and further in awe of you!

You told me if I would give you "everything," you wouldn't waste "anything." I hold that proof in my hands.

I will never fully understand why you chose me for this great work until I see you face-to-face. Until then, I just want to say, "Thank you, Lord, for using a sinful person like me to do it! May you, and you alone, receive all the glory!"

To Dr. Tony Evans, Christian author, speaker, Senior Pastor of Oak Cliff Bible Fellowship, President of the Urban Alternative, former chaplain for the NFL Dallas Cowboys, and the longest-standing chaplain of the NBA Dallas Mavericks:

As one of the finest Bible teachers and theologians of our day and all time, no one has had a more profound influence and impact on my spiritual growth in the last several years than you. I feel confident when I say that if you had not answered the call to full-time ministry over forty years ago, it's highly unlikely this book would have ever been written for the church! I can't thank you enough for your outstanding teachings, powerful illustrations, and daily inspiration in my life, Dr. Evans!

In a day when so many Christian leaders are compromising the truth of God's Word to appease the culture, you will not! I am more grateful for that than you will ever know at this critical juncture in our nation's history.

Please accept my deepest prayers and sympathy for the loss of your beloved wife, Lois, of many years on December 30, 2019. While our tears of sadness were nothing in comparison to yours, those of us all across the nation who see you as "our pastor" too wept when you wept because of the way you have loved and ministered to us! Now, we stand with you!

Thank you, Dr. Evans, for being "The Kingdom Man" among all kingdom men on this side of eternity!

To my three children—Lauren, Brandon, and Kristen:

Stand firm. Let nothing move you. Always give yourselves fully to the work of the Lord (1 Corinthians 15:58 NIV)! May this book live on through you and be a testimony and memorial to your children and your children's children to the things I hold dear. I love you more than you'll ever know!

INTRODUCTION

Our nation is in trouble. However, contrary to what many Christians believe, God is not holding Satan, demons, unbelievers, past and present administrations, Congress, Republicans, Democrats, moderates, progressives, liberals, conservatives, the alt-left, the alt-right, the "deep state," "fake news," special interest groups, lobbyists, underground operatives, social media, or even Hollywood responsible. He is holding *His people* responsible. Darkness is just doing what it knows to do. Have we forgotten that we fellow believers are the light of the world (Matthew 5:14)?

Instead of being "light" in the midst of a crooked and perverse nation (Philippians 2:15) that dispels the darkness around us, many of us have forgotten who we are, why we're here, whose kingdom we're supposed to be building, and whose word has the final word. Instead of ruling our worlds under God's hand to advance His kingdom and bring Him glory in the earth, many Christians are allowing their worlds to rule them while they advance their kingdoms and bring Satan glory in the earth.

Our problem is not numbers. More and more Christians are attending more and more megachurches than ever. While certain denominations are seeing a drastic drop-off in attendance, nondenominational church growth is at an all-time high. God has Christians on Wall Street, "Main Street," and most likely on your street. Thus, it begs the question, with Christians in all the right places in every institution in America from our house to the White House, why aren't we transforming our culture? Worse yet, why is the culture transforming us?

While I, like many of you, love the church of Jesus Christ in America (hereafter referred to as "the church"), I do not like what we've become. Not only is the nation divided, but the church is divided. Instead of being part of the solution, we are now part of the problem. Tolerance at all costs, prosperity theology, "cheap grace" that leaves His people trapped in their sins, unholy living, watered-down gospel messages that don't require repentance, rejection of God's divine order for the family and church, mission statements that do not reflect the primary mission of the church, and mission statements that do but are not being executed, alarming statistics that reveal that 95 percent of all Christians have never won a soul to Christis;[1] and the widespread acceptance of gay marriage and homosexual ordinations are just a few of the "sins" plaguing the church today that are not only breaking the moral and spiritual back of our great nation but, more importantly, the heart of God.

Many of our churches have become more politically correct than biblically correct. Instead of the church operating like a hospital that helps people "get well" spiritually by making disciples who will "go" and make more disciples in fulfillment of the Great Commission, most churches in America today are operating like hospice centers that give people what they want to keep them comfortable while they "die."

The problems facing our nation today are not first social, moral, political, geopolitical, economic, racial, or cultural problems. They are spiritual. Spiritual battles, however, can only be fought and won by spiritual people using spiritual weapons. That would be us! At least that's the way it's supposed to work. While much of the church is waiting to see what God is going to do amid the cultural chaos that surrounds us, God is waiting to see what we're going to do before He will bring desperately needed healing and revival to our land. His requirements to make this our present-day reality have not changed in all these years.

God declared, "If my people will humble themselves and pray, and seek my face, and turn from their wicked ways, then I will hear their prayers, forgive their sin, and heal their land" (2 Chronicles 7:14). In the Old Testament, God's covenant people were the Jews.

In the New Testament, God's covenant people are the body of true believers, called the church, who have accepted Jesus Christ as their sin-bearer, Savior, and Redeemer.[2]

While this certainly isn't the first time someone has urged every Christian in America from our house to the White House to fulfill the terms of 2 Chronicles 7:14 so God would hear our prayers, forgive our sin, and heal our land to be glorified on the earth as it is in heaven, it is the first time that God has provided a detailed national plan that every Bible-believing church and believer in America could easily follow to achieve it! This is what you hold in your hands.

When the Holy Spirit first told me He wanted to take my thirty-six years of operational experience as a Naval Academy graduate, Navy pilot, and FBI Agent; and thirty-two years as a follower of Jesus Christ and worship leader to write an Operation Order (OPORD) for the church, centered on 2 Chronicles 7:14 which, if followed, would result in the healing of this nation, I told Him He must have made a terrible mistake. I said, "This needs to be done by an 'insider.' And oh, by the way, I never went to Bible college."

There was silence from heaven. What followed was the most fabulous set of orders I have ever received. I now give them to you since these same orders include all of us! I'm convinced that God allowed me to become a Special Agent with the FBI so I would know how to be His Special Agent in the earth with you for such a time as this!

I asked God to allow me to conduct an investigation that would lead to the truth about the spiritual crisis we are facing in our nation and, more importantly, the solution. Investigations often reveal the good, bad, and ugly about those they are targeting. This one is no different, except this time we, the church, are the target. The hard-hitting truths I expose about what we've become, and more importantly, our willingness to deal with them in accordance with God's Word, however, hold the key to receiving the healing that God has for our lives and every institution in America we comprise from our house to the White House!

In the first seven chapters of this book, we will go on a journey where few "believers" dare to go; that is, many fathoms below

11

the surface of mainstream Christianity in America to learn why God, despite all of our praying, fasting, church attendance, small groups, Bible-studies, conferences, workshops, chest-beating, and hand-wringing has not only *not* healed America spiritually but has allowed the culture to get progressively worse.

Then, in chapter 8, I will unveil the highly anticipated long overdue but right on time five-part OPORD that, if followed, will cause God to unleash spiritual healing and revival to every institution in America from our house to the White House.

If there's one thing that I've learned about God after all these years, it's this. When He's "got your number," you'd better take the call! While the results of my investigation are not "pretty" and the road to spiritual healing in America will come with fierce opposition, we now have everything we need in one place to usher in the greatest healing and revival America and the world have ever seen for God's glory!

Though I am humbled beyond words that God would use a sinful person like me who is "guilty" of virtually everything I uncover to write an OPORD for the healing and revival of our nation, I do not hold the key to its success. You, my beloved brothers and sisters, me, and Bible-believing pastors all across America underneath the leadership and authority of Jesus Christ and His Word hold the key.

While all will benefit tremendously from this book, it was primarily written for Christians and church leaders who have been involved in and around the "local church" for many years. We are the ones I believe God will hold most accountable and who will be without excuse.

It is my earnest prayer that God would give you ears to hear and a heart to receive what I am about to share with you and that each of us would, more importantly, have the courage to act upon it. May it never be said of this generation that we had the opportunity to see God unleash spiritual healing and revival throughout our land to advance His kingdom and glory but didn't have the heart to make it happen!

With everything you and I now need to make this dream a reality, only one question remains: Will you answer God's call with me since He now has both of our numbers?

CHAPTER 1

◆◆◆◆◆

Let Them Rule!

It was Saturday night. Unless I'm doing this, it is highly unlikely you will ever find me at a mall, much less a mall on Saturday night! Little did I know, however, that this was about to be one of the best nights of my life! My good friends, Paul and Jenna, were shadowing me on "Soul Patrol" for their first time. Paul works in the business information field, and Jenna is a schoolteacher. Married and in their late-twenties, Paul and Jenna are a precious Christian couple who love Jesus Christ with all their hearts and who desire to use their gifts, talents, and abilities to fulfill the Great Commission.

"Soul Patrol" received its name from my former pastor in Jacksonville, Florida, who loved sharing the Gospel with unbelievers more than life itself. For me, Soul Patrol is not only one of the most important uses of my time on this side of heaven, but it's the most fun I can have on this side of heaven! It is a walk by faith where the Holy Spirit directs me and others to "patrol" areas for "lost souls" that we can share the Gospel message with in fulfillment of the Great Commission. While some go to Africa, China, and the Middle East, I go to local malls, casinos, restaurants, and festivals. While I know God wants us to do both, He told me a long time ago that I have no business going around the world to proclaim the Good News at great expense to myself and others until I've been faithful to do it with those in my back yard at no expense.

While I knew the Holy Spirit had something special in store for us tonight, I could have never imagined this in a million years! After Paul, Jenna, and I met up inside the mall entrance, I explained to them the friendly approach I like to take to Soul Patrol. After I did this, we took some time to pray and then put the entire evening into the hands of God.

As we began walking, I told Paul and Jenna that while God always did amazing things on Soul Patrol, there was a place in this particular mall where many young people liked to congregate and, more importantly, respond to the Gospel. I refer to it as holy ground.

As you know, malls not only have an endless array of retail stores but numerous kiosks that shoppers have to carefully navigate around lest they get "sucked in" and overspend before they make it to their intended destination. Unless, of course, a particular kiosk is your intended destination. We had just finished talking to my friend, Tyler, a young unmarried dad in his early twenties who I had shared the Gospel message with weeks prior. He was working a dessert kiosk with one of his friends, Marv, who had accepted Christ on Soul Patrol just a few weeks earlier.

I introduced them to Paul and Jenna, and we engaged in some light conversation. Tyler has a great sense of humor and is very street smart! At the end of our short chat with Tyler, I would always ask him the same thing, "Ty, you ready to accept Jesus Christ as your personal Lord and Savior yet?"

He would typically say the same thing, smiling, "Aw, man, I told you God is using you to get to me, but I'm not ready yet. When I get *in*, I want to be *all in*, and I'm not done playing yet, man, but please keep asking me, okay? I know you care about me. I'm feelin' ya. I like the way you roll."

I always appreciated Tyler's honesty despite his decision to put his salvation off another day. I assured him I would keep asking him but not to delay it because one day, it would be too late. He would almost always say, "I know, man, I know. My mom and grandma been working on me for a long time. I'm getting there. Be patient with me, okay?"

Before we left, the Holy Spirit told me to give Tyler enough money so that the next five people who came up to the kiosk could get a free dessert. The only condition I had was that Tyler had to tell the customers that the free desserts were a gift from God to them. Tyler said, "You got it, man."

Tyler and His girlfriend had just started the business a short time ago. I wanted to help them succeed. His girlfriend makes the dessert cups, and wow, they're good! I gave Tyler and Marv a hearty handshake and a "man hug" before saying goodbye. With a smile, I told Marv to watch Tyler and keep working on him. They both smiled back at Paul, Jenna, and me. The night had already been a massive success for the kingdom!

As Paul, Jenna, and I took a few steps away from Tyler's dessert kiosk, I motioned for Paul and Jenna to stop. I said, "There it is. The spot where God always shows up 'big' that I told you about earlier." I proceeded to tell Paul and Jenna that more people have gotten "saved" in this one spot than anywhere else in the mall. The "holy ground" was an area to the left of a popular coffee chain about twenty-five steps away from where we were standing. Specifically, it was the area around an eight-by-four-by-six kiosk filled with high-end limited-edition basketball shoes.

The kiosk looks like something you would see in an arcade. For a small fee, the player gains access to a joystick that moves a large three-prong hook that opens and closes. If the operator can lower and successfully grab one of the items in the kiosk, they win a pair of basketball shoes. As you might guess, it's a lot harder than it sounds. What I love about this kiosk is that it's a magnet for young people—and tonight was no exception!

I noticed that on this particular night, there was a young new kiosk manager here that I had never seen before. Paul, Jenna, and I introduced ourselves and struck up a friendly conversation with him. His name was Dallas, age seventeen, a senior in high school who had ambitions of owning his own business one day. The kiosk was his first business venture. As Paul, Jenna, and I talked to Dallas and began to share the Gospel with him, four very excited "tatted" young males between the approximate ages of sixteen to nineteen came up to the kiosk to check out the shoes. The typical frenzy began as they got a good look at the pumps—loud talking, rapid pacing in circles, and lots of shoe pointing. At that moment in time, nothing else mattered to them!

The Holy Spirit said, "Yes." These guys would be in the wind very shortly if I didn't move quickly. I asked Dallas if he would please excuse us for a moment. Paul, Jenna, and I walked over to them. I invited Dallas to listen in if he wanted to but not to feel obligated if he had customers that He needed to help. I didn't want to get in the way.

Dallas said, "Sure." Besides hoping to make a sale, Dallas was as curious as the rest of us to see how this was going to play out with the guys.

I turned to the group and said, "Hey guys, what's up?"

Silence. No eye contact.

I said, "Pretty amazing shoes, right?"

I got the "You think?" look before they looked away.

I said, "I'll tell you what I'm going do." Eye contact. "If you guys can tell me who the greatest salesman in the world is that has ever lived, I'm going to buy one of you a pair of these shoes. All I'm asking for in return is a few minutes of your time—nothing else. Interested?"

In disbelief, they each gave their response, which, as I recall, was something like, "You're gonna do what? Really? You're kidding! Oh yeah!"

We introduced ourselves to them, chatted a bit, and then the game was on. Two of the boys were siblings, and all of them close friends. Three of them were still in high school. The fourth, closest to me, had graduated from high school the previous year. However, basketball was their common love! Needless to say, at this point, they were not interested in anymore of my small talk.

I said, "Great, there are just a few rules, so listen, because if you break any of them, the offer is off the table, okay?"

They nodded. The Holy Spirit had their undivided attention. I told them that before I shared the three rules with them, they needed to select a spokesman from the group who would give me the "final answer" to the question I asked them moments ago. Unsurprisingly, they chose the young man closest to me who was the oldest and most vocal of the bunch, Mike. I smiled at Mike and said, "I had a feeling it would be you."

He smiled back.

I turned to all of them and said, "Okay, here are the three rules. Ready? First, you only get one shot, meaning the first answer Mike gives me is your final answer. Second, you have to provide me with the first *and* last name of the greatest salesperson (male or female, dead or alive) that ever lived. Third, you get one 'lifeline' each. This means you can call your mom, grandfather, text a friend, or Google it if you want."

Before I could finish, they were saying, "Oh, man, we got this! We got this!" As is typical, they started shouting out some answers in their excitement "Is it Bill Gates?"

"Steve Jobs?"

I immediately stopped them and reminded them of the first rule—that they only get one try and it had to come through Mike. I encouraged them to "huddle up" like a football team, use their lifelines if they wished, and then give their unified answer to Mike who would then give it to me. Finally, I told them that they only had ten minutes to give me the correct answer!

Sidebar: The main reason why I allow lifelines is to cast the Gospel net as far and wide as possible as family members and friends are always curious to know what the correct answer is, especially after they hear how we met and what the offer is. Some of the lifeline participants on the other end of the cell phone even ask to be put on speakerphone to hear the correct answer. Somewhere in the exchange (usually early), I tell those who are physically present with me, "While I will offer you no clues other than what I've said already, I promise you one thing, and then I need you to promise me one thing, okay? Number one, I promise you that none of us are ever going to forget this evening. Number two, I need you to promise me that you will tell at least three people what happened tonight." I've never had anyone turn me down. Again, the purpose of doing this is to impact as many lives as possible for Christ with every encounter.

As I recall, two of the four young men called family members on their cell phones, another texted a friend, and one was Googling it. Usually, by this point, because the participants know they are up against the clock, you can cut the tension and excitement with a knife as they go back and forth, feverously discussing and debating the answer. I usually get a few attempts for additional clues but typically don't budge.

At this point, I looked down at my watch and noticed it was about 8:45 p.m. The mall closed at 9:30 p.m., but I knew the stores themselves started closing around 9:15 p.m. It was time for my five-minute warning. I looked at the guys and said, "Five minutes left."

The tension and excitement rose to a new feverish pitch. By this time, we started gathering a small curious crowd around us of about seven to ten people. Some stayed for seconds, others minutes. One older gentleman walked past me, smiled, and said, "Greatest salesman in the world, huh?" Demonic opposition was in the house. I was having the time of my life, yes, at the mall on a Saturday night! During the remaining five minutes, Paul, Jenna, and I turned our attention back to Dallas before the timer went off on my cell phone.

I said, "Time's up, guys. Mike, do you have an answer for me?"

He said, "We got the answer." After taking a deep breath, Mike said, "The greatest salesman in the world is God because He showed us how much He loved us when He died on the cross for us, and people are still talking about it."

The Holy Spirit said, "Close enough. Give it to him."

I said, "There's good news and bad news. Which do you want first?"

No reply.

I said, "The bad news is that you didn't give me the first and last name and, therefore, broke one of the rules." [Sidebar: The reason I tell people that they have to give me the first and last name (even though Christ isn't Jesus's last name) is because while most people don't get the answer right, some have said "God," and after further discussion, I learned that it was the God of their understanding, not

Jesus]. "The good news is that the Holy Spirit told me to give it to you because of your explanation. So, congratulations, you won!"

They went berserk! One of them said, "I told you, bro, it was God. I knew it! I knew it!"

Mike said, "When I heard one of the guys say what I was thinking—God—I knew it was right."

I looked down at my watch. In all the excitement, we had lost track of time. It was now 9:05 p.m.

I said, "Before we figure out which one of you is going to walk away with a pair of these limited-edition basketball shoes, you promised me a few minutes, remember?"

They agreed.

I said, "The greatest salesman in the world is Jesus Christ, but He is much more than that to me. When I was twenty-four-years old, I asked Him to be my Lord and Savior in Pensacola, Florida, while in flight school. My life has never been the same, and I love to tell people like yourselves what He means to me. However, practically speaking, Jesus is also the greatest salesman that ever lived. Did you know that the Bible is still the number one best-selling book of all time and that no one has had more songs written about them than Jesus? Quite a salesman, wouldn't you agree?"

They said, "You know that's right!"

I said, "Did you know, like many great salesmen, that whenever anyone ever asked Jesus a question, He often responded with a question? That's a pretty effective sales technique, wouldn't you agree?"

They nodded yes.

"Well, guess what? He sent Paul, Jenna, and me out here tonight to ask you guys a question, and if you get it right, you get to 'stay,' and that will be the biggest sale you'll ever make! Any idea what He sent us out here to ask you?"

One of them said, "If we believe." The others were anxiously waiting to hear my response.

I said, "Great answer. God sent us out here to ask you if you have ever heard the Gospel message before. Have you?"

All of them responded, "No."

One of them said, "I love gospel music."

I said, "No, not gospel music, the Gospel message?"

He shook His head, "No."

I said, "Let me explain it to you as quickly and simply as I can. I will give you a short sentence for each letter in the word *gospel*: G-O-S-P-E-L. I hope you never forget this and will share it with as many people as you can. G: *God* created us to have a relationship with Him. Do you believe this?"

All of them nodded their heads. "Yes."

"O: *Our* sin separates us from God because God is holy and cannot dwell with we who are unholy until we deal sufficiently with our sin. Does this make sense?"

They said, "Yes."

"S: *Sin* cannot be removed by good deeds alone." I further explained to them that if we could get to heaven and have our sins forgiven through "good works," Jesus would not have needed to die on the cross for our sins. I asked them if this made sense.

They said, "Yes."

"P: *Paying* the penalty for our sins, Jesus Christ became our sin-bearer when He died on the cross for our sins." I asked them if they understood this and believed it.

Each one of them said, "Yes."

"E: *Everyone* who puts their faith and trust in Jesus for the forgiveness of their sins will inherit eternal life. "Do you believe this?"

They nodded, "Yes."

"L: *Life* that's eternal means we will forever be with Him. Do you believe this?"

Again, they responded, "Yes."

I said, "Awesome." Then I told them that if they were okay with it, I would love to lead them in a simple prayer of faith. I asked them to listen to it first, and then, if they wanted, I would be honored to pray it again with them where they could repeat it after me. They smiled and nodded their heads. I said, "Great, just listen to it first to make sure you understand what I'm saying and that you're 'good' with it. If you have any questions about the prayer, I want to answer them upfront before you pray with me, okay?" I told them that I would rather that they not pray with me than to pray something that they didn't mean, understand, or believe.

They nodded.

I asked them again to just listen to the prayer first. It went something like this:

> Lord Jesus, I know that I'm a sinner, and I
> can't save myself. But you can, and you did, when
> you died on the cross for my sins. Please forgive
> me for sinning against you. I turn from my life
> of sin now to receive the free gift of salvation you
> made possible as my Sin-bearer and substitute. By
> faith, I'm asking you to be my Lord and Savior.
> My heart is yours. Thank you for loving me and
> saving me. Now help me to follow you and live a
> life that is pleasing to you, in Jesus's name. Amen!

I asked the guys if they had any questions about the prayer. They responded, "No." I told them that I would be honored to pray that same prayer with them right now if they would like to but that it was critical that they understood that the prayer was between them and God and not between them and me. I told them that it was no accident that all of us were in the mall tonight and that if they believed that God had sent Paul, Jenna, and me to find them and tell them about God's amazing love for them and were ready to turn from their sin and follow Jesus, then they really should respond to it.

They couldn't wait to pray! A couple of them started closing their eyes. I said, "Now you don't have to close your eyes if you don't want to, but I believe this is a holy moment, and I, like your buddies here, like to close my eyes so I don't get distracted and can focus on what I'm saying. If you want to keep your eyes open, no problem. All I ask is that you repeat the prayer loud enough so that I know you heard me and understood me. Most importantly, it is critical that you believe the words you are about to pray. Ready?"

They nodded.

It was all I could do to fight back the tears and get through the prayer. All seven of us prayed (four of them and three of us) a prayer very close to the one above, and the four young men became our brothers in Christ. It was a miracle!

I told them how Jesus says, "Behold, I stand at the door and knock. If anyone hears my voice and opens the door, I will come in to him and dine with him, and he with me" (Revelation 3:20 NKJV). I told them that this is what they did tonight. They heard Jesus knocking at the door of their lives and they opened the door for Him. I said, "Did you know that when you open the door for Jesus, the Bible says that He will open doors for you that no man can shut?" (Revelation 3:8).

I encouraged them to find a good Bible-believing church, read God's Word every day, and get baptized. I also told them that I would like to send them Bible verses every day if they were comfortable giving me their cell numbers. They did. I've been sending them the Word every day ever since. I also invited them to church and my small group. I told them that it was critical that they became followers of Jesus or disciples and that I was my desire to help them do that!

I said, "Now, is one of you ready to get some shoes?" As if I even needed to ask. I looked back at Paul and Jenna and asked them if they had an idea of how we could determine who would get the shoes.

Jenna's occupation as a school teacher saved the day. Jenna said, "I have some pieces of white paper in my purse and a yellow highlighter. How about if I tear four small pieces of white paper off into strips and color the tip of one of the pieces of paper with the yellow highlighter? Then, whoever draws the piece of balled-up white paper with the yellow highlighter on the tip wins."

I said, "Jenna, you're a genius! Perfect."

She put highlighter on the tip of one the strips of paper, crumpled all four pieces of white paper up into four white paper balls, and then, with an open hand, allowed each of the guys to pick one. I felt like I was watching a scene from *Willy Wonka and the Chocolate Factory*. Each young man quickly opened their candy bars to see who had the golden ticket.

Hernandez, in spot number three (from left to right), shrieked! He couldn't believe it! By this time, I had noticed that some of the shoes were much more expensive than the $200–$300 price tag I had previously observed. There were several pairs in the kiosk that went for as much as $700! I gasped. I said, "Look, dude, I originally said any pair of shoes, and I'll stick to my bargain, but if you can keep me at or below $300, I'd be forever grateful!

He graciously smiled and said, "No problem."

By this time, it was about 9:20 p.m. We had about ten minutes to complete the transaction. I was thinking, *No problem.* I said, "Dallas, you do accept a credit card here, right?"

He said, "Normally, yes, but my credit card machine is busted tonight. Sorry, I can only take cash. But if you quickly run down to the other end of the mall, there is an ATM machine."

I looked down at my watch. It was now 9:25 p.m. There was no time for that.

Hernandez hollered out the name of a popular shoe store.

I said, "What?"

Hernandez said, "It's an athletic shoe store just a couple of stores down this way." He pointed to our right.

I said, "Let's go, hurry!" I apologized to Dallas for not being able to give him the sale.

He said, "That's okay, I understand. You guys better hurry."

Seconds later, we arrived at the store. The glass doors were locked, and the security bars lowered halfway. There was one light still on inside the store. Thank God! I could see two employees still working near the counter. All seven of us were knocking on the outer glass when I motioned for someone to let us in. Imagine what that looked like from inside the store! I would soon learn that the two employees that were still there were, unsurprisingly, the manager and the assistant manager. The assistant manager walked toward the front door and stopped at a distance where he could be heard and said, "Closed. The register is closed, sorry. You need to come back another day."

We kept knocking.

The manager moved toward us and said the same thing, "We closed the register, sorry."

We said, "Please, please, you don't understand, we have to get these shoes tonight. Please open the door. It will just take a minute, please." By this time, Hernandez had noticed the pair of shoes he wanted that just happened to be on display to the right of the door. He started pointing at them. He said, "Please, these…please!"

The manager, beginning to get frustrated with us again, said, "We're closed. Come back another time."

We said, "Please, please, it will just take a moment. We know what we want."

The manager looked at the assistant manager and said, "Let them in, but only two of them. The one who is paying for the shoes and the one who wants the shoes."

Hernandez and I raised our hands, and I said, "That would be us!"

The manager motioned for the assistant manager to let us in. We walked in.

I glanced down at the assistant manager's name tag to see what his name was so I could thank him. That's when my jaw dropped. His name was none other than… Jesus! A big grin came across my face. I asked Hernandez to look down at his name tag. The others couldn't hear us nor see his name tag. I said, "Hernandez, do you remember when I told you earlier that when you open the door for Jesus, Jesus will open the door for you that no man can shut? Did you see what just happened?"

You should have seen the smile on his face! The others outside the store who had no idea what just happened would soon learn.

Little did I know, however, that God was still not done putting His glory on display! Yes, really! The manager who was halfway wondering what had just happened hurriedly asked Hernandez what pair of shoes he wanted to buy. Hernandez told him the candy-apple red "Foams" in the display window.

The manager said, "Son, those shoes are not going to be 'rolled out' for another two weeks. That's just the display model. I have one pair of them in the back, and they are a lot bigger than the size you're wearing! I think they're size eleven. What size do you wear?"

Hernandez said, "Eight-and-a-half."

The assistant manager, Jesus, was standing right by my side. Everyone else was still standing outside of the store, watching our every move. I asked the manager if he wouldn't mind bringing out the pair of "Foams" that he had in the back anyway.

He said, "Sure, but they're not going to fit."

The Holy Spirit had already told me he was wrong. After all, Jesus had let us in!

After returning from the back, the manager said, "Kid, I don't know what's going on here tonight, but you're not going to believe this!"

I looked at him and said, "Try me."

He said, "I have this one pair in the back, and I was wrong, it's a size eight."

With a smile on my face, I told Hernandez to sit down and try the shoes on. I already knew they were going to fit. The second he unlaced them and popped his first foot down, a big smile came across his face, and his eyes began to fill with tears. I asked him how it felt. He very quietly said, "It's perfect."

I told him to put the other shoe on just to make sure, and again, he said, "Perfect." He jumped up and hugged me and said, "Thank you, sir, thank you, sir, thank you so much for these shoes!"

It was the first time all night that he had called me "Sir." At that moment, he felt like my son. The love of the Father was flowing through me to my new brother in Christ whose life had just been radically transformed by the power of God. I said, "Hernandez, thank Jesus because it was Jesus who made this evening possible!"

I waited for him to ask me, "Which one?"

The manager who was listening just shook his head. And Jesus never stopped smiling. I couldn't stop smiling either. I looked at the manager and said, "We'll take 'em!"

While the manager was ringing up the purchase, I asked Jesus if he was a born-again believer in Christ. He smiled and said, "Yes, sir!"

I said, "I knew it!" I told him that Hernandez and the three young men outside of the store had just given their hearts and lives to Jesus Christ moments ago as Lord and Savior and that God had powerfully used him to create a moment that none of us would ever forget! He was speechless!

I turned to the manager who was anxiously waiting for me to pay for the shoes so I would get out of his store. I asked him if he had ever heard the Gospel before. He said, "Look, man, I appreciate what you're doing here tonight for this young man, and I'm not going deny that something bigger than me is going on here, but I need to close this store and go home."

I said, "I understand. God bless you." I completed the purchase and turned to Hernandez who hadn't stopped rubbing his eyes. He was overwhelmed by the love of God! Now my eyes began to fill with tears. I hugged Hernandez and told him how special he was to God and me and that God had great plans for his life! He kept saying, "Thank you, sir, I'll never forget this!"

I said, "Do you remember when I told you guys at the beginning of our conversation that none of us would ever forget this evening?"

He said, "Yes, sir."

I said, "Was I wrong?"

He smiled and said, "No, sir."

Hernandez sat down and began taking his new shoes off to put them in the box. I said, "Oh, no, you don't. Put those shoes back on your feet and wear them right out of this store as a testimony to the great things the Lord has done for you, man!"

Hernandez couldn't have been any happier! He laced up his new shoes, put his old ones in the box, and thanked the manager and Jesus with tear-filled eyes.

He still couldn't believe these shoes were his! The manager said, "Now you guys need to leave so I can close this store."

I shook the manager's hand and said, "Thank you for allowing God to use you tonight."

He said, "You're welcome."

I turned to Jesus and said, "It is only appropriate, if you're willing, that you walk out of this store with us right now to meet the rest of our friends and lead us in a closing prayer."

Jesus said, "Absolutely!"

When we walked out of the store into the mall, I introduced everyone to Jesus. They couldn't believe it! So at approximately 9:40 p.m. outside of this now famous store, in a very popular mall in Pennsylvania, with security guards circling the area like sharks, the eight of us peacefully formed a circle, held hands, and bowed our heads. Then Jesus led us in a powerful closing prayer of thanksgiving to our Lord and Savior, Jesus Christ, for demonstrating His love for us on the cross and putting that love on display tonight. It was the perfect ending to a perfect evening! We all thanked Jesus and said our goodbyes. God had touched many hearts this night, numbers of which we will only know on the other side of heaven! And to Jesus Christ be all the glory!

As we started walking away, Hernandez's brother and two friends kept "high-fiving" Hernandez and telling him how much they liked his shoes and how happy they were for him. While initially overjoyed with their excitement, strangely, it started to seem a bit excessive. I would now learn why. Hernandez said, "You're not going to believe this, but last weekend, all of us were at a sleepover at a friend's house with several others. When I woke up the next day, I couldn't find my basketball shoes. Someone stole them. I just bought them with my own money, and they were expensive! No one else had their shoes stolen that night but me. All four of us were there. God gave me my shoes back tonight and an even better pair! That's why my friends are so happy for me!"

I covered my mouth, closed my eyes, lowered my head, and wept. It was more than I could bear.

By this time, we had moved toward the exit doors of the mall. I knew we still had a few minutes before security would ask us to leave. Paul, Jenna, and I took this opportunity to ask our new friends another question. I said, "If you guys have another couple of minutes, I would like to explain to you why God created us in the first place. Next to what happened earlier this evening, this is the next most important discussion we can have. It's important because if we don't know why we're here, we can waste a lot of time." I told them it's wonderful to obtain an education, have an exciting career, build a "dream house," start a family, go on vacation, volunteer for a worthy cause, be part of a local church, or (fill in the blank), but we will have wasted our lives if we never fulfill the primary reason for which we were created. "It's good to know why you're here, wouldn't you agree?"

They nodded.

I asked them if they wanted to take a shot at the answer before I told them what it was and not to feel bad if they didn't know. Silence. Finally, one of them blurted out, "To give God glory!"

I said, "Great answer! God's Word says that everything comes from Him and exists by His power and is intended for His glory (Romans 11:36). Another scripture says, 'Give to the Lord the glory He deserves' (1 Chronicles 16:29)." I told them that we were created in God's image to know Him, love Him, worship Him, and bring Him glory in the earth. Isaiah 43 says, "Bring my sons from afar and my daughters from the ends of the earth, everyone who is called by my name, whom I created for my glory, whom I formed and made" (Isaiah 43:6–7 ESV).

"But how do we give Him glory?" I asked.

Silence. More silence. I told them that one of the primary ways we give God glory besides praising and worshipping Him for who He is (Psalm 67:3–5) is by fulfilling His eternal plan in the earth. God gave us a clue on what that plan is when He taught us how to pray:

> Our Father in heaven, hallowed be Your name. Your kingdom come, your will be done, on earth as it is in heaven. (Matthew 6:9–10 ESV)

I asked them, "But what does Jesus mean when He says, 'Your kingdom come?'"

Silence. I said, "First, notice the word *Your*. Whatever this 'kingdom' is, Jesus is telling us that it is the Father's kingdom and not our kingdom that needs to come to the earth." I explained to them that so many Christians want to bring God glory but spend the majority of our lives building their kingdoms instead of God's kingdom. I told them that we can't "hallow" (honor as holy) His name when we're trying to elevate our names and our kingdoms above His name and His kingdom. "Make sense?"

"Yes," they said.

"Then there's this word *kingdom*," I explained, "a whole book could be written on it and was. It's called the Holy Bible." I quickly explained the difference between the Old and New Testaments to them. "What ties the Old Testament to the New Testament is this theme of the kingdom of God. Think of the kingdom of God as 'territory' owned by God, delegated to the people of God, to demonstrate the comprehensive rule of God in every area of life, underneath the authority of God's son, Jesus, who is 'the King' of this kingdom. The King's manual, called the Holy Bible, is God's rule book for how this kingdom is supposed to operate. All good?"

They nodded, "Yes."

I explained, "We can't bring God glory with our lives, regardless of how many good deeds we do, if we are going to operate by the rules of *our* kingdom. Said another way, in God's kingdom, there is only one King, Jesus, and one set of rules—His. The sooner we realize that neither of these roads leads back to us, the sooner we can begin bringing God glory with our lives. In other words, if God's Word doesn't have the final word in the kingdom we are modeling, then it is *not* His kingdom."

I told my new friends that Satan had deceived many Christians into believing that they could serve two masters, two kingdoms, and two kingdom manuals while somehow bringing glory to God! No dice. I told them that while it is beautiful to be "kind," for example, God cannot receive glory from kind people who have no interest in operating by the rules of God's kingdom.

"That brings us to the next phrase in the Lord's prayer, 'your will be done.'" I explained to them in so many words that God's kingdom manual, the Holy Bible, outlines the totality of God's will for our lives, but that we can't execute it if we don't know it or operate contrary to it. And if we don't execute His will, we will never be able to bring God glory. They got it.

I then turned to the phrase "[o]n earth as it is in heaven." I told them that God is looking for us to model His kingdom on earth as it is in heaven as His earthly ambassadors. I explained, "While God could do it Himself, He chose to do it through us. Do you know why?"

Silence.

I told them that when God created man on the sixth day (Genesis 1:26–31), He created us to have dominion over the fish of the sea, over the fowl of the air, over the cattle, and "*over all the earth*" (Genesis 1:26 KJV). In essence, He said, "Let them rule." I told them that standing in opposition to God's plan for us to rule over all the earth under God's hand to advance His kingdom and bring Him glory, however, is an angel who is equally interested in having us rule under His hand. I asked them if they have ever heard of an angel by the name of Lucifer before.

Two of the young men said, "Yes."

I told them that I hoped they never forgot what I was about to tell them because it had the power to change their lives forever. The same is true of you if you have never heard this before!

"Lucifer is Satan," somebody said.

I said, "Yes, but not at first." I proceeded to tell them that God didn't give Lucifer His new name, Satan, until Lucifer rebelled and fell like lightning from heaven (Luke 10:18). Before that, Lucifer was one of God's archangels who was specifically in charge of the worship of God in music (Isaiah 14:11). Ezekiel 28 says the following about Lucifer:

> You were the seal of perfection, full of wisdom and perfect in beauty. You were in Eden, the garden of God; every precious stone was your covering. (Ezekiel 28:12–13 NKJV)

The same young man said, "That's right. He 'fell' from heaven because he wanted to be like God."

I said, "Good." Isaiah 14 and Ezekiel 28 capture the account of His fall from heaven. I encouraged them to check it out. I included it here for your benefit:

> How you are fallen from heaven, O Lucifer, son of the morning! Oh, you are cut down to the ground, you who weakened the nations! For you have said in your heart: "I will ascend into heaven I will exalt my throne above the stars of God; I will also sit on the mount of the congregation on the farthest sides of the north, I will ascend above the heights of the clouds, I will be like the Most High." Yet you shall be brought down to Sheol, To the lowest depths of the Pit. (Isaiah 14:12–15 NKJV)

> You were perfect in your ways from the day you were created, Till iniquity was found in you. By the abundance of your trading You became filled with violence within, And you sinned; Therefore I cast you as a profane thing Out of the mountain of God; And I destroyed you, O covering cherub, From the midst of the fiery stones. Your heart was lifted up because of your beauty; You corrupted your wisdom for the sake of your splendor, *I cast you to the ground*; I laid you before kings, That they might gaze at you. (Ezekiel 28:15–17 NKJV)

I then asked them if they knew where Lucifer, now Satan, ended up after God cast him out of heaven? A couple of them said, "Hell." I said, "No. That's what most people think, including many Christians." I explained to them that hell was prepared for Satan and his demons as their ultimate sentence (Revelation 20:10), but that Satan and approximately one-third of the "bad" angels (we call demons) were cast out of heaven and hurled into the earth (Revelation 12:3–4, 12:9). I said, "You know what that means?"

They said, "What?"

I said, "This means Satan was already on the earth before Adam and Eve existed."

They said, "What?"

I said, "Do you remember where Satan was when Adam and Eve first appeared together in scripture, and Satan inhabited the serpent and began talking to Eve?"

Silence.

"He was already in the Garden of Eden," I said. I asked them if they knew where the Garden of Eden was on the earth? No response. I said, "In the days of the Old Testament, it was in ancient Mesopotamia. Ancient Mesopotamia is modern-day Iraq." You should have seen the expressions on their faces.

"So picture this," I said. "God's Word says that angels were present and rejoiced when God laid the foundation of the earth (Job 38:4–7). This means that all angels, including Lucifer, existed on or before Day 1 of the creation story, which also means that angels existed before man came into existence on Day 6. Good so far?"

"Yes," they said.

Sidebar: Many theologians agree that the fall of Lucifer likely occurred before Adam and Eve existed since angels existed before man and since Satan, a fallen angel, was present in the Garden of Eden when Adam and Eve first appeared together in the garden. One highly respected national Bible teacher, speaker, writer, and theologian states that the proof that Satan was already in the earth before Adam and Eve were created is in the opening of Genesis 1:2. He contends that the reason the earth was without form and an empty waste, and darkness was upon the face of the very great deep was because Satan and his demons were already here.[3] If this is correct (and I believe it is), this means that Satan was "large and in charge" of the earth before God created man a little lower than the angels to have dominion over the works of God's hands and to put everything (including Satan) in subjection under his [man's] feet (Psalm 8:5–6 ESV; Hebrews 2:6–8 ESV).

I told my new brothers in Christ that this explains why Satan "moved in for the kill" right after Adam and Eve became "one flesh" in the garden. I asked them, "How would you like it if someone moved into your house and slept in your bed, ate your food, watched your flatscreen TV, put their feet up on your coffee table, and told you that your house was now their house?" I said, "Now you know how Satan felt when Adam and Eve took over His house! Satan wanted his house back!"

I said, "So check this out. God has just created man a little lower than the angels who, when submitted to Him, would crush the power of a bad angel (Satan and his demons), created above man but who were unsubmitted to God. Pretty amazing, right?"

I told them that man, in Genesis 1:26, was given instructions to rule over all the earth as God's ambassadors under His hand for the advancement of His kingdom to bring Him glory in the earth. While we know how that turned out, it didn't change God's assignment for humanity. He still wants us to rule over all the earth under His hand to advance His kingdom and bring Him glory. But something else happened when Adam and Eve disobeyed God and "sin" entered the world. It is hardly ever mentioned, and the devil would like to keep it that way. In fact, in all my years of attending church, I never heard one sermon on it! Ready? Adam and Eve transferred the title as "Rulers of the Earth" (under God's hand) and all of earth's kingdoms over to the devil (Luke 4:6). In other words, Satan became the ruler of the earth (John 14:30)!

I said, "So picture this. You have this big chess game going on in heaven to see who's going to be the ruler of the earth. Move, counter-move. Move, countermove. Move, countermove. In the beginning, it was God (move)! When Satan rebelled and got cast out of heaven with one-third of the angels (demons) and into the earth, it was Satan (countermove). When God created man a little lower than the angels, it went back to humanity (Adam and Eve; move). When Satan got Adam and Eve to 'fall' and eat from the tree of the knowledge of good and evil, Satan and his demons reclaimed it (countermove). Finally, after watching His people go through seemingly endless cycles of disobedience and repentance, God fulfilled the prophecy that He would use a man (i.e., the seed of the woman, that is, Jesus Christ, from Eve's descendants) to crush the head of Satan (Genesis 13:15). God said, in essence, 'Enough is enough. I'm going to send myself, the second person of the Trinity, Jesus Christ, fully God and fully *man* to crush the head of Satan once and for all (final move).' Satan never anticipated this move! This move on the part of God the Father in sending His Son, Jesus Christ, to be our sin-bearer, not only made a way for God to reconcile man unto Himself but made a way for man, in unity with Christ, to crush the power of Satan in the earth through the advancement of God's kingdom!"

I said, "In the same way that God laid claim to heaven from Satan who wanted to be worshipped just like God in heaven when He (God) cast Satan to the earth, God wants to use us to lay claim to earth from Satan before Jesus fully reclaims it and casts Satan into hell forever. Amazing, right?" You should have seen their jaws drop.

In summary, I told them that when Adam and Eve showed up, Satan came up to them and said, "I want my planet back." And Adam and Eve gave it back! And now you and I, in Christ, are in the process of taking it back all for God's glory! That's why you and I are here, brothers! Had Lucifer, now Satan, never fallen from heaven, you and I would not even exist!

I told my new brothers that it is critical, however, to understand a few things if you expect to rule well and give God glory with your lives. I told them while Jesus Christ has given every believer legal authority and, therefore, the power to tread on serpents and scorpions and over all the power of the enemy (Luke 10:19); Satan is still the ruler of this present world (Matthew 4:8–9; John 12:30–31; John 14:30; 2 Corinthians. 4:4; 1 John 5:19).

God's Word says that He wages war with those who keep God's commands and hold fast to their testimony of Jesus (Revelation 12:17). Because Satan has already blinded the minds of those who don't believe (2 Corinthians. 4:4), He's after us (believers) because He knows we're the only threat to the preservation and expansion of His kingdom in the earth. Said another way, we, in Christ, are the only thing standing in the way of Satan getting the whole earth to follow and worship Him! The good news is that he is powerless as long as we rule our worlds (e.g. our relationship worlds, our financial worlds, our career worlds, our stewardship worlds, our emotional worlds, our spiritual worlds, our sexual worlds, etc.) under God's hand, God's way!

I explained to them that while God allowed Satan to reclaim his title as "Ruler of the Earth" when Adam and Eve turned the earth back over to him, Satan knows full well that we, in Christ, and not he (Satan) have legal right to it because of the cross! I asked my new brothers in Christ if they understood what this means.

Silence.

I said the following: "When you accepted Jesus Christ as Lord and Savior tonight, you became part of God's Army to reclaim 'territory' from the devil to advance God's kingdom and bring Him glory in the earth! Every time you share the Gospel with others like I did with you tonight and someone responds to it (like you did) by turning from their 'sins' to accept what Jesus did for them on the cross, you, in Christ, have just reclaimed some 'territory' from Satan in the earth for God's glory. This is why Jesus could have said anything He wanted to say before He ascended to heaven. Yet, He said, 'Go therefore and make disciples of all nations, baptizing them in the name of the Father and of the Son and of the Holy Spirit, teaching them to observe all that I have commanded you. And behold, I am with you always, to the end of the age' (Matthew 28:19–20). You see, God knows it takes true disciples to reclaim God's kingdom and bring Him glory…on earth just as He did in heaven with Lucifer!"

I told them that whether or not they believe that Satan fell to the earth and was in the Garden of Eden before or after, Adam and Eve having existed is irrelevant; we have all been placed in the middle of an angelic conflict (Ephesians 6:12; Job 1–2; Daniel 9) to reclaim "territory" from Satan for the expansion of God's kingdom and glory in the earth.

I told them that one day, Jesus is going to return for His church (us!), lay claim to the earth, and fully establish His kingdom here. Then, after a seven-year period known as the Great Tribulation (Daniel 7; Revelation 13), we will rule and reign with Christ on the earth for 1,000 years, referred to as the Millennial Reign (Revelation

20:4). The Bible says that our assignments as "believers" in the Millennial Reign will be tied to how well we ruled on God's behalf in the earth now (Matthew 25:23). I told them that God is getting us ready to rule with Him in the Millennial Reign by allowing us to model His kingdom in the earth as His legal tenants now! I said, "Isn't that amazing?"

They couldn't believe it!

Our time together had ended. We exchanged contact information, "high-fived," and said our goodbyes. No words could express the immeasurable gratitude and joy Paul, Jenna, and I felt toward the Holy Spirit for what He had done.

Now I'd like to share some remaining thoughts with you that I didn't have time to share with them.

Yes, God wants to receive glory from our lives. Even the end of the Lord's prayer, which we did not discuss above, confirms this:

> For thine is the kingdom and the power,
> *and the glory*, forever. Amen. (Matthew 6:13)

What I hope you now see is that the amount of glory God receives from our lives is directly proportional to the amount of "kingdom-building" we accomplish in this angelic conflict we are in middle of.

You may be asking yourself, "But how do I become a kingdom-builder so my life brings God glory?" Answer: By becoming intimately familiar with the King and His kingdom manual, the Word of God, and doing what it says in every area of life that applies from your house to the White House.

It has been very sobering and troubling for me to learn that, to date, none of the Christians I have encountered on Soul Patrol, young and old, when asked, have been able to explain, even remotely, what I by God's grace just shared with you. Satan has done a masterful job at blinding the hearts and minds of many of God's people (who have been in church for years!) in a concerted effort to keep us from building God's kingdom! When it became apparent to me that this was a massive scheme against the body of Christ, I asked God to show me how I could create a powerful in-the-moment situation that would cause us to learn how we fit into God's eternal plan right now.

A few years ago, the Holy Spirit told me to give $1,000 to anyone on Soul Patrol who could explain to me why God created mankind (them). The only condition I gave them (and no, this does not apply to you since you now know the answer) is that their response must include a discussion about angels. I do the same thing in restaurants with workers I come in contact with during my dining experience. The first one who can give me the correct answer, "wins."

Some ask, "Why $1,000? Why not just do $20 instead? In fact, why even introduce money at all?"

Answer: Because I don't want them to ever forget the experience. A $1,000 prize has the uncanny ability to not only get people's undivided attention but to create a memory that will never be forgotten. While an extra $20 sometimes gets the attention of a young waiter or waitress hoping to make a few extra bucks than they might otherwise, $1,000 gets the attention of the whole restaurant. However, it doesn't stop there. The offer also spreads like wildfire to coworkers, friends, and family members outside of the restaurant! I do not seek to draw attention to myself but to draw in as many people as possible to put Jesus Christ on display to impact as many lives as possible with the Gospel.

It has been my experience that people tend to give undivided attention to, remember, and share with others the unusual, especially when it involves fun, excitement, adrenaline, and, yes, money! God has given me the means and ability to create such an environment in a culture that is not only "done" with traditional church and Christianity but that has become increasingly hostile toward Christians and Christianity. With the average attention span being between eight to ten seconds for most people, the opportunity to make some fast money and satisfy an overwhelming curiosity for why I would be willing to make such an extreme offer draws them in instantaneously almost every time. When many come to realize that I am there for no other reason but to allow them the opportunity to have their sins forgiven and to have a personal relationship with Jesus

Christ as their Lord and Savior, the love of God leaves many of them speechless.

To those of you who think I'm somehow "buying" salvation, please understand that 95–99 percent of those I share the Gospel with and who receive Jesus Christ as their personal Lord and Savior never receive a penny from me. I use the money for no other reason but to capture their undivided attention so they won't miss a word of what the Holy Spirit wants to say to them through me. And guess what? It works like a charm—a snake charm. Did you forget that Jesus told us to be as wise as a serpent and harmless as a dove (Matthew 10:16)? In the end, it is the kindness of the Lord demonstrated to them by Christ, through me, that leads them to repentance (Romans 2:4) every time. Nothing more, nothing less.

For those of you who wish to remain judgmental and critical toward me, nonetheless, enjoy your First Amendment right to do so. However, may I ask you a question with my First Amendment right as well? When was the last time you allowed yourself to be used by the Holy Spirit in any way to rescue anyone from the hellfire that awaits them by sharing the Gospel with them as Jesus instructed us to do? It sure is quiet in this Presbyterian Church.

Now the sad part. While many Christians do understand that they are in the middle of an angelic conflict, not one person to date, as stated, including many professing Christians, have been able to explain, even remotely, what I just shared with you above. It saddens me to think how so many of us Christians are just drifting through life spiritually "blind" and/or unengaged in the angelic conflict we have been placed in the middle of with good angels and Jesus against unbelievers, bad angels, and Satan to advance God's kingdom and miss out on the joy and the future crowns that would otherwise await them for fulfilling the reason for which we were created. However, none of this compares to how God must feel after all He's done for us!

When Jesus left the earth, He gave us our assignment. He expects us to do it! I ask some I meet, "Can you imagine being an attorney and never getting around to practicing law? Can you imagine becoming a CPA and never performing any accounting functions? Can you imagine being a firefighter and never responding to a fire? Can you imagine being a doctor and never seeing a patient?"

I can't imagine being an FBI agent who never conducted an investigation! But what if we're the nicest, kindest, friendliest, gracious, selfless, and generous lawyer, CPA, firefighter, doctor, or FBI agent that ever lived; however, never got around to doing what we were educated and trained to do? Surely our bosses would say, "Well done, thou good and faithful servant," right? Hardly. If they were good bosses who had the back of their boss, they'd say, "You're fired!" You see, there are a lot of nice, kind, friendly, gracious, selfless, generous Christians out there who never get around to doing what Jesus told us to do before He left the earth. That's the issue, beloved.

Brothers and sisters, what I just described is the greatest tragedy in the church of Jesus Christ today and why I believe the world is transforming us instead of the other way around! Given all God has done, this should cause each of us to weep to the core of our beings. And if it doesn't, to have the courage to ask ourselves, "Why?" And then when the Holy Spirit tells us to have the courage to walk by faith (2 Corinthians. 5:7), not merely talk by faith. Talk is cheap, isn't it, husbands and wives? Something tells me Jesus feels the same way when He listens to many of us!

You see, in case you and I have forgotten, Jesus is looking for a return on His investment with us. Have we forgotten the parable of the talents? It was about building God's kingdom, not ours! Like any good coach, Jesus wants to know what He can expect from us. The good news is that if we don't like what we've been able to accomplish for God's kingdom and glory up to now, it's not too late! How do I know? We're still breathing!

Before closing this chapter, I would like to define a critical term that I have used several times already and will continue to use throughout this book but have not yet fully explained. The word is *territory*. As we discussed, when God created man, He said now I want you to rule over all the earth and subdue it (Genesis 1:26–28). In other words, I have assigned "territorial rights" over all the earth to you, humanity. We discussed that God's intent in doing this was for man to begin reclaiming the earth, through Christ, from Satan as God did in heaven since Adam and Eve were not up to the task.

The extent of man's "territory" from God's perspective, however, has never changed—all the earth! All the earth consists of all the nations, and in the case of America, all the states, cities, counties, communities, churches, homes, and individuals in America. In other words, while Christians have the collective responsibility to take back "territory" from the enemy throughout the nation for Jesus Christ for His glory, we are each responsible for the "territory" in our respective gardens (i.e., our spheres of influence and control).

In the FBI, there are fifty-six field offices centrally located in major metropolitan areas all across the United States and Puerto Rico and sixty-three legal attaché offices (known as "legats") situated in the US. Embassy or consulate of the host country.[4] Additionally, there are more than two dozen smaller sub-offices in key cities around the world, providing coverage for more than 180 countries, territories, and islands.[5] Within these fifty-six field offices, there are about 380 resident agencies located in smaller cities and towns.[6] Collectively, all of these offices are responsible for covering the FBI's "territory" around the globe.

This means, for example, that the Special Agent-in-Charge of the Phoenix Division has authority and responsibility for His or her "territory" for that division but does not have jurisdiction over or responsibility for investigating Federal crimes in Los Angeles' "territory" or division. We refer to our different "territories" as Areas of Responsibility or "AORs." In our previous example involving the Phoenix Division, we would say this particular FBI investigation is in "Phoenix's AOR."

Did you know that each of us, like the FBI, have our own spiritual "territories" or "AORs" that God has given us spiritual authority over and responsibility for that He expects us to rule for Him to expand His kingdom and bring Him glory? It's everything in our respective "gardens," as previously stated.

God's AOR in a nation encompasses His three divine institutions—Family, Church, and Government (local, city, state, and federal). Thus, believers who operate on God's behalf in each of these three divine institutions, where applicable, cover God's AOR!

There are two types of "territory"—present-day territory that's already in our "gardens" and future territory that's going to be in our "gardens" if we'll go out and get it because the Lord has already given it to us. We see a great illustration of this in the passage below where God is addressing Joshua following Moses' death (*italics* used for emphasis):

> Moses my servant is dead. Now, therefore, arise, go over this Jordan, you and all this people, to the land which I am giving to them—the children of Israel. *Every place that the sole of your foot will tread upon I have given you, as I said to Moses. From the wilderness and this Lebanon as far as the great river, the River Euphrates, all the land of the Hittites, and to the Great Sea toward the going down of the sun, shall be your territory.* (Joshua 1:2–4)

You see, the territory in your garden (present and future), plus the territory in my garden (present and future), plus the territory in the garden of every other "believer" (present and future) equals a "whole bunch" of territory for the kingdom of God in preparation for our Millennial reign with Christ (Revelation 20:4). In this 1,000-year reign, Satan will be bound (Revelation 20:1–3), and Jesus will reclaim all the land ("territory") promised to the Jews under the Palestinian Covenant (or Land Covenant) that went unclaimed under the Abrahamic and Mosaic Covenants (Genesis 15:18–20; Numbers 34:1–2). In fulfillment of the Davidic Covenant, Jesus, during the Millennium, will take His rightful place on the throne of Israel forever (2 Samuel 7).

Also, in complete fulfillment of the New Covenant, the nation of Israel will return to God and worship their Messiah forever (Jeremiah 31:31–34). Jesus will be given dominion over all the nations (Daniel 7:11–14), and His faithful followers (us) will receive positions of authority based on our faithfulness in the here and now (Luke 19:12–27; 1 Corinthians 6:2; Revelation 5:10). All this involves occupying, seizing, and reclaiming "territory" in time and history that belongs to its rightful heir, Jesus Christ! In other words, this life, for the believer, is but a mere "dress rehearsal" for the life to come. And just like any director, Jesus doesn't like it when His "cast of characters" (us!) don't take our dress rehearsal before opening night seriously!

An excellent illustration of claiming territory occurs during the execution of an arrest warrant where law enforcement officers (LEOs), like myself, have probable cause to believe that the subject(s) of the arrest warrant is (are) located inside a particular residence or location. Many times, this lawful entry may involve clearing several rooms, hallways, stairwells, and closets to find subjects and effect their arrest.

The deeper we have to penetrate into the subject's "territory," the more territory we have to occupy until we locate our arrestee. Moreover, if we have probable cause to believe that "fruits and instrumentalities" of a particular crime may be in the subject's residence, we will also obtain and execute a search warrant for that location. The search warrant not only gives us the legal authority to enter that location but legal authority to search the premises and seize evidence named in the search warrant. This evidence may even include stolen items that can now be returned to their rightful owner(s).

As God's "Special Agents" in the spiritual realm, we have, similarly, been given legal authority by God to "lawfully" move into the enemy's "territory" from our house to the White House to occupy, seize, and reclaim what rightfully belongs to the kingdom of God! This is what happens, spiritually, when you and I fulfill the Great Commission!

Another critical point to understand about "territory" is that God will only expand our territory when He knows we intend to use it for the benefit of God and others. Some of you recall the New York Times bestseller that took the church by storm in 2000, *The Prayer of Jabez*, written by Bruce Wilkinson.[7] Take a look at the prayer of Jabez here in the following (*italics* used for emphasis):

> And Jabez called on the God of Israel saying, "Oh, that you would bless me indeed, and *enlarge my territory* that your hand would be with me, and that you would keep me from evil, that I may not cause pain!" So God granted Him what He requested. (1 Chronicles 4:10 NKJV)

God enlarged Jabez's territory because Jabez aligned His will with God's will, and God knew it! Jabez not only wanted God's presence, but He wanted God to help him live in such a way that he wouldn't cause pain to God and others. In other words, when God knows that He has our hearts and that we are concerned about representing Him well and advancing His kingdom, He knows He can trust us with more territory.

This illustration may help. As I type this, I am glancing outside my kitchen window, which gives me a view of my backyard. I can't help but notice that there are several children joyfully playing in my yard. None of them, however, are my children. You see, I have an end unit townhome, which has a bit more yard than my neighbor who owns the middle unit.

Now, if I wanted to, I could go outside and tell the neighbor's children and the other children from across the street to get off my property. If you say I would be justified in doing so because they are on my property, you'd be right. I could do the same thing with the middle and high school children that use my yard as a shortcut to their bus stop. My neighbor even asked me if I was going to make them stop so they wouldn't destroy my grass.

I said, "No, it's just grass." Again, I would be entirely justified telling them not to trespass through my yard since this is part of my "territory." However, the Holy Spirit told me a long time ago that everything I possess belongs to Him. He told me that He wanted me to use my "territory" to advance His kingdom. If I allowed others to benefit from my property in ways many others would not, they might see Jesus in me. This was more important than having "nice grass."

Shortly after purchasing my home, I asked God to give me opportunities to use my home and the small yard it sits on to bless those around me. I asked Him to show the neighborhood children that the reason that I allowed them to play in my yard and use it as a shortcut was because God loved them. I wanted them to experience His love through me.

God not only allowed me to extend His love to children who play in my yard and their parents who hear about it, but also to children and their parents from other communities. You see, my next-door neighbor came to me several years ago and said that he was having a small outdoor barbeque with family and friends. He wanted to know if it was okay if his friends and their children could use my yard to play games and spread out a bit.

I said, "Sure, please do."

He asked if the "grownups" could set up a horseshoe pit on the side.

I said, "Sure."

He asked if he could dig up all my trees with a backhoe and plant them in his yard. I said, "Okay." Just kidding. I just wanted to make sure you're still with me. Yes, I do have a sense of humor as warped as it may be as well as limits with my neighbors. I did, however, say "yes" to all his prior requests. While these simple acts of kindness blessed my neighbors and their children, they had the most impact on my neighbors' friends and their children who did not live in our community. They couldn't believe that one neighbor could be such a good neighbor to another neighbor who wasn't "family." It was merely the love of God for the glory of God!

I was so grateful that God used my territory to expand God's territory that day...and so were they! The following day, I told my neighbor that his kids were free to use my yard whenever they wanted, and they have. God just smiles. The impact of this simple act has been enormous and the "fruit" endless. It allowed me to witness and experience *The Prayer of Jabez* firsthand in my life.

As stated earlier, the primary way God expands His territory is through the fulfillment of the Great Commission. In real estate development, you cannot build on land ("territory") you do not "own," right? The same is true in the spiritual realm. Kingdom construction cannot begin until God first owns and occupies the hearts of His construction crew. You see, this is why Jesus needs disciples versus converts. Disciples use their salvation to expand the kingdom of God. Mere converts just watch everyone else do it!

In light of what I just said, please understand something as we return to my backyard illustration for a second. The reason I turned my yard (i.e. territory) over to my neighbor and his family and friends to use was not because I wanted to be a "nice" Christian who does "nice" Christian things. I did it because God radically transformed my heart with the love of Christ. And because God radically transformed my heart with the love of Christ, I want to see others' hearts radically transformed with the love of Christ. And if allowing people to use what God has given me will help God radically transform their hearts with the love of Christ so God's kingdom will expand, how could I refuse such an opportunity as one who claims to be a true disciple of Jesus Christ?

This raises a critical point that we mustn't overlook in a chapter called "Let Them Rule," which is that before we can rule well from our house to the White House to advance God's kingdom and glory, the Word of God and God Himself must first be ruling our hearts. Said another way, our greatest attempts to reclaim every institution in America from our house to the White House for Christ will be futile at best until we have allowed Jesus Christ to reclaim the territory in our hearts. Thus, it is only fitting that we spend the rest of this chapter discussing how we do this so we can all become kingdom-building disciples.

Contrary to what many believers think, only one-third of us (spirit, soul, and body) gets "saved" at conversion...and it isn't our souls. It's our spirits.[8] The remaining two-thirds of us—that is, our souls—are "being saved" through the process known as sanctification (referred to above). As for our bodies (the remaining one-third)... stay tuned.

At conversion, a seed of the Spirit, if you will, gets transferred into our hearts, where our spirit resides by the Spirit of God (1 Peter 1:23).[9] Spirit to spirit. God's Word says that we are born again of an incorruptible seed through the Word of God which lives and abides forever (1 Peter 1:23 KJV). Don't miss that key phrase—*through the Word of God.* This incorruptible seed of the Holy Spirit that brings life to our dead spirits is incorruptible because it, like the Word of God it passes through, is perfect, meaning it cannot be polluted or corrupted by "sin." Not only can sin not dwell within this incorruptible seed, but sin can no longer stay where this incorruptible seed got deposited (i.e., in our spirits) since this is now where the Holy Spirit resides. Thus, at conversion, our spirit, which now houses the Holy Spirit and the incorruptible seed of the Holy Spirit can never get "more saved." Nor can it ever get unsaved, which explains why true believers can never lose their salvation (Ephesians 4:30).

Psalm 119 says, "The entirety of Your word is truth" (Psalm 119:60 NKJV). As stated above, the Holy Spirit and truth (i.e., the Word of God) can "hang together" because both are incorruptible. Now you understand why our Spirit is the only part of us that can dwell with Christ forever in its present state. Said another way, since our spirits are the only part of us that is sinless and contains 100 percent truth (i.e., the Word of God and the Holy Spirit), it is the only part of us in its present state that can live with Christ (a.k.a. "The Truth"; John 8:31–32) in heaven where sin is not permitted.

That leaves our soul, which is our mind, will, and emotions, and our body. Our souls and bodies still need to "get saved." How? Well, the first thing you and I need to know is that the moment we were physically born, our souls were fully contaminated with sin. Not until our Spirit gets saved do we have the capacity and ability to begin the process of "soul sanctification." That's right. What we call sanctification is, technically, soul sanctification since our spirit is already fully sanctified at conversion. Please allow me to explain what I mean with this vivid illustration.

Imagine, if you will, three glass bowls (small, medium, and large), one inside the other. The small bowl represents our spirit, now saved, that houses the incorruptible seed of the Spirit. The medium bowl represents our souls, and the large bowl represents our bodies. If you have these glass bowls or something like it at home, I will encourage you to do this along with me. It's very powerful! I recommend doing this in your kitchen sink so, one, you never forget it and, two, you don't flood the rest of your house unless you want to for effect!

If you haven't already done so, place the medium bowl (soul) inside the large bowl (body) and then the small bowl (spirit) inside the medium bowl (soul). So from the inside out, you have the "spirit bowl" inside the "soul bowl" and the "soul bowl" inside the "body bowl." Now center your spigot over the top of the small bowl (spirit). Feel free to use a large pitcher of water instead of your faucet if you wish.

The water that will flow out of your spigot (when you turn it on) gets there by way of a pump and delivery system that you cannot see. Let's assume your water is drinkable and 100 percent pure, even if it isn't! The water coming out of your faucet will represent the continuous flow of God's Word that gets pumped up from a pump that you cannot see called your heart. In Scripture, the word *heart* refers to the totality of man's being. It includes our spirit and our soul (Hebrews 4:12).

While the job of our physical heart is to "pump" life-giving blood throughout our bodies, the role of our spiritual hearts is to pump God's life-giving truth into our spirit. Remember the Word, which is 100 percent truth, always gravitates to the Spirit, which contains 100 percent truth (i.e., the Holy Spirit). The Word of God never bypasses our spirit and goes straight to our souls. It goes into the Spirit first before it gets transferred to the soul from the spirit.

What you are about to observe is what happens in the spirit realm when God's Word (truth) gets pumped into our spirits from our hearts. Now slowly turn your spigot on and begin filling up the small bowl (spirit) with water until the water in the small bowl (spirit) begins to overflow into the medium bowl (soul). Don't turn off the spigot. Continue filling the small bowl (spirit) with "truth" until the water in the medium bowl (soul) begins flowing over the edge into the large bowl (body). Don't turn off the spigot. Continue filling the small bowl (spirit) until the water in the large bowl (body) begins to flow over the edge of the large bowl into your sink! Got it?

What you just witnessed in the physical realm is what happens in the spiritual realm when "soul sanctification" takes place. We begin to think and act differently when we're committed to getting the truth of God's Word into our hearts so it can be pumped into our spirits until it overflows into our souls. You see, the Holy Spirit (small bowl) loves and craves truth because it knows that if it can receive enough of it from our hearts, it will eventually "spill out" and overflow into our unsanctified souls (medium bowl).

This is an exciting time because this is where God's Word begins "taking over" our minds (thoughts), wills (choices), and emotions (feelings), which are all part of our souls. But wait, there's more! As we saw, if the believer can keep pumping more truth from their heart into the spirit (small bowl) so that it ultimately flows out of their soul (medium bowl) and into their body (large bowl), the soul (medium bowl) can now tell the body to go "right" instead of "left." It is here where strongholds that have existed for years get broken! Amazing, right? And it was all made possible *through the Word of God!*

King David understood this principle long before we did when He said, "I have hidden your word in my heart so that I would not sin against you" (Psalm 119:11). Yes, beloved, there's nothing new under the sun! I just helped you unwrap it a bit.

Now you correctly understand that the real "war" for our souls doesn't stop at justification (i.e., at salvation through the finished work of Jesus Christ on the cross) but sanctification. Said another way, while the Holy Spirit has sealed our spirit until the day of redemption (Ephesians 4:30), the territory of our souls is still "up for grabs." In the angelic conflict we have been placed in the middle of, the devil knows that if he *can't* keep our spirits from becoming fully sanctified at conversion (and he can't!), he has to keep our souls from becoming sanctified after conversion. He accomplishes this by stopping or polluting the flow of God's Word (a.k.a. truth) to the heart so truth cannot be pumped into the spirit and overflow into the soul. Got it? Awesome! Ha ha, devil! If you don't like it, talk to Jesus. We're with Him!

Here's the full passage of scripture I referred to above that high-lights what I have attempted to communicate to you taken from 1 Peter 1:22–23 (*italics* and brackets [] used for emphasis):

> *Since you have purified your souls in obeying*
> *the truth through the Spirit* [allowed the process
> of soul sanctification to take place as described
> above] in sincere love of the brethren, love one
> another fervently with a pure heart, *having been*
> *born again, not of corruptible seed but incorrupt-*
> *ible, through the Word of God* [truth] *which lives*
> *and abides forever.* (1 Peter 1:22–23 NKJV)

Maybe some of you are saying, "Okay, great, but wait a minute. The Bible also says the heart is deceitfully wicked, who can know it (Jeremiah 17:9)? It also says that out of the heart flows all the issues of life (pure and impure; Proverbs 4:23; Matthew 12:34–35). What happens in the spirit realm when my heart is pumping out dirty water because of the garbage I've exposed it to (e.g., violent video games, illicit streamed content, social media envy, and nonstop negative news)?"

Great question! I alluded to this above. When polluted or impure "water" enters our hearts by way of the polluted and impure things we expose it to, our spirits, which can only accept what is true and pure, see it coming and close in the spirit realm. Again, our new spirits, where the Holy Spirit resides, can only accept pure and unadulterated truth. Thus, in the spirit realm, this "impure water" that enters our hearts bypasses the spirit.

In our three-bowl illustration, dirty water is now hitting an imaginary lid that is affixed to the top of the small bowl and gets redirected toward the soul. Instead of our soul getting sanctified with the Word of God, it gets further contaminated with "sin" (i.e., the "impure" water). While our souls are already "contaminated" with sin at birth and get more contaminated until the Word becomes "alive" and "active" in our lives, no soul sanctification can take place until truth flows into our souls from our spirits *through the Word of God.* If we continue to allow impure water (i.e., "sin") to fill our hearts and be pumped into our souls, it will eventually overflow into our bodies (large bowl; i.e., tell our bodies to act in ways that are unholy and impure).

Concerning our bodies, they cannot nor will ever experience any level of sanctification on this side of eternity. Period. While every saint will be given a sinless glorified body at the Second Coming of Christ (1 Thessalonians 4:16; 1 John 3:2), the only way we can get our bodies to act "right" and not "turn left" in the here is now is with the help of a soul that is being sanctified by a spirit that tells it to go "right."

Thus, the Spirit's job is to release life into the soul, and the soul's job is to release life into the body.

Jesus himself said, "Anyone who is thirsty may come to me! Anyone who believes in me may come and drink! For the Scriptures declare, '*Rivers of living water will flow from His heart*'" (John 7:37–38 NLT).

Now you understand how someone can be a Christian and be an alcohol, drug, sex, or food addict. While the incorruptible seed through the Word of God may have got planted in their spirit, soul sanctification has not yet taken place in that particular area due to the absence or lack of God's Word (truth) reaching the soul from the spirit in that specific area. Thus, instead of the Spirit directing the soul to direct the addict's body, for example, to walk in righteousness, the soul directs the addict's body to go "left" because there's no truth reaching that particular soul compartment from the Spirit.

This is why "deep" and "continuous" study of God's Word is critical and not optional for the Christian who seeks deliverance from an addiction. James says it this way, "So get rid of all uncleanness and all that remains of wickedness, and with a humble spirit receive the word [of God] which is implanted [actually rooted in your heart], which is able to save your souls" (James 1:21 AMP).

Jesus similarly said, "Sanctify them in the truth; your word is truth" (John 17:17 AMP).

This is, incidentally, why most "counseling" (Christian or otherwise) and 12-step secular recovery programs are a total waste of time and money when it comes to *spiritual* healing and recovery. The operative word here is *spiritual* healing and recovery. Why? Because most counseling, and all 12-step secular recovery programs, are focused on correcting behavior from the outside in (body to heart), not from the inside out (heart to body) as God designed.

While 12-step secular recovery programs clearly have physical, mental, and emotional value, the devil loves when we decide to "keep coming back" to focus on what our bodies are doing (and not doing), instead of focusing on what's going on in our hearts and souls. He loves it when we keep coming back to places where Jesus and His Word are not permitted to have the final word. Why? Because he knows we will never find complete healing and always be in bondage to him.

Here's the issue: If the "God of [our] own understanding" is not Jesus, then we don't have resurrection power living on the inside of us to help us overcome sin. Said another way, no Jesus, no Word. No Word, no resurrection power. No resurrection power, no deliverance. No deliverance, no healing. Conversely, know Jesus, know Word. Know Word, know resurrection power. Know resurrection power, know deliverance. Know deliverance, know healing!

Spiritual battles of the mind can only be fought and won with spiritual weapons. In other words, until our "higher power" is the Highest Power where Jesus and the truth of His Word get to have the final word and are allowed to take over more and more "territory" in our souls, by way of the Spirit, the stronghold of addiction can never be fully broken. Who wants to stay in the recovery room for the rest of their lives? Not any patient I know! There's way too much kingdom business to do!

Did you ever notice that whenever Jesus healed someone spiritually or physically, it always happened *immediately*? The invalid, whoever it was, didn't hang out in recovery for the next thirty years. It's time for some of us to receive the spiritual healing that Jesus has for us through His Word and take up our mats and walk in Jesus's name!

Now you and I can fully understand why there's chaos all around us and why we, the body of Christ, have not been ruling well. The world is out-of-control because our souls (Christian and non-Christian) are out-of-control. And because our souls are out-of-control, our bodies are out-of-control. Have you seen the headlines today?

Maybe you say, "Okay, already, but how do I practically get the Word into my heart so it can be 'pumped' into my spirit and released into my soul to tell my body to go 'right' instead of 'left?'" Great question!

Answer: Through consistent study, reflection, meditation, and prayer centered on God's Word. Notice, I didn't say by merely reading God's Word. Paul said, "Study to show thyself approved unto God, a workman that needeth not to be ashamed, rightly dividing the word of truth" (2 Timothy 2:15 KJV). This involves getting the Word down deep. I mentioned the importance of this moments ago. Let's spend a critical moment here.

To get the Word down deep, it is essential to understand the difference between three Greek words that describe Scripture, which is translated "word" in the New Testament—*graphe, logos,* and *rhema.* Many of you know this already. Bear with me for the many who don't.

Graphe, very simply, refers to the writings of God contained in the Bible. This is the Bible under your car seat or on your living room table that contains the Word of God. Nothing more, nothing less. *Logos* refers principally to the total inspired Word of God. It is the God-inspired message that comes from the *graphe*. Whenever we find ourselves saying, "Oh, that's what that means," we just received *logos* or the meaning of the *graphe*. *Logos* is where the Word of God becomes "alive" and "active." Sharper than any double-edged sword, it penetrates even to dividing soul and spirit, joints and marrow; it judges the thoughts and attitudes of the heart" (Hebrews 4:12 NIV).

This is what Paul is referring to in 2 Timothy 2:15. While *graphe* stays on the surface where the words of the Bible appear on the pages, *logos* goes deep. *Logos* gets pulled into our spirits and transferred into our souls where it remains "alive" and "active," waiting for us to apply it. You'll know you have *logos* operating in your life when you are able to correctly discern whether what others are telling you is, in fact, God's Word. Said another way, with *logos* comes understanding.

This brings us to our final Greek word for the Word of God, *rhema*. This is where demons tremble. Why? Because now we are a threat to hell! At least this is the way it's supposed to work! I firmly believe the reason why the culture is transforming the church instead of the other way around is because the overwhelming majority of God's people never get beyond *graphe* and *logos* to the application of *rhema* word. Read that again, beloved.

Rhema refers to a word that is spoken and means "an utterance." We use *Rhema* word when we declare and apply the message of the word (*logos*) that we get from the written word (*graphe*) to a given situation. The sword that the Spirit uses is the *Rhema* of God (Ephesians 6:17). Rhema plunges in and draws blood. It is what Jesus used against Satan in Matthew 4. This is where demons tremble because this is where the spoken word unleashes the power needed to reclaim "territory" that the devil has stolen from us or the power needed to defend territory we have already possessed and occupied for God's kingdom and glory.

Thus, when we say someone is spiritually mature, what we are really saying is, "Here's a 'believer' who has allowed the 'territory' of their soul to be transformed by the truth of God's Word (*logos*), resulting in a glorious walk by faith *(rhema)*." One of the evil lies of the devil is when he can convince Christians that they can become mature without God's Word. Did you know that many Christians believe this? I meet them all the time. I used to be one of them.

Really "nice" men and women who do not nor will not allow God's Word to tell them what to do, instead, their word or another's word gets to have the final word. The Word of God is all *graphe* and *logos* to them—no *rhema*! Easy day for Satan! How this must break God's heart when He has given us everything we need in His Word to be victorious over Satan!

Therefore, Satan has two goals for every individual when it comes to the Word of God to keep us from ruling well. Number one, and most importantly, he wants to do all he can to prevent the incorruptible seed that leads to salvation from getting implanted into our hearts. Number two, if he can't stop number one, he wants to keep the truth of God's Word from reaching our souls *(logos)* so our souls will never be able to tell our bodies to go "right" through the application of *rhema* word. In this way, Satan can prevent us from occupying and reclaiming "territory" from him in every institution from our house to the White House.

You see, beloved, a Christian whose soul (i.e., mind, will, and emotions) is being controlled by Satan is no real threat to Satan, regardless of what we may think, which is just evidence of soul contamination (i.e., deception)! Said another way, if God's Word cannot tell our souls what to do so our souls can tell our bodies to go "right," Satan can get us to go "left" to expand his kingdom and glory! Have you looked around lately? There are a lot of Christian marriages, homes, and churches doing the work of the devil! More on that later.

Thus, while we in Christ have won the battle in our spirits, we have not yet won the battle in our souls (mind, will, emotions, and conscience) or bodies. Therefore, when Christian pastors and leaders say that the battleground for the Christian is in the mind (a component of our souls), are they right? One hundred percent (1 Peter 1:13; 2 Corinthians 10:5; Romans 7:23, 8:6, 12:2)!

God's Word says that we are transformed by the renewing of our minds (Romans 12:2). The only way we can present our bodies as a "living sacrifice" holy and acceptable to God is if our minds (part of our souls) tell us to (Romans 12:1)! Other key scriptures that validate that the battleground is in our minds (souls) include 2 Corinthians 10:3–5, Isaiah 26:3, Philippians 4:8, Ephesians 4:23, Romans 7:25, Proverbs 3:5, Colossians 3:2, Romans 1:28, and Nehemiah 4:6.

No truth, no territory. Know truth, know territory! Now you and I can finally understand the magnitude of the spiritual crisis we have in America today. It's a little tough to reclaim territory for God in our nation when many of us have reclaimed little to no "territory" in our souls!

When God said, "Let them [us] rule" (Genesis 1:26), He meant it. When God said, "[t]hy kingdom come and thy will be done on earth as it is in heaven" (Matthew 6:10), He meant it. When the Psalmist said, "You have given [man] dominion over the works of your hands and you have put all things under His feet," they weren't just words. When Jesus said, "Behold, I have given you authority to tread on serpents and scorpions and over all the power of the enemy," he wasn't kidding. When he said, "The Son of God came to destroy the works of the devil," it wasn't just to make us feel good.

When Paul said, "For we wrestle not against flesh and blood, but against principalities and powers and spiritual wickedness in high places," it wasn't for informational purposes only. When John said, "Then the dragon was enraged at the woman and went off to wage war against the rest of her offspring *those who keep God's commands and hold fast their testimony about* Jesus" (Revelation 12:17), he wasn't fearmongering. And finally, when Jesus said, "You have made them [us] to be a Kingdom and priests to serve our God and they [us] will reign on the earth" (Revelation 5:10), it wasn't just to make us feel good!

Beloved, His kingdom cannot come and His will cannot be done on earth as it is in heaven during our lifetimes for His glory if we never get around to ruling our worlds under His hand His way from our house to the White House. Again, every war fought, whether it's in the Middle East, inside the Beltway, or inside our homes is about territory! Now that you know this, who's ruling the territory in your heart, home, church, city, and nation? And if it's not God, what are we prepared to do about it?

Thus, the real crisis in America is not a moral one, a political one, a social one, an economic one, or a military one. It's a spiritual "ruling" one.

Some of you are about to have a breakthrough. You didn't fully understand why God created you before reading this chapter. Now you do! Yes, I, like you, wish I had known this years ago, but praise God, we know it now! Ha ha devil! Talk to our attorney, Jesus, if you don't like it! Surely you know Jesus, the One who defeated you at Calvary and the One who represents us flawlessly before the Father, day and night, when you come to accuse us? By the way, that's how you use rhema!

May we never make our lives, first and foremost, about our happiness again, which is what Satan wants us to do. However, even with that said, here's what's so cool about God's master plan. When we rule well under His hand for His kingdom and glory, we will experience a joy that goes far beyond any earthly happiness. Why? Because it doesn't depend on how well people are treating us or how much money we have in the bank. Good luck beating that on the open market!

You are now positioned and energized for kingdom business and represent a direct threat to Satan in your region. Tell at least three people what you've learned as you rule your world under God's hand, His way.

Finally, do not ever forget how much you are loved by the Savior! Though we are all in different places in our walks with God, the key to moving from where we are to where we now know we need to be is the inexhaustible love that God has for each one of us as demonstrated on the cross. It never loses its power! If that doesn't motivate you to rule well, nothing will.

Now you know the rest of the story! May each of us, from this day forward, begin ruling our worlds under His hand to expand His kingdom and bring Him glory so that "[t]hrough the church the manifold wisdom of God might be made known to the rulers and authorities in the heavenly places. This was according to the eternal purpose that He has realized in Christ Jesus our Lord, in whom we have boldness and access with confidence through our faith in Him" (Ephesians 3:10–12 ESV).

Prayer of Repentance (if applicable)

> Heavenly Father, until now, I never fully understood why you created me and, as a result, have wasted much time—your time. I recognize by not ruling my world well under your hand for the advancement of your kingdom and glory that I have contributed to the chaos I am witnessing today in my individual life, home, church, community, city, and nation. As a result, I have not brought glory to your name but shame and have grieved your heart. I have allowed Satan to use

me to advance his kingdom by not realizing that you placed me in the middle of an angelic conflict with you and good angels against Satan and bad angels (demons) to seize and occupy spiritual territory for you. No words can express the level of sorrow I have in my heart for what my actions have done to you. Will you please forgive me, Lord?

I now turn from my independent way of thinking and operating to willingly place myself underneath your authority in *every* area of life. Allow the same resurrection power that rose Jesus from the grave that lives on the inside of me (Ephesians 1:19–20) to empower me to rule well from this point forward so that I might reclaim in and through you what I have foolishly relinquished to the enemy through my ignorance and willful disobedience.

While I don't deserve it, please restore the years that the moth and locust have eaten (Joel 2:25) in my life and in every institution I have negatively impacted from my house to the White House.

Help me to seek forgiveness with those I have hurt where I did not rule well and extend forgiveness to those who have hurt me (whether they seek it or not) because they did not rule well with me.

Thank you for your steadfast love and mercies toward me that never cease and are new every morning (Lamentations 3:22) and for standing more prepared to forgive my sins than I am to commit them, more willing to supply my needs than I am to confess them.

Finally, help me never again to forget why I'm here, so through me, your kingdom would come, and your will would be done on earth as it is in heaven (Matthew 6:10) for your glory. Amen!

Verses to Remember

1. And God said, "Let us make man in our own image, after our likeness; and let them have dominion over the fish of the sea, and over the fowl of the air, and over the cattle, and over all the earth..." (Genesis 1:26 KJ21)

2. You were the seal of perfection, full of wisdom and perfect in beauty. You were in Eden, the garden of God; every precious stone was your covering. (Ezekiel 28:12–13 NKJV)

3. How you are fallen from heaven, O Lucifer, son of the morning! Oh, you are cut down to the ground, you who weakened the nations! For you have said in your heart: "I will ascend into heaven I will exalt my throne above the stars of God; I will also sit on the mount of the congregation on the farthest sides of the north, I will ascend above the heights of the clouds, I will be like the Most High." (Isaiah 14:12–14 NKJV)

4. Yet you have made Him [man] a little lower than the heavenly beings and crowned Him with glory and honor. You have given Him dominion over the works of your hands; you have put all things under His feet. (Psalm 8:5–6 ESV)

5. Then the serpent said to the woman, "You will not surely die. For God knows in the day that you eat of it your eyes will be opened, and you will be like God, knowing good and evil." (Genesis 3:4 NKJV)

6. And the devil took Him up and showed Him all the kingdoms of the world in a moment of time, and said to Him [Jesus], "To you I will give all this authority and their glory, for it has been delivered to me, and I will give it to whom I will." (Luke 4:5–6 ESV)

7. We know that we are from God, and the whole world lies in the power of the evil one. (1 John 5:19 NASB)

8. I will make you and the woman hate each other. Your children and her children will be enemies. Her son will crush your head. And you will bite His heel. (Genesis 3:15 NIRV)

9. He [Jesus] disarmed the rulers and authorities and put them to an open shame, by triumphing over them in Him. (Colossians 2:15 ESV)

10. Then the dragon became furious with the woman and went off to make war on the rest of her offspring, on those who keep the commandments of God and hold to the testimony of Jesus. (Revelation 12:17 ESV)

11. God may perhaps grant them [us] repentance leading to a knowledge of the truth, and they [us] may come to their senses and escape from the snare of the devil, after being captured by Him to do His will. (2 Timothy 2:25–26 ESV)

12. Behold, I give unto you [disciples] power to tread upon serpents and scorpions and over all the power of the enemy, and nothing shall by any means hurt you. (Luke 10:19 KJV)

13. But thanks be to God who gives us the victory through our Lord Jesus Christ. (1 Corinthians 15:57 ESV)

14. Our Father which art in heaven, hallowed be thy name. Thy kingdom come, thy will be done on earth as it is in heaven. (Matthew 6:9–10 KJV)

15. You have made them into a kingdom for God to rule, to serve Him; and they will rule over the earth. (Revelation 5:10 CJB)

16. For we wrestle not against flesh and blood, but against principalities, against powers, against the rulers of the darkness of this world, against spiritual wickedness in high places. (Ephesians 6:12 KJV)

17. [s]o that through the church the manifold wisdom of God might be made known to the rulers and authorities in the heavenly places. This was according to the eternal purpose that He has realized in Christ Jesus our Lord, in whom we

have boldness and access with confidence through our faith in Him. (Ephesians 3:10–12 ESV)

18. Well done, good and faithful servant; you have been faithful over a few things, I will make you ruler over many things. (Matthew 25:23 NKJV)

19. Then I saw thrones, and seated on them were those to whom the authority to judge was committed. Also, I saw the souls of those who had been beheaded for the testimony of Jesus and for the Word of God, and those who had not worshipped the beast or its image and had not received its mark on their foreheads or their hands. They came to life and reigned with Christ for 1,000 years. (Revelation 20:4 ESV)

CHAPTER 2

* ✦ ✦ ✦ ✦ ✦ *

The Great Role Reversal

Its origin extends back to where human life began—the Garden of Eden. We know that after the Lord God planted a garden in Eden, He placed the man He created, Adam, in it. Adam, unlike some men today, was not confused about his gender, his sexuality, his identity, or his purpose. God told him to tend and care for the Garden of Eden (Genesis 2:15). We also know that at the center of the garden, God placed two trees, not one—the tree of life and the tree of the knowledge of good and evil (Genesis 2–3). Then came God's warning to Adam to never eat from the tree of the knowledge of good and evil (Genesis 2:17). There's no indication that Adam questioned God's authority or tried to reason with Him like many of us do. All was well with the world.

We remember that Eve had not yet arrived on the scene when Adam received his assignment from God to tend and care for the garden and name every living thing. Certainly, God could have reversed their birth order and given this responsibility to Eve before creating Adam, but He didn't. God could have created Adam and Eve at the same time and given the responsibility to both of them, but He didn't.

We know that before Eve entered the world, God formed every kind of bird and animal from the soil (Genesis 2:19). Then God brought them to Adam to see what Adam would name them, and

Adam chose a name for each one (Genesis 2:20). God gave the full responsibility to Adam before Eve ever arrived, and whatever Adam called them, that was their name! Again, God could have waited and given the responsibility to Eve or to both of them, but He didn't. God asked Adam to do it...before He ever created Eve. As you may recall, Adam also named his wife—Eve (Genesis 3:20)!

The responsibilities of caring for the garden and naming every bird and animal was placed squarely on Adam's shoulders by God before God would make a "helpmate" suitable for him. But why would God choose to do it this way? Women are just as capable as men at maintaining a garden and naming things, right, ladies? So why would God give the ultimate responsibility to "the man" only?

While the Bible doesn't specifically say, there are several verses throughout God's Word that suggest He did it this way for at least four reasons. First, He did it to illustrate God's spiritual hierarchy or divine authority structure for the family. Secondly, to demonstrate the divine transfer of ruling authority from himself to man to define man's leadership role as chief ruler under God in the earth and who God would ultimately hold accountable for it. Thirdly, to reveal man's distinct role as the "priest," protector, and provider for his family. Finally, to show Adam his need for a helpmate (Genesis 2:18) who would help him rule over all the earth under God. A closer look at each of these will lay the necessary foundation for the rest of the chapter.

The first reason why God gave the primary responsibility of caring for the garden and naming every animal to Adam before Eve arrived was to illustrate God's spiritual hierarchy; that is, God's divine authority structure for the family. While husbands and wives are equal in being to one another in every way (1 Peter 3:7), God designed them to be functionally different. Functionally, the head of every husband is Christ, the head of every wife is her husband, and the head of Christ is God (1 Corinthians 11:3 ESV). God intended from the very beginning until now for the husband to be the spiritual leader of the family under God's authority, the wife to be her husband's "helper" under his spiritual authority, and for unmarried children to be under their parents' authority.

In other words, God has a "chain of command" for the family, and He expects husbands and wives to follow it. But why? So we can maintain order and peace in the family. God is a God of order and peace, not a God of disorder and chaos (1 Corinthians 14:40). I will, hereafter, refer to this "chain of command" as God's "divine order" for the family.

Men, we didn't decide this, God did. Ladies, we men didn't choose this. God did. Therefore, if anyone has a problem with it, please take it up with God. There is only one opinion that counts at the end of the day. And in case you were wondering, it's not yours or mine. Do you still want to rule your world under His hand His way (chapter 1)? Yes, I know, this is countercultural, but we belong to another kingdom, remember? Whose word will get to have the final word in your house?

Certainly, God could have named the animals and birds himself. Still, instead, He chose to delegate that responsibility to Adam before Eve ever arrived to illustrate that in terms of God's divine order—Adam, not Eve, was directly underneath God "positionally." How do you think Adam must have felt when God gave him this responsibility, knowing God could have done it himself? While the Bible doesn't say, I can't help but think it must have been a serious "wow" moment for Adam as he realized his incredible value and worth in God's eyes.

While we don't know what Adam was thinking, I would have been thinking, "Wow, God must really love, trust, and believe in me. The Creator and Ruler of the universe is asking me to exercise rulership over the earth as His ambassador (2 Corinthians. 5:20). What an honor, what a privilege, what a responsibility, what a God!"

God, in essence, handed the keys of the earthly kingdom over to Adam and said, "Here, while it belongs to Me, I'm appointing you as the chief steward, ruler, and guardian over it. All power and authority to rule over creation I give you, Adam. Rule well, my son."

Without Eve present, there was no chance Adam could be confused about his role or abdicate his responsibility as spiritual head to anyone else. There was no chance he would be confused about who was next in line under God. Next to God, he was at the top of the ladder. And so are we men. I can't imagine Adam saying, for example, "I wonder if God wants me to be in charge? I wonder if God shouldn't consult with the feminist movement first or consider what impact this might have on gender equality, affirmative action, political correctness, or the tolerance movement before asking me to do this? I wonder if God wants to use someone else? I wonder." To Adam, Eve's absence left no doubt who God had appointed to be the spiritual leader of the family.

Secondly, God gave the responsibility of naming the animals to Adam to illustrate the divine transfer of ruling authority from God to man as God's primary ruler in the earth under God's authority. God wanted Adam to know that with the authority God gave him comes responsibility. And because Adam, like every man, is the spiritual leader of his family, God will always come looking for "the man" first since the expansion of God's kingdom is dependent upon how well the spiritual leader of the family is ruling his world.

After the Fall, we remember who God called out to when Adam and Eve were hiding from Him in the garden. It was Adam, not Eve. Eve was with him, but God called Adam's name. Why didn't God call Eve's name also, especially since Satan deceived Eve (1 Timothy 2:14)? Because Adam was "on the hook" as the spiritual leader of his family and primary ruler over what God created. In God's divine order for the family, Adam, not Eve, was "next in line."

Aren't you glad, ladies? It was Adam who had forsaken his leadership role when the serpent came to Eve and deceived her. It was Adam who allowed his wife's human viewpoint, orchestrated by Satan, to overrule him and God! It was Adam who listened to his wife instead of God when it came to eating from the forbidden tree (Genesis 3:17). While Eve usurped Adam's authority by listening to the serpent, it was Adam who went "passive" and allowed it to happen right under his nose. Thus, it was Adam who God came looking for first as the spiritual leader of their family and chief ruler over all God created.

Men, did you know that we are God's ruling ambassadors, primary caretakers, and chief stewards over everything in our "gardens" (e.g., wives, children, careers, property, possessions, money, time, choices, gifts, talents, abilities, and service to others)? How are you doing at exercising authority over and responsibility for these things?

Men, we also need to rule over the "sin" in our gardens. So are you ruling it? Or is it ruling you? Are you, for example, ruling over the streamed content in your home? Or is it ruling over you and your family? Are you ruling over your thought life? Or is your thought life ruling over you? Are you ruling over how you spend your time away from your wife? Or is it ruling over you? Are you ruling over where you allow your feet to go? Or is where you allow your feet to go ruling over you? Are you lovingly and responsibly ruling over all God has placed in your "garden" under Christ's authority? Or have you gone passive like Adam and allowed all God has placed in your garden and those in your garden to rule over you?

Again, God will come looking for us first, men. Remember what God said to Cain in Genesis 4 right after God accepted Abel's offering and rejected Cain's offering? Sin is crouching at the door. Its desire is for you [Cain], *but you must rule over it* (Genesis 4:7 ESV*)*.

You see, God wants men to name things because He knows if we do, we will exercise rulership authority over it and responsibility for it. At least, that's the way it's supposed to work. Did you know that God hard-wired men to name things for this very purpose? Yes, even still. Ladies, it's why guys instinctively name their "stuff" such as their cars, boats, motorcycles, pets, and, yes, even you. Hopefully, not in that order. It's why Adam named Eve and why you, lady, took your husband's last name when you were married. At least that's the way it's supposed to work.

Sidebar for single men: Any single woman who wants to keep her last name after she is married to you should keep her life! That was extra. How can the two become one when one wants to remain as two? I don't care what the reason is. I've never heard a good one, including the ever-popular "for professional reasons." This dynamic recently played out in my garden. A man (I'll call Sam) who was attending the men's small group I facilitated at my home recently confessed, after this teaching, that his son's wife refused to take his son's last name when they were married. After hearing this teaching, Sam believes this is the reason why they are getting a divorce. The two refused to become one from day one. Whenever we violate God's principles, we invite "chaos" into our lives!

The third reason why I believe God gave Adam the assignments of tending to and caring for the Garden of Eden and naming the birds and animals before Eve arrived was to leave no doubt in Adam's mind, and us men, that husbands are responsible for being the priests, protectors, and providers for their families. Let's take a look at each of these responsibilities. For those of you men, like me, who wondered for many years (or still do) what it truly means to be a man, you are about to find out!

In the same way that God expected Adam to tend to, care for, and serve the things that God entrusted unto him in his garden, God expects us men, as the "priests" of our households, to tend to, care for, and serve the things that God has entrusted to us in our gardens. This would include anything God has given men authority over and responsibility for, such as the provision, protection, and spiritual guidance of his family. While wives "help" their husbands with these and other things, God intended for the primary responsibility to fall on us men.

Note that even after Eve arrived on the scene to "help" Adam rule everything under God's hand for the expansion of His kingdom, God never directly asked her to "tend to" and "care for" the garden or to have *primary* dominion over anything. Not because she wasn't capable, but because God didn't create her for that reason! God created her to *help* her husband with these things! Why? Because the man needed help!

Men, how would your wives and children say you're doing at tending to, caring for, and serving them as the "priest" of your household? Guess what, guys? If your wife is out serving you, then she's the husband ("priest"), and you're the wife! And guess what? God is going to come looking for you first!

In the same way that Adam knew God created him to be the "priest" of his household, Adam also knew it was his job to be the protector of what God had entrusted to him. After all, he had been doing it before Eve arrived. The English Standard Version of Genesis 2:15 says that "the Lord God took the man and put Him in the

Garden of Eden to work it and *keep it.*" While the Bible doesn't specifically say what *keep it* means, the International Standard Version of the same verse says, "to work it and *guard it*" (Genesis 2:15 ISV, 2012). This translation implies that God wanted Adam to protect the garden. Against what? The evil that was already there—Satan and his demons (chapter 1).

Thus, God told Adam what He expected of him (Adam) well before Eve ever arrived on the scene. Again note, at no time between Eve's creation and Adam and Eve's ex-communication from the garden after the fall did God tell Eve it was her job to protect the garden. No, it was Adam's responsibility. Without Eve present, there again could be no confusion regarding who God holds accountable for protection in the family.

Incidentally, do you know why God kicked Adam and Eve out of the garden after the fall? He did this to *protect* his holiness and the tree of life (Genesis 3:24). In the same way that God places separation between us who are unholy and He who is holy until we receive the forgiveness Christ offers, God put separation between himself and Adam and Eve (i.e., via excommunication) after they sinned to signify a change in their relationship. Even after Adam and Eve's relationship with God was restored, they ceased to have direct access to the Father for the forgiveness of sin.

The same is true for us. While Old Testament saints went through priests who sacrificed animals on their behalf to have their sins forgiven, New Testament saints have to continually go through Christ, our sacrificial Lamb, to have our sins forgiven. Not having direct access with the Father is a consequence of the fall. However, this will all change when we get to heaven because there will be no sin in heaven just as it was in the Garden of Eden before the Fall.

The other reason Adam and Eve were excommunicated from the garden was to protect the tree of life from them. If they ate from the Tree of Life in their fallen state, it would have forced mankind to have to live forever cut off from God (Genesis 3:22). By expelling them from the garden (i.e., placing separation between himself and man) and guarding the way to the Tree of Life (Genesis 3:24), God was protecting future generations from eternal separation from God before God's plan of salvation would be fulfilled through the death, burial, and resurrection of Jesus Christ! Oh, how He loves us, church! So as you can see, men, God takes protection very seriously. Do you?

Ladies, the primary protection of your family rests with your husband, not you. Men, did you know you can place the burden of protecting the family on your wives by being unnecessarily absent? Men, one of the main reasons why your wife doesn't want you working late or being away on business trips or temporary assignments unless you have to be is because she needs to feel protected. Yes, she's a "big girl," and her mother hen instincts will kick in to defend herself and her chickadees, but she needs to know that you're protecting her so she can spend her greatest energy on what God created her to do—helping you fulfill God's vision and purpose for your family!

And for you ladies who are okay with your husband being unnecessary absent or even encourage them to do so when it isn't necessary, it is not only a sign that your marriage is in trouble but a sign that you are aiding and abetting the enemy. What? How? By leaving yourself unnecessarily unprotected and more vulnerable to the schemes and strategies of the devil. Also, by indirectly communicating to your husband and God that you would rather be "two" than "one." Or that what you want (e.g., more money or a more extravagant lifestyle to enhance your self-image) is more important to you than maintaining God's priorities.

Also, please don't hear what I'm not saying. I am not saying that husbands should spend every waking minute with their wives when they are not working to ensure their protection. Husbands (and wives for that matter) must have the freedom to pursue other healthy hobbies, interests, and Godly friendships (with the same sex) apart from their spouses that contribute to their overall spiritual, mental, and emotional health. It's a win-win for everybody. However, in the case of husbands, these pursuits should never result in him abdicating his responsibility to protect his wife to the best of his ability.

In the same way that Secret Service Agents protect our presidents from harm so the president can focus on what he was created to do, wives need to know that their husbands are protecting them so they can focus on what they were created to do. Some husbands are great with presents but not with their presence, thus creating unnecessary fear, loneliness, anxiety, and insecurity in their wives. When it comes to protection, *Godly* wives will always desire your presence over your presents if given a choice. However, I should warn you that if you get her a present now and then with your presence, you better give your boss a head's up that you'll probably be a little late for work in the morning!

While most men know it's their job to protect their wives and families physically, few men understand that it is also their job to protect their wives emotionally, sexually, and spiritually. What?

Husbands emotionally protect their wives, for example, by encouraging them not to take on too much responsibility and by taking an active role with parenting, meals, cleanup, and the maintenance and upkeep of the home. Husbands also protect their wives emotionally by not degrading or poking fun at them in public or private and by listening to them without trying to "fix" them. Another way is by helping them carry their burdens and by defending them when friends, family, relatives, or others attack or disrespect them.

I once told one of my children, "While you may feel you have the right to talk to your mom that way, you will not speak to my wife that way. Do we understand each other?" That's emotionally protecting your wife. Do you do this, mister? The biggest complaint my mom had with my dad growing up that she sadly shared with me, unsolicited, was that my father didn't protect her emotionally—a sad commentary for two people who had been married for fifty-five years at the time! What's your definition of a successful marriage? I hope it's more than time.

Men, emotionally protecting your sons and daughters means being emotionally present and available to love, listen, validate, encourage, correct, train, and instruct them so they know *who* they are and *whose* they are. The goal is that this will hopefully culminate into a rich friendship between you and them and between them and God one day. Children who feel emotionally protected by their fathers know that they are loved, that they matter, and that they are valuable and precious to God, their family, and the church of Jesus Christ.

While some men understand that it is their job to protect their children emotionally, I find even fewer men (Christian or otherwise) know that it is their responsibility to protect their wives and children sexually. What do I mean by this? It's every man's responsibility before God and other mature men to not only raise the purity bar in their own lives but also in the lives of their wives and children. Men, are you not only faithful to your wives sexually but faithful to your wives with your thought life? Or do you allow your eyes and affections to wander at work, on the Internet, or while on business, fishing, or hunting trips with the "boys"?

Unfortunately, many men are unable to raise the purity bar in their own families because they're entangled in their own webs of sexual impurity involving internet pornography, social media flirting, sexually suggestive material, and various forms of live and streamed "adult" entertainment. Men, we cannot export to our wives and children what we have not first imported ourselves. If sexual purity is not important to you, I can guarantee you it will not be important to your children. You will have already lost your impact in the battle for their souls. Don't let this be you. The good news is that if you have compromised in this area, today is a new day, and God's mercies are new every morning (Lamentations 3:22). If you need help, I urge you to get it today!

Other reasons why I believe men will not protect their families sexually by raising the purity bar in their own lives is because (in their minds) they already have enough battles to fight. Secondly, they don't want to feel the wrath or rejection of a wife who may not share their more modest wardrobe convictions (as was the case in my first marriage). Thirdly, they have bought the cultural lie of free expression. Fourthly, they have already pushed this responsibility off on their wives. Fifthly, they are more interested in being their children's friend than their parent. Finally, they have believed the lie that a lukewarm Christ-compromising relationship with their son or daughter is better than a tough-love relationship centered on Christ's truth and love, regardless of the outcome.

A "bad" relationship with your son or daughter doesn't necessarily mean that you are a "bad" parent, dad, or mom. It may just mean that the child has chosen against you and God because of what you will allow and not allow in the home. I am in the throes of this right now with my adult son whom I love and miss dearly. While it is painful, compromising God's standards for the happiness of our children will always be "sin" (i.e., a form of idolatry). Our desire to see their spirit saved in the day of the Lord (1 Corinthians 5:5) should always be greater. In the meantime, I get to trust God, lean on Him, and stand on His promises! I trust some of you can relate. Be encouraged. God is not finished with any of us yet!

Husbands, if sexual purity is important to you but not important to your wife, or vice versa, my heart goes out to you. Your marriage is divided, and the devil has a foothold in it. There are countless Christian marriages like this. However, this is no time to take off the pack and fold up your tent. Get help from a mature Christian couple or counselor right away.

Children, like adults, will almost always take the path of least resistance where there's division. I know this factually and personally. Because sexual purity wasn't important to my parents, it wasn't important to me. In fact, "safe" promiscuity was encouraged by both of my parents. So what did I become? Promiscuous. That is until God finally got a hold of me in 1988 and began to show me that I was no longer a slave to my sexual desires and that women were God's valuable and precious gift to me to be esteemed and honored. Again, men, here's the bottom line: If you expect to be able to protect your family sexually, you have to have won this battle yourself first.

Something that I try to do when I'm not sure whether or not I am on the right side of a particular issue after considering what God's Word has to say on the subject is to default to whoever's position is more conservative. This means to try and lay my ego aside and agree to take whichever path provides the least chance for sin, danger, spiritual harm, or an opportunity for the devil to get a foothold into my life and family. Another way to say the same thing is that I try to choose the path that has the greatest likelihood of making God smile, closing the door on the enemy, and protecting myself and those I love.

As I observe the Christian landscape today, I am shocked at what Christian parents and church leaders allow teens and older congregants, respectively, to wear at church. No, I'm not a prude. I like stylish clothes as much as the next person, but modest, stylish clothes. I believe this is one of the quickest ways to determine the spiritual health of an individual and church—a barometer if you will. I can walk into a church I've never visited before, and with a glance at the way the youth and ladies dress, determine how serious the leadership of that church is about purity, secular infiltration, and protecting the flock.

God's Word says that we are known by our "fruit." Our dress reflects what's in our hearts. If I'm looking for a new church and the congregation is immodestly dressed, this one just got eliminated regardless of the worship and teaching. Again, lest I come across as a legalistic prude, I am not talking about the dress of those who have not yet professed the name of Jesus Christ as Lord and Savior and are seeking Him out just as they are. I'm talking about the dress of professing Christians, and more specifically, Christian teenagers and adult Christian women who have been "churched" for many years.

Parents aside for a moment, any church leader who will not address this issue head-on with parents, children, youth, or anyone else in their flock who profess the name of Christ, have abdicated their responsibility under an umbrella of "cheap grace." They have communicated that they either don't care about purity or are more concerned with offending their flock where money, status, power, and popularity are at stake than they are in offending God. Said another way, they are more concerned with building their own kingdoms (or preserving the one they already have) than they are in building God's kingdom. Yes, as you can see, I am very passionate about this issue given the degradation of our society due to the degradation of many of our churches that have become heavy on tolerance and light on holiness and righteousness.

I, too, was guilty of not always confronting immodest dress with my teenage girls in order to keep the peace. I know the battle well. After all, who wants to have to deal with another "issue" on Sunday morning when you're trying to get everyone up, fed, cleaned, dressed, out the door, and in the family car to arrive at church on time? Yet, the decision to take the easy way out is cowardly, weak, and harmful given what's at stake.

Gentlemen, what lengths will you go to protect your children sexually? Unfortunately, many Christian parents sadly and tragically take the position that "it's just not a big deal," which leads to the next generation thinking, *It's just not a big deal*, which leads to the next generation thinking, *It's no big deal*. And so on. And we wonder why we live in such a sexually saturated society and why we, the church, are as bound up in sexual sin as the rest of the world.

While there are many reasons, I believe one of them is because few parents are telling their kids "no" anymore when it comes to their dress. If we don't say "no" to their immodest dress today, statistics show they will say "yes" to someone other than their husband or wife with their bodies tomorrow. We see the results of sexual sin every day—porn addictions, teen pregnancies, abortion, STDs, adultery, divorce, rape, premarriage cohabitation, and intimacy-hijacked marriages from "ghosts" of the past. Still no big deal?

Men, we not only have a responsibility to teach our children about modesty to protect them against testosterone-driven boys (in the case of our daughters) and aggressive girls (in the case of our sons) but also to protect others from our testosterone-driven boys and aggressive girls! While the best intentions to protect your wife and family sexually are no guarantee they or you will not become another statistic in our sexually-saturated society, it is highly unlikely. However, if you don't make it a priority, it's all but guaranteed.

Many men also do not understand that it is their job to protect their wives and children spiritually. Men, is Bible reading, prayer, and spiritual growth a daily priority in your life? Do you build yourself up in your most holy of faith (Jude 1:20) in order to lead your family well and to see God's purpose and plan fulfilled in their lives? Again, no man can export what he has not first imported.

Guys, do you help your wife carve out time for herself to spend with God and other like-minded ladies? Have you ever offered to send her on a Christian women's retreat or prayer breakfast? Have you ever attended a Christian marriage retreat with her? Do you make devotions and prayer a daily priority for you to do together? Do you take an active role in ensuring that your family attends weekly worship services and that they are growing in their faith? Or do you leave this responsibility to your wife? Do you protect your wife and children from the schemes of the devil through prayer and fasting? Do you protect your children from violent or sexually explicit video games? Or are you just glad to have them out of the way for a few hours? If all this talk is just "noise" to you, Satan would like to thank you!

God expected Adam to protect Eve from the devil. Something tells me Eve also expected Adam to protect her from the devil once the devil began to dialogue with her about what God said. While we know how that turned out, did we learn anything from it, guys? Or was it just a good Bible story with a tragic ending for all humanity? How would your wife say you're doing at protecting her from the schemes and strategies of the devil? When was the last time you prayed a protective covering over her and asked God to cancel every assignment and strategy of the devil in her life so that no weapon formed against her would prosper (Isaiah 55:7)?

It should come as no surprise that many Christian wives do not feel spiritually protected by their husbands. But, hey, no big deal, right, mister? After all, you just celebrated another wedding anniversary. No, my friend, it's a huge deal if you've been married for twenty-five years, for example, and your wife has felt spiritually unprotected for the last twenty-four of them! It is a very big deal when Christian men can recite the lyrics of their favorite pop, country, rock, and even Contemporary Christian charts but have no idea what God's Word has to say about spiritual protection! It's a huge deal when Christian men know more about fantasy football, politics, power tools, guns, vacation spots, fishing, golf, company earnings, and their retirement portfolios than they know about the angelic conflict they and their families are in the middle of.

Husbands and fathers, you are the "spiritual gatekeepers" for what comes into your home ("garden"). Ladies, a husband or father who decides it's time to reel in or eliminate altogether certain video games, streamed content, cable TV, movies, is not to be "cursed," just because you don't agree with him or don't like his decisions; but it should be praised, especially in a day and age when home after home and marriage after marriage are being destroyed by sexual content, violence, and worldly influences that tell us life is all about us and our happiness and not about God and others. It is staggering to me the number of Christian women who want their husbands to protect them and the children but only if they protect them their way, showing a complete disregard and disrespect for their husband's position, authority, responsibility, and Judgment Day!

Men, while God is not looking for domineering autocrats in the home when it comes to what you will allow and not allow, you are to be commended for your desire to protect your family spiritually, even when your wife does not share your convictions. I know what I'm talking about. I lived it. Do not cave in to your wife's opposition if she does not share your convictions based on God's Word. Remember, God will come looking for you first, not her. And if you do cave, God—not your wife—just became your biggest problem! Trust me, blaming your wife on Judgment Day for the reason why you couldn't protect your family didn't work for Adam, and it won't work for us! Obey God and leave the consequences to Him.[10]

For those of you who live in "la-la land" and think Christian husbands and wives should be able to agree on these things out of their love for Christ, you're right. We should, but we don't because we live in a fallen, selfish world, which is why adherence to God's divine hierarchy in the family is of paramount importance if we expect to maintain order and fulfill God's purpose and plan for our lives (chapter 1).

While few men have difficulty understanding what an absence of physical protection means to their wives and families, I believe most men have no idea what a lack of spiritual protection means to them. In fact, most men I have found don't even understand what spiritual protection is. Yes, even in the church! If God's Word is true (and it is!), and the enemy prowls around our homes in the spiritual realm each day seeking whom he may devour (1 Peter 5:8), unimpeded, and we could somehow wear spiritual 3-D glasses to see the effects of our negligence, I believe many would see hunks of spiritual flesh missing from their wives and children.

We have been given legal authority in the name of Jesus Christ to bind the works of Satan in our homes, churches, cities, and nation; that is, to bind sin, iniquity, perversion, sickness, disease, infirmity, death, destruction, curses, witchcraft, sorcery, divination, poverty, lack, divorce, strife, lust, pride, rebellion, fear, torment, and confusion. The question is…are we doing it? It's quiet in this Pentecostal church.

The battleground for the devil is, has always been, and will forever be in the mind. When the spiritual leader of the family does not protect the mind and heart of his wife and children through prayer, intercession, and loving confrontation, family members are left vulnerable to various strongholds, "imaginations," and "high things" that exalt themselves above the knowledge of God (2 Corinthians 10:4–5). Can you imagine how different our homes, churches, cities, and nation would be if men began to take spiritual protection seriously?

Now, where were we? Oh yeah, Adam and Eve. Without Eve on the scene yet, it was also clear to Adam that God not only wanted him to be the protector of his family but also the *provider* for his family. But what family would Adam provide for as the only human inhabitant of the earth? While the family of God only consisted of God and him before Eve, I believe God was showing future generations of men, through the work assigned to Adam by God, that God expected men to work. God's Word says that he who does not work does not eat (2 Thessalonians 3:10).

No work, no provision. Thus, by fulfilling God's call for Him, the garden and animals not only got cared for and protected, but future generations of men learned that work was necessary to provide for their families and the family of God. Through Adam, God was showing us that it takes good providers (i.e., hard work) in this generation to advance God's kingdom in the next generation.

While things are drastically improving in this regard under the Trump administration, there is a work crisis in our nation today as the government continues to offer "handouts" to many who won't work because quite frankly, they don't have to. Incentives for healthy men to do what God created them to do have been eliminated in some cases, leaving men feeling depressed and confused about who they are and why God created them.

According to the United States Office of Management and Budget (OMB), the fiscal year 2015 became the first year that means-tested entitlement spending (i.e., welfare spending) exceeded national defense spending.[11] While some cases are legitimate, many are not, causing great spiritual, emotional, marital, and financial fallout to families, churches, government, the American taxpayer, and our nation!

The Bible says that he who does not provide for his family has denied the faith and is worse than an infidel (1 Timothy 5:8). Pretty serious, wouldn't you agree? Notice it doesn't say "she" who does not provide for "her" family; it says "he" who does not provide for "his" family.

Men, we are responsible for the financial provision in our families regardless of what the culture says or how much the government disincentivizes men who are otherwise physically able to work with government entitlements. While I believe this role as provider includes providing for our wives emotionally (as discussed similarly with "protection" above), physically (with our presence), sexually (by not denying one another sexually, except perhaps by agreement for a limited time that you may devote yourselves to prayer; 1 Corinthians 7:5 ESV), spiritually (as discussed similarly with "protection" above), and financially, I will continue to focus the remainder of our discussion on financial provision.

Men, here's the bottom line. Can you be counted on to meet the financial needs of your family according to your means and ability to see the kingdom of God advanced? Or do you place this burden unnecessarily on your wife? I know every situation is different. I'm not referring to a man who lost his job and needs his wife to help out while he seeks employment. Nor am I talking about the wife who must work to supplement her husband's income to meet the *basic* needs of the family or the wife who has decided to return to work now that their children are older. Nor am I referring to the family who, for whatever reason, does not have children or the children are no longer at home, and the wife desires to work.

I am referring to the lazy or irresponsible man who won't work or a man who purposely "jumps" from job to job when he doesn't like something about his current employer to the detriment of his family. I'm referring to a man who makes only half-hearted attempts to obtain employment or the man who abdicates his role as financial provider and forces his wife to work so he can "retire," be a "professional student," or be in "full-time ministry" with no income for the rest of his life. I'm also talking about a man who agrees to stay home with the kids because his wife makes more money than him or a man who is otherwise physically able to work but would rather rely on a government handout. Last but not least, I'm referring to the man who forces his wife to work for material gain above and beyond the basic needs of the family while other aspects of their home life, including their children and marriage, get neglected.

Any man who forces his wife into the *primary role* as provider is out of order. Not because she can't do it, but because that's not the role God gave her. I didn't say it, He did. It is better to have less with God's priorities than to have more without them. Mature believers understand this. Immature believers don't. Which are you? Do you still want to rule under God's hand His way (chapter 1)? Great, because this is His way!

Ladies, after God, your priorities, according to God's Word, are to be your husband, then your children, your home, and your work in that order. Your primary place of duty, occupation, and ministry is at home, even when you must work! Notice I said must work, not want to work. Add to these often-misplaced priorities the "modern-day husband" who also believes his wife should be at home but expects her to go there immediately after work! Then maybe, you and I will begin to understand why there's so much chaos in our homes! In other words, too many men are "forcing" their wives to work when they don't have to, and far too many women are choosing to work when it is unnecessary to the detriment of their homes.

This is the sin. And why? So we can keep up with the Joneses or project a particular image to others that make us feel "good" about ourselves. Really? Really. As the primary provider, it is every husband's job to free his wife up to be the wife and mother God has called her to be without placing an unnecessary burden on her to work unless it is needed to meet the *basic* needs of the family.

For those of you who do not agree with this and think it doesn't matter who the primary provider of the family is, you have just told God that you know better than He. Not a good idea. Whose word did you say gets to have the final word?

To further illustrate God's design for the family, have you ever noticed how deeply a job loss affects men compared to women? Ladies, it "rocks" our world and makes most men feel worthless. While we can say it shouldn't affect us because God defines us, not our jobs (correct!), God is with us (right again!), and God will provide (ditto); the truth is, it does affect us profoundly because God has "hardwired" men to be the providers for their families, and when we can't, we feel like we've failed you and God. While it is the rare exception, men have even tragically committed suicide (as we saw in the 2007–2008 financial crisis) when the only way out they saw for their families after losing their jobs was a "payout" on their life insurance policy. While it may have occurred, I'm not aware of one instance where the wife committed suicide for the same reason.

With respect to this issue of financial provision, I have already told each of my daughters (now ages twenty-two and twenty-six at the time of writing) that I will ask each man who seeks their hand in marriage one question among many others, which will be, "How do you intend to provide for my daughter and your future family?" I have already told my daughters that if I don't like his answer, they will not have my blessing to marry him, no matter what a "great guy" he is, how much they love him, or how much he loves God. Ladies, you are foolish if you marry a man who cannot or will not provide for you and the future needs of your family. If he says he can't now but will be able to later, wait. If he can't provide for you now, you have no business marrying him now! I trust God gave you a good mind—use it! There are a lot of irresponsible "boys" (not men) out there with good intentions and raging hormones that have no plan. Yes, even in the church. Beware, sisters!

Now that we've finished with the man's role in marriage from God's perspective, we will turn our attention to the ladies for a bit.

You're welcome, men! Surely you didn't think that I would forget about you, did you, ladies?

Remember when God created mankind, male and female, on the sixth day, He created them to rule over all the earth. Ladies, you don't stop ruling when you get married, but how you rule and where you rule does change. As your husband's "helpmate," you are called to use your gifts, talents, abilities, mind, and influence to "help" your husband rule everything in your collective garden under God's hand to advance His kingdom and bring glory to His name. How, you ask? By blending your calling with your husband's calling. Notice, I didn't say by getting your husband to blend his calling with your calling. Remember, Adam had his calling before Eve ever arrived!

Though wildly unpopular and more countercultural now than ever, the Bible says that God created the woman for the man (1 Corinthians 11:9), not the other way around. Not to give men license to be an authoritarian dictator in the home, but to highlight the fact that God created a wife to be her husband's "helper," not vice versa.

Again, Adam was "the man" with God's "orders" before Eve ever arrived on the scene. While husbands should serve their wives in the ways I have described above, the job title of "Helper" was given to wives in scripture, not to husbands. The female empowerment movement, formerly called the feminist movement, in the culture (and now in the church!) has profoundly influenced many Christian women today. These women not only demand to operate as the ordained leader at home, like Eve (though most would ever admit it!), but as the ordained "overseers" over men (e.g., pastors and elders) in the church in violation of scripture (1 Timothy 2:12–14; Titus 1:5–9; 1 Peter 5:1–4) while the male leadership of the church, like Adam, allow it! Truly remarkable, though not surprising, given the tactics and strategies of the enemy. Ladies, concerning the home, did you forget that Christ is the head of every man, the man is the head of a woman (i.e., his wife, not "all" women), and God is the head of Christ (1 Corinthians 11:3)?

Immature Christian women like the fact that everyone is under divine authority, except when it comes to her. While many Christian women understand the concept of divine order biblically, few Christian women model the concept practically. It doesn't work that way, ladies. Instead of wives helping their husbands rule their (collective) world by fulfilling the vision and purpose God gave *him* for the family (with her help!), many Christian wives expect their husbands to "help" them rule (their) worlds by fulfilling the vision and purpose God gave her for the family. Mature, biblical wives understand this is wrong and "help" their husbands in their roles. Immature wives don't understand this and reject it outright as they "buck" their husband's authority and invite chaos into their homes and churches.

Proverbs says that a virtuous and capable wife will not hinder her husband but *help* him all her life (Proverbs 31:12 NLT). Sadly, what we have in so many Christian homes today are wives who are not only *not* helping their husbands but hindering them from fulfilling the vision and purpose that God gave him for their family, church, and community. How, you ask? By using their husband and their marriage as vehicles to get what they want (i.e., the image and lifestyle they feel they deserve). Then, when it doesn't happen or deliver to them what they thought it should, they begin viewing him not as their partner in love and ministry but as an obstacle standing in front of what they want. Welcome to most homes in America!

In the same way that husbands are to love their wives like Christ loved the church (Ephesians 5:25), women are to respect and honor their husbands (Ephesians 5:33) whether he deserves it or not. Read that last part again, ladies, whether he deserves it or not. Yes, I know it is hard to respect a man who's not loving you the way you think he should, but that doesn't change the standard or God's expectation of you. Read that again, precious sister. While husbands earn the respect of their wives, God also commands wives to respect their husbands, whether he earns it or not, just as God commands men to love their wives whether their wives respect them or not.

It's incredible to me how many Christian wives do not understand this simple truth and make the demonstration of their respect contingent on their husband's display of love. We are guilty of the same thing, guys, when it comes to loving our wives. The day wives stop making their respect contingent on their husband's demonstration of love for them and the day husbands stop making their love contingent on their wife's respect for them is the day God heals our marriages, homes, and churches of all this self-centered garbage! And we wonder why God isn't answering our prayers. Aren't you glad God doesn't make His love for us contingent on how well we love and respect Him? Forgive us, oh God!

Ladies, God is calling you to use your gifts, talents, abilities, and influence to help your husband rule your collective "world" under God's hand for the expansion of God's kingdom and magnification of His glory, according to the blueprints God gave him. If you say, "I would help him, but he doesn't have any blueprints or plan." Then guess what? It's your job to *help* him find his plan from God through prayer, intercession, and discussion; and then *help* him develop it. Note, I didn't say help him find *your plan*. I said *help* him find his plan (from God) for your family, church, and community with your desperately needed input. Then, it's your job to *help* him execute that plan for the rest of your life!

The day you deviate from the plan God gave him (with your help) to your plan with his help is the day you invite chaos and disaster into your life and marriage—maybe not from the world's perspective, but from God's perspective, which, if you recall, is the only one that counts!

This is why a wife's prayer life is so powerfully important. Your husband needs your input! Not your nagging, your input. And if your husband foolishly won't take your input, pray that God would change his heart in a new direction. Not in your direction, though, God's direction. Maybe you're asking, "But how do I know if it's my direction or God's direction?"

Great question! You'll know it's your direction and not God's direction if you're the only one who benefits from the answered prayer. God's direction not only involves God's glory, God's purposes, and God's Word, but greater territory that goes beyond just you (chapter 1)!

Again, I can't overstress this point enough. While your husband should be modeling servant-leadership to you, God did not design him to be *your helper*. God created him to be your servant leader and you to be his *helper*. I firmly believe most, if not all, marriage problems would get fixed overnight if we would just stay in our God-ordained "lanes."

We've all played "Follow the Leader" as children before. Except according to the Bible, your husband is always the leader, and you're always the follower. Read that again, please. A wise husband may delegate leadership authority to his wife in a particular area because of a strength she may have, say in finances or home remodeling. Still, a *mature, godly woman* recognizes two things in situations like these. First, in God's divine order, her husband is still her spiritual leader, even though he has delegated leadership authority to her in this particular area. Secondly, God is pleased when she yields to her husband's headship.

Ladies, the only time you need not follow your husband is if he is leading you or your children in a direction away from God. That's your only "out." Said another way, if he's making decisions in the "flesh" that are contrary to the Word of God, you do not have to follow him. But if he's in his lane under Christ doing what God has called him to do (not perfectly, but faithfully) according to the Word, God expects you to follow him, even if he is not leading you in a way or in a direction you like or agree with. If you ignore this warning, your biggest problem just became God, not your husband! Did you hear me, precious sister?

Too many wives want to lead instead of follow because they either believe it is their right to lead or because their husbands don't (or won't) lead them in the way or direction they think they should. Not only do these wives expect their husbands to follow them against God's divine order (though they seldom see it this way) but then get angry with their husbands when their husbands don't follow them, declaring, "He's not loving me as Christ loves the church." Why, because he refuses to abdicate his role as the spiritual leader of the family to you? No, he's loving you precisely the way Christ loves the church by not forsaking his position under God to you, assuming he's not asking you to do something immoral or unbiblical.

Though many men are sadly and tragically "happy" to upset God's divine order by allowing their wives to usurp their authority under counterfeit labels of "service" and "sacrifice," this is entirely out of God's will as we saw with the first marriage between Adam and Eve. Recall what God said, "Adam, *because you listened to your wife*" (Genesis 3:17). That's right, ladies, sometimes it's good for your man to listen to you and do what you say, and sometimes it's not! It all depends on whose back you have first—yours or God's! There's the dividing line, men!

Many, if not all, men who allow their wives to operate as the spiritual leaders (or as "co-spiritual leaders," which is equally unbiblical) of their families (consciously or unconsciously) have bought in to the cultural lie, which has also permeated the church that says, "If Momma ain't happy, nobody's happy." I've heard many Christian men, including several pastors, say this to me over the years. What many don't realize is that at the core of this attitude is cowardly self-centeredness; that is, the husband's own happiness. In other words, many men think (I know because I did it myself!) that if I give her what she wants, even if have to become the follower instead of the leader, I'll "survive" this marriage, my life will be easier, and I can get what I want every once in a while. Sounds like a wonderful marriage made in heaven, doesn't it? Hardly!

Men, however, are not the only ones who have bought in to this self-centered lie and existence. For in many cases, it is being perpetrated by women who truly believe that it is their husband's primary responsibility to make them happy at all costs! In other words, if they are not happy, it is their husband's fault! This "at all costs" mindset is where the marriage is cooked on two fronts, whether divorce occurs or not.

First, while God calls a husband to love, nourish, and cherish his wife, he is not called nor designed to meet *all* of his wife's needs. Did you hear me, ladies? Only Christ can do this, which is why Christ must be at the center of your marriage! Secondly, the relationship is cooked because the husband and wife have declared, in essence, that his wife's happiness is more important than the husband's obedience to Christ. By way of example, what happens when the wife has an eating or prescription drug addiction and refuses to get help? What happens if she decides one day that she no longer believes in tithing or consistently and unrepentantly spends hundreds of dollars beyond your agreed-upon budget, resulting in massive, unsustainable credit card debt? What happens if she believes that both of you are the spiritual leaders of the family, and it's your responsibility to submit to her authority in areas of disagreement?

I'll tell you what happens. Nothing, if you're a cowardly husband who has forsaken your role as the spiritual leader of your family to survive or "keep the peace" and think the best way to serve your wife is by giving her what she wants. Incidentally, mister, did you ever stop to consider that God may want you to create the necessary crisis in your marriage that could result in the healing and restoration of your marriage as you both begin to operate by God's blueprints for marriage instead of your own? But immature women love this cowardly behavior from weak men who have forsaken their roles because they can continue to get what they want without having to bear the consequences of their "sin" that could make them holy.

Are you ready for an Ephesians 5:25 wake-up call, husbands? "Husbands love your wives as Christ loved the church and gave himself for her" does not mean that it is your responsibility to you give your wife whatever she wants whenever she wants it. A husband who truly loves his wife and wants to love her like Christ loved the church asks himself, "What does God have to say about what she wants?" Maybe what she wants is not good for her, you, your marriage, your family, your testimony, or the legacy you and she hope to leave to the next generation for Christ.

What would have happened to the Corinthian church if Paul had given them everything they wanted whenever they wanted it at the height of their rebellion and disobedience? Better yet, what would have happened to the human race if Adam had denied his beloved Eve what she wanted instead of giving in to it?

Did you know that even a "good thing" that your wife may want can become a "bad thing" when it becomes a "ruling thing?"[12] Read that again. The same is true of us, men. Guys, while your denial of a "good thing" in your wife's life may become a "bad thing" between you and your wife (because it became a "ruling thing" in her life and now she's unhappy with you), you answer to a higher authority.

You will not answer to her on Judgment Day, but Christ and she will not be standing with you. In light of this, sometimes the most loving words we can say to our spouses to ensure they have the best Judgment Day possible is "no." And while we're here, you should also know that if God can't overrule what's ruling us, it's probably because someone else is ruling us! Hello, it's quiet in this nondenominational megachurch.

Thus, if the truth be known, it is probably more accurate *not* to say, "If Momma ain't happy, nobody's happy," but say, "If Momma is always happy, God's probably unhappy." And guess who He is unhappy with? You, mister, because you have forsaken your role as the spiritual leader of your family by making your wife's happiness more important than her holiness[13] and God's calling on your life.

Some of you men can convince yourselves that you're the servant leader of your family all you want, but if you're the one who's following instead of leading, you, like Adam, have abdicated your role as the spiritual leader of your family. Real men reject passivity, accept responsibility, lead courageously, and live for God's rewards,[14] regardless of the consequences or whether others like it or not. Does this describe you, mister?

While we must never excuse the oppressive actions of authoritarian and dictatorial men, I have found that few women, not unlike men, really understand their God-ordained roles as outlined in the Bible to the detriment of their marriages, families, churches, and this nation. Far too many women (non-Christian and Christian), for example, want the financial and societal benefits of being married without the responsibility of operating under the authority marriage brings. Pretty self-centered, lady, considering the ultimate responsibility for the family falls on your husband and not you!

Most of the confusion and "pushback" from women that ushered in the feminist movement and now the female empowerment movement centers, as most of you know, around the hated word *submission*. While there are many books, teachings, and sermons available on the topic, one of the best explanations of *submission* I've ever heard may be found in the following explanatory note from the

New Living Translation on Ephesians 5 (*italics* and brackets [] used for emphasis):

> Submitting to another person is an often-misunderstood concept. It does not mean becoming a doormat. Christ, at whose name 'every knee will bow, in heaven and on earth and under the earth' submitted His will to the Father, and we honor Christ by following His example. When we submit to God, we become more willing to obey His command to submit to others, that is, to subordinate our rights to theirs. In a marriage relationship, both husband and wife are called to submit. For the wife, this means willingly following her husband's leadership in Christ. For the husband, it means putting aside His own interests in order to care for His wife. Submission is rarely a problem in homes where both partners have a strong relationship with Christ and where each is concerned for the happiness of the other.[15]
>
> Although some people have distorted Paul's teaching on submission by giving unlimited authority to husbands, *we cannot get around it.* Paul told wives to submit to their husbands. *The fact that a teaching is not popular is no reason to discard it.* According to the Bible, the man is the spiritual head of the family and His wife should acknowledge His leadership. But real spiritual leadership involves service. Just as Christ served the disciples, even to the point of washing their feet, so the husband is to serve His wife. A wise and Christ-honoring husband will not take advantage of His leadership role, and a wise and Christ-honoring wife will not try to undermine her husband's leadership. Either approach causes

disunity and friction in marriage (Ephesians 5:22–24).[16]

Paul devotes twice as many words to telling husbands to love their wives as to telling wives to submit to their husbands. How should a man love His wife? (1) He should be willing to sacrifice everything for her [unless it runs contrary to the Word of God], (2) make her well-being of primary importance [after God, and assuming that what she wants does not run contrary to the Word of God], and (3) care for her as He cares for His own body. No wife needs to fear submitting to a man who treats her in this way (Ephesians 5:25–30).[17]

Again, while wives are equal to their husbands in every way in the eyes of God (i.e., "joint-heirs" with Christ; Romans 8:17), they are functionally different. Functionally, wives are underneath their husbands' authority when it comes to their roles to maintain divine order and structure in the family and not invite chaos as stated earlier.

God created lines of authority in the home so that it will function smoothly (1 Corinthians 11:9–11).[18] Two people cannot lead in two different directions at the same time and expect to fulfill God's mission for them. It's why corporations, nonprofits, the government, the military, sports teams, the NFL, and yes, even the church have one person who is known as the commanding officer, head coach, commissioner, or senior pastor, respectively. It is also why so many churches are "messed-up." Instead of pastors leading after hearing from the "sheep," many pastors allow the "sheep" to "call the shots" to ensure that bills, salaries, missions, and building projects get fully-funded by a "happy" congregation. While wise leaders take input and feedback from their "sheep" before making significant decisions, leaders lead, and sheep follow as long as where their shepherd is leading them does not run contrary to the Word of God.

The same principle is true in a family. Ladies, when God changes the rules and holds wives responsible for being the "priest," protector, and provider for the family, then husbands who earnestly desire to please the Lord will gladly step aside and come under your authority. When God changes the rules to allow you to answer for your husband on His Judgment Day for why He abdicated His leadership role to you, then you can have His position. Until then, God expects you to yield to your husband's authority in *everything* (Ephesians 5:25) as long as what he is asking you to yield to is not immoral, unholy, illegal, unethical, or otherwise unbiblical.

Remember, that's your only out! He has to be out of his lane. If, for example, he is asking you to sign a joint tax return that you know contains false entries so you can get a larger refund or he wants you to watch some porn with him to spice up your sex life, then he's out of his lane. You need not submit to him or follow him in that particular area. The same is true if he, for example, no longer wants your family to go to church or tithe anymore. However, if he is in his lane under Christ, not perfectly, but characteristically, then God expects you to stay in your lane under him.

If you don't stay in your land under him, several devastating consequences will occur. I will cover two of them now and the rest later. Number one, in the spirit realm, you have tragically moved out from underneath your husband's spiritual covering and protection that God designed for you, as previously discussed. Two, you are now hindering, not helping, your husband fulfill God's vision and purpose for your family. If you are single and desire to be married one day and this is either "no big deal" to you or irritating to you, please do yourself, the man you would like to marry, the church, society, our nation, and most importantly God a favor and don't get married! If this upsets you, it is a clear indication that God's Word does not have the final word in your life. The exact opposite is true of kingdom men and kingdom women.

Biblical authority always comes with responsibility. Your husband is responsible to be your "priest," protector, and provider, not the other way around. Since this is the case, make his job a blessing, not a burden!

The holy women of old understood their place, and trusted God, accepting the authority of their husbands (1 Peter 3:5–6). Does this describe you, lady? Or have you bought into the cultural lie that times are different now? Is your husband's Judgment Day as important as yours? It is for the holy woman of old.

Note that the devil never came to Adam while Adam was by himself in the garden. Why? While the Bible doesn't say, I believe one of the reasons was because the odds of getting Adam to usurp God's authority was next to none, given the perfect closeness and intimacy God and Adam shared. In my "sanctified imagination," I believe the devil knew it would be easier to work on man through a woman than to go to Adam directly himself. It's an ingenious plan that Satan still uses in marriages today the moment men and women say, "I do."

We know, however, what mature Christian women would have done in Eve's situation because God's Word tells us. She would have displayed a gentle and quiet spirit (1 Peter 3:4) and engaged Adam as her spiritual leader. If he wasn't protecting her, she would have encouraged him to step up and take his rightful place. She would have listened to her husband and not eaten fruit from that tree nor entered into a conversation with the serpent in the first place. A godly woman would have hidden under the Lord's protection whether her husband was protecting her or not. She would have been silent and not taken matters into her own hands. So why didn't Eve? For the same reasons women today aren't doing it. Like Eve, they're focused on what they want instead of what God wants!

As tragic and frustrating as it is, ladies, when your husband will not exercise his God-given authority as the proper priest, protector, and provider for your family, it's never an excuse to usurp his authority and take matters into your own hands. Unless, as stated earlier, what he is asking you to do is wrong, illegal, unethical, immoral, or otherwise unbiblical. Besides being flat out wrong and sinful, the consequences of usurping his authority couldn't be any more severe as we saw with Adam and Eve.

I try to imagine what Eve might have been thinking while Adam was committing dereliction of duty offenses against her by not being her proper priest, protector, and provider. One possibility may have been, "Well, supreme leader, since you're not going to say something to the serpent, I will."

"Why aren't you protecting me, Adam? Do something."

"I want to be like God, Adam, so if you're not going to take the fruit and give some to me, then get out of my way. Do I have to do everything?"

"If you really loved me, Adam, you would do what the serpent is telling us to do."

Wow. Nothing like aiding and abetting the enemy!

"This is good for us, Adam; here I'll show you."

"Adam, I feel guilty. Here, now eat so that I won't be the only one feeling like this."

Any of these lines sound familiar, lady?

While some of you ladies couldn't picture yourselves saying some of these things, if any of them strike a chord with you, beware, you may be prone to usurping your husband's spiritual authority and therefore causing *The Great Role Reversal* (as I will hereafter refer to it) to occur, where you become the leader and your husband becomes the follower. If this sounds good to you, lady, you may already be in trouble as you're about to see!

You see, the devil has done a masterful job at blinding the eyes of many wives who have no trouble yielding or submitting to their bosses, pastors, the police, or the IRS, for example, but who refuse to submit to the authority of their husbands as God requires. In other words, they willingly play by the rules of authority in every other conceivable area of life, except when it comes to their marriages. While wives clearly know that things will not go well for them if they do not submit to their boss or the IRS, for example, they somehow believe they will be immune from any consequences for not yielding to the authority God has placed over them for their spiritual protection, provision, and guidance. In other words, while lines of authority exist outside of the home (and corresponding consequences for disregarding them), many wives believe they do not exist at home. Yes, even Christian wives. Easy day for Satan!

Maybe you're thinking, "Did God really say in this day of equality between men and women that wives are still to be 'underneath' the spiritual authority of their husbands?" Yes, precious sister, He did. Why? I told you earlier, but it's worth repeating so we never forget it! Besides, being the safest place for you to be because it is the place where God meets needs for provision, protection, and spiritual guidance (assuming your husband is doing what he is supposed to be doing!), it keeps things from "crashing" around us. God is a God of order and peace (1 Corinthians 14:33). Abiding by His divine order for the family is how we keep it.

Mature wives don't have to understand or agree with their husbands to submit to their authority; they just do it out of respect for the position God has given him and the responsibility he has to uphold it. More importantly, however, they do it out of their love for God so that the name of God will not be blasphemed (Titus 2:5). Does this describe you?

Ladies, your best weapon will always be prayer if your husband is not leading you (or the children) in the direction you feel is right or better. Again, this assumes he is not leading you (or your children) immorally, illegally, or away from God and His Word. If he is in his lane, I would encourage you to consider asking God for two things when you pray. Neither of which is easy. First, pray that God would help you to trust Him (God) more and your husband more so that you would stop usurping your husband's authority while you wait on God to change the heart of your husband. Secondly, that God would give you a supernatural grace (above that which you are able) to be content in all things (Philippians 4:11), even if God doesn't change the heart of your husband. This is the mark of a true kingdom woman!

If you have assumed your husband's role, I implore you to repent precious one! The devil finds few things more gratifying than when he can get a husband and wife to swap roles with one another. I will hereafter refer to this as *The Great Role Reversal*. Allow me to explain with this powerful helicopter illustration.

Many years ago, I used to fly the US Navy SH-2 Lamps Mk-I Seasprite helicopter. Its primary mission was anti-submarine warfare, which means that the Navy designed it to "hunt," detect, and destroy enemy submarines. The Seasprite, not unlike all navy helicopters, has two sets of identical flight controls next to each other in the cockpit. One set of controls is for the pilot, and the other set is for the copilot.

In the military aviation world, at least five things are inherently understood by a pilot and copilot before they ever step foot in the aircraft together. First, the mission is being directed by a higher authority, that is, the Commanding Officer (CO); secondly, the aircraft commander (pilot) is ultimately responsible for the mission and the safety of the crew and aircraft. Thirdly, he cannot transfer his authority and responsibility to the copilot. Fourthly, both pilot and copilot will be flying the same mission given to the pilot by the CO. Finally, only one person (pilot or copilot) will operate the flight controls at any given time.

Regarding this last point, there are strict protocols that pilot and copilot must follow each time control of the aircraft is transferred between them. This procedure is known as "positive three-way change-of-controls," or "change of controls" for short, and it is always initiated by the individual seeking to take control of the aircraft. Let's assume that the copilot is the one who is flying the helicopter, and the pilot is the one who is seeking to take control. To begin the change of controls, the pilot would say (over the internal communications system), "I have the controls."

This announcement tells the copilot that he or she is now free to "let go" of the controls because the pilot now has them. When the copilot relinquishes control to the pilot, the copilot will say, "Roger, you have the controls."

The pilot is then required to acknowledge that he heard the copilot, so there's no confusion on who is currently flying the aircraft. Thus, the pilot says, "Roger, I have the controls," reaffirming to the copilot that he (the pilot) is, in fact, the one who is now flying the aircraft. This protocol leaves no doubt in the pilot and copilot's mind who is flying the aircraft at any given time. In a typical mission, it is not uncommon for the pilot and copilot to change controls multiple times with one another.

It's critical to understand, however, that the chain-of-command never changes, regardless of who is flying the aircraft. In other words, the aircraft commander never ceases being the aircraft commander-in-charge of the crew, aircraft, and mission. If something goes wrong, regardless of who is flying the aircraft at the time, it is common knowledge by everyone onboard the aircraft that the pilot or aircraft commander is ultimately responsible and will, therefore, be the one the CO will come looking for once on the ground.

Now, imagine what would happen if the copilot decided, mid-flight, that he or she wanted to be the aircraft commander (i.e., commit *The Great Role Reversal)* and fly a different mission than the one that was given to the aircraft commander (pilot) by the CO? How well do you think the aircraft commander and CO would receive that? If the aircraft commander (pilot) allowed it, do you think the CO would have the aircraft commander's "back" when it came time to recommend him for a promotion? What if there was an aircraft incident and the aircraft mishap board investigation revealed that the mishap was caused by "pilot error?" Specifically, the "black-box" or Flight Data Recorder retrieved from the incident revealed that the copilot was fighting the aircraft commander for control of the aircraft. Do you think the CO would have the copilot's back if she and the entire crew were fortunate enough to walk away from the incident? What are the odds the pilot would fly with her again?

You see, friend, when you and I became Christians, we got a new set of "orders" (i.e., mission) from the Commanding Officer of the fleet, Jesus Christ Himself, who calls all the shots from His Word. Jesus delegates His authority to carry out His mission to each "aircraft commander" (husband) and then expects the aircraft commander (husband) to brief his copilot (wife) on his mission and then, with her help, pass on his mission to the rest of the crew (children) for execution. Thus, it is every husband's primary responsibility not only to see that Christ's mission is received and accepted but that he executes it safely and correctly within the boundaries and limitations of God's Word.

To this end, a well-trained copilot (godly wife) knows before she ever steps foot in the aircraft (i.e., says "I do") that she is operating under the authority and direction of her aircraft commander (her husband). She also understands that her aircraft commander (her husband) is operating under the authority and direction of the CO (Jesus Christ). At least this is the way it's supposed to work. She also knows that no aircraft commander worth his "salt" will ever fly with (i.e., marry) a copilot who doesn't understand this. Furthermore, all good aircraft commanders (husbands) and copilots (wives) know that they will be subject to discipline by the CO (Jesus) if they do not abide by His "chain-of-command." The same is true if they fly any mission other than the one given to the aircraft commander by the CO.

Additionally, every good aircraft commander (husband) relies on his copilot (wife) to be an integral part of every aspect of the mission, which may include flying, responding to in-flight emergencies, employing tactics, activating weapon systems, navigating, communicating, and monitoring the weather, altimeter, and duty runways.

Unlike real flying, however, the copilot (wife), according to God's Word, never "graduates" to become the aircraft commander though she may be smarter, more capable, or an even better "stick" (pilot) than her husband. Why? Because that is not the role God gave her as stated at the beginning of the chapter.

Tragically, when it comes to men, what we have in so many marriages and families today are husbands and fathers who never report for duty or who prefer to fly solo without any input or feedback from their copilots (wives); or men who haven't the faintest idea what it means to be an "aircraft commander" or even what their mission is (chapter 1). Because many men don't know who they are or what God's mission is for them and their family, if they do report for duty, they end up flying a mission that was never given to them by God or never leaving the ground because they don't know where God wants them to go. Now, add to this mess the number of husbands who *do* understand that they are supposed to be the aircraft commanders of their family but who won't accept God's mission or properly execute it within the boundaries of His Word, and you and I will begin to understand (not excuse) why so many families are an absolute mess and why so many wives feel empowered and burdened to be the aircraft commanders of their families.

Then, there are those wives who, from the moment they step foot in the cockpit, have no intention of supporting any other mission but theirs, regardless of God's chain-of-command or what the CO says. In the Navy, she would be grounded and possibly never fly again. She would be subject to discipline, perhaps demoted, or even dishonorably discharged. Why? Because she is now more of a liability and safety hazard to the Navy than an asset.

The number of Christian marriages operating in one of the scenarios I just described above is staggering, all because the pilot or copilot either do not understand their roles and responsibilities or refuse to operate in accordance with them.

The devil knows that two people who attempt to fly the same "aircraft" in two different directions will not only not complete God's mission for the family but will eventually "crash." Ladies, I know this can be very difficult. However, when you refuse to yield to your husband's authority on something that he feels strongly about (assuming it isn't contrary to God's Word) because you think it's "silly," "wrong," or unreasonable, it is not only disrespectful and disobedient but *dangerous*. In the spirit, you are fighting with him for control of the aircraft, which will not only lead to an inevitable "crash" at some point in time in the future, whether divorce occurs or not, but get you permanently "grounded" by God until you can be trusted to assume your proper role! This has nothing to do with losing your salvation but everything to do with severe consequences to make you holy. In fact, God may tell your husband to not "fly" with you anymore until you can be trusted to maintain good order and discipline in the cockpit by submitting to his authority since he will ultimately be held accountable by Jesus for the success or failure of the flight. Love him and his Judgment Day enough to yield to what he, not you, will have to answer for on that day by being the best copilot you can be.

No family can accomplish the mission handed down to them by God when the pilot (husband) and copilot (wife) are constantly fighting for control of the aircraft. However, we can accomplish Satan's mission. It's partly why so many fathers are missing-in-action, why 50 percent of all the marriages inside and outside of the church end in divorce, and why the vast majority of remaining marriages are not advancing God's kingdom and bringing Him glory (chapter 1)!

So the next time you see the bumper sticker that reads "God is my copilot," now you ladies can say, "No, He's not. I'm the copilot, and my husband is the pilot, and I'm going to trust that where God is leading my husband is where God wants us to go. Meanwhile, I'm going to do everything I can to help him get there. And if I think my husband is going in a different direction than where I believe God wants us to go (assuming he is not "flying" outside of the parameters of God's Word), I may inquire and make a suggestion. However, I'm not going to take control of the aircraft without permission. I will, however, be praying that God gives him a new flight plan! In the meantime, I'm going to be the best copilot I can be!" Now that's a wife who understands her role!

With the proper foundation now laid regarding the roles and responsibilities of husbands and wives from God's perspective, which is the only perspective that counts, I am finally ready to turn toward the heart of this chapter. Yes, I know, that was quite the introduction!

Up to this point in time, I have only discussed consequences in the physical realm when we commit *The Great Role Reversal* with one another. We will now move to what happens in the spirit realm, which is where the real damage occurs! For this, we must go back to the Garden of Eden.

Where was Adam was when the devil came to Eve? Where was Adam when the devil was filling Eve's mind with lies and deception? Where was Adam when his beloved Eve responded to the devil? Where was Adam when Eve reached for the apple? Where was Adam when she placed her hand around it? Where was Adam when she moved it toward her mouth? Where was Adam when she took her first bite. We know. He was right next to her (Genesis 3:6)—silent. Adam, who had been God's man of power for the hour up to this point in time, had nothing to say, like many men today. But this is just the beginning of the story. For as Adam remained silent as Eve's God-ordained priest, protector, and provider, Satan, as stated earlier, moved in for the "kill" to get Eve to become the leader and Adam to become the follower.

When this *Great Role Reversal* took place between Adam and Eve in the Garden of Eden, a Great Exchange took place in the spirit realm. We discussed it, if you recall, in chapter 1. Adam and Eve not only relinquished rulership of the earth over to Satan after God gave it to them, but they relinquished rulership of their world over to the devil and got a new leader—him! In the spirit realm, they shifted kingdoms! They moved out from underneath God's spiritual covering and authority where Satan had no power over them and unknowingly placed themselves under Satan's spiritual covering and authority where Satan had all power over them! Game over.

Tragically, however, this scheme didn't end with Adam and Eve. It's been playing out in homes worldwide ever since. Every time husbands and wives allow Satan to orchestrate *The Great Role Reversal* with them successfully, we, like Adam and Eve, get a new leader, lose our ability to rule our world under God's hand, and begin advancing Satan's kingdom! Now imagine what a different world it would be if we, the bride of Christ, were as committed about staying in our lanes (i.e., assuming our proper roles) as Satan is about getting us out of them?

Did you just hear loud screeching in the spirit world? I did. Satan is furious that you now understand this! I told you we were in the middle of an angelic conflict, didn't I (chapter 1)?

While I know this has been incredibly difficult for some of you to read, believe, and accept, you must know the whole truth. Ready? It only takes one of you to switch roles for *The Great Role Reversal* to occur, giving the enemy immediate and unfettered access to your home and family until the spouse that is out of their lane gets back in their lane! Why? Because when you got married, you became "one." Therefore, when one of you is out of order, your marital unit is out of order." You are now a house "divided" against itself, which *will* fall (Mark 3:25), whether divorce occurs or not. Why? Because every day a marriage is divided is a day we allow the devil to rule it and run it however he pleases. I know. You should have seen my face when God first revealed this to me!

Now you know how the devil has been destroying countless Christian homes without ever firing a shot! If this describes your home, it's time for you to "sound the alarm!" You, your spouse, or both of you may have invited "hell" to take over your family! The good news is that God can immediately reverse this when the spouse who is out of their lane gets back in their lane! In every healed marriage I've ever known (not just those that escaped divorce court), this is what happened! One or both spouses got back in their lanes! Conversely, the opposite was true when one or both spouses refused to get back in their lane(s) whether divorce occurred or not. Don't let this happen to you. If you and your mate are "out of order," I urge you to get back in your lane(s) today! If you need help, don't wait a day longer! Every day you wait is another day the devil is running the show in your marriage and another day God is your biggest problem!

Each of us must understand that the reason Satan takes over when we commit *The Great Role Reversal* with God and one another is because Jesus will not co-lead with anyone, especially Satan! We saw that in heaven before Satan fell, remember? Jesus knows that no man can serve two masters: for either he will hate the one and love the other; or else he will hold to the one, and despise the other (Matthew 6:24). You see, there's no such thing as a "leaderless" saint or a leaderless marriage. So if Jesus is not the leader of our marital units because one or both of us are out of our lanes, then guess who is? I know!

I sense some of you are still not convinced that *The Great Role Reversal* applies to a marriage when only one of you is out of your lane. Okay. Answer this. If only one of you lets a "little fox" into your marital garden, is there a little fox in *your* marital garden? You bet. Maybe you said, "Yes, but I'll have a talk with my spouse."

Okay, great, but what if your spouse says, "I don't know what you're talking about, honey."

Is the little fox still in your garden? You better believe it! In the meantime, while your spouse refuses to acknowledge the "little fox" in your garden, do you think it will be a "nice little fox" and not destroy your garden? Great, now, after thirty-plus years of being married to someone who refuses to join you in the fight against the "little foxes" in your marital garden and home, what do you think your garden is going to look like after thirty-plus years? How effective do you think you will have been *as a couple* at "ruling your world" under God's hand to advance God's kingdom and bring Him glory in a home that Satan has divided for thirty-plus years? How effective do you think you will have been as a couple at reclaiming territory from the devil in the earth before Jesus's return (chapter 1)? How often do you think your marriage will have made God smile while it was in a perpetual state of chaos and disorder because you as a couple refused to deal with the "little foxes" in your garden? How many people will you and your spouse lead to Christ and disciple *as a team* while the "little foxes" are wreaking havoc in your home? How close and intimate do you think you'll want to be with your spouse who is allowing the "little foxes" to destroy your home? I trust I have painfully and necessarily made my point.

Please understand, my goal is not to hurt or discourage anyone but to show us the seriousness of our "sin" so we will be motivated to lovingly, prayerfully, and courageously get back in our lanes so we can rule well (chapter 1). Pain is God's gift to us to tell us something is wrong! Please don't ignore it.

Thus, since so many of us, like Adam and Eve, turn our worlds over to the devil, it begs the following question starting with us men. Remember, God always begins with the men. Why do so many husbands abdicate their responsibility to be the spiritual leaders of their families and allow their wives to usurp their authority leading to *The Great Role Reversal*? I believe there are several reasons for this—ignorance, immaturity, selfishness, rebellion, fear, and because some men have what is known as the Spirit of Ahab. You may want to fasten your seat belt before we begin!

The first reason why husbands forsake their role as the spiritual leader, allowing their wives to usurp their authority, causing *The Great Role Reversal* to occur and "hell" to take over their home is out of ignorance. Sadly, many men don't have the slightest idea what it means to be a spiritual leader, which is one of the main reasons why I spent significant time on it earlier in the chapter. Now you do. Many men, like me, grew up without a spiritual compass that only a Christ-following father can provide. The devil knows this. The world gives men a good "grade" if they are good providers, pay their taxes, coach something, do some occasional volunteer work, don't drink or do drugs excessively, and don't beat or cheat on their wives.

However, the world places little to no emphasis on a husband's need to provide spiritual leadership, protection, and guidance. Thus, a husband who doesn't know that he is supposed to be the spiritual leader of his family, won't be. This, tragically, not only leaves his wife and children spiritually unprotected, but it makes the marriage a prime target for Satan to successfully orchestrate *The Great Role Reversal*.

The second reason why husbands forsake their role as spiritual leaders and allow their wives to usurp their authority, causing *The Great Role Reversal* to occur and "hell" to take over their home is because they are immature. If the godliest man in the world has further to go in his walk with God than he's already gone (and he does!), where does that leave spiritually immature husbands and their families where "the man" refuses to mature? You guessed it—vulnerable as a prime target for *The Great Role Reversal*.

The third reason why husbands forsake their role as spiritual leader, allowing their wives to usurp their authority, causing *The Great Role Reversal* to occur and "hell" to take over their home is because they are selfish. Very simply, they don't want the job. It requires too much time that could be better spent serving themselves. It also requires them to come under God's authority, which they know could stand in the way of what they want. Being the spiritual leader of the family requires husbands to be God-centered and other-centered. The self-centered husband has no time for this "nonsense" since it gets in the way of his real interest—himself!

The fourth reason why husbands forsake their role as spiritual leader and allow their wives to usurp their authority, causing *The Great Role Reversal* to occur and "hell" to take over their home is because they are rebellious. All of us are rebels to the core. Yes, beloved, even you. I know. That's why we need Jesus. Unlike the husband above who is ignorant of his spiritual leadership responsibilities, the rebellious husband knows what they are but refuses to do them. In the case of the rebellious husband, it's more than just selfishness; it is outright defiance! Maybe he's angry at God, the church, his wife and children, or for some other reason, but it is not because he doesn't know what he is supposed to do or what God expects of him. The devil loves this one! Men, hear me, you and I have not reached biblical manhood until God can tell us what to do![19]

The fifth reason why husbands abdicate their responsibility as spiritual leaders, allowing their wives to usurp their authority, causing *The Great Role Reversal* to occur and "hell" to take over their home is because of fear. Very simply, men fear their wives' rejection more than they fear God's rejection—a form of idolatry. This is a "biggie" in the church and even for many pastors! For many cowardly men, it is easier not to lead than to lead and risk their wife's disapproval for the way they are leading. While many wives are desperate for their husbands to lead them, some husbands instinctively know that their wives are even more desperate to lead them their way!

For the fearful or cowardly man, it is just easier to do nothing (in the name of "love" that's not love) than to face rejection from the one he fears can make his life a "living hell." Who knows? But this may have been the reason why Adam folded. It's not like he had many other options! Immature women know this about men and use it to control and manipulate them into getting what they want or use it as a way to punish men who become obstacles in the way of what they want. Mature women, on the other hand, know this about men and use it as a "vehicle" to encourage their husbands to be kingdom men!

For a more in-depth discussion on this topic of man's greatest fear, the fear of rejection, I would encourage you to pick up my first book, *Do You Want to Get Well?* I spent a whole chapter on this. It's a must-read if you desire to have healthy Christ-centered relationships, regardless of marital status.

The last reason why men abdicate their responsibility as the spiritual leaders of their family and allow their wives to usurp their authority, causing *The Great Role Reversal* to occur and "hell" to take over their home is because they have the Spirit of Ahab. This is the most serious scenario.

The Spirit of Ahab gets its name from King Ahab, son of Omri, who reigned over the Northern kingdom of Israel for twenty-two years (1 Kings 16:29). It was Ahab who did evil in the sight of the Lord more than all who were before him (1 Kings 16:30 ESV). In violation of God's Word, King Ahab intermarried with a pagan woman named Jezebel, daughter of Ethbaal, king of the Sidonians, and went off and served Baal and worshipped him. This activity set off a chain reaction of further disobedience to God's Word and passivity that plunged the whole nation of Israel into sin. For a more detailed account of the life of King Ahab, see 1 Kings 16–22.

While the Ahab spirit can infect women, it is more predominant in men and more common than we realize or would like to admit. For this chapter, I will limit my discussion to men. In twenty-seven years as a Christian, I have no recollection of hearing one sermon taught on the Spirit of Ahab from the pulpit. Not surprising, however, since it's not exactly "feel-good ear-tickling" sermon material. While Paul says we are not ignorant of the devil's devices (2 Corinthians. 2:11), I believe most of the church is totally unaware of this device…and the devil would love to keep it this way to bring more and more homes, churches, and nations under its "curse." It is time to expose it for what it is—pure unadulterated evil.

So what exactly is the Spirit of Ahab? The Spirit of Ahab is a demonic "spirit" that trivializes the things of God. While many men with the Spirit of Ahab go to church and fellowship with other believers, they genuinely have little interest in spiritual matters. Like the self-centered husband we discussed above, Ahab views spiritual growth as a distraction, obstacle, or hindrance to self-gratification. As long as "the Ahab" can have his porn collection, for example, or other pleasures of the world, he is content. His wife can do whatever she pleases.

The typical Ahab wants his wife to go to church and get involved so he can "play." "Ahabs" are happy to give their leadership position in the home to their wives to pursue their self-centered interests, which often come at great peril to their families. Hollywood has even picked up on him. Have you noticed how many husbands and fathers today are portrayed as weak, lazy, "clueless," "in the way," irrelevant, or without vision or purpose? Some of you think this is funny. Trust me when I say that Satan is the only one laughing!

Ahabs willingly give spiritual authority to their wives to remain passive or to "keep the peace." Even when she "acts out," he will not confront her out of fear. We see an example of Ahab's passivity in 1 Kings 19:1–2 when Ahab would not restrain his wife, Jezebel, from sending a death threat to Elijah who had just killed all the prophets of Baal on Mt. Carmel. Instead of confronting her, Ahab arose, ran for his life, and asked God to kill him. Some man of God he was!

The Spirit of Ahab in a man is generally seen as a vacillating spirit that transfers more and more spiritual authority and responsibility to his wife until he becomes weaker and weaker.

The Ahab seeks the destruction of God-ordained authority, roles, and family responsibilities. Emptying the garbage can, for example, is the only responsibility he wants. He not only does not want to lead, but he criticizes those who do. He is not a man of strength and would rather hide who God has created him to be than exercise his God-given authority.

We see an example of this in 1 Kings 22 when King Ahab and Jehoshaphat, King of Judah, go into battle together against the King of Syria to take the land of Ramoth-Gilead from Syria. When have you ever known a battle commander to be "out of uniform" on the day of the battle? Never. The warrior's uniform, with rank and insignia prominently displayed for all to see, tells his men and the enemy who he is and who's in charge. King Ahab not only abandoned his men, his "post," and didn't wear his uniform, but he asked his "buddy," King Jehoshaphat, to wear his (Ahab's) uniform so the enemy would think Jehoshaphat was him. And it worked like a charm. Though Jehoshaphat cried out and the Syrian army eventually retreated, it nonetheless highlights what great self-centered and cowardly lengths an Ahab will go to in order to avoid being the man God has called him to be.

Not only will a husband with the Spirit of Ahab not be the proper priest and protector of his household, but he will not be the proper provider for his family either. If there's not enough money to meet the basic needs of the family, it's not his problem.

A man with the Spirit of Ahab lives for worldly peace at all costs and will gladly sacrifice future good for it, even when it results in unholy alliances. We saw this in Ahab's decision to marry Queen Jezebel, as discussed above. Ahab married Jezebel to satisfy his flesh "today" rather than wait and trust God for a godly wife who would help him lead the Israelites into a better tomorrow.

Parenting for "the Ahab" is often relegated to playing or "gaming" with the children but not correcting them. He would rather be out with the "boys."

An Ahab generally doubts his abilities and, unsurprisingly, holds marriage in low-esteem. Men with the Spirit of Ahab are unable to cope with their wife's problems and, therefore, "tune them out."

Ahabs are classic workaholics to avoid confrontation and responsibilities at home. Their goals are simple—wealth, success, status, greed, and self-gratification at all costs.

The Ahab is usually an insecure individual subject to withdrawal and low self-esteem. Ahab loves the human body, which makes him prone to things like pornography addictions. He also loves sports and will go to great lengths to see them "live" or on TV in excess if he can't participate in them to escape his leadership responsibilities.

The Ahab is not physically weak as Ahab himself was a warrior, but the Ahab is emotionally and spiritually weak as described. Men with the spirit of Ahab enjoy a good temper tantrum, sulking, and childish things (1 Kings 20:43, 21:1–15). He may even call his wife "Mama" or "Mom."

Before leaving the Ahab, while it is not quite the same, I do believe when it comes to parenting and raising children that a father and mother can exhibit Ahab-like qualities together. From birth, nobody has to teach us to seek our self-centered interests. Parents and others have to teach us to share, take turns, serve, sacrifice for the benefit of others, esteem others higher than ourselves (Philippians 2:3), and to exercise self-control when it comes to things we want or things that might be harmful or unsafe for us.

Ahab parents in stark contrast, however, could care less about such spiritual mumbo-jumbo. After all, Ahab parents are not in charge; the kids are, and everyone knows it, but it's okay because everyone's happy, right? Ahab parents, like King Ahab, are weak, passive, and "peacekeepers" at all costs. Having happy children today outweighs whatever negative consequences they may have to experience tomorrow. Since Ahab parents allow their children to usurp Mom and Dad's authority, virtually anything goes (e.g., disrespect, sexually-suggestive dress, promiscuity, "partying," violent video games, sexting, and even a little Internet porn for the boys). Instead of the family's priorities being God, family, and the church, the priorities of Ahab parents are themselves. If God is fortunate enough to be in the picture at all, he is usually at the bottom of the barrel, near the marriage.

And we wonder why so many youths today have little, if any, respect for authority and walk around "trash-talking" their parents and teachers with their pants halfway down their backsides, cleavage exposed, and eyes buried into their smartphones. Ahab parents, however, are "all good" with this because the more entertainment outlets and electronic devices their kids have, the less they have to parent, and the more they are able to pursue their own self-centered interests.

Lest you hear what I'm not saying, I'm not talking about parents who allow their children to utilize electronics safely or who need a short break from the often-chaotic life of raising children. I'm talking about parents who allow their kids to spend several hours a day, several days a week, using these things because parenting interferes with their pursuit of self-gratification.

Ahab parents are not raising their children. Smartphones, social media, YouTube, video games, and Hollywood are raising them. But, again, it's "all good" because everyone's happy, right?

I can hear some of you saying, "Wait a minute, I'm not an Ahab parent. But my spouse is. They give the kids, not Christ, center stage of our family, and as a result allow them to dictate what our priorities will be. My spouse gives them whatever they want while our marriage continues to suffer. What do I do in this case?"

The same thing you do when he is out of his lane for any reason. Speak the truth in love with him (Ephesians 4:15) about what you need, then give it some time. Husbands should do the same with wives who allow their children to take center stage. If things don't improve, seek help from a trusted Christian counselor as a couple or by yourself if your spouse refuses. Get a healthy support system of people around you who will take God's side, not yours.

No action is no option if you want to keep the devil from taking over your family! As long as the Ahab Spirit is allowed to exist, the devil has unfettered access to your family. Don't become another one of his casualties even if speaking the truth in love causes things to get worse. The devil wants to destroy you. Let God and His Word fight for you, and you will keep your peace (Exodus 14:14), regardless of what happens to your marriage.

The problem with Ahab-parents in this chapter on *The Great Role Reversal* is that Ahab parents allow their children to usurp God's ordained spiritual authority structure for the family. A mom who lets her children's happiness to set the priorities for the family, for example, places herself and the children above God's appointed spiritual leader of the family, her husband, committing *The Great Role Reversal* against God, her husband, and her children. A dad who allows the children's happiness to set the priorities for the family abdicates his responsibility and does the same thing.

The Spirit of Ahab is one of the most serious problems facing not only our marriages and families but also our churches. I have personally observed pastors and church leaders form unholy alliances with Christian men and women in their congregations who refuse to leave lifestyles of systemic, unrepentant, sexual sin. I'm not talking about a member of the flock who has sinned, confessed, and repented of the "sin." I'm talking about church leaders who embrace or ignore those in their congregations who willfully and unrepentantly continue in lifestyles of sin. I'm talking about church leaders who knowingly leave their "sheep" stuck in their "sin" because they are afraid to lovingly confront them out of fear of the impact it might have on church tithing, attendance, and the "unity" of the church. I'm talking about church leaders who leave their "sheep" unprotected because they are not willing to deal with the "wolves" in sheep's clothing that are seated in the pews of the church who give handsomely every week. It's the spirit of Ahab.

I believe one of the greatest weakness among church leaders today comes from the spirit of Ahab. We have even given it a cute title—*Overwhelming Grace*. In the name of "grace," I have personally observed church leaders turn a blind eye to persistent and unrepentant false teaching, idolatry, criminal conduct, promiscuity, and adultery. For those of you who know me, if I should ever find myself in a similar situation, please don't "love" me like this. Find me and love me enough to confront me with truth and love so that I would repent. And if I refuse, love me enough to "boot" me out of the church and hand me over to Satan for the destruction of my flesh so that my spirit may be saved on the day of the Lord (1 Corinthians 5:5). Yes, beloved, that's biblical love and biblical discipline!

To the Ahab in church leadership, false peace with the unrepentant that allows for the advancement (or preservation) of their kingdom today is more important than the pursuit of righteousness and justice that will allow for the advancement of God's kingdom tomorrow. Does this describe your church? If so, it is operating under the Spirit of Ahab. If I were you and this was my church, I'd be looking for another church! For those of you who feel "stuck," remember, our first loyalty should always be to Jesus Christ and the truth of His Word, then to a church family that worships God *in spirit and truth* (John 4:24).

We can also see the Spirit of Ahab alive and active on the world stage. We saw it under the Obama Administration when it came to our foreign policy practices with countries like Saudi Arabia and Iran, for example. In the case of Saudi Arabia, we would rather be friendly with a nation that sponsors terrorism to keep the oil flowing today (especially while they remain our number one purchaser of military arms![20]) than to "take our medicine" to reduce our dependence on foreign oil tomorrow. In the case of Iran, we would rather give the most active state sponsor of global terrorism the agreement they want today for "improved diplomatic relations" that has "no teeth" to prevent them from obtaining a nuclear weapon than reject such an agreement today for improved odds of a nuclear weapons-free Iran tomorrow. Thank God the current administration "gets it."

Similar unholy alliances have also existed between the US and Russia and China. I think you get the idea. In all of these cases, what the Ahab fails to see or just simply dismisses out of hand is that it is impossible to have peace with someone who is trying to you kill you or conquer you. I wish more of our liberal elected officials understood this simple reality. Though some of you may say that this is no place to be airing political opinion, I say it is precisely the place as this last point captures the essence of who the Ahab is. It is someone who will form an unholy alliance with anyone to get what they want *today*, even when they know the consequences could be devastating *tomorrow*.

Incidentally, do you remember what happened to the people of Israel who formed unholy alliances with foreigners from the east who practiced magic and communicated with evil spirits as the Philistines did? God rejected them (Isaiah 2:6)! He did the same thing with Adam and Eve when they formed an "unholy alliance" with Satan. He drove them out of the garden (Genesis 3:24), remember?

Our discussion on why husbands forsake their role as the spiritual leader of their families and allow their wives to usurp their authority, causing *The Great Role Reversal* to occur and "hell" to take over their home is almost complete. The critical point to remember is this—regardless of why we men do it, the result is always the same. We're no longer under God's spiritual covering and protection, and we get a new leader!

Now it's your turn, ladies. The reasons why wives usurp their husband's spiritual authority, causing *The Great Role Reversal* to occur are very similar to those we've already discussed with men, as you might expect.

The first reason why wives usurp their husband's authority, causing *The Great Role Reversal* to occur and "hell" to take over their homes is because they are spiritually ignorant. God says that His people perish for lack of knowledge (Hosea 4:6). In other words, many Christian women usurp their husband's authority because they don't understand God's hierarchy for the family, as previously discussed. They don't understand that Christ is the head of the husband, the husband is the head of a woman (his wife), and God is the head of Christ (1 Corinthians 11:3). Because these wives do not understand their God-given roles from scripture, they are equally ignorant of the consequences of not following them (i.e., *The Great Role Reversal*). Easy day for the devil!

Other Christian women believe their husband is the spiritual leader of the family and willingly give him that "title" but are spiritually ignorant (or spiritually blind) to the fact that his title comes with responsibility *and* authority. Crazy, right? Another scheme of the enemy. What leader doesn't have responsibility *and* authority? These women lack knowledge of the scriptures we discussed earlier (1 Corinthians 11:3; Titus 2:5; and 1 Peter 3:5–6). In other words, while immature Christian women are happy to give their husbands the title of "spiritual leader," many of them have no intention of yielding to it in practice (i.e., following him), especially where disagreements or conflicts exist. Mature Christian women, on the other hand, honor their husband's role as the spiritual leader in title *and* practice, even where disagreements and conflicts exist.

Then there are those wives who, because they lack scriptural knowledge and understanding, believe that they *share* the role of spiritual leader with their husbands with no one having higher spiritual authority than the other. Satan loves this one. It's very slick! It's now in churches. It's called the husband-wife pastoral team. In other words, some wives believe, for example, that their husbands have the "final say" during disagreements when it comes to the family's finances, but not when it comes to the children. Have you ever heard the devil whisper something like this to you, lady? "Did God really say your husband has authority over you in *every* area of life?"

Yes, He did (Ephesians 5:25)! Because he is responsible for *your* protection, provision, and guidance. You're not responsible for his, remember? Responsibility always comes with authority. Just ask the CEO of any major corporation or the President of the United States for that matter.

Then there are those wives who use the term "spiritual leader" when referring to their husbands but have a distorted, inaccurate, or incomplete view of its true meaning from scripture. Another form of spiritual blindness. This was my last wife. Because these ladies do not understand what the term "spiritual leader" means, they decide when and where their husbands will be permitted to exercise their authority. I call this "wildcard submission" because you never know when it's going show up, causing the marriage to become a breeding ground for *The Great Role Reversal* to occur with all of the uncertainty, insecurity, chaos, disorder, and evil that accompanies it.

The second reason why women usurp their husband's authority, causing *The Great Role Reversal* to occur and "hell" to take over their homes is because they are immature. While everything I said above applies to immature woman as well, immaturity can also manifest itself in other ways. For example, immature women (like men) may lack the discipline, motivation, or desire to acquire and apply biblical knowledge and are thus prone to seek ungodly counsel from others. For example, someone else's interpretation of the facts is all some women need to justify their actions, especially when this person tells them what they want to hear. Even where some immature women do apply scripture, it is often wrongly used to achieve their immature objective(s).

Immature women do not hunger and thirst after righteousness. They are content to remain like little children who get "tossed to and fro by the waves and carried about by every wind of doctrine, by human cunning, by craftiness in deceitful schemes" (Ephesians 4:14 ESV). Because of this, immature wives are, therefore, prone to "dialogue" with the devil, like Eve was, which eventually leads to usurping their husband's authority without thinking twice about it, especially if they do not like how or where their husband is leading them.

The third reason why women usurp their husbands' authority, causing *The Great Role Reversal* to occur and "hell" to take over their homes, is out of frustration or desperation. This is a "biggie" in churches today for women. Ask any pastor. One of the biggest complaints Christian wives have about their husbands is that their husbands will not be the spiritual leader of their homes.

I'll never forget it. I was leading a discussion on spiritual leadership at a church who was using my first book, *Do You Want to Get Well?*, in their marriage ministry small group. One of the wives of an older couple who had been married for over twenty years said, "Jim, I know I am supposed to follow my husband's lead, but how do you follow a parked car?"

Ouch! Between nervous laughter and an embarrassed and disrespected husband, I attempted to answer the question so many Christian women are asking.

First and foremost, ladies, remember, it was God, not your husband, who declared him (your husband) to be the spiritual leader of your family, whether he wants to be or not. The moment you disregard God's divine order for the family is the moment in time that God opposes you (James 4:6). Did you hear me? God just became your biggest problem! I said your biggest problem, no matter what happens from this point on in your life, just became the Creator of the universe, the One who will judge the quick and the dead (you and me) when Christ returns (2 Timothy 4:1). And the moment that God opposes you is also the same moment that Satan becomes your master. Why? I said it earlier. Because no man can serve two masters, for you will love the one and hate the other, or else you will hold to the one and despise the other (Matthew 6:24). To oppose God is to say "yes" to Satan. Don't ever forget this!

So many women get duped by the devil into thinking they have to "lead" when their husbands won't. Says who? You are his helper, right? When was the last time you offered to help him become the leader God called him to be out of your obedience to Christ and love and respect for Him?

"Fine, Jim, but what am I supposed to do if my husband won't lead after I've offered to help him?" the lady asked.

Great question. "Does God really expect me to follow a parked car?" Another great question. If this is you, I know this must be extremely difficult, and you're right, it's a big problem, but this is no time to throw in the towel or to take matters into your own hands by usurping your husband's authority as Eve did. Pray and have an honest discussion with your mate and get others involved for support, if needed. If this terrifies you, or you don't know how to begin, again, get a copy of my first book, *Do You Want to Get Well?* It will greatly assist you in knowing what to do and how to do it. After you tell him that you are committed to him, love him, and desire to follow him, tell him what you need.

"But what if he still won't 'step up' after I give it some time?"

Come back to the table, admit you're "stuck," and get some help from another mature couple, church leader, or counselor. But do not assume his role as spiritual leader in the interim. If you do, you provide little incentive for him to change, cause God to oppose you (more importantly), and invite the devil to take over your life, marriage, and home. If your husband refuses to address the issue or refuses to allow others to get involved, you are now dealing with a much more serious problem—rebellion. Get help and support for yourself, pray, and begin to ask God and others, according to His Word, what your next step is.

There's a big difference between someone who cannot lead (due to a health limitation) and someone who will not lead (rebellion). If your husband is truly a "will not," this is no time to minimize, rationalize, or usurp his authority. He will never become what God has called him to be as long as you keep rescuing him, nagging him, or trying to fill his shoes. Don't do it, precious one! Help him to help himself, but don't nag or belittle him. Again, the only time you do not need to follow him is when his action or inaction causes health, legal, ethical, or safety issues for you, your children, others, or him. If you're going to "hang your hat" on any of these, however, make sure there is indeed a biblical basis for your departure from his position versus something he's doing that you just don't like. If there is truly a *biblical* basis for your departure from his position, then act, but do so from a supported position with others who can offer up prayer, biblical wisdom, confirmation, accountability, encouragement, and support along the way.

Wives who usurp their husband's authority out of frustration are not hard to find. Wives who will trust God and submit to their husband's authority in all things out of their love for Christ (barring the above exceptions) *are* hard to find. Which one are you, lady?

Men, if you want to bless your wife today, go to her and say, "Baby, I want to lead you well, and know it's my responsibility, but I don't know how. However, I am committed to learning how and getting help. Will you please be patient with me and help me as I begin the process of becoming the man God called me to be? Will you please forgive me for not being the spiritual leader of our family?"

Wow, after your wife, let me be the first to congratulate you on that bold, yet humble and courageous step. Now follow through and get someone to walk with you and hold you accountable. How about that, ladies?

Women also usurp their husband's spiritual authority out of frustration or desperation, causing *The Great Role Reversal* to occur and "hell" to take over their home because they do not like how he is leading. I touched on this earlier. In this case, he is not guilty of being a "parked car," he is guilty of driving in a direction or in a way that she doesn't like, agree with, or understand. As I've said, while Christian wives do not have to follow a husband who is asking them to do something evil, wrong, abusive, or unholy, they are required to follow them, even when their husbands are going in a different direction than they prefer. Husbands, while a mature and godly wife will seek to follow you, even if she doesn't agree with you or like your approach (as long as you are not asking her to do something unbiblical), a good leader will listen to his wife, strongly consider her viewpoint, and treat her with tenderness.

If you do this, the odds are good (though still no guarantee) you will have the humbling privilege of watching your wife blossom under your leadership. If you don't, however, odds are equally good you will have the sad misfortune of watching her wilt under what feels like controlling authoritarian leadership. Make it a blessing for her to follow you.

However, ladies, even if he isn't making it a blessing for you to follow him and you don't agree with the direction he is taking you and the family or agree with his methodology, you are still called to honor and respect his position as spiritual leader and yield to him, just as you would a boss you didn't like as long as where your husband is taking you is not wrong, abusive, unholy, or otherwise unbiblical. Again, that's your only out! I can't emphasize this enough! So few Christian women sadly understand this to the detriment of their homes, and more importantly, the advancement of God's kingdom. Note the scriptural support for this in the following passage (*italics* and brackets [] used for emphasis):

> You who are slaves must accept the authority of your masters. *Do whatever they tell you* [unless what they are asking you to do is immoral, unholy, illegal, unethical, or unbiblical]—*not*

114

only if they are kind and reasonable, but even if they are harsh. For God is pleased with you when, for the sake of your conscience, you patiently endure unfair treatment. Of course, you get no credit for being patient if you are beaten for doing wrong. *But if you suffer for doing right* and are patient beneath the blows, God is pleased with you. This suffering is all part of what God has called you to. Christ, who suffered for you, is your example. *Follow in His steps.* He never sinned, and He never deceived anyone. He did not retaliate when He was insulted. When He suffered, He did not threaten to get even. He left His case in the hands of God, who always judges fairly. He personally carried away our sins in His own body on the cross so we can be dead to sin and live for what is right. You have been healed by His wounds! Once you were wandering like lost sheep. But now you have turned to your Shepherd, the Guardian of your souls.

In the same way, you wives must accept the authority of your husbands, even those who refuse to accept the Good News. Your godly lives will speak to them better than any words. They will be won over by watching your pure, godly behavior. (1 Peter 2:18–3;1–2 NLT)

Lest you hear what I am not saying, I am in no way suggesting that a wife should tolerate a husband who is being physically or verbally abusive to her as some slave owners were of that day to their slaves. This is never acceptable. The purpose of highlighting this scripture is to simply communicate that from God's perspective, even when husbands are not kind and reasonable, God expects wives to stay in their lanes and honor His position as "head." Notice that God not only expects wives to do this with their Christian husbands but also with their non-Christian husbands! Do you get the impression that God takes maintaining divine order in the family seriously? You bet He does! Ladies, make it easy for your husband to love you and obey God by respecting his position, even when you don't agree with him or like his approach. Yes, I know this is incredibly difficult, but it doesn't change God's standard and expectation of you.

The fourth reason why women usurp their husband's authority, causing *The Great Role Reversal* to occur and "hell" to take over their homes is out of fear. Very simply, some wives fear what their husbands might do if they submit to their authority. Instead of seeing this as a beautiful way to imitate her husband's submission to Christ and Christ's submission to the Father, these women allow their fear to keep them from becoming a willing participant in helping their husband fulfill God's vision and purpose for their family. Instead of trusting, obeying, and honoring God by following their husbands in whatever direction God is calling him (as long as it isn't away from God), many wives allow their fears (orchestrated by the devil) to "call the shots." Satan convinces them it will be much safer in they are in control. In other words, "following" is way too risky. This can be in many areas of the marriage or just one. Satan could care less. All he needs is one to successfully orchestrate *The Great Role* Reversal, *neutralize* you as a couple, and get you to follow him.

Fear is a powerful motivator. If maintaining power and control by usurping her husband's authority is what a wife needs to do to deal with her fear in a particular area, this is what she'll do. Even though some of these Christian women know what the Bible has to say about fear, they allow their fear to conquer their faith.

Note the last sentence in the passage of scripture from 1 Peter we looked at (in part) earlier (*italics* used for emphasis):

> You should clothe yourself instead with the beauty that comes from within, the unfading beauty of a gentle and quiet spirit, which is so precious to God. That is how the holy women of old made themselves beautiful. They trusted God and accepted the authority of their husbands. For instance, Sarah obeyed her husband, Abraham,

when she called Him her master. *You are her daughters when you do what is right without fear of what your husband might do.* (1 Peter 3:4–6)

Now ask yourself this. Is the woman who does *not* do what is right because she is afraid of what her husband might do a *daughter* also? No. A true daughter of the King does what is right without fear of what her husband will do because she knows God has her back if she does! Her desire to please her Lord by being obedient to His Word trumps any fear she has of what her husband might do.

The fifth reason why women usurp their husband's authority, causing *The Great Role Reversal* to occur and "hell" to take over their home, is because they are self-centered, prideful, or rebellious. The origin of this "sin" may be seen following the "curse" God spoke to Eve in the garden after Adam and Eve fell (*italics* used for emphasis):

> I will sharpen the pain of your pregnancy,
> and in pain you will give birth. *And you will desire*
> *to control your husband,* but He will rule over you.
> (Genesis 3:16 NLT, EXB)

It is incredible to me how many times I've read Genesis 3 over the years and never picked up on this. Nothing has changed since the days of Adam and Eve. Women, as a consequence of the fall, are hardwired to control their husbands! That's right, ladies. The desire to control your husband is a "curse" handed down to you as a consequence of the fall! Don't ever forget this! Only Jesus can help you break this chain. And if you don't, it's a breeding ground for *The Great Role Reversal* to occur!

The self-centered, prideful, or rebellious woman will take a "backseat" to no one because, in her mind, she's the more capable leader. Whether this is fact or fiction is irrelevant to God or Satan. In her heart, she declares, not unlike Eve, "I want his position," "I deserve his position," "I'm entitled to his position," or "I'm more qualified for his position." The self-centered, prideful, or rebellious wife knows, in most cases, that she is supposed to be underneath the authority of her husband but will often refuse to do it and not think twice about it. Even when she is "sitting down" outwardly (i.e., has the appearance of yielding to her husband), she is "standing up" inwardly (i.e., not submitting to him in her heart).

The selfish, prideful, and rebellious wife, not unlike a similar husband, is not interested in anyone else's version of truth (including God's) but her own to get what she wants. It could be as simple as the image she wants (or demands) to project to others. Think about Eve for a second. Had she been more interested in building God's kingdom than in building her kingdom, which is really Satan's kingdom, she would never have usurped Adam's authority. The devil played right in to her pride, proving that pride did, literally, come before "the fall" (Proverbs 16:18).

The final reason why wives usurp their husband's spiritual authority, causing *The Great Role Reversal* to occur and "hell" to take over their home, is because they have the Jezebel spirit. Still have your seat belt on, right? While this spirit can also work through men, including pastors, we will focus on how it operates through women. Like the Ahab spirit, this is the most serious scenario.

The Jezebel spirit is a spirit born of witchcraft and rebellion. It is a "man-hater" that seeks to emasculate all men (i.e., deprive them of their effectiveness, spirit, or force) and divest them of their authority and power over others.[21] Jezebel is first seen in scripture as the rebellious and manipulative wife of King Ahab. She is a picture of female dominance and witchcraft. The Jezebel Spirit is a controlling, manipulative, and "bossy" spirit. It was the spirit of Jezebel that caused ten million Hebrews (all but ~7,000) to bow down in idol worship to Baal, break their covenants with God, tear down God's altars, and kill all of God's prophets (1 Kings 19:14).

The Jezebel spirit inhabits women who are embittered by men either by misuse of authority or neglect.[22] The spirit of Jezebel generally attaches itself to women who, through their insecurity or vanity, seek to dominate others.[23] Here's what one author had to say about the Spirit of Jezebel (*italics* added for emphasis):

[The] Jezebel [Spirit] is fiercely independent and intensely ambitious for pre-eminence and control. The name Jezebel literally means, "without co-habitation." This means that she refuses to "live with" or "co-habit" with anyone. Jezebel will not dwell with anyone unless she can control and dominate the relationship. When she seems submissive or slave-like, it is only for the sake of gaining some strategic advantage. From her heart, she yields to no one. *The Spirit of Jezebel enters the family situation whenever God's divine order of authority is either not known or ignored. It causes women to forsake the protection and place given to them in God's Word.*[24]

Did you catch it? The Jezebel spirit enters the family whenever God's divine order of authority is unknown or ignored! Said another way, it enters the family where God's "chain of command" is disregarded. Homes and churches are full of men and women today who either do not know or reject God's divine order for the family and church, creating a breeding ground for the Jezebel spirit to flourish!

As long as the Jezebel spirit gets its way at home, everything is fine; however, when it doesn't, a series of determined maneuvers begin that are calculated to get what she wants. She has no desire to cheerfully submit, and her all-out campaign to get what she wants eventually provokes the one she dwells with to anger.[25] Check this out:

Rather than believing that God will give her husband wisdom to lead the family, she sets out to accomplish things in her own deceptive ways. Her husband begins a silent, but furious retreat to get involved in anything. Her proud looks, sharp tongue, emotional outbursts and bedroom blackmail results in a silent retreat to sports, newspaper, hobbies, alcohol, or anything

He can find appreciation and satisfaction in. If He attends church, He seldom does more than sit back, fearful of the sharp and critical tongue of His wife. She speaks out for the family in spiritual matters and He becomes more silent. The Jezebel Spirit does not always assume a brash, bossy, and aggressive stance, openly overbearing or dominant. There is a more subtle manifestation. The woman is outwardly sweet and unassuming, a picture of demure helplessness and feminine flutterings. Feigned sickness or injury is another convenient way of dodging responsibility and gaining sympathy at the same time. Actually, there is a mauled fist of fiercest determination and rebellion under that velvet glove.[26]

Pretty evil, huh? The Jezebel spirit is in more homes and churches than most of us realize or would like to admit. In fact, many of you reading this have never heard of the Jezebel spirit, and again, the devil would have loved to keep it that way. Our ignorance is his bliss! None of us can overcome something that we're spiritually blind to, right? Satan knows that's right!

I have personally witnessed the Jezebel Spirit. It is demonic to the core. These women not only seek to wear the pants in the relationship but the shirt, socks, and every other article of clothing. What the feminist movement was born out of and sought to overcome (passive and abusive men) has given rise to a new kind of American Christian woman who calls all the shots and will, inwardly, come under the authority of no man. This is the Jezebel spirit. It has a form of godliness, which is why it is so deceptive, but it is an enemy of the cross of Jesus Christ because it feeds on power, control, and manipulation.

There's good news and bad news for anyone married to someone with the Jezebel spirit. The good news is that I've exposed it. The bad news is that it is a very fierce spirit. The only hope for a godly man married to a woman with the Jezebel spirit is deliverance and healing through the power of the Holy Spirit because Jezebel hates repentance, humility, and intercessory prayer. Without deliverance, godly men will be unable to dwell with this spirit because Jezebel will not allow it. Holy men will either have to develop an "Ahab spirit" and yield to Jezebel to survive as Ahab did (i.e., allow *The Great Role Reversal* to occur) or separate from it if they expect to rule their world as God intended (chapter 1).

Jesus also recognized this when He was addressing the church of Thyatira. He not only issued a stern rebuke to the church who was tolerating Jezebel but showed us how to treat her and those who commit spiritual adultery with her where there's no repentance as seen here in the following:

> Nevertheless, I have a few things against you, because you allow that woman Jezebel, who calls herself a prophetess, to teach and seduce my servants to commit sexual immorality and eat things sacrificed to idols. And I gave her time to repent of her sexual immorality, and she did not repent. Indeed, I will cast her into a sickbed, and those who commit adultery with her into great tribulation, unless they repent of their deeds. (Revelation 2:20–22 NKJV)

The principle we are to take from this passage regarding Jezebel is simple. Jesus does not want us to tolerate the spirit of Jezebel. If Jesus held the church of Thyatira accountable for tolerating Jezebel, He will hold us accountable for tolerating Jezebel. Jesus expects us to separate ourselves from the spirit of Jezebel if Jezebel will not repent. And why? So she will no longer be able to wield her power and demonic influence over us. In this way, we can get back to kingdom business unhindered.

Regardless of how it occurred, remember what you're left with after Satan orchestrates *The Great Role Reversal* as we saw with Adam and Eve—a marriage that God opposes and that Satan is leading until everyone gets back in their lanes!

It is my firm belief that a marriage that God opposes and that is doing the work of the devil is far worse than a marriage that ends in biblical divorce (chapter 3) after every effort at restoration has been made. No, I'm not advocating divorce. I'm advocating for Christ-centered marriages that advance God's kingdom and bring Him glory, not marriages that advance Satan's kingdom and bring him glory (chapter 1)!

Years ago, I used to live in military base housing onboard Naval Air Station Pensacola (NAS Pensacola) in Pensacola, Florida, which is home to the world-famous Blue Angels Flight Demonstration Team, founded in 1946. Affectionately known as "the Blues," they are the second oldest formal flying aerobatic team (under the same name) in the world after the French Patrouille de France formed in 1931.[27] I was a lieutenant (O-3) at the time teaching "ground school" to Navy, Marine Corps, and Coast Guard flight students, which included introductory courses in aerodynamics and meteorology.

This, however, was not my first assignment in Pensacola. I had been a flight student there about four years earlier. Thus, I had become quite accustomed to seeing "the Blues" zoom by in their F/A-18 Hornets and hearing the unmistakable sound of those twin General Electric F-404 turbofan engines. To this day, few things stir me as deeply as the sight and sound of the Blues.

I had the pleasure of witnessing the Blues in action, however, even before flight school. I was incredibly blessed to have them commence graduation ceremonies for my class at the US Naval Academy with a precision "flyby" in perfect Delta formation (all six planes) above the Navy-Marine Corps Memorial Stadium in Annapolis, Maryland.

While learning to land a helicopter at night on the flight deck of a pitching and rolling frigate or destroyer requires a certain skill set, it doesn't compare to the skill set needed to "fly the ball" (i.e., maintain the proper angle of attack during descent for landing) and "hit the wire" (i.e., "grab" a cable stretched tightly across the flight deck with the tailhook on the aircraft) at night at approximately 160 mph. Though many of my fellow helicopter buddies ("bubbas") might jokingly disagree (and do!), and others be unwilling to "face the music," flying jets require a far superior skill set because everything happens much more quickly! Margins of error are smaller and less forgiving, and jets, with a few notable exceptions (e.g., V-22 Osprey, AV-8B Harrier, and the F-35B Lightning II), do not have the luxury of reducing their groundspeed to zero (i.e., pulling into a hover) before landing. However, this aside, what is unique about navy flight training is that every Navy, Marine Corps, and Coast Guard pilot goes through the same primary flight training syllabus (known as "Primary") as every Blue Angel pilot did on their way to becoming a "Blue."

During Primary, every navy student pilot is required to fly a series of precision aerobatic flights and then a series of formation flights after their first solo. This inescapable, stressful, and thrilling opportunity allows each student pilot to get a "taste" of what it's like to fly in formation with other aircraft before they do it in the "Fleet." The squadron I was assigned to was known as the "Lamplighters." Did God have my number or what? While the fundamentals of flying in formation in the T-34C Mentor during Primary, or in a helicopter, are the same fundamentals employed by the Blue Angels, employing them at 120 knots or less with one or two other aircraft requiring small course corrections is very different than employing them at airspeeds of up to 400 knots with five other aircraft doing aerobatics! The Blues are truly amazing! If you've never seen them at a live air show, I highly recommend putting it on your "bucket list" today!

Even after all these years, whenever I see the Blues, I am immediately flooded with feelings of patriotism and gratitude to those who fought (and fight) to secure the liberties and freedoms I enjoy and so often take for granted. Regardless of what is going on in my life, when I witness the Blues' astonishing display of power, command presence, expert precision, unrivaled self-control, unparalleled unity, and unwavering commitment to excellence, I know that God is still large and in charge of my life and world events. Simply put, whenever I witness the Blues' jaw-dropping beauty, elegance, and grace, "It Is Well with My Soul!"[28]

Spontaneous reactions I have had to the Blues over the years (as "corny" as this may sound) have included salutes, shouts of "yes," silent prayers, singing of the National Anthem, or just standing at attention as my eyes filled with tears. Regardless of my reaction, one dominating thought always flooded my mind, then and now: *This is the way it's supposed to be.*

While some of you may not be able to relate to how deeply the Blues affect me, others of you know exactly what I'm talking about. It's how you feel after seeing a well-executed play in the NFL or NBA or how you feel after taking that first bite of your favorite entrée at your favorite restaurant. Or it's how you feel when you drive a well-engineered automobile. Or it's how you feel when you listen to your favorite songs, play eighteen holes on your favorite golf course, or when some of you ladies get your hair done at your favorite salon or find the perfect outfit with the perfect pair of shoes to match! Have you ever said to yourself, "Now, this is the way it's supposed to be!"? Okay, now you know what I'm talking about!

While this should come as no surprise, Blue Angel pilots are among the Navy and Marine Corps' finest pilots who get nominated and selected from among the best jet pilots in the aircraft carrier community. Said another way, the Blue Angels are, in the military aviation world, what Seal Team Six is in the "Spec Ops" world—the very best of the best! Yes, I'm admittedly a bit biased! Go Navy, beat Air Force!

During my research, I came across what is commonly known to every Blue Angel as the "Blue Angel Creed," written by J01 Cathy Konn between 1991 and 1993, which is spoken over every new "Blue." It goes as follows (*italics* used for emphasis):

> Today is a very special and memorable day in your military career that will remain with you throughout your lifetime. You have survived the ultimate test of your peers and have proven to be completely deserving to wear the crest of the US Navy Blue Angels. *The prestige of wearing the Blue Angels uniform carries with it an extraordinary honor—one that reflects not only on you as an individual, but on your teammates and the entire*

squadron. To the crowds at the air shows and to the public at hospitals and schools nationwide, *you are a symbol of the Navy and Marine Corps' finest. You bring pride, hope, and a promise for tomorrow's Navy and Marine Corps in the smiles and handshakes of today's youth.* Remember today as the today you became a Blue Angel; look around at your teammates and commit this special bond to memory. "Once a Blue Angel, always a Blue Angel," rings true for all those who wear the crest of the US Navy Blue Angels. Welcome to the team.[29]

As stated in the Blue Angel Creed, every Blue Angel understands that their actions (or inaction) not only affect them individually but also affect every member of the team. Each Blue, like a professional athlete, also understands that their reputation is always on display for the world to see whether they want it to be or not. Furthermore, they know that one serious lapse of judgment cannot only affect them and the other Blues for the rest of their lives but how the public perceives the Blues for the rest of their lives. The Blues thus take their jobs seriously both on and off the field because they know they represent something much greater than themselves to present and future generations.

During their air shows, it is commonly understood that the Blues "own" the airfield and the airspace where they happen to be operating. All six demonstration aircraft may be seen together during taxi, takeoff and, of course, when flying together in formation. The Blues fly two different formations, the famous Diamond Formation, consisting of four planes (Blue Angel Nos. 1 through 4), and the stunning Delta Formation, consisting of all six demonstration aircraft. I will primarily focus on the Delta Formation (hereafter referred to as "the Delta") during my remaining discussion.

Though each of the six Blue Angel demonstration pilots in the Delta is equally valuable, each member has their own function. For those of you who go bowling or who may be familiar with the numbering system of the ten pins when "in formation," when the Blue Angels are in the Delta, they are numerically positioned the same way as the first six bowling pins on the bowling alley. The only exception is that Blue Angel Nos. 4 (pin #4) and 5 (pin #5) switch positions in the formation. Thus, Blue Angel Nos. 1, 3, and 5 fly the left side of the Delta and Blue Angel Nos. 1, 2, and 6 fly the right side of the Delta with Blue Angel No. 4 in-between Blue Angel No. 5 and Blue Angel No. 6. Got it?

Blue Angel No. 1 (bowling pin #1 in formation) is the Commanding Officer (CO) or Flight Leader of the Blues. To the rest of the team, however, he is affectionately known as the "Boss." Not surprisingly, he's the most senior member of the team responsible for the overall leadership, training, safety, and guidance of the team. To be considered for the position of "Boss," pilots must have a minimum of 3,000 tactical jet flight hours and must have been the former CO of a tactical jet squadron.

As the senior member of the Blues, the boss "calls all the shots," directly or indirectly, through delegated authority to the other Blues on the team. Like a caller singing out the steps at a square dance, the boss methodically tells the other pilots in the Delta everything he is about to do just before he does it. Then, on the next radio call, he and Blue Angel Nos. 2 through 6 simultaneously execute his instructions.[30] When he speaks, they follow him. Why? Because they know his voice.

As the Flight Leader, the boss is ultimately responsible for not only leading the other Blues but protecting them against things like excessive fatigue, bad weather, and other flight hazards.

The Boss is usually a Navy Commander (0–5), but it is not uncommon for him to "make" Captain (0–6) while on assignment. While he may be the one "in-charge" in formation, it is common knowledge by every member of the Blues that he operates under the authority of a "bigger boss," known as the Chief of Naval Operations (CNO). The CNO, in turn, operates under the authority of the "biggest boss," the Commander in Chief or President of the United States. In other words, everyone knows that everyone on the team is under authority.

Said another way, the boss is under the CNO, Blue Angel Nos. 2 through 6 are under the boss, and the CNO is under the commander-in-chief. Thus, the job of every boss is to follow the CNO while the job of every Blue is to follow the boss. Said another way, while Blue Angel No.1 (hereafter referred to as "#1") is in charge and ultimately responsible for every aspect of the Blues, he knows he is operating under a higher authority at all times. This higher authority determines is based upon how well the boss fulfills his duties and responsibilities, whether the boss will complete his tour of assignment or be relieved of duty "for cause." Thus, the boss understands that while he has great freedom, his freedom comes with great responsibility that is restricted to, and governed by, the provisions and guidelines of the CNO.

In addition to these requirements, the boss also understands that he and his Blues are bound by the limitations of the Naval Air Training and Operating Procedures Standardization (NATOPS) manual for the F/A-18 Hornet. In fact, the cover of every NATOPS manual says that it is issued "*by authority of the Chief of Naval Operations* and under the direction of the Commander Naval Air Systems Command."

The NATOPS manual, which exists for all Naval aircraft, is affectionately referred to as the pilot's "bible." Seriously, I'm not kidding! It's also common knowledge by every naval aviator that every NATOPS manual was written in "blood" from the lessons learned of those who lost their lives so others wouldn't have to. It sounds like the Holy Bible and our Jesus, doesn't it? While some of the sections of NATOPS vary depending upon the type of aircraft and its respective mission, two standard sections found in every NATOPS manual are the *Operating Limitations* and *Emergency Procedures*. In the *Operating Limitations* section of NATOPS, engine, airspeed, weight, and angle of attack limitations are discussed, among many other limitations, as well as all prohibited maneuvers for that aircraft type.

The "Emergency Procedures" section of NATOPS, as one might expect, lists step-by-step procedures to employ during every conceivable ground or in-flight emergency encountered by that aircraft type. The correct application of emergency procedures requires every pilot to have an in-depth knowledge of every system in their aircraft, including, but not limited to, the power plant, fuel, flight performance, electrical, lighting, oxygen, hydraulic, flight control, avionics, and landing gear systems. The consequences of not operating within the boundaries and limitations of NATOPS can be fatal. Said another way, operating outside of NATOPS can result in damage to the aircraft, serious bodily injury, or even death.

To meet the minimum flight qualifications, every Navy, Marine Corps, and Coast Guard pilot must "pass" a NATOPS "check ride" with a grade of "Conditionally Qualified" every year. In other words, they have to continually demonstrate that they can safely and effectively operate their aircraft within the boundaries and limitations of their "bible."

Thus, every Blue Angel understands that they are only under the authority of their "Boss" and "Big Boss" (the CNO), but also their "bible" (NATOPS). While the Blues have great freedom, each Blue understands that their freedom is limited to the boundaries set forth by their Boss, Big Boss, and their NATOPS manual. Let's now take a look at the boss's role a little more closely.

The boss's role involves detailed planning, instruction, training, guidance, correction, and lots of practice and communications to ensure that the Blues bring as much "glory" as possible to the big boss (i.e., the CNO). The boss's attention to detail ensures, to the greatest extent possible, that each team member of the Blues properly executes their roles and responsibilities correctly, and under authority. While the boss extends "grace" to team members who are learning new maneuvers or fine-tuning their skills and precision on existing maneuvers, there is zero-tolerance for any pilot who operates outside of their function or who usurps the boss's authority in any way.

Needless to say, the boss is not a passive individual when it comes to his role and responsibilities, knowing abdication of them could be fatal to the team. Unlike Adam, a good boss makes things happen. He doesn't watch things happen or say, "What happened?"

Additionally, a good boss knows what's going on in his formation, good and bad, at all times. For example, when it is time for specific team members to conduct solo maneuvers, it is the boss who authorizes "breakaways" from the Delta for this purpose. The boss also authorizes "join-ups" once solo maneuvers are complete. No one in formation acts independently of the boss, and he expects nothing less.

Every good boss is also a nice balance of grace and truth. He knows that too much grace can lower the standards and expectations while too much truth can take the joy out of flying. So even when things don't go well, and correction is necessary, the boss has a beautiful way of extending grace without lowering the standards of the big boss. Maintaining these standards of excellence while giving the Blues the freedom to fail communicates to every Blue just how valuable they are and how much they are needed, accepted, and loved by the boss.

A good boss is a joy to follow, and Blues who understand their roles are a joy to lead! Now, let's take a look at the other Blues.

Blue Angel No. 2 (hereafter referred to as "#2") is known as the "Right Wing" or the boss's right "wingman." The right wingman's job is to support the boss at all times. While the boss has two wingmen, she, #2, is his primary wingman. Next to the big boss, the boss's greatest loyalty and allegiance is to #2. She "watches the back" of her boss in formation by staying functionally behind, underneath, and to his right to help him complete the big boss's mission. In combat, the big boss, boss, and #2 understand that the boss and #2 have more firepower, better situational awareness, and a superior ability to employ dynamic tactics against the enemy together than they each have on their own.

Blue Angel No.2 maintains her proper place in formation behind and underneath the boss by maintaining the same sight picture she sees when she lines up the leading edge (front part of the wing) of her left-wing with the nearest part of the boss's aircraft. She maintains this relative position to the boss at all times by making continuous adjustments to her airspeed and flight path. Every time a boss and his primary wingman (#2) begin a relationship, boss and #2 practice this over and over until they are flying "as one." Then, and only then, can the rest of the Blues assume their proper positions behind them in formation.

The boss is in constant communications with #2 so that #2 knows what #1 is going to do before #1 does it to make it easier for #2 to follow him. Blue Angel No. 2, similarly, is in constant communications with #1 so that #1 knows that #2 heard what #1 just told her and is ready to execute his instructions. Because there is a trusted history, sense of loyalty and duty, and a keen understanding and adherence to their specific roles and responsibilities, #2 knows that #1 will never leave her. Additionally, #1 trusts that #2 will stay in formation behind and underneath him at all times for the benefit of the entire formation.

Even when #2 gets out of position ever so slightly, #1 has complete confidence that she will make whatever "course corrections" are necessary to get back into her "lane" because she knows her role and understands what's at stake. Therefore, every #2 is happy to submit to #1's authority because she knows he is responsible for her and will do his best to protect her and provide for her the necessary leadership, provision, and guidance that she needs to be successful!

Though there are five other aircraft in the Delta, #2 only takes instructions from and follows the movements of the boss to maintain her proper position behind him in the Delta. And #1 expects nothing less, since the ability of Blue Angel No. 6 to maintain his position, behind, and underneath #2 in the Delta is dependent on #2's ability to maintain her position, behind, and underneath the boss.

Blue Angel No. 3 (hereafter referred to as #3) is known as the "Left Wing" or #1's left wingman. Number 3 does on the left side of the formation behind and underneath #1 what #2 does on the right side of the formation behind and underneath #1. Everything stated above between #1 and #2 above applies equally between #1 and #3, except that the relationship between #1 and #3 is junior to the relationship between #1 and #2 as outlined above. The relationship between #1 and #3, however, is still critical to the success of the team since the ability of Blue Angel No. 5 to maintain her proper position in the Delta behind and underneath #3 is dependent on #3's ability to maintain their proper position behind and underneath #1.

Flying Blue Angel No. 4 (hereafter referred to as "#4") behind and underneath #1, #2, and #3 is the "Slot." The "Slot" pilot is the boss's designated "Safety Officer" because of the Slot's unique position in formation that enables him to see all of the other Blues in formation. One Blue Angel Slot pilot had this to say about his role. "Number 4 has to have the "big picture." He keeps an eye on weather, emergency field status, fuel, altitude, and airspeed. He can even call for more room between wingtips or advise the boss to increase roll rate. Everyone depends on you for backup."[31]

One boss had this to say about his slot: "Number 4 sets the formation and has to be rock solid. He's a safety valve behind [me]."[32] However, just like #2 and #3, #4's job is to stay focused on #1's every movement to maintain his proper alignment behind and underneath the boss in formation at all times. Again, the boss expects nothing less.

Flying Blue Angel No. 5 (hereafter referred to as "#5") is the "Lead Solo," positioned to the left, behind, and underneath the Left Wing (#3). The job of the Lead Solo is to demonstrate what the F/A-18 Hornet is capable of doing. One Lead Solo said, "We bring in the low, the fast, the loud, and the vertical maneuvers. The Lead Solo is responsible for adjusting the Solo's timing to offset the Formation[33] during an air show." This minimizes "dead space" during their performance and keeps the pilots safe. Everything stated above between #1 and #3 applies equally between #3 and #5. And #1 expects nothing less, knowing that the success of #5 depends on the success of #3, which depends on the success of #1.

Flying Blue Angel No. 6 (hereafter referred to as "#6") is the "Opposing Solo," positioned to the right, behind, and underneath #2. The job of the Opposing Solo is identical to #5 but on the opposing side, hence, the name. Everything stated above between #1 and #2 applies equally between #2 and #6. And #1 expects nothing less, knowing that the success of #6 depends on the success of #2, which depends on the success of #1. Are you starting to see a pattern here?

As mentioned earlier, Lead Solo (#5) and Opposing Solo (#6) are not authorized to commence "breakaways" from the Delta for solo maneuvers without prior authorization from the boss. All unauthorized breakaways are subject to immediate disciplinary action.

Among the many fascinating discoveries about the Blues in doing my research was realizing that their functional names in formation are also what they "go by," even when they are not flying. For example, Blue Angel No. 4 is never introduced to the public as just "Blue Angel No. 4." His function is always included during his introduction which goes like this: "Flying Blue Angel Number 4, *the Slot pilot*, from (City, State), (Rank), (Name)." Thus, each Blue Angel is known by the function they serve in formation, whether flying or not. Why? Because it's "who they are."

The tour of duty for each Blue Angel pilot is typically two years. However, the two-year period begins and ends at different times for different Blues, so there are not too many new Blues beginning at once or too many senior Blues leaving at once. This rotation allows the Blues to maintain as much continuity and seniority as possible at all times. After the first year a team flies together, some of the demonstration pilots get promoted into more senior assignments within the Blues formation while certain section leaders rotate out. For example, Opposing Solo (#6) moves up into the Lead Solo (#5) position and becomes responsible for training the new #6. Another significant "jump" that occurs within the formation is that the Left Wing (#3) moves into the Slot (#4) position and trains the new Left Wing (#3). Only the Right Wing (#2) remains in her position for the entire two years. And #1 expects nothing less. As stated earlier, their relationship is very special, and the rest of Blues know it and wouldn't have it any other way!

Like a fantastic band that makes a lead singer sound better than he is, when all the Blues are properly aligned behind and underneath the boss in formation, they make the boss look better than he is! And when the boss looks good, the big boss looks good. Said another way, when everyone is operating under authority in their proper positions as established within the guidelines established by the CNO and NATOPS, everyone makes the "big boss" look good! However, the opposite is also true. When just one Blue is "out of line," not only does it make the big boss look "bad," but it makes the whole team look bad, especially in the eyes of those who look to them for hope in present and future generations. Such an out of order Blue can quickly find themselves grounded if it is determined that their actions posed a threat to the safety, morale, or welfare of the team.

The Blues sometimes come to within eighteen inches of one another while in the Delta and Diamond formations. It is not uncommon for their wingtips to overlap! The trust and loyalty that exist between each member of the Blues that allows them to fly like this is unprecedented.

However, this trust and loyalty can also be a double-edged sword when Blues "blindly" follow a boss who is operating outside of the boundaries and limitations of the big boss or NATOPS. Such was the case in 1982 in a tragic incident involving the Thunderbirds, the Air Force version of the Blue Angels, when they lost four jets and their pilots during a training "run," known as the "Thunderbirds Indian Springs Diamond Crash." In this horrific mishap, while in the Diamond Formation, the boss experienced a problem with his aircraft that he could not recover from in time and flew his plane into the ground. Tragically, the other three pilots followed his lead to their deaths.[34] While many details of this tragic incident are still unknown to date, I share it with you for one primary reason: Every boss loses his authority to lead and have others follow him when he is knowingly or even unknowingly operating outside of the boundaries and operating limitations of his NATOPS manual.

So why would I go into such detail about the Blue Angels and their amazing Delta formation in a chapter about the Great Role Reversal? I'm sure it is obvious by now. It is so you and I would have a powerful and vivid illustration of what a Christ-centered family looks like when everyone is functioning in their proper roles underneath the authority of the Big Boss (Jesus) and His NATOPS manual (God's Word). You see, every family, from God's perspective, is in its own family "formation" where each member, like the Blues, has also been given a distinct role subject to the authority of the Big Boss (Jesus) and His NATOPS manual (the Bible). Every Christian family that has a husband/father, wife/mom, and children have a "big boss," "boss," primary wingman, and one or more "Blues" who, by God's design, function figuratively and spiritually in ways similar to Blue Angels #3 through #6. While this is a far from perfect illustration, there are many striking similarities, as you've seen, between the way the Blues operate and the way God expects our families to operate.

In case you didn't make all the connections, let me do it for you now. It's worth every bit of repetition so that we never forget it! Thank you, Holy Spirit!

In the same way that the head of every Blue Angel Boss is the big boss (CNO), the head of every primary wingman is her boss, and the head of every big boss is the biggest boss (Commander in Chief); the head of every husband is Christ, the head of a wife is her husband, and the head of Christ is God (1 Corinthians 11:3 ESV). Everyone is under authority!

Like the boss of the Blue Angels, every husband and father has been appointed by the big boss (Jesus) to lead his family through the angelic conflict we have been placed in the middle of for the expansion of God's kingdom and glory (chapter 1). "Bossman," you "own" the "airspace" ("territory") the Big Boss has given you to execute His flight plan. He expects you to rule it well!

The Big Boss (Jesus) then declared that every wife (primary wingman) would follow and operate underneath the authority of her husband (the boss) and that children (Blue Nos. 3–6 as applicable) would follow and operate underneath the authority of the boss (Dad) and primary wingman (Mom).

While every husband and father is the God-appointed flight leader of his family, it is common knowledge that if he expects his wife and children to follow him, he better be following the big boss (Jesus Christ). Every husband and father, like every boss, thus understands that while he has been given great freedom, his freedom comes with great responsibility that is restricted to and governed by the boundaries and operating limitations of God's Word. Therefore, like the boss of the Blue Angels, the responsibility for provision, protection, and guidance by God's design rests squarely on the shoulders of the spiritual leader and his ability to be the kind of leader, under Christ, that the rest of his family can trust and follow.

Also, like the boss of the Blue Angels, the husband's leadership role at home with the help of his wife (primary wingman) involves planning, instruction, training, guidance, correction and of course, lots of practice and communication to ensure everyone stays in formation. While the boss (husband/dad) extends grace to family members who get out of line, there is zero-tolerance for any family member who gets out of formation and refuses to get back in formation. Why? Because pleasing the Big Boss (Jesus) is of utmost importance to the boss (husband/dad) who will be held accountable by the Big Boss (Jesus) for how He carried out His leadership duties and responsibilities.

In the same way that the boss's role with the Blues is not passive, the role of husband and father at home is not passive. Every boss (husband/father) understands that the abdication of his responsibility could be fatal to the survival of his family formation. It is, therefore, the job of every husband and father, like the boss of the Blue Angels, to "make things happen," not watch things happen or simply say, "What happened?"[35] For example, when it is time for certain family members to conduct solo maneuvers (e.g., begin dating, driving, or living on the college campus), the family boss authorizes these breakaways with help from his primary wingman (wife).

Now let's look at the similarities between the role of the wife and Blue Angel No.2 in the family formation.

Functionally behind and underneath the authority of her husband, by God's design, is his "primary wingman" or wife. Like Blue Angel No. 2, it is the job of every wife to "watch the back" of her husband as he leads the family. She does this by staying in formation functionally behind, underneath, and to the right of "her man," thus helping him fulfill the mission the Big Boss (Jesus) gave him, using her gifts, talents, skills, and abilities. Just like the Blues, every flight leader recognizes that his wife brings more firepower, better situational awareness, and an improved ability to employ dynamic tactics than he would ever have by himself. Thus, her presence dramatically increases the odds that they will complete God's mission. Similarly, every godly wife, like Blue Angel No. 2, makes whatever course corrections are necessary to maintain her proper place in the family formation relative to her leader at all times.

Like the boss of the Blue Angels, every family boss (husband) stays in constant communications with his wife so that his wife knows what he would like to do before he does it to make it easier for her to follow him. Every wife in the primary wingman position is, similarly, in constant communications with her boss (husband) so that he knows she heard him and is ready to respond after providing him her desperately input and feedback. Like Blue Angels No. 1 and No. 2, because there is a trusted history, sense of loyalty and duty, and a keen understanding of their individual functions and responsibilities, every godly wife knows that her husband will never leave her. Moreover, every godly husband knows that he can count on his wife to stay in her lane underneath his authority even when she doesn't like or agree with the direction he's going. Even when his wife veers slightly off course, her husband (#1) has complete confidence she will make whatever course corrections are necessary to get back in her lane because she knows her role and what's at stake.

Because the future of God's glory is at stake, every godly wife knows (like every right wing) that to stay correctly aligned under Christ, she must stay properly aligned under "her man." Thus, she doesn't take instructions from anyone else inside or outside of the formation but him nor does she follow anyone else's movements but his. Her husband expects nothing less since the ability of Blue Angel #6 (i.e., one of your children) to maintain their proper position in the family formation behind and underneath Dad is dependent on her (#2's) ability to maintain her proper position behind and underneath Dad. Therefore, it is common knowledge in Christ-centered families, as with the Blue Angels, that any wife (primary wingman) who can't follow her husband (boss) as he follows the Big Boss (Christ) poses a grave danger and threat to the integrity and survival of the family formation, the success of the mission, and the amount of glory the Big Boss (Jesus) receives.

Now, let's take a look at the similarities between the roles of children (between the approximate ages of eight to eighteen) in the family formation and the roles of Blue Angel Nos. 3 through 6 in the Delta formation.

Symbolically, representing Blue Angel No. 3 in the family formation as left wing would be an older, more mature child in the family. While it is the job of every wife or primary wingman to watch the back of her leader, she can't possibly see every "enemy combatant" that threatens the family formation from the other side of the formation given her own "blind spots" and limitations. Therefore, it is the job of every older, more mature child to help Mom watch Dad's back from the other side of the formation to ensure the successful completion of the family mission for God's glory.

Christ-led families do this by training their older children (when they are younger) to not only follow Dad and Mom as they follow Christ but to "get outside of themselves" long enough to see and respond to potential threats to other members of the family formation (e.g. alcohol, drugs, porn, gangs, etc.). This is a far cry from the many teenagers who come home from school each day and play video games or hang out on their smartphones and social media accounts for hours and rarely "check in" with Dad, Mom, or their siblings to see how they can help or serve the family.

Symbolically representing Blue Angel No. 4 in the family formation (assuming other children exist) by delegated authority from Dad is a spot typically reserved for the oldest child—ideally, a son—who receives training from Dad to be his "Safety Officer." While everyone knows Dad is ultimately responsible for everyone's safety, Dad and Mom can't possibly see everything going on behind them. Since the slot has the best view of everyone else in the family formation, Dad and Mom rely on him to help them make sure everyone is operating safely within the boundaries and limitations of the family.

In giving his oldest son this responsibility, the boss is using his superb leadership skills to accomplish two essential goals in # 4's life. First, if the oldest child is a boy, he is preparing him to be the boss of his own family one day by giving him "safety" and "protection" practice. Secondly, Dad is multiplying his training efforts by using his oldest child to help him train the child in position #3 to be the next "Safety Officer." This frees Dad up, with Mom's help, to remain focused on the vision and execution of the family mission while and eliminating any safety "vacuum" that would otherwise exist when the slot "breaks away" for college or their chosen career. Even with all of this responsibility, the oldest child (No. 4) knows that he can only be successful in this role when he maintains his proper alignment behind and underneath Dad's authority.

Again, this is a far cry from the many fourteen to eighteen-year-olds at home who have to be continually reminded to clean up after themselves, help out around the house, finish their homework, get off their smartphones, stop playing video games, serve others, or to get back in their lanes.

Even when a daughter must fulfill the slot position due to the age and maturity of the children, it is wise for Dad and Mom to allow her to do this. Besides satisfying the "safety backup" requirement needed, her interaction with the boss helps her to know what to look for in her future husband who will lead her one day! Additionally, she gets a "front-row" seat to see how Mom (#2) helps Dad fulfill the mission God gave him for the family so she will know exactly what to do when she becomes a primary wingman herself!

Symbolically representing Blue Angel No. 5 (Lead Solo) in the family formation (assuming multiple children) would also be an older child, but not "senior" to #3 or #4. In the same way that the slot has the responsibility of assisting Dad and Mom in training, guiding, familiarizing, and equipping the younger sibling in position #3 for the slot position one day, #5, who just "graduated" to the #5 position from the #6 position, has the responsibility for "grooming" #6 to take the #5 position after him. Again, this is all by design. Dad and Mom are flying with the long-term view of making sure all their Blues know how to be the future lovers, leaders, and followers they need to be in their own family formations one day.

The child in position #5, like Blue Angel No. 5, is behind, underneath, and to the left of #3 in the family formation. Even when the boss chooses to put an older child in position #5 than in position #3 because of #5's responsibility to train #6, it is a strategic and powerful reminder to the rest of the Blues of the ongoing need to esteem others higher than ourselves (Philippians 2:3). And one guess who taught them this? Dad and Mom. For years, they have watched Dad deny himself and "fly" behind Jesus and Mom deny herself and "fly" behind Dad! What a beautiful picture of true submission! Now this is the way it's supposed to be!

For children in the Blue Angel No. 6 position, where applicable, everything stated between #1, #3, and #5 on the left side of the family formation symbolically applies to #1, #2, and #6 on the right side of the formation. The only thing I would like to say regarding the youngest ("newest") member of the family formation, #6, is that Dad and Mom should not be the only ones praying for them, encouraging them, watching out for them, and helping them stay in their lane. Again, this is a far cry from the average family in America who struggles to have dinner together once a week because everyone is "jetting off" in their own directions to fly their own missions. Good luck getting people to come to that air show!

Like the real boss of the Blue Angles, not only does every family boss expect his Blues (children) to obey, honor, and show respect for him and his primary wingman (wife and Mom) but also to one another to promote good order, discipline, peace, unity, and teamwork within the family formation. And woe to the Blue (child) who doesn't!

Whenever media personnel interview a Blue following an air show, the Blue said what you would expect them to say. It is similar to what a championship athlete says after a "big win" or what you would expect a member of Seal Team 6 to say after killing Osama Bin Laden. What is it? It goes something like this. "What happened today was not the result of one person or even a few but was the direct result of the hard work, dedication, and sacrifice of every member of this team who decided a long time ago that they would be committed to something greater than themselves!"

Now imagine how differently our marriages, homes, churches, communities, cities, and nation would be if our family formations flew behind Christ with this level of dedication for no other reason but to make the Big Boss (Jesus) look good?

Maybe some of you, after reading this and considering the Blue Angel illustration I have provided are saying, "While it would be great if our family looked and operated like this Jim, our family is not a military flight demonstration team. Who wants to be part of a family where the boss is barking out orders like a general, and everyone has to obey with expert precision or else?"

I couldn't agree more. After all, this is not how the Father leads Christ, how Christ leads men, how husbands are to lead their wives, or how Dads and Moms are to lead their children. Nor is it how the boss leads his Blues. I would encourage you to watch some of their videos for yourself—it's beautiful how the boss lovingly leads his Blues. However, as countercultural as it may be, God does have a "chain of command," beloved, and it is nonnegotiable if husbands and wives expect to rule well on God's behalf in the earth to advance His kingdom and bring Him glory. In the words of Paul, "If anyone is inclined to be contentious [about God's divine order for the family], we have no such practice, nor do the churches of God" (1 Corinthians 11:16 ESV). Thus, if you still have an issue with the Big Boss's divine order for the family, I suggest you take it up with Him!

Now, given all I've said, what do you think would happen to the Blue Angels in Delta formation if all of a sudden, the boss stopped following the big boss by refusing to operate within the boundaries and operating limitations of the big boss and his NATOPS manual? I'll tell you: The same thing that is happening in Christian families all across America because family bosses are refusing to follow Christ and His Word. First and foremost, we unknowingly get another leader, as stated earlier. Secondly, wives and children are left without a spiritual leader to lead, protect, provide, and guide them in fulfilling God's mission for their family. Thirdly, wives and mothers are being forced into roles that they were never designed to have, resulting in chaos, confusion, bitterness, resentment, and every evil work. (James 3:16) Welcome to the overwhelming majority of American families!

That's right. While none of us could imagine the boss of the Blue Angels ever rejecting the big boss and his NATOPS manual to fly his own mission leaving his Blues without his provision, protection, and guidance, men, through passivity, ignorance, abdication of responsibility, abuse, neglect, misplaced priorities, rebellion, and abandonment are rejecting their "Big Boss" Jesus and His Word every day to fly their own missions, leaving the "Blues" in his family without his provision, protection, and guidance. Wives are not only left assuming a role that God never intended for them to have but raising a generation of kids who don't know the distinct roles Dad, Mom, and they play in the family formation because it was never modeled for them. The cumulative impact of this leadership vacuum over many generations has resulted in the unprecedented level of chaos we are experiencing in society today as family after family passes on the same destructive model that was modeled to them.

Conversely, however, note what happens when men (bosses) all across a nation appear together before the Lord God (the Big Boss) and submit themselves to His lordship and authority in every area of life as shown here in the following (italics used for emphasis):

> God told the Israelites, as described in Exodus 34:23, that three times a year all of their males were to appear together before Him to receive instructions from Him. Yet when God told them to appear, He specifically called them out before the "*Lord, God, the God of Israel.*" He called them to submit themselves to His complete authority. *If the men submitted, they were told that they, and those connected to them, would receive God's covering, protection, and provision. But they would receive this only if they positioned themselves under His absolute rule.*[36]

This is, incidentally, why so many men never get their own flight plans from God. They are unwilling to come before the Lord God and submit themselves to His complete authority first. God says, in essence, "No, no, you have it all backward. Come before me first. Submit yourself to my complete authority first, and then I will give you instructions." To use a football illustration, when you, Coach, are willing to come under the authority of the NFL rule book, I, the NFL Commissioner, will allow you, Coach, to have your own playbook. In other words, while every team must operate under the same rule book, the NFL Commissioner gives each team the freedom to have their own playbook.

God wants to give every man His own playbook, but He can't because we're unwilling to play by His "rule book!" The process begins when we're willing to come before the Lord thy God and submit to Him.

Now add to the above problem, primary wingmen (wives) who refuse to submit to their boss's (husband's) authority and follow him and the number of bosses who take instructions from their wingmen (instead of the big boss) that run contrary to God's instructions. Maybe then we will begin to understand the magnitude of the spiritual crisis we're in as a nation!

By the way, "Bossman," could all hell be breaking loose around you as it did for Adam because your primary wingman (wife) just told you to eat the apple from the forbidden tree, and you said, "Yes, dear"? Please tell me this isn't your idea of "mutual submission."

You see, what happens in the spirit realm whenever Blue Angel No. 2 decides that she wants to be the "boss" or that she will only follow the boss if he goes in her direction is that the Big Boss, Jesus, "grounds" the whole family formation! The same thing happens when the boss (husband/Dad) decides he no longer wants to follow the Big Boss (Jesus). Maybe you're wondering why the whole family gets "grounded" when just one Blue is "out of order." Because when one Blue is out of order, the entire formation is out of order. Like the Blue Angels, the family unit can no longer complete the mission that was given to the boss (husband and Dad) by Jesus Christ. Any boss (Dad) who tolerates such open rebellion to continue by even just one Blue is not flying God's flight plan! He might as well be called the flight leader of the Blue Devils since that's whose flight plan he's flying. Good luck with that air show on Judgment Day, "Bossman."

Remember, when you and I are out of order with God and one another, we are not flying God's mission no matter how "happy" we are or how much we read the Bible, pray, or go to church. Religious activity has never been nor will ever be a threat to Satan. However, I'm sure he finds it amusing, especially when many of us return to flying his mission and building his kingdom before we even leave the church parking lot!

How about this scenario? What do you think would happen if Blue Angel No. 2 decided that Blue Angel No. 5 should get to call the shots, set the pace, and choose the direction for the family?

What would never happen in a million years on the Blue Angels Flight Demonstration Team is happening in Christian homes all across America in the name of "love." What do I mean? Dads and Moms—but mostly Christian Moms because of their nurturing "mother hen" instincts that seek the happiness and well-being of her "chickadees"—are elevating the needs, wants, and desires of her children above God's flight plan and His chain of command. Grounded!

Sadly, many Christian women, once they have children, go into "Mommy mode" and never come out.[37] I experienced this personally. Instead of the family flight plan revolving around the expansion of God's kingdom and His glory, it revolves around the needs, wants, and desires of the children. What this means, practically, is that if Johnny's soccer schedule or Brittany's dance schedule prevents the family from having dinner and family devotions together regularly or there's no opportunity for a date night anymore, oh well. "Sorry, honey, we'll be at dance practice again. There's some cold chicken in the fridge. See you later."

Really? Really. Guess who the Boss OF this family is and guess who God is looking for, mister. Clue: The first answer is different than the second. Have I found you yet? No? Okay, let's try this next one.

What do you think would happen if Blue Angel No. 5 or Blue Angel No. 6 were permitted to authorize their own breakaways from the rest of the family formation whenever they wanted? Better yet, what if #2 (Mom) authorized their breakaway without ever consulting #1? After the Big Boss spiritually grounds the whole family formation and cancels all of their upcoming "air shows" because they are no longer operating His way, He will again come looking for the Boss to see what he authorized. He will then come looking for you, lady, to see why you got out of your lane and invited chaos to your family formation and, more importantly, made the boss (your husband) and Him (the Big Boss, Jesus) look bad!

What if you're the boss (husband and Dad) and one of the Blues (your children) needed to be corrected and disciplined for a repeat "flying offense," and Blue Angel No. 2 (your wife) routinely undermined your role and told the Blues behind your back that you (#1) were the one out of line? Cringe. Need I even answer?

Can you imagine a Blue Angel (child) ever going "rogue" on his boss (Dad) and Big Boss (Jesus) without getting disciplined? No way! A good boss, just like Jesus, our Big Boss, disciplines those he loves. Why? So they will become holy. Every good leader knows that left to our own devices, rogue Blues pose too high a risk to themselves and the entire family formation.

Finally, what do you think would happen if the boss and Blue Angel No. 2 allowed the rest of the Blues to come and go as they please without any rules or limitations? After all, that's what a tolerant, freedom-loving family does that does not want to limit their Blues' freedom of expression, right? Again, good luck finding someone to attend that chaotic air show.

While comparing the Blue Angels in Delta Formation to our family formations is in no way a perfect illustration, I trust you can now see how out of order we are, how far we are from God's standard, and how easy it is for Satan to orchestrate *The Great Role Reversal* with us so he can take over our homes. Yes, even Christian homes!

Let me put it to some of you this way. If you don't care about reclaiming, through your family, what has been stolen by the devil in the earth (chapter 1), then disregard God's chain of command. If you could care less about advancing God's kingdom and bringing Him glory, then let your wife be the boss, mister; usurp the authority of your husband, ma'am; follow the "other" leader so you can live your best life now, and be prepared to answer for it all on Judgment Day! Don't worry, I got my toes too.

Make no mistake. Our nation is in trouble because the family formation is in trouble. And our family formations are in trouble because many bosses and primary wingmen (husbands and wives) have committed *The Great Role Reversal* with God and one another, showing a complete disregard for God and His Word. And because many of us are out of order, our children and the culture are out of order.

In summary, Satan can easily orchestrate *The Great Role Reversal* with present and future generations of families, inviting "hell" to take over our homes, when we:

1. Don't know why we were created or what our purpose is from God's perspective;
2. Don't know what our role is (and isn't) from God's perspective;
3. Don't know what our mate's roles is (and isn't) from God's perspective;
4. "Fly" our own missions, which is really Satan's mission, instead of flying God's mission outlined for us in His Word;
5. Operate outside of the boundaries and limitations of the Big Boss (Jesus) and His Word;
6. Only follow the Big Boss (Jesus) when we like the direction He is going;
7. Elevate the parent-child relationship above the husband-wife relationship;
8. Do not partner with our spouse to fulfill God's vision and purpose for the family;
9. Do not train and equip our children to be the future bosses and primary wingmen of their own families.

While it would be nice if all of our family formations operated like the Blue Angels to maximize our impact for the kingdom of God in every area of society, I clearly recognize that this is not possible for some of us. One reason is that we cannot control how others choose to "fly" in our family formations. I get it! However, we can control how *we* are going to fly and *what* we are willing to accept and not accept from others. We can also, where appropriate, dispense appropriate consequences (like God does with us) for "flight violations" so others will get back in their lanes or decide against God and us! Additionally, we can humble ourselves and ask for forgiveness for not leading or following well where appropriate.

While Scripture commands us to forgive at all times and make allowances for "faults" (Colossians 3:13), annoyances, and misdeeds, it does not command us to abdicate our responsibilities or to make allowances for those who refuse to get back in their lanes. Additionally, it does not command us to trust those who cannot be trusted to stay in their lanes.

Please allow me to be blunt (as if I haven't been already). Since God will come looking for you and me first, sir, make sure if your family, God forbid, "crashes," it is not "crashing" because you were unwilling to follow Christ and operate by the boundaries and limitations of His Word. While doing the right thing doesn't guarantee that others will follow you and do the right thing, it certainly improves the odds. But since God's love and eternal assurance in Christ are the only guarantees we have in life, build your life around these as you extend that love to others within the framework of His Word, then leave the consequences to God! This is what it means to "seek ye *first* the kingdom of God and His righteousness" (Matthew 6:33) and what I believe God is calling every man to do whether others follow them or not.

The same goes for you, lady. Do not allow the "sins" of your boss (husband) to be your excuse for promoting yourself to a position you were never created to have or entitled to assume (i.e., boss)! If your husband is "out of order," follow your Big Boss (Jesus) until your boss (husband) places himself back underneath the Big Boss's authority. However, the reality is your husband may not. While God commands you to respect your husband's position, whether he deserves it or not, you do not have to follow him if he is not following Christ. However, if your husband *is* following Christ as I have said over and over again (though it may not be the way you like), you will be "on the hook" if you choose not to follow him and usurp his authority in *any* area of life. Therefore, if your family is going to "crash," make sure (as previously stated with men) it is not crashing because you insist on being the boss through your actions, attitudes, or beliefs.

While I tried to hit the "biggies," there are countless other ways Satan can get us to commit *The Great Role Reversal* with God and one another should the ones I have highlighted fail to materialize. Be keenly aware of this! The good news is we don't have to fear any of them as long as we stay in our lanes!

So why is it such a struggle to stay in formation with God and one another? Simple. We want the glory, just like Lucifer, and don't want to share it with anyone else, not even God. We, as a consequence of the fall, instinctively want to be the center of our worship and control others. Yes, even Christians, and the devil knows it! How does he know it? Because that's what he wanted, remember? Silently and internally, while the choice of our words may be different, many of us, in essence, declare (if we were truly honest) that "Nobody is going to tell me what to do, including God. I will be the center of my worship, and if you get in my way, you will feel my wrath!"

The only way out of this self-centered demonically influenced "hell" that plagues all of us to varying degrees is submission to Christ and His Word through the ongoing process of sanctification. Nobody has to worry about "jockeying" for positions in a family formation where every member of the family seeks to be under Christ's authority and is concerned about obeying and pleasing Him.

So tough questions (honesty required). What do people see when they look at your family formation? Do they see a spiritual leader who, in spite of his sin, is constantly adjusting his life to follow Jesus Christ? Do they see a wife and mom who, despite her sin, is frequently adjusting her life to follow her husband as he follows Christ? Do they see children who, despite their sin, are continually adjusting their lives to follow Dad and Mom? Boss, I dare you to ask your wife, your kids, and others mature believers (who know you well, not just casually) to truthfully tell you what they see when they look at your family formation. Wives, same thing. You might be surprised at what you hear! The real question, however, is if you don't like their answer, are you and I willing to do something about it? Knowledge alone never saved anything. You and I must take action.

Maybe some of you are saying this is all well and good for traditional families, Spence, but I'm a single parent. How does all this apply to me? Simple. If you're a single mom with your children living at home with you, Jesus is your Boss and Big Boss. You are married to Him. He is your leader, and you are His primary wingman. If their father is still alive, he is still their spiritual leader, not you. However, if he is out of his lane, your children do not have to follow him.

While it may feel like you have to assume his position as the spiritual leader of the children because their father is no longer in the home, do not do this. Besides committing *The Great Role Reversal* with your spiritual leader Jesus, first and foremost, you have just programmed yourself for future failure should you get married again. How? Simple. Because you have allowed yourself to function as the boss, you will instinctively want to continue being the boss, which just became your new husband's role if your children are living under his roof.

Think about it. How easy do you think it's going to be for you to allow your new husband to function as the boss when you've been the boss all these years? Meanwhile, who's fulfilling the role of primary wingman? Not you! And if your new husband is, he's out of his lane! While you absolutely have a critical role to play in your biological children's spiritual training and development, whether single or married, you will never, by God's design, be their spiritual leader. To assume a role that doesn't belong to you is to tell God that He doesn't know what He's talking about. Not a good idea, sister! Guess who just became your biggest problem? Clue: Not your new husband!

If you teach your children that you, not your new husband, are their spiritual leader (i.e., boss), other than what I already said above, you have just programmed their future families to be immediately hijacked by the devil! Why? Because your boys will grow up thinking it's normal to follow the women in their lives, and your girls will grow up thinking it's normal to be the leader instead of the follower. Have you looked around lately? Satan doesn't even have to show up to do his job in most cases because the current generation has already programmed the next generation to do it for him! Yes, even in the church! And some of you thought the consequences of ordaining women as pastors and elders stopped at the front doors of your home. Good luck with that one on Judgment Day to all the men in our churches all across America who are allowing it! We operate by the rules of another kingdom, remember?

This is one of the main reasons why so many blended families fail. The biological mom refuses to give the role of spiritual leader to her new husband because she says, "These are my children." No, actually, precious sister, they belong to Jesus, the Giver of life and, therefore, are subject to His spiritual hierarchy and ethics. We say the same thing about our money and our possessions (at least we should) that "it all belongs to God," right? Somehow, we think this doesn't apply to children. While you (like Mary was with Christ) were hand-picked by God to give birth to them and partner with Christ in the stewardship of their soul by training them up in the nurture and admonition of the Lord (Proverbs 22:6), our children exist for God's glory, not ours!

God didn't give us children so we would have "lookalikes" who simply become productive members of society as necessary as this is; He gave us children to replicate His image and glory worldwide. Sadly, single moms who do not understand any of this unknowingly commit *The Great Role Reversal* with God and their new husband on day one by assuming his role over "her" biological children. Easy day for Satan!

If you are a single Dad with your children living with you, you are still flying in the same position you were flying in before, just without a primary wingman. Jesus is your leader, not your copilot or primary wingman. If you have a daughter at home, this is an ideal time to train her on how to be the primary wingman for her future husband. Teach her, her role and let her practice "watching your back" as one of your boys (if you have one) "watch your back" from the other side of the "formation." They need to see you following Christ as they follow you. All the dynamics I have described above are still "in play." Despite not having a primary wingman, you, as a family, can still fly God's flight plan and fulfill His mission for you! I have been doing that for years! Don't let the devil convince you otherwise!

Additional Warnings to Single Parents and Blended Families

While everything I've said in this chapter applies to non-blended and blended families, I need you to know something vital if you are a single parent who desires to be married again. Ready? It's the same thing I want you to see if you are in a blended family now. While it should be obvious given what I've said already, I do not wish to assume anything given the schemes and strategies of the enemy. Ready?

While the devil is flawlessly orchestrating *The Great Role Reversal* over countless first-time marriages (non-blended families), it is even easier for him to do it in a blended family where stepchildren exist. Why? Two reasons primarily. First, there is often great parental "guilt" over divorcing the child's other parent. Number two, there is an overwhelming desire to "protect" children from future hurt (also tied to guilt). Both of these realities, unless they are nailed to the cross and brought under God's authority, often result in that spouse being more loyal to his or her biological children than they are to their new spouse, especially when those two worlds collide. And trust me, they will collide!

It is very easy for the devil to turn things "upside down" when guilt is driving decision-making. And there is no shortage of it in "blended families." Satan knows that. Now you do! Be very mindful of this. This is one of the major reasons why divorce statistics increase roughly 10 percent with each succeeding marriage.[38] The good news is that if the devil tries this scheme on your blended family, you now know what it is and how to defeat it by getting back in your lane!

Ladies, to eliminate all "wiggle room" for the devil to exploit you, please allow me to be very direct. If you have biological children from a previous marriage and you can't let your new husband be their spiritual leader under the "roof" where you and they will reside, you have no business getting married. It doesn't matter if you're their biological parent or not. God's role for your new husband also applies to stepchildren.

We are all adopted children of God. In the same way that God doesn't distinguish between Jew and Gentile concerning "His children," God doesn't differentiate between biological and stepchildren when it comes to your new husband's role as the spiritual leader of the family. Therefore, lady, if you have no intention of operating under God's divine order for your family, don't get married. If you do, your new husband, if he's truly a man, will occupy the position as the spiritual leader of your children, period. This means that in areas of disagreement, as long as he is not "out of order," God expects you to "yield" to his spiritual authority *in everything* when it comes to your biological children.

Read this again, precious one. Again, if you cannot do this while your children are living under your marital roof, do yourself, your man, your children, and most importantly, God and society a favor and do not get married! If you ignore this warning and do not recognize his position as the spiritual leader over you and your biological children, you have just invited Satan to take over your family!

Single moms, have you ever heard Satan whisper:

"Nobody loves your children like you."

"Your new husband is not going to protect them like you."

"After all the pain they've been through, they deserve to be happy."

"If you don't take the lead, he's going to abuse his position with your children. Where does that leave you then?"

"You're the one in control. You didn't need him before. You certainly don't need him now."

"Don't yield. You'll regret it and never get what you want."

"You know what's best for your kids."

"You take the lead. Remember how your mother 'called the shots' in your house when you were growing up? That's you! No man gets to 'call the shots' when it comes to your children!"

If you routinely have thoughts like these I described above as a single mom, then I would highly recommend you not get married as it is all but a guarantee that you and your new husband will become victims of *The Great Role Reversal!* Stay single and raise your kids to love God and follow Him as you complete His mission. No shame. In fact, it's a very high calling to be commended. If it's too late, and you already got married and are out of your lane, I strongly encourage you to seek your husband's forgiveness and assume your proper role today. Order your priorities around God first, your husband second, and your children third.

Ladies, God is not looking for selective obedience on this spiritual leadership issue with your biological children depending upon your mood, feelings, or your husband's tone of voice, choice of words, and/or facial expressions. God is looking for you to obey Him because you love God and want to make the Big Boss look good!

Please understand ladies that if your husband is not the spiritual leader of *all*, including your biological children (i.e., his stepchildren), he is not your spiritual leader at all. Did you catch that? The minute you elevate the parent-child relationship with your biological children above the husband-wife relationship out of fear, guilt, or for any other reason, your Big Boss (Jesus) just became your biggest problem!

Single dads, I give you a similar warning. If you are considering marrying a woman who has children from a previous marriage, I urge you to do everything in your power, through Christ, to ensure that your future wife understands your role *and hers* concerning *her* children *before* you get married. This is why a long courting period (one to two years) is critical. If there is any indication during this time that your future wife may have struggles allowing you to be the spiritual leader of her biological children, I would urge you not to marry her and end the relationship immediately! If you don't, the odds are nearly 100 percent you will end up as a statistic of *The Great Role Reversal*, whether you divorce or not. More importantly than that, however, is that you will never be able to rule your world under God's hand as one to fulfill the purpose for which you and she were created (chapter 1)!

Men, equally, if you are not willing to assume the role of spiritual leader over your future stepchildren, don't get married! If you marry her and abdicate this responsibility to her to "keep the peace" in your home, you, like Adam, will have to answer to God for why you allowed *The Great Role Reversal* to occur, especially since you knew better after reading this!

Similarly, single dads, if you're going to be more loyal to your biological children than your new wife, you equally have no business getting married. Be honest with yourself and your future wife if you are in a relationship like this and end it. Save yourself, her, and your children a lifetime of misery and regret that will surely come if you put your children in the #2 position in the family formation and push your new wife to the back of the formation. God will "ground" you, remember?

I can hear some of you saying, "I would never put my biological children ahead of my husband." That's the same thing my former wife and countless others say until real-life situations arise that involve that very choice. Remember, divided loyalty between a new spouse and biological children from a previous spouse over guilt you carry for the divorce from their other parent is a strong "disobeyer."

Since approximately 50 percent of all families in the church today involve blended families, I would like to share a real-world example of how easy it is to become a victim of *The Great Role Reversal* with a Christian married couple I will call Dave and Megan. Note, as you go, how masterfully Satan orchestrates his every move.

Dave and Megan, both professing believers in Christ, were both been previously married before. Megan brought four children into the marriage, and Dave three! I know! At the time of their story, Dave had two teenage girls (ages sixteen and twenty) and one teenage boy (eighteen). Megan had one adult son (twenty-two), a teenage boy (eighteen), and fraternal boy-girl twins (eight)!

Dave and Megan dated for approximately two years before getting married. During their courtship, they talked extensively about spiritual growth, goals, ministry interests, expectations, "triggers," finances, sex, schedules, vacations, conflict resolution, parenting, time management, holiday management, ex-spouse management, and how their blended-family would operate. They discussed what each of them believed was the best course of action in the event of a sick or aging parent who could no longer care for themselves and a host of other complicated but necessary topics. Of particular importance to Dave was significant discussion around what each of them understood to be their role as husband and wife in marriage from God's perspective. What came from that discussion was a shared understanding and belief that the husband was the spiritual leader of the family under Christ's authority and that the wife, while equal to her husband in every way, was functionally under the authority of her husband; and finally that their children (biological and step) were underneath the authority of both of them, with Dave being the spiritual leader of the family.

Both of them correctly understood that this was God's design for how a Christian family (blended or not) should operate. This meant, for example, that if the two of them disagreed on a particular spiritual issue that both of them felt strongly about involving biological or stepchildren that Dave would have the "final word" as long as his position wasn't unbiblical.

Generally, the way this would practically play out was that if both Dave and Megan agreed that Megan's spiritual concerns were greater than Dave's, Dave would "yield" to Megan as long as her position was not unscriptural. If Dave's spiritual concerns were more significant than Megan's, Megan would yield to Dave as long as his position was not unscriptural. However, in instances where both of them had equal concerns, spiritually, or in cases where Dave felt more strongly about his spiritual concerns, even when Megan didn't necessarily understand or agree, Megan would yield to Dave as the spiritual leader of the family.

Both also agreed before marriage that when it came to their respective biological children, each biological parent would make the functional day-to-day decisions regarding them with input from the nonbiological parent when requested or necessary. Where there were disagreements on non-spiritual issues, each agreed that they would yield to the other. This was very important to both of them, given the complexities of dealing with ex-spouses and child visitation schedules. Plus, each parent already knew what "worked" and "didn't work" for their children.

Sounds good so far, right? They thought so too. Feeling God's favor and blessing, Dave and Megan decided it was time to "tie the knot."

Their transition into married life was both amazing and miraculous for a blended family with seven children between them. Megan's twins (Tyler and Madison) and her teenage son, Jeff, lived with them full-time. Megan's oldest son, Michael, would periodically stay with them for days or weeks at a time in between job contracts. Two of Dave's three children lived at college, and his youngest child at the time (sixteen) lived with their biological mother about twenty minutes away with a fairly traditional visitation schedule for Dave. It was a very workable arrangement that allowed Dave the time and opportunity to love and serve his new wife and the opportunity to provide spiritual training to Megan's children as the spiritual leader of the family. It also afforded Dave's youngest daughter the wonderful opportunity to bond with her new siblings while Dave got to enjoy her last two years of high school before she would leave for college.

The first eighteen months of Dave and Megan's marriage were marked with great love, trust, respect, honor, kindness, and lots of laughter! Quite frankly, it seemed miraculous! Each of them was thrilled to be married to someone who loved Jesus Christ more than anything, understood their role, and were focused on kingdom business in every area of life!

Then one day, everything changed. Out of nowhere, the devil fired his first torpedo, scoring a "direct hit" on their marriage and family.

Just before the "hit," Dave said that he began noticing that one of the twins, Tyler (eight), starting spending what Dave believed to be an unhealthy amount of time on the couch pursuing his new hobby, crocheting. Dave said Tyler's interest in crocheting blossomed into a "mild obsession." According to Dave, Tyler spent hours a day, every day, with a bag of yarn at his feet and multiple crochet hooks at his side. Other activities that he enjoyed began to take a "backseat." Dave said it was "nothing" at first, but when it started to become excessive and he stopped doing some of the other things boys typically enjoy, it concerned Dave.

Dave thought Tyler's behavior seemed highly unusual for a boy his age. Dave said in a day where boys are surrounded, for the most part, by women, instead of men at home, at church, and in school, Dave was getting concerned that Tyler was spending too much time on an activity typically enjoyed by girls his age. Additionally, Dave confessed that he pictured Tyler a few years from now, crocheting in his middle-school cafeteria with a small "army" of boys around him saying, "Hey, Tyler, will you crochet me a blankie too?" Dave knew how ruthless kids could be and didn't want Tyler to have to experience that cruelty.

Dave finally had an opportunity to speak with Megan. Dave explained that while he didn't think there was anything inherently wrong, immoral, or unbiblical with Tyler's crocheting, Dave thought it was overly excessive and had the potential of causing some problems for Tyler later in life. Needless to say, Dave saw this as a spiritual matter. Dave also admitted that he believed God would hold him responsible if he abdicated his responsibility to address the issue.

Megan, however, did not share Dave's concerns. She angrily told Dave, in essence, that he was unreasonable, absurd, "out of touch with the times," and a "killjoy" for an activity that she and Tyler were enjoying together. He said she also cited, in her defense, different professional male athletes that were expert knitters, "crochet-ers," and seamstresses. In the end, Megan refused to yield to Dave's authority and told Dave that Tyler would continue to crochet as much and as often as he wanted. Dave told her in the "heat" of the moment that while he had no intentions of "going there," if Megan willfully and consistently refused to yield to his position as spiritual leader of the family, he considered this to be grounds for a divorce. Though he had no intention of "going there," He wanted Megan to understand the seriousness of matter.

Dave asked if they could go to counseling to work on the issue. Megan agreed. While they eventually found a "middle ground" in counseling, Dave began to get concerned that Megan saw herself as the spiritual leader of her biological children. He began to wonder if her loyalty to her biological children was, in fact, greater than her loyalty to him and, more importantly, the Word of God. Megan also began to get very fearful and insecure about their future, given what she perceived to be the threat of divorce by Dave.

For Dave, it was no longer about crocheting. For Megan, it was only about crocheting and Dave's unreasonable attempt to be a "control freak" and a "cosmic killjoy."

While their marital "ship" definitely took on some water, they eventually came to an understanding in counseling and were able to move on. Dave said, "Then, about six months later, Satan fired an even bigger torpedo at us." It was another direct hit in the same spot as before, only this time the damage was much greater, and they were taking on a lot more water! Dave said that while he was in "damage control" mode after the hit, Megan again seemed oblivious to what had caused it! Dave said her denial fueled his anger as ownership of her behavior would be essential to the restoration and reconciliation of their relationship.

Forgiveness was never the issue for Dave. Dave said he had forgiven her for her unwillingness to yield to his authority regarding the crocheting. In his mind, it was now about restoration and trust. Dave said for the first time in their marriage, it felt like Megan did not have his back.

This particular "hit" from Satan came by way of a T-shirt that Tyler's biological father had given him (Tyler) for Tyler's gymnastics team, which read, "The Next Big Thing." Dave remembered the first time he saw Tyler wearing the T-shirt, thinking, *Wow, I like the shirt, but I do not like the message it's sending*. Dave felt that it was a very prideful statement that worked against his desire to see Tyler walk in humility as an exceptionally gifted child of God.

Dave thought that it would not be wise to react to the shirt but instead pray about the situation and how to correctly and wisely address it with Megan. Dave wanted to do everything he could to encourage Tyler's relationship with his biological father but did not want to abdicate his spiritual responsibility to address the matter with Megan.

Dave said that he and Tyler had gotten very close with one another up to this point in time. They spent time in Bible study, on nature bike trail rides looking for turtles and honeysuckles, playing chess, practicing pull-ups, push-ups, sit-ups, and "V-ups" for gymnastics; talking about Tyler's favorite snakes, severe weather, or what cloud formations were in the sky. Dave said, most of all, Tyler liked it when Dave taught him about God. Dave said Tyler's favorite book was the Bible. Megan attributed that to Dave and was very grateful for the time Dave spent with Tyler studying God's Word.

Dave said Tyler was a happy, energetic, sensitive, and extremely bright boy who loved God and loved learning about all the creatures

God made for his enjoyment. Tyler enjoyed sharing his knowledge on the make and model of different automobiles, random facts about God and the Bible, weather patterns and cloud formations, as well as random facts about snakes and different reptiles, among other things. Dave said that Tyler also found great satisfaction in knowing that the people around him noticed how bright he was on certain subjects. Whenever Tyler shared something he knew, Dave said that Tyler would often anxiously and eagerly await others' response and "praise." However, whenever he didn't get that praise, he would sometimes pout or get very quiet. This was the part that concerned Dave. Dave thought that while Tyler's behavior was totally normal for a boy his age, he was beginning to show some early signs of pride in his desire to impress others with his knowledge.

Dave, wanting to make sure that pride wasn't trying to rear its ugly head into Tyler's amazing little life, decided that it was time to talk to Megan about Tyler's T-shirt. While Dave said he dreaded this conversation with Megan, he knew he couldn't be silent about something so severe given his love for Tyler and his responsibility to protect him against the spirit of pride as the spiritual leader of the family. Dave said that the potential consequences of allowing pride to manifest itself in Tyler's life would be too great if he didn't "step up" now at this critical stage in Tyler's spiritual development.

Dave remembers the conversation well. Dave, in essence, told Megan that while he (Dave) wanted to honor Tyler's father by allowing Tyler to wear the T-shirt, he (Dave) did not think the shirt was sending the right message to Tyler or others about their family. Dave believed it was important for Tyler to walk humbly before God and "shine the light" on Christ, not on himself. Tyler's T-shirt, "The Next Big Thing," in Dave's mind was "shining the light" on no one but Tyler and a prideful set of parents that had allowed him to wear it for the world to see. This was not the kind of witness that Dave wanted Tyler or their family to have for God.

Curious, Dave asked Megan if Tyler had been getting any reactions from anyone on Tyler's gymnastics team regarding the T-shirt. Megan said (paraphrase), "As a matter of fact, his coaches were saying (paraphrase), 'Oh yeah, so you think you're the next big thing, huh, Tyler? Well, we'll see about that.'" While Megan thought it was funny, Dave didn't. It only confirmed his concerns that, number one, the T-shirt was being noticed and was sending the wrong message and, number two, that it was hurting Tyler's Christian witness and the Christian witness of their family in the community. At least that's how Dave saw it. After much thought and prayer, Dave's concerns over the T-shirt did not subside.

Dave began to lovingly and gently share his concerns again with Megan one day. Dave said Megan was unresponsive and irritated. Dave, getting frustrated and angry with Megan's lack of concern, said to Megan, "So, if Tyler's 'The Next Big Thing,' Megan, does that mean that God doesn't already think that Tyler is a 'Big Thing' right now?" Dave said there was silence from heaven. Dave continued, "If Tyler is 'The Next Big Thing,' Megan, does that mean that the other boys on the team aren't a 'Big Thing' to God?" Dave said. A look of disgust began to form on Megan's face. "And what if someone else on the team or another team become 'The Next Big Thing' instead of Tyler, Megan? How does wearing the T-shirt serve Tyler now?"

Megan was fuming.

Dave continued, "Megan, you and I know from God's Word that Tyler (and all those boys for that matter) are already a 'Big Thing' in God's eyes. To communicate anything else through this T-shirt or in any other way is not only inaccurate and unscriptural but an arrogant, 'worldly' perspective that doesn't reflect well on him, our family, or Jesus Christ. It sends a prideful message from us that we think our son is better than everyone else's son. Tyler should be letting another man praise him, not praising himself (Proverbs 27:2). It's a poor reflection on Tyler and a poor reflection on us. The Bible tells us that we should abstain from even the appearance of evil (1 Thessalonians 5:22), and to me, this T-shirt has an appearance of 'evil'—pride. Please support me on this. I love your son. I'm only trying to protect him. I do not want him to wear this T-shirt anymore. Please. As the spiritual leader of the family, I, not you, will be held accountable."

Dave was desperately hoping Megan would yield to him, even if she didn't agree, remembering the damage from the first "torpedo." Dave said he was holding his breath.

Megan, furious and irritated, said, "Dave, I don't agree with you. It's just a T-shirt! His father gave it to him. I am not going to tell him he can't wear it, and I'm not going to deny Tyler's father the opportunity to bless his son with a T-shirt. Tyler is my child, not yours! You're not going to tell me what to do! We agreed that each of us would make our own decisions concerning our biological children. You agreed. This is not a spiritual issue, Dave. Therefore, he's wearing the T-shirt." Their two worlds had finally collided!

Dave was totally blown away! To him, it was most definitely a spiritual issue, and more importantly, one that he, not she, would be held accountable for as the spiritual leader of the family since Tyler was living under their roof. "And it was just because I wanted to protect Tyler," he said.

Back to counseling they went. Each of them had always agreed that they would go to counseling when either party requested it. Three things came out of counseling this time. First, a confirmation that Megan definitely believed that Dave was *not* the "*primary*" spiritual leader of her biological children, contrary to their premarital discussions. Two, Dave and Megan would "meet in the middle" and allow Tyler to wear the T-shirt at home, but not in public, which Dave still didn't like or agree with but was willing to do for the sake of the marriage. Three, Dave would continue to appeal to Megan to yield to him on future spiritual issues involving her children where disagreements existed.

Up to this point in time, Dave and Megan's counselor still had not addressed Megan's unbiblical belief that she believed she, not Dave, was the spiritual leader over her biological children. Dave said the counselor never told Megan that she needed to stop usurping Dave's authority unless he was asking her to do something wrong or immoral. Dave said that he left this counseling session feeling defeated and hopeless. Dave believed the counselor had left Megan "trapped in her sin" and the relationship vulnerable to future damage because the counselor was unwilling to confront Megan's false theology. Dave was equally "blown away" from the experience in a totally different way. He said their counselor was also a well-known Christian author and speaker with decades of Christian counseling experience, yet seemed to be "clueless" of the underlying issue.

While the counselor thought Dave was a bit "over-the-top" with his concerns over the T-shirt, it was clearly not a case where Dave was asking Megan to do something that was immoral, illegal, or unbiblical. Conversely, Dave said in both cases, he was just trying to spiritually protect Tyler whether Megan agreed or not. At the end of the counseling session, the counselor told Dave, "You just have to love her." Dave said that he had been loving her since the last "attack" and it wasn't working. In fact, things had gotten much worse. Dave believed Megan clearly did not understand his role in their marriage or hers. He said it began to affect all of the other relationships in the house as distance grew between them.

Dave told me that things would have been fine if Megan would have simply owned the fact that she was not the spiritual leader of her biological children and "yielded" (not perfectly, but to the best of her ability) to his role. Dave said she had plenty of room to fail as long as she understood her role and his and was willing to yield to him on spiritual matters regarding her children. Until she agreed to do this, things would likely get much worse. And they did. Dave said that the spiritual warfare and demonic presence in their home increased exponentially with each passing day.

Dave indicated that as incomplete, deficient, and harmful as the counseling was, he and Megan had a game plan going forward. However, admittedly, it was more or less the same game plan as before! Dave had the freedom to "appeal" to Megan on issues involving her children and, specifically, Tyler. In the meantime, he would love her the best way he knew how. Dave concluded that the reason why the counselor didn't confront Megan's false theology (i.e., Megan's belief that she was the spiritual leader of her biological children) was because the counselor either didn't believe it was wrong or didn't have the courage to do so.

Meanwhile, the enemy had done enormous damage to their marriage, and the root problem was still there. Dave said fear and insecurity about the future of their relationship were at an all-time high. Battle-weary, both Dave and Megan were desperately seeking calmer waters. Satan, however, was just getting started. Not even two months later, the devil launched his third and final death blow to their marriage. I don't have to tell you where it "hit." The damage would be unsustainable.

Dave said one night while Dave was getting an evening snack ready for Megan, Tyler, and Madison (Tyler's twin sister), Tyler came through the front door from gymnastics and excitedly ran into the kitchen. When Dave turned around to give Tyler a hug, Dave was mortified! Tyler was wearing the T-shirt! Dave was speechless. He couldn't believe it after he and Megan had agreed that he would only wear the T-shirt at home. Dave was furious. When Dave could gain some composure, Dave asked Megan if she could please come upstairs so they could talk privately.

Once upstairs, Dave asked Megan if she knew Tyler had been wearing the T-shirt tonight, giving her the benefit of the doubt that Tyler may have slipped it on without her knowing it. Megan confirmed that she knew Tyler was wearing the shirt and had allowed it!

Dave's worst fear had become a reality. In Dave's mind, Megan not only believed that she was the spiritual leader of her biological children but was communicating to him that this was how she intended to operate going forward, regardless of Dave's concerns, hurts, or role as the spiritual leader of the family. After Dave stopped speaking, Megan said, "Tyler is my son, not yours. While you are the spiritual leader of this family, I am his mother. I am not going to tell him he can't wear the T-shirt, and neither are you."

Dave was speechless. Dave said to Megan, "But I thought we agreed that he could wear the T-shirt but just at home."

Megan said, "He's going to wear the T-shirt wherever he wants and whenever he wants, Dave. I'm not going to deny him or his father the pleasure of wearing that shirt, and neither are you. He's my child, Dave, not yours."

The Great Role Reversal was complete and there was no denying it, except in Megan's mind! Satan had been given a direct invitation to take over their family formation and did so without ever firing a shot. All it took was just a bit of good old-fashioned "spiritual blind-ness." Another family "grounded" by God and unable to complete its mission because this primary wingman demanded to be the boss when it came to her biological "Blues." It was a horrible "air show."

Righteous and unrighteous anger began to "spill out" every-where in their marriage as the spiritual battle around Dave and Megan intensified. Dave said he created a crisis for the purpose of restoration. Megan "dug in," refusing to repent. Dave confessed that while the same thing happened in his first marriage, it was much more intense this time because he now understood the spiritual con-sequences of being out of order. He also felt that Megan had been dishonest with him before they were married when she told him that she considered him to be the spiritual leader of her children. Dave said, clearly, her understanding of his role when it came to her chil-dren was very different than God's.

Dave said hell and chaos took over their entire family as the devil began sifting them like wheat (Luke 22:31). He said you could cut the demonic presence in their home with a knife. Megan's chil-dren began disrespecting Dave, and for the first time, Megan allowed them to do it. Megan and Dave barely acknowledged one another's presence for days at a time. It was a "free-for-all," and the only one winning was the one who orchestrated it all—Satan! Dave said that in the spirit realm, he saw Satan smiling.

From the first torpedo to this point in time, Dave said that nothing in his Christian arsenal had worked—not prayer, fasting, avoidance, loving confrontation, unloving confrontation, righteous anger, unrighteous anger, counseling, or church intervention. Dave said his next step was a biblical separation with the goal of restoration.

Dave told Megan that he would not return to the marriage until Megan was willing to renounce her role as her children's spiritual leader and give that role to him in title and practice. Dave said that to accept anything less would be to consent to idolatry—acceptance of Megan's divine order above God's divine order. No option. In Dave's mind, Megan had replaced Dave as the spiritual leader of the family with herself. She had elevated herself ("I am Tyler's spiritual leader"), her ex-spouse ("I'm not going to do that to Tyler's father"), and her children ("I am not going to do that to Tyler") above Dave and God.

Dave felt totally betrayed by Megan. Megan felt equally betrayed and abandoned by Dave when he decided to separate. Dave said, "Megan can't get past the fact that I left over a disagreement about a T-shirt." Dave said, "To this day, she still doesn't get it!"

Dave confessed that one of the most difficult aspects of this tragedy is that, in both cases, whether she agreed with him or not, Dave was just trying to protect "her" children. To this day, Dave has great difficulty understanding (even though Megan believes Dave's concerns were unfounded, "controlling," and absurd) why she was unable to see that Dave's motivation in all of this was his love and concern for Tyler. "Unless, of course, the devil blinded her to that as well," he said.

Dave shared that at one point between counseling sessions, the Holy Spirit told him to ask Megan if he (Dave) was the spiritual leader of her biological children. Megan responded, "Yes."

He said then the spirit told him to ask her if he was the *primary* spiritual leader of her children. Megan responded, "No, I am because they are my children." Satan's lie was finally exposed!

Dave and Megan are now divorced. Dave said, "As long as Megan believed she was the 'primary' spiritual leader of her biological children, we would always be a house divided against itself, unable to stand (Mark 3:25). More importantly, we would be unable to fulfill the purpose for which marriage and family were created." Dave further said that for him to stay in the marriage union, he would have to allow the willful and unrepentant practice of idolatry in the home (i.e., Megan to elevate her divine order above God's divine order) and answer for it on Judgment Day. He said, "No way!"

In helicopter terms, Dave knew that under these circumstances, she would never stop fighting him for control of the aircraft when it came to her biological children, preventing them from reaching God's intended destination for their family!

Agreed. It's kind of tough to make the Big Boss look good under these flight conditions, wouldn't you agree?

So why the sad story? To share what the devil is orchestrating in homes all across America every day and not just in blended families. Here me, saints. If the devil *can't* get you upside down using big things, he'll get you upside down using little things like crocheting and T-shirts. He knows exactly what buttons to push. Even as I write this now, I can think of very few marriages that haven't fallen prey to *The Great Role Reversal*, whether it ends in divorce or not! Weak, passive, or abusive husbands who refuse to lead their wives and children biblically that are married to wives who refuse to follow or who selectively follow their husbands are sadly the norm outside in most Christian families!

And just like Megan, most of us don't even know we're upside down because we've believed the lie that a true biblical partnership means that God intended for there to be two bosses with equal spiritual authority in every family formation. Great lie, right? Incidentally, besides the fact that women are not supposed to be in "overseer" positions over men in the church (i.e. pastors or elders), this is another reason why husband-wife co-pastoring is unbiblical, no matter how "big" and "successful" the church (e.g., Hillsong Church, Lakewood Church, etc.). That was extra!

Please don't ever forget what I am about to say! If while reading Dave and Megan's story you found yourself taking "his side" or "her side," you have absolutely missed the point of this entire chapter up to now, which is precisely what the devil was hoping. If all you and I can say is, "Wow, that Dave sure is a hyper-sensitive religious fanatic 'weirdo' or 'control freak'" or "Yep, if I were Megan, I would have said and done the same thing" or "Megan should have known that Dave was the spiritual leader of her children," then guess what? The devil almost kept you from the truth, which is that God absolutely has a divine order for every family, and the moment we disregard it because we don't like it or agree with it is the moment we invite hell to take over our homes. Don't ever forget this! Yes, you and I can ask Adam and Eve all about their fumble when we get to heaven, but shame on us if we drop the ball like they did in the here and now!

Why, some of you may not have liked Dave's position, and he certainly could have handled things better; he was not out of his lane.

Dave never asked Megan to do anything illegal, immoral, unethical, or unbiblical. Remember, this would have been Megan's only "out." On the contrary, his motives were pure (i.e., trying to protecting Tyler), whether you and I agree with Dave's methodology or not. Instead, she, like Eve, took matters into her own hands, elevating her divine order for the family above God's divine order. Remember, one of the purposes of marriage is the replication of God's image through the raising of godly offspring. Again, God is always looking at the remnant seed. Pride is one of the greatest obstacles, if not the greatest obstacle, to the raising of godly offspring. When we sow seeds of pride into the lives of our children (or allow it through our passivity), we are doing the work of the devil!

Remember, while divorce can be useful to advance Satan's kingdom and glory in the earth, Satan is equally "happy" to use families that have been "grounded" by God for "flight violations" to accomplish the same objective. In fact, it can be a very efficient use of his time when he can get the current generation of bosses and primary wingmen (inside and outside of the church) to train the next generation of bosses and primary wingmen (inside and outside of the church) on how to commit *The Great Role Reversal*. Why? Because he doesn't even have to show up. We do his work for him. Have you looked around lately?

Remember, precious one, a "dead" tree can stand in the forest for a long time. So can a "dead" marriage. Therefore, make sure if your marriage is still "standing," you're standing on the rock, Christ Jesus, and the reason for which God created it. Remember, the job of every boss and primary wingman is to make sure the Big Boss looks good!

When it comes to submitting to God's divine order for the family, it is critical that we check our likes and dislikes at the door. Said another way, when our ways disagree with God's ways, He's always right, and we're always wrong!

Please also understand that the devil can't orchestrate *The Great Role Reversal* until he can get a husband or wife to *accept* one of his lies as their truth. The operative word is *accept*. As long we can expose and reject his lie in the suggestion, "consultation," or consideration phase, *The Great Role Reversal* cannot occur. This requires "casting down imaginations and every high thing that exalts self above the knowledge of God" (2 Corinthians 10:5).

You see, lies start as "imaginations." If the devil can get us, like Eve, to "imagine" how glorious things would be if we would just act independently of God and His Word, he's got us. If he can get us to elevate "high things" (i.e., proud things he erects in our minds) above what God has already said on a matter, we're done!

Ladies, you must realize, as the "weaker vessels" (1 Peter 3:7) that you are significantly more prone to being deceived by the devil and committing *The Great Role Reversal* than your husband (all else being equal), and the devil knows it. That's why many religious scholars and theologians believe Satan waited until Eve arrived on the scene before he came to Adam and Eve in the garden.

While my discussion on *The Great Role Reversal* up to now has been intentionally confined to heterosexual marriages, I would be remiss in a chapter about role reversals if I didn't discuss the other great role reversal occurring in society today—gay marriage. Men and women are not only reversing roles in traditional families, but they are abandoning their roles altogether in the pursuit of homosexual unions and marriages. Have you ever considered, for example, that gay marriages can't operate in their God-ordained marital roles as God intended when the opposite sex does not even exist in a two-man or two-woman relationship? However, for gay marriage to allegedly "work," according to them, one partner has to be the "leader" and the other the "follower." This means at least one of the partners are operating in a role that God never designed for them. I do find it fascinating, though not surprising, that some gay couples, however, understand the importance of order in the family better than some heterosexual couples as misplaced as it is!

No, for the record, I'm not a homophobe. In fact, I worked civil rights cases for the FBI, which included investigating hate crimes against gay individuals. I value all human life equally and know that God loves us all the same; however, when what God has to say about a matter (i.e., the sin of homosexuality; Leviticus 18:22, 20:13; Romans 1:26–27; 1 Corinthians 6:9–10; 1 Timothy 1:9–10) differs from what society and the courts have to say about the matter, I'll go with God every time! How about you, Christian? Now, where was I?

We are now at the most important part of the entire chapter and one of the most critical sections of the whole book. Up to now, I've discussed only some of the consequences of *The Great Role Reversal* in a marriage. I would like to cover the rest of them with you now for two reasons. First, so you will never forget them, and secondly and more importantly, so you would never have to experience them. In this way, we can all get back to making the Big Boss look good!

The list below comes from the excellent teachings of none other than Dr. Tony Evans, Christian author, speaker, Senior Pastor of Oak Cliff Bible Fellowship, President of the Urban Alternative, former chaplain for the NFL Dallas Cowboys, and the longest-standing chaplain of the NBA Dallas Mavericks.

Whenever husbands or wives commit what I have been referring to as *The Great Role Reversal* in their marriage, the following devastating consequences occur *until* God's divine order is restored:[39]

1. The husband and wife lose their ability to rule their world as "one;"
2. The marriage no longer functions underneath God's spiritual covering and authority;
3. Satan becomes our new leader, inviting "hell" to take over our home;
4. God holds the "out of order" husband or wife in "contempt of court;"
5. God can no longer help or work for the marriage;
6. God stops participating in the marriage;
7. God opposes the "out of order" spouse(s);
8. The "out of order" spouse cancels God on His or her behalf;
9. The marriage loses God's blessing because God will not operate in, or bless, chaos;
10. The marriage lives in the environment of a "curse" (Genesis 3:17).

If you are experiencing *The Great Role Reversal* right now, do not ignore, deny, minimize, rationalize, blame, or hide the fact that it has occurred. Get help now if you need it! There are a lot of marriages doing the work of the devil! Don't let yours be one of them!

If you're stuck in an out of order marriage with someone who, unrepentantly, refuses to get back in their lane, my heart goes out to you. I know exactly how you feel. While this is where the devil wants you to stay so he can continue to "call the shots" in your family formation, it is not where God wants you to stay. Again, this is not an invitation for divorce. But it is time for you and your mate to get some help. There's a big difference between righteous suffering—that is, suffering for doing what is right as Christ did—and unrighteous suffering, which is suffering for doing what is wrong, unlike what Christ did.

You may feel powerless to speak the truth in love to your mate in your desire to stand up for righteousness. In moments like these, it is critical that each of us ask ourselves the following questions. One, does Jesus want me to elevate man's divine order above God's divine order (idolatry)? Two, what does this say about my heart? Three, is my unwillingness to do what is right helping or hindering my spouse (or me) from becoming holy? Four, is this the kind of legacy I want to leave to those behind me after all Jesus has done for me? Finally, what will my Judgment Day look like if I refuse to stand up for righteousness in this hour and fail to fulfill God's purpose and plan for my life (chapter 1)?

For those of you who say, "Have you ever considered that *The Great Role Reversal* may be God's will for me in my marriage?" to this, I respond, how can you possibly read the list of ten consequences above for committing *The Great Role Reversal* and believe that any of them is God's will for you? While Satan would love for you to believe this, don't confuse consequences for "sin" with God's will, beloved. God's will is that we would not sin so that we would not have to bear the consequences of our sin. Secondly, go back and reread chapter 1. You have already forgotten why you are here! How can you, as a couple, rule your world under God's hand to advance His kingdom and bring Him glory when your marital unit refuses to operate under God's hand because one or both or you are out of your lanes?

Again, please understand, I am not advocating divorce; I am advocating obeying God and leaving the consequences to Him![40]

If you are the one who's out of your lane with no intention of getting back into it, please know that going to church, praying, fasting, or being part of a Bible study is a total waste of time! If you don't believe me, take a look at what the Lord God said through the prophet Isaiah to the Israelites who, like you, were elevating their ways above God's ways (committing idolatry; *italics* used for emphasis):

> Tell my people Israel of their sins! Yet, they act so pious! They come to the Temple every day and seem delighted to hear my laws. You would almost think this was a righteous nation that would never abandon its God. They love to make a show of coming to me and asking me to take action on their behalf. "We have fasted before you!" they say. "Why aren't you impressed? We have done much penance, and you don't even notice it!"
>
> I'll will tell you why! It's because you are living for yourselves even while you are fasting. You keep right on oppressing your workers. *What good is fasting when you keep on fighting and quarreling? This kind of fasting will never get you anywhere with me.* You humble yourselves by going through the motions of penance, bowing your heads like a blade of grass in the wind. You dress in sackcloth and cover yourselves with ashes. *Is this what you call fasting? Do you really think this will please the Lord?* (Isaiah 58:1–5 NLT)

Similarly, recall the words of Samuel when he said the following (*italics* used for emphasis):

> What is more pleasing to the Lord: your burnt offerings and sacrifices or your obedience to His voice? Listen! *Obedience is better than sacrifice and submission is better than offering the fat of rams*. (1 Samuel 15:22 NLT)

If you are the one causing *The Great Role Reversal*, "own it," repent, and "go and sin no more" (John 8:11). Now that you know the truth, you and I are now accountable to God to do something about it! Aren't you glad you read this book? However, out of my great love for you and the church, you should also know that if you reject this truth and continue to operate out of your lane, you are completely out of God's will. You will sadly and tragically experience all of the consequences I have outlined above if you haven't already. It is my earnest prayer that this would not have to happen to you and that you would humble yourself, get back in your lane, and receive the forgiveness and healing that God has for you.

If, on the other hand, you are the one enabling or allowing *The Great Role Reversal* to occur (as Adam did), please understand that you are just as culpable for the loss of God's favor in your marriage as your spouse and even more if you're the "boss."

Wives, if you enable, rescue, or follow a husband who is "out of order," you will bear the consequences outlined above. You are not loving him, serving him, or bringing glory to God if you do this and may even be placing yourself and your children in danger. If this is you, I urge you to get help now!

In his forty-plus years of counseling married couples as the senior pastor of Oak Cliff Bible Fellowship, Dr. Tony Evans says the one common denominator that *every married couple* he counsels has is that one or both spouses are "out of their lanes."[41] The only marriages that received healing were those where the spouse or spouses who were out of their lanes got back in their "lanes!"[42] Wow, right?

The Bible says that he who sows to the flesh shall of the flesh reap corruption, but he who sows to the Spirit shall of the Spirit reap everlasting life (Galatians 6:8–9 NKJV). This principle holds true not only for the one who is causing *The Great Role Reversal* to occur (like Eve) but to the one who is allowing *The Great Role Reversal* to occur (like Adam). In other words, whether we are sowing seeds of "activity" that cause *The Great Role Reversal* to occur (like Eve) or are sowing seeds of "inactivity" that allow *The Great Role Reversal* to occur (like Adam), we *will* reap the devastating consequences of *The Great Role Reversal.*

You must know that while many Christians know when they are out of their lanes, many Christians do not as you saw with Megan. This is the main reason why I shared their story. And because most of us don't look to "fix" something that isn't broken (at least in our minds), the most serious out of order scenario is when an out of order husband or wife genuinely believes they are in their lane when they aren't.

"Spiritual blindness" is a form of bondage. Think about it. If the devil is slick enough to convince a spouse that they are in their lane when they aren't, how hard do you think it is for him to convince us that everything is "all good" when it's not?

Maybe you're saying, "Great, but what do I do if my mate has committed *The Great Role Reversal,* and he or she refuses to get back in their lane?

Great question. Shine a brighter light on the problem by bringing other witnesses into the situation as outlined in Matthew 18:15–17. While this is a very familiar passage of scripture to most, Christians seldom use it in the context of marital conflict. It is Jesus's instructions to us on how to deal with a brother or sister which includes a Christian spouse who has "sinned" against us. See for yourself:

> Moreover, if your brother sins against you, go and tell Him His fault between you and Him alone. If He hears you, you have gained a brother. But if He will not hear, take with you one or two more, that 'by the mouth of two or three witnesses every word may be established.' And if He refuses to hear them, tell it to the church. But if He refuses even to hear the church, let Him be to

you like a heathen and a tax collector. (Matthew 18:15–17 NKJV)

Sadly, however, few husbands, wives, friends, family members, and church leaders are willing to apply this scripture to marriages and exercise church discipline like this, where appropriate, for reasons I will discuss later in this book. For now, it suffices to say that none of them are good!

As we come to the close of this chapter, maybe you realize you have committed *The Great Role Reversal* with God as an individual or with your spouse and God if you are married. If you are prepared to get some help, please allow me to be the first to congratulate you. Your life and marriage now have a chance of being everything God intended. Additionally, you have unselfishly made our nation stronger. Most importantly, by agreeing to do life on God's terms and not your own, God is no longer opposing you, and the devil can no longer rule over you. Your marriage is now able to build God's kingdom for His glory! However, the fight for your life and home has just begun. The good news is that you and I have the victory in Jesus Christ, and the devil knows it! He just doesn't want you to know it. Too late for that!

Please remember, no matter what you are going through, precious one, God always gives greater grace (James 4:6). For those married, even if your mate sadly doesn't want to assume his or her biblical role, you can assume yours. While your marriage may be "grounded," you are not individually "grounded." Do not allow your spouse's disobedience to be an excuse for your disobedience. After all, your obedience may be the very catalyst God uses to cause your mate to get back in their lane. But then again, it may not (1 Corinthians 7:16), contrary to all the bad Christian counseling out there that "guarantees" it will.

Nevertheless, let your obedience either drive them to you and God or away from you and God. In this way, they are the ones deciding against you and God, not the other way around. Though you are still a house divided in your marriage, you are no longer part of the problem. More importantly, however, God is no longer your biggest problem!

Husbands, God would never ask you to forsake His truth or divine order as the way to demonstrate love to your wife. This is not how Jesus loves the church. Contrary, it was Jesus's submission to the Father's will, against His disciples' desires I might add, that led to the greatest demonstration of love the world has ever known!

Similarly, wives, you cannot place yourself underneath the authority of your husband in every area of life until you have first placed yourself underneath the authority of the Lord Jesus Christ in every area of life (Ephesians 5:22). The same is true of you, single Christian lady who desires a husband one day. Until you're willing to do this, do yourself, your future mate, society, and God a favor and don't get married.

Additionally, husbands and wives, God would never ask you to elevate your or your spouse's "chain of command" above God's chain of command to "save" your marriage. That's not only "bad" theology, it's idolatry!

As you may have guessed, the ten devastating consequences of *The Great Role Reversal* I have outlined above are not confined to marriage. They apply to every institution in America from our house to the White House.

In the case of churches, the consequences of *The Great Role Reversal* would apply to a pastor, for example, who is not shepherding his flock under God's authority. Maybe it's because he is engaging in false teaching or perhaps it's because he is allowing his "sheep" to lead the church where they want to go, instead of him leading the church where God has instructed him to go. Maybe it's because your church allows women to hold the office of senior pastor (in the case of husband-wife co-pastoral teams), pastor, associate pastor, or elder in violation of 1 Timothy 2:11–14, 3:1–13; Titus 1:5–9; 1 Peter 5:1–4; Acts 6:1–6. Did you just hear plates crashing?

By the way, what other "outdated" "no longer applicable" New Testament verses have some of you conveniently kicked to the curb because they are no longer politically correct? Or maybe you're concerned about the effect they could have on tithing and, God forbid, "your" church growth if you don't kowtow to the culture? I've heard all the spiritual mumbo-jumbo. And for those of you who wish to wrongly judge me as a chauvinist or misogynist to justify your rebellion to God's Word, good luck with that on Judgment Day. I also wish you luck with the many superb female FBI agents and federal prosecutors I have had the pleasure of working with and under (in some cases) during my career. I don't recommend getting on their bad side! The workplace is not a divine institution, beloved. However, the home and the church are!

Now, where was I? Oh, yeah. Maybe the church is out of order because the senior leadership of the church is really only interested in building (or preserving) their kingdoms or because church leadership is continually and unrepentantly making allowances for evil because they want to be embraced by the culture. The result is the same. "Out of order" churches are now being transformed by an "out of order" culture!

Instead of God's priorities being God, family, church, then work (ministry), many pastors (because their occupation and ministry are the same) make their first priority all three—God, church, and the ministry (all wrapped up in one) and then family when it should be God, family, and then the church. This is the great challenge for every pastor and why it is so easy for the devil to get pastors "upside down" without them even knowing it, subjecting themselves, their families, and their flock to "fallout" from the consequences of committing *The Great Role Reversal* against God and others.

If we can't get it right at home and in our churches, how can we expect our communities, cities, states, government, and nation to get it right? Simple. We can't!

You see, our nation is upside down morally, socially, and spiritually because many of our homes and churches are upside down. Elected officials, at every level of government, for example, have, through demonic influence, orchestrated *The Great Role Reversal* with God himself by elevating themselves, their policies, and their party politics above God and His Word. Instead of us being one nation under God, we've become one nation, in many cases, who thinks it's above God. What many of us don't realize, however, is that God will share His glory with no one, including those inside the Beltway who think that they know more than God when it comes to things like gay marriage, taxpayer-funded LGBTQ education, The Equality Act, abortion, harvesting baby parts for profit, and open borders. And poppycock to those of you who claim to be Christians inside the Beltway and have the spineless arrogance to push these off as "state matters" and not voice your opposition out of fear of how your constituents might perceive you! Step up or resign!

These are not state matters, friend, these are God matters, and guess who God is going to hold accountable at every level of government for making sure they stay God matters? Every Christian who holds a position in government, at every level of government, and every Christian voter in America who has the ability to make these God matters in the office they held (or hold) or in the voting booth but didn't. Real Christians obey the laws of the land *unless* those laws run contrary to God (i.e., gay marriage, abortion, etc.). Selah.

Every knee will bow and every tongue will confess that Jesus Christ is Lord (Philippians 2:10–11). We can do it now with actions that show this is true in the offices we hold, or we can do it later when, one day, it will be too late. But one thing is for sure. We will all do it! If you've never heard this before, take this as your official warning from God through me to you. No, we are not behaving as one nation under God but as one nation that thinks that it is above God and is somehow exempt from the consequences of committing idolatry against God!

> Do not be deceived: God is not be mocked;
> for whatever a man sows, that He will also reap.
> For He who sows to the flesh will of the flesh
> reap corruption, but He who sows to the Spirit
> will of the Spirit read everlasting life. (Galatians
> 6:7–8 NKJV)

Haven't we reaped enough chaos and corruption from our house to the White House?

Thus, God not only "grounds" individuals, marriages, families, and churches that commit *The Great Role Reversal* by getting out of their "lanes" but also entire cities, states, and nations.

Look now, if you will, at the same ten consequences I covered earlier that have been modified for America to show what happens to any nation (like ours) that commits *The Great Role Reversal* with God. In other words, when this great nation, America, commits *The Great Role Reversal* with the Lord God, the following devastating consequences will occur *until* God's divine order is restored:[43]

1. America loses its ability to "rule," that is, to exercise *godly* rulership and dominion over its "sovereign territory" within its sovereign boundaries;
2. America no longer operates under God's spiritual covering and authority;
3. Satan becomes America's leader, causing "hell" to take over our nation;
4. God holds the "out of order" nation, America, in "contempt of court;"
5. God can't help or "work" for America;
6. God stops participating with America;
7. God opposes America;
8. The "out of order" nation, America, cancels God on their behalf;
9. America loses God's blessing because God will not "bless" chaos;
10. America lives in the environment of a "curse."

Have you looked around lately? If this doesn't motivate us to "repent" and get back in our lanes, nothing will!

As a retired military veteran and public servant of this great country for nearly thirty-six years, I, like many of you, am proud to be an American. However, I am not proud that this nation has elevated man's law, in many cases, above God's law. Additionally, I am not proud that we have elevated man's ways above God's ways, and man's worship of country, flag, and its founding documents *above* man's worship of God, the cross, and God's founding document, the Holy Bible. I am not proud that our nation, allegedly founded on Judeo-Christian values, has kicked Jesus Christ and His Word out of every conceivable institution in America from our house to the White House while some of these same "so-called" Christians "jam" a radical "far-left" agenda down the throats of the American people. Please, if you're going to gain power and enrich yourself at the expense of those you swore to represent, at least have the decency to leave God out of your rousing hypocritical speeches that you arrogantly conclude with "God Bless America."

If you remember nothing else from this book, remember this: As I said earlier, the fundamental problem with our lives and every institution in America we comprise from our house to the White House comes down to one question, "Whose word will be final?" Will God's Word have the final word? Or will the Supreme Court, our political party, pollsters, professional athletes, pop-culture, social media, Hollywood, friends, or (fill in the blank) have the final word? Satan wants to know!

Please understand that when it comes to committing *The Great Role Reversal* at any level in society, we are talking about characteristic behavior, right? All of us get out of our lanes from time to time. The Bible says that the godly may trip seven times but will get up again (i.e., get back in their lanes). But one disaster is enough to overthrow the wicked (Proverbs 24:16). Why? Because the wicked refuse to get up and get back in their lanes. All of us have moments when we do not submit to God's authority. The question is, what are we characterized by, individually, as the people of God and as a nation? But more importantly than that, what do we do when we find ourselves out of our lanes? Do we "man up," take ownership, and get back in our lanes? Or do we refuse (rebellion) or deny (spiritual blindness) that we're even out of our lanes?

We cannot expect our nation to get back in its lane under God until we, God's people, in every institution in America from our house to the White House get back in our lanes!

Can you imagine how different our homes, churches, cities, states, and nation would be if the 80 percent of us who profess to be

Christians would get back in our lanes to become one nation that is truly under God in every area of life?

Do you know what I love most about this chapter? Knowing the devil hates it! He is absolutely furious that you now know about *The Great Role Reversal!* Please don't let it go to waste. Share it with as many people as you can—your family, church, community, small group, men's group, ladies' group, and Bible study so we, by God's grace, can all receive the healing God has for us and give Him all the glory!

For those of you who just decided to "do life," "family," and church God's way, you not only dealt a death blow to Satan and the power of *The Great Role Reversal* in your life, your family, and your church, but you gave Jesus Christ and this nation the greatest gift possible—your heart!

To celebrate your decision, I give to you the below-revised version of the Blue Angel Creed, written especially for you (*italics* and [] used for emphasis):

> Today is an amazing and memorable day in your life and the life of your [family] that will remain with you forever. You have agreed to take the narrow road in a world that is content to take the wide road because you wear His name. The humble privilege of being a child of God in this, your new family formation, carries with it an extraordinary honor, privilege, and responsibility—one that reflects not only on you as an individual, but on the rest of your family and the entire family of God around the world. To you who seek to follow Christ and are willing to make that sacrifice, you are the truest of heroes. The Kingdom of God and it's King, Jesus, applaud you. You bring encouragement, hope, and a promise for tomorrow's families and churches in the smiles and handshakes of those who look to

you to show them the way of our Lord and Savior Jesus Christ.

Remember today as the day you committed yourselves to following Jesus Christ His way and in accordance with His Word; look around at the rest of your family and church and commit this special bond to memory. "Once a follower of Jesus Christ, always a follower of Jesus Christ rings true for all who proudly wear His name and are willing to follow Him to the ends of the earth. Welcome to the family!

Prayer of Repentance (if applicable)

Lord Jesus, I confess I've been "out of order" and "out of my lane" with you and my spouse. In doing so, I have forsaken you as my leader and invited Satan to take over my home. I have allowed my word and others' word to have the final word in every aspect of my life. I recognize that in doing this, I have advanced Satan's kingdom in the earth instead of yours, contributing to the cultural chaos around us.

I repent, first and foremost, for sinning against you and, secondly, for sinning against my spouse, children, church, city, state, and nation (where applicable). At this time, I turn from my prideful and self-centered way of operating to align myself behind and underneath you, my spouse (for the married ladies), and your word in this most crucial area of life whether my spouse gets back in their lane or not.

Grant me the courage to humble myself and ask those (where appropriate) to forgive me for committing *The Great Role Reversal.*

I now willfully choose to get in my lane and assume my proper role within the family formation as you designed. Help me from this day forward to stay in my lane and never again elevate my divine order above your divine order, committing idolatry against you.

Thank you for your steadfast love and mercies toward me that never cease and are new every morning (Lamentations 3:22) and for standing more prepared to forgive my sins than I am to commit them, more willing to supply my needs than I am to confess them.

May my "family formation" bring you great honor and glory from this day forward as I seek to follow you and operate within the boundaries and limitations of your word to advance your kingdom and bring glory to your name! In Jesus's name. Amen.

Verses to Remember

1. And the Lord God took the man and put Him in the Garden of Eden to tend and guard and keep it. (Genesis 2:15 AMPC)
2. The man gave names to all livestock and to the birds of the heavens and to every beast of the field. But for Adam there was not a *helper* fit for Him. (Genesis 2:20 ESV)
3. Then He said to the woman He said, "I will sharpen the pain of your pregnancy, and in pain you will give birth. And you will desire to control your husband, but He will rule over you." And to the man He said, "Since you have listened to your wife and ate from the tree whose fruit I commanded you not to eat, the ground is cursed because of you." (Genesis 3:16–17 NET)

4. Pride goes before destruction and a haughty spirit before a fall. (Proverbs 16:18 AMP)

5. But I want you to know and realize that Christ is the Head of every man, the head of a woman is her husband, and the Head of Christ is God… Now if anyone is disposed to be argumentative and contentious about this, we hold to and recognize no other custom [in worship] than this, nor do the churches of God generally. (1 Corinthians 11:3,16 AMPC)

6. Wives submit to your own husbands, as to the Lord. For the husband is the head of the wife, as also Christ is the head of the church; and He is the Savior of the body. Therefore, just as the church is subject to Christ, so let the wives be to their own husbands in everything. Husbands, love your wives, just as Christ also loved the church and gave Himself for her, that He might sanctify and cleanse her with the washing of water by the word, that He might present her to Himself a glorious church, not having spot or wrinkle or any such thing, but that she should be holy and without blemish. (Ephesians 5:22–27 NKJV)

7. To be discreet, chaste, keepers at home, good, obedient to their own husbands, that the Word of God be not blasphemed. (Titus 2:5 BRG)

8. All things must be done decently and in order. (1 Corinthians 14:40 KJV)

9. No man can serve two masters: for either He will hate the one and love the other; or else He will hold to the one and despise the other. Ye cannot serve God and mammon. (Matthew 6:24 KJV)

10. And if a house is divided against itself, that house will not be able to stand. (Mark 3:25 ESV)

11. Lest Satan should get an advantage of us; for we are not ignorant of His devices. (2 Corinthians 2:11 KJV)

12. My people are destroyed for lack of knowledge. (Hosea 4:6 ASV)

13. Therefore, submit to God. Resist the devil and He will flee from you. (James 4:7 KJV)
14. Perhaps God will grant them repentance leading them to the knowledge of the truth. Then they may come to their senses and escape the devil's trap, having been captured by Him to do His will.(2 Timothy 2:26 HCSB)

CHAPTER 3

◆◆◆◆◆

Whose Covenant Is It Anyway?

"A marriage covenant is a very serious thing and it should never, ever, be broken under any circumstance." Really? That's it? Please tell me there's more. Welcome to the chapter where there's more—much more! And for a good reason. You see, we, the church, are not only being transformed by the culture because we don't know why we're here (chapter 1) and because we are committing *The Great Role Reversal* with God and one another (chapter 2), but also because we thought we wrote the book on marriage, divorce, and remarriage!

To have a proper and complete biblical understanding of marriage, divorce, and remarriage, it helps to understand why God created marriage in the first place. Before you "tune" me out because you think you've heard this before, trust me when I say that most of you, including pastors, have not heard all I am about to say, which is why I devoted an entire chapter to it. How do I know this? Because I have been listening to many of you for years and never heard it before! For those of you who are looking for some new premarriage counseling material, you just found it! And yes, many of you, like me, will wish you had known this years ago! That's okay. God's ways are higher than ours, and He doesn't waste anything! Allow me to kick things off with a question.

Have you ever stopped to consider why, after creating man, God said, "Be fruitful and multiply" (Genesis 1:28 KJV)? Was it just about populating the earth with offspring that look like us who could fund Social Security? Or did God have something else bigger in mind? Welcome to the first reason why God created marriage.

The first reason why God created marriage was to replicate His image worldwide through the spread of Godly offspring (Malachi 2:15) who would, as image-bearers of the King, spread God's glory far and wide through the expansion of His kingdom! You see, offspring that do not become godly offspring do not accomplish this objective and are of no use to God when it comes to kingdom business, which is the only business that counts; remember (chapter 1)? I used to think this "procreation thing" was just about "numbers." How about you?

The second reason why God created marriage was for divine illustration. In the same way that a husband, a wife, and their offspring make up one unit, known as the family, Father, Son, and Holy Spirit make up one unit, known as the Godhead, and who we commonly refer to as the Trinity. Both "units" are three-in-one divine relationships.

We also know that marriage is a divine illustration of Christ's (our heavenly bridegroom's) relationship to the church ("His bride"). This is the more common teaching you hear in churches and at marriage conferences. It is absolutely true and accurate. The commonly-quoted biblical support for this is found in Ephesians 5 which says, "Husbands, love your wives, just as Christ also loved the church and gave himself up for her, that He might sanctify and cleanse her with the washing of water by the word, that He might present her to Himself a *glorious church*, not having spot or wrinkle or any such thing, but that she should be holy and without blemish" (Ephesians 5:25–27 NASB).

The home, as a unit of the church, also has a part in God's plan for the church in the earth (chapter 1). As a husband and wife live together in unity within the framework of their God-ordained functions (chapter 2), their home becomes an outpost of God's rule for defeating Satan and his demonic forces in the earth to expand God's kingdom and bring Him glory (chapter 1).

The third and final reason why God created marriage was for self-*realization*. He wanted the first man, Adam, and every man after him to *realize* that it is not good for man to be alone. Note, He didn't say it's not good for man to be *single*; He said it is not good for man to be alone—without a "helper" suitable for him (Genesis 2:18). To help him do what? To help him rule over all that God created to advance God's kingdom and bring Him glory on earth as it is in heaven (chapter 1).

The Apostle Paul, as you know, has much to say about the benefits of singlehood. Thus "alone" and "single," from God's perspective, must be very different. And they are. Our status, whether single or married, is not fulfilled in our calling. Our calling is fulfilled in our status, whether single or married. Please read that again. We get it all backward and believe the lie that we're not complete until we're married. In fact, it's no secret that many Christian spouses feel "alone" in their kingdom-building efforts because their husband or wife is either disinterested in kingdom business or more interested in building their kingdom than God's. Thus, a marriage must have its spiritual roots in something far more significant than mere companionship. And it does.

While companionship was and is an added benefit to marriage, it was not and is not the *primary* reason why God created woman for man (1 Corinthians 11:9). Again, the boy needed help ruling everything God gave him to advance God's kingdom (chapter 1). While there are exceptions, like Paul, who have the gift of singleness and rely on *help* from others to fulfill this purpose and calling, God wanted Adam, and now us men, to *realize* that most men receive their greatest *help* from their wives since most men, by God's design, do not have the gift of singleness. And thank God we don't—again, by design—since God knew among other things that procreation would be needed to replicate His image far and wide through the spread of godly offspring. At least that's the way it's supposed to work!

Singles, you'll know you've found the right one when the one you are considering marrying not only has kingdom expansion for God's glory as their primary goal but has the track record as a single to prove it! Are you thinking about marrying him? Ask him to tell you the last time he shared the Gospel with someone. Ask her to tell you who she is currently discipling? If they haven't done this as a single, and it's not a top priority now, expect more of the same after marriage. If you do not end the relationship, you just elevated your primary reason for marriage (i.e., personal happiness) above God's primary reason for marriage (i.e., the expansion of His kingdom in history by replicating His image through godly offspring and exercising dominion over the earth). Not good.

How can our families and churches become outposts of God's rule in the earth if the marriages in them never become outposts of God's rule in the earth? Said another way, how can our families and churches advance God's kingdom and bring Him glory if the marriages in them never advance God's kingdom and bring Him glory?

Is this why you got married? Sadly, it is not why most people get married. Yes, even Christians. Come on, tell the truth and shame the devil. Most of us, if we were honest, get married for no other reason but our own personal happiness, which is why so many marriages fail or never become what God intended them to be whether divorce occurs or not. This "low bar" for Christian marriage, which is no different than the "world's" bar, is also one of the main reasons why I believe the church is having very little impact in the culture but why the culture is having tremendous impact on the church!

Now that we know why God created marriage, we now have some context from which to begin a discussion on marriage covenants. First, allow to provide some brief background on what a covenant is, generally, from God's perspective which, if you recall, is the only perspective that counts.

In essence, a *covenant* is a divinely ordained contract predicated upon a relationship to God.[44] In his book, *Kingdom Man*, Dr. Tony Evans says the following about every covenant (brackets [] used for emphasis):

Every covenant always includes three fundamental facets: transcendence, hierarchy, and ethics. Transcendence simply means that God rules above as sovereign over the covenant. He is in charge. Hierarchy represents the specific order in which the covenantal components and participants are to function [chapter 2]. And ethics, which are the rules that govern the operation of the covenant, include three interdependent elements: rules, sanctions, and continuity.

When a marriage functions according to the components of a covenant, the blessings of the covenant are the ultimate result. However, when a marriage functions outside the components of the covenant, the negative consequences attached to the covenant will result. Because marriage is a sacred covenant and not just a social contract, it entails sanctions and continuity that have generational repercussions. A contract is a legal agreement that does not carry within it a spiritual and divine component, while a covenant engages God in relationship to His kingdom and the spiritual benefits and losses that occur because of that agreement.[45]

So as you can see, God's covenants are no joke. But that's not all. For example, did you know that every covenant is established and inaugurated by the shedding of blood (Hebrews 9:18)? The word *covenant* comes from the Hebrew word meaning "to cut."[46] This explains the strange Old Testament custom of two people passing through the cut bodies of slain animals after making an agreement (Genesis 15:10, Jeremiah 34:18). Before the coming of Christ, we know that God established His covenant with man through the shedding of blood from bulls, goats, rams, and lambs. Without the shedding of animal blood, there could be no atonement for sin. In the New Testament, God established a new *covenant* between God and man through the shedding of Christ's blood on the cross for the forgiveness of sins. Jesus said, "This cup is the new *covenant* sealed by my blood, which is being poured out for you" (Luke 22:20 ISV). The book of Hebrews says it this way: "[t]hrough the blood *that sealed and ratified* the eternal covenant" (Hebrews 13:20 AMP). Love it!

God also demonstrated this principle in the way He designed a virgin's body to respond to intercourse with her husband for the first time. When the hymen is broken, there is the shedding of blood "[a]nd the two shall become one flesh" (Mark 10:8 NIV). Finally, even the cowboys and Indians understood that promises, agreements, and brotherhood weren't binding until blood from the cowboy's wrist touched blood from the Indian's wrist during a forearm shake.

God established eight different covenants with man. While I will not dive too deeply into them as it would take another book to do it, it is critical for our remaining discussion to understand that some of these covenants are conditional and some of them are unconditional. In essence, God's conditional covenants say the following, "If you do this, then I, God, obligate myself to do that. If, however, you don't do this, then I, God, no longer obligate myself to do that." In other words, if we don't do what God tells us to do, God renders the covenant invalid or broken. In the case of an unconditional covenant, however, God obligates to fulfill His promise to us, even when we don't fulfill our promise to Him.

Five of the eight major covenants that God established in the Bible were made with the Israelites. He established the other three with all of mankind. Two of the eight covenants are conditional, the Edenic Covenant and the Mosaic Covenant, while the other six are unconditional and include the Adamic Covenant, Noahic Covenant, Abrahamic Covenant, the Palestinian or Land Covenant, the Davidic Covenant, and the New Covenant (in part). Let's take a look at a few of them now.

As mentioned above, the Edenic Covenant is a conditional covenant. Here, God promised Adam eternal life if he would abide by the terms of God's covenant and not eat from the tree of the knowledge of good and evil located in the Garden of Eden. God told Adam, however, that in the day he disobeyed, he would surely die

(Genesis 2:15–17). A condition was placed on Adam. His future and the future of all mankind would be tied to Adam's obedience. We know how that turned out. The record of Adam breaking the Edenic Covenant is found in Genesis 3:1–8.

The other conditional covenant is the Mosaic Covenant. It is the only conditional covenant that God established with the nation of Israel. Unlike the unconditional covenant God made with Abraham, wherein God would bring forth a great nation through Abraham regardless of what Abraham did or didn't do (Genesis 12:1–3), the covenant between God and Israel (the Mosaic Covenant) was a conditional covenant. In essence, it said that God would keep His promise to bless the nation of Israel if the nation of Israel remained faithful. God established it at Mount Sinai with Moses, Israel's leader at the time. It is sometimes referred to as the Sinai Covenant.

Under the Mosaic covenant, God said *if* you will indeed obey my voice and keep my covenant, *then* you shall be my treasured possession among all peoples, for all the earth is mine (Exodus 19:5 ESV). While the people agreed to the covenant when they said—"All that the Lord has spoken, we will do" (Exodus 19:8 ESV)—their hearts to obey didn't match their wills to obey when God said, "But like Adam, they [Israel] have transgressed the covenant. There they have dealt treacherously against me" (Hosea 6:7 NASB).

The blessing and cursing associated with adherence to and rejection of the Mosaic covenant may be found, among other places, in Leviticus 26 and Deuteronomy 28, respectively. In short, when Israel was obedient, God blessed them. When Israel was disobedient, God disciplined them.

Daniel, the Hebrew prophet, acknowledged the conditional nature of God's Mosaic Covenant in a prayer of confession and repentance when he said, "Oh, Lord, the great and dreadful God, who keepeth covenant and lovingkindness *with them that love Him and keep His commandments*" (Daniel 9:4 NLT). While the nation of Israel eventually reached the Promised Land, Canaan, under Joshua, first-generation Israelites who had been freed from Pharaoh and led out of Egypt under the leadership of Moses were relegated to wander in the wilderness for forty years due to their unbelief and disobedience. While God continued to meet their physical needs, Joshua and Caleb were the only ones from the first generation that God permitted to enter into the Promised Land (Numbers 14:30). Those who believed God's promise of long ago were freed from spiritual death ("Egypt") to abundant life in the Promised Land to receive their spiritual inheritance while those who didn't believe in God's promise died in the wilderness.

The Noahic Covenant, unlike the two previous covenants, however, is an example of an unconditional covenant that God made with man, wherein God said no matter what you (man) do, I will never destroy the earth by way of flood again (Genesis 9:11). Every time we see a rainbow (the sign of the Noahic covenant), we are reminded of God's faithfulness to uphold His covenant promise to us, even though we continue to sin.

While the New Covenant that God made with man involving the free gift of salvation offered through Jesus Christ's death on the cross for the forgiveness of sin is an unconditional covenant to Jew and Gentile alike. There is a conditional component to it. In other words, action is required on our part for it to become our experience and reality. No action. No reality. Thus, a condition. The action necessary requires us to call upon the name of the Lord (Romans 10:13). It requires us to confess with our mouth, the Lord Jesus, and believe that God has raised Him from the dead (Romans 10:9). It requires us to repent and be converted that our sins may be blotted out (Acts 3:19). It requires us to acknowledge and accept the payment that Jesus Christ made on our behalf as our personal sin-bearer and substitute on the cross (1 Peter 2:24) and the only acceptable means whereby men can be saved (Acts 4:12).

The conditional component of the New Covenant also appears in John 3:36, which says, "He who believes and trusts in the Son and accepts Him [as Savior] has eternal life [that is, already possesses it]; *but He who does not believe the Son and chooses to reject Him*, [disobeying Him and denying Him as Savior] will not see [eternal life], but [instead] the wrath of God hangs over Him continually" (John 3:36 AMP). My point in sharing this background on a few of God's covenants is to simply highlight the fact that God does not always bind or obligate himself to a contract when others reject His terms and conditions. Therefore, those church leaders and Christians who say (and many do!) that God never breaks His covenants with man wrongly divide the truth (2 Timothy 2:15).

With this critical background now laid, we are now ready to turn to the heart of the chapter. God's marriage covenant or divinely ordained contract with husbands and wives predicated upon their relationship to Him, contrary to what many believe in mainstream Christianity is a conditional covenant. Did I just hear plates crashing again? Now, before you start "hatin'," I suggest you read on, brothers and sisters. Again, let God be true and every man a liar (Romans 3:4), including me!

While marriage should be honored by all (Hebrews 13:4) and always placed on the "high shelf," making divorce hard to reach and always the last option, God does, in certain circumstances, allow the marriage covenant to be broken (i.e., divorce to occur). Why? He allows it to happen to protect innocent parties from the ravages of sin that entered the world through the fall of Adam and Eve. As long as we are faithful to abide by God's "rule book" for marriage, the Holy Bible, God's marriage contract (covenant) with us remains valid. If, however, we violate God's rule book for marriage, God, depending on the circumstances, will allow His covenant with us to be broken to protect and preserve life.

God's Word says that our wives are our companions *by covenant* (Malachi 2:14). There it is. All marriages, from God's perspective, as stated in our definition of covenant above, are designed to operate under a divinely ordained contract predicated upon a relationship to God. God gave us the terms and conditions of the marriage covenant (transcendence, hierarchy, and ethics) in His Word, asked us to study it (2 Timothy 2:15) and then "sign" His terms and conditions (by His Spirit) on our wedding day if we are willing to abide by them. At least, that's the way it's supposed to work! If only more of our pre-marital counseling focused on this! If you're engaged to be married and do not fully "get" what I just said, I urge you to put on the brakes now until you do!

Most of us thought we got to draft the terms and conditions of our "marriage contracts" with God and one another for how marriage was going to work for God to sign. No, no, friend. God wrote the terms and conditions of our contract with Him in His Word for our signature! Hear me. Most marriages fail or never become what God meant for them to be from day one, whether divorce occurs or not, because of what I just said. Again, it's His contract and His terms with us, not our contract and our terms with Him! If you and I are going to sign it, it would be a good idea to know what's in it, wouldn't you say? What we would never do in any other area of life (i.e., sign a contract without first reading it and agreeing to its terms and conditions), men and women routinely do in the second most important contract they enter into on earth. Yes, God is our first! And we wonder why things don't work out the way we planned.

While wedding days in all their elegance and beauty should be days we never forget, when it comes to our contracts with God, it should also be a day we never forget! When God said that wives are bound to their husbands as long as He lives (1 Corinthians 7:39; Romans 7:2), He wasn't kidding—contractually bound! Therefore, since God makes the rules on how marriage covenants are supposed to operate, we would all do well to abide by *His* terms and conditions, wouldn't you agree? Unfortunately, most of us are selfishly doing the latter, and our families, churches, cities, and nation reflect it!

The same concept is true in the game of football or any sport, right? What do I mean? Each sport has its own set of rules found in that sport's respective rule book. If the player knows and abides by the rules, things go well for them and their team, assuming the rest of their game is up to "snuff." However, if the players don't know the rules or continually violate them, things do not go well for them and their team, even when the rest of their game is solid. Breaking the rules of the game routinely costs teams and players playoff opportunities, divisional titles, and championships.

Head coaches don't take too kindly to players who violate the rules. Some of these players become more of a liability to the team than an asset, resulting in fines, bad publicity, and suspensions. Some players get permanently suspended if the violations are egregious enough. Therefore, every good player understands at least three things when it comes to the rules of their game. Number one, what the player thinks the rules should be doesn't matter. Number two, the quicker the player operates under all of the rules established by the creator of their game (not just the ones he likes), the better things will go for him and his team. And number three, if a player desires to operate by his or her own set of rules, they have no business playing the game.

Rules establish order and structure and prevent anarchy and chaos. Can you imagine the game of football without rules? It wouldn't be football. It would be mayhem—grown men running around, grunting without function or purpose. I recognize that some of you reading this book think that's what football is anyway, even with the rules, but trust me when I say it would be a very different game! Its popularity and future would die overnight without rules. Rules define a sport and make it what it is.

Allow me to take this illustration one step further. None of us like it when the rules of our favorite sport or activity get violated, especially when it is by someone from the opposing team, or worse yet, a team that happens to be competing with our son's or daughter's team. Right, Dad and Mom? We've all seen the ranting, screaming parent demanding justice from the "ref" for the infraction committed by an opposing team member against their child's team. Maybe you've been that crazed parent. Don't worry, I can relate. Or maybe, like me, you weren't outwardly crazy but inwardly crazy.

Why do we get so upset? Because we like the order that comes with rules and value justice when rules get violated. To a real sports enthusiast, there are few things, if any, more respected and beautiful than a referee who knows how to correctly "call" a game. Even when a call goes against our team, if it's a "good call," we not only respect the "call" but the one who made the "call" because they were able to maintain order by correctly enforcing the rules of the game.

God's Word says, "An athlete is not crowned unless he competes according to the rules" (2 Timothy 2:5 ESV). Love it! Now, infinitely more important than the game of football (or any sport), for that matter, are a set of rules established by the Creator himself for how a marriage covenant is supposed to operate, contained in God's rule book for marriage, the Holy Bible. How many fewer marriages and unbiblical divorces would there be if we applied the same logic to marriage (and God's rule book for marriage) as we do to our favorite sport and its set of rules? In fact, I believe many who stay married their whole lives but who refuse to operate by God's rule book for marriage (i.e., those who are doing the work of the devil) are going to be in for a big surprise on Judgment Day. The good news is that if there is still breath in your lungs—and there must be or you wouldn't be reading this—there is still time to change! Clearly, it's no accident that you're reading this book!

Have you ever wondered why there are so many husbands and wives willing to "play by the rules" when it comes to every other conceivable area of life, except marriage? What we would never tolerate in the game of football, we routinely tolerate in the most important relationship in life next to our relationship with God. And we somehow think we can routinely "foul" one another without consequences? Football is not the only thing that "dies" without adherence to the rules. In other words, don't assume your marriage is still "alive" just because you're still married. Remember, a "dead" marriage, like a "dead" tree, can stand in the forest for a long time!

So why do so many of us not play by God's rules when it comes to marriage? I believe one of the reasons, besides not knowing what God's rule book says (which is a huge problem!) is because we don't like anyone telling us what to do, including God. After all, it's our marriage, right? Wrong! She is your wife and your companion *by covenant*—His covenant! So many of us are "happy" to let God marry us but then expect to operate our way after the wedding. No dice, that is, if you and I expect to fulfill the divine reasons for why God created marriage.

God says that if we operate according to the covenantal rules contained in His rule book, things will go well for our marriage "team" and us. If we don't, they won't. Jesus Christ, our Head Coach, is greatly grieved when we choose to operate by our rule book instead of His rule book. While God is the Divine Gentleman who will not force us to play by the rules of His covenant, neither will He spare us from the consequences of operating outside of them. Why? Because He loves us and wants us to grow up in every way like Christ (Ephesians 4:15).

Incidentally, singles, this is why sex before marriage is wrong. It's a covenantal lie. You're saying "yes" with your body but "no" with your life. When you have sex with someone outside of marriage, you become "one flesh" with them, whether you intended to or not. I didn't say it, God did (*italics* used for emphasis):

> Do you not know that your bodies are members of Christ himself? Shall I then take the members of Christ and unite them with a prostitute? Never! Do you not know that He who unites himself with a prostitute is *one with her in body?* For it is said, *"The two will become one flesh."* (1 Corinthians 6:15–16 NIV)

While this verse has to do with a prostitute, indeed, if it's true with a prostitute, then it's true when we have sex with our boyfriend or girlfriend. Spiritually, we become one flesh with them. Now ask yourself this, single, do you think it's God will that you become one flesh with someone else before you become "one flesh" with your spouse? Or ask yourself this. Does God want me to establish multiple "one flesh" relationships with others before I establish the "one flesh" relationship with the one I intend to spend the rest of my life with? Is it God's will that I become "one flesh" with someone who may not be my wife or husband? "But what if she (or he) is going to be my wife or husband?" you ask.

This is what a Christian brother said to me. "We're engaged," he said.

I said, "Fine, but it's still a covenantal lie. At this point, she is not yet your wife and companion by covenant, even if you go on to be married."

And what happens if you don't get married? I'll tell you. You have just become "one flesh" with someone else's future wife! But even if you do go on to marry her, you have not led well, for you told

God and your mate that your happiness is more important than your holiness and the holiness of your future mate. This is not the kind of trust and respect foundation you want to establish your married life on. While God will always forgive us when we repent, premarital sex will always be one of the most selfish acts we can ever commit against God, others, and ourselves. Now, back to our discussion.

The next thing that is critical to understand about a marriage covenant, which may now be evident given the above discussion but is nonetheless worthy of repeating is that without God, there is no marriage covenant. While husbands and wives are certainly active participants in their marriage contract with God, without God, there is no marriage covenant. To use the football analogy again, had Walter Camp, known as the "Father of American Football," never created a set of rules for football, there would be no game of football.

A discussion on establishing marriage covenants would be incomplete without a discussion on breaking marriage covenants. Remember, the marriage covenant is a conditional covenant subject to the terms and conditions of God's rule book (the Holy Bible) for how marriage is supposed to function. Incidentally, if you have been married to the same person your whole life and are beginning to "check out" of this chapter because you think I'm about to air a commercial for divorce, number one, you're incorrect. Number two, you are about to be robbed of a tremendous opportunity to verify whether or not you are correctly operating under God's set of rules for your marriage and not yours or someone else's. Lastly, you will be robbed of the opportunity to fortify your covenant with God and your mate and help countless other couples who are either contemplating divorce, currently getting a divorce, or trying to make sense out of the divorce they had.

Also, while it's a sad reminder, it is a present reality that the statistics inside and outside of the church indicate that half of you reading this book have either been divorced one or more times or *will* be divorced one or more times. Not knowing God's rule book for marriage, divorce and remarriage has cost us greatly, brothers and sisters. So if you don't know them or even if you think you do, stay with me. We all need to get this right once and for all if we expect to transform the world around us for Jesus Christ.

While some Christians think they know what the Bible says about marriage, even fewer understand what it says about divorce. Said another way, many of us are confused about divorce because we're confused about marriage. While God hates divorce (Malachi 2:16), He also hates certain sinful marriages (not the people) as you will soon see. As mentioned earlier, everything changed when sin entered the world.

Before I cover the few exceptions whereby God does allow the marriage covenant to be broken (i.e., divorce to occur), please understand that I believe in the sanctity of marriage now more than ever. Marriage should always be honored, protected, held in high esteem, and therefore never easily discarded. It should always be the last option, even in situations where God does allow the divorce.

I realize saying that a marriage covenant should never be broken sounds noble to some and flies just under the radar of piety and self-righteousness to Christians who have never had their spouse commit adultery on them or forge their name on bank documents to obtain personal loans without their knowledge; but what does God's Word really say about divorce? You're about to find out!

Contrary to what many in the church believe, God does *allow* the marriage covenant to be broken (i.e., divorce to occur) in three cases—adultery, abandonment, and death. As stated before, everything changed when sin entered the world. Let's look at each of them more closely from God's Word.

In Matthew 19, when the Pharisees came and tried to trap Jesus with the question, "Should a man be allowed to divorce his wife for any reason?" note the first thing Jesus said: "Haven't you read the Scriptures" (Matthew 19:4 NLT)? Apply brakes now! *Screech!* Come to a complete stop! Consider the enormity of what Jesus just said to us.

The problem with many of us today is that we haven't read the scriptures; therefore, we don't know what God has said about marriage, divorce, and many other matters. Many of us just accept what other people say as long as it sounds good or makes us feel good about ourselves or our decisions. Jesus, through Paul's writing in 2 Timothy, warned us to study (not merely read) His Word to show ourselves approved workmen that need not be ashamed, *rightly* (not wrongly) dividing the word of truth (2 Timothy 2:15). Sadly, and with grave consequences, many of us are not only *not* reading God's Word but wrongly dividing it on this and many other critical areas of life to the detriment of our families, churches, cities, and nation.

Now, without interruption, let's look at the entire passage of Matthew 19 here in the following (italics and brackets [] added for emphasis):

> Now when Jesus had finished these say-ings [the parable of the unforgiving debtor], He went away from Galilee and entered the region of Judea beyond the Jordan And large crowds followed Him, and He healed them there. And Pharisees came up to Him and tested Him by asking, "Is it lawful to divorce one's wife for any cause?" He answered, "Have you not read that He who created them from the beginning made them male and female, and said, 'Therefore a man shall leave his father and his mother and hold fast to his wife, and the two shall become one flesh?' So, they are no longer two but one flesh. What therefore God has joined together, let not man separate." They said to Him, "Why then did Moses *command* one to give a certifi-cate of divorce and to send her away?" He said to them, "Because of your hardness of heart Moses *allowed* you to divorce your wives, but from the beginning [before the Fall] it was not so. And I say to you: whoever divorces his wife, *except for sexual immorality*, and marries another, commits adultery." (Matthew 19:1–9 ESV)

One of the first things I would like you to see is that Jesus corrected the Pharisees when He said that Moses did not *command* them to divorce their wives. Instead, He said Moses "*allowed*" them to divorce their wives and send them away. Big difference! One of the most important things to remember about this whole discussion on divorce that we're about to have is that God never *commands* divorce, even where biblical grounds exist. He "allows" or "permits" it but leaves the choice with us.

While Jesus's discussion above focuses on sexual immorality and physical adultery, what many don't realize is that God also has a lot to say about spiritual adultery as seen here in the third chapter of Jeremiah (italics added for emphasis):

> During the reign of King Josiah, the Lord said to me, "Have you seen what fickle Israel has done? *Like a wife who commits adultery, Israel has worshiped other gods on every hill and under every green tree.* I thought that after she had done all this, she would return to me. But she did not come back. And though her faithless sister Judah saw this; she paid no attention. *She saw that I had divorced faithless Israel and sent her away.* But now Judah, too, has left me and given herself to prostitution. Israel treated it all so lightly—*she thought nothing of committing adultery by worshiping idols made of wood and stone. So now the land has been greatly defiled.* But in spite of all this, *her faithless sister Judah has never sincerely returned to me. She has only pretended to be sorry.*"
>
> Then the Lord said to me, "Even faithless Israel is less guilty than treacherous Judah. Therefore, go and give this message to Israel." This is what the Lord says:
>
> "Oh Israel, my faithless people, come home to me again, for I am merciful. I will not be angry with you forever. Only acknowledge your guilt.

Admit that you rebelled against the Lord your God and committed adultery against Him by worshiping idols under every green tree. Confess that you refused to follow me. I, the Lord have spoken!" (Jeremiah 3:6–13 NLT)

I hope you noticed at the beginning of this passage that God, through the prophet Jeremiah, compares spiritual adultery (i.e. idol worship) to physical adultery saying, "*Like* a wife who commits adultery." In other words, God puts spiritual adultery (idolatry)—that is, worshiping any created thing more than the Creator himself—on the same plane as physical adultery.

Since I will continue to use these terms, *idol* and *idolatry*, it is critical that we have an accurate and complete biblical understanding of them to avoid any confusion in light of our topic. In addition to what I have already said, an idol in our day, as in Jeremiah's day, is further defined as anything we "worship" or elevate above God and His established will. This could include things like "happiness," money, fame, power, notoriety, our careers, our political party, education, spouses, children, celebrities, sports teams, athletes, or a sinful lifestyle. Said another way, it's the person, place, or thing that we allow to take God's primary place in our hearts or the person, place, or thing that gets to ride in the "front seat" with us instead of God.

Note, God himself issued a bill of divorcement to His "wife," Israel, for all of her adulteries (not just physical adultery) and then sent her away (like He did with Adam and Eve) because He did not want His land to be defiled. *The Message* says, "[b]ecause of Israel's loose morals I threw her out, gave her her walking papers" (Jeremiah 3:17 MSG). When was the last time you heard that at a Christian marriage conference?

God said He would not accept simply being one of Israel's many lovers as stated here in the following:

"But like a woman unfaithful to her husband, so you, Israel, have been unfaithful to me," declares the Lord. (Jeremiah 3:20 NIV)

Note the sobering consequences God had for Israel for all her "adulteries" as spoken here through the prophet Hosea (*italics* used for emphasis):

> *But now, call Israel to account, for she is no longer my wife, and I am no longer her husband.* Tell her to take off her garish makeup and suggestive clothing and to stop playing the prostitute. If she doesn't, I will strip her as naked as she was on the day she was born. I will leave her to die of thirst, as in a desert or a dry and barren wilderness. (Hosea 2:2–3 NLT)

In Ezra 9–10, when Ezra heard the report that the men of Israel had intermarried with the pagan women, causing the holy race to become polluted by these mixed marriages, *all who trembled at the words of the God of Israel* came to sit with Ezra because of the *unfaithfulness* (spiritual adultery) of the Jewish people (Ezra 9:2,4). Note the following taken from Ezra 10 (*italics* and brackets [] used for emphasis):

> While Ezra prayed and made this confession, weeping and throwing himself to the ground in front of the Temple of God, a large crowd of people from Israel—men, women, and children—gathered and wept bitterly with Him. Then Shecaniah son of Jehiel, a descendant of Elam, said to Ezra, "We confess that we have been *unfaithful* to our God [spiritual adultery], for we have married these pagan women of the land. But there is hope for Israel in spite of this. *Let us now make a covenant with God to divorce our pagan wives and to send them away with their children.* We will follow the advice given by you and by the others who respect the commands of

203

our God. We will obey the law of God." (Ezra 10:1–3 NLT)

A covenant with God for divorce? Really? Yes, really. Within three days, all the people of Judah and Benjamin gathered in Jerusalem before the Temple of God. Those who failed to come to Jerusalem as Ezra demanded would have to, if the leaders and elders decided, forfeit all their property and be expelled from the assembly (Ezra 10:5, 8–9). Ezra explained the charges and told them that they were under God's condemnation even more and told them to confess their sin to the Lord *and do what God demands*, saying:

> Separate yourselves from the people of the land and from these pagan women. (Ezra 10:11 NLT)

Approximately three months later, the matter was finished, and all the Israelite men were divorced from their pagan wives (Ezra 10:16–17). Why did God take this so seriously? Because He's always looking long-term at the remnant seed. These idolatrous marriages, if God had allowed them to continue, would have resulted in generations of offspring that would have worshipped and served other gods instead of the one true God.

Also note, while we're here, that the Hebrew and Greek translations for the word *divorce* mean to "be separated," "driven out," "put away," or "free fully," which was the same thing that God did with Adam and Eve when they broke God's covenant and were unfaithful to Him (Hosea 6:7 NLT). God drove them out of the garden and, in doing so, put "separation" between himself and them.

Examples of spiritual adultery are certainly not confined to the Old Testament. In the book of Mark, Jesus says, "If anyone is ashamed of me and my words in this *adulterous* and sinful generation, the Son of Man will be ashamed of them when He comes in His Father's glory with the holy angels" (Mark 8:38 NIV).

James says, "Adulterers and adulteresses! Do you not know that friendship with the world is enmity with God? Whoever therefore wants to be a friend of the world makes himself an enemy of God" (James 4:4 NKJV). Here, we learn that copying and modeling the behavior and customs of this "world" (i.e., conforming to the world; Romans 12:2) is a form of spiritual adultery. I wonder how many of us are unknowingly committing spiritual adultery. It's quiet in this Baptist church!

In Revelation 2, Jesus is addressing "The Loveless Church" at the church of Ephesus. He praises them in verses two and three and then rebukes them in verse four, saying, "Nevertheless I have this against you, *that you have left your first love.*" We have already discussed that idolatry (anything we love above Him) is a form of spiritual adultery.

Sadly, married men and women are "leaving" Jesus and their mates for different "lovers" all across America committing not only physical adultery but spiritual adultery, weakening our families, churches, communities, cities, and nation. Thus, if God's character never changes (and it doesn't because He never changes; Hebrews 13:8), would it not be possible for Him to break His "marriage covenant" with us and "send us away" as He did with Adam and Eve, Israel, and Judah if He thought we had committed "spiritual adultery" against Him by having a heart that was more loyal to another "lover?" And if He would break His marriage covenant with us and send us away for committing spiritual adultery against Him, why would He not *allow* one spouse to do the same thing with another spouse "guilty" of the same thing?

Lest there be any confusion, I'm not talking about anyone losing their salvation where belief in the finished work of Jesus Christ on the cross exists. Recall, even after God sent Adam and Eve away, Adam and Eve never ceased being God's children, but there was most definitely a change in their relationship with one another in terms of the closeness and intimacy they shared.

Thus, it is clear from God's Word that He does allow (not command) divorce to occur wherever physical or spiritual adultery exists. For those of you who remain skeptical about whether or not this is true in cases of spiritual adultery (idolatry), stay tuned.

Secondly, God allows or permits the marriage covenant to be broken (i.e., divorce to occur) in cases of abandonment by an unbeliever. I have found that even fewer Christians recognize this as a situation wherein God allows for divorce than those who believe that divorce is only permitted in cases of physical adultery. The scriptural support for this second biblical grounds for divorce may be found in 1 Corinthians 7:15, which says that if the unbeliever desires to depart, let them leave. A brother or sister is not bound in such cases. God has called you to live in peace (1 Corinthians 7:15 NET).

This passage basically says that if a non-Christian spouse doesn't wish to be married to their Christian mate anymore, then the Christian mate is free to get a divorce. I used to believe, because of false teaching in the church, that God only allowed a divorce in this case if the unbeliever initiated the divorce. This is not what this passage says, beloved. God allows either party, the believer or the unbeliever, to initiate the divorce when the unbelieving spouse does not wish to dwell or function as mate with the believing spouse any longer.[47] Note the physical act of "leaving" by the unbelieving spouse is not a requirement for this biblical grounds for divorce to attach itself.

An unbeliever can depart physically, emotionally, sexually, or functionally. The unbelieving spouse departs physically by being routinely absent or physically abusive. They depart emotionally by being emotionally absent or emotionally abusive. They depart sexually by persistently refusing to have sexual relations with their mate when they are, otherwise physically able to barring sexual abuse or sexual sin by their spouse. And finally, an unbelieving spouse departs a believing spouse, functionally, by refusing to function in their God-ordained role. While the unbeliever may not have verbalized that they desire to depart, their actions demonstrate that they not only desire to depart but that they have departed, whether they physically leave the home or not.

Finally, God allows the marriage covenant to be broken (i.e., divorce to occur) in the case of death. The Bible says that a wife is married to her husband as long as he lives, but that if her husband dies, she is free to marry whomever she wishes, provided he is a Christian (1 Corinthians 7:39). Well, that makes sense, right? It's kind of hard to be married to someone who isn't alive!

However, while I'm here, I've also met many who believe they are still married to their spouse, even after their spouse dies. These widows and widowers wouldn't think of marrying another because, in their mind, they are still married to their deceased spouse. Again, while this may seem understandable or even noble and admirable to some, it is not scriptural. For those of you who think you are going to be married to your earthly spouse in heaven, whether they are currently dead or alive, take a look at Luke 20:35. We're not! There will be no marriage in heaven because we will be married to Him! So if you wish to remain unmarried under these circumstances, fine, but understand you are free to marry whomever you wish, but only in the Lord (1 Corinthians 7:39).

A similar scripture to the one I just cited above (1 Corinthians 7:39) comes out of Romans 7, which says that a married woman is bound by law to her husband as long as he lives, but if her husband dies, she is released from the law of marriage (Romans 7:2 ESV). In both verses, 1 Corinthians 7:39 and Romans 7:2, it is important to highlight that Paul is addressing Christians. Here, similarly, in Romans 7:2, Paul is saying that a Christian woman is bound by law to her Christian husband, for example, as long as he lives, but if her Christian husband dies, she is released from that marriage.

Now, here's where the discussion really gets interesting and where much of the church is divided. For example, many understand that God allows divorce in the case of physical adultery. Even less, as previously stated, understand that God allows divorce in cases of spiritual adultery and in cases when an unbeliever "departs" from their believing spouse physically, emotionally, sexually, or function-ally. However, it has been my experience that even fewer understand what God's Word says about divorce among two Christians where adultery doesn't exist.

So the question on the table is this. Can one Christian divorce another Christian for reasons other than adultery or physical death? To find the answer, we have to take a deeper dive into God's Word. Incidentally, what I am about to share with you did not come from any church sermon, marriage retreat, or marriage seminar I've ever attended. It didn't come from any Christian book I've ever read or from any marriage or divorce counseling session I've ever attended. The truth came straight from God's Word and the marvelous teachings of none other than Dr. Tony Evans. Yes, by now, you have correctly gathered that I believe he is one of the greatest Bible scholars, teachers, and theologians of our day! Are you ready?

What did God say would happen to Adam and Eve (two "believers") on *the day* they ate the fruit from the tree of knowledge of good and evil? God said they would die, right (Edenic Covenant)? But did they? No, they lived for hundreds of years after they "fell." So then, is God a liar? Or was He talking about another kind of experiential death besides physical death? God knew the day they ate from that tree they would experience *spiritual death!* While God graciously provided "child support" to Adam and Eve in the form of food to eat and clothes to wear since they never ceased being His children ("believers"), there was no doubt that they entered the realm of spiritual death.

The prophet Isaiah describes Israel's *spiritual death* experience like this:

> But your iniquities *have made a separation between you and your God*, and your sins have hidden His face from you so that He will not hear. For your hands are defiled with blood and your fingers with iniquity; your lips have spoken lies; your tongue mutters wickedness. (Isaiah 59:2–3 AMPC)

We see the "label" of *spiritual death* being placed on a "believer" again in the famous story of the father and prodigal son. When the prodigal son, a believer, finally got to the end of himself and came home seeking forgiveness and restoration with his father, the father declared, "This son of mine who was dead [spiritually dead] is now alive" (Luke 15:24).

Jesus, when He was speaking to the church in Sardis in Revelation 3 ("believers"), said, "I know all the things you do, and that you have a reputation for being alive—but you are dead" (Revelation 3:1).

While "believers" are not spiritually dead, technically, since our spirits became alive with Christ at conversion, these scriptures, and many others like them, give credence to the fact that Christians can become spiritually dead "experientially." In other words, we Christians can *experience* many of the same consequences as those who are truly dead spiritually ("unbelievers") when we give ourselves over to willful, persistent, and unrepentant lifestyles of sin.

Maybe you have this question: "So are you saying that if a Christian woman is married to a Christian man and that Christian man or woman enters the realm of spiritual death, then their Christian mate is no longer bound to their mate who entered the realm of spiritual death?"

Yes, that's precisely what I'm saying, only God said it first, not me. A married woman is bound by law to her husband as long as he lives, but if her husband *dies,* she is released from the law of marriage (Romans7:2). This death can be physical or spiritual.[48] And why is this? Because when one living Christian spouse enters the realm of spiritual death, they *illegitimately* break God's covenant (Hosea 6:7), like Adam and Eve did with God's covenant when they entered the realm of spiritual death. Said another way, illegitimate breakage of the marriage covenant "uptown" (against God) by the Christian mate who enters the realm of spiritual death *allows* (doesn't command) the other Christian mate to legitimately break the marriage covenant "downtown" (in court with man).[49]

Remember, this is no different than what God did with Adam and Eve ("believers") *after* Adam and Eve illegitimately broke God's covenant with God "uptown" and entered the realm of spiritual death. God legitimately "put them away" downtown.

So if marriage is God's covenant (and it is!) and He's the only one who can *legitimately* break it (and He can!), when does a Christian spouse enter the realm of spiritual death, experientially, wherein God (uptown) allows the other spouse to legitimately break the marriage covenant downtown? That's the question, isn't it? To answer it, we need to go to 1 Corinthians 5, where Paul is chastising the Corinthian church for allowing a man, who was engaging in sexual immorality with his stepmother, to remain in the church. Note, this man is a Christian.

While this scripture doesn't pertain to marriage per se, it nonetheless highlights what types of sinful behavior cause Christians to enter the realm of spiritual death and how we are to treat those who do when they refuse to repent. I said when they refuse to repent. This is key. Paul's concern in 1 Corinthians 5, if you recall, is that the whole church would be affected by this man's behavior if he were allowed to go on sinning (1 Corinthians 5:6). Here again, we see God's concern for His remnant seed. Note the key verses here below (*italics* used for emphasis):

> When I wrote to you before, I told you not to associate with people who indulge in sexual sin. But I wasn't talking about unbelievers who indulge in sexual sin, or who are greedy or are swindlers or idol worshippers. You would have to leave this world to avoid people like that. What I meant is that you are not to associate with anyone *who claims to be a Christian yet indulges in sexual sin, or is greedy, or worships idols, or is abusive, or a drunkard, or a swindler. Don't even eat with such people.* It isn't my responsibility to judge outsiders, *but it certainly is your job to judge those inside the church who are sinning in these ways.* God will judge those on the outside; but as the Scriptures say, "*You must remove the evil person from among you.*" (1 Corinthians 5:9–13 NLT)

Did you hear what Paul said? Do not associate with anyone who claims to be a Christian, yet indulges (continuously and unrepentantly) in these types of sin. Don't even eat with them. Remove the evil person from the church (i.e., excommunicate them). Sound familiar? Adam and Eve. Again, please note that this passage involves Christians.

So again, if one Christian spouse is behaving in ways like this against their Christian spouse persistently and unrepentantly and has thus entered the realm of spiritual death, does God *allow* (not command) the other spouse to break the marriage covenant that God established? Yes. In the same way that God sent Adam and Eve "away" when they entered the realm of spiritual death and the Corinthian church sent this Christian man "away" when he entered the realm of spiritual death, God allows one Christian spouse to send the other Christian spouse "away" when that spouse enters the realm of spiritual death and refuses to repent.

While we are commanded to forgive an unrepentant spouse who has entered the realm of spiritual death, we are not commanded to trust them and would be foolish to do so without genuine repentance and a track record that may be trusted. Note, the paramount issue with God (as it should be for us) for those who enter the realm of spiritual death and will not repent, therefore, is trust. Recall, the Lord's words through the prophet Hosea to the nation of Israel (*italics* used for emphasis):

> But like Adam, you broke my covenant *and betrayed my trust.* (Hosea 6:7 NLT)

With this in mind, let's now look more closely at each group of individuals who Paul considers to have entered the realm of spiritual death wherein God will allow (not command) the marriage covenant to be *legitimately* broken by one Christian spouse against another Christian spouse.

Christians who enter the realm of spiritual death include those who, number one, are engaging in sexual sins. We've talked a bit about this already; however, today, sexual immorality includes not only physical adultery, homosexuality, bestiality, fornication, orgies, and molestation but also those engaging in partner swapping ("swinging"), webcam sex, and various other pornographic addictions. Many books have been written on this topic. I will, therefore, not elaborate on this any further here other than to say that if you or your Christian mate have given yourselves over to these or other sexual sins, habitually and unrepentantly, you or they have entered the realm of spiritual death.

Other Christians who enter the realm of spiritual death, according to 1 Corinthian 5, include those who pursue a lifestyle of greed. Socrates said, "He who is not contented with what he has would not be contented with what he would like to have."

Jarod Kintz said, 'The only gift I have to give is the ability to receive. If giving is a gift, and it surely is, then my gift to you is to allow you to give to me."

When will the greedy be satisfied? When they get just one more! The Bible says that hell and destruction are never full, so the eyes of man are never satisfied (Proverbs 27:20 KJV). Greedy people enter the realm of spiritual death because their hearts and loyalties to Christ are divided between the riches of this world and the riches of God. In their never-ending pursuit of "more," they are unable to pursue what God wants (in this case, a Christ-centered marriage), causing them to live a double and divided life apart from God and their spouse.

Colossians 3:5 says, "So put to death the sinful, earthly things lurking within you. Have nothing to do with sexual sin, impurity, lust, and shameful desires. Don't be *greedy* for the good things of this life for that is *idolatry*" (Colossians 3:5 NLT).

"For a greedy person is an idolater, worshipping the things of this world. Don't be fooled by those who try to excuse these sins, for the anger of God will fall on all who disobey Him" (Ephesians 5:5–6 NLT).

Note in every one of these verses, Paul, a Christian, is writing to other Christians regarding their conduct, not the conduct of "unbelievers."

Thus, God also considers those who willingly and persistently pursue idolatry as we saw earlier with spiritual adultery, and here again with the greedy, to be among those Christians who enter the realm of spiritual death, wherein God will allow the marriage covenant to be legitimately broken. While the saints of old bowed down to Baal and other false gods and intermarried with pagan women

(Ezra 10:2–3), Christian idol worshippers of today "bow" down to fame, fortune, power, popularity, and prominence. Because all covenants operate under divine order (spiritual hierarchy), when we "mess" with His divine order by replacing Him with an idol, we not only "mess" with *His* covenant, but we mess with Him![50]

Idols cause our loyalties to be divided between God and other things. Remember, God will not share His glory with anyone, including you and me. When we allow *our* feelings (e.g. pride, self-sufficiency, jealousy, and fears) to drive *our* decision-making (love of self) instead of allowing God's Word to drive our decision-making (love of God), we commit idolatry. Paul calls this dining at the table of demons (1 Corinthians 10:21).

Did you know that the way we interact with our children can even be a form of idol worship? What? That's right. If we, for example, as parents are characteristically *more* invested in our children's happiness, academic success, or weekly activity schedule than we are in their Godly character and spiritual training, for instance, we are guilty of idolatry. If our children consistently get our "best" while God and our spouses consistently get our "worst" or our "leftovers," the same is true.

The good news is that it is not too late to "fix" it today if we're willing to repent. However, God will not compete with us or our children for first place in our lives. Although phrases like "My children mean everything to me," "My kids are my world," "My children come before anything or anyone else," and "My kids are the most important thing to me" may sound noble and admirable, this can very often reflect a divided and idolatrous heart that has elevated "love of child" above "love of God" and "love of spouse."

Ladies, if your desire to be a good mother *exceeds* your desire to be a good disciple of Jesus and wife, your heart is divided, and you have entered the world of idolatry to the joy of Satan. The same applies to us, guys. Need we all be reminded of the words of Jesus himself when He said, "And He that loves son or daughter more than me isn't worthy of me" (Matthew 10:37 NKJV)?

The number of Christian marriages and families operating under this powerfully orchestrated scheme of the devil is staggering.

It is especially deceptive because the devil masquerades "child-centered parenting" as the ultimate earthly example of sacrificial "love." While raising children in the nurture and admonition of the Lord arguably requires daily demonstrations of sacrificial love, these demonstrations should never exceed those we express toward God (first) and our spouses (second).

If you were like me when your children came along, you said something like this: "God, please help me to be the best parent I can be and not to mess them up!" Most of us honestly and appropriately desire to be good parents, but somewhere along the way in our desire to be good parents, the desire to become good parents can get elevated above our desire to be good spouses and, most importantly, good disciples of Jesus. Said another way, the desire to be a good parent, which is a "good thing," can become a "bad thing" when it becomes a "ruling thing."

Society tells us that our priorities should change when we have children, and they should! However, instead of making our children the beautiful new additions to our families who are worthy of our love, time, affection, and attention, we too often make them the center of our universe. This is the sin of idolatry.

If some of you are saying, "Look, this is no big deal. My spouse and I both enjoy putting our kids first;" my loving question to you in response is, "Okay, while you and your mate have both agreed to commit idolatry, did you ever stop to consider that your biggest problem just became God because you made your children, instead of God, the center of your worlds? Not exactly a marriage made in heaven, wouldn't you agree?"

A quick way to know if you have elevated the parent-child relationship above the husband-wife relationship and your relationship to God is to examine how you handle conflict. When your spouse has an issue with one of your children or your child has a problem with your spouse, do you *consistently* take up the offense of your child over your mate and God? Do you *consistently* dishonor your spouse because your children's happiness means more to you than your mate? Do you allow your children to *routinely* circumvent your spouse (their other parent) and come to you to get what they want because they know your spouse will say "no" to them?

When it comes to the training, correction, and discipline of your children, do you consistently have your spouse's "back" first or your child's "back" first? How about when you and your spouse disagree? Do you routinely allow conflicts with your children to divide your marriage? Or do you let your marriage be God's "force to reckon with" for a child who is being used by the enemy to divide you? Are the priority relationships in your family, as I said earlier, God first, your mate second, and your children last? If not, your loyalties are divided, and you have forsaken your first love (God) and your second love (your spouse) for your third love (your children), committing idolatry.

Sadly, the intense desire to be our children's friend instead of their parent in those critical adolescent and teenage years can cause us to place our relationships to God and our mates on the "back burner," leading to idolatry. Beware, parent: If the fear of losing your relationship with your child is more important than maintaining your relationship to God (as evidenced by consistently compromising God's standards for the "happiness" and welfare of your child), you have crossed the line into idolatry. Solution: Obey God and leave the consequences to Him!

Now you know the spiritual reason behind why so many "empty nesters" desperately struggle to reconnect with their mates once their children leave home. For the last eighteen to twenty-plus years, they have allowed their children to occupy center stage of the family, and now, for the first time, the consequences of doing so are staring them square in the face, namely a spouse whom they no longer know or can relate to anymore.

It is never good when the husband-wife relationship has to "die" for the parent-child relationship to "live," especially when adherence to God's divine order for the family brings life and life more abundantly for all! Not only do we negatively impact this generation of families, but we program the next generation of families to do the same thing. And they have! We must break this generational curse if we expect to see our homes, churches, cities, and nation healed.

In summary, whenever a husband or wife willingly, consistently, and unrepentantly elevates the parent-child relationship above the husband-wife relationship, and thus, their relationship to God, they are committing idolatry and behaving as one who has entered the realm of "spiritual death."

Christians who have given themselves over to various addictions (alcohol, drugs, sex, pornography, prescription drugs, gambling, food, day-trading, gaming, smartphone, social media, etc.) are also among those who commit idolatry. It's impossible to love God and our mates the way we are supposed to when we are "in love" and in bondage to the things that replace them in our hearts.

Does this mean you have grounds for a biblical divorce if your husband likes sports or the stock market or if your wife likes chocolate and has a glass of wine with dinner? Absolutely not! But if they have persistently forsaken their relationship to God and you to be "married" to a real addiction, they have entered the realm of "spiritual death," and it's most certainly time to sound the alarm!

Christians can also be guilty of idol worship by worshiping a false or watered-down version of Jesus Christ instead of the real Jesus. It should be obvious that if you're worshiping Buddha or Mohammad instead of the God of Abraham, Isaac, and Jacob that you are involved in idol worship. However, what I am talking about are churches today who portray a different Jesus than the one in the Bible. In many American churches today, Jesus is a God of grace and mercy, but not a God of justice, truth, and righteousness. The "Jesus" in many churches today doesn't judge sin or require holiness. He accepts everyone's version of "truth." He gives everyone a "green light" into heaven based upon their plan of salvation versus God's plan of salvation through the finished works of Jesus Christ on the cross. Any Christian who is willingly, consistently, and unrepentantly worshipping a false or "watered-down" version of Jesus is committing idolatry and has entered the realm of spiritual death.

An even less obvious form of idol worship is worshiping Jesus for what He can do for us versus worshiping Jesus for who His is— our Savior, Lord, and King. The devil loves it, for example, when he can get Christians more interested in their healing than in their

Healer, their gifts than in their Giver, their deliverance than in their Deliverer, their redemption than in their Redeemer, their blessing than in their "Blesser," their creation than in their Creator, and in their benefits than in their Benefactor. How about you? Do you worship Jesus for who He is or to see what He will do next?

Rebellion and stubbornness are also forms of idolatry. We discussed this in chapter 1. God's Word says, "Rebellion is as sinful as witchcraft, and stubbornness as bad as worshiping idols" (1 Samuel 15:23 NLT). I like what Dr. Charles Stanley, senior pastor of First Baptist Church in Atlanta, Georgia has to say about rebellion:

> Rebellion is an act against established order and authority. It can be defiance against God's will or resistance to leadership He has ordained. When we insist on doing things our way, we reveal our pride and selfishness.[51]

Rebellion and stubbornness are idolatry because they elevate self-will above God, making fellowship with God impossible. As we saw in chapter 2, this can be a husband who refuses to come under God's authority or a wife who refuses to come under the authority of her husband.

Psalm 68:6 says that God makes the rebellious live in a sun-scorched land (Psalm 68:6 NLT). In the Bible, water signifies life, and the lack of water, death. "Those who rebel against God are not 'brought out' of dry land but are left to 'die' in the dry land of their own shamelessness and self-will" (Psalm 68:6, Pulpit Commentary). This is a true picture of what it looks like to enter the realm of *spiritual death*.

Rebellion, not unlike other forms of idolatry, is an open door to the demonic world. God's Word warns us that rebellion darkens our spiritual eyesight (discernment) and deafens our ears to hear God's voice.[52] It allows the god of this world, Satan, to "blind" us to the reality of God and His Word and deceive us.

The rebellious spouse stares good (God's Word) in the face, smirks, and turns to embrace evil. Rebelliousness is pride on "parade."

The Bible says that if anyone repays evil for good, evil will not depart from his house (Proverbs 17:13). This is precisely what happens in a home where a spirit of rebellion is permitted to flourish. Pretty serious, wouldn't you say? If only more of us believed it.

Remember, rebellion is very different than immaturity. Rebelliousness is "sin" by willful intent in the face of knowledge and truth. While this can be the case with some who are spiritually immature, it is not always the case. Some of us are immature but want to mature. Others of us are immature but refuse to grow despite knowing what we need to do. It is this latter group of individuals that enter the realm of *spiritual death* because of their willful disobedience and refusal to repent.

The Bible is clear that a rebellious man or woman is someone whose heart is not right with God. In Psalm 78, Asaph retells of the history of the Jewish nation from the time of slavery in Egypt through David's reign. He urges the current generation of Israelites to not be like their ancestors, a *stubborn* and *rebellious* generation, a generation *whose heart was not steadfast, whose spirit was not faithful to God* (Psalm 78:8 ESV). Note, Asaph is not referring to unbelievers but the people of God.

Ezekiel, who was used by God to play the role of a captive being led away into exile to highlight what was about to happen to King Zedekiah and the Jews who remained in Jerusalem, received this word from the Lord (*italics* used for emphasis):

> Son of man, thou dwellest in the midst of
> a *rebellious house*, which have eyes to see, and see
> not; they have ears to hear, and hear not; for *they*
> *are a rebellious house*. (Ezekiel 12:2 KJV)

The true heart of a rebel may also be seen here in Isaiah 30:8–11 in God's warning to rebellious Judah (*italics* used for emphasis):

> Now go and write down these words con-
> cerning Egypt. They will then stand until the
> end of time as a witness to Israel's unbelief. *For*

> *these people are stubborn rebels who refuse to pay*
> *any attention to the Lord's instructions. They tell*
> *the prophets, "Shut up! We don't want any more of*
> *your reports." They say, "Don't tell us the truth. Tell*
> *us nice things. Tell us lies. Forget all this gloom. We*
> *have heard more than enough about your 'Holy One*
> *of Israel.' We are tired of listening to what He has to*
> *say."* (Isaiah 30:8–11 NLT)

Is this not reflective of the attitude of many in our American culture today, including many inside the church who reject the truth but in the same breath hypocritically claim to be "One Nation under God?" What a number the enemy has done on the people of God!

Psalm 107 was written to celebrate the Jews' return from exile in Babylon. Here we see that while some of the Jewish people cried out to God for help during this dark period in Jewish history, others "sat in darkness and in the shadow of *death*; prisoners in affliction, and in iron, *for they had rebelled against the words of God, and spurned the counsel of the Most High*" (Psalm 107:10–11 ESV). While they, too, eventually cried out and the Lord saved them, it nonetheless emphasizes the fact that until we are willing to repent, the persistent and unrepentant rebellious one enters the realm of *spiritual death*.

God additionally says that if we keep turning away and refusing to listen, He will allow us to be destroyed by our enemies (Isaiah 1:20; Nehemiah 9:26–27), and even cause himself to become our enemy and fight against us (Isaiah 63:10). Could this be one of the many reasons why God allows bad things to happen to some good people; that is, because those same "good" people reject God and His Word in all of their "goodness" and refuse to be "God's people?"

The truly rebellious will not repent barring spiritual deliverance because, in their mind, you, not they, are the problem. Thus, until they repent, God casts the shadow of spiritual death upon them.

Note, regardless of whatever is drawing our hearts away from God, true idol worship in whatever form it takes is not occasionally flirting with idols; it is giving ourselves completely over to them.

Did you know that having fun can also be a breeding ground for idolatry? Please hear me out before you tune me out. I love fun as much as the next person, but what if having fun becomes more important to us than having a relationship with God and fulfilling our God-ordained role as a husband or wife? In other words, what if a Christian husband, for example, is more committed to his new boat, golf clubs, fishing gear, and sporting events then he is God, his marriage, and kingdom business?

Similarly, what if a Christian wife is more committed to her friends, travel, hobbies, and shopping than she is to God, her marriage, and kingdom business?

I'll tell you. In both cases, having fun has become an idol, and both of them have entered the realm of spiritual death. It's impossible to build God's kingdom as a couple when one or both spouses are *more* committed to having fun than they are to God, their spouse, and kingdom business. By the way, do you have any idea how much fun it is to walk in the Spirit and do kingdom business? Many of you know exactly what I'm talking about!

Maybe you're saying, "Wow, you just described my marriage to a T above, except it's no big deal because we both like it that way" or "We do the same fun things together. In fact, Jim, it's one of the main reasons why we're still married after all these years!"

Did you just hear what you said? In so many words, you just said that the reason why you're still married and never got around to kingdom business, individually and as a couple, is because you both worship the same idol! Good luck with that one on Judgment Day, beloved, if you're not willing to change. Satan is not called the Great Deceiver for nothing! If you're angry with me, that's okay, but please know that if what I have just said describes you or your mate—your biggest problem is not me but God. I didn't write the book. I just try to follow it.

Maybe you're trying to figure out whether you or your spouse is engaged in idolatry. Perhaps this will help. Idolatry is the one thing you, or they, will willfully, consistently, and unrepentantly lie about, conceal, or be irresponsible about! Again, it is the person, place, or thing that has taken God's place. "It," not Jesus, is their (or your) all-consuming fire.

I hope you can see the clear relationship between idolatry and abandonment. In every case, idolatry involves abandoning God and His will for the idol.

So here's the question for every husband and wife in light of our discussion on idolatry. Is there anyone or anything that you've elevated above God or that has taken the place of God? If there is, I urge you to lay it and them at the foot of the cross today so God can resurrect you from the realm of spiritual death.

Now that we've concluded our discussion on idolatry, next in line from the list in 1 Corinthians 5 that causes a Christian to enter the realm of spiritual death where God will allow (not command) one Christian to divorce another Christian is abusive behavior. Just to be clear, this is not a father or mother who "spanks" their young children for willfully defiant behavior or a spouse who is biblically standing up for righteousness and justice in their marriage by speaking the truth in love (Ephesians 4:15) out of love of God, spouse, and others. This is a spouse who exhibits a characteristic pattern of physical or verbal abuse as a means of domination, manipulation, control, or intimidation. Again, the motive is everything.

One who commits verbal abuse, for example, is known in scripture as a *reviler* (1 Corinthians 5:11 ASV, AMP). A reviler is a reproachful person—a man or woman of coarse, harsh, and bitter words who vilifies or attacks another's character. Many excellent books have been written on the topic of verbal abuse as well as physical abuse. I will, therefore, not elaborate on them any further here other than to again say that for a Christian to enter the realm of spiritual death because of any type of abuse, it must be the abuser's characteristic behavior.

Warning: If you are constantly living in fear of being belittled or physically beaten by your mate because that has been the "norm," then you are living with an abuser. While verbal abuse from one spouse never warrants physical abuse from the other, be aware that verbal abuse is often present where physical abuse is present sometimes by the same party, the other party, or both parties. Own what you need to own and do not "own" what you don't "own." Realize, however, that both of you may have entered the realm of spiritual death. Either way, it's time to sound the alarm, get out, and get help to stop the cycle of abuse!

Drunkards, Christians or otherwise, as listed in 1 Corinthians 5, also operate in the realm of spiritual death (1 Corinthians 5:11). Instead of getting drunk on the Holy Spirit, drunkards get drunk on beer, wine, and other liquid "spirits." Again, I am not talking about someone who drinks but someone who has given themselves over to the "sin" of drunkenness. A drunkard's heart is divided because their all-consuming fire is not God but getting "drunk." The same rules apply to those who have given themselves over to drug addictions (illegal or prescription).

And while we're on the subject of drunkenness, poppycock to those of you who have bought into the lie that alcoholism is a disease. Picking up a drink requires a personal choice. It's a self-control issue, and last time I looked, self-control was a fruit of the spirit (Galatians 5:23). "Picking up" Lou Gehrig's disease or cancer, however, is not a self-control issue. Disease chooses us. We don't get to choose it. It attacks whoever and whenever it wants as a consequence of living in a fallen world. Still not convinced? If I decide not to go to work for a year straight, is that disease too? Give me a break! It's called laziness. Or to use the biblical term, being a sluggard, which is another self-control issue that God calls "sin."

While the sinner is powerless, we who have the greater one living on the inside of us have been given all power over all the power of the devil (Luke 10:19)! Drunkards, however, who have given themselves over to the spirit of drunkenness willingly and unrepentantly have no interest in being raised from the "dead" to live a victorious life in Christ.

Christians who are swindlers or "fraudsters" as they are often referred to in my line of work have also entered the realm of spiritual death as seen in 1 Corinthians 5. As a white-collar crime investigator for the vast majority of my FBI career, I had the privilege of investigating various complex financial crimes. Many of my cases involved victims who either lost money by relying on material misrepresentations (or lies) made to them by one or more fraudsters or victims who lost money they would not have otherwise invested had they known the fraudster had intentionally withheld certain information from them that a reasonable investor would want to know before investing, referred to as "material omissions of fact."

What distinguishes a swindler from someone who simply loses someone's money due to poor business decisions or external forces beyond their control (e.g., an unanticipated downturn in the stock market) is the swindler's "intent to defraud" his victims. To prove criminal intent, the prosecution must show that the defendant intentionally lied to the victim investor(s) and that the victim investor(s) relied on these misrepresentations when deciding to invest their money with the defendant.

Swindlers make their living trying to convince people that they and their investment "opportunity" are "legit." The fifty-plus billion-dollar Ponzi scheme perpetrated by Bernie Madoff was a perfect example of how many people can be duped by the actions of one swindler. Swindlers are often very charismatic, outgoing, and glib. The best fraudsters not only have all the answers to all of the questions you will ask them, but they already know the questions you will ask them even before they know your name.

While all of us have told lies before, technically, making all of us liars, lying is a way of life for the swindler. Every aspect of their life is one big lie. Their consciences have been seared with a "hot iron." Swindlers have a distorted view of life that rejects truth for the lie until they can hardly, if at all, recognize truth anymore. Contrary, when a Christian who is spiritually "alive" in Christ lies, the Holy Spirit goes to work on them immediately until they "come clean." While true believers seek to live for Christ every day, yet sin, swindlers have completely given themselves over to a double life.

Because a swindler is behaving as one who is spiritually dead, God will allow one Christian mate the option of divorcing another Christian mate who is behaving this way. While the vast majority of us are not married to fraudsters, I have known many Christian men and women who routinely lie to their mates to either get what they want or conceal what they already have. Some of these men and women have secret bank accounts, social media and e-mail accounts, expense accounts, cellular telephone accounts, credit card accounts, secret "lovers," alternate living arrangements, and post office boxes that their spouses know nothing about. Yes, even Christians! In some cases, it is to conceal a secret relationship; in others, it is to hide an addiction. In every case, it is to conceal a double life, which casts the shadow of spiritual death on them.

One Christian attorney whose wife, according to him, "never looked at their credit card statements," told me that he had been purchasing very expensive fishing reels ($500–$1,000) for years that he had mailed to his office to conceal them from his wife. So while these Christian men and women may not be running sophisticated Ponzi schemes, per se, they routinely "swindle" their mates by lying to them or concealing the truth about different aspects of their lives with little regard, if any, given to the consequences of their actions.

Sadly, financial secrecy (e.g. hidden saving, credit card, or checking accounts) as one recent article pointed out, is widespread in many marriages. One in five spouses view it as being worse than infidelity.[53] Given these statistics, which are probably low due to underreporting, some of you who host marriage conferences need to make sure you are applauding the "right kind" of marriages and not just those that haven't ended in divorce. Tragically, there are plenty of Christian marriages like those mentioned above doing the work of the devil!

Recently, a Christian man told me that his Christian wife in their blended family had been falsifying tax, student loan, and bank records for years without his or his stepdaughter's (the student loan applicant) knowledge. His wife had been successful in "diverting" thousands of student loan dollars to accounts she controlled. Her Christian husband came to learn that his wife's criminal conduct was proceeded by a wave of similar criminal conduct with others before him that spanned several years. He was totally "blown away." To this day, she continues her double life and remains unrepentant, even after intervention and counseling. The two of them are now divorced. The prosecutor's office in the county where they reside is currently pursuing that matter.

Most people are surprised when I tell them that the majority of the white-collar defendants I investigated as an FBI agent who were subsequently charged, arrested, convicted, and sentenced were men and women of professing faith in Jesus Christ. They are even more surprised when I tell them that some of the defendants also used the cross of Christ as a means to fraudulently obtain the trust of their victims. I will discuss two such cases later.

Christian husbands and wives who behave like swindlers (whether their actions are criminal or not) have entered the realm of spiritual death because they refuse to walk in truth, making honest, safe, and healthy "connection" with their mates impossible.

Christians who are self-indulgent have also entered the realm of spiritual death. In 1 Timothy 5, Paul discusses the responsibility that we, the church, and children of widows have in caring for widows. Paul goes on to say how godly widows, while desolate, set their hope on God and continue in supplications and prayers night and day (1 Timothy 5:5 ESV). Then, in the very next verse, he contrasts this widow with the self-indulgent widow saying, "But the widow who lives for pleasure *is dead although she is still alive*" (1 Timothy 5:6 GW). While this verse does not deal with marriage per se, it certainly suggests that anyone who lives, first and foremost, for pleasure has entered the realm of spiritual death. The self-indulgent person is not merely someone who enjoys pleasurable things; it is someone who has given themselves over to the worship of pleasurable things.

Finally, those who will not provide for their families enter the realm of spiritual death. The Bible says that he who does not provide for his family has denied the faith and is worse than an infidel or unbeliever (1 Timothy 5:8). This would include a man who refuses to work or a lazy or irresponsible man under any of the other scenarios I previously discussed in chapter 2.

Recall, however, that this abandonment of responsibility above is not merely limited to financial provision. The same principle would apply, for example, to a husband or wife who willingly, persistently, and unrepentantly refuses to provide *for his or her mate* emotionally, physically, sexually, or spiritually.

Remember, in all of the scenarios I've described above wherein God considers the Christian to have entered the realm of spiritual death, this must be the Christian mate's normal pattern of behavior (i.e. those who willingly, persistently, and unrepentantly do what I have described above) for God to allow the marriage covenant involving two Christians to be broken. We can't simply reach over and touch our Christian mates in bed one night because we want a divorce and say, "Yep, they're dead![54] No, no, friend. Only God, based upon what He says in His Word, gets to play "coroner."

Again, does this mean you have to divorce your mate if you're a Christian, and your Christian spouse has entered the realm of spiritual death? No. Remember, God never commands divorce. Here, a Christian has three options. It is the same three options in any case where God permits divorce. First, they can remain in the home (if safe) and become an evangelist to their "spiritually dead" spouse through sacrificial love (in the case of the husband) or their holy and respectful behavior (in the case of the wife). While this first option, as I said earlier, is no guarantee that God will raise your mate from the "dead," it does happen. Just remember that if you stay in the home, God's standard is not merely a better version of spiritual death. He's looking to resurrect husbands and wives from the "dead." This will always involve biblical confession and repentance on the part of the offending party.

The second option a Christian couple may exercise, instead of divorce, when one mate has entered the realm of spiritual death is what is referred to as a biblical separation for the purpose of restoration. Please read that again—for purpose of restoration! We looked at this earlier with Dave and Megan, if you recall. If you and your mate do not have this as the goal of separation, it is not a biblical separation but a worldly separation.

Lastly, the couple may get a divorce. However, this should always be the last option after much prayer, fasting, counseling, and only after a biblical separation has occurred (minimum of three to six months) where the Christian spouse who has entered the realm of spiritual death remains unrepentant.

Warning: True repentance should never be based merely on what someone says but rather on observing a new direction over some time by the offending spouse that shows the offended spouse that real change has taken place. The offended spouse should be able to see "fruits of repentance." To go back into a relationship with someone who continues to perpetrate evil, rebellious, idolatrous, or abusive behavior is not only foolish, but it can also be dangerous. Beware!

Besides observing real "fruits of repentance," the Bible also speaks of restitution to innocent parties. We saw this as kids. If we accidentally threw a baseball through the neighbor's window, our parents, if they were good parents, not only required us to take ownership of the deed and seek forgiveness from our neighbor (i.e., confess and "repent") but pay for the window. The matter was not fully resolved with our parent and our neighbor until we had made full restitution for our "sin." For those who went through something similar as a child or parent, do you remember how much better everyone felt after restitution occurred? Why? Because this is how God hardwired us.

In the Bible, when David committed adultery with Bathsheba and had Bathsheba's husband, Uriah, killed in battle to cover up David's sin, God required the death of David and Bathsheba's son that had been conceived in their adultery as "payment" for restitution. Note, before this, no amount of praying, fasting, confession, nor repentance by David saved the child or provided an adequate payment of restitution to God by David for what he had done. It wasn't until David satisfied God's requirement for restitution that David's relationship with God was fully restored. The beautiful thing about God is that once restitution is paid, God opens up the floodgates of heaven to dispense grace upon the offending party.

Do you remember what happened to David and Bathsheba after restitution was made? God allowed Bathsheba to get pregnant again, and from this birth came the wisest man who ever lived—King Solomon!

In the case of marriage, restitution by the offending spouse to the offended spouse could involve many things such as a sacrifice of time, money, or service that says to the offended party, "I am so sorry for what I've done. To show you how sorry I am, I commit to (fill in the blank) over the next (fill in the blank)." It's hard to beat that on the open market if you're the spouse who has been "sinned" against. Many husbands and wives who experience this kind of restoration say that they are better off afterward than they were before the offense occurred.

You should know that even in cases where God does allow for divorce, it is seldom the mate who is spiritually "alive" who will have to initiate it. By simply standing up for what is right and refusing to allow, condone, or participate in the spiritually "dead" behavior of the mate, the spiritually "dead" mate will, in most cases, choose against their spiritually "alive" mate and end the marriage because they have no desire to change.

Thus, in summary, God only allows divorce (i.e., the marriage covenant to be legitimately broken by the offended party) in three instances—adultery (physical or spiritual), abandonment (by an unbeliever), and death (physical or spiritual). I hope you can now see that "thou shalt never divorce" is not only unscriptural but, in some cases, dangerous because it can leave innocent parties needlessly exposed to the ravages of sin without a means of escape.

While divorce should always be on the high shelf where it is hard to reach, far too many inside the church have made marriage the "sacred cow" that you never "mess with" under any circumstances. Nowhere in scripture did God ever declare the institution of marriage to be more important than the people in that institution! While God hates divorce (Malachi 2:16), He also hates any marriage that is doing the work of the devil! Remember, when sin entered the world, it changed everything. And for those of you who like to use this verse (God hates divorce) as a means of justification for never getting (or sanctioning) a divorce under any circumstances, we would all do well to remember that divorce is not the only thing God hates.

A quick look at the list of six things the Lord hates from Proverbs 6 doesn't' even include divorce. "A proud look" and "a lying tongue" are at the top of the list! Thus, those who are quick to trumpet the "God hates divorce counsel" to someone who may very well be in an "evil" or abusive marriage would do well to keep their "wisdom" to themselves until they have the facts, not merely the church gossip disguised as "prayer."

How many of you have ever heard this teaching on divorce before? For years, I thought that God only allowed divorce in the case of physical adultery. Somebody lied on God. Sadly, it continues today in pulpits all across America.

Again, lest you hear what I am not saying, the discussion above is in no way intended to be a "commercial" or endorsement for divorce even in cases where God allows it. Remember, God never commands divorce. And even when He does allow it, we should always hate it like He does.

So in cases where God does allow the marriage covenant to be broken legitimately (i.e. divorce to occur), who is permitted to break it? Let us now examine this most important question and put it to rest forever! You should already know the answer.

Since God establishes all marriage covenants, only God can legitimately break them.[55] Please read that again, slowly. Because it is God who establishes all covenants and "sits" above them all (transcendence), only God has the power to legitimately "overrule" or "cancel" them (Hebrews 10:9). Sadly, many Christians invite God to their wedding but tell Him to stay home for the divorce while they go to a local judge ("man") to get *their* (notice the pronoun) divorce "legalized" before God has "legitimized" it based upon His biblical grounds for divorce outlined in His Word.

Listen, beloved, just because man has legalized a divorce doesn't necessarily mean that God has legitimized it. What? That's right. Just because husbands and wives go downtown to the local courthouse and obtain a judgment of divorce from a judge, dissolving the marriage doesn't necessarily mean that God has dissolved their marriage covenant! God's Word tells us in Mark 10:9 that what, therefore, God has joined together, let no man (i.e., judge) separate (Mark 10:9). Said another way, what God has joined together, only God can *legitimately* separate.

This brings up an interesting question. Since God is the one who establishes all covenants and God is the only one who can *legitimately* (the operative word) break them, does God recognize man's ability to *illegitimately* break God's covenant (against God's will) with their spouse? You bet. We saw this earlier in the chapter, remember? Back to that free will thing.

In Jeremiah 31, God uses Jeremiah to proclaim God's hope for the restoration of Israel and Judah under the new covenant He will make with them, declaring how Israel broke the former covenant seen here in the following (italics added for emphasis):

> "The day will come," says the Lord, "when I will make a new covenant with the people of Israel and Judah. This covenant will not be like the one I made with their ancestors when I took them by the hand and brought them out of the land of Egypt. *They broke that covenant, though I loved them as a husband loves a wife,*" says the Lord. (Jeremiah 31:31–32 NLT)

Comparing His relationship with Israel to that of a husband with His wife, God says that even though He loved His wife (Israel) as a husband loves his wife, His wife (Israel) chose to break His (God's) covenant. Certainly, if Israel (God's "wife") can illegitimately break God's covenant, husbands and wives can illegitimately break God's covenant. We see it every day, even in the church!

In Jeremiah 34, God shows us, generally, how serious the consequences of illegitimately breaking God's covenants can be with Him. Here, God proclaims through the prophet Jeremiah that He (God) made a covenant with Israel's ancestors long ago that when He (God) rescued them from slavery in Egypt that every Hebrew must be freed after six years. Up to now, in Jeremiah 34, no Hebrews had been released. Babylon has laid siege to Jerusalem, and the city is about to fall. King Zedekiah of Judah, who tries to appease God, finally decides to listen to Jeremiah and free the slaves, making a solemn covenant with God in His Temple that He would not make them slaves once again. King Zedekiah then disobeys the terms of his covenant with God by making them slaves once again. The Lord gives

Jeremiah the following message for King Zedekiah (*italics* used for emphasis):

> You freed your slaves and made a solemn covenant with me in my temple. *But now you have shrugged off your oath and defiled my name* by taking back the men and women you had freed, making them slaves once again. Therefore, this is what the Lord says: "Since you have not obeyed me by setting your countrymen free, I will set you free to be destroyed by war, famine, and disease. You will be considered a disgrace by all the nations of the earth. *Because you have refused the terms of our covenant,* I will cut you apart just as you cut apart the calf when you walked between its halves to solemnize your vows. Yes, I will cut you apart, whether you are officials of Judah or Jerusalem, court officials, priests, or common people—*for you have broken your oath.*" (Jeremiah 34:15–19 NLT)

As you can see, God takes the illegitimate breaking of His covenants very seriously. There are a couple of critical principles we can take from these Old Testament passages and apply to our New Testament situations. First, whenever we break God's covenants illegitimately—that is, whenever he does not allow us to break them—we defile His name and experience enormous consequences. Secondly, these consequences may include setting us free to be destroyed by the world around us where we will be seen as a disgrace. If only more of us truly believed this, I firmly believe we would see fewer *illegitimate* divorces.

In Hosea 6, the prophet Hosea issues a call to repentance to Israel for its sins against God, showing them that what they have done in illegitimately breaking God's covenant is no different than what the first man, Adam, did (*italics* used for emphasis):

"O Israel and Judah, what should I do with you?" asks the Lord. "For your love vanishes like the morning mist and disappears like dew in the sunlight. I sent my prophets to cut you to pieces. I have slaughtered you with my words, threatening you with death. My judgment will strike you as surely as day follows night. I want you to be merciful; I don't want your sacrifices. I want you to know God, that's more important than burnt offerings. *But like Adam, you broke my covenant and rebelled against me.*" (Hosea 6:4–7 NLT)

God highlights some other examples of illegitimate covenant breaks involving Israel in the books of Ezekiel and Joshua.

God tells the prophet, Ezekiel, to say this to the house of Israel:

And say to the rebellious house, to the house of Israel, Thus says the Lord God: "O house of Israel, enough of all your abominations, in admitting foreigners, uncircumcised in heart and flesh, to be in my sanctuary, profaning my temple, when you offer to me my food, the fat and the blood. *You have broken my covenant*, in addition to all your abominations. And you have not kept charge of my holy things, but you have set others to keep my charge for you in my sanctuary." (Ezekiel 44:6–8 ESV)

At the end of Joshua 6, Joshua has just captured the city of Jericho and burned it to the ground. Before the siege, he gives the Israelites instructions that the city and everything in it must be destroyed entirely as an offering unto the Lord. Joshua tells them not to take any of the things set apart for destruction or they would be destroyed and bring trouble to Israel (Joshua 6:17–18).

Following the victory, it is discovered that one man, Achan, is unfaithful to the instructions and steals some of the items set apart for the Lord. The Bible says that the Lord was very angry with the Israelites (Joshua 7:1). Achan's "sin" subsequently resulted in the death of about thirty-six Israelites by the men of Ai—the battle right after Jericho. Joshua questions the Lord and asks Him why He brought them across the Jordan River if He (God) was just going to let the Amorites kill them. The Lord provides the following powerful response to Joshua:

> Get up! Why are you lying on your face like this? *Israel has sinned and broken my covenant!* They have stolen the things that I commanded to be set apart for me. And they have not only stolen them; they have also lied about it and hidden the things among their belongings. That is why the Israelites are running from their enemies in defeat. *For now Israel has been set apart for destruction. I will not remain with you any longer* unless you destroy the things among you that were set apart for destruction. (Joshua 7:10–12 NLT)

In Joshua's farewell address to his leaders in Joshua 23, after many years of conquering their enemies in Canaan, Joshua underscores the importance of obeying God and what will happen to *them if they break the covenant of the Lord* by worshiping and serving other gods as seen here in the following:

> Soon I will die, going all the way to the earth. Deep in your hearts you know that every promise of the Lord your God has come true. Not a single one has failed! But as surely as the Lord your God has given you the good things He promised, *He will also bring disaster on you if you disobey Him. He will completely wipe you out from this good land He has given you. If you break the covenant of the Lord your God by worshiping and serving other gods, His anger will burn against you,*

*and you will quickly be wiped out from the good
land He has given you.* (Joshua 23:14–16 NLT)

What I want you to take from this discussion is that from the creation of the first man, Adam, until now, man has been illegitimately breaking God's covenants. Secondly, the consequences for doing so have been great, resulting in nothing less than a holy mess today!

So the question that those contemplating divorce should be asking themselves (because it's God's covenant and not ours) is not what the judge downtown says about the grounds for divorce, but instead, "What does God's Word say about the grounds for divorce?" In other words, does God allow *His* covenant to be *legitimately* broken under the grounds for which I or my mate are seeking a divorce?

Read that again, saints. That's the question all married couples considering divorce should be asking themselves. It's not what others say. It's "What does God say in my situation?" Sadly, very few of us ask this question, including Christian counselors, leading to many selfish, unbiblical divorces. Even in rare instances where a Christian counselor is involved and does ask this question, I have found it to be equally rare that they know what God's Word says on the subject or how to apply the word correctly.

So in cases where God does allow divorce, how is it decided? And where is it decided if not by a judge downtown? Great questions!

Because marriage and divorce are kingdom matters, they should only be decided by kingdom people applying the king's word in the kingdom's courthouse, the local church. The local church was never supposed to be a meeting place where people went just once or twice a week. The New Testament church was, and is, supposed to be the daily meeting place for prayer, fellowship, discipleship, evangelism, training, discipline, and among other things, deciding kingdom matters by those who have been appointed by God as overseers. Primarily, this role belongs to the senior pastor and associate pastors or elders (i.e., "overseers") who, incidentally and contrary to our politically correct culture, are all *men* (not women) of mature Christian character (Titus 1:5–9, 1 Peter 5:1–4).

So why don't the vast majority of churches "step up" and adjudicate on issues of divorce? Easy. It's a ton of work! Untangling "bad" or broken relationships is a full-time job that requires more time and dedication than most church leaders are willing to commit, given their responsibilities, challenges, and problems. I understand. I also understand that the number of those who flood the doors of a church on any given Sunday in bad or broken marriages is enormous. However, this does not excuse church leaders who will one day give an account for their actions and inactions (Romans 14:12; 2 Corinthians 5:10) on kingdom matters like divorce, in kingdom's court using the king's word.

The second reason why most churches don't adjudicate on matters of divorce is that they lack the knowledge and, therefore, don't know what to do. So many do nothing, leaving the offending party trapped in their "sin" and the offended party vulnerable and unprotected in many cases.

The third reason why church leaders will not adjudicate on matters of divorce is out of fear. Church leaders fear that their decisions will alienate and divide the "flock," causing some to leave and take their money with them.

Church leaders who will not adjudicate on matters of divorce or on other kingdom business for that matter, using the King's word, have just told God, their church members, and all relevant "parties" involved, the following:

1. Protecting innocent parties and exercising church discipline is not a top priority.
2. It is okay that the "back door of the church" is open to the devil.
3. Church leadership is ill-equipped to shepherd the flock.
4. Divorce is a matter of the local government in violation of 1 Corinthian 6:1–8.
5. The expansion (or preservation) of their kingdom is more important than God's kingdom.
6. God's Word will not have the final in this church.

The purpose of such a "family court" in our local churches is not for "beating up sheep" who step out of line but for administering God's truth and grace in the given situation. It is for teaching, reproofing, correction onto righteousness, repentance, healing, and restoration so that the man (or woman) of God may be thoroughly equipped for every good work (2 Timothy 3:16–17).

Note, while the below passage of scripture doesn't specifically deal with the issue of divorce, it nonetheless highlights who, how, and where God expects kingdom issues to be handled—by kingdom people using the King's word in kingdom's court, the local church. We looked at this same passage earlier but were focused on a different section of it. Again, a Christian man has been found to be engaging in sexual immorality with his stepmother. Paul is addressing the Corinthian church who was ignoring it (italics added for emphasis):

> I can hardly believe the report about the sexual immorality going on among you, something so evil that even the pagans don't do it. I am told that you have a man in your church who is living in sin with his father's wife. And you are so proud of yourselves! Why aren't you mourning in sorrow and shame? And why haven't you removed this man from your fellowship? Even though I am not there with you in person, I am with you in the Spirit. Concerning the one who has done this, I have already passed judgment in the name of the Lord Jesus. *You are to call a meeting of the church,* and I will be there in spirit, and the power of the Lord Jesus will be with you as you meet. Then you must cast this man out of the church and into Satan's hands, so that his sinful nature will be destroyed and he himself will be saved when the Lord returns. (1 Corinthians 5:1–5 NLT)

Paul tells them to call a meeting of *the church*. He does not say to push the problem off on someone else, ignore it, or to let the judge "downtown" decide the matter. Call a meeting of the church. Also, note that this isn't one guy (i.e., the senior pastor) shouldering the responsibility alone but multiple Christians *meeting* to discuss the matter at the local church. God, through Paul, also gives us a glimpse at what the church's position should be involving the man or woman who is in sin but who will not cease the behavior or come under the authority and leadership of the church and repent. He or she should be cast (or excommunicated) from the church into Satan's hands.

Wow! Really? We say, "My loving God would never do this." Reread it, saint. Yes, our loving God will do this because He loves us and hopes that, in doing so, our sinful nature would be destroyed, and we would be saved when the Lord returns. Whose rule book are you operating under? Here, we have a hard but excellent example of tough love from Paul who loved the sheep and understood what was at stake. Do you, Pastor?

But again, you say, "Operating as kingdom's court is a lot of work." Yes, and quite unpopular, I might add. It's the reason why so many churches avoid it and also why so many churches in America today are spiritually "anemic." How can any church walk in God's power and authority when its back door is open to the devil? However, a faithful shepherd will "step up" and do what God requires, regardless of the consequences.

Why is this so necessary? Besides restoring broken marriages, where possible, the sheep need to know that the leadership of the church is protecting them from the ravages of sin that entered the world during the fall and hold people accountable. To not do this is a form of spiritual abandonment by the pastor and the leadership of the church. However, the most important reason pastors and church leaders need to "step up," if what I have already said isn't compelling enough, is because we promised God we would advance His kingdom and glory. If we are unwilling to do what He requires, it is evidence that we are more invested in our kingdoms and glory than His. It is also evidence that we are operating in pride or fear and not faith.

Any pastor or church leader who will not protect His "sheep" in these ways has a warped concept of grace, and is in the wrong profession. While there are no perfect churches, many churches are a lot "sicker" than others because its leaders are more interested in being politically correct than biblically correct. Some churches are more interested in being peacekeepers than peacemakers. If you are in a church whose leaders will not protect you or others by removing, through the process of biblical discipline, those who seek to harm others in the flock with their evil, harmful, and unrepentant behavior, you're in the wrong church!

Just one chapter later, in 1 Corinthians 6, we see yet another example of where God expects kingdom people to use the King's word to make kingdom decisions. Again, while this scripture doesn't specifically relate to marriage covenants and divorce, per se, it clearly illustrates who is responsible for deciding kingdom matters like divorce and remarriage. As referenced earlier, Paul tells us that Christians should not be filing lawsuits against other Christians in front of unbelievers in the secular court. These matters should be decided by the local church as seen here in the following (*italics* added for emphasis):

> When you have something against another Christian, why do you file a lawsuit and ask a secular court to decide the matter, instead of taking it to other Christians to decide who is right? Don't you know that someday we Christians are going to judge the world? And since you are going to judge the world, can't you decide these little things among yourselves? Don't you realize that we Christians will judge angels? So you should surely be able to resolve ordinary disagreements here on earth. If you have legal disputes about such matters, why do you go to outside judges who are not respected by *the church*? I am saying this to shame you. Isn't there anyone in all *the church* who is wise enough to decide these argu-

ments? But instead one Christian sues another—right in front of unbelievers! To have such lawsuits at all is a real defeat for you. (1 Corinthians 6:1–7 NLT)

Matthew 18:15–17 is another passage that points to the responsibility churches have to handle kingdom matters. If our brother offends us, we are supposed to go to them. If they still don't listen, we're supposed to bring one or two others with us so two or three witnesses may confirm the matter. And if they still don't listen, we are supposed to bring the issue *before the church*. When was the last time your church did that? No, brothers and sisters, it seems we are more interested in "pushing" matters of the kingdom off on secular courts downtown than we are in upholding the integrity of God's Word. May God have mercy on us.

Though this may be obvious, I do not wish to assume anything on such a critical topic. The goal of the local church should never be to pursue divorce as the first step, even in cases where God does allow it. The purpose of the local church should always be, as stated earlier, the restoration of the relationship where possible. However, when the offending party refuses to repent, churches must take the unpopular step and do what Paul admonished the Corinthian church to do (i.e., deliver this man to Satan for the destruction of the flesh so that his spirit may be saved in the day of the Lord; 1 Corinthians 5:5). Again, the restoration of the individual should always be our motive. If it's not, the church is not exercising real biblical discipline.

Church leaders must be equally courageous with husbands and wives who initially do come into kingdom's court for such a kingdom matter but abandon the process to pursue a divorce in man's court. This departure typically occurs before kingdom's court has ruled on the issue or after kingdom's court has ruled that biblical grounds for a divorce do *not* exist. Again, in cases like these, church leaders must remove husbands and wives from the church who will not come under the authority of the church so that their sinful nature will be destroyed, and they will be saved when the Lord returns.[56]

Beware, saints, while kingdom decisions should be decided by kingdom people in kingdom's court, kingdom people don't always render decisions based upon the King's word—yes, even in kingdom's court! I believe this is part of the crisis that exists in Christian churches in America today. I've seen this tragedy over and over again at local churches. For example, a Christian wife may have biblical grounds for a divorce from her unrepentant Christian or non-Christian husband who continues to be physically or verbally abusive to her. However, instead of counseling her to get out of the "danger zone" and pursue a biblical separation and ultimate divorce if her mate refuses to repent, church leaders encourage some wives to stay in the home, pray, and to be "more loving."

The hope is that he may be won to Christ through her holy and respectful behavior (1 Peter 3:2). While the witness of a holy and respectful wife is undeniable and does change some hearts, again, it's no guarantee. Meanwhile, she exposes herself to more abusive behavior. For a pastor, church leader, or anyone to "encourage" such a woman to go back into the "lion's den" is not only lousy counsel but dangerous counsel. While we should always pray, Jesus, our Good Shepherd and Protector, does not want us to become anyone's "prey."

Warning: If the counsel you are receiving from kingdom's court doesn't line-up with the King's word, this is no time to abandon the faith and go to man's court. It is time, however, for a change in venue. Bring your matter before another kingdom's court. Yes, you could take things into your own hands and save a lot of time by filing for divorce downtown because you now know what God's Word says on the subject of divorce and whether God allows divorce in your situation, but there are at least four things wrong with this.

First, your judgment may be impaired because you're too close to the situation causing you to make a foolish decision that you would have not otherwise made if the local church were involved. Secondly, you cut yourself off from those who could support you, challenge you, and hold you accountable to God's Word. Thirdly, you eliminate a valuable resource of influence and godly leverage where more than just you (the offended spouse) may be needed to intervene and communicate to the offending party that what they are doing is wrong. Lastly, and most importantly, by bypassing kingdom's court and taking matters into your own hands, you are directly opposing God and His Word on how these matters are to be handled.

However, once kingdom's court has ruled that biblical grounds for divorce exist and restoration is not possible because the offending party is unwilling to repent, the offended party may then, if they choose, legalize "downtown" what God has legitimized "uptown." Thus, it is critical to understand that in cases where God does allow divorce, marriage covenants are legitimately broken by God in kingdom's court, the local church, "uptown," before they are ever legally broken in man's court "downtown." At least, that's the way it's supposed to work!

I'll never forget the torment one Christian woman was experiencing who approached me after a *Do You Want to Get Well?* marriage conference. Her husband was not with her. She was tormented because her Christian husband was demanding his "biblical right" to have sex with her, though he was knowingly, admittedly, and presently committing adultery with other women. For years, the woman, who had received unbiblical counseling from her former pastor and Christian friends, was convinced it was her "wifely duty" to meet her husband's sexual needs, though he continued to be unfaithful and unrepentant.

Unreal, right? I saw this woman again about a year later after telling her the year prior that she had received some very unbiblical counseling and that while divorce should never be her first option, she did have biblical grounds for a divorce based on adultery if what she was saying was true. I encouraged her the year prior to get supported, stop having sex with her husband until there was genuine repentance with a track record that could be trusted, and finally to bring the matter before kingdom's court since her repeated attempts with him had failed.

When I saw her a year later, she ran up to the driver's side window of my vehicle and said, "Hey, Jim, I don't know if you remember me, but I was the lady who took your advice and got the church involved."

I remembered her instantly. Her countenance was completely different. The veil of oppression had been lifted from her face. The love of Christ was in her eyes. She said that she took my advice and brought the matter before a new "kingdom's court" and that the church heard the matter and told her that God did allow her to divorce him based on her circumstances. She was free from the ravages of her husband's sin and finally able to see her worth as a daughter of the King! A great victory for one woman who had believed the "lie" that you should never, ever get a divorce under any circumstance!

The scripture says that whatsoever is bound on earth is bound in heaven and whatsoever is loosed on earth is loosed in heaven (Matthew 18:18). The job of the local church, as representatives of heaven's court on earth, is to render "binding" and "loosing" decisions on kingdom matters. In the case of marriage and divorce, it is the church's job to decide when husbands and wives are still "bound" to one another in marriage and when husbands and wives may be "loosed" from one another in marriage for reasons allowed by God where restoration of the marriage is not possible.

One church that understands that kingdom matters, including but not limited to divorce, should be decided by kingdom people in kingdom's court using the King's word is none other than Oak Cliff Bible Fellowship (OCBF), located in Dallas, Texas. Check out this excerpt taken from OCBF's Church Mission Campaign Contract titled "Memorandum of Understanding, Oak Cliff Bible Fellowship Kingdom Agenda Mission Campaign Contract":

> By signing this contract, I am indicating I am a Christian and believe that the Bible commands to make every effort to live at peace and to resolve disputes with each other in private or within the Christian church (see Matthew 18:15–20; 1 Corinthians 6:1–8). Therefore, I agree that any claim or dispute arising from or related to this Contract or any campaign in which I participate shall be settled by biblically based mediation and, if necessary, legally binding arbitra-

tion in accordance with the Rules of Procedure for Christian Conciliation of the Institute for Christian Conciliation. All such mediation and arbitration shall take place in Dallas, Texas. Judgment upon an arbitration award may be in any court otherwise having jurisdiction. I understand that these methods shall be the sole remedy for any controversy or claim arising out of this Contract or any such campaign and I expressly waive any rights I have to file a lawsuit in any civil court for such disputes, except to enforce an arbitration decision.[57]

Also noteworthy as a model to churches everywhere is their following policy on Christian conduct, which would certainly include but not be limited to matters of divorce and remarriage and the exercise of church discipline where warranted:[58]

1. OCBF's members' conduct, whether on or off church premises, that is criminal, dishonest, immoral in nature, unbiblical, or detrimental to the best interest of the church, may be subject to corrective action, which could include Church discipline.

2. In harmony with the scriptural teaching of the Christian faith, discipline must be a functional part of the local church (Matthew 18:15–0; Galatians 1:8–9; II Thessalonians 3:11; I Corinthians 5:1–13). The Board of Elders shall discipline any unrepentant member who knowingly holds false or heretical doctrine, who knowingly lives inconsistently with their Christian profession, or who knowingly would disturb the unity and peace of the church.

3. The goal of discipline is to restore the person to the church whenever there is repentance and evidence of spiritual change.

May this become the standard of every church in America. I love it, Dr. Evans. Thank you!

While I take no joy in saying this, only two of the many churches I have been associated with over the last three decades have ever attempted to model this or anything even close to this to the detriment of our marriages, homes, churches, cities, and nation. While I know others churches do, there aren't nearly enough, especially when this is God's standard for the church! The devastating result is that kingdom matters are being decided by "man" downtown, resulting in nothing less than a holy mess!

One of the reasons I wrote this chapter was to equip church leaders with the tools they need to deal with this issue of divorce and remarriage head-on, armed with the truth. If we're supposed to come to the church and the church won't decide on such kingdom matters for whatever reason or cannot be trusted to decide correctly, where does that leave us? I'll tell you—forced to take matters before the unrighteous instead of saints in violation of 1 Corinthians 6. Pastors, you will be without excuse. If there was ever a time that the church and the culture needed you to do your job in this area, it is now!

We have not represented Christ well concerning this issue of divorce, brothers and sisters. It's time for all of this to change if we want to see our homes and nation healed.

Now that you know that God allows divorce to occur in certain circumstances and also know where matters of divorce are to be decided, please let me discuss remarriage briefly. What may have seemed like a very complex topic to some of you before this discussion is now quite simple. And since approximately 50 percent of all marriages in the church experience divorce and the vast majority of the remaining 50 percent of marriages consist of those who remain married not because they "want to" but because they believe they "have to,"[59] it is certainly worth a bit of extra time.

Simply put, biblical grounds for divorce are automatic grounds for a biblical remarriage. Read it again slowly. Make sense? In other words, if God allows a person to get a divorce for a reason recognized by Him, then that person is free to marry again in the Lord. Similarly, those who get a divorce for reasons not allowed by God, if they marry another, commit adultery because in God's eyes, they are still married to their former mate, regardless of what the court downtown says.

Many have been divorced and remarried one, two, three, or more times for reasons not allowable by God, resulting in nothing less than a holy mess from our house to the White House. If this is you, ask God to forgive you, and He will. Do not divorce your current mate. There is no need to compound the "mess" any further. I believe Jesus would tell each of us to make our current marriage count for the kingdom of God and go and sin no more.

The compounding effects of playing by our own set of rules for marriage, divorce, and remarriage have had a devastating impact on not only our homes but our communities, churches, cities, and nation. The majority of Christians I have known personally through the years have *not* married, divorced, and remarried according to God's rule book but have taken matters into their own hands. Many of us ask God to bless our unbiblical decisions and then get angry with Him when things don't work out the way we wanted. How arrogant, ignorant, and foolish are we to reject God's rule book for marriage, divorce, and remarriage and expect any other outcome but utter chaos? How can the rest of the world get it right when we can't even get it right?

As stated before, God does not operate by our set of rules for marriage, beloved. Remember, it is His covenant. He makes the rules, and He will share His glory with no one by allowing us to modify His rule book to suit our needs, wants, or desires.

Some married couples may want to consider doing the following on their next wedding anniversary. Instead of "patting yourselves on the back" and announcing to the world how many years you've been married, honestly and courageously consider asking your mate the following tough questions:

1. Do you think our marriage advanced God's kingdom and glory more this year than in the previous year? Or were we more interested in advancing our kingdoms and glory?

2. Is the level of closeness and intimacy we share greater than it was a year ago? Or are we settling for marital détente where we're not devouring one another but where there is little evidence of tenderness and sweetness in our relationship?
3. Do you trust and respect me more than you did a year ago?
4. Do you think the last year of our marriage caused God to smile more or less than it did in the previous year?

If the thought of asking your spouse one or more of these questions terrifies you (men), than you already have your answers. Be honest with yourself and your mate, and get help if you need it. Finally, if these questions don't matter to you, I would ask you to honestly search your heart and ask yourself whether you and your mate are truly living for Christ. As I said earlier, a "dead" marriage, like a dead tree, can stand in the forest for a long time! And we've got a lot of "dead" marriages out there—Christian couples who are smiling on the outside but who are "dead" on the inside.

The consequences of violating the rules of God's marriage covenant have been severe, wouldn't you agree? I hope you now see that whether we're talking about a marriage, a football team, a corporation, or how the government should run, for example, whenever we play by our own set of rules, we stop advancing God's kingdom, give up more territory to the enemy (or the "competition"), and invite more chaos into our lives. Some of you reading this book have already experienced this chaos in your marriage directly as a result of your actions or indirectly as the result of someone else's actions (i.e., your current or former spouse). Yet, others are sadly experiencing it now in their current marriages. Ignorance and self-centeredness have cost us much. It's time for all of this to change!

Operating under Godly marital covenants must be one of our top priorities if we expect God to use us to reclaim territory in the earth through the expansion of His kingdom and magnification of His glory (chapter 1)!

Can you imagine what impact we would have in society today if the 80 percent of us who profess to be Christians allowed God's

Word to have the final word on every issue relating to marriage, divorce, and remarriage?

If you're ready to join me and countless others who are committed to this already, please allow me to be the first to congratulate you! You and I are no longer part of the problem. We just became part of the solution! May God be glorified and every demon terrified as you go from this place with the knowledge you have gained and the courage to live it out.

Prayer of Repentance (if applicable)

> Lord Jesus, I confess that I have been arrogant and self-righteous to think that I knew more than you about marriage, divorce, and remarriage when it was you, not me, who wrote the book on it. You, not me, established the marriage covenant from the beginning of time and the framework upon which it was, and is, to operate (transcendence, hierarchy, and ethics). My ignorance up to now on these things has resulted in nothing less than a "holy mess" in my life and in every institution I impact from my house to the White House.
>
> Instead of ruling my world under your hand to advance your kingdom and glory, I have violated the terms of your marriage covenant, allowing the devil to rule my world to advance His kingdom and glory.
>
> I repent of this conduct now, Lord, and allow your word to have the final word on marriage, divorce, and remarriage in my life from this day forward. Help me now to go and sin no more (John 8:11).
>
> Thank you for your steadfast love and mercies toward me that never cease and that are

new every morning (Lamentations 3:22) and for standing more prepared to forgive my sins than I am to commit them, more willing to supply my needs than I am to confess them. A love like this compels me to obey you in this most crucial area of life to see your kingdom come and your will be done on earth as it is in heaven, in Jesus's name. Amen!

Verses to Remember:

1. [S]he is your marriage partner and your wife by covenant. (Malachi 2:14 LEB)
2. Jesus said, "This cup is the new covenant between God and His people—an agreement confirmed with my blood." (1 Corinthians 11:25 NLT)
3. Now therefore if you will indeed obey my voice and keep My covenant (agreement), then you shall be My own special possession and treasure from among all peoples [of the world], for all the earth is Mine. (Exodus 19:5 AMP)
4. Then I said, "O Lord, God of heaven, the great and awesome God who keeps His covenant of unfailing love with those who love Him and obey His commands." (Nehemiah 1:5 NLT)
5. And the Lord God commanded the man, saying, "You may surely eat of any tree of every tree of the garden, but of the tree of the knowledge of good and evil you shall not eat, for in the day that you eat of it you shall surely die." (Genesis 2:16–17 ESV)
6. And bring the fatted calf here and kill it and let us eat and be merry; for this my son was dead and is alive again; He was lost and is found. (Luke 15:23–24 NKJV)
7. But like Adam, you broke my covenant and betrayed my trust. (Hosea 6:7 ESV)

8. I say to you whoever divorces His wife, except for sexual unfaithfulness, and marries another woman commits adultery. (Matthew 19:9 CEB)

9. But if the husband or wife who is not a believer decides to leave, let them leave. When this happens, the brother or sister in Christ is free. God chose you to have a life of peace. (1 Corinthians 7:15 ERV)

10. For a married woman is bound by law to her husband while He lives, but if her husband dies she is released from the law of marriage. (Romans 7:2 ESV)

11. What I meant is that you are not to associate with anyone who claims to be a Christian yet indulges in sexual sin, or is greedy, or worships idols, or is abusive, or a drunkard, or a swindler. Don't even eat with such people. It isn't my responsibility to judge outsiders, but it certainly is your job to judge those inside the church who are sinning in these ways. God will judge those on the outside; but as the Scriptures say, "You must remove the evil person from among you." (1 Corinthians 5:11–13 NLT)

12. Therefore what God has joined together, let not man separate. (Mark 10:9 NKJV)

13. Follow the Lord's rules for doing His work, just as an athlete either follows the rules or is disqualified and wins no prize. (2 Timothy 2:5 NLT)

CHAPTER 4

❖❖❖❖❖

What Took You So Long?

Some say it was the worst intelligence disaster in US History.[60] At the time of his arrest on February 18, 2001, in Vienna, Virginia, "Ramon," age fifty-six, was observed clandestinely placing a package of highly classified information for pick up by his Russian handlers at a prearranged "dead drop" site at Foxstone Park, one mile from his Vienna, Virginia, home.[61] In exchange for the information he provided the KGB, his Russian handlers gave him two Rolex watches and paid him cash and diamonds in excess of $600,000 over a nearly twenty-year period.[62] Additionally, they placed funds in an escrow account in Moscow that were allegedly valued at or above $800,000.[63] As fellow FBI agents were arresting him, he simply said, "What took you so long?"[64]

On July 6, 2001, Robert Philip Hanssen pled guilty to fifteen counts of espionage in the United States District Court for the Eastern District of Virginia and was sent to prison without the possibility of parole.[65] Hansen currently resides at ADX Supermax in Florence, Colorado—the same maximum security prison that holds 9-11 terrorist Zacarias Moussaoui.[66]

Former FBI Agent Robert Philip Hanssen was born on April 18, 1944. He graduated from William Howard Taft High School in Chicago in 1962. He later attended Knox College in Galesburg, Illinois, where he graduated in 1966 with a bachelor of science degree in chemistry.[67] While at Knox, Hanssen pursued his interests and took courses in Russian.[68] He applied for a position with the National Security Agency (NSA) as a cryptographer but was later denied due to budgetary setbacks.[69] With his original goal of becoming a doctor, he instead enrolled in dental school at Northwestern University.[70] While he excelled, he also discovered that "He didn't like spit that much"[71] and changed his focus to business after three years. In 1971, he received an MBA in accounting and information systems from Northwestern University.[72] From 1971 to 1972, he took a job with an accounting firm in Chicago but later quit to work as an investigator in the Financial Section of the Inspection Services Division of the Chicago Police Department[73]—the same police department that his emotionally abusive father worked in during Hanssen's childhood.[74]

Robert met his wife, Bernadette "Bonnie" Wauck, while in dental school in Chicago.[75] Bonnie was one of eight children from a strict Roman Catholic family.[76] After marrying Bonnie in 1968, Robert zealously converted to Catholicism from the Lutheran Church and became extensively involved in Opus Dei,[77] an institution in the Catholic Church primarily composed of lay members. Secular priests operate under the governance of a bishop who is elected by specific members and appointed by the pope.

As a member of Opus Dei, Hanssen was responsible for organizing and assisting other members with, among other things, training in Catholic spirituality for application into daily life.[78] Opus Dei members are not only involved in personal charity and social work, but they are also involved in running universities, university residences, schools, publishing houses, and technical and agricultural training centers.[79] Opus Dei, which in Latin means *Work of God,* requires its members to attend mass daily and participate in weekly confessions.[80]

Hanssen took the oath of office to become an FBI Agent on January 12, 1976, serving an initial two-year tour in Gary, Indiana, as a white-collar crime agent.[81] Hanssen sought out counterintelligence assignments in Gary and, after being unsuccessful, requested a transfer to the New York Field Office.[82] Within six months of arriving in New York, Hanssen was assigned to a Soviet counterintelligence squad.[83]

Hanssen continued to work foreign counterintelligence matters for most of his twenty-five-year FBI career from 1976 to 2001, serving primarily in the New York and Washington DC field offices.[84] However, in the 1980s and 1990s, Hanssen also held positions at FBI Headquarters and the State Department, which gave him access to a broad range of highly sensitive counterintelligence and military information.[85] It was this access that enabled Hanssen to discreetly and effectively commit espionage against the United States for over twenty years. The following is a summary of Hanssen's espionage career:

> Hanssen's espionage spanned three separate periods: 1979–1981, 1985–1991, and 1999–2001. Over more than twenty years, Hanssen compromised some of the nation's most important counterintelligence and military secrets, including the identities of dozens of human sources, three of whom were executed. Hanssen gave the KGB thousands of pages of highly classified documents and dozens of computer disks detailing US strategies in the event of nuclear war, major developments in military weapon technologies, information on active espionage cases, and many other aspects of the US Intelligence Community's Soviet counterintelligence program.[86]

Hanssen's personal life offered few clues that he was working as a double agent for the KGB. In his community, Hanssen was known as a devoted husband and father who spent considerable time teaching his children how to excel at academics.[87] To fellow FBI agents, Hanssen held politically conservative, anti-Communist views and, according to those closest to him, had no issues with alcohol, drugs, or gambling. Moreover, he was not a big spender.[88]

Other aspects of his personal life, however, did reveal signs that Hanssen was living a "double life." For example, while Hanssen went to Catholic mass, had a crucifix on his office wall, possessed an icon of the Virgin Mary on his desk, and knelt during the workday at 4:00 p.m. to offer up novena prayers to Mary,[89] Hanssen routinely attended strip clubs and had a great affinity for a Washington DC stripper named Priscilla Sue Galey who later traveled with him to Hong Kong.[90] Hanssen lavished money and gifts on her that included cash, jewels, an AMEX card, and a Mercedes Benz.[91] In an interview following Hanssen's arrest, Galey admitted that while she repeatedly offered Hanssen sex, Hanssen always declined, saying he was much more interested in trying to convert her to Catholicism.[92]

Federal law enforcement agents have the great privilege, duty, and honor of investigating violations of the laws of the United States, which involve collecting evidence in cases in which the United States is or may be a party in interest and for performing other duties imposed by the law.[93] We act on behalf of our government. Our allegiance and loyalty is to the government we represent, in this case, the United States of America. We vow allegiance and loyalty to no other government.

"Double agents," however, vow secret allegiance and loyalty to other governments while feigning allegiance and loyalty to their government to obtain a personal benefit for themselves. In other words, double agents "play" both sides of the fence. However, no double agent can be loyal to a foreign government until they first decide to be disloyal to their own government. Such was the case with Robert Philip Hanssen.

God's Word says that no man can serve two masters for either he will hate the one and love the other or else he will hold on to the one and despise the other (Matthew 6:24 KJV). In other words, if someone tries to serve two governments faithfully, this scripture says they will end up, in this context, "loving" one government and hating the other government or else holding to one government and despising the other government.

In the case of Hanssen, he could not serve both governments. His contempt for the US government and desire for significance and power, however, created the perfect environment for him to "hold on" to the Russian government and "despise" the US government.

I'll never forget it. The day the FBI arrested Hanssen, I had only been an FBI agent for about a year and a half. The shock wave of disbelief, anger, and betrayal surrounding his actions reverberated throughout our organization before reaching the rest of the intelligence community, and finally, you, the beloved American people.

As a Christian, and now retired FBI agent, I find myself periodically reflecting on the story of Robert Hanssen and continue to be confronted with one sobering question, which is this: "From God's perspective, am I, and are we, the church of Jesus Christ really that much different than Robert Philip Hanssen?"

What? Hold on before you start "hatin'" a fellow special agent-in-Christ. What I mean is this. While the vast majority of us reading this book would never commit an act of espionage or treason against the United States or any act of crime for that matter, how many of us are in some way, large or small, living a double life like Robert Philip Hanssen?

God's Word says that the heart is deceitful above all things and desperately sick; who can understand it (Jeremiah 17:9)? Guess who it deceives first? That's right, us! Don't agree? I have a few questions for you.

How many of us Christians, for example, are more loyal to our self-centered interests than we are to God's interests; more loyal to our money, eating, spending, drug, alcohol, social media, or sexual addictions than we are to Christ? It's quiet in the Evangelical Free Church?

How many of us say we want to advance God's kingdom but at the end of the day are really only interested in advancing (or preserving) our kingdoms despite all of our prayers, Bible reading, and weekly church attendance? Be more specific? Okay.

How many of us husbands and dads profess loyalty to Christ, yet consistently make decisions that take us unnecessarily out of the home and away from our families?

How many of you Christian moms say you are more interested in your children's holiness but routinely compromise it for the sake of their happiness?

How many of you Christian husbands are faithful to not commit physical adultery against your mate but routinely commit emotional adultery against them through your ongoing exposure to internet pornography?

How many of you Christian wives would never "cheat" on your husbands sexually but have bank accounts, investment accounts, social media accounts, cell phones, credit cards, and cash stashed away that your husbands know nothing about?

How many of us Christian singles say we love God with our mouths but act just like the culture when it comes to our bodies?

How many of us Christians boldly identify with Jesus on Sunday but become "Secret Agents" in the workplace on Monday?

Sadly and tragically, our "double lives" go well beyond our homes.

For example, how many of you Christian attorneys, for example, have "sold your souls" to win the "big case?" How many of you have sought to acquit a defendant that you knew was guilty? How many of you have taken a position that you knew was improper or unethical to continue bilking a wealthy client or make it to the national stage where the "big bucks" and notoriety are? I've sat across the table from some of you!

How many of you Christian dentists and physicians have fraudulently billed Medicare, Medicaid, and private insurance companies for services (or equipment) not needed or rendered, driving up the cost of health care for us all?

How many of you Christian local, state, and national politicians take actions that reflect a greater interest in securing your reelections than in defending the constitutional rights, freedoms, and liberties of the people you swore to represent? How many of you have used your public offices to enrich yourselves at the expense of the American taxpayer or, worse yet, used "God" and the "Christian label" to get elected with no intention of allowing His Word to have the final word in the performance of your duties?

How many of you Christian senior FBI, DOJ, and State Department officials have misused your positions of trust and power in an attempt to control the outcome of a presidential election? What about to undo the appointment of a duly-elected president by way of a baseless special counsel investigation (i.e. "insurance policy") to divert the attention of the American people away from the real crimes you committed? You know, the crimes against the FISA Court and an American citizen (2016 Trump campaign aide, Carter Page). You know, the crimes you committed against the United States by knowingly allowing or utilizing an unsecured private e-mail server to store and transmit classified communications improperly? You know, the private e-mail server later determined to have been compromised "by unauthorized individuals to include foreign governments or intelligence services via cyber intrusion or other means?"[94] And why? Just please don't tell the American people it was tied to special favors and privileges some of you would have received had your 2016 presidential candidate won the election.

How many of you Christian media personnel have printed or "aired" a story that you knew was factually inaccurate to save your job, make a name for yourself, or advance a particular political narrative or agenda?

How many of you Christian entertainers thank your "Lord and Savior Jesus Christ" on awards night for the opportunity you've been given to, in reality, destroy the moral fabric of our society with your sexually explicit movies, violent and vulgar rap and hip-hop lyrics, and shameless online videos?

How many of you Christian educators go to church on Sunday but support, defend, tolerate, and even promote LGBTQ education in your school on Monday?

How many of you Christian corporate executives and company officers of publicly-traded companies falsify, direct others to falsify, or have knowledge of false entries or material omissions-of-fact in your "books and records" to meet or exceed Wall Street's earnings expectations for the quarter, thereby artificially inflating the price of your stock?

How many of you Christian managers of privately held hedge funds act one way on Wall Street and another way on "Main Street?"

How many of you Christian coaches teach your players that winning is more important than Godly character by screaming at or belittling your players? How many of you encourage your players to cheat or "bend the rules" whenever necessary, "curse out" the "ref" when you don't like a particular "call," or "look the other way" when your players engage in unsportsmanlike conduct?

How many of you pastors have forsaken your first love and so watered-down the Gospel message and the truth of God's Word to keep the dollars and popularity flowing that you're not even sure who you are or what you believe anymore?

How could the same America that prides itself in being a Judeo-Christian nation who undeniably gives more money and aid to alleviate human suffering around the world than any other country be the same America that murders just under one million unborn children per year?[95] How could the same America that has "In God We Trust" on its money and whose citizens identify themselves as being predominantly Christian be the same America to legalize gay marriage in clear violation of scripture (Leviticus 18:22, 20:13; Romans 1:26–27; 1 Corinthians 6:9–10; 1 Timothy 1:9–10)?

What do all these people in all these institutions from our house to the White House have in common? Answer: Evidence of a divided heart—just like Robert Philip Hanssen! May God have mercy on us all!

As a career FBI agent, I had the opportunity to witness the very best and worst in humanity. Had someone told me at the start of my career that the overwhelming majority of the individuals I would investigate and ultimately see convicted of federal crimes would be men and women of "faith," I would have said, "Impossible." Yet, this was my experience! Not only were many of my criminal subjects professing "believers," but some of them even used their "religious labels," religious practices, and religious speech to gain the trust of their victims and, ultimately, access to their money. Two such investigations of mine, now public information, were United States v.

Ralph Romero and the United States v. Donald Gridiron Jr., both in the District of New Jersey.

In United States v. Ralph Romero, defendant Romero used his faith and daily mass attendance, among other things, to gain the trust of dozens of victims who ultimately gave him over two million dollars from retirement accounts, credit card advances, home equity lines of credit, and various brokerage accounts in a nearly eight-year Ponzi-scheme.[96] While a small portion of the victims' money was returned to them to further perpetuate the fraud (known in the fraud world as "lulling" payments), defendant Romero spent the victims' money on gambling, drinking, car rentals, and "clubbing," among other things.[97]

One of the primary factors that heavily contributed to the 150-month prison sentence that defendant Romero received was the "extreme psychological injury" that he caused to many of his victims.[98] Some of the victims told me that before Mr. Romero took their money, he repeatedly asked them to attend religious services with him so that they could get to know him. Some agreed. When interviewed, some victims stated that this action alone on Romero's part was one of the most significant factors that caused them to invest their money and lives with Romero.

In United States v. Donald Gridiron Jr., defendant Gridiron used his Christian faith and good family name (Donald Gridiron Sr., father and current senior pastor and 1987 founder of Faith Center ministries in Walnut, California) to gain trusted access to the finances of Agape Family Worship Center (Agape), located in Rahway, New Jersey. As their certified public accountant, defendant Gridiron used his position of trust to secretly embezzle over four million dollars from the church during a seven-year period to accounts he controlled.[99] Gridiron then used the funds for his expenses, including mortgage payments, luxury car payments, and gambling expenses.[100]

Agape's senior pastor, Lawrence Powell, said, "And personally, I feel betrayed because this man used to be my friend. It hurts, but we serve a God who will get us through this."[101]

Note the following excerpts taken from a New Jersey press release following defendant Gridiron's sentencing. (*italics* used for emphasis):

> *Donald Gridiron admitted he was living a double life* from 2007 to 2014. To the public, his wife, and family, he was an accountant and a church-going man. But starting sometime in 2007, he was also a compulsive gambler, until 2014, when his crimes were exposed.
>
> But, by that point Gridiron had taken more than $4 million from the Agape Family Worship Center in Rahway [NJ], which had paid him a monthly salary, and [from] the Western States Golf Association, for which he served as treasurer.
>
> "I caused severe devastation," he read from a statement in court Tuesday. "I'm extremely remorseful."
>
> Gridiron who pleaded guilty to one count of wire fraud and one count of filing a false tax return, was sentenced to 57 months in prison by US District Judge Kevin McNulty, who added three years of supervised release following his prison term.
>
> He will also be responsible for making $5.1 million in restitution to the entities he defrauded.
>
> According to Gridiron's public defender, Candace Hom, Gridiron started out gambling by betting a few dollars while playing golf. That blew up into an all-consuming gambling addiction at casinos, where he spent as much as $230,000 in one day, she said. According to court records, Gridiron also used the embezzled funds to pay his home mortgage and for a luxury car.
>
> Assistant United States Attorney Andrew Kogan acknowledged Gridiron's problem but

said the devastation Gridiron caused was greater than he admitted, because the church couldn't pay down its building debt and the [golf] association lost the funds it had to issue scholarships.

Gridiron's family, as well as members of the church attended the sentencing Tuesday.[102]

While these cases may be difficult for some of you to read, they beg the following question in light of our topic? What does God see when He looks at your heart and mine. While our actions may not be criminal, would there be enough "evidence" to convict us in heaven of living a double life on earth?

Can the people we encounter each day tell which kingdom we belong to? Or do we "shift our halos" from one kingdom to another, depending on who we're talking to, where we are, or what's at stake?

The only thing worse than living a double life is "throwing stones" at others for doing the same thing. In God's world, a "first-degree" double life is no worse than a "third-degree" double life. A double life is a double life. There's no better example of this hypocrisy anywhere in scripture than when Jesus encountered the woman about to be stoned to death by her accusers for committing adultery in John 8.

According to Mosaic law, before someone could stone another person to death for adultery, two critical elements had to be satisfied, none of which were present. First, both the man *and* the woman had to be brought before their accusers (Deuteronomy 22:22–24) to prevent false allegations. It's a little hard to commit adultery by yourself, wouldn't you agree? If the woman was "caught" in the act of adultery, then her accusers must have known who the man was, right? So where was he? This violation of Jewish law alone would have precluded her from being stoned. Certainly, Jesus could have exposed this, but he didn't. Have you ever wondered why? While the Bible doesn't say, I can't help but think that Jesus kept quiet to let the drama build for what was about to be done!

Secondly, Mosaic Law required that the stone "thrower" could not be guilty of the same type of offense as the stone "receiver."[103]

If the stone "thrower" were guilty of a similar offense as the stone "receiver," then after the stone "receiver" was stoned to death, the stone "thrower" would have to get in the "quarry."

While the Bible doesn't say what Jesus wrote in the sand during those divinely orchestrated moments of silence, which probably seemed like an eternity to the religious teachers and Pharisees who knew they had not met the requirements of Jewish law, we do know that as they continued to question Jesus about what should be done to her. Jesus stood up and publicly declared, "Let him who is without sin among you be the first to throw a stone at her" (John 8:7 ESV).

Incidentally, this scripture has been grossly misinterpreted and misused by many church leaders and Christians to this day. Many Christians love to use this scripture to "turn the tables" on those who are lovingly confronting them with their sin so they don't have to change. Jesus did not mean you, who have never committed *any* sin, cast the first stone; otherwise, a judgment could *never* be rendered on *any* issue at *any* time, according to Jewish law. He meant you, who are without any notorious sin, having committed *a similar scandalous sin*, and *particularly this sin of adultery*,[104] cast the first stone.

You see, Jesus knew where the "boys" had been and what they'd been doing. He was exposing their double lives. Note what else Jesus says to them in Matthew 23:

> What sorrow awaits you teachers of religious law and you Pharisees. Hypocrites! For you are so careful to clean the outside of the cup and the dish, but inside you are filthy—full of greed and self-indulgence! (Matthew 23:23–25)

Christians living double lives are *only* concerned about the outside of the cup, like the Pharisees, *not* the inside of the cup. The following passage of scripture taken from 2 Timothy 2 captures the heart of what I will hereafter refer to as a Christian Double Agent (CDA):

> For men will be lovers of themselves, lovers of money, boasters, proud, blasphemers, disobedient to parents, unthankful, unholy, unloving, unforgiving, slanderers, without self-control, brutal, despisers of good, traitors, headstrong, haughty, lovers of pleasure rather than lovers of God, *having a form of godliness,* but denying it's power. And from such people turn away. (2 Timothy 3:2–5 NKJV)

This brings us to one of the most significant consequences of being a CDA—a powerless life! The single greatest reason why most of us are not seeing God's power on display in our individual lives, churches, and in society is because most of us, if the truth be known, are living double lives!

Because all believers still sin, all of us will behave like CDAs from time to time. The question is, what are you and I characterized by? What is our usual pattern of behavior? Ask someone who really knows you, loves you, but is not afraid to be honest with you if there is an area of your life that is *routinely* inconsistent with your Christian faith. Yes, it will take great courage, but we must do it if we want to see our families, churches, cities, and nation healed and fulfill the reason for which we were created!

You see, we all have blind spots, which is why it is so critical to be in community with other believers. We cannot always tell when we are living double lives. Others can. If we truly desire to please the Lord, we will welcome this kind of open and honest feedback and repent where necessary. If, however, we care more about getting what we want or looking "good" to others to continue our sinful lifestyles, then we will be more like the Pharisees who honored Christ with their lips but whose hearts were far from Him; who worshiped Him in vain, with teachings that are merely human rules (Matthew 15:8–9).

Notice how seriously God takes this issue. Paul says in the passage quoted above from 2 Timothy 2 "*[f]rom such people turn away.*" God warns us to stay away from those who live double lives. He doesn't say to "go after them," evangelize them, encourage them to repent, or fellowship with them; He says to stay away from them! Why? Because they have no interest in changing, and He knows that bad company corrupts good morals (1 Corinthians 15:33 ASV). God is afraid that if we don't come out from among them and be ye separate 2 Corinthians. 6:17), we will become like them. It's the same thing we told our children when we learned they were "hanging out" with the wrong crowd and the same thing our parents told us when they learned we were hanging out with the wrong crowd.

The Bible says that a double-minded man is unstable in all His ways (James 1:8).

> *Double-minded* literally means "double-souled," or one who has two souls. It also means one who is wavering or inconsistent. It is applicable to a man who has no settled principles, who is controlled by [worldly] passions, and who is influenced by popular feeling. (James 1:8; Barnes Notes on The Bible)

> *Unstable in all His ways* denotes those without any fixedness or consistency of spirit, who are as ready to depart from God as [they are] to cleave to Him; [loud], troubled, and/or full of inward tumults. (James 1:8; Matthew Poole's Commentary)

While Hanssen's double agent work for the Russians resulted in exceptionally grave damage to the United States, CDA work for the kingdom of darkness has also resulted in exceptionally grave damage to the United States—spiritually. I don't know about you, but the thought that my double life would bring "aid and comfort" to the enemy by helping him build his kingdom, while at the same time hindering me from building God's kingdom leaves me breathless! How about you? Men, listen carefully. If the devil can get us to play both sides of the fence, he "owns" us. The same is true of you, ladies.

So what causes Christians to live double lives? Very simple. Pride and self-centeredness. Just like Adam and Eve, we want the best of both worlds and, in many cases, believe we deserve it! We want the best the earth has to offer and the best God has to offer. We want to preserve the right to advance our kingdom and His kingdom. We want the societal benefits of having the Christian label without having to operate under the authority it brings! As long as God is helping us get what we want, we love Him. When He stands in the way of what we want (e.g. premarital sex), we reject Him. And the moment we reject Him (knowingly or unknowingly) or His Word (since they are inseparable!) in any area of life is the moment we are no different than Robert Philip Hanssen!

While Hanssen vowed his loyalty to God, the Catholic Church, his wife, children, and the United States government, his true allegiance was to himself, the KGB, and his Russian handlers—all for ego, excitement, and a few pieces of silver. Sound familiar? Hanssen, just like Judas, betrayed those he loved and those who loved him for a world that would not (and could not) ever satisfy. Herein lies the truth to Satan's big lie that has now been exposed for the world to see. Living a "double life" at any level will never satisfy, but in the end, leave us feeling more defeated and empty than ever.

James "takes off the gloves" to say this about living a double life to the Christians of his day and to us today, "You adulterers! Don't you realize that friendship with the world makes you an enemy of God? I say it again, if you want to be a friend of the world, you make yourself an enemy of God" (James 4:4 NLT).

If you were like me, it was the kindness of Christ that led you to repentance (Romans 2:4). It was the realization that God loved me so much that He sent His only Son, Jesus Christ, to experience the most brutal death on earth imaginable—death by slow asphyxiation on the cross—to atone for every sin (past, present, and future) I would ever commit. I yielded my heart and life to Him like so many of you. But as time goes by, if you're like me, you allow the circumstances of life like a demanding career, marriage, raising children, bills, difficult relationships, sickness, religious activity, service to others, and even the pursuit of theological knowledge to sabotage the love you once had for Christ!

The cross that once meant so much, if you're like me, can get slowly pushed to the back of the bus. Not intentionally, of course. It's a slow fade. But what you and I must understand in this angelic conflict we have been placed in the middle of (chapter 1) is that it is absolutely intentional on the part of Satan. He will do whatever he has to do to get us to forget what happened on the cross and what happened early Sunday morning just a little while before day!

The death and the resurrection of Jesus were not only the key to Jesus's victory over him but are the key to *our* victory over him because of our union with Christ! The moment Satan can get us to forget this or to only think about it twice a year (i.e., at Christmas and Easter) is the moment he can get Christians to live double lives! And the moment he can get us living double lives is the moment he can use us to build his kingdom instead of God's kingdom (chapter 1).

Listen, beloved. I believe this with all my heart! To the extent that you and I are ungrateful to Christ for what He has done for us on the cross is the extent to which you and I are vulnerable to living a double life. Thank you, Holy Spirit! Please read that again. Why is this? Because we were made to worship, and if we're not grateful to Christ for what He's done, we won't worship Him. And if we don't worship Him, we will worship something else, and that something else is always tied to the "other" kingdom!

Thus, daily gratitude to Jesus for the cross and resurrection is the key to living a victorious Christian life! A man or woman like this will have no desire to work for the other kingdom. How grateful are you to Christ daily for what He's done for you on the cross? When was the last time you told Him and demonstrated it by sharing the Gospel with someone? That's the test!

Can you imagine the impact we could have in our homes, families, churches, cities, and nation if the 80 percent of us who profess to be Christians in the United States daily demonstrated our gratitude to Christ for what He's done for us?

The most loving, joyful, peaceful, and powerful Christians I have ever known are those who routinely express gratitude, inwardly and outwardly, for the cross and the resurrection of Jesus Christ. For them, all of life is filtered through this prism. Not perfectly, but characteristically. They are indebted to Christ for what He has done for them and have committed to spending the rest of their lives, wherever God has placed them, joyously satisfying a debt to Him they know they will never be able to repay—all because they're grateful! Does this describe you? To the extent it doesn't, you and I are vulnerable to becoming CDAs—just like Robert Hanssen.

So what is God calling the double-minded to do? James tells us here in the following (*italics* added for emphasis):

> Cleanse *your* hands you sinners and purify *your* hearts *you double-minded*. Lament and mourn and weep! Let your laughter be turned to mourning and *your* joy to gloom. Humble yourselves in the sight of the Lord and He will lift you up. (James 4:7–10 NKJV)

Paul says it this way (*italics* used for emphasis):

> Dear brothers, pattern *your* lives after mine, and notice who else lives up to my example. For I have told you often before and I say it again now with tears in my eyes, *there are many who walk along the Christian road who are really enemies of the cross of Christ their future is their eternal loss for their God is their appetite*. (Philippians 3:18)

Now how about a little practical application pop quiz? Christian husbands, if your wife had a GPS read-out of where you've been over the last three months, would she be surprised, hurt, or outraged? Christian wives, if your husband had unfettered access to your credit card purchases as well as your smart phone and social media accounts, would he raise an eyebrow? Christian employees, if your boss contacted the IT department for a list of all the websites you've visited at work over the last year, would you be embarrassed or fearful about losing your job? Pastors, if the associate pastors, elders, or leaders of your church asked for the same thing, would you all of the sudden feel sick to your stomach? Does the name Ashley Madison ring a bell to some of you?

Christian husbands, if your wife suspected that you were being "unfaithful" to her and told you that she had hired a private investigator (like some do!) to follow and photograph your movements over the last six months, would you have anything to fear? How's that thirty-five-year marriage working out for you now?

It's time for some of us to come out of the closet and "man up."

Reputation is what others believe about us. Character is what our spouses, children, and those closest to us believe about us. As Christians, there should be no difference in the two. Our public and private lives should match. And poppycock to elected officials (many of who claim to be Christian), mainstream media, Hollywood, and many in society who say that what we do in our private lives has no bearing on our public lives. A lack of character in our private lives will always show up and impact our public lives.

Surely you're familiar with the #MeToo movement that's resulted in countless resignations all across America, right? Yes, I know many allegations are bogus and unfounded, but I also know many are not! Certainly, the names Jeffrey Epstein and Harvey Weinstein ring a bell, no?

It's not a difficult stretch for a "cheating spouse" who lies and conceals his adultery from his wife, for example, to be a "cheating politician" who lies and conceals his true intentions and conduct from the American people to get elected. A cheat will always be a cheat, and a liar will always be a liar no matter where you put them until they are ready to do "business" with God.

What many CDAs don't realize in their "undercover" capacity is that God's Word says that our "sin" will always eventually find us out as seen here in the following:

> Therefore, whatever you have said in the dark shall be heard in the light, and what you have whispered in private rooms shall be proclaimed on the housetops. (Luke 12:3)

Please understand that this chapter is not about guilt or condemnation; it's about conviction and repentance so that each of us would receive the healing that God has for us so we can begin fulfilling the reason for which we were created (chapter 1)!

Please also understand that if you have been living a double life, you are not alone. I also stand guilty before a holy God without excuse for thinking I could advance the kingdom of God while I advanced the kingdom of self. The question is, what are you and I characterized by? And what are we willing to do about it if we're living a double life now?

If you are in any way living a double life, I plead with you to renounce it now, in Jesus's name. A house divided against itself will fall (Mark 3:25). And your fall will not just affect you. It will affect every person in your "garden" and every institution you are a part of from your house to the White House.

There's nothing new under the sun, precious one. The reality is sin causes all of our hearts to be divided, and the sooner we get "real" with ourselves, others, and God, the sooner God can use us to advance His kingdom and bring Him glory. If Moses, Jonah, David, Peter, and Paul (who referred to himself as the "Chief Sinner") had hearts that were divided at different times in their ministries, who are we to think we're immune from it?

May we not be like the Pharisee who, in Luke 18:11–14, proudly and hypocritically stood by himself and prayed, "God, I thank you that I am not like other people—robbers, evildoers, or adulterers, or even like this tax collector."

Remember? This Pharisee boasted about fasting twice a week and giving one-tenth of all his income. Then, in contrast, was the tax collector who stood off in the distance, unable to even look at heaven, beating his breast, saying, "God have mercy on me, a sinner."

Recall, it was the tax collector, not the Pharisee that went home justified before God (Luke 8:14). Who do you more closely resemble?

Before concluding this chapter on CDAs, I would be derelict in my duties if I didn't devote an entire chapter—in this case, the next one—to exposing what I believe to be one of Satan's most wicked schemes and strategies to get Christian men to live double lives. And if recent statistics are correct, Christian women aren't lagging far behind. Before we go there, join me in this prayer of repentance if you feel the Holy Spirit tugging on your heart.

Prayer of Repentance (if applicable):

> Lord Jesus, I confess that I have been living a double life. My loyalties are divided between what I want and what you want. They are divided between my kingdom and your kingdom, and between my glory and your glory.
>
> My greatest loyalty has not been to you and your word, but to my self-centered interests and my word. My double life has wreaked havoc on my family, church, community, city, state, and nation, but more importantly, has grieved your heart and prevented me from building your kingdom.
>
> I understand that a house divided against itself cannot stand and that while I may be "standing" on the outside, I have "fallen" on the inside. I don't want to live like this anymore. But more than anything, I don't want to grieve your heart anymore!
>
> I have sinned against you and others and brought great shame and dishonor to your name. The consequences of my actions against others have been great. I willingly bow my heart and bend my knee before you and beg for your for-

giveness. I repent of my double life and now submit every area of my life underneath your rulership and authority.

I know you have no secret agents and that there is nothing hidden that will not be disclosed, and nothing concealed that will not be known or brought out into the open (Luke 8:17). Nonetheless, help me to confess my sin to those I have sinned against while acting as a CDA (where appropriate and safe to do so) and ask them to forgive me.

Thank you for your steadfast love and mercies toward me that never cease and are new every morning (Lamentations 3:22), and for standing more prepared to forgive my sins than I am to commit them, more willing to supply my needs than I am to confess them. A love like this compels me to want to live an authentic, Christ-centered life from my house to the White House for your glory. Amen!

Verses to Remember

1. The Lord detests people with crooked hearts, but He delights in those with integrity. (Proverbs 11:20 NLT)
2. I hate the double-minded, but I love your law. (Psalm 119:113 ESV)
3. Ye adulterers and adulteresses, know ye not that the friendship of the world is enmity with God? Whosoever therefore will be a friend of the world is the enemy of God. (James 4:4 KJV)
4. A double-minded man is unstable in all His ways. (James 1:8 KJV)
5. For I have told you often before, and I say it again with tears in my eyes, there are many who walk along the Christian

road who are really enemies of the Cross of Christ. Their future in their eternal loss for their god is their appetite: they are proud of what they should be ashamed of; and all they think about is this life here on earth. (Philippians 3:18–19 TLB)

6. Therefore whatever you have said in the dark shall be heard in the light, and what you have whispered in private rooms shall be proclaimed on the housetops. (Luke 12:3 ESV)

7. And if a house be divided against itself, that house will not be able to stand. (Mark 3:25 ASV)

8. Woe to you [self-righteous] scribes and Pharisees, hypocrites! For you clean the outside of the cup and of the plate, but inside they are full of extortion and robbery and self-indulgence (unrestrained greed). (Matthew 23:23–25 AMP)

9. For men will be lovers of themselves, lovers of money, boasters, proud, blasphemers, disobedient to parents, unthankful, unholy, unloving, unforgiving, slanderers, without self-control, brutal, despisers of good, traitors, headstrong, haughty, lovers of pleasure rather than lovers of God, having a form of godliness, but denying its power. And from such people turn away. (2 Timothy 3:2–5 NKJV)

CHAPTER 5

✦✦✦✦✦

In My Church?

The rest of the world will stop talking about it when we stop doing it!

In November 2006, Ted Haggard, founder and former pastor of New Life Church in Colorado Springs, Colorado, and leader of the National Association of Evangelicals (NAE) from 2003 to November 2006, paid his masseur, Mike Jones, for sex over three years and also purchased and used crystal methamphetamine.[105] The church's internal investigation and public statements issued by Haggard additionally revealed that Haggard had committed sexually immoral conduct.[106] Days later, "Pastor Ted," as his congregation affectionately knew him, resigned from the ministry, bringing disgrace to himself, his wife, "his flock" and, most importantly, the name of Jesus Christ.

In 2009, Joe Barron, a former minister at megachurch Prestonwood Baptist Church in Plano, Texas, received a seven-year jail sentence for attempting to engage in sexual behavior with a thirteen-year-old girl.[107] During a search incident to his arrest, authorities found Barron in possession of a webcam, condoms, and a cellular telephone.[108]

In November 2009, Christian evangelist Tony Alamo of Tony Alamo Christian Ministries was sentenced in Texarkana, Arkansas, to 175 years in prison after being convicted on ten counts of transporting minors across state lines to engage in sex.[109] While the age of the defendant usually plays a mitigating factor during sentencing, US

273

District Judge Harry Barnes handed down the maximum sentence possible to this seventy-five-year old pastor, citing Alamo's position of trust as the primary reason for the hefty sentence.[110]

On June 8, 2011, Bishop Eddie Long, founder of New Birth Missionary Baptist Church, issued a private apology and paid nearly $25 million dollars to settle claims out of court that he had sexual relationships with four young male parishioners in return for money and gifts Long gave them.[111]

In March 2013, Jack Schaap, former pastor of northwest Indiana megachurch, First Baptist Church of Hammond, received a twelve-year prison sentence for sex crimes involving a seventeen-year-old female church member.[112] In letters filed with the court, Schapp said his relationship with the girl was "God's plan" and discussed how he "helped save her from self-destruction by putting her on a better path of living, that's what we call righteousness."[113]

On September 21, 2013, Geronimo Aguilar, founding former pastor of Richmond Outreach Center in Virginia, was indicted by a Texas grand jury on two counts of aggravated sexual assault involving a child under the age of fourteen and two counts of indecency with a child.[114] On June 24, 2015, a Texas jury found Aguilar guilty of sex crimes against two sisters that he started to abuse in his capacity as their pastor in the 1990s when they were eleven and thirteen years old.[115] While Aguilar denied the sex crimes at trial, CBS 6 legal analyst Todd Stone said that testimony from women in Richmond who said they had affairs with "Pastor G" revealed inconsistencies in Aguilar's testimony that ultimately led to his conviction.[116] On October 13, 2015, Aguilar received a forty-year prison sentence.[117]

On November 10, 2013, five Colorado church leaders from VineLife Church in Boulder, Colorado, were charged with attempting to conceal a sex-abuse scandal involving allegations that their youth pastor, Jason Roberson, had sexually assaulted a female church attendee when she was fifteen years old according to Boulder police officials close to the situation.[118] On July 23, 2015, for failure to report the child abuse, VineLife pastors Walter Roberson and Robert Young were sentenced to serve ten days in jail or on work crew.[119]

Elder Edward Bennell was sentenced to serve two days in jail or on work crew; elder Warren Williams was sentenced to perform forty hours of community service.[120] The sentencing took place nearly one year after ex-VineLife youth pastor Jason Roberson, thirty-six, was sentenced to two years of incarceration and ten years of probation for the seven-year relationship he initiated with the then fifteen-year-old female congregant.[121]

On August 19, 2015, the hacked database of Ashley Madison, a "go-to website for infidelity," publicly released the identities of thirty-two million customers, making it easily searchable on several websites.[122] On August 24, 2015, six days after learning that his name was on a list of exposed Ashley Madison customers, Baptist pastor and seminary professor John Gibson sadly and tragically committed suicide.[123] On August 27, 2015, it was estimated that at least four hundred church leaders (pastors, elders, staff, deacons, etc.) would resign that Sunday,[124] sending a shockwave of guilt, shame, and devastation through hundreds of churches and families nationwide.

From 1950 to early 2013, approximately 6,900 Catholic priests were found guilty of sexually abusing nearly 17,000 children.[125] As of March 2013, the Catholic church has paid out over $2.5 billion in settlements.[126]

On August 14, 2018, a Pennsylvania grand jury report released stated that internal documents from six Catholic dioceses in Pennsylvania revealed that more than 300 "predator priests" have been credibly accused of sexually abusing more than one thousand child victims.[127] Grand jurors believe the real number is in the thousands due to lost records and numerous victims who were afraid to come forward.[128] Note the following excerpt taken directly from the grand jury report:

> Priests were raping little boys and girls, and the men of God who were responsible for them not only did nothing; they hid it all. For decades. Monsignors, auxiliary bishops, bishops, archbishops, cardinals have mostly been protected;

many, including some named in this report have been promoted.[129]

On December 20, 2018, more accusations of child sex abuse emerge against at least 500 Roman Catholic priests and clergy members in Illinois, which have never been made public according to a preliminary investigation by the Illinois Attorney General's Office.[130] This brings the total number of members in the Illinois dioceses accused of sexually abusing minors to approximately 690.

In February 2019, during his return trip to Rome from Abu Dhabi, Pope Francis reported for the first time that priests and bishops had been sexually abusing nuns, including a case in which some clergy used women as sex slaves.[131] Furthermore, the pope did not deny that there were reports of sexual abuse by clerics resulting in nuns having abortions or giving birth to children fathered by priests.[132]

On February 28, 2019, an Independent Advisory Group (IAG) report was released following the April 13, 2018, resignation of Bill Hybels, senior pastor and founder of Chicago-area Willow Creek Community Church with nearly 26,000 attendees every weekend, confirming multiple allegations that Hybels had engaged in "sexually inappropriate words and actions" with numerous women over many years.[133] The claims were deemed "credible" following a six-month investigation by the IAG.[134] The matter became public in March 2018 when a group of former Willow Creek pastors and staff accused Hybels of a pattern of sexual harassment and misconduct including, but not limited to, suggestive remarks, invitations to his hotel rooms, prolonged hugs, and an unwanted kiss.[135]

While many Christians would rightly argue that the egregious conduct of those cited above is rare among church leaders, some of these same people might be surprised if I told them that approximately 40 percent of pastors have admitted to having an extramarital affair after entering the ministry,[136] 57 percent of pastors and 64 percent of youth pastors confess that Internet pornography is a current or was a former struggle for them,[137] and that 75 percent of pastors are not accountable to anyone for their Internet use.[138]

Additionally, you may be surprised to learn that at least eight major church denominations now sanction gay marriage (Conservative Jewish Movement, Episcopal Church, Evangelical Lutheran Church in America, Presbyterian Church USA, Reform Jewish Movement, Society of Friends (Quaker), Unitarian Universalist Association of Churches, and United Church of Christ),[139] while nearly forty-six Christian congregations consider themselves to be "LGBTQ-affirming" (i.e., where homosexuality is not viewed as a "sin") within the Anglican, Baptist, Catholic, Lutheran, United Methodist, Pentecostal, Mennonite, Seventh-Day Adventist, Charismatic, and United Church of Christ denominations in the US and around the world.[140]

If you're like me, the shocking information and statistics I just shared with you give rise to even deeper questions. First, if many Christian leaders are losing the battle to maintain their sexual purity and uphold traditional family values, what does that say about the battle that the average Christian is facing all across America? Secondly, if you're a pastor or church leader, what are you doing about it? Thirdly, given the fact that we can't even get it right, why are we surprised by the level of sexual deviancy and immorality in our culture? Finally, when will we stop blaming the "world" for the mess we're in and "clean up" our side of the street?

While most Christians would like to believe that sexual sin stops at the front doors of their church, this couldn't be further from the truth. Just listen to a sample of what some "good Christian men" have told me over many years, spanning multiple congregations all across America.

"Yes, it's a struggle, Jim, but I really don't see a problem having sex since we're engaged to be married. After all, no one is perfect."

Another Christian man told me, "She's a great Christian woman, Jim. I know we shouldn't be having sex until we're married, but we worship and pray together, and I even have an opportunity to lead her children in devotions. I'm happy for the first time in my life."

"I just need to feel like a man, Jim. I'm not attracted to my wife anymore. When I get this kind of a massage, I feel validated!"

"I'm lonely," said one Christian man. "Porn and adult movies fill a deep void inside of me."

"It started with porn," another said, "and before I knew it, I was sleeping with her and allowing her son to disrespect me. When I tried to leave, she got even more controlling. I felt utterly trapped and hopeless in a circle of sexual sin."

Another brother told me, "I'm living with my girlfriend to save some money. We plan on getting married anyway, so it's no big deal. It's hard to get by on your own these days."

"She cheated on me first. I wasn't unfaithful to her until I found out she had been unfaithful to me."

One Christian husband and father for twenty-plus years said, "I recently got arrested for lewd conduct while I was watching women in my car at the local supermarket. I have to go to court next week. My wife is 'done,' and I'm probably going to jail. Would you please pray for me?"

What do all of these men have in common? They are all men who have professed to be followers of Jesus Christ. All of these men, at the time, were either husbands, fathers, pastors-in-training, elders, deacons, lay leaders, worship team members, and/or weekly "servants"/attendees at their local churches. And if you think the average Christian church in America is any different friend, you are sadly mistaken.

Knowing these men, many others like them, and my personal battle to maintain a life of sexual purity in this sexually saturated culture that knows no boundaries causes me to wonder. How will this nation ever be able to survive the compounding effects of such perversion when we, the church, can't even get it right?

With the explosion of the Internet, streamed content, smartphones, and social media, the volume of sexual material infiltrating our homes, schools, churches, cities, and nation has never been greater. And so is the "fallout." Just take a look at these alarming statistics and trends:

- 50 percent of all Christian men and 20 percent of all Christian women say they are addicted to porn.[141]

- 60 percent of all Christian women admit to having significant struggles with lust.[142]
- Among "born again" Christians, 49 percent believe sexual thoughts and fantasies are "morally acceptable."[143]
- 70 percent of all men and 60 percent of all women will commit adultery.[144]
- A boys' first exposure to pornography occurs at the average age of twelve (12).[145]
- 71 percent of teens hide their online behavior from their parents.[146]
- Nearly 40 percent of all teenagers have posted or sent sexually suggestive messages.[147]
- 32 percent of boys and 18 percent of girls have viewed bestiality online.[148]
- 39 percent of boys and 23 percent of girls have viewed sexual bondage online.[149]
- 83 percent of boys and 57 percent of girls have viewed group sex online.[150]
- 69 percent of boys and 55 percent of girls have seen same-sex intercourse online.[151]
- $3,075.64 is spent on internet porn every second.[152]
- 25 percent of all search engine requests are for porn.[153]
- The top US websites with the most traffic following Instagram (#5) and Twitter (#6) are porn sites.[154]
- One out of every five mobile searches is for porn.[155]
- 57 percent of pastors say that addiction to pornography is the most sexually damaging issue they are facing.[156]
- 29 percent of "born-again" Christians say porn is morally acceptable.[157]
- 51 percent of "born-again" Christians believe sex outside of marriage is "morally acceptable."[158]
- The largest consumers of porn are twelve to seventeen-year-old boys.[159]

I'll never forget it. Many years ago, I attended a Christian Men's stadium event conference with approximately 80,000 men from around the nation. During a pivotal point in the conference, the keynote speaker challenged every man in attendance to stand up if they were currently struggling to maintain a life of sexual purity. As far as the eye could see, no man in the stadium was seated, including many pastors in attendance. It was a very sobering and defining moment in my life as a young Christian. While it was comforting to know I wasn't alone, it shocked me to learn how pervasive the lust problem was among men who genuinely sought to please God.

In the words of Steve Arterburn and Fred Stoeker, authors of *Every Man's Battle*, sexual sin is truly *every* man's battle. Not until we men (and women) are willing to admit we're vulnerable (at least at some level) and not "above" sexual temptation will we ever begin ruling our worlds as God intended (chapter 1).

I just mentioned women. The rise in porn-watching among women has also reached epidemic proportions. According to the anti-porn advocacy group, Fight the New Drug, Pornhub released information in 2017 revealing that women had spent more time watching porn than men.[160] Women were also more likely to search for harder versions of porn than men.[161] Surprised?

So if it's such a problem in the church today, why don't you hear more about it from the pulpit? I have my theories. While I respect the fact that many church leaders do not want to preach about the speck of sexual sin in their congregation's eye when they may have a log of sexual sin in their own eyes (Matthew 7:3), it does nothing to address the problem. I don't know about you, but I've never heard even one sermon fully dedicated to the topic in all my years of church attendance. While most men's conferences dedicate appropriate time and attention to the subject, it has been my experience that most Christian men in America do not attend Christian men's conferences. And since the problem is now becoming as much of an issue for ladies as it is for men, church leaders who are serious about holiness and fulfilling the primary mission of the church must address it.

I try to think of other reasons why more church leaders do not address the problem of sexual sin from the pulpit, none of which are good. One possibility is that church leaders are *more* concerned about building their kingdoms instead of God's kingdom. It's no surprise that this topic has the potential to offend and alienate many congregants who view themselves and their families to be "above" this type of "sin" or who view this topic to be inappropriate for church. So pastors, not wanting to see a decline in church attendance and tithing, stay away from the topic to ensure the advancement (or preservation) of their kingdoms.

If you're a pastor or church leader, honestly ask yourself this question: "Am I more concerned with the number of sheep in 'my' house or in protecting the sheep under my care in God's house?" If it's the former instead of the latter, I implore you to repent and begin addressing this issue in your church immediately.

The only other reason I can think of for why church leaders do not address the subject of sexual sin in their churches is that they honestly feel ill-equipped. These leaders want to do something but don't know where to start. It's too overwhelming to them, given the other challenges of church leadership. Some feel they have neither the knowledge or the resources to deal with it. So instead of calling on the help and getting the resources they need, they remain paralyzed by the topic and, therefore, derelict in their duties as the "shepherd" of the flock God has given them.

I can't imagine standing before God on Judgment Day as a minister of the Gospel and using any of the above excuses for why I didn't do everything I could to expose this evil and protect my sheep. In the corporate world, such ignorance and inaction on the part of a CEO gets you fired. Some pastors need to be fired or resign. Others need to be praised and rewarded for the exemplary job they have done. For the pastors in this latter camp, you have my greatest respect and admiration. Keep it up! We need you like never before!

If you are reading this book and are experiencing victory in this area of your life, you are truly blessed. Please prayerfully consider coming alongside your pastor or another man if you're a man or another woman if you're a woman so that no man or woman walks through this battlefield alone.

Many books have been written, Christian and secular, on the effects of and recovery from various sexual sins. I will, therefore, not spend time here on the subject. However, in a later chapter, I will address what I believe to be the key to gaining victory from this sin and all sin, for that matter, which I have found to be virtually absent from most Christian material published today. Only by the grace of God did I come across this very powerful teaching! Stay tuned.

Rest assured, that if we don't take our sexual sin seriously fellow believers, there is one who will and does daily—Satan. If you have a computer, tablet, smartphone, TV, gaming device, or other similar electronic devices with access to the Internet, the devil has an "open road" to your mind, heart, and home. This is all he needs to neutralize God's purpose and plan in our lives and in every institution we comprise from our house to the White House. We, not he, have been given the victory in Christ! It's time we started acting like it!

Warning for Singles

God's Word says that it is "better to marry than to burn" (1 Corinthians 7:9) if you can't control your passions. This verse is often taken out of context, resulting in some very bad counseling from pastors and church leaders. While it is true that it is better to marry than to burn, God's Word also tells us that it is better to control ourselves than to marry the wrong person. Check out, for example, what God has to say about marrying a nagging wife (Proverbs 21:9), or about marrying a man who will not provide for his family (1 Timothy 5:8), or about marrying someone who is an unbeliever (2 Corinthians. 6:14). None of it is good. God would much rather we flee youthful lusts (2 Timothy 2:22) than marry the wrong person. But once we've found the right person, it is better to marry than to burn if we can't control our passions. Now you have the proper context for that scripture.

With the above foundation, I am now ready to make a point that I pray you never forget. Here it is. If you have not been able to control your passions up to now and are currently being held hostage by sexual sin that is a daily or frequent part of your life, you have no business getting married until you, in Christ, have overcome it. Men who are addicted to pornography and promiscuity before marriage will be men who are addicted to pornography and promiscuity after marriage. Women who dress seductively to access "the power" to turn a man's head before marriage will do the same thing after marriage. You get the message, and if you doubt it, review the above statistics again.

Warning for Married Couples

Sex should never be the "power" of your relationship but the "follow-through." When two people are individually and as a couple experiencing God's amazing love in profound and powerful ways, His love will automatically overflow into every other area of the relationship. Why? Because His love cannot be contained. This is why so many relationships dry up sexually. Husbands and wives are not individually and as a couple drawing "water" from the life-giving well of His love that never runs dry (Isaiah 58:11)! Now some of you may be able to understand why the research shows that husbands and wives who are deeply in love with Jesus Christ have the best sex lives.[162]

Couples who don't understand this will go to great lengths to "spice" up their sex lives. For example, I have tragically and sadly known many Christian couples who have introduced pornography into their bedrooms, hoping it would take them to the "next level" or help them with the boredom, frustration, or desperation they are experiencing in the bedroom—bad idea.

Men, let me be frank and direct. I know it's not my style. If you are the instigator in introducing porn into your marriage, this is not honoring your wife or bringing glory to God. It is, however, opening you and her up to the demonic world that feeds on lust, power, and control. Stop it. Ladies, if you are instigators or if you are allowing or encouraging it, the same warning goes to you. If you feel powerless to overcome this "sin" on your own, get help now!

Your sexual relationship should only involve you and your spouse and the God who created it, not images of others for either of you to fantasize about, try to emulate, or compare yourself or your mate to. The number of Christian men I have met over the years who have said to me that "porn has really helped their sex lives" is staggering. One Christian man even told me, "Don't knock it until you try it." Wow!

Satan has done a masterfully good job at deceiving and seducing the minds and hearts of God's people into believing that something as destructive as pornography is good for marriages. Besides being a direct violation of scripture and a path for the demonic world, research shows it's only a matter of time before your increased attempts to "spice" things up eventually fail, leaving you even more empty and defeated than ever. Like a heroin addict who has to take greater doses of heroin over time to get the same "rush," porn addicts have to "inject" heavier and harder doses of porn into their minds and hearts to get the same "rush." And all it will cost us at the end of the day is the sanctification of our souls and ability to be used by God to advance His kingdom and glory (chapter 1)! Not the kind of Judgment Day I want. How about you?

Dealing with sexual sin in the church must be one of our top priorities if we want to experience spiritual healing in every institution in America from our house to the White House.

If you are currently engaged in any sexual sin, please get the help you need today. Don't wait. Your God, your family, your church, and this nation desperately need you to be healthy and well if we're going to reclaim what the enemy has stolen from us to further God's kingdom and glory (chapter 1).

Can you imagine how different every institution in America would be from our house to the White House if the Christians in America would repent and use the time and money they are spending on porn and other sexual addictions to build the kingdom of God?

Prayer of Repentance (if applicable):

> Heavenly Father, I confess that I am embroiled in the midst of sexual sin. It consumes me every day. It has not only cost me time, but it has cost me money, relationships, job/career

advancement, spiritual vision, the expansion of your kingdom, and most importantly, closeness and intimacy with you.

Up to now, my greatest loyalty has not been to the Spirit, but to my flesh. You have called me to walk in the spirit and fulfill not the lust of the flesh (Galatians 5:16). My sexual sin has not only wreaked havoc in my home but has also infiltrated the church through me, impacting the church's ability to transform our community for your glory.

I understand that as long as I am unwilling to deny my will for your will and take up my cross in this key area of life, I cannot follow you (Matthew 16:24). This breaks my heart and now brings me to my knees.

I have sinned against you and others and brought great shame and dishonor to your name. The consequences of my sin have been severe, not only in my life but in the lives of others who depend on me to stand firm and give myself fully to the work of the Lord (1 Corinthians 15:58). Like a California wildfire out-of-control that burns everything in its path, my sexual sin has been out-of-control and burned everything and everyone in its path, including the people I love and those who love me.

I this most desperate hour in our nation where all manners of sexual sin and deviancy are becoming morally and socially acceptable, I surrender to your will and ask you to do in me through the power of the Holy Spirit that which I have been unable to do for myself. Specifically, I repent for [state your specific sexual sin(s)] and bring this area of my life into complete submission beneath you and the authority of your word.

Forgive me Lord! Now create in me a clean heart, oh God, and renew a right spirit within me (Psalm 51:10).

Where I have hurt others, and it is safe to do so, please grant me the courage, humility, and grace to seek forgiveness and make restitution where applicable and possible.

Thank you for your steadfast love and mercies toward me that never cease and are new every morning (Lamentations 3:22), and for standing more prepared to forgive my sins than I am to commit them, more willing to supply my needs than I am to confess them. A love like this compels me to want to flee youthful lusts and pursue righteousness, faith, love, and peace, along with those calling on the Lord out of a pure heart (2 Timothy 2:22 NIV) to see my individual life, family, church, community, city, and nation healed for your glory.

Verses to Remember:

1. But I tell you that if you look at another woman and want her, you are already unfaithful in your thoughts. (Matthew 5:28 CEV)
2. Flee from sexual immorality. All other sins a person commits are outside of the body, but whoever sins sexually, sins against their own body. (1 Corinthians 6:18 NIV)
3. For all that is in the world—the lust of the flesh, the lust of the eyes, and the pride of life—is not of the Father but is of the world. (1 John 2:16 NKJV)
4. For this is the will of God, your sanctification: that you should abstain from sexual immorality; that each of you should know how to possess his own vessel in sanctification

and honor, not in passion of lust, like the Gentiles who do not know God. (1 Thessalonians 4:3–5 NKJV)

5. So put to death the sinful, earthly things lurking within you. Have nothing to do with sexual immorality, impurity, lust, and evil desires. (Colossians 3:5 NLT)

6. If our minds are ruled by our desires, we will die. But if our minds are ruled by the Spirit, we will have life and peace. (Romans 8:6 CEV)

7. The Lord will guide you continually, and satisfy your soul in drought, and strengthen your bones; you shall be like a watered garden, and like a spring of water, whose waters do not fail. (Isaiah 58:11 NKJV)

8. How can a young man keep his way pure? By guarding it according to your word. With my whole heart I seek you; let me not wander from your commandments! I have stored up your word in my heart, that I might not sin against you. (Psalm 119:9–11 ESV)

CHAPTER 6

❖❖❖❖❖

Big Lies the Church Believes

"America's hope lies in the hands of evangelical Christians who will have the courage to live what they believe."[163]

What? Are you're kidding me? I couldn't believe what I was hearing. While this statement might not surprise you if I told you it came from another Christian, it might surprise you if I said it came from a well-known nationally syndicated *secular* radio talk-show host. I wanted to scream for joy, but my joy quickly turned to sorrow as I reflected on the likelihood that this would occur in our generation given the level of compromise that exists in the church today. Instead of being places where God's power, manifest presence, and glory are transforming the hearts and minds of people into true disciples of Jesus Christ who will "go" and make more disciples of Jesus Christ, many feel that the average church in America today is little more than a social meeting place of comfort, compromise, predictability, political correctness, and tolerance. If you're lucky, you get five pounds of Jesus sprinkled in.

Please don't misunderstand me. I love the church of Jesus Christ now more than ever, but I do not like what we've become. Instead of being hospitals where people get well, spiritually, to fulfill the

289

Great Commission (Matthew 28:18–20), many of our churches have become hospice centers that give people what they want so they will be comfortable while they "die." Is it any wonder why the culture is transforming the church instead of the other way around? What has happened to us?

The answer is so simple most of us will miss it. And most of us have. Satan has gotten us, like Adam and Eve, to exchange the truth about God for lies and to worship and serve the creature [ourselves] rather than the Creator who is blessed forever! Amen (Romans 1:25).

What many of us fail to understand, or routinely forget—which is why I dedicated an entire chapter to it, chapter 1—is that when you and I were created, God placed us "smack-dab" in the middle of an angelic conflict. This means that everything "good" and "bad" that is going on from our house to the White House is the direct result of who's winning the angelic conflict. While some of you reading this may be "winning" your personal battles with Christ and "good" angels against Satan and "bad" angels (chapter 1), one look at the number of casualties in our homes, churches, communities, cities, and nation tell a different story.

But what I want you to see is this: The reason we are losing the angelic conflict in our nation is because we are losing the angelic conflict in our states. And the reason we are losing the angelic conflict in our states is because we are losing the angelic conflict in our cities. And the reason we are losing the angelic conflict in our cities is because we are losing the angelic conflict in our communities. And the reason we are losing the angelic conflict in our communities is because we are losing the angelic conflict in our churches. And the reason we are losing the angelic conflict in our churches is because we are losing the angelic conflict in our homes. And the reason we are losing the angelic conflict in our homes is because we are losing the angelic conflict in our individual lives. And the reason we are losing the angelic conflict in our individual lives is because Satan has gotten many of us to accept his lies as our truth.

In "scrambling up" the Word of God in our lives, Satan has "scrambled up" our lives and every institution in America we comprise from our house to the White House. You would have thought we would have learned something from Adam and Eve's encounter with Satan in Genesis 3 with all our megachurches, small groups, retreat centers, conferences, cruises, trips to Israel, and weekly Bible studies! Nope.

You see, in the "game of life," which is no game, whoever's word gets to have the final word gets to "call the shots;" and whoever gets to "call the shots" gets to set the agenda; and whoever gets to set the agenda gets to control the outcome. What Satan knows that most of us don't know, however, is that if he can "call the shots" and set the agenda by getting us to accept his lies as our truth, he can control the outcome (i.e., get us to build his kingdom)! However, he also knows that the opposite is true. If we one day "wake up" as the body of Christ in America and allow God's Word to "call the shots," set the agenda, and control the outcome in every area of our lives from our house to the White House, he's out of a job!

You see, Satan knows that we cannot worship God "*in spirit and in truth*" (John 4:24) and build God's kingdom when the foundations of our lives, families, churches, cities, and nation have been built upon "lies." Said another way, Satan knows that we cannot reclaim, through Christ, what Adam and Eve turned over to the devil (Luke 4:6) if we, the church, are "living a lie." Thus, Satan's primary job as the "Father of Lies" (John 8:44) is to make sure that we never build our foundations upon the truth. If Satan can keep us focused on "fixing" the fruit of the problem in the physical (i.e., what we can see, hear, touch, smell, and taste—our five senses), he can prevent us from "fixing" the "root" of the problem in the spiritual realm.

This reminds me of a story about a homeowner who, after having the same contractor patch, repair, and re-paint cracks on his walls and ceiling three times in the same spot, decided it was time for a "real professional." The new contractor comes over and looks at the job. While he is inspecting the cracks carefully, the homeowner informs him that the area where the cracks continue to resurface has been patched, repaired, and painted three times in the last six months. The contractor looks up at the cracks on the walls and ceiling, then looks down. No response. He looks up, then down. Again, nothing. He looks up one final time, down, shakes his head back and forth, and begins walking toward the front door.

The distraught homeowner says, "Hey, where are you going?"

The contractor says, "Sir, your problem is not cracks on your walls and ceiling. Your problem is a shifting foundation. Until you fix your foundation, you will forever be repairing the cracks on your walls and ceiling! Goodbye!"

Fellow believers, what we are witnessing all across America today are the consequences of shifting foundations beneath every institution in America from our house to the White House. Up to now, the best we've been able to do is "patch and repair" a broken marriage here and a broken family there, a broken church here and a broken educational system there, a broken city council here and a broken state budget there. Until we are willing to address our "foundation" problem with spiritual solutions, the best the current administration can hope to do is temporarily "patch and repair" a broken immigration system here and a broken welfare system there, a broken health care system here (i.e., Obamacare) and a broken social security system there, a broken Supreme Court confirmation process here and a broken Special Counsel investigation there.

Barring spiritual solutions to our earthly problems, the best we'll be able to do is temporarily "patch and repair" a broken FBI (at the highest level) here and a broken Department of Justice (at the highest level) there, a corrupt "deep state" here, and a corrupt deeper state there. While we need to continue to make these repairs in the physical realm, there will be no end to this insanity until we are finally ready to address the "foundation" problem we have in the spiritual realm!

In just one generation, I, like many of you, have watched the shifting foundations beneath every institution in America from our house to the White House give rise to the widespread acceptance among many Christians of abortion, gay marriage, marijuana legalization, salvation without repentance, prosperity theology, homosexual ordinations, women pastors and elders ("overseers"), and illegal immigration all in the name of "compassion" while drugs, violent crimes, and terrorists continue pouring across our borders.

Nobody addresses our "foundation" problem better than Jesus as seen here in this familiar passage of scripture (*italics* used for emphasis):

> Why do you call me, "Lord, Lord," and do not practice what I tell you? *Everyone who comes to Me and listens to My words and obeys them,* I will show you whom He is like: He is like a [far-sighted, practical, and sensible] man building a house *who dug deep and laid a foundation on the rock*; and when a flood occurred, the torrent burst against that house and yet could not shake it, *because it had been securely built and founded on the rock.* But the one who has [merely] heard and has not practiced [what I say], is like a [foolish] man who built a house on the ground without any foundation, and the torrent burst against it; and it immediately collapsed, *and the ruin of that house was great.* (Luke 6:47–49 AMP)

So how much more moral, social, and spiritual ruin will we have to experience from our house to the White House before we listen to Jesus? In this passage of scripture, Jesus tells us that three things are necessary if we want a sure foundation. First, we must come to Him. Please allow me to add one word to the end of this sentence. Jesus uses it in Matthew 6—*first* (Matthew 6:33). If we want to guarantee a sure foundation, we must come to Him *first,* especially since He is the sure foundation. You see, some of us come to Him but not first. We come to Him second, last, or when nothing else works. Then when we do come, we come on "our terms," not His. No dice. Jesus plays "second fiddle" to no one.

Coming to Jesus first means that we see what His Word has to say about the matter first before we go to anyone else; then we allow His Word to have the final word! Is this what you do, Senator? How about you, Congressman? If this is not what you're doing, maybe you should consider changing the focus and format of your weekly prayer meetings inside the Beltway. You know, the ones you've been having for decades while our nation continues to be ravaged by chaos and compromise!

Secondly, if we want a sure foundation, we have to *listen* to Jesus's words. Did you know that it is possible to come to Jesus first but not listen to Him first or even at all, especially when we do not like what He has to say about a matter? Husbands and wives do this with one another all the time. So do parents and children. One comes to the other, but no listening occurs because one party isn't interested in hearing anyone else's viewpoint but theirs. Jesus says, in essence, that if we want to fix the foundation of our *nation*, for example, the leaders of that *nation* must come to Him *first* and listen to His Word *first*.

So how's this working out for our nation so far, Congressman, from the fine state of (fill in the blank)? We know. From God's perspective, which is the only perspective that counts, it's not. Why? Because many of you who profess to be Christians refuse to listen to what God has already said about a matter by elevating what you have to say above what He has to say! But, hey, "God Bless America," right? Yeah, right.

Lastly, a sure foundation requires biblical obedience. It does no good to come to Jesus first and listen to Him first if we're just going to do what our political party, "most Americans," our favorite celebrities, constituents, friends, parents, or what we want to do in the end, no? We saw this with Adam and Eve. Everything was "all good" until it came time to obey. News Flash: Satan could care less if we come to Jesus first and listen to Jesus first as long as we obey him (Satan) first!

Now you know. The devil "piggybacks" on lies to gain access into our lives to destroy every foundation we comprise from our house to the White House. I'd say he's done a pretty good job so far, wouldn't you?

We are now about to come face-to-face with some of the biggest, most deceptive lies that Satan has gotten us, the church, to believe in our day causing unprecedented levels of chaos in our homes, churches, government, and society. If we're ever going to fix the "foundation" problem we have in this most desperate hour in our nation's history, we must replace these lies with God's truth immediately!

By design, we have already exposed and obliterated many of Satan's lies. Many of you, until now, for example, didn't even know why you were here (chapter 1). Satan lied to you and told you that life was, first and foremost, about your happiness. Well, now it's time to kick it into "high gear." The sooner we repair the foundations from our house to the White House with God's truth, the sooner we'll be able to stand against any "hell" that Satan can manufacture against us to become one nation that is truly "under God." I don't know about you, but I'm ready to step on the neck of the enemy (Romans 16:20) and proclaim victory in Jesus's name!

As a white-collar crime investigator with the FBI for most of my career, it was my job to uncover the lies that victim investors relied upon before investing with the "bad guy." Little did I know that God was going to use this experience to help me to uncover the "big lies" that Satan has gotten us to rely on before "investing" with him so he could use us to build his kingdom instead of God's (chapter 1).

It should be no surprise that the very best high-yield investment frauds are those perpetrated on victims who have no idea they were defrauded until it's too late. The better the lies and deception, the better the scam. The best deceivers, not unlike the Great Deceiver, Satan, conceal their "lies" (i.e., their intent to defraud you) in "kindness," "care," "concern," "compassion," "religion," "spirituality," "service" "past performance," "guarantees," "years of experience," and yes, even "love." That's right. The very best deceivers, like Satan, know exactly how to "love" you.

Because it would take another book to cover them adequately, you should know that the "big lies" I am about to cover with you do not include the "big lies" that many Christians are already aware of, such as salvation through some other means than Christ, for example. While this lie and others like them have had devastating consequences in our society and must be addressed, I will instead focus on the "big lies" that most Christians are totally unaware of that have caused us to "invest" our lives with Satan and build his kingdom!

Again, what makes these lies so powerfully destructive is not only the fact that they have "wormed" their way into Christian homes and Bible-believing churches all across America causing us to be spiritually impotent in the culture but the fact that Satan has gotten us to act upon them, like Adam and Eve, for his benefit. Like a nuclear-powered ballistic missile submarine in "stealth" mode, these "hidden" lies run "silent," "deep," and undetected by most Bible-believing Christians. It's time for that to change!

While these big lies clearly impact all the nations of the world— that is, all the earth—I will spend the bulk of our discussion focused on the impact they have had from our house to the White House. I am confident that any spiritual transformation realized in America as a result of replacing these "big lies" with God's truth will be exported by God's people to the uttermost ends of the earth for God's glory!

Jesus said, "And you shall know the truth, and the truth shall make you free" (John 8:32 NKJV). I'm ready to be free. How about you? I hope your seatbelt is still locked.

So what "big lies" has Satan gotten us to believe and "invest in" to destroy the foundations of our lives and every institution in America we comprise from our house to the White House?

One of the "biggest," most sinister lies that Satan has gotten many of us in the church to believe to destroy the foundations of our lives and every institution in America we comprise from our house to the White House is that he, Satan, doesn't even exist! I know some of you have heard this before, but stick with me as I'm confident you're about to learn something new.

You see, as long as Satan can be a little red cartoon character with a pitchfork and long tail or a figment of our imagination, he can accomplish his mission without ever firing a shot. He cannot only block salvation to unbelievers, but he can bring maximum chaos and confusion to "believers" to get us to build his kingdom instead of God's (chapter 1).

As stated in chapter 1, the devil's goal is to steal as much of God's glory in the earth as possible through the expansion of his earthly kingdoms. As you may recall, he uses unbelievers and deceived believers to accomplish this (chapter 1). What I want you to see is that one of the biggest ways he pulls this off is by convincing both groups of people that he doesn't exist! Maybe some of you are saying, "What Christian would believe this nonsense?" Some of you are about to be shocked!

Barna polling data reveals that approximately 40 percent of all professing Christians in America strongly agree that Satan is not a living being but merely a symbol of evil.[164] Another 19 percent of Christians said that they somewhat agree with this.[165] That's means approximately 59 percent of all Christians in America agree or somewhat agree that Satan is not real!

When I say that approximately 59 percent of Christians in America agree or somewhat agree that Satan is not real, I'm not even factoring in the number of non-Christians who don't believe the devil exists (unless of course, they're practicing Satanism!). I'm only talking about Christians in America. With this in mind, let's do some quick math. If approximately 300 million Americans live in the US today and 83 percent of them profess to be Christian,[166] then there are about 249 million Christians (83 percent of 300 million people) living in America. If approximately 59 percent of them (as highlighted above) do not believe that the devil exists, then there are nearly 147 million Christians (59 percent of 249 million) living in America who don't believe Satan exists.

If we add the remaining 17 percent of Americans, or 51 million people (300 million - 249 million) who are not Christians and, therefore, unlikely to believe in Satan, to the 147 million Americans previously mentioned, then there are approximately 198 million Americans (147 + 51) or nearly two-thirds (63.7 percent) of all Americans totally oblivious to the schemes and strategies of the devil. Now maybe some of you can begin to understand the magnitude of the spiritual crisis we're facing today?

In the event I haven't made my case yet, this means that your adversary and mine, the devil, prowls around like a roaring lion in nearly two-thirds of all homes, churches, and cities across America seeking whom he may devour (1 Peter 5:8), totally undetected and unhindered! Said another way, if Satan comes to steal, kill, and destroy (John 10:10), this means that he is stealing, killing, and destroying nearly two-thirds of our homes, churches, communities, cities, states, and nation without any opposition! How wickedly powerful is that? Yet, this is what is happening. Belief in this "big lie" is one of the main reasons why I believe there are so many Christian "casualties" in the church today!

Incidentally, two-thirds is probably a conservative estimate given the number of Christians in America who *do* believe the devil exists, just not in their homes. For those of you from this "camp," guess what? If you have a smartphone, smart TV, and high-speed Internet access, then the devil has high-speed access to your home. The question is, what are you doing about it? Unfortunately, many of us, even most Christians, are doing nothing about it, and our culture reflects it. Have you looked around lately?

So what kind of moral and spiritual "fallout" have our homes, churches, cities, and nation experienced as a result of this undetected, unopposed demonic activity? For starters, divorce rates inside and outside the church are nearly identical. Moreover, more than one in four children are being raised without a father,[167] homosexual ordinations and women pastors are now the "norm" in many mainstream church denominations, and gay marriage has become the law of the land. Polygamy is next. Yes, the devil has done a masterful job convincing Christians that he doesn't exist while he destroys our lives and every institution in America we comprise from our house to the White House without ever firing a shot!

Again, it's easy to deceive those who don't believe you exist. Just ask an expert criminal hacker what they enjoy most about gaining illegal access to network servers. On the dark web, they generally say the same thing, which is something like, "While we love taking over your accounts and stealing your personal information, money, and trade secrets, what we really get off on is knowing that you have no idea we did it until it's too late! It's so easy and so much fun!"

Does that alarm you or make you angry? Why? It's no different than what Satan is doing in many of our homes all across America! Does that also alarm you or make you angry? It should! If it doesn't, you and I have a bigger problem!

Can you imagine how different our world would be today if we had denied the existence of Joseph Stalin or Adolf Hitler? Maybe you need a more modern-day example. Okay. Can you imagine how different our world would be if the United States and Israel denied the existence of Iran's nuclear program or had denied the existence of the Islamic State of Iran and Levant (ISIL)?

Fellow believers, it's time to wake up and recognize that the devil does exist and emphatically declare that he is powerless over the blood-bought born-again believer who knows who he or she is in Christ! I dare to say that our homes, churches, cities, and nation would be much different if the nearly 80 percent of us who profess to be Christians really understood that the battle we are fighting is not against flesh and blood but against principalities, against powers, against the rulers of the darkness of this age, against spiritual hosts of wickedness in the heavenly places (Ephesians 6:12 NKJV) operating under Satan's authority.

Jesus said that we have been given all power over *all the power* of the devil (Luke 10:19). Did you hear me? The devil is powerless over you because you belong to Christ, regardless of how inadequate you may feel. God declared that no weapon formed against you can prosper if you are in Christ (Isaiah 54:17)! Do you believe that? Really? Then tell someone else who doesn't. There's no shortage.

If you're in a church that doesn't believe that Satan exists and doesn't proclaim the victory that you have over him in Christ, then I urge you to leave immediately and find one that does! We have no more time for "church games," brothers and sisters!

As many acknowledge, there is a battle being waged against the Christian faith in America like never before. The devil and his legions of demons whose time is limited are unleashing an unprecedented attack through the souls of willing men and women, saved and unsaved, against every imaginable institution and entity in our society including, but not limited to, the home, the church, academia, the press; local, city, state, and federal government; the military, our legal system; and world banks, markets, and economic institutions. Only those who know who they are in Christ and understand the spiritual battle they have been placed in the middle of will be able to make sense out of the unprecedented evil and chaos to come and stand victoriously.

Contrary, those who continue to deny the existence of Satan and, therefore, the angelic conflict that they have been placed in the middle of will sadly and tragically continue to be spiritual casualties of this war! Now you know the truth! The good news is that it is not too late. How do I know? Because we're still breathing!

If you have believed this lie, reject it now. Replace it with the truth that Satan does exist. Then, stand fast in the victory you've been given in Christ, rebuild every foundation from your house to the White House upon this truth, advance God's kingdom, and give Him all the glory!

Moving right along. The next big lie that Satan has gotten many in the church to believe to destroy the foundations of our lives and every institution in America we comprise from our house to the White House is that *tolerance is more important than righteousness*. Read it again, s-l-o-w-l-y. Today, many churches in America are embracing the "sinner" and their "sin" because they don't want to offend anyone. What we don't realize is that we have offended a holy God by "tolerating" the very thing He hates—sin.

Christians who are willfully and unrepentantly engaged in immoral, illegal, and/or unethical lifestyles may sit comfortably in most church pews all across America week after week and never be appropriately warned (Colossians 3:16), rebuked (Titus 1:13), corrected (2 Timothy 3:16), or disciplined (Matthew 18:15–18; Hebrews 12:6). And it's not because church leaders don't know what's going on. In many cases, they do. It's because they refuse to deal with it for the reasons I discussed in the last chapter. Comments I have routinely received over the years by those who have been legitimately victimized by the evil and abusive actions of others (i.e., offenders who will not repent) are almost always the same. "I made the leadership of the church aware of my situation after confronting the individual, and they did nothing!" The result is always the same—sheep who get devoured because there was no one there to protect them. Why? Tolerance. Why? Because it draws a crowd and preserves/expands man's kingdom. Why? Because people can come, hear a sermon, "feel good," leave, and "happily" give to the work of that "ministry" without ever having to change.

Have you ever stopped to consider where we would be if Jesus had tolerated our sin instead of dying for it on the cross? We would all be dead in our trespasses and sins and without hope. While Christians have the "blessed assurance" of spending eternity in heaven with Christ after we die, the "tolerance movement" has left many Christians "dead" in their trespasses and sins without hope in the here and now.

While I hate giving the devil "props," you have to admit that "tolerance above righteousness" is a pretty slick lie to keep God's people in chains to advance his agenda in the earth (chapter 1), wouldn't you agree?

I can already hear some of you saying, "But Jesus was a friend of sinners. If He tolerated sin in order to be a friend of sinners, shouldn't we?"

Before answering that, I have a question for you. Was Jesus "tolerant" with their "sin," or was He tolerant with the "sinner" while He confronted their "sin?" Big difference, friend! A study of Jesus's life in the four Gospels, and also in Revelation 2 (Jesus's letters to the seven churches), will clearly reveal that it was the latter. Before we look at a few examples, let's finish addressing this common argument that Jesus was a "friend of sinners" as the basis for why many Christians elevate tolerance above righteousness.

What many don't realize (I sure didn't!) is that the title "friend of sinners" was *not* a title given to Jesus by Jesus or by any of His followers (us) for that matter. That's right. This alone should have the "tolerance camp" rethinking their position. Just as the term *Methodists* was used in a sneering way by the enemies of Methodists who followed Wesley's *methodical* system of Bible study, prayer, and fellowship and was later adopted by those being sneered at, so it was with this title, "friend of sinners." That's right. The title *friend of sinners* was given to Jesus *by His* enemies, the Pharisees and the experts of religious law who rejected the will of God for themselves and refused to be baptized by John (Luke 7:30). Like those in Wesley's day who adopted the term *Methodists* given to them by their enemies, Jesus accepted the sneering term, "a friend of sinners," given to Him by His enemies that we recognize today!

Before I break this down a bit further, let's take a moment to look at the relevant passage of scripture together that contains the actual phrase, "a friend of tax collectors and sinners." In Luke 7, John the Baptist has sent His messengers to Jesus with instructions to confirm that Jesus "is the one who is to come" at a time when Jesus's miracles had begun spreading throughout Judea and the surrounding country. After John's messengers find Jesus and confirm that Jesus is the one who is to come, Jesus tells John's messengers to return to John to tell John what they have seen and heard regarding the miracles Jesus performed in that very hour.

When John's messengers left Jesus, Jesus began to speak to the crowds about John and how it was prophesied that John would be sent as a messenger to prepare the way of the Lord. Then comes the critical part of the chapter for our purposes, beginning in verse 29, where Jesus says the following (*italics* used for emphasis):

> When all the people heard this, *and the tax collectors too, they declared God just, having been baptized with the baptism of John, but the Pharisees and the lawyers rejected the purpose of God for themselves, not having been baptized by Him.*
>
> To what then shall I compare *the people of this generation*, and what are they like? They are like children sitting in the marketplace and calling to one another, "We played the flute for you, and you did not dance; we sang a dirge, and you did not weep." For John the Baptist has come eating no bread and drinking no wine, *and you [the people of this generation] say*, "He has a demon." The Son of Man has come eating and drinking, *and you [the people of this generation] say*, "Look at Him! A glutton and a drunkard, *a friend of tax collectors and sinners!*" (Luke 7:29–34 ESV)

It is critical to note that the "tax collectors and sinners" Jesus was "hanging out" with weren't just any old "tax collectors and sinners." They were "tax collectors and sinners" who willingly sat under Jesus's teaching in that hour and *declared God just* and followed that declaration with "believer's baptism," if you will. I will, hereafter, refer to this group of "sinners" as "Camp 1." Camp 1 was notably different than the Pharisees and the religious lawyers who rejected Christ. I will, hereafter, refer to the Pharisees and religious lawyers as "Camp 2." My point is simply this. Christians in the "tolerance movement" make no distinction between "sinners" from Camp 1 and "sinners" from Camp 2. In other words, many Christians believe that they should be a "friend of sinners" in both "camps" because that is what Jesus did. I hope you now see that this is *not* what Jesus did and thus not what He expects us to do!

Jesus himself said, "You are my friends *if* you do whatever I command you" (John 15:14 ESV). And think about this, if Jesus is a "friend of sinners" without distinction (i.e., a friend to sinners in both Camps) then why didn't He befriend the Pharisees and religious lawyers of the day—that is, the "sinners" who gave Him that title (Camp 2)? Again, because they refused to declare Him just and to do whatever He commanded.

Do you recall when Jesus said to His disciples, "I no longer call you servant, because a servant does not know what His master is doing. But I call you friends, because I have made known to you everything I heard from my Father" (John 15:15 NCV)? *Friend* is a term that Jesus reserves for those closest to Him, not for those who are interested in "killing Him," "mocking Him," "tricking Him," "playing games," being His "fan," or in merely "hanging out" at a distance to see what He will do next.

God's Word tells us in many different places that we are only to pursue fellowship with "sinners" in Camp 1, not in Camp 2. Let's look at a few of these verses.

"What fellowship can light have with darkness?" (2 Corinthians. 6:14 ISV)

Bad company corrupts good morals. (1 Corinthians 15:33 AMP)

Come out from among them and be separate touch not the unclean thing and I will receive you. (2 Corinthians. 6:17)

"He who walks with wise man will be wise, but the companion of fools will be destroyed." (Proverbs 13:20 NKJV)

"Hear, my son, and be wise; and guide your heart in the way. Be not among drunkards or among gluttonous eaters of meat." (Proverbs 23:20 ESV)

"You adulterous people! Do you not know that friendship with the world is enmity with God." (James 4:4 NKJV)

"And if any place will not receive you and they will not listen to you, be their friend anyway. They just need someone to be kind to them and show them how to live their best life now." Oh. That's not what it says? Just making sure you're still with me since this is what so many Christians believe. No, warrior, what the passage actually says is the following:

> And if any place will not receive you and they will not listen to you, when you leave, shake off the dust that is on your feet as a testimony against them. (Mark 6:11 ESV)

What? Did you say leave? Shake off the dust as a testimony *against* them? I thought we are supposed to be "for" them no matter what? That doesn't sound very loving to me, Jesus. In fact, it seems mean and offensive! So did Jesus have it all wrong? Or is it possible that we are the ones who have it all wrong? I can assure you it's the latter, friend!

Jesus's friendship with "sinners" always has this goal—"Your sins have been forgiven" (Luke 7:48 NASB). Church leader, does your "friendship" with the "sinners" in your community and in the church God has given you have the same goal? Or do you encourage those in your congregation to be a "friend to sinners" from both camps without distinction? Brothers and sisters, do you "shake off the dust" with Christians and non-Christians who have no interest in turning from their sins and doing what Jesus commanded? Or do you "hang out" with them anyway because "that's what Jesus did?" Now you know the truth. That's not what Jesus did!

Whose word will have the final word, Jesus's or ours? Yes, Jesus loves all people, but He is only a "friend who sticks closer than a brother" (Proverbs 18:24 AMPC), to those who declare Him just and follow Him.

All through God's Word, we see Jesus turning "toward" the broken ("unbelievers" and "believers") and "away" from the unbroken ("unbelievers" and "believers"). Yet so many pastors and church leaders "encourage" us to turn "toward" both groups of people. The unintended consequence of this sin is that we, the church, waste time and get "sicker" and "sicker" over time because we continue to lower the standards of holiness to accommodate those who have no interest in following Jesus. Show me where Jesus made people comfortable while they "die." No, friend. Jesus was and is the King of the uncomfortable so that we may live!

If Jesus Christ is to be that Special Someone and speak for us, we must first recognize our need and turn toward Him. Similarly, if we are to be a friend to "tax collectors and sinners," those "tax collectors and sinners" must recognize their need and turn toward Him. I like what this author says:

> God so loved the world that He sent His only begotten Son, not to His friends, but to His enemies that they might be reconciled to Him; that they might obtain to the glorious and awesome privilege of truly becoming His friends. This privilege is granted exclusively to His sanctified sons (and His daughters) in Christ. To express the notion to the unbelieving world that "Christ was a friend of sinners," to assign this holy privilege to those who are at enmity with Him, is indeed to "give what is holy to the dogs (Matt 7:6)."[168]

To further deal with this big lie that Satan has gotten many in the church to believe (i.e., that tolerance is more important than righteousness), please allow me to explain a term I have already used several times. This term, which is at the heart of every church that elevates tolerance above righteousness, is known as "cheap grace." Just reading it should make you cringe. Lest there be any confusion, it is we, the church, through Satan's influence, who have made it "cheap," not God. Why? Why else? So Satan can use us to advance his kingdom and bring him glory (chapter 1). How? You're about to see.

The best way to define cheap grace is to compare and contrast it with real grace. Simply defined, real grace is unmerited favor. It is getting what we don't deserve and could never earn. However, it's anything but cheap! It cost God the death of His Son on the cross to redeem us from the penalty of our sins. Now contrast cheap grace with real grace. Cheap grace says, "I get to sin, since grace will abound," while real grace says, "Shall [I] continue to sin that grace may abound" (Romans 6:1 ASV)?

Cheap grace says, "God will forgive me; therefore, I don't need to change," while real grace says, "Because God has forgiven me, I want to change." Cheap grace accepts a lower standard despite what Christ has done, while real grace aims for a higher standard because of what Christ has done. Cheap grace lowers God's standard to our standard so we don't have to experience any "guilt," while real grace motivates us to raise our standard to God's standard so we can experience joy. Cheap grace leaves us trapped in our "sins," while real grace frees us from the bondage of sin. Cheap grace says, "I owe you nothing for what you've done for me," while real grace says, "I am your bondservant forever, Jesus, for what you've done for me!"

Cheap grace tramples the Son of God underfoot, insulting the Spirit of Grace (Hebrews 10:29), while real grace exalts the Son of God, magnifying the Spirit of Grace. Cheap grace requires no confession and repentance to be "activated," while real grace requires confession and repentance to be "activated." Cheap grace causes us to labor for Christ less, while real grace, out of gratitude, causes us to labor for Christ more (1 Corinthians 15:10). Cheap grace says, "Go, and sin some more," while real grace says, "Go, and sin no more" (John 8:11).

I trust you see that "cheap grace" is an utter disgrace! Sadly, this is the kind of grace that Satan has gotten most churches in America today to embrace, regardless of denomination. Many churches have become heavy on grace but light on holiness. Is it any wonder why we are not experiencing God's power and presence in our individual lives, churches, cities, and nation?

Cheap grace is nothing new in Satan's arsenal. Before Dietrich Bonhoeffer was executed by hanging at a Nazi concentration camp on April 9, 1945, he said this about "cheap grace" (*italics* used for emphasis):

> *Cheap grace* is the deadly enemy of our church. We are fighting today for costly grace. Cheap grace means grace sold on the market like cheapjacks' wares. The sacraments, the forgiveness of sin, and the consolations of religion are thrown away at cut prices. Grace is represented at the church's inexhaustible treasury, from which she showers blessings with generous hands without asking questions or fixing limits. Grace without price; grace without cost! The essence of grace, we suppose, is that the account has been paid in advance; and because it has been paid, everything can be done for nothing... In such a church the world finds a cheap covering for its sins; no contrition is required, still less any real desire to be delivered from sin. Cheap grace therefore amounts to a denial of the living Word of God, in fact, a denial of the incarnation of the Word of God. Grace alone does everything they say, and so everything can remain as it was before.
>
> Cheap grace is the grace we bestow on ourselves. Cheap grace is the preaching of forgiveness, without requiring repentance, baptism

without church discipline, Communion without confession… Cheap grace is grace without discipleship, grace without the cross, grace without Jesus Christ, living and incarnate.[169]

The "deadly enemy" of the church in Gerhard Leibholtz's day remains the "deadly enemy" of the church today. However, what you and I must know is that it's a much greater threat to us today because Satan has had generations to perfect it through us! We've even given it a slick label—*overwhelming grace*!

I love this passage from Titus which portrays real grace as a "trainer" and "teacher" that purifies us for God (*italics* used for emphasis):

> *For the grace of God* has appeared, bringing salvation for all people, *training us to renounce ungodliness and worldly passions, and to live self-controlled, upright, and godly lives in the present age*, waiting for our blessed hope, the appearing of the glory of our great God and Savior Jesus Christ, *who gave himself for us to redeem us from all lawlessness and to purify for himself a people for His own possession who are zealous for good works.* (Titus 2:11–14 ESV)

For those of you who still insist on elevating tolerance above righteousness to not offend others under the banner of "cheap grace," ask yourself this question. How concerned do you think Jesus was with offending the money changers in the temple when He drove them out with a whip for turning God's house into a den of thieves (Matthew 21:12–13)? He wasn't. He took a necessary stand for righteousness at that moment because He knew God's kingdom and glory were at stake (chapter 1).

Incidentally, this is precisely when you and I need to take a stand for righteousness—whenever God's kingdom and glory are at stake. Jesus's barometer is our barometer. By taking a righteous stand in the temple, Jesus demonstrated His love for the Father, His love for the church, and His love for us!

We saw the same demonstration of love in Jesus's encounter with Peter in Matthew 16 after Jesus tells His disciples that He must suffer many things, be killed, and be raised again on the third day. See it for yourself here in the following (*italics* used for emphasis):

> From that time Jesus began to show His disciples that He must go to Jerusalem and suffer many things from the elders and chief priests and scribes, and be killed, and on the third day be raised. And Peter took Him aside and began to rebuke Him, saying, "Far be it from you, Lord! This shall never happen to you." *But He turned and said to Peter, "Get thee behind me, Satan! You are a hindrance to me. For you are not setting your mind on the things of God, but on the things of man."* (Matthew 16:21–23 ESV)

I don't know about you, but I don't see a tolerant Jesus here either. Do you? I don't even see a gentle Jesus, a kind Jesus, a patient Jesus, a loving Jesus, or a merciful Jesus. Do you? Could it be that the real Jesus is significantly different than the one we've concocted in our minds? Could it be that when Jesus walked the earth, He displayed whatever aspect of His character was most appropriate at the moment to ensure fulfillment of the Father's will? Notice, Jesus did not mince words with Peter. He called Him Satan. Name-calling—really, Jesus? And also notice that Jesus wasn't rebuking a religious leader, scribe, or a Pharisee this time but one of His own, a "family member" if you will.

You see, Jesus understood that some of the greatest opposition He would face would come from His very own "family." If you're a pastor, you also know this to be true. Jesus, unlike the "tolerance crowd," understood that at that moment, Peter was doing the work of the devil by trying to keep Jesus from going to the cross where Satan would be defeated.

Imagine how differently this scene would have played out if Jesus had tolerated Peter's "caring" and "compassionate" attempt to block the Father's will? Did you ever stop to consider that we needed Jesus to be intolerant with Peter's "sin" at that moment? We needed Jesus to rebuke Him! And did you ever stop to think that we too could be vehemently opposing the Father's will and doing the work of Satan, even when we're being "caring" and "compassionate," depending on the circumstances? Blocking the Father's will is blocking the Father's will, whether we're "kind" when we are doing it or not. Our churches today are full of some of the most "caring" and "compassionate" people hindering the plans and purposes of God (e.g., prosperity theology, LGBTQ-affirming, etc.) that have ever existed. Pretty scary, right?

So why do I tell you all of this? Because if we expect to rule well under Jesus's hand for the expansion of His kingdom to bring Him glory in the earth (chapter 1), God knows it will never happen as long as we are hindering the plans and purposes of God by tolerating sin in ourselves and others from our house to the White House! Said another way, we can't fulfill the Father's will on earth as it is in heaven if we're setting our mind on the things of man instead of the things of God (Matthew 16:23).

Jesus wants us to know that if we truly want to follow Him and fulfill the Father's will, nothing nor anyone can be permitted to hinder the plans and purposes of God in our lives, including the actions of those closest to us. Hence, if that requires, at times, a warning, rebuke, correction, or discipline from us to others and others to us to ensure the Father's will (not our will) is being fulfilled according to God's Word, then so be it. However, don't expect to hear any of this from the pulpit of a "tolerance above righteousness" church. They'll have none of it. It's way too "unloving" and way too risky to the preservation and expansion of their kingdoms.

Another wonderful example of Jesus's righteousness and "intolerance" with sin is in Revelation 2. Here, beginning in verse 18, after commending them for their works, love, service, faith, and patience, Jesus rebukes His "bride," the church of Thyatira, for "tolerating" the woman Jezebel. Notice, Jesus even uses the word *tolerating*. Could

Jesus be any clearer on how He feels about tolerating sin? Recall, as previously discussed in chapter 2 of this book, Jezebel sought to thwart the plans, purposes, and will of God just like Peter did in Matthew 16. Are you starting to see a pattern here? That is, what "triggers" Jesus to stand up for righteousness?

I don't know about you, but considering how Jesus loved His "bride," in this case, *the church* of Thyatira, this adds a whole new dimension to the words of Paul in Ephesians 5:25–27 when He says, "Husbands, love your wives, as Christ loved *the church* and gave himself up for her, that He might sanctify her, having cleansed her by the washing of water by the word, so that He might present the church to himself in splendor, without spot or wrinkle or any such thing, that she might be holy and without blemish." (Ephesians 5:25 ESV) What do I mean? Maybe the best way to explain what I'm trying to say is to rewrite Ephesians 5:25–27 in light of how Jesus loved "His bride," the church of Thyatira in Revelation 2:

> Husbands, sometimes it will be necessary to love your wife, just as Christ loved the church of Thyatira. Giving yourself up for her includes not only rejoicing in what is good, but biblically confronting, when necessary, any evil she may be tolerating, that you might sanctify her, having cleansed her by the washing of water by the word, so that you might present her in splendor, without spot or wrinkle or any such thing, that she might be holy and without blemish.

Maybe you're saying, "Wait a minute, are you suggesting that there may be an appropriate time for a husband to rebuke His wife [i.e., a "family member"] who has her mind on the things of man and not on the things of God like Jesus did with Peter and the church of Thyatira?"

Yes, that's precisely what I'm saying, but good luck hearing this at a marriage conference or in a Sunday sermon about marriage. Why? Because *we* want to be able to define the way "Christ loved the church" instead of examining *all the different ways* Christ loved the church. Think about that for the rest of your life. We like to emphasize the "sacrificial love" part but deemphasize (or totally ignore) the truth, warning, correction, rebuke, or biblical discipline part as Jesus demonstrated with the seven *churches* in Revelation 2–3.

Unlike many of us, Jesus understood that if He was going to present the church of Thyatira to Himself, a glorious church, not having spot, wrinkle, or blemish, then He needed to deal with the spots, wrinkles, and blemishes of "His bride," the church of Thyatira...*with the washing of water by the word.*

Now, before some of you "shout me down" and wrongly judge me a misogynist, chauvinist, or autocrat, note how Jesus told husbands to do it...*by the word.* He didn't tell husbands to *scrub* their wives with their opinions or *beat them up* with the truth. He told husbands to wash their wives with the Word of God! Gently. But it goes even deeper than this. Notice *why* Jesus wants husbands to do it. Not so husbands can be controlling demagogues in the home but so that husbands will be able to present their wives holy and blameless before Christ upon His return. Husbands who are not dealing with the "spots, wrinkles, and blemishes" of their wives this way, and for this purpose, forfeit the right to do so. I trust that was for somebody!

Remember what Job as an honest and innocent man that honored God and stayed away from evil (Job 1:1) said to his wife when she told him "to curse God and die" after God allowed Satan to bring devastation upon them?

Job rebuked her, saying, "You're talking like an empty-headed fool. We take the good days from God—why not also the bad days" (Job 2:10)? Did Job have it all wrong too? Notice the same thing that "triggered" Jesus to rebuke Peter ("a family member") in Matthew 16 was the same thing that triggered Job to rebuke his wife ("a family member") here! What was it? They were both "guilty" of setting their minds on the things of man and not the things of God (Matthew 16:23).

Sadly, we live in a day where many Christian spouses not only hinder the plans and purposes of God in the home by tolerating their sin and the sin of their mate but also where many pastors and church leaders hinder the plans and purposes of God in the church by tolerating their sin and the sin of the "flock."

If we love Jesus, we should hate what He hates, "sin," and not tolerate it, ignore it, or make unholy allowances for it in our or others' lives; assuming, that is, we care about advancing God's kingdom and bringing Him glory (chapter 1)!

Before the world will be interested in our Jesus, they must see a noticeable difference in us. This will never occur as long as Christians are heavy on tolerance and light on righteousness and holiness.

Many of us like to forget (or conveniently ignore) the sobering, intolerant words of Christ Himself who said the following (*italics* used for emphasis):

> Do not think that I came to bring peace on earth. I did not come to bring peace but a sword. For I come to set a man against His father, a daughter against her mother, and a daughter-in-law against her mother-in-law; *and a man's enemies will be those of His own household.* He who loves father or mother more than Me is not worthy of Me. And He who loves son or daughter more than Me is not worthy of Me. (Matthew 10:34–37 NASB)

If Jesus knew that this message and others like it—e.g., "If anyone would come after me, let Him deny himself and take up His cross and follow me" (Matthew 16:24 ESV)—would be an offense to others, yet didn't "bow" to the culture and even to those closest to Him, then why are so many Christians quick to do it with things like gay marriage, homosexual ordinations, prosperity theology, salvation without repentance, and a host of other sins?

Answer: Because Satan has so "scrambled up" the Word of God in many of our lives that we actually believe giving people what they want is advancing God's kingdom!

Work with me for a minute. If John the Baptist were alive today and preaching inside one of our churches in America, do you think

Jesus would tell him to "tone it down a few notches" so he doesn't offend anyone? Oh, you weren't a John the Baptist fan? Jesus said, "[a]mong those born of women none is greater than John" (Luke 7:28).

Okay, then let's try Paul. If the Apostle Paul were alive today, do you think Jesus would tell Paul to temper his zeal a little bit so he doesn't offend anyone who doesn't believe that there is no other name among heaven and earth whereby men can be saved (Acts 4:12)? If Jonah were alive, would Jesus tell Jonah that he (Jonah) should not have gone to Nineveh to warn the people to repent out of fear of offending them? How about Peter in the house of Cornelius?

How about us today? Would Jesus ask us to remove the crosses from the walls of our churches so we don't offend anyone? Would He ask us only to use the name "God" and not "Jesus" to create a more "seeker-sensitive" environment? What do you think? Yet, this is exactly what many churches are doing, and we wonder why the culture is transforming us instead of the other way around! And by the way, if you happen to be an advocate for churches that "tolerate" whatever society "tolerates," you have just demonstrated intolerance to every true disciple of Jesus Christ. Just curious, are you equally troubled that you have offended us?

Who should be our example? Jesus or the latest church fad or business model that promises to increase the size of your congregation and help you live your best life now? Jesus required change from those who wanted to follow Him. Shouldn't we, who desire to be like Him, expect the same of one another? Go back and examine Jesus's encounter with the Samaritan woman at the well (John 4), the paralytic at the pool of Bethesda (John 5), and the woman caught in the act of adultery (John 8). You'll see that in each case, Jesus called each of them to a life of holiness. He didn't leave them trapped in their sins by tolerating the very sin that He knew would destroy them and be a hindrance to fulfilling His will.

This leaves us with only two choices. One, we can speak the truth in love with one another becoming in every way more like Christ (Ephesians 4:15) and fulfill the purpose for which we were created (chapter 1); or, two, we can continue to push a religious tolerance message that leaves people trapped in their sins while we continue to advance Satan's kingdom and glory in the earth. Which will you choose?

It's not hard to see that tolerance has had grave consequences. While these consequences have been around since Adam *tolerated* Eve's sin by listening to her instead of confronting, correcting, and rebuking her during her dialogue with Satan in Genesis 3, what I believe is distinctly different in our day is the rate in which we are experiencing them. In a nation that used to look to the church to help it determine right and wrong in society, most of our churches are now looking to society to help them determine what is right and wrong in the church! How messed up are we?

We cannot change what we are willing to tolerate. Thus, we shouldn't expect to be able to transform our communities, cities, states, and nation for Jesus Christ until we are ready to allow God's Word to have the final word in our hearts and homes.

Tolerance is the enemy of faith. Satan knows it. Do we? Satan knows the longer he can get us to tolerate sin, the more enslaved we will become to it, and the less likely we will do anything about it. Only when we become more concerned with offending a holy God than we are in offending people by speaking the truth in love will our homes, churches, cities, and nation be healed!

Now you know the truth. We should never elevate tolerance above righteousness. May we build the foundations from our house to the White House upon this truth as we advance God's kingdom and magnify His glory!

Weaved into the fabric of this big lie that tolerance is more important than righteousness is another big lie that Satan has gotten many of us to believe to destroy the foundations from our house to the White House, which is that we're not supposed to judge. The "religious" mantra goes like this: Everybody should keep quiet about everyone else's sin because we're not supposed to judge. The famous verse that Christians love to quote to support Satan's "big lie" is a gross misinterpretation of Jesus's own words in Matthew 7:

> Judge not, that you be not judged. For with
> what judgment you judge, you will be judged;
> and with the measure you use, it will be measured
> back to you. And why do you look at the speck in
> your brother's eye, but do not consider the plank
> in your own eye? (Matthew 7:1–3 NKJV)

Note, nowhere in this passage of scripture does it say "Don't judge." Period. It says, if you are going to judge someone in a particular area, you better be living right in that area yourself because the same judgment you render out is coming back to you (i.e., the "boomerang effect"). Christ's words specifically deal with hypocritical judgment; that is, judging others for the same "sin" that we have in our lives. We looked at this a bit earlier in chapter 4, if you recall, when we talked about the woman brought before Jesus who was caught in the act of adultery.

Another translation of the same verse above, which makes it even more clear, says it this way (*italics* used for emphasis):

> So why do you see the piece of *sawdust* in
> your brother's eye and not notice the *wooden beam*
> in your own eye? How can you say to another
> believer, "Let me take the piece of sawdust out
> of your eye," when you have a beam in your own
> eye? You hypocrite! First remove the beam from
> your own eye. Then you will see clearly to remove
> the piece of sawdust from another believer's eye.
> (Matthew 7:3–5 GWT)

I like this translation better because sawdust is produced from wood, and so is a wooden beam! Thus, we're not talking about two different sins that the one doing the judging and the one being judged are engaged in. We're talking about varying degrees of the *same sin*, that is, a little speck of *wood* in the eye of the one being judged versus a *wooden* beam in the eye of the one doing the judging.

Written another way, we could say, "Why do you see a speck of sin 'x' in your brother's life and not notice the beam of sin 'x' in your own life?" Or by way of a real-life example, "Why do you judge someone for their porn addiction when you produce pornographic videos for profit?" In other words, in this example, before you lovingly confront someone else about their porn addiction (i.e., render a judgment), deal with your own deep porn addiction. Got it?

We see this concept again in Romans 1. Here, Paul has just finished describing the fate of the unbelieving pagan Gentiles, and in Romans 2, has moved on to admonish God's people regarding hypocritical judgment here in the following [*italics* and brackets []] used for emphasis]:

> Therefore you have no excuse, O man, every one of you who judges. For in passing judgment on another you condemn yourself, because you, the judge, *practice the very same things.* (Romans 2:1 ESV)

> You tell others not to steal [render a judgment on those who steal] but do you steal? You say it is wrong to commit adultery [render a judgment on those who commit adultery] but do you do it? You condemn idolatry [render a judgment on those who commit idolatry], but do you steal from pagan temples? (Romans 2:21–22 NLT)

God's Word tells us over and over again that it is not only proper to judge but that it's our responsibility to judge as long as we do so correctly and righteously. Here are just a few of them:

1. The mouth of the righteous speaketh wisdom, and His tongue talketh of judgment. (Psalm 37:30 KJV)
2. With my lips have I declared all the judgments of thy mouth. (Psalm 119:13 KJV)

3. Open thy mouth, judge righteously, and plead the cause of the poor and needy. (Proverbs 31:9 KJV)

4. Moreover the word of the Lord came unto me saying, Now, thou son of man, wilt thou judge, wilt thou judge the bloody city? Yea thou shalt show her all her abominations (Ezekiel 22:1–2 KJV)

5. But He who is spiritual judge all things, yet He himself is rightly judged by no one. (1 Corinthians 2:15 NKJV)

6. Do ye not know that the saints shall judge the world? And if the world shall be judged by you, are ye unworthy to judge the smallest matters? (1 Corinthians 6:3 KJV)

7. For I indeed, as absent in body, but present in spirit, have already judged (as though I were present) Him who has so done this deed. (1 Corinthians 5:3–4 NKJV)

8. It isn't my responsibility to judge outsiders, but it certainly is your responsibility to judge those inside the church who are sinning in these ways. God will judge those on the outside. (1 Corinthians 5:12–13 NLT)

9. The king speaks with divine wisdom; He must never judge unfairly. (Proverbs 16:10 NLT)

10. For it is time for judgment to begin at the house of God; and if it begins with us, what will be the outcome for those who do not obey the Gospel of God? (1 Peter 4:17 ESV)

11. For if the correct time for circumcising your son falls on the Sabbath, you go ahead and do it so as not to break the law of Moses. So why should you be angry with me for healing a man on the Sabbath? Look beneath

> the surface so you can judge correctly. (John 7:23–24 NLT)

12. Simon answered, "The one, I suppose, for whom He cancelled the larger debt." And Jesus said to Him, "You have judged rightly." (Luke 7:43 ESV)

As you can see, even Jesus himself acknowledges the importance of proper, righteous judgments.

According to Webster, "to judge" means to discern, to distinguish, to form an opinion of, to compare facts or ideas, to distinguish truth from falsehood. Therefore, when you say your neighbor is a "good" person and that a particular thief is a "bad" person, you are rendering a judgment. Someone with the gift of discernment has been given the gift of judging someone or a situation correctly and biblically.

Just imagine, if we were not supposed to judge, there would be no need for pulpits, prophets, prisons, probation, courts, law enforcement, or a military. You could not discipline your children or lovingly challenge their decisions. You couldn't tell your twelve-year-old daughter to stop pursuing a romantic relationship with a nineteen-year-old boy and vice versa. You couldn't discipline your children for willfully defiant behavior. Failing students would advance to the next grade. Colleges would have to accept anyone who applied.

You couldn't vote in any election. You would have to marry the first person who asked you regardless of their character or external appearance. An employer would have to hire every applicant that applied. False teaching would be allowed to run rampant in the church. Immoral laws could not be reversed. Church leaders would never have to "step down" for sexual sin. There would be no need for accountability groups. The United States could not place economic sanctions on countries like Iran and North Korea, and the Trump administration could not impose tariffs on Chinese goods coming into America to level the "playing field."

The list is endless. I trust you get the idea. Pretty silly, right? Yet, this is precisely what so many Christians believe declaring. "You know, brother, you're not supposed to judge." Give me a break! Just stop and think about all the judgments you made in the last twenty-four hours. It would take most of us another twenty-four hours to list them!

This "big lie" has even weaved its way into the gay marriage debate among Christians. To not appear judgmental, well-meaning Christians say something like, "Well, if that's what they want to do behind closed doors, that's their business;" or "It's not for me to judge someone else." Besides kicking God's truth to the curb where He has declared homosexuality to be an abomination (Leviticus 18:22, 20:13), despite His love for the homosexual, they commit idolatry by elevating their word above God's Word on the matter. Oh, you need a New Testament example on God's view of homosexuality? Did the Apostle Paul, under the inspiration of the Holy Spirit, also have it wrong in Romans 1:26–27, 1 Corinthians 6:9–10, and 1 Timothy 1:9–10? God has spoken on the subject of homosexuality, beloved, and He did not stutter. He expects us to do the same thing, respectfully and unapologetically, on clear matters of sin. This requires righteous judgments on all matters.

I love what this author has to say about the big lie that "we're not supposed to judge" [parenthesis () and brackets [] used for emphasis]:

> The devil has been successful to push the church further and further into a corner, while everyone else comes out of the closet with their sins. Most often, those who tell you "not to judge" them do so because they are either hiding something [themselves] or want to continue doing it without reaping negative effects for it. In the campuses where we have been, students say that we shouldn't judge (form an opinion of) fornicators, drunkards, liars, homosexuals, or the like. However, they fail to realize that sin harms them and their neighbors. A caring loving Christian will judge all situations according to the Word of God and call sinners to repentance.

The church has become intimidated by the opinions of the world as they [the world] scream, "You religious bigots, hate-mongers, and intolerant people [which are judgments in themselves] do not judge me!" However, God clearly commands us to judge so we won't be deceived. Obviously, if the church stops judging and using our common sense, we will no longer be able to distinguish good from evil, we will buy into the politically correct idea of moral relativism, and we will bow down to the devil's wishes to deceive us, our family, and our [nation].

Even more disturbing is to see church leadership saying, "Do not judge." Many pastors lead their sheep astray and keep them under their manipulative control by telling them that they have a "critical spirit," they are "prideful," or "judgmental," while all they [the sheep] are trying to do is to discern the truth. If you find yourself in such a church, *flee* for your (spiritual) life![170]

Matthew 18, which I discussed earlier, is all about the church rendering proper judgments; in this case, when one believer sins against another believer. Let's look at it together (brackets [] used for emphasis):

If another believer sins against you, go privately and point out the fault [render a judgment]. If the other person listens and confesses it, you have won that person back [by correctly judging them]. But if you are unsuccessful, take one or two others with you and go back again [so that you may collectively render a judgment], so that everything you say may be confirmed [judged] by two or three witnesses [who will render their judgments]. If that person still refuses to listen, take your case to the church. If the church decides you are right [by rendering a judgment], but the other person won't accept it, treat them as a pagan or a corrupt tax collector [judge them in this manner]. Whatever you prohibit on earth [by way of judgment] is prohibited in heaven [by way of judgment], and whatever you allow on earth [by way of judgment] is allowed in heaven [by way of judgment]." (Matthew 18:15–18 NLT)

This also means that we should listen to the proper righteous judgment of others who come to us because we have "sinned" against them. If we love God, we should want to confess our sins, turn from our wicked ways (i.e., "repent"), and be restored unto God and one another.

Finally, it is critical to remember that even when judgment is proper and righteous, there is a correct way to do it and an incorrect way to do it. In Galatians 6, Paul tells us the correct way (*italics* used for emphasis):

> Brothers, if anyone is caught in any transgression, you who are spiritual should restore Him *in a spirit of gentleness*. Keep watch on yourself, lest you too be tempted. (Galatians 6:2 ESV)

Matthew says that we should judge others in the same way we would want to be judged (Matthew 7:12).

Thus, in an effort to obliterate the big lie that we're not supposed to judge, let God's Word be true and every man a liar (Romans 3:4). The truth is, when it comes to judgment, God expects His people to judge righteously (Proverbs 31:9), not hypocritically. As discussed in chapter 2, God expects kingdom people ("His church") to make kingdom decisions in kingdom's court using the King's word. This requires proper, Godly judgments to be rendered by the church.

Only when we judge righteously and allow others to judge us righteously will we come to our senses and escape the snare of the devil after being captured by him to do his will (2 Timothy 2:26).

I don't know about you, but I already sense a lot less "shaking" going on in our foundations after addressing these first three "big lies;" how about you? Great! Let's keep the party going!

The next big lie that Satan has gotten many in the church to believe to destroy our lives and every institution in America we comprise from our house to the White House is that *unity is more important than theology*. Read that again. In other words, this "big lie" says that if biblical truth has to be compromised or overlooked in order to maintain "unity," then so be it.

That's right. Many believers today would rather be *unified* around a lie than *divided* over truth. For example, if the vast majority of believers in your church were united around the belief that repentance is not necessary for salvation, that hell does not exist, that God supports gay marriage, or that women should be "overseers" in violation of 1 Timothy 2:12–14, 3:1–13; Titus 1:5–9; 1 Peter 5:1–4; and Acts 6:1–6, would you continue attending that church for the sake of "unity"? Or would you be looking for a new church? Sadly, many Christians are choosing the former in the name of a "false" unity, grieving the heart of God.

While the "unity crowd" rightly proclaims that a house divided against itself cannot stand (Mark 3:25), churches that unify themselves around lies have already fallen. Why? Because the Holy Spirit, who only inhabits truth, departs when truth departs. Remember, a "dead" church, just like a "dead" tree, can stand in the forest for a long time; and we have plenty of "dead" churches all across America!

I, like you, have heard many sermons on the topic of unity. One pastor says, "We need to be unified in this church." Another declares, "We must not become divided over this issue, saints." The following are some familiar Bible passages pastors use when discussing unity:

> Behold, how good and pleasant it is for brethren to dwell together in unity!" It is like the precious oil upon the head, running down

on the beard, the beard of Aaron, running down
of the edge of His garments. It is like the dew
of Hermon, descending upon the mountains of
Zion; for there the Lord commanded the blessing—Life forevermore. (Psalm 133:1–3 NKJV)

I appeal to you brothers, in the name of our
Lord Jesus Christ, that all of you agree with one
another so that there be no divisions among you
and that you may be perfectly united in mind
and thought. (1 Corinthians 1:10 NIV)

I in them and you in me that they may be
perfected in unity, so that the world may know
that you sent me, and love them, even as you
have loved me. (John 17:23 NASB)

Finally, all of you, have unity of mind. (1
Peter 3:8 ESV)

Who could argue on the importance of unity after reading these
verses? Not me. Our problem is not unity. Our problem is that we are
comprising truth in order to achieve it!

It is shameful, detestable, and staggering to me how many
Christians today, for example, are unified around the belief that
homosexuality is not a sin and that God takes no issue with gay
marriage, homosexual ordinations, abortion in every circumstance,
women "overseers," and disobeying the laws of the land (Romans
13:2; e.g., illegal immigration) that were put in place to protect us.

I just want to ask them, "What Bible are you reading?" I am
much less burdened over churches that are *divided* over these issues
than I am over churches that are *united* over them so they can be
more like the culture. How about you? You should be if you're a true
disciple of Jesus Christ who seeks to obey all of God's Word and not
just the parts you "like" or that are "politically correct."

Did you know that maintaining unity at the expense of theology is idolatry? Read that again, beloved. Remember our earlier definition of idolatry—anything, including unity in this case that gets elevated above God and His Word is an idol. Remember, precious ones, God and His Word are inseparable. To reject His Word (correct theology) is to reject Him. To reject Him is to reject His Word.

Church leaders, if maintaining unity in the church that God has given you to lead is more important to you than preserving the truth of His Word, you are engaging in idolatry and have the back door of the church open to the devil! I don't care how big "your" church is or how much money you take in on a given Sunday for the work of the ministry. Some of the "biggest" and most "successful" churches in America are doing the work of the devil! May God help us!

The devil has many "loyal followers" too, you know. In fact, I would argue that he has a greater number of loyal followers in America than Jesus has true disciples in America. What? Did you forget that approximately 64 percent of Americans support gay marriage?[171] Yes, some of his most loyal followers are even in the church. Were you aware that, for the first time, the majority of Protestants support gay marriage?[172] Did you now know that the number of US adults who say that abortion should be legal in all or most cases remains as high as it has been in two decades at 61 percent?[173] He isn't called the *Great Deceiver* for anything!

Many in our culture, including many Christians, would rather believe the "majority opinion" on a particular issue than what God's Word has to say about it. Have we forgotten that there is only one opinion that counts at the end of the day, regardless of what the "unified" masses say? The apostle Paul said it this way, "Let God be true and every man a liar" (Romans 3:4 KJV).

That reminds me of the time I asked my "Introduction to Aerodynamics" class of approximately forty Navy, Marine Corps, and Coast Guard flight students to point in the direction of magnetic north on the count of three. "One... Two... Three!"

What followed was nothing less than utter chaos, followed by piercing silence and tension that you could cut with a knife. Why? Because nearly everyone in the class was pointing in a different direction. I decided to let another ten seconds go by, which must have seemed like an eternity, to see if anyone would change their minds based on "majority opinion." Many did. Then I slowly pulled out a magnetic compass from behind the podium, held it out in front of me, and said, "You three are correct. The rest of you are wrong."

You should have seen their faces. Before the compass, everyone believed they were right. It reminded me of our culture. Sadly and tragically, we are living in a day where "everyone thinks they're right" and few have the one True Compass, Jesus Christ, and His Word guiding them! News Flash: If you and I are not pointing in the same direction as God and His Word, God's right and we're wrong, regardless of what the majority says!

What is truth? Very simply, truth is what God has to say about a matter. If only the people of this great nation, supposedly founded upon Judeo-Christian values believed it, we would truly be one nation under God! Another News Flash: We will never be one nation under God until God can tell us what to do in every area of life!

In a church I used to attend, my former wife and I were participating in a Sunday Church class whose primary goal was to get church members connected through the study of God's Word. We liked the idea, especially being in a larger church, and looked forward to getting to know other like-minded believers. The first few classes were especially enjoyable as we began to cultivate new friendships.

The leader was a friendly fellow I will call Ron who we later learned was also one of the elders of the church. His format usually involved leader-led discussions that centered on a particular passage of scripture with interpretation, humorous anecdotes, and application followed by a "break-out" session into small groups to discuss the scripture and its application further. Then, for the last fifteen minutes of class, we would reassemble and share group insights with the rest of the class. Nice format.

On week 4, however, "the bottom fell out." While there are many mysteries and unanswered questions in the Bible, God's omniscience is *not* one of them. In a nutshell, Ron had taken the position that when Jesus told the young rich ruler that he had to sell all of his possessions after he asked Jesus what he must do to inherit eternal life, Jesus wasn't necessarily asking him to sell his possessions because He (Jesus) knew that the young rich ruler was struggling with the love of money. Ron said that while Jesus is omniscient, Jesus wasn't necessarily omniscient in this situation, which led to a further assertion from Ron that "Jesus is not necessarily omniscient in every situation."

I couldn't believe what I was hearing! After others began to question the basis of his theology respectfully, the class quickly became polarized. At this point, Ron got flushed and defensive and then began to lecture the class (about thirty of us) on the importance of being unified. "Unified on what?" I wanted to ask. He further told us that it was wrong and divisive to judge, which is the big lie we just finished discussing.

In the spirit of Matthew 18:15–17, I brought this matter to the attention of Ron and then another elder (I will call Dave) after Ron refused to repent. I told Dave that I liked Ron but that Ron was causing great confusion among the "sheep" and should, thus, be removed as the leader of the class. Had I known Ron was an elder at the time, I would have also recommended that he be removed as an elder. I told Dave, who agreed with me, that this was a significant issue that needed to be addressed with Ron right away and that in keeping with Matthew 18, I would go with Dave if he agreed. Dave indicated that he would handle the matter and did not need me to go with him. Not only did Dave not address the issue with Ron, but after my family and I left the church for this and other significant leadership deficiencies, we learned that Ron was now overseeing the entire youth ministry in this nearly 1,500-member church!

What sadly stuck out in my mind about this whole experience, however, and the point I wish to make with you given our topic was the number of people who were willing to "look the other way" at Ron's "bad" theology for the sake of some kind of sick unity and loyalty to Ron while further subjecting themselves to false teaching that could take years, if not a lifetime, to untangle. I don't know about you, but I'm still untangling theological "messes" from the pulpit, which is why it is so critical for each of us know God's Word for ourselves!

If you're from the "unity at all costs camp," ask yourself this—when did Christ ever compromise biblical truth for the sake of unity? Then why are so many of us so quick to do it? I believe there are at least six reasons: ignorance, arrogance, laziness, apathy, cowardice, and guilt tied to misplaced loyalties.

Some of us (even those who have been Christians for a long time) are sadly unable to discern the lie that "unity is more important than theology" because we, very simply, don't know God's Word! This is one of the greatest crises in the church today. These are the spiritually immature who sadly, I believe, represent many professing Christians in America who have worn the Christian label for years but do not know His Word. While the spiritually mature are not ignorant of the schemes of the devil (2 Corinthians 2:11), the spiritually immature are and are thus easily deceived by man.

Is anyone, including the devil, "playing" on your ignorance, intentionally or unintentionally? How do you know? The only way you'll know is to know the truth in God's Word for yourself. While other Christians can be a great source of counsel, nothing can substitute for God's Word. Why? Because even well-intentioned Christians, like Ron (above), are subject to bad theology. God's Word should always be every believer's *first* line of defense.

Another reason why some Christians believe the lie that unity is more important than theology is because we think we're smarter than God. Oh, we don't say it, but deep down, many of us believe "our theology" is flawless, don't we? After all, how could God be as knowledgeable as we are on the latest social media, fashion, Hollywood, technology, business, medical, engineering, construction, and, yes, even church trends, right? How could God possibly know more than us about the latest economic and polling data, American sentiment, partisan talking points, scandals, or Supreme Court decisions, right? Certainly, God doesn't understand politics like we do.

Really? Give me a break! Who do we think we're kidding? It's very sad to think that many of us believe we know more than the One who created the universe and the galaxies (Genesis 1), who commands the wind and the waves to be still (Mark 4:39), and who knew us before we were formed in our mother's womb (Jeremiah

1:5). Even sadder, however, is how it must make God feel. Some of us need to be reminded of the following words God spoke to Job:

> Where were you when I laid the foundations of the earth? Tell Me, if you have the understanding. Who determined its measurements? Surely you know! Or who stretched the line upon it? To what were its foundations fastened? Or who laid its cornerstone when the morning stars sang together, and all the sons of God shouted for joy? (Job 38:4–7 NKJV)

> Have you commanded the morning since your days began, and caused the dawn to know its place? (Job 38:12 ESV)

> Have you entered the springs of the sea? Or have you walked in search of the depths? Have the gates of death been revealed to you? Or have you seen the doors of the shadow of death? Have you comprehended the breadth of the earth? Tell Me, if you know all this? (Job 38:16–18 NKJV)

> Have you entered the treasury of snow, or have you seen the treasury of hail, which I have reserved for the time of trouble, for the day of battle and war? By what way is light diffused, or the east wind scattered over the earth? (Job 38:22—24 NKJV)

What blows me away is that even after reading this, there will still be some Christians who continue to embrace bad theology for the sake of unity because they believe they (or someone else) know more than God. Don't be one of them! Hear me. If you do, God will oppose you. I didn't say it. James did when he declared, "God opposes the proud but gives grace to the humble" (James 4:6 ESV).

Other Christians elevate unity above theology because they are too spiritually lazy to learn the truth for themselves. This is similar to our first reason. After all, it's a lot quicker and easier to get our theology from someone else, especially if it sounds good and makes us feel good, right? In the same way the sluggard is too lazy even to lift a fork of food to his mouth (Proverbs 26:15), the spiritually lazy person would rather "die" than expend the time and energy needed to feed themselves the Word of God. Another easy day for Satan!

Others elevate unity above theology because they are simply apathetic, neither cold or hot on the issue (Revelation 3:16). It has been my observation that this group, frankly, just wants a nice, safe, comfortable, "happy" church where they can "unplug" from the world for an hour or two and maybe even get a break from their children.

This brings me to the fifth reason I believe people elevate unity above theology—they're cowards! They know in their hearts that someone's theology (or their theology) is wrong, but they are afraid to lovingly confront them (or be confronted) because they fear that person's rejection more than they fear God's rejection—another form of idolatry. Instead of allowing the love of God and His Word to drive their decision-making, cowards allow the fear of being rejected by a spouse, other Christians, or a pastor who may "correct" them for being "judgmental" or "divisive," to drive their decision-making. Rocking the "unity boat" is simply too risky for the coward who cares more about their personal comfort, "peace," and preservation of their kingdom than upholding the truth of God's Word. What a "servant leader!"

Another reason I believe people elevate unity above theology is out of guilt. The loyalty some of us have to our pastors and church leaders, for example, is greater than our loyalty to Jesus Christ and the truth of His Word. Said another way, we would rather betray God and His Word than have to face any guilt we might feel over "betraying" man (e.g., a pastor to whom we've been loyal to for many years). Yes, another form of idolatry. I actually had one Christian brother tell me that once you become a member of a church, you are "married" to that church forever. Wow, really? Really! Run, Forrest, run!

What many don't realize is that division in a church can be a good thing. Paul acknowledges this in 1 Corinthians 11 in discussing the purpose of the Lord's supper. He said that "[t]here must be divisions among you so that those of you who are right will be recognized" (1 Corinthians 11:19 NLT). In other words, division is sometimes necessary to differentiate between those who are walking in the truth and those who are not! Good luck hearing this on a Sunday morning.

I like what this author had to say regarding the present-day "push" for unity above theology among many church leaders today (*italics* used for emphasis):

> Today, many are calling for "unity meetings" and efforts to end religious division. These might be productive if everyone involved had the same respect for God's authority and interest in seeking absolute truth. But too often the agenda is to compromise truth and agree to disagree. This does not promote biblical unity and is very harmful to the church.[174]

Amen and amen, my brother! I couldn't agree more. The unintended consequences of this big lie that unity is more important than theology have been enormous. Individuals that are willing to compromise God's truth for the sake of unity become marriages, homes, churches, cities, states, and ultimately, a nation that is willing to compromise God's truth for the sake of unity (e.g., legalization of gay marriage nationally).

Remember, if the devil can get us unified around bad theology (i.e., a lie), he "owns" us. He gets to "call the shots," set the agenda, and control the outcome. Have you looked around lately?

Lastly, please don't hear what I am not saying. I love unity. Few things are more beautiful than true biblical unity centered on God's truth. However, I imagine only a few things being more detestable to

God than "fake" unity around a lie. There's a fancy name for it—ecumenism. Ecumenism is cooperation that results in a dilution or compromise of the essential truths of the Bible or an organized attempt to bring about the cooperation and unity among Christians.[175] This is not Holy Spirit-breathed biblical unity.[176] Welcome to the church of Jesus Christ in America!

So if the big lie is that unity should never be elevated above theology, what's the truth? The truth is that biblical unity can only exist where there is correct theology. Being disunified around the truth will always be better than being unified around a "lie."

The next big lie that Satan has gotten many in the church to believe to destroy the foundations of our lives and every institution in America we comprise from our house to the White House is that our individual sin only affects us.

When I was a freshman (plebe) at the United States Naval Academy, one of the many pieces of trivia I was required to memorize and regurgitate back to my upperclassmen were *The Laws of the Navy*, written in 1896 by Rear Admiral Ronald Arthur Hopwood, Royal Navy, while he was a lieutenant (O-3). To this day, *The Laws of the Navy* continue to be one of the most famously quoted pieces of naval literature of all time. The fifth law of the Navy, out of twenty-seven, is particularly relevant to our discussion and goes as follows:

> On the strength of one link in the cable,
> dependeth the might of the chain, who knows
> when thou mayest be tested? So live that thou
> bearest the strain![177]

Many of us have heard the expression that a chain is only as strong as its weakest link. It's 100 percent true, whether we're talking about a Navy Seal team, a sports team, a dance team, a sales team, a corporation, a marriage, a family, a church, a government, or a nation. When one Seal team member misses a designated checkpoint by seven seconds, for example, the mission of the entire team, and even lives, can be lost. When just one NFL lineman jumps "offside," the whole team gets penalized. When one dance team member's timing is even slightly "off" during a competition, the score of the entire team is negatively impacted. When one publicly traded corporation misses their "numbers" for the quarter, every shareholder "suffers."

For those of you who still don't believe that your sin or another's sin only affects you or them only, respectively, I wouldn't recommend telling this to a husband whose wife has been unfaithful to him with another man. Nor would I recommend telling this to a wife that has been devastated by her husband's pornography addiction. Don't say this to a parent who lost a son to a drunk driver in a head-on collision. Spare the teenage girl who will soon give birth to a child whose father is MIA.

Additionally, I wouldn't recommend telling this to the parent whose son or daughter is addicted to heroin (laced with fentanyl) brought in from the Southern border or to the member of a congregation who just learned that their beloved pastor of many years was living a "double life." Good luck telling this to the American taxpayer who longs for the day when they will no longer be victimized by the lies and actions of corrupt politicians. Nor would I recommend telling the Iranian people who have been oppressed by their government for centuries that the "sins" of their government don't affect them.

Can you imagine how different we would behave as Christians if each of us in the body of Christ believed that we were a critical "link" connected to another critical "link" (another Christian) connected to another critical "link" (another Christian) that, in the end, comprised the "chain of believers" known as the church? Imagine if we lived like the overall strength of our collective chain was dependent on the strength of our individual "links" in the chain. Imagine what a force the church would be to reckon with in the earth today. Jesus can. Can you?

Spiritually weak Christians make spiritually weak families, churches, cities, states, and a spiritually weak nation. We're like a Navy Seaman (junior position) telling a Navy Chief who ultimately reports to the "CO" who is responsible for the safety of each crewmember that one of the links on the anchor chain is "rusting out," but that it's "no big deal" because the rest of the links are fine. Yeah, right. People lose limbs or die that way—Google "anchor chain snapback" some time. When that chain "gives way," it takes out everything and everyone in its path.

What a good Navy Chief would never allow in the "kingdom" of the Navy, we routinely allow in the kingdom of God through our unwillingness to conduct "preventative maintenance" (PM) on ourselves and others (i.e., biblically deal with our sin and the sins of others). And we wonder why people keep getting hurt and why the church keeps drifting further and further into moral and spiritual obscurity with each passing day. Said another way, we'd see more spiritual transformation in our culture and a lot fewer "casualties" in the body of Christ today if we conducted PM on our "links" like the Navy does on its links.

Our sin not only affects present generations but future generations, that is, until the current generation cancels it—another reason why this "big lie" is such a "big deal." I have a personal example of this.

I grew up in a family engulfed by alcoholism with all of the normal dysfunction that accompanies it. My father, mother, and two of my three siblings were alcoholics. While all of them eventually stopped drinking by the grace of God, I found myself headed in the same direction by age twenty-four; that is, until God rescued me from myself. While in flight school, I turned my will and my life over to Jesus Christ and asked Him to be my Lord and Savior. While that was, and is, the greatest thing that ever happened to me, it also resulted in breaking the generational "curse" of alcohol addiction in my "family tree."

You see, when I got "saved," Jesus Christ delivered me immediately from any desire I would ever have to drink alcohol again! Today, by God's grace, none of my three adult children are alcoholics. While some of you may be thinking, "Well, isn't that nice?" Trust me when I say that this isn't just a "nice thing," but it's a Jesus Christ generational curse-busting thing! Our and others' actions, "good" and "bad," absolutely impact others to many generations. The good news is that Jesus's blood never loses its power! It will do the same thing for you! Many of you have already experienced it! Go ahead and praise Him if you want—we've got time!

Maybe you're thinking, "Yeah, but my sin is not as 'bad' as some of the 'sins' you just described. How much impact could my sin have on others?"

So glad you asked. First, remember who went home justified before God in Luke 18:11–14 as we discussed in chapter 4. Secondly, Jesus Christ's death on the cross is as much for the person who struggles with gossip or unkind thoughts as it is for the murderer (Romans 6:23). Does gossip only affect the gossiper? No way. God's Word says that the unbridled tongue is a fire that corrupts the whole body, setting on fire the entire course of life (James 3:6). In other words, it "burns" everything and everyone in its path!

I can hear some of you saying, "But how can my sin affect others if no one else knows about it but me and God?" In other words, what if I, as a Christian husband, by way of example, have successfully kept my porn addiction a secret from my wife? That's like saying, "What if the tenth link in the chain doesn't know that the fifth link has a significant rust problem?" Is that chain any less vulnerable to breakage? Hardly.

God's Word says we are all members of one body (1 Corinthians 12:12), and we belong to each other in Christ (Ephesians 4:25; Romans 12:5), right? If the leg didn't know that the arm was broken because the arm kept quiet about it, is the body somehow not handicapped? Ridiculous, right? Under Christ, who is the head of His body, the church, the whole body, under His direction, is jointly fit together perfectly. As each part does its own special work, it helps the other parts grow so that the whole body is healthy, growing, and full of love (Ephesians 4:15–16). At least this is the way it's supposed to work!

Please hear me. The degree that I, as a member of the body of Christ, remain in bondage to sin is the degree to which I "handicap" the body of Christ since we're connected. The same is true of you. It's the height of self-centeredness and cruelty to the rest of the body. While the body can still function with a broken arm, it works much better with two healthy arms. And so it is with the body of Christ. Each of us, out of our love for Christ and one another, should want to go through whatever "sin overhaul" and PM are necessary to ensure that we, in Christ, are "mighty to save" and able to bear up under any "load" that this evil and hostile world can bring against us.

However, putting this all aside for a second, let's assume, as some say, that no one but God knows about your sin. Does it at least matter to you that your actions are grieving the heart of God and causing your relationship with Him to suffer? In other words, even if you can't see that your "sin" is affecting others and weakening the impact that we, the body of Christ, are having in the world today, are you at least willing to acknowledge that your sin is grieving the heart of God and affecting your relationship with Him?

As we come to the end of this "big lie" that Satan has gotten us to believe, please allow me to solidify our discussion with a short story. About three years ago, a Christian brother and close friend of mine told me that after his upcoming wedding, he would be relocating to Washington, DC, without his future wife for eighteen months. He wanted to pursue a promotion that, in the end, would result in a salary that would, otherwise, take him many years to achieve. He explained to me that his fiancé currently made about $90,000 a year and that they had agreed to forfeit her salary once they had children so she could stay home and raise them. He stated that taking this assignment now would make up for her lost wages later once their first baby came.

I said, "I understand, but at what cost?"

A puzzled look came across his face.

"The two of you are about to become 'one' (Mark 10:8). Why? So you can become 'two' again? I understand the temptation, but you make a good salary that more than meets the basic needs of your family. While I know the extra money would be nice and would speed up the salary clock, you don't need it. But your future wife will need you once you get married."

He said, "What do you mean?"

I said, "Who's going to physically, emotionally, and spiritually protect her while you're away? Jeff, you're not only called to be her provider but her protector."

He said, "But DC is close enough for me to come home on the weekends."

I said, "Okay, and who is going to protect her the other five days of the week? This is your responsibility. Do you think God is calling you to protect your wife to the best of your ability or only as long as it doesn't impact your ability to make more money?"

After two similar discussions like this one, he decided to go to DC anyway. His desire to replace her lost wages later had totally blinded him to his responsibility to protect his wife to the best of his ability today. Besides God opposing him and his wife being unprotected, he also made himself more vulnerable to sexual temptation while apart from her—something he struggled with as a single. And if that weren't enough, the vital role he fulfilled in his church would soon be vacant.

His "sin" would clearly affect more than just him. Unfortunately, like so many others, he didn't see it that way! Satan had blinded him. And for what? A few more shekels of silver.

Maybe you're thinking about a similar decision. I know you're out there. I run into men like Jeff all the time. Take this as God's warning to you, through me, and don't do it! It is better to have less with your priorities than more without them!

The story is not over. About eighteen months later, I ran into Jeff again. We had lunch together. He informed me that he was on the brink of divorce and should have listened to me. He said that his wife was full of anxiety and was insecure about his love for her. Their marriage had taken a "major hit," and all of it was avoidable if he had only maintained God's priorities.

We, as the Body of Christ, will be tested in these prophetic days in which we live. It has already begun. As things get darker and darker, Satan and his well-ordered legions of demons will continue to look for weak links in the chain who are willing to compromise God's Word for "his" word so he can further divide us and use us to advance his kingdom.

On the strength of your link (and mine) will depend the might of our "chain." The current state of our chain is not good. What I hope you now see is that one of the main reasons for this is because we have allowed Satan to convince us that our sin only affects us.

This, in turn, has decreased, and in many cases eliminated our desire to be victorious over it, hurting the entire body of Christ.

If the Holy Spirit, like the Navy, made an announcement beginning tomorrow that He was going to send a representative to your house and mine to conduct PM on our links, what condition would He find us in? If He found some unaddressed sin in our lives, causing the "chain of believers" to be vulnerable to breakage and casualties, would we work with Him to receive the healing He has for us or "brush" it off? Satan and the other links in the "chain" want to know.

As the "world" seeks to pull the church of Jesus Christ apart all across America and at every corner of the globe, it is my earnest prayer that each of us would seek to be strong links in the chain that Jesus and the rest of the body can count on!

Now you know the truth. Our sin does affect others since we are all members of one body, the body of Christ!

God's Word says that he who the Son sets free is free indeed (John 8:36)! For those who were bound by this "lie" like me and are now free, enjoy your newfound freedom. From this day forward, may each of us "live that though bearest the strain" not only for our individual lives but for every institution in America we comprise from our house to the White House for God's kingdom and glory!

The next big lie that Satan has gotten many in the church to believe to destroy the foundations of our lives and every institution in America we comprise from our house to the White House is that the demonstration of the Gospel eliminates the need for proclamation of the Gospel. You've heard this. "Preach the Gospel always and, if necessary, use words."[178] Maybe you've even said it yourself. While this quote often receives a confident "nod of approval" by many, it couldn't be any more unbiblical. Did you know that even the Catholic church attempted to remedy this false theology under Pope Paul VI in his 1974 encyclical on Evangelization, *Evangelii Nuntiandi*, when he penned the following (*italics* used for emphasis)?

> Nevertheless [witness without words] always remains insufficient, because even the finest witness will prove ineffective in the long run if

it is not explained, justified…and made explicit by a clear and unequivocal proclamation of the Lord Jesus. *The Good News proclaimed by the witness of life sooner or later has to be proclaimed by the word of life.* There is no true Evangelization if the name, the teaching, the life, the promises, the kingdom and the mystery of Jesus of Nazareth, the Son of God are not proclaimed.[179]

Spot on, but you have to admit, it's a great lie if your goal is to keep God's people from sharing the Gospel and becoming true disciples who will "go" and make more disciples to transform the world around them for Jesus Christ!

Perhaps you're more familiar with this version of the same "big lie" that I use to promote, which goes like this, "I just try to live like Christ so people will want to know Him." Sounds very "nice," "proper," and "religious," doesn't it? While many, including me, have cowered away from opportunities to preach the Gospel to avoid rejection, all of us will be without excuse on Judgment Day when God rewards us (or doesn't reward us) for doing (or not doing) what Jesus commanded us to do.

Jesus told us all, whether we have the gift of evangelism or not, to "go into all the world and *preach* the Gospel to every creature" (Mark 16:15 NKJV). Clearly, this has a nonspeaking component, "go," and a speaking component, "preach." While many of us do a great job at "going" on vacation and "going" to the movies, and even "going" to church or small group, we do a horrible job of "going" to share the Gospel with those who will spend eternity in hell if we don't. This is the great tragedy in the church today.

Have you forgotten that 95 percent of all Christians have never won a soul to Christ?[180] And we're going to "beat our chests" and "wring our hands" about the current social, moral, and political chaos of our day? May God forgive us!

Remember "show and tell" in grade school? Our teachers all told us the same thing. "I not only want you to *show* the class what you bring in, but I want you to *tell* them about it also, okay?" Those who remembered to do both always got the best grade, remember? And those who had little or nothing to say didn't fair very well. That was me. "Shyness" was no excuse. At least that's the way it used to be when everyone didn't get a trophy for just showing up! That was extra.

The same is true in parenting and marriage, right? In parenting, we can, and should, for example, allow our children to see us behaving in financially responsible ways. However, at some point, we need to explain to them the difference between a credit card and a debit card. In marriage, wives like demonstrations of their husbands' love for them, but they also like to hear that you love them. Ladies, your husband loves it when you're respectful, but he also loves it when you grab him by the collar, kiss him, and say, "Wow, baby, I really respect the way you're leading our family!" Show and tell!

On New Year's Day 2015, the Holy Spirit had been leading me to begin the new year by witnessing to a contractor named Brian who was in my home, repairing a large three-by-four-foot opening in my living room ceiling. You see, I had a persistent hidden water leak from an upstairs bathroom toilet that began to show itself as a wet six-inch diameter circle on my living room ceiling downstairs! I had the leak fixed and replaced my toilet. Brian was at my house to patch and paint the living room ceiling...for the second time!

His first patch job didn't "hold" and required him to come back to do it over again. He felt bad. I felt bad. However, he couldn't have been more gracious.

The rework began on December 30. He graciously returned the following day on December 31. That day, New Year's Eve, the Holy Spirit prompted me to share my faith with him on New Year's Day since he, once again, graciously agreed to return to finish the job. I thought, *Wow, what a great way to begin the New Year.* By this time, I had developed good rapport with him. Additionally, we each had a teenage child attending the same high school with ties to the wrestling team. His son was a wrestler. My daughter was friends with someone else on the same wrestling team that Brian and his son knew well.

While I had tried to be the best "witness" for Christ I could be to Brian up to now, for all he knew, I was just a "nice" atheist or agnostic. To allow him to respond to the Gospel message, it would require me to tell him about the Gospel, which I did. While in the end, he did not choose to receive Jesus Christ as his personal Lord and Savior, my job was done, and I trust God was pleased with my obedience. I would like to say that I am obedient to share my faith whenever the Spirit prompts me, but it would be a lie. Nonetheless, I know I have the responsibility to show and tell others the "good news."

The Apostle Paul says it this way in Romans 10 (*italics* used for emphasis):

> For everyone who calls upon the name of the Lord will be saved. How then will they call on Him in whom they have not believed? And how are they to believe in Him of whom they have never heard? *And how are they to hear without someone preaching?* And how are they to preach unless they are sent? As it is written, "How beautiful are the feet of those *who preach the good news!*" (Romans 10:13–15 ESV)

Demonstration of the Gospel, beloved, will never eliminate the need to preach the Gospel. Remember my four friends from chapter 1? They would have never had the penalty of their past, present, and future sins canceled forever if I had not opened my mouth and shared the Gospel message with them and asked them to respond.

Someone once said to preach the Gospel and not use words is like telling someone to wash but not use water. So the next time you hear someone say, "Preach the Gospel always, and if necessary, use words;"[181] you can politely tell them, "Thanks, but I prefer to 'preach the Gospel always and, because it's necessary, use words.'"

By the way, remember Dallas from chapter 1? Two weeks later, I went back to visit him with my good friend, Mike, who just happens to be Jenna's dad (Paul's father-in-law). Dallas was still there, thank

God. In all the commotion, I never allowed Dallas to respond to the Gospel. By the time the seven of us got done praying outside of the shoe store that night, Dallas was long gone. I felt so bad. After introducing Dallas to Mike, I said, "Dallas, do you remember me and what happened a couple of weeks ago?"

Dallas said, "How could I forget?"

I smiled and said, "I'm so sorry I couldn't give you that sale, but more importantly, I'm sorry Paul, Jenna, and I didn't have the opportunity to get back to you so you could respond to the Gospel message. Please forgive me, man."

He said, "Oh, that's okay."

Then I looked him straight in the eyes, smiled, and said, "The Holy Spirit told me you're ready to respond to the Gospel message right now. Am I right?"

He said, "Yes, sir, you're right!"

We bowed our heads, closed our eyes, and Dallas received Jesus Christ as his personal Lord and Savior. That night, my friend, Dallas, became my brother-in-Christ with my other brother-in-Christ, Mike, standing right by my side on "holy ground." However, none of this would have been possible unless Mike and I were willing to "show" *and* "tell."

As an aside, one of my greatest concerns about sharing a testimony like the one I did above about Dallas is that many of you will do what I used to do and say, "I could never do that." First of all, the same is true of me, that's why I ask God to speak through me. So instead of doing what you could do, many of you don't do anything like I used to do. That's what the statistics show. God knows we're all wired differently, and your approach doesn't have to be my approach and vice versa. God just wants to see if we'll do what He's asked us to do using any approach.

People ask me all the time, "How do you get past the fear of rejection?"

I say, "First, I'd be lying to you if I told you I never took someone's rejection personally. The truth is, I have. However, that doesn't change another truth, which is that when they choose to reject the opportunity to accept Christ, they are not rejecting me but Christ.

Furthermore, Jesus told us that if we followed Him, we would experience rejection."

I, like many of you, have experienced great rejection by even those closest to me. While it is very painful, it will always greatly pale in comparison to the rejection Christ experienced for you and me. This is what helps me to overcome my fears as I do what is foolish in man's eyes for my Jesus! Incidentally, when He was just "Jesus," it was really hard; when He became "my Jesus," it got a lot easier! Sharing the Gospel from your heart and not your head makes all the difference! It's always the same thing that causes people to respond to the Gospel message over and over again—the love of God demonstrated for them on the cross!

Still, some will say, "I know that, but it is still really hard for me."

To that, I would say, remember the verse we covered earlier that talked about the fellowship of His suffering, being made conformable even unto death (Philippians 3:10)? Here's where you and I get the awesome privilege and opportunity to really know Him, not only in the power of His resurrection, *but* in "the fellowship of His suffering." Jesus will know you felt what He felt when man rejected Him, and it will make you love Him even more, causing the closeness and intimacy between you and Him to become greater and greater. Now, what man or woman who truly desires to know Christ like this would deny themselves that opportunity? None.

My other great concern about sharing such testimonies like this is that some will read this and say, "Well, you clearly have the gift of evangelism, and since that is not my gift, I'll just let you and the other evangelists do it while I volunteer at the local food bank and try to be a good spouse, parent, and provider. That's how I serve God."

Great, but your back to being a lawyer without a client. You forgot your primary mission—the Great Commission. You're great at legal research, writing legal briefs, filing motions, and presenting arguments in front of a "mock" jury. You have all the right clothes, office space, staff, equipment, but you've been a lawyer for twenty years and still haven't advocated for your first client. No, we're not all evangelists; some will sow, and others will reap, but shame on us if we never get around to doing what Jesus commanded us to do.

The Great Commission requires demonstration and proclamation. The day we begin to care about others' Judgment Day as much as we care about our own Judgment Day is the day all this will change!

Over the last three years, by God's grace, I have shared the Gospel with over 1,500 people. Approximately 500 people at the time of this writing have responded to God's love and asked Jesus Christ to forgive them of their sins and be their Lord and Savior. Some have gotten baptized, and some have even invited family members to church who, in turn, have accepted Christ and been baptized. It is not uncommon for waiters and waitresses to accept Jesus Christ right at my restaurant table when confronted with the love of God and their need for a Savior. One night, five out of seven gang members received Christ right in front of their gang leader who didn't, which is unheard of in the gang world; that is, unless Jesus does it!

As previously mentioned, while 95–99 percent of the people I share the Gospel with never receive one penny from me, some have given it back when they realized why I was there. One young man (age fifteen) who won $100 for correctly guessing that Jesus Christ was the greatest salesman in the world that ever lived, said, "Sir, I can't take this money from you. It wouldn't be right. Thank you for doing what you did tonight. Please don't stop. More kids need to hear this message. God bless you."

I said, "Please keep it. What happened tonight was a multimillion-dollar transaction in heaven. I'd like to bless you."

The young man said, "No, sir, I can't take it, but thank you so much!"

Blown away once again by the love of God, these young people who I had just shown Jesus to were showing Jesus to me—all because I was willing to "show" and "tell." Some nights when Soul Patrol is over, it's all I can do just to get back to my car and weep. None of this, however, would be my reality and experience if I believed that the demonstration of the Gospel eliminated the need for proclamation of the Gospel. Many of you who faithfully share the Gospel with others know exactly what I'm talking about.

For those of you in law enforcement with children, the closest thing I can compare Soul Patrol to is how you feel when you can track down and successfully return an unharmed kidnapped child to their parent. When someone you share the Gospel with accepts Jesus as Lord and Savior, you are literally being used by God to "rescue" them from the most dangerous "felon" in the earth, Satan, and safely return them (i.e., reconcile them) to their heavenly Father. And we're going to allow our demonstration of the Gospel to eliminate our need to proclaim the Gospel? May God help us!

The consequences of believing that the demonstration of the Gospel eliminates the need to proclaim the Gospel should be obvious—the Gospel message does not go forth, and Satan gains more territory in the earth (e.g., homes, churches, schools, cities, states, government, and nation) to expand His kingdom and glory (chapter 1).

Don't be like so many who say, "I'll tell people about Jesus when God opens the door." Praise God for that, but what happens if the door never opens or it takes twelve years to open? You and I have wasted all that time! Remember, God has already declared that right now, the harvest is plenty, but the laborers are few (Luke 10:2). This means that while a family member might not be ready, a coworker might be ready. While the door may be closed with your neighbor, it could be wide open with the person in your check-out line. And by the way, none of us know if a door is unlocked unless we check it. I say that because sometimes we wrongly assume it's a closed door that can't be opened when we don't even check to see if it's closed. Another lie from the devil to stop us.

Don't allow yourself to become part of the statistic I shared earlier. I often wonder how many of those same Christians who never led one person to Christ over their entire life didn't do so because they were waiting for God to "open doors?" Remember, on Judgment Day, we will all be without excuse!

While the devil would like to convince us otherwise, the Gospel message is not about the number of conversions. It's about consistent obedience and faithfulness to do what Jesus told us to do, regardless of the outcome. For example, I believe Jesus will count those who are physically able and faithful to share the Gospel with 1,000 people over their lifetime where no conversions occur as being more faithful than those who share the Gospel with ten people over their lifetime where eight conversions occur. Since the Holy Spirit, operating through us, is responsible for every conversion, I believe God is much more interested in our faithfulness to do what He told us to do than in the outcome, which belongs to Him. When we are faithful to "show and tell," some of us may be tilling the ground, planting the seed, watering someone else's seed, adding fertilizer, removing weeds, or harvesting. May this encourage all of us to begin sharing the Gospel like never before!

In the age of social media, where virtually every Christian I know has a Facebook, Twitter, Instagram, Snapchat, or Pinterest account, it is an utter disgrace that the majority of us are using these accounts for every other reason but the Great Commission! May God have mercy on us!

For those of you—hopefully, fewer in number than before—who are still convinced that demonstration of the Gospel eliminates the need to proclaim the Gospel, please allow me to ask you this tough question. How much do you and I really love the people we are demonstrating the Gospel to when we are willing to let allow them to go to hell? Allow me to share a brief true story to drive this point home.

It is a story of a married couple who I will call Gary and Ann-Marie. This godly couple understood that the purpose of their marriage went far beyond their "personal happiness" and included using their home for hospitality, discipleship, and evangelism. No longer newlyweds and with two children, they befriended a non-Christian married couple, Chuck and Sue, to demonstrate the love of Christ to them and their family.

Over four years, Gary and Ann-Marie invited them over for meals, watched their children, worked on home projects together, and attended various birthday and anniversary events involving one another's family members. Their families even began to go on vacation together as their friendship, closeness, and love for one another grew.

Then one night, everything changed. After dinner at Gary and Ann-Marie's home, Chuck said, "Sue and I have some incredible news we would like to share with you!" With childlike excitement in his voice, Chuck said, "Gary, Ann-Marie, you're never going to guess what happened to Sue and me yesterday. We heard the Gospel message and accepted Jesus Christ to be our Lord and Savior. We wanted you to know because we consider you to be our closest friends. It's so exciting! Have you two ever heard the Gospel message before?"

Before Chuck could finish His last sentence, Gary said, "Oh my gosh, Chuck, that's great, Ann-Marie and I are Christians! We're so happy for you! That's wonderful! Praise God!" Gary and Ann-Marie were smiling from ear to ear as their eyes filled with tears of joy. As Gary and Ann-Marie moved toward Chuck and Sue to hug them. Chuck took a step back just before Gary reached him with a confused look on his face. Sue did the same thing with Ann-Marie. You could have heard a pin drop. Chuck and Sue looked at one another in disbelief. Then Chuck dropped the "bomb" on them. Chuck said, "Gary, let me get this right. You and Ann-Marie have been Christians this whole time our families became best friends and did virtually everything together, including vacations, and you and Ann-Marie were willing to let us go to hell by not sharing the Good News with us?"

Silence.

"We need to go. Goodbye."

Gary and Ann-Marie were mortified and speechless. While both had been in Christian ministry for years, they said that the first day of their ministry began that night!

Demonstration of the Gospel will never eliminate the need to share the Gospel. Gary and Ann-Marie had masterfully demonstrated the Gospel to their friends but never got around to sharing it. Chuck and Sue just thought they were a "really nice" family. If the truth be known, their story is no different than many of ours who are loving our neighbors as ourselves but not enough to share the one thing that has the power to rescue them from eternal damnation. Thus, it begs the question. If we're unwilling to do this, how much do we really love those around us?

If we want to expand God's kingdom and glory like never before, we must "show" and "tell" like never before. Imagine the transformation that would take place from our house to the White House if every Christian would "show *and* tell" those they come in contact with from their house to the White House. We'd be one nation under God comprised of states that are under God, consisting of cities that are under God, consisting of communities that are under God, consisting of churches that are under God, made up of families that are under God! In other words, one nation under God would be our reality instead of something you hear every election cycle. So what are we waiting for?

The next big lie that Satan has gotten many in the church to believe to demolish the foundations of our lives and every institution in America we comprise from our house to the White House is that the Great Commission is more important than the Great Commandment. How could I say anything is more important than the Great Commission after spending all that previous time on the importance of proclaiming the Gospel in our last "big lie?" You're about to find out!

The Great Commandment is to love the Lord our God with all of our heart, soul, mind, and strength (Mark 12:30; Matthew 22:37). Think about the compounding effect of what I just said in light of the previous "big lie." Satan has not only been successful in keeping most Christians from doing what Jesus commissioned us to do (the Great Commission), but he has been successful in getting us to elevate it above what he commanded us to do (the Great Commandment).

I like what this pastor and author says on subject (*italics* used for emphasis):

> There are a lot of churches that focus on the Great Commission more than the Great Commandment. And I'm all for the Great Commission, but I'm more concerned about the Great Commandment. Here's my logic: If you take care of the Great Commandment, then the

Great Commission will take care of itself. How? Well, you can't love God with all your heart, soul, mind, and strength and not be sold out to the mission He's called you to. But if your missional without the relational component, it won't sustain itself. I'm concerned that some of us are more missional than relational and it actually short circuits what God wants to do *in us* and *through us*. Why? Precisely because we're more focused on what God wants to do *through us* than *in us*. It's the difference between ministering *for* and ministering *to* the Lord.[182]

Love it! Our love for Christ, in response to His love for us, provides the necessary "fuel" for us to express that love to others through the Great Commission. Without this, it is only a matter of time before fulfilling the Great Commission becomes a burden instead of a blessing. If you're already there, your turn-a-round is here!

Love rescued us from *love* so that we would be able to *love*.[183] What? The sacrificial *love* of God, demonstrated through Jesus's death on the cross *rescued us* from the *love* of self so that we would be able to *love* others the way God intended.[184] In other words, "We love because He first loved us" (1 John 4:19).

Thus, when it comes to the Great Commandment and the Great Commission, the two are very much related. The divine order should never be ignored. But here's the catch—it really doesn't begin with either one. What? That's right. We must have a "Great Exchange" with Jesus if we ever expect to be able to fulfill the Great Commandment and the Great Commission. In other words, until we have a Great Exchange with Jesus that causes gratitude and thanksgiving for what He's done to flow from us to others, we'll never be able to love Him (the Great Commandment) and others (the Great Commission) the way He intended. This is one of the main reasons why Jesus wants us to seek His kingdom first (Matthew 6:33).

Wouldn't it be great to live your Christian life "wanting to" share your faith instead of feeling like you "have to" share your faith?

Loving out of duty is very different than loving out of devotion, wouldn't you agree? Those of you who have been married for any length of time know the difference. So does God. He wants us to love Him and others out of devotion, not duty. Having a Great Exchange with Him every day makes this possible. When we are truly grateful to God for what He has done for us, it is only natural to want to extend this love to Him (The Great Commandment) and others (The Great Commission).

The key to everything in the Christian life is the cross of Jesus Christ. The greatest demonstration of love that the world has ever known occurred at the cross. The penalty for all of our sins (past, present, and future) was paid-in-full at the cross, making a relationship with God that was previously impossible, possible. At the cross, Jesus defeated death, hell, and the grave. At the cross, we were given, through our union with Christ, all power over all the power of the devil (Luke 10:19 ESV) to reclaim territory in the earth from Satan for God's glory (chapter 1).

When you and I begin to realize how much we are loved, how much Christ has given us, and how valuable and precious we are to the plans and purposes of God, we will not be able to contain the gratitude and thanksgiving we have in our hearts to our Lord and others. Some of the greatest exchanges I have with Jesus is when I very simply and quietly tell Him that I can't believe He loves me. The Holy Spirit living on the inside of me confirms the reality of this truth. When this happens, all I can do is praise Him! Thus, the Great Exchange I just experienced with Jesus causes me to love God back (the Great Commandment) and be motivated to love others by sharing the Gospel with them (the Great Commission). However, again, none of this would be possible without the cross of Jesus Christ. If you take nothing else from this book but what I just said, your life will never be the same!

Mary understood this truth; Martha didn't. Mary wanted to "be" with Christ out of devotion. Martha wanted to "do" for Christ out of duty. Mary had a Great Exchange with Jesus, Martha, "distracted with much serving" (Luke 10:40 NKJV), didn't. Mary had chosen the better part (Luke 10:42 CEB). Who do you more closely resemble?

Each of us needs to have a Great Exchange with Jesus every day if we want to fulfill the Great Commandment and the Great Commission. When Jesus tells us to come to Him all who are weary so that He can give us rest (Matthew 11:28), He is inviting us to have a Great Exchange with Him. When we do this, we will not only find rest because His yoke is easy and His burden is light (Matthew 11:30), but we will find that the Great Commandment and the Great Commission are now something we want to do. In His presence, obedience is no longer a burden but a blessing. What used to be "heavy" is now light.

Do you have "friends" who only call you or come around when they want something? We all do. Do you, in turn, have "friends" who only hear from you when you want something? If we were honest, some of us would also admit that this is also true. Sadly, too many of our relationships with Jesus are like this. Jesus only hears from us when we want something. These are not great exchanges. I repeat, these are not great exchanges! God knows the difference. Do we?

A Great Exchange with Jesus also involves telling Him, even when it costs us things like relationships, favor, fame, position, or promotions, that we are going to allow His Word to have the final word in our situations. Satan has deceived too many of us in believing that we have our daily "Great Exchange" with Jesus when Jesus knows we have no intention of allowing His Word to have the final word in our lives. These are what the Bible calls, "Great Exchanges" at the wrong table—the table of demons (1 Corinthians 10:21). Thus, it is critical for each of us to understand that it is impossible to have a Great Exchange with Jesus until His Word can have the final word in every area of life!

The consequences of believing this lie that the Great Commission is greater than the Great Commandment should be evident if it wasn't before. We cease to advance God's kingdom and glory with our lives due to "burn out" because no Great Exchange is fueling the Great Commandment and, therefore, the Great Commission. We're back to being transformed by the world because there's no power flowing out of the church to transform the world.

On the other hand, can you imagine the impact we would have in our homes, churches, cities, and nation if the 80 percent of Americans who profess to be believers were having a daily Great Exchange with Jesus that was fueling the Great Commandment, which was, in turn, fueling the Great Commission? Me too!

The next big lie that Satan has gotten many in the church to believe to destroy the foundations of our lives and every institution in America we comprise from our house to the White House is that Christians are "sinners" saved by grace, not "saints" who still sin. This is a really "good" lie because it's partially true. However, many of us have forgotten that a partial truth is a total lie! Yes, we have been gloriously saved by grace through faith, but we are no longer "sinners" contrary to what Satan would love us to believe.

Contrary to popular belief, there are only two groups of people in the New Testament—"sinners" and "saints." The two terms are never used interchangeably *by God* (whose opinion is the only one that counts, remember?) and are total opposites.

Sinners are the unredeemed who have not accepted Jesus Christ's sacrifice on the cross for their sins and, therefore, do not have their names written in the Lamb's Book of Life (Revelation 13:8). Saints, on the other hand, are the redeemed who have accepted Jesus Christ's sacrifice on the cross for their sins and do have their names written in the Lamb's Book of Life. Sinners who don't accept Christ's sacrifice for their sin will be separated from Him in hell forever (Matthew 13:42; Luke 13:28). Saints will be with Him forever in heaven though they still sin here on earth (Matthew 25:46). Sinners need to repent unto salvation. Saints have already repented (Luke 15:7). Saints practice holiness; sinners do not. Sinners are comfortable with sin. Saints are grieved by sin. Saints have a fundamental understanding that their life is not their own and that it was bought with a price (1 Corinthians 6:19–20). Sinners have a fundamental understanding that their life is their own, and then they die. Saints have resurrection power living on the inside of them (Romans 8:11); sinners do not.

Saints are not forsaken but preserved forever. The seed of sinners, however, shall be cut off (Psalm 37:28).

"Sanctification," or the process from which we get the word "saint," means to be set apart for God, not sinless perfection.[185] In scripture, saints are called, among other names, the elect (1 Peter 1:1), faithful brothers (Colossians 1:2), beloved (John 2:7), new creations (2 Corinthians. 5:17), children of God (John 3:2), royal priesthood (1 Peter 2:9), believers (1 Corinthians 14:22), the godly (Psalm 4:3), friends of God (John 15:15), disciples, and Christians (Act. 11:26). Sinners, on the other hand, are called wicked (Psalm 10:4), unholy (1 Timothy 1:9), infidels (1 Timothy 5:8), unrighteous (1 Corinthians 6:9), and "spiritually dead" (Ephesians 2:1). Quite a contrast, wouldn't you agree? Terms Christians like to use, such as "carnal Christian" or "super Saint," are all man-made labels to categorize Christians according to their maturity level, but they do not exist anywhere in scripture.

I have found that many Christians have great difficulty with the term "saint" because we confuse the world's definition of a "saint" with God's definition of a saint. The "world" typically defines a saint as someone who is admired or respected because of their exemplary virtues or character. We say things like, "Wow, that person is such a saint!" However, when the word *saint* is used in scripture, it means one thing and one thing only—what each of us have done with the finished works of Jesus Christ on the cross for our sins. That's it! A "saint" in the world is a title that is *earned*. A "saint" in the Bible is a title that is *given* to those who repent and accept Christ's sacrifice on the cross as payment for their sin. To "smuggle" anything else into God's plan of salvation in an effort to earn the title of "saint" disqualifies us from being a true biblical "saint." Not the case, however, when it comes to the world's definition of a "saint." The more "good" you do, the more "saintly" you are.

I can hear some of you saying, "Wait a minute, what about Paul, who in 1 Timothy, referred to himself as "The Chief Sinner" (1 Timothy 1:15). How do you reconcile this statement with what you are saying?"

So glad you asked. While there are few exceptions, the over-whelming majority of Bible scholars agree that this verse, when taken in full context, was Paul referring to his life before conversion. As you recall, before conversion, he killed Christians. And if he believed we were all a bunch of "sinners" after conversion, then why did he begin every epistle with "Paul, an apostle of Jesus Christ, by the will of God to the *saints* of..." Incidentally, what kind of impact for Christ do you think Paul would have had in those same churches if he began every epistle with "Paul, an apostle of Jesus Christ, by the will of God to the *sinners* of (fill in the blank)?"

Words have power, beloved—the power to define us. Many of us know this to be true and have spent years allowing others to define us instead of God. I, like many of you, had to remind my children when they were growing up that "because God had already defined them, no one else could define them—not friends, peers, teachers, social media, Hollywood, pop-culture, or even their parents!" The same is true of us saints. In Christ, we have been redefined. We are no longer sinners but saints. It's about time we start seeing ourselves the way God sees us. While we will never be sinless, the same res-urrection power that rose Jesus from the grave lives on the inside of every believer (Ephesians 1:19–29; Romans 8:11) and gives us the ability to sin less! This is not true of an unredeemed sinner. Let the redeemed of the Lord say so (Psalm 107:2)! Yes, saints, by God's grace, we are very different than the sinners we used to be!

Secular psychologists confirm that people behave on what they and others believe about them. Sadly, this is also true inside the church. Studies show that when people think they're "losers," they generally respond as "losers," even when they "win." However, when they believe they are "winners," they usually respond as "winners," even when they "lose." Many believers act the same way. While few of us have difficulty understanding that we will be "winners" in eter-nity, few of us understand (by Satan's design) that God sees us as "winners," not "sinners" in the here and now. God is waiting for us to "live up" to who God says we are, not "live down" to who we, Satan, or others say we are.

This reminds me of a story about a young girl who kept slouching at the British Royal feast table. Her mother kept saying, "Girl, sit up." The girl sat up, but within seconds, she began to slouch again. Again, her mother said, "Did you hear me? I said sit up. You're slouching!" The girl momentarily snapped to attention in her chair, but not less than a minute later, she began to slouch again. Finally, her mother had enough of her slouching. She said, "Girl, I said sit up! Don't you know who you are? You are the daughter of a queen! It's time you started acting like it!"

Jesus is asking us the very same question. Don't you know who you are? Do you not know that you are the son (or daughter) of the King? It's time for some of us to "sit up" and start acting like it! I guarantee we would "sit up" a lot more and give ourselves license to slouch down into sin a lot less if we would remember who we are!

My children attended a K-8 school whose sports teams were known as the "Saints." If they were playing the Cavaliers, for example, it was the Saints versus the Cavaliers. Can you imagine what it would have been like for my children if their team was known as the "Sinners" instead of the Saints? Would you want your child attending a school where the students are known as the "Sinners?" Why not? That's what many of you call yourselves at church and in your Christian circles. Well, if you're like me, it's because you don't want your son or daughter to identify themselves with that name, and you probably don't want other people calling your son or daughter a "sinner" either, even though they still "sin," right? You and I should feel the same way about ourselves. Did you ever stop to consider that God the Father could feel the same way about us as we feel about our children when they (our children) or others refer to our children as "sinners?"

Just imagine overhearing the following conversation from two dads one Saturday morning at the local hardware superstore. Each of them have seventh-grade sons who play basketball at two different schools but in the same league as the Saints.

"Hey Mike," says Terry, "who does your son play this afternoon in basketball?"

Mike, whose son plays for the Eagles, tells Terry, whose son plays for the Hawks, "We play the "Sinners" at 2:00 (chuckle)."

At 2:00 p.m., you go to watch your son's game against the Eagles, and from the bleachers on the home side, everyone is screaming, "Go, Sinners, go! You can do it."

From the bleachers on the visitor's side, fans are screaming, "Fly, Eagles, fly."

Which team do you wish your son was on in that instant? Which team do you think is more likely to view themselves, win or lose, as a "winner?" Which team do you think has a greater desire to pursue excellence? Which team do you think feels more valued by their coaching staff and school faculty? Which team do you think feels more honored to represent their school?

It must sadden Christ to see Christians not accepting their new identity and even defending their right to continue to call themselves a sinner when Jesus saved us for so much more! When the believer falls down, he is like a dancer who falls down against his nature to dance. He is *not* like a dancer who falls down against his nature to fall.

To continue to view ourselves as a sinner (post-conversion) is to tell Jesus that His sacrifice on the cross for our sins was not sufficient for us to become a new creation where the old has passed away and the new has come (2 Corinthians 5:17). While Satan loves it when he can convince us that we're no different than we used to be, it's one big lie!

I grew up near the Severn River, which is a tributary of the Chesapeake Bay in Maryland. On unusually cold winters, "The Severn" (as we affectionately call it) would sometimes freeze over and allow for some amazing sleigh-riding and ice-skating. I was around twelve years old when the Severn froze over this particular winter. I couldn't wait to get out on the ice with my friend Michael to "test" it out. We knew we had no business being on the ice yet because it wasn't thick enough, but we didn't care.

Typically, five inches of thickness or more was all you needed for ice-skating to ensure safety. We were looking at about one three inches, depending on the spot. It was at this moment that I said, "Hey, Mike, let's come back another day. It doesn't look safe."

He said, "Okay."

Yeah, right! Are you kidding me? No, what I really said was something more intelligent like, "Hey, Mike, let's see who can walk across the most ice without falling in."

I knew he would accept the challenge. It was one of the reasons I liked hanging out with him. He was as daring and foolish as me. Each of us began inching our way out onto different sections of the ice, trying not to get too close to each other where the weight would be too great in one spot to support us. After a successful few minutes, we starting getting bored. Mike started walking toward me, saying "No worries, dude, it's good."

Then I heard it. When Mike got within three steps of me, I heard a loud crack in the ice, then another, and then many more in rapid succession. I shouted at Mike to back up and put some distance between us. He thought it was funny and kept walking toward me. Needless to say, he was the only one laughing at this point. His next step would cause the ice to quickly give way around me.

Down I went into the frigid Severn waters that quickly engulfed every inch of my flesh. I was breathless, in over my head, and about fifty yards from shore with nothing but ice and Mike between me and the shore. Fortunately, for both of us, Mike had not fallen through the ice. About twenty pounds lighter than me, he was able to approach me on a thicker section of ice and pull me out. I'm convinced to this day that he saved my life. That's the good news.

The bad news was that we were still a long walk up a steep hill to get home. With numbness in all my extremities, it wasn't but a few seconds before my feelings of joy and gratitude toward Mike would be overcome by fear, anxiety, anger, and hopelessness as my body began to "shut down." Mike told me to lean on him, and he would help me get up the hill. After what felt like an eternity, I eventually made it home to a warm house and did not sustain any injuries beyond some bumps, bruises, and minor frostbite. However, this day would forever be etched into my mind. Little did I know what a great illustration it would provide decades later for what I am attempting to communicate to you now. God truly doesn't waste anything!

You see, this story reminds me of so many Christians who still think of themselves as "sinners." No sooner do we get rescued by Christ from "death" after conversion do we begin exchanging our gratitude to Christ for fear, anxiety, anger, hopelessness, and other sins that leave us feeling "numb," "cold," and distant from God.

Make no mistake. What I have just described is by design, Satan's design, to keep us from ever realizing who we are and what we've been given in Christ. His greatest fear is that we will one day "wake up" and begin acting on our true identity and reclaiming territory he has stolen from us (chapter 1)!

With this in mind, let's examine how Satan gets Christians to accept the "sinner" label so we can demolish this lie once and for all!

The first way Satan gets us to accept the "sinner" label is through guilt. Many Christians are happy to keep their pre-conversion "sinner" label because, quite frankly, it's hard to feel like a saint when you're still sinning. Having the "sinner label" conveniently lessens the guilt many of us carry due to an ongoing, unrepentant, sinful lifestyle. You see, if we Christians are nothing but a bunch of sinners at the end of the day, then what's the big deal with getting drunk on occasion, spending beyond our means, hiding money from our spouses, nursing an eating addiction, flirting with someone at the office, or looking at a little porn now and then, especially when every other "sinner" in the church is doing the same thing, right? Sadly, this is the very mindset and attitude that keeps so many of us in bondage to sin, grieving the heart of God. Satan knows this. Do we?

Satan wants us to name ourselves based on our "sin" versus who God says we are, regardless of our sin. Don't get me wrong. Obedience and holy living are critically important to our success as a kingdom builder, but they do not define us. We are sons and daughters of the King, whether we're slouching in our chairs or not, remember?

Let me free all of us up right now! Did you know that the most Godly man or woman in the world has further to go than they have already gone? In mathematical terms, this means that the most Godly man or woman in the world you know is not even 50 percent sanctified. That's right. You know what this means? It means that being a "saint," from God's perspective, must not be dependent on reaching a certain level of sanctification. While this certainly isn't a license to sin so that grace may abound (Romans 6:1), it does suggest that our identity must rest on a righteousness that is not of our own! And it is. His name is Jesus Christ! God's Word says, "For He made Him, who knew no sin to be sin for us; that we might become the righteousness of God in Him" (2 Corinthians 5:21 KJV 2000).

You and I were not "sinners" before we accepted what Christ did for us on the cross because we sinned; we were sinners because we were born "sinners." Similarly, we did not become saints by behaving "saintly," we became "saints" because we were "reborn" that way. Got it?

> For as by one man's disobedience many were
> made sinners, so by the obedience of one shall
> many be made righteous. (Romans 5:19 KJV)

Satan has also gotten many believers to keep their pre-conversion "sinner" label by convincing them that it is a mark of humility to do so. Many Christians believe that calling themselves a "saint" sounds "prideful," but calling themselves a "sinner" displays humility. So instead of calling themselves what God calls them, they commit heresy and idolatry. What? You see, for us to see ourselves as a "sinner" after salvation is to say that Jesus's blood wasn't sufficient to redeem us from the penalty of our sins. Without realizing it, we can make God out to be a liar, declaring that we, better than He, know who we are! Please tell me where the humility is in that? It sounds like the work of the devil to me to keep us in chains so we will continue building his kingdom!

It has been my experience that much of our false humility around this big lie is rooted in biblical ignorance and pride. Many Christians genuinely believe that they are still "sinners" after conversion because they believe that this is actually what the Bible teaches! Others believe that they are still sinners because it's what their pastors or other "mature" believers "humbly" proclaim.

Beloved, it is absolute humility to say about yourself what God has said about you. Why? Because you didn't do it to you. You and I are royal priesthood (1 Peter 2:9) because He said so, not because we said so!

Finally, by Satan's design, I believe many Christians continue to see themselves as sinners so they don't have to raise the standard of holiness in their own lives. It's simply way too much work and, frankly, no fun! Why pursue excellence and train in righteousness (2 Timothy 3:16) to jump over a "high bar" and possibly hit it when we can just step over the same bar at ground level and act like we did something great? We're back to "cheap grace" whose standard is no higher than the culture's standard.

Believing the lie that Christians are still sinners has resulted in a light attitude toward sin in the modern church. Take a look at what this author said:

> According to the modern-day church's Gospel, the only difference between a sinner in the church and a sinner in the world is that the sinner in the church may not sin as much, their sin may be more secretive, and they may feel guilty after they sin. The sinner of the world looks at this and says there is no real difference. The only difference they see is that the sinner in church doesn't have as much fun as they do.[186]

Another author made this observation:

> If we think of ourselves as only "sinners" then our sins are seen as something ordinary and inevitable. They are just the result of who we are. Sure, we wish we didn't do it, but that's just what sinners do. If we instead view ourselves as saints, then we will begin to see our 'sin' in a whole new light. If we really are 'holy ones' then whatever sins we commit are a deeper, more profound, and

more serious departure from God's calling then we ever realized. Our sin, in a sense, is more heinous because it is being done by those who have new natures and a new identity.

And it is this "cognitive dissonance" between our identities as saints and our sinful actions that leads us to repentance. We repent because these sins are not ordinary and expected. They are fundamentally contrary to who God has made us to be. It is this tension between our identities and our actions that is lost when we cease to think of ourselves as saints.

In the end, I am not suggesting that Christians can never refer to themselves with the word "sinner." If rightly understood, this can be fine. But we should also be keen to think of ourselves as saints. After all, when Christ returns that is what we will be. In glory, there will be no sinners. Only saints.[187]

By Satan's design, when we view ourselves as "sinners saved by grace" versus "saints who still sin," we accept limitations that God never designed us to take. This reminds me of how a young elephant is trained to be a circus elephant.

Before an elephant can be used in the circus, its mind has to be programmed to accept a limitation. When the elephant is young, the elephant trainer begins this process by securing one end of a thick heavy chain to a hook that is deeply embedded into the top of a large cement block that gets buried deep in the ground. The other end of the chain is attached to one of the front ankles of the elephant. The weight of the cement block is typically two to three times that of the elephant.

When the young elephant begins walking away from the cement block in any direction, it is only a matter of time before the elephant feels a "tug" on his ankle toward the direction of the hook. At first, the young elephant fights against the annoying tug of the chain until eventually, the elephant realizes it's useless and quits trying. This is the day every circus elephant trainer anxiously awaits—the day his "new recruit" accepts his limitation. The elephant trainer can now swap the thick heavy chain on the elephant's ankle for a thin piece of rope that only needs to be tied to a peg, like those you see in the circus. While the strong elephant could easily break this rope with minimal effort if it tried, he's already been programmed to accept this limitation for the rest of its life! Yes, a lifetime of bondage.

I wonder how many of us have been programmed by Satan to accept a lifetime of bondage because he has programmed us to accept the limitation that we'll never be anything more than a lowly sinner. It's time for some of us to break free in Christ from that silly little rope that Satan has had around our ankles.

Lest some of you think I am in some kind of denial, I absolutely understand, first hand, that there remains an intense struggle with the power of sin. I, like you, experience it every day. Our justification has resulted in a battle for our sanctification. In other words, peace with God has started a war! However, this does not change how God sees His children, regardless of how we may feel or behave on any given day as Paul expresses here in the following:

> You, however, are not in the flesh, but in the Spirit, if in fact the Spirit of God dwells in you. Anyone who does not have the Spirit of Christ, does not belong to Him. But if Christ is in you, although the body is dead because of sin, the Spirit is Life because of righteousness. (Romans 8:9–10 ESV)

Paul talked about the constant struggle between his new self and his old self. He spoke about the thorn in the flesh (2 Corinthians. 12:7), saying the things I don't want to do I do, and the things I do I don't want to do (Romans 7:15). Yes, we absolutely sin, but we don't allow our sin to define us. We allow Jesus and who He says we are to define us! It's time to stop being such an easy target for Satan! Many of us have given him way too much power. He's defeated, remember?

As my children were growing up, we, like most of you, watched different family movies together. While some were better than others, virtually all of them provided excellent opportunities to discuss the application of different biblical principles. My children loved these interruptions. Not!

While my family enjoyed many of the Disney classics together like many of yours, my all-time personal favorite was *The Lion King*. One particular scene stood out head and shoulders above the rest and will hopefully serve as a powerful illustration to deal a final "death blow" to the lie that Christians are sinners saved by grace versus saints who still sins.

To refresh your memory, or in the event you're unfamiliar with the story, Mufasa, the Lion King of Pride Rock, was just murdered by his jealous brother, Scar, who, in an attempt to secure Mufasa's royal throne, devised a plan to kill both Mufasa and Mufasa's son, Simba, the rightful heir to Mufasa's throne. Cleverly trapping Simba in a vast gorge, Scar signals his hyena minions—Shenzi, Banzai, and Ed—to trigger a massive wildebeest stampede. When Scar informs Mufasa that Simba is trapped in the gorge, Mufasa makes a desperate but successful rescue of Simba. Placing Simba in a safe location, Mufasa begins his exit climb out of the gorge, but not before the sides give way as he makes his way to the top of the canyon. Near the top, and in close proximity to his brother, Scar, Mufasa desperately pleads with Scar to pull him to safety. Scar sinks his claws into Mufasa's front paws, looks Mufasa squarely in the eyes, and with a most sinister voice declares, "Long…live…the King"[188] as he thrusts Mufasa from the edge of the cliff to his death by stampede below.

Instead of killing Simba right after Mufasa's death to avoid suspicion from the rest of the pride that Scar had orchestrated Mufasa's death and now Simba's death to secure Mufasa's throne for himself, Scar brilliantly and diabolically pins Mufasa's death on Simba. He then orders young naive Simba to run away and never come back. And this is exactly what Simba does. As Simba runs through the elephant graveyard, alone, scared, and overwhelmed at having just witnessed his father's death, Scar expects Simba to be eaten by a pack of ferocious hyenas. However, against all the odds, Simba makes it to the other side where he, over time, assumes his new "worry-free" identity with his new friends, Timon and Pumbaa, captured in a song called *Hakuna Matata*.

Meanwhile, Simba is maturing into the adult lion. From heir to the king, and rightful owner to his father Mufasa's throne to a life of ease, pleasure, and predictability, Simba is content to never become what he was created to be. Even when his friend, Nala (a lioness), joyfully reunites with him later in a desperate attempt to have him return to Pride Rock to claim his throne in a land now plagued with famine under Scar's reign and rulership, Nala quickly notices how different Simba has become. She says, "You're not the Simba I remember."[189]

Simba replies, "You're right. Now are you satisfied?"[190]

She says, "No, just disappointed."[191]

It's not until Rafiki, a wise mandrill, shows up and tells Simba that his father is still alive do things start to change for Simba. Simba, who can't believe that his father is still alive, is speechless. Rafiki says, "Come, I show you"[192] and takes off quickly through the jungle. Simba frantically follows after Rafiki until Rafiki abruptly tells him to stop. Rafiki then motions for Simba to stoop down and look into a still pool of water. Simba, discouraged, doesn't see anything but his own reflection. Rafiki touches the water and tells Simba to look again.

This time, Simba miraculously sees his reflection slowly morph into that of his father. Rafiki tells Simba, "You see…he [your father] lives in you."[193] Then comes the most powerful verbal exchange in the entire movie, capturing the essence of what I have been trying to communicate to you. Mufasa (in Simba's vision) says, "Simba, you have forgotten me."[194]

Simba says, "No, how could I?"[195]

Mufasa replies, "You have forgotten who you are and so have forgotten me. Look inside yourself, Simba. You are more than what you've become. You must take your place in the circle of life."[196]

Simba says, "How can I go back? I'm not what I used to be?"[197]

Then comes the most powerful line in the whole movie. Mufasa says, "Remember who you are. You are my son and the one true king. Remember who you are. Remember. Remember. Remember…"[198]

Sadly, many of us, like Simba, have forgotten who we are and, in doing so, have forgotten Jesus, the one true King. Many of us are more than what we've become. Instead of taking our rightful places as heirs of the King in every institution in America from our house to the White House, we, like Simba, have allowed ourselves to get comfortable in a "foreign" land that is not our home! We have not only forgotten who we are and forgotten Him, but we've forgotten why we're here. It's time to take our place in the kingdom of God and stop allowing our "sin" to define us and start allowing God to define us as the kings and priests He says we are as seen here in the following (*italics* used for emphasis):

> To Him who loved and washed us from our sins in His own blood, and has made us *kings and priests* to His God and Father, to Him be glory and dominion forever and ever. Amen. (Revelation 1:6)

So the next time you're tempted to believe you're nothing but a lowly sinner saved by grace, remember, what we do doesn't determine who we are; who we are determines what we do![199] Remember who you are. Remember. Remember. Remember…[200]

The next big lie that Satan has gotten many in the church to believe to destroy the foundations of our lives and every institution in America we comprise from our house to the White House is that Jesus Christ will never leave or forsake anyone. I don't know about you, but I have never been to a funeral where the deceased wasn't in heaven; have you? Is this because everyone's going to heaven or because someone lied on God? In the land of make-believe, where God doesn't leave or forsake anyone and man gets to make all the rules, everyone gets to go to heaven. The famous "religious" argument goes like this: "Why would a loving God forsake anyone?"

First, allow me to provide some brief background. The words *leave* or *forsake* in Greek and Hebrew mean to reject, desert, abandon, disown, discard, renounce, give up, or to cast aside (*Strong's Greek and Hebrew Lexicon*).

As just discussed, from God's perspective, all of us are either "saints" or "sinners." We've either accepted Christ's sacrifice on the cross for our sins or we haven't. Those who haven't, "sinners," live separate lives from God because they have rejected the only way by which the penalty of their sins may be satisfied; that is, by accepting Jesus Christ as their personal sin-bearer on the cross. The Bible says that Jesus is the "bridge" between sinful man and a sinless God who enables those who put their faith and trust in Jesus for the forgiveness of their "sins" to "crossover" from spiritual death to spiritual life into a relationship with God. Without putting our faith in what Christ did for us on the cross, the Bible says there is no way to bridge this gap and, thus, no way to get to God. Though many falsely believe they can get to God by "crossing over" on their "good works," their parent's faith, or their choir or church attendance, the Bible declares that we are "saved" not by works of righteousness but by Christ's mercy through the washing of "rebirth" and renewal by the Holy Spirit (Titus 3:5).

Jesus told Nicodemus that "unless one is born again, He cannot see the Kingdom of God" (John 3:3 NASB). Jesus goes on to explain that which is born of the flesh is flesh, but that which is born of the Spirit is spirit (John 3:6 KJV). Paul explains that all of us have sinned and fallen short of the glory of God (Romans 10:13), and only those who confess with their mouth the Lord Jesus and believe that God raised Him from the dead will be saved (Romans 10:9).

Paul also says in the book of Romans that whosoever calls upon the name of the Lord will be saved (Romans 10:13; Acts 2:21). Thus, being "born-again" or "saved" involves a declaration by the unbeliever that they believe that Jesus Christ paid the penalty for their sins when He became their sin-bearer on the cross. However, when we refuse to do this and reject the free gift of salvation made available to us through Christ, it is we who forsake Him. And if we forsake Him, God's Word says that He will, in turn, forsake us, contrary to the opposing views of many Christians in America. Don't believe me? See it for yourself.

In Luke 12, as Jesus observed the huge crowds waiting to hear Him, He warned His disciples about hypocrisy. After He told them to beware of the "yeast" (hypocrisy) of the Pharisees (Luke 12:1) and not to be afraid of those who can merely kill the body but to fear God who can kill the body and the soul (Luke 12:4–5), He says the following to them (*italics* used for emphasis):

> And I tell you, whoever declares openly and confesses that He is My worshipper and acknowledges Me before men, the Son of Man also will declare and confess and acknowledge Him before the angels of God.
> *But He who disowns and denies and rejects and refuses to acknowledge Me before men, will be disowned and denied and rejected and refused acknowledgment in the presence of the angels of God.* (Luke 12:8–9 AMPC)

This teaching is so central to the Christian faith that when Paul leaves Timothy with instructions that He wants Timothy to pass on to other trustworthy people who will, in turn, pass them on to others, Paul similarly says the following (*italics* used for emphasis):

> If we die with Him, we will also live with Him. If we endure hardship, we will reign with Him. *If we deny Him, He will deny us.* (2 Timothy 2:11–12 NLT)

While Paul was desperate for Jews and Gentiles alike to know God's grace and mercy, He was equally emphatic about them understanding the consequences of rejecting Christ.

God's Word says that He is longsuffering toward us, not willing that any should perish but that all should come to repentance (2 Peter 3:9). However, while God will not force us to come to Him His way, neither will He spare us of the consequences in this life and the next if we don't (Matthew 13:40–42).

While the description of hell involving the weeping, wailing, and the gnashing of teeth and a fire that cannot be quenched (Matthew 13:42) is certainly real, I do not believe this will be the worst part of hell. I believe true "hell" will be having to live with the moment by moment reminder for all eternity that the opportunity we once had to have our sins forgiven through Christ is no longer available to us and we will now live forever separated from God with this realization.

God's Word says that unbelievers will not only be rejected in all eternity for rejecting Christ in the here and now, but they will also be "abandoned" by God to their evil desires in the here and now as seen in Romans 1. Here, Paul is writing to Jewish and Gentile believers in Rome (Romans 1:7 ESV) so that they would not be ignorant regarding God's wrath on the unrighteous ("unbelievers") this side of eternity. Beginning in verse 18, He says, "The wrath of God is revealed from heaven against all ungodliness and unrighteousness of men, who hold the truth in unrighteousness; because that which may be known to God is manifest in them; for God hath showed it unto them" (Romans 1:18–19 KJV). They knew God, Paul said, but they wouldn't worship Him as God or even give Him thanks (Romans 1:21 NLT). Note what Paul says next here in the following (*italics* used for emphasis):

> And they began to think up foolish ideas about what God was like. As a result, their minds became dark and confused. Claiming to be wise, they instead became utter fools. And instead of worshipping the glorious, ever-living God, *they worshipped idols* made to look like real people and birds and animals and reptiles.
>
> *So God abandoned them* to do whatever shameful things their hearts desired. As a result, they did vile and degrading things with each other's bodies. They traded the truth about God for

a lie. So they worshipped and served the things God created instead of the Creator himself, who is to be praised forever. Amen.

That is why God abandoned them to their shameful desires. Even the women turned against the natural way to have sex and instead indulged in sex with each other. And the men, instead of having normal sexual relationships with women, burned with lust for each other. Men did shameful things with other men and, as a result, suffered within themselves the penalty they so richly deserved.

When they refused to acknowledge God, *He abandoned them to their evil minds and let them do things that should never be done.* Their lives became full of every kind of wickedness, sin, greed, hate, envy, murder, fighting, deception, malicious behavior, and gossip. (Romans 1:21–29 NLT)

Another group of individuals who will also be forsaken by God despite what many Christians believe are known as "apostates." As surely as apostates were a part of the church during Jesus's day, they exist today and thus, are worthy of some time and attention.

The word *apostate*, from the Greek, *apostasia*, means "a falling away" (*Strong's Greek and Hebrew Lexicon*) or to renounce or disassociate one's self from a particular religion or set of religious beliefs.[201] Apostasy is the abandonment or defiance of what was previously held to be true and practiced, rebelling against those same beliefs and practices.[202]

Apostates and "backsliders" are terms that are sometimes used interchangeably in Christian circles but are very different! *Backsliders*, a term that appears nowhere in scripture, commonly refers to those who have made a true "inward" profession of faith in Jesus Christ in their hearts but who are not "outwardly" living it. Apostates, on the other hand, are those who have made an "outward" profession of faith through adherence to a set of rituals and religious practices but who have never made an "inward" profession of faith in their hearts, and thus, "fall away." "Backsliders" are concerned about the "inside of the cup" and the "outside of the cup" before "backsliding," while apostates are never concerned with the "inside of the cup" (Matthew 23:26). Apostates are "wolves in sheep's clothing" who follow Christ for what they can gain. "Backsliders," on the other hand, are legitimate members of the flock who follow Christ but are drawn away by their own lust and are enticed (James 1:14 KJV). "Backsliders" sometimes return to the "fold" after "backsliding" while apostates never return to the "fold" after apostatizing.

Many Bible scholars consider Judas Iscariot, one of Jesus's apostles, to have been an apostate, for he knew, believed, and walked with Jesus "outwardly," but he never knew, believed, and walked with Jesus "inwardly;" otherwise, he would have never betrayed Jesus.

Other examples of apostasy that you can read about in the Bible, according to various theologians, include Amaziah (2 Chronicles 25:14,27); Hymeneus and Alexander (1 Timothy 1:19–20); Demas (2 Timothy 4:10); and many Old Testament Kings such as Saul (1 Samuel 15:11); Jeroboam (1 Kings 12:28–32); Ahab (1 King 16:30–33); Ahaziah (1 Kings 22:51–53); and Manasseh (2 Chronicles 33:1–9).

A brief look at King Saul, the first King of Israel, will allow us to see some additional characteristics of an apostate. In 1 Samuel 15, the Lord, through the prophet Samuel, told King Saul that He wanted to deal, once and for all, with the nation of Amalek for opposing Israel during their exodus from Egypt. King Saul received instructions from the Lord, through Samuel, to "go and completely destroy the entire Amalekite nation—men, women, children, babies, cattle, sheep, camels, and donkeys" (1 Samuel 15:3 NLT). In disobedience to God's instructions, King Saul not only spared Agag, the Amalekite king's life, but he kept the best sheep and cattle, among choice calves and lambs, as plunder from the war to be used for a sacrificial offering. As a result of King Saul's disobedience, the Lord told Samuel that He [the Lord] was sorry that He [the Lord] ever made Saul king for he [Saul] had not been loyal to the Lord and had again refused to obey the Lord (1 Samuel 15:10–11).

As you just read, this was not the first time that King Saul disobeyed the Lord's instructions through Samuel. The first time was back in 1 Samuel 13 when Samuel instructed King Saul to wait for him (Samuel) at Gilgal seven days before advancing on the Philistines. When Samuel did not appear on the seventh day, King Saul, watching his men begin to scatter, fearfully and impatiently took matters into his own hands and sacrificed the burnt offering that was supposed to have been done in Samuel's presence, only to be rebuked by Samuel when he arrived shortly thereafter.

As a result of King Saul's two acts of disobedience, Samuel tells King Saul in 1 Samuel 15 that because He [Saul] has rejected the word of the Lord, God has rejected him from being king (1 Samuel 15:23). Just a few verses later in 1 Samuel 16, after the Lord instructs Samuel to find a new king from among the sons of Jesse, Samuel privately anoints David as the new king. Note the very next verse (*italics* used for emphasis):

> *Now the Spirit of the Lord had left Saul,* and
> *the Lord* sent a tormenting spirit that filled Him
> with depression and fear. (1 Samuel 16:14 NLT)

Note, it wasn't the devil who did this, it was God—hardly the picture of a loving God who never forsakes anyone, wouldn't you agree?

The pinnacle of King Saul's apostasy, however, occurred when he did what he forbade others to do. Because God would no longer speak with him, Saul traveled to Ednor in 1 Samuel 28 to consult with a "witch" who had access to a "familiar spirit." Saul asked her to summon Samuel, who had since died, from the dead. The surprise appearance of Samuel from the dead was not the result of the woman's power but God's way of pronouncing His final judgment on this apostate.

The final chapter of 1 Samuel captures the sad and tragic ending of King Saul's life who, after being wounded by an arrow in a battle with the Philistines, committed suicide by falling on his sword out of fear he would be captured and abused by the Philistines.

While Judas and King Saul may be extreme cases of apostasy to some of you, a common thread that runs through every apostate then and now is the rapid deterioration of the life of an apostate once they "fall away."

Paul said this about apostasy in 1 Timothy 4:

> Now the Spirit expressly says that in latter times some will depart from the faith, giving heed to deceiving spirits and doctrines of demons, speaking lies in hypocrisy, having their own conscience seared with a hot iron. (1 Timothy 4:1–2 NKJV)

Jude, brother of Jesus and James, also warned of the realities and consequences of apostasy here in the following (*italics* used for emphasis):

> Dear friends, although I have been eager to write to you about our common salvation, I now feel compelled instead to write to encourage you to contend earnestly for the faith that was once for all entrusted to the saints. *For certain men have secretly slipped in among you—men who were long ago marked out for the condemnation I am about to describe—ungodly men who have turned the grace of our God into a license for evil and who deny our only Master and Lord, Jesus Christ.*
>
> Now I desire to remind you (even though you have been fully informed of these facts once for all) that Jesus, having saved the people out of the land of Egypt, *later destroyed those who did not believe.* You also know that the angels who did not keep within their proper domain, but abandoned their own place of residence, He has kept

in eternal chains in utter darkness, locked up for the judgment of the great Day. (Jude 3–7 NET)

In the first passage below, known as the "Judgment of Pretenders" in Matthew 7, Jesus pronounces His judgment on apostates, then again through the Apostle John in Revelation 21 (*italics* used for emphasis):

> Not everyone who says to me, "Lord, Lord," will enter into the kingdom of heaven—only the one who does the will of my Father in heaven. On that day many will say unto me, "Lord, Lord didn't we prophesy in your name, and in your name cast our demons and do many wonderful deeds?" Then I will declare to them, "I never knew you. Go away from me you lawbreakers!" (Matthew 7:21–13 NET)

> But cowards *who turn away from me*, and unbelievers, and the corrupt, and murderers, and the immoral, and those who practice witchcraft, and idol worshipers, and all liars—*their doom is in the lake that burns with fire and sulfur.* This is the second death." (Revelation 21:8 NLT)

If you, as a Christian, still have difficulty believing that God would leave or forsake anyone, allow me to bring it a little closer to home. Let's assume you have a son for a moment and that he's your only son. Imagine how you would feel if the Surgeon General of the United States contacted you and told you that your son had a rare gene-type and that if you would be willing to sacrifice his life for cancer research, his death would guarantee a cancer-free world! Against every natural desire you have, you finally agree to sacrifice him.

Now, imagine how you would feel if, after your son died, the medical community and the world rejected him and the cure he provided to rid the world of cancer. Tell me, would you want to have a relationship with those who rejected your son? Now maybe you and I can begin to understand how God feels when we openly reject what He made possible through the death of His Son, Jesus, so we could be "cured" from the "cancer" of "sin" that dwells in our hearts! You see, to reject God's Son, Jesus, is to reject God the Father, which is why, in the end, those who do not accept Jesus as the cure to their "sin problem" will be rejected by God for all eternity. You see, beloved, the reason why God's Word declares that today is the day of salvation (2 Corinthians 6:2) is that one day we will all be out of tomorrows on this side of eternity.

Maybe after reading this, you're not sure if you've ever dealt with your "sin problem" by turning from it (i.e., repenting) and accepting what Christ did for you on the cross as the only acceptable cure. If you feel the Holy Spirit "tugging" on your heart right now, I would encourage you to accept Christ as the only acceptable form of payment for your sin problem! I know I gave you an opportunity earlier, but if you're like me, you needed several!

Please don't wait any longer. If you just did this, let me be the first to congratulate you! Not only are you now "cancer-free" before God the Father because you accepted the cure He provided through Christ the Son on the cross, but you just entered into a loving relationship with the one who made you! Oh, and if that wasn't enough, you also just became an heir to a retirement plan that's out of this world! I couldn't be happier for you on every front! Welcome to the family!

Finally, we get to the only group of people that Jesus promises never to leave or forsake as seen here in the following:

> For the Lord will not reject *His people*; He
> will never forsake *His inheritance*. (Psalm 94:14
> NIV)

While God loves everyone, His promise to never leave or forsake anyone only belongs to those who have put their faith and trust in Jesus Christ for the forgiveness of their sins. This includes all the Old Testament saints who believed that Jesus was their Messiah and

King as well as every New Testament believer. I also recognize that it may now even include some of you!

The promise that God will never leave nor forsake "believers" appears, among other places, in Genesis 28:15; Deuteronomy 31:6–8; 1 Chronicles 28:20; Haggai 1:13; Joshua 1:5; Isaiah 41:10, 57:17; Psalm 9:10, 37:25, 28; John 14:18; 2 Corinthians 4:9; and Hebrews 13:5.

But what about "backsliders" or "prodigals"? Will God leave or forsake them? Though I briefly touched on "backsliders" earlier when discussing apostates, let's examine God's Word to see what the future holds for them, especially since Satan has created much confusion in the Christian "ranks" over this issue.

While there are enormous consequences to those who stop "walking" with Christ (i.e., "backsliders" or prodigals) to pursue lifestyles of "sin" as we saw with King David, Samson, the prodigal son, and Peter, none of them were in jeopardy of being eternally forsaken by God. Why? Because none of them apostatized. In other words, each of them was a true believer. Even Peter who, out of fear, denied Christ "outwardly" three times, never "inwardly" denied Him, declaring that Jesus was the Christ, the Son of the living God (Mark 8:29). In other words, his conversion was real.

What is in jeopardy, however, for the "backslider" or prodigal, which can "feel" the same as being forsaken by God (as David felt in Psalm 22:1) is fellowship with God (John 1:3). When the prodigal son "left" his father to pursue his own self-centered life, fellowship with his father was broken. However, what is critical to see is that it was he (the prodigal son) who caused the separation to occur. It wasn't until he was willing to come home and restore what had been "broken" with his father did fellowship with his father return. Said another way, when any true believer feels "far away" from God, it's not because God moved!

The Apostle John had this to say about fellowship with God when we, His children, walk in darkness (*italics* used for emphasis):

> This then is the message that we have heard
> of Him, and declare unto you, that God is light,

and in Him is no darkness at all. *If we say that we have fellowship with Him, and walk in darkness, we lie, and do not the truth:*

But if we walk in the light as He is in the light, we have fellowship one with another and the blood of Jesus Christ His Son cleanseth us from all sin.

If we say that we have no sin, we deceive ourselves, and the truth is not in us. If we confess our sins, He is faithful and just to forgive us our sins, and to cleanse us from all unrighteousness. (1 John 1:5–9 KJV)

"Believers" don't confess their sin (post-conversion) to ensure eternal life; we confess our sin (post-conversion) so we can enjoy fellowship (i.e., closeness and intimacy) with God. Said another way, our relationship with God is secure, but our ongoing fellowship with Him (and others for that matter) is dependent upon confessing our sin (i.e., owning it) and repenting of our sin (i.e., turning away from it and turning back toward God).

As believers, God gives us the freedom to obey Him and enjoy the blessings of fellowship with Him or the freedom to disobey Him and reap the consequences of "disfellowship" with Him. As many of us know, the longer we wait to confess our sins, the farther we get from "home" and the farther we get from home, the harder it is to find our way back (i.e., repent).

While some, like the prodigal son, are fortunate enough to find their way "home," other "backsliders" do not, though their belief in Christ remains intact. Our heavenly Father longs for the day when all of His children will return to Him so that He and we can experience the wonderful benefits of fellowship and intimacy once again.

Nevertheless, God's elect will never be forsaken by Him. I love what the late Billy Graham had to say on the subject:

One reason God will never forsake us [believers] is because His Son was forsaken in our place. All our sins were placed on Him. He became guilty in God's eyes for every sin ever committed. God made Him who had no sin to be sin for us (2 Corinthians 5:21). In that moment, Jesus fell under the judgment of God—because of our sins on His shoulder. [203]

One of the most comforting and familiar verses in all of scripture for every believer is the following taken from Romans 8 to drive home further this point that true believers will never be forsaken:

> For I am persuaded, that neither death, nor life, nor angels, nor principalities, nor powers, nor things present, nor things to come, nor height, nor depth, nor any other creature, shall be able to separate us from the love of God, which is in Christ Jesus our Lord. (Romans 8:38–39 KJV)

Okay, but what about nations? In other words, does God leave or forsake nations? More specifically, has God "left" or forsaken this nation? Before we look at this most pressing question, let's first consider how God treated the nation of Israel, His covenant people, in the Old Testament in light of what we've already discussed.

Recall, under the Mosaic Covenant, God promised to "bless" His covenant people, the nation of Israel, if they (Israel) remained faithful to Him. While their eternal future was secure based upon their belief in Jesus Christ as their coming Messiah and King, their present-day "blessings" in the Old Testament were tied to their present-day obedience in the Old Testament.

In the Book of Deuteronomy, written by Moses around BC 1406, the Israelites have just endured forty years of wandering in the wilderness after leaving Egypt under Pharaoh. They are on the east side of the Jordan River in view of Canaan, the Promised Land. Moses is preparing the sons and daughters of this faithless generation to possess the land. In the first nearly four chapters of Deuteronomy (1:1–4:43), Moses reviews the mighty acts God has performed for the nation of Israel. In the next several chapters (4:44–29:1), he reviews the law and renews God's contract with the nation of Israel (the Mosaic Covenant) for the new generation about to enter the Promised Land. Moses reviews the Ten Commandments, the Great Commandment, laws for proper worship, laws for ruling the nation, laws for human relationships, and the consequences of obedience and disobedience. He then calls the people to commit in his third and final address (29:2–30:20) before passing the leadership "baton" on to Joshua who will lead the nation of Israel into the Promised Land after Moses' death (31:1–34:12).

In Deuteronomy 28:1–14, Moses tells the nation of Israel that if they fully obey the Lord, God will exalt them above all the nations of the world (v. 1). They will be blessed in their towns and country (v. 3); they will be blessed with many children and productive fields (v. 4). They will be blessed wherever they go, both in coming and going (v. 6). The Lord will conquer their enemies when they attack them (v. 7). The Lord will send rain at the proper time from His rich treasure in the heavens to bless all the work they do. Moses tells them they will lend to many nations, but they will never need to borrow from them (v. 11).

Moses further tells them that the Lord will make them the head and not the tail, and they will always have the upper hand (v. 13). Then, after warning them not to turn away from any of the commands He is giving them, including following after other gods and worshipping them (v. 14), Moses tells them what the consequences will be if they do here in the following:

> But if you will not obey the voice of the Lord your God or be careful to do all His commandments and His statutes that I command you today, then all these curses shall come upon you and overtake you. Cursed shall you be in the city, and cursed shall you be in the field. Cursed shall be your basket and kneading bowl. Cursed shall be the fruit of your womb and the fruit of your ground, the increase of your herds and the

young of your flock. Cursed shall you be when you come in, and cursed shall you be when you go out. *The Lord will send on you curses, confusion, and frustration in all that you undertake to do, until you are destroyed and perish quickly on account of the evil of your deeds, because you have forsaken me.* (Deuteronomy 28:15–20 ESV)

There it is. God, in essence, says, "You, Israel, my covenant people, will experience all of these 'curses' from me in the here and now *because you have forsaken me.*" Said another way, "While I will not eternally forsake you, Israel (Psalm 94:14), because of the unconditional covenant I made with your father Abraham (the Abrahamic Covenant), there will be severe consequences in the here and now if you forsake me."

In the very next book of the Bible, Joshua, chapter 24, Joshua gathers all the tribes of Israel to Shechem. He reminds them how far God has brought them from the days of Abraham's father beyond the Euphrates to Abraham through all the land of Canaan, from Isaac to Jacob, whose children went down to Egypt. He reminds them of how God, through Moses, brought them out of Egypt and how God destroyed the Egyptians at the Red Sea. Joshua reminds the Israelites how they took possession of the Amorite land, how they were victorious at Jericho, and how God had given them a land on which they had not labored and cities that they had not built where they now dwell (Joshua 24:13). He then charges them, in verse 14, to fear the Lord and serve Him in sincerity and faithfulness by putting away the gods that their fathers served beyond the Euphrates River and in Egypt in order to serve the Lord. After the people recite all the great things the Lord has done that Joshua brings to account, God's covenant people declare, "Far be it from us that we should forsake the Lord to serve other gods" (Joshua 24:16 ESV). Before Joshua renews the covenant with them and puts in place statutes and rules for them at Shechem, he gives them the following warning in verse 20:

> If you forsake the Lord and serve foreign
> gods, then He [the Lord] will turn and do you
> harm and consume you, after having done you
> good. (Joshua 24:20 ESV)

After settling in Canaan, you may recall that Israel fails to clear some of the enemy from the land. Instead of enjoying their new found freedom and prosperity in the Promised Land, the Israelites, through a government leadership vacuum brought about through the death of Joshua and the elders, abandoned God and engaged in intermarriage and idolatry. Every time the nation of Israel found itself in captivity due to their sin and disobedience, God, in the book of Judges, would raise up a judge to deliver them when they cried out for help.

In Judges 10, we get to the newly instituted judge, Jair, who is the second judge after Gideon in Israel's fourth period of oppression and deliverance among six that last approximately 325 years. Beginning in verse six, the Israelites again did what was evil in the Lord's sight, committing idolatry with various gods and abandoning God, refusing to serve Him at all (Judges 10:6). In response, the Lord hands them over to their enemies, the Philistines and the Ammonites, who oppress the Israelites for the next eighteen years.

In Judges 10:10, the Israelites finally cry out, saying, "We have sinned against you because we have forsaken our God and have served the Baals" (Judges 10:10 ESV). Note the Lord's response (*italics* used for emphasis):

> And the Lord said to the people of Israel,
> "Did I not save you from the Egyptians and
> from the Amorites, from the Ammonites, and
> from the Philistines? The Sidonians also, and the
> Amalekites and the Maonites oppressed you, and
> you cried out to me, and I saved you out of their
> hand. *Yet, you have forsaken me, you have served
> other gods, therefore I will deliver you no more. Go
> and cry out to the gods you have chosen. Let them*

deliver you in the time of your distress." (Judges 10:11–14 ESV)

Note, every time God accuses the nation of Israel of forsaking Him, whether it comes through Moses in the book of Deuteronomy, Joshua in the book of Joshua, or the prophet Samuel in the book of Judges, it's always in response to Israel's refusal to acknowledge God and put away their idols.

We see the same thing here in Psalm 81 (*italics* used for emphasis):

> Hear me, *my people*, and I will warn you—if you would only listen to me, Israel! *You shall have no foreign god among you; you shall not worship any god other than me.* I am the Lord your God, who brought you up out of Egypt. Open wide your mouth and I will fill it. *But my people would not listen to me; Israel would not submit to me. So I gave them over to their stubborn hearts to follow their own devices.* If my people would only listen to me, if Israel would only follow my ways, how quickly I would subdue their enemies and turn my hand against their foes! Those who hate the Lord would cringe before Him, and their punishment would last forever. But you would be fed with the finest of wheat; with honey from the rock I would satisfy you. (Psalm 81:11–16 NIV)

In Hosea 4, the Lord accuses Israel of being unfaithful to Him, referring to Israel by the name of Ephraim saying, "Ephraim is joined to idols" (Hosea 4:17 ESV). The rest of this verse says, "[l]eave Him [Ephraim] alone" (Hosea 4:17 ESV).

Note again with Asaph (author of Psalm 81) and Hosea, the reoccurring sin that causes God to "give Israel over" to their enemies and stubborn hearts is idol worship. Are you starting to see a pattern here?

We are now almost prepared to answer the question I posed to you earlier, "Could God forsake America or, worse yet, has He?" I said we're almost prepared because it is also critical to remember that God, at no time in history, has ever made a covenant with the United States as He did with the nation of Israel. Recall from chapter 3, five of the eight major covenants that God established in the Bible were all made with the nation of Israel. The other three, as you may recall, were made with mankind of every nation.

While the New Covenant in Jesus Christ is the fulfillment of the Abrahamic and Mosaic Covenants to Jew and Gentile alike, a fundamental principle of the Mosaic Covenant that applies to every nation today, including the United States, is that obedience and disobedience will always have consequences. God's Word reinforces this in many New Testament scriptures like Galatians 6:8–9, which says, "For He who sows to His flesh will of the flesh reap corruption, but He who sows to the Spirit will of the Spirit reap everlasting life" (NKJV).

We are now ready to address this most serious and sobering question regarding America. Has God "left" or forsaken America? Consider this in light of what I've said up to this point. If God, through cycles of oppression and deliverance brought "cursing" instead of "blessing" on the nation of Israel under Moses, turned and harmed Israel under Joshua and gave Israel over to a stubborn heart in Judges when, in each of these three instances, Israel refused to acknowledge God, listen to Him, and put away their idols...how much more would God cause and allow to occur to a nation like the US in whom He has no covenant relationship with and who refuses, unlike Israel, to acknowledge God, listen to Him, and put away their idols? At least Israel understood that their greatest problem was spiritual and repented. Many of us in America, including many Christians, believe our greatest problem is the "other" political party, radicals from both sides of the political aisle, a two-tiered justice system, the deep state, or fake news and don't repent!

The wisest man who ever lived, King Solomon, tells us to "keep our hearts with all diligence, for out of it springs the issues of life" (Proverbs 4:23 NKJV). In other words, the deep state is corrupt because the hearts of those in the deep state are corrupt. Fake news is fake because the hearts of the journalists covering the fake news are "fake." And so on. You see, unlike so many of us in America from our house to the White House, the nation of Israel in Moses and Joshua's day understood that their greatest problem was not outside of them but inside of them (i.e., their hearts). We still don't get it. It's why we, in America, continue to fight spiritual problems (e.g., racial division, class warfare, and liberalism) with earthly weapons (i.e., focus groups, "expert panels," meetings, conferences, and leadership summits).

Maybe some of you have been wondering, "Can't we all just get along?"

Answer: We will never get along until we acknowledge that the greatest problem we have is in the walls of our chests—our lustful, deceitful, and self-centered hearts that want to act independently of God and His Word.

We caught a glimpse of the consequences of unbelief, rebellion, and idolatry in Romans 1 earlier. As previously mentioned, Paul is addressing Christians in Rome and believers everywhere regarding the sinful state of unbelievers in a gentile region that was plagued with idol worship, homosexuality, and violence, not unlike the United States. Rome was the capital of the Roman Empire, which had spread across most of Europe, North Africa, and the Near East.

In Paul's day, Rome was experiencing a golden age. The city was wealthy, literary, and artistic—a cultural center of sorts. However, it was also morally decadent. The worship of pagan gods and even some emperors stood in stark contrast to the followers of Christ who believed in only one God. Many argue, and I wouldn't disagree, that what was occurring in that region at the time is not much different than what's occurring in America today. I rewrote Paul's letter so you could see what it would look like if we substituted in our nation or Americans, where appropriate, every time Paul used the pronouns "they" or "them" (*italics* and brackets [] used for emphasis):

And [the US] began to think up foolish ideas about what God was like. As a result, the minds [of Americans] became dark and confused. Claiming to be wise, [Americans] instead became utter fools. And instead of worshipping the glorious, ever-living God, [America] *worshipped idols* [self-promotion, self-image, and self-gratification—fame, materialism, riches, pleasure, and power]…

So God abandoned [the U.S] to do whatever shameful things [its] heart desired. As a result, [Americans] did vile and degrading things with each other's bodies. [America] traded the truth about God for a lie. So [Americans] *worshipped and served the things God created instead of the Creator himself,* who is worthy of eternal praise! Amen.

That is why God abandoned [the US] to their shameful desires. Even the women turned against the natural way to have sex and instead indulged in sex with each other. And the men, instead of having normal sexual relationships with women, burned with lust for each other. Men did shameful things with other men, and as a result of this sin, they suffered within themselves the penalty they deserved.

Since [the US] thought it foolish to acknowledge God, *He abandoned [the US] to their foolish thinking [a reprobate mind (KJV)] and let them do things that should never be done.* Their lives became full of every kind of wickedness, sin, greed, hate, envy, murder, quarreling, deception, malicious behavior, and gossip." (Romans 1:21–29 NLT)

Now, make your own judgment based on what you've just read in light of the current culture as to whether or not you think God has abandoned this gentile nation that refuses to repent of its unbelief, rebellion, and idolatry. While none of us can pretend to know the heart of God, we can learn much about God's heart through the study of His Word. Let's go a little deeper.

In Acts 14, Paul, at Lystra, a city then located in what is now known as modern-day Turkey, a gentile nation, had just healed a man who had been crippled since birth, when Paul, who was preaching the Gospel, observed that the man had faith to be healed. The crowds attributed the miraculous healing to the gods "who have come to us in human form" (Acts 14:11 AMPC). When Paul and Barnabas learned that the people wanted to offer sacrifices unto them, they tore their clothing and inquired unto the men why they were doing this. Paul assured them that he and Barnabas were mere men just like them and that they were simply bringing the Gospel to them so they would turn away from these foolish and vain things to the living God (Acts 14:15).

Then we come to the applicable verse for our discussion where Paul tells the people that in generations past "God allowed *all the nations* to go their own ways" (Acts 14:16 NLT). Bible commentaries on Acts 14:16 contend that this reference to "the nations" refers to "heathen"[204] or "gentile"[205] nations, which brings me to my main point. If God allowed gentile nations in generations past "to go their own way" for worshipping other gods, it wouldn't be inconsistent with God's character to allow this gentile nation to go "its own way" for worshipping its many gods (e.g., wealth, power, status, physical beauty, self-image, self-promotion, self-gratification, fame, materialism, and athleticism), wouldn't you agree?

For those of you who may be wondering if I believe God has left or forsaken America, please allow me to share a few thoughts. Based on God's Word, I believe that we, in America, are living in a post-Christian era because we, as a nation, refuse to acknowledge Jesus Christ as the one true God, listen to Him (i.e., allow His Word to have the *final* word), and put away our idols. We are living in a day when the majority of Americans, including many who profess to be Christians, have made it abundantly clear that they do not want God in any institution from our house to the White House (e.g., gay marriage, LGBTQ-affirming congregations, tolerance above righteousness, prosperity theology, salvation without repentance, abortion, etc.). Instead of being one nation that worships the one true God, we are a nation, not unlike Old Testament Israel, that worships many gods. Thus, I believe it is we who have forsaken God. And because we have, God has given us over to our own devices and their consequences; hence, the spiritual crisis we're in today.

While America still leaves a little room on its shelves for a generic brand of God that is "light" on holiness and "heavy" on tolerance, the shelf-life of even this God will expire by the time the children of this generation reach adulthood if we don't "wake up" and repent! As I previously said, no one else has the power to correct spiritual problems but spiritual people!

Incidentally, did you know that the widespread acceptance and practice of homosexuality is one major sign that a nation is in rapid decline?[206] Don't believe me? Do your own research.

While the United States of America continues to be a model nation to the rest of the world when it comes to providing aid and assistance around the globe to alleviate human suffering, none of these "good works," while necessary, will save us from the consequences of our unbelief, rebellion, and idolatry. Never mind the fact as stated earlier that while we are alleviating human suffering around the world, we are simultaneously inflicting unfathomable human suffering to hundreds of thousands of unborn babies each year through abortion.

While some of you would prefer me to simply say what many say in pulpits all across America each week, which is, "Smile, God loves you and has a wonderful plan for your life," regardless of how we live, I'd prefer to ask a few questions. How has this 'sermon' been working out for us so far? How's it working out for the divorce rate inside the church? How's it working out for the 80 percent of our Christian youth who go off to college and never return to church?[207] How's it working out for the 95 percent of Christians who have never won a soul to Christ?[208] How's it working out for pastors who seek to unify with other pastors from other denominations but can't because more and more churches are more interested in being politically correct than biblically correct? Are we closer to God as a nation or further from God as a nation? Have these "ear-tickling" sermons made us more God-centered or more self-centered? Have these messages caused us to believe that we exist for God or that God exists for us? Has it gotten us, as a nation, to acknowledge God, listen to Him, and put away our idols?

You see, Jesus does love us and have a wonderful plan for our lives, brothers and sisters, but it's tied to the advancement of His kingdom and glory, not ours! He didn't die on the cross to give *us* a better kingdom; He died on the cross so we would forsake our kingdoms for His! That's His wonderful plan for our lives as I have tried to communicate throughout this book! Until we understand this, repent, and begin to walk in it in every institution from our house to the White House, I firmly believe God will continue to give this nation over to its own devices until the curses we have brought upon ourselves are unsustainable and we cease to exist as a nation!

Many of you already know that the United States of America is not specifically mentioned in end-times prophecy in the Bible. That means that God can "pull the plug" on us anytime He wants between now and the second coming of Christ, regardless of who wins the next election! God's Word makes it clear that no man knows the hour or the day of Jesus's return (Matthew 24:36). Thus, we do not know when we will cease to exist as a nation. However, we do know that it would not be the first time that a gentile nation, like America, ceased to exist in the here and now when that nation continued to do what was right in their own eyes (Judges 21:25).

Remember the Roman Empire we looked at earlier? While there were arguably many factors that contributed to the fall of the Western Roman Empire in 476 AD, it is an undisputed fact by most historians and theologians that one of the major reasons was due to great instability caused by the worship of many gods. While many in the Roman Empire worshiped one God under Roman Emperor Constantine, who was responsible for making Christianity legal in Rome in 313 AD, others worshipped gods that came to the region through social and economic instability created by the rise and fall of emperors and Germanic invasions. Do we, in America today, arrogantly believe we can similarly worship many "gods" and somehow escape similar consequences?

While I do believe God's passive wrath and judgment are being manifested in America at an accelerated rate at this time in history due to our increasing unwillingness to acknowledge God in every area of life, listen to Him, and put away our idols, I also believe God is exercising a level of sovereign restraint, mercy, and patience toward us so we will repent before it's too late. How do I know? Easy. We're still here!

Right now, our nation is in the midst of the Coronavirus pandemic. Currently, the total number of confirmed world cases and deaths are 2,394,278 and 164,938, respectively (at the time of writing).[209] The total number of confirmed US cases and deaths are 755,533 and 40,449, respectively (at the time of writing).[210] In just a few short weeks after the pandemic erupted, the Dow Jones Industrial Average was down approximately 10,000 points from record highs in the longest "bull market" in history (at the time of writing). Now consider this. If God is sovereign (and He is!) and nothing is allowed to happen unless He causes (or allows) it to happen, that means that God has either caused or allowed this pandemic to occur. Now if this is not God in His mercy trying to get our attention so we will "repent," I don't know what is!

Could it be possible that God has allowed us to continue to exist as a nation because God believes we will repent so He can use our vast wealth, might, resources, generosity, and compassion to build His kingdom worldwide before Jesus returns (chapter 1)? If you said "yes" like me, that means we believe *that God believes* our nation can still be used around the world for kingdom business! I don't know about you, but that makes me want to shout!

Okay, but maybe you're asking yourself, "How does believing the lie that God is not going to leave or forsake anyone, including our nation, cause us to destroy the foundations of our lives and every institution in America we comprise from our house to the White House?" The best way to answer this question is with another question. What incentive is there for any of us (unbeliever, believer, or "backslider") to repent and live a transformed life on this side of eternity if aiming for a higher standard (God's standard) doesn't matter? In other words, if the "big lie" says that no one (and no nation) is going to be forsaken or abandoned by God on this side of heaven or in eternity, why take "sin" seriously? Why not just do whatever feels good and makes us happy? Life is hard enough. Why should anyone deny themselves anything if God is not going to leave or forsake anyone in the end? Let's get drunk, do drugs, indulge in some porn, sleep around, mortgage our children's futures, live one life in public and another in private, commit fraud on the FISA Court, utilize an unsecured private e-mail server to store and transmit classified communications, and pursue wealth, fame, popularity, and self-gratification at all costs!

If we're going to reduce God to someone who won't leave, forsake, or bring "curses" upon any individual or nation, why not legalize gay marriage? Oh, we have!. Why not let women become pastors and elders in our churches (oh, we have!), especially since many Christian men are "following" their wives at home anyway? Why not organize a vote to legalize online gambling, marijuana, and prostitution to bring in more revenue for the state? Makes economic sense, right? Indulge in some porn. Have a cell phone, credit card, checking account, or secret "stash" of cash that your spouse doesn't know about. Have a fling or two. Teach your congregations that "bigger is better" and that repentance and self-denial are not necessary as a follower of Christ. After all, "God wants you to be happy."

If you're a politician, use race, class, warfare, and the Second Amendment to divide the nation. Build your kingdom first. "Sell your soul" if necessary. Be more loyal to your political party and the flag than to God, His Word, and the American people. It doesn't matter in the end, right? Apply one legal standard to one presidential candidate and Supreme Court nominee and another legal standard to "your people." Destroy someone else's reputation to enhance yours.

If God is not going to leave or forsake anyone and there are no spiritual consequences for unbelief, rebellion, idolatry, obstruction of justice, treason, or corruption in this life or the next, what's the harm in misusing your public office for political or economic gain? After all, God will forgive us, right?

In other words, if there are no consequences on this side of eternity or the next, let's get it on! While I am clearly not serious, I firmly believe it is this very thinking from the "pit of hell" that has led to the social, moral, and spiritual crisis we're facing from our house to the White House.

I trust you clearly and painfully see the "fallout" from believing this "big lie." If you, as an unbeliever, do not want God to forsake you in the here and now and for all eternity, you must receive Jesus Christ as your personal Lord and Savior now. I showed you how to do this earlier. Don't wait!

If we don't want God to continue to forsake us as a gentile nation and continue to give us over to a depraved mind to do things that should never be done, we'd better acknowledge God, listen to Him (i.e., allow His Word to have the final word), and put away our idols while we still have a nation.

Finally, if we as "believers" don't want to continue living in the environment of a curse like the Israelites did when they forsook God and His Word, we, His people of the New Covenant, better acknowledge God, listen to Him, and put away our idols!

The next big lie that Satan has gotten many in the church to believe to destroy the foundations of our lives and every institution in America we comprise from our house to the White House is that Christians should not be involved in politics. While Christians are called to be excellent in all things (2 Corinthians. 8:7), somehow many in the church believe that this doesn't apply to politics. Some Christians say, "It violates the separation between church and state." Others say, "It detracts from kingdom business." Yet, others say, "It's not a good use of time since God's is going to do what He wants to do anyway" or "It's unnecessary given the prophecy that things are going to get worse."

Then, there are the Christian masses that say, "It creates too much division in the church" or that "the church could lose its tax-exempt status." Lastly, some Christians say that Christians should not be involved in politics because "Jesus is the hope of the world, not the government." Let's take a closer look at each of these reasons so we can demolish this big lie once and for all while we still have a nation!

Many in the church believe Christians should not be involved in politics because "it violates the *separation between church and state*." Really? Really! Where's this in the Bible? It's not. Many Christians don't realize that the original intent of this phrase was to keep the government out of the affairs of the church, not the other way around! So how did everything get so scrambled up? Did you forget who our adversary is, Satan, the Great Deceiver (Revelation 12:9), a.k.a. the author of confusion (1 Corinthians 14:11)?

A brief history lesson will help. The phrase, "separation between church and state," first appeared on the scene shortly after Thomas Jefferson became President on March 4, 1801. The Danbury Baptist Association (DBA) of Danbury, Connecticut, was concerned with intrusion by the government on their free exercise of religion with a new duly elected presidential administration. The DBA penned their concern to Jefferson on October 7, 1801. On January 1, 1802, Jefferson, with the hope of alleviating their fears and concerns, offered them his comforting interpretation of the First Amendment of the Constitution in what is famously known as "Jefferson's Danbury Letter." In this letter, Jefferson reassured the DBA that they do not need to fear intrusion by the government on their free exercise of religion, declaring the following:

> I contemplate with sovereign reverence that act of the whole American people which declared that their legislature should "make no law respecting an establishment of religion or prohibiting the free exercise thereof," thus building a wall of *separation between Church and State*.[211]

There it is—the first use of the expression "separation between Church and State." It's not in the Constitution, contrary to what many believe, including many trial lawyers and judges! It's in Jefferson's Danbury Letter. Jefferson believed that the government was to be powerless to interfere with religious expression for one simple reason.

He had long witnessed the unhealthy tendency of government to infringe upon the people's free exercise of religion.[212] While I don't cover it here, Jefferson offered similar language in a letter to Noah Webster Jr. (hereafter referred to as "the Webster letter"), a lexicographer known as the "Father of American Scholarship and Education."

After Jefferson's Danbury letter and the Webster letter, there was no doubt where Jefferson stood on the issue as captured by this author in the following (*italics* used for emphasis):

> Jefferson believed that God, not government, was the Author and Source of our rights and that the government, therefore, was to be prevented from interference with those rights. Very simply, the "fence" of the Webster letter and the "wall" of the Danbury letter were *not to limit religious activities in public; rather they were to limit the power of the government to prohibit or interfere with those expressions.*[213]

Little did Jefferson know that nearly 145 years later, the true meaning and context of his phrase, "separation between church and state," would be tragically and forever altered following a 1947 US Supreme Court decision involving the landmark case, Everson versus Board of Education, also known as the New Jersey School Bus Case. In this case, humorously known as The Most Important Church-State Decision You Never Heard Of,"[214] the Plaintiff, Everson, asserted that taxpayer funded subsidies to pay for bus transportation for children attending Catholic school in his town violated the constitutional prohibition against state support of religion (i.e. the Establishment Clause of the First Amendment of the Constitution) as well as the Due Process Clause of the Constitution, which prohibits governmental deprivations of "life, liberty, or property, without due process of law."[215]

In his majority opinion, US Supreme Court Justice Hugo Black declared, "The First Amendment has erected *a wall between church and state.* That wall must be kept high and impregnable. We could not approve the slightest breach."[216] While the Supreme Court found that the New Jersey law was not in violation of the Establishment Clause breaching the "wall between church and state" since all school-aged children had the right to taxpayer-funded bus transportation regardless of the type of school they attend, it was, nonetheless, the first time the Establishment Clause was cited in a judicial opinion involving a case of this nature and, more importantly, the first time this language, "a wall between church and state," was wrongly associated with the Constitution.

Since future case law decisions are based on interpretation of the Constitution and precedent established by prior case law, this Supreme Court decision paved the way for individuals and liberal action groups from any state to misuse and misapply the Constitution to sue anyone who was merely enjoying their constitutional right to the free exercise of religious liberty in public, or in taxpayer-funded programs, organizations, and institutions without governmental interference. Yes, Jefferson was way ahead of his time. His battle has now become our battle!

Thus, from Jefferson's Danbury letter to the 1947 US Supreme Court decision in Everson v. Board of Education, the "separation between church and state" legal argument continues to be taken out of context and used, unconstitutionally, by liberal trial attorneys, judges, and courts all around our nation to rewrite the law. The result has been one devastating "blow" after another to Christians who have historically enjoyed the free exercise of religious freedom and liberty in public and in taxpayer-funded programs, organizations, and institutions.

Two of the more prominent organizations who have been successful in using their legal scare tactics involving unconstitutional "separation between church and state" lawsuits to suppress the free exercise of religion in public and in publicly funded programs, organizations, and institutions have been, as many of you know, the American Civil Liberties Union (ACLU) and Americans United for the Separation of Church and State.

One such Christian organization, however, who has not been afraid to "take them on" in defense of religious freedom and liberty in the public square is the American Center for Law and Justice (ACLJ). This outstanding Christian organization, who has had countless victories under the leadership of Chief Counsel Jay Sekulow, legal counsel to President Donald Trump, makes it their mission to advocate in the courts, in Congress, and in the public square for religious liberty, freedom, and democracy. Thank you for your outstanding work, ACLJ! Keep it up!

The "vacuum" created in our nation's law schools and courts through the retreat of Christians who wrongly believe that they should not be involved in politics because "it violates the *separation between church and state*" has now been filled by those who do not share our convictions or the convictions of our forefathers and framers of the Constitution. We are left with no one to blame but ourselves!

Our Christian forefathers believed it was necessary to involve themselves in politics and thank God they did, for it was their involvement in government and politics that gave rise to hospitals, civil liberties, the abolition of slavery, modern science, equal rights for women, regard for human life, a workable system of justice, education for common people, the free-enterprise system, and much, much more.[217]

Historically, Christians have understood the importance of staying involved in politics and government as captured here by Dr. Wayne Grudem in a Q&A video segment titled "Should Christians Be Involved in Politics and Government?":

> When Christians began to gain influence in the Roman Empire they brought about the passage of laws that prevented infanticide, child abandonment, and abortion in AD 374. In 1829 Christians brought about laws that prohibited the burning of Indian widows with their dead husbands. In England, William Wilburforce had a tremendous amount of influence on the British Empire that campaigned, argued, and debated for 40 years, but His efforts resulted in the out-

lawing of the slave trade and then slavery itself in
the British Empire in the early part of the 1800s.
Two-thirds of the abolitionists against slavery
were Christians who preached that slavery was
wrong from the pulpit and that the laws of the
nation needed to be changed because these laws
were contrary to God's moral laws found in scripture. Martin Luther King preached against racial
segregation and discrimination from the pulpit
and that laws needed to be changed.[218]

Do some of you still think Christians shouldn't be involved in
politics? Take a look at what this author had to say about the relationship between church and state:

> While the Gospel is essential for lasting
> change, God has also ordained that righteous
> laws protect our society. Thus, the relationship
> between church and state is not one of total sep-
> aration nor one of total identification. Rather
> it is education and confrontation. The Church
> must educate and confront the state on matters
> of morality and justice. In the Old Testament,
> the prophets called the kings to account on these
> matters. In the New Testament, John the Baptist
> and Jesus confronted the religious and political
> leaders. In Acts 24:25, the apostle Paul confronted
> Felix, the governor, concerning righteousness,
> self-control, and the judgment to come.[219]

Did John the Baptist, Jesus, and Paul somehow get it all wrong
too, saints? I think not. Long before we would ever have a nation
and a Constitution, they already understood it was the government's
responsibility to stay out of the affairs of the church but that it was
not the church's responsibility to stay out of the affairs of the government when it came to issues of morality and justice.

God's Word says that when there is moral rot within a nation, its government topples easily. But with wise and knowledgeable leaders, there is stability (Proverbs 28:2). Thus, as Christians, we have a moral responsibility to ensure that wise and knowledgeable leaders are leading this country. Maybe one of them needs to be you!

Another reason why Christians believe that they should not be involved in politics is that "it detracts from kingdom business." Since when is standing up for righteousness and justice against those who seek to perpetrate evil in our society not "kingdom business?" Like the Good Shepherd who not only loves and cares for His sheep but protects them from harm, the government's job is to do the same for its citizenry—physically, morally, and legally. And if this is not happening, it is every Christian's responsibility to make sure that it does, beginning at the ballot box.

It is both staggering and alarming to me how many Christians, when asked why they don't vote, simply say, in essence, "It's not kingdom business." In the 2012 reelection of Barack Obama, nearly 40 percent of all evangelical Christians stayed home.[220]

Equally troubling than the many Christians who don't vote are the number of Christians who vote for the candidate that exhibits fewer Christian values and ethics than their opponent because they either haven't adequately educated themselves on the candidate's voting record or are unable to accurately reconcile a particular candidate's voting record with the Word of God. To drive this point home even further, take a look at how "religious" people voted in the 2012 presidential reelection of Barack Obama against Mitt Romney (Romney):[221]

1. Evangelical and non-Evangelical Protestants: Obama, 42 percent; Romney, 57 percent
2. Catholics: Obama, 50 percent; Romney, 48 percent
3. Jewish: Obama, 69 percent; Romney, 30 percent
4. Other faiths: Obama, 74 percent; Romney, 23 percent
5. Religiously unaffiliated: Obama, 70 percent; Romney, 26 percent

Of the 117 million people who voted in the above election, about thirty million (or 26 percent) were white "born-again evangelicals."[222] Of this thirty million, approximately 6.4 million (or 21 percent) voted for Obama's reelection. While that's down from nearly 7.8 million votes they gave to Obama in his 2008 election win against John McCain, it is still an alarming number of Christians who voted twice for someone who became directly responsible (by way of Supreme Court appointments) for gay marriage becoming the law of the land, unconstitutional health care, more debt than all of other presidents combined before him,[223] and nearly 100 million Americans (approximately one-third of our population) on welfare programs not including Social Security, Medicare, or unemployment.[224]

In case some of you wish to take this as your golden opportunity to "label" me as a "right-wing racist" or "homophobe" because that is your standard response when you do not have any facts, you should know that I am not a fan of either political party. I vote along God's party line. As far as the "racist" part goes, good luck convincing all my African-American friends with that one! Lastly, on the "homophobe" front, while homosexuality is a sin (Leviticus 18:22), every person that has chosen this sinful lifestyle is equally valuable and precious to God and is in no less or greater need for a Savior than you and me!

There is also a fascinating, though not surprising, correlation between how "religious" people voted in the same 2012 election (above) and how often they attend religious services. Note the following "Presidential Vote by Religious Attendance" statistics:[225]

1. Religious attendance at least once a week: Obama: 39 percent; Romney: 59 percent
2. Religious attendance a few times per month or year: Obama: 55 percent; Romney: 43 percent
3. Never: Obama: 62 percent; Romney: 34 percent

Note, the less "religious" people attend their respective houses of worship, the less biblical values and principles they require of their president. Again, not surprising.

Can you imagine what impact we the church could have on laws of morality in our nation if even just 10 percent of all Christians in America (approximately twenty-four million people) would leave "party" politics behind and vote God's conscience? And yes, while the late former Arizona Senator John McCain was maybe not your top pick to run against Obama in the 2008 Presidential election, I am confident, for example, that the two liberal Supreme Court Justices that Obama appointed in May 2009 (Judge Sonia Sotomayor) and May 2010 (Solicitor General Elena Kagan) who were later confirmed by the Senate and voted with justices Kennedy, Ginsberg, and Breyer to make gay marriage the law of the land on June 26, 2015, in a 5–4 split decision, would not have been the same two Supreme Court Justices that former Senator McCain would have nominated given the same opportunity. Incidentally, I have a question for those Christians who stayed home in 2008 and 2012 because you didn't want to get involved in politics. How did that work out for God's people?

Since when is electing presidents who will appoint Supreme Court justices that uphold Christian values *not* kingdom business? Same question regarding the election of Senators who confirm these Supreme Court justices. Since when are moral issues like abortion, gay marriage, taxpayer-funded LGBTQ education, and building a "wall" on the southern border to reduce the flow of illegal immigration, drugs, disease, and terrorism across our borders, not political issues that require Christians to stand up and be counted at the ballot box and in the public square?

The third reason why many Christians believe the "big lie" that they should not be involved in politics is because they say, "It's unnecessary given the sovereignty of God." In other words, because "God sits on the throne, holds the world in His hands, and knows how things are going to play out from beginning to end," it is a total waste of time for Christians to get involved in the affairs of "man." Sounds very spiritual, doesn't it? Some even quote the following scripture in defense of this position:

> He changes times and seasons; He removes kings and sets up kings; He gives wisdom to the wise and knowledge to those who have under-standing. (Daniel 2:21 ESV)

It's true. So why should Christians bother with politics or with anything else, for that matter, in light of God's sovereignty? Because God created us to rule the earth under His hand within His sovereign boundaries to advance His kingdom agenda, remember (chapter 1)? Last time I looked, having dominion over all the earth (Genesis 1:26) included the realms of government and politics too, no?

We must not forget that though God is sovereign, He uses man to accomplish His will and purpose in the earth. This means that God is going to remove and raise up kings, in space and time, through us to fulfill His will in the earth.

When you and I choose to sit on the sidelines and not, for example, vote on kingdom matters, educate our congregations on kingdom business at the local, state, and national level, or peacefully confront immoral laws and legislation, we just made a choice! We chose not to rule our world well on God's behalf in these critical areas. We also chose to reap the grave consequences of our disobedi-ence. Welcome to America!

God's sovereignty has been the perfect excuse for many Christians to reject all things political, and thus, become part of the problem. You have heard the famous quote that says, "The only thing necessary for the triumph of evil is for good men to do nothing!"[226] Far too many Christians want to triumph over evil while they do nothing in the political realm to achieve it!

One author and speaker had this to say about political apathy:

> Benjamin Franklin and the other founding fathers understood the peril of apathy. If citizens don't get involved, elected representatives quickly

begin to express their own interests or the interest of those who are willing to pay them money
and attention. Apathy and greed soon give way to
corruption and injustice which give way to tyranny and misery.[227]

Does this not describe how many in Congress operate to a T or
what? Wow! If heaven and earth were witnessing against us today for
our involvement in kingdom matters in the political realm, would
there be enough evidence to convict us? Or would we be found innocent of all charges because we believed that the sovereignty of God
relieved us of our duty and responsibility?

The fourth reason why many Christians believe the "big lie"
that they should not be involved in politics is because they say, "It's
a total waste of time given the prophecy that things are just going to
get darker and darker anyway." In other words, "What good does it
do to polish brass on a sinking ship?"[228] Sounds pretty logical, doesn't
it? That is, until the cross-examination begins (Proverbs 18:17).

While it is clear from God's Word that things will get darker
around us in anticipation of Christ's return and the Great Tribulation,
this does not absolve us of our responsibility to be "salt" and "light"
in the midst of a crooked and perverse nation (Philippians 2:15) that
gets more crooked and perverse with each passing day. Is it possible
that one of the reasons why the world around us has gotten so dark is
because so many Christians have refused to be salt and light? Could
it also be that many Christians have counted the cost of true discipleship and decided it's way too expensive to represent Christ's interests
in government and politics?

Remember, we are in the middle of an angelic conflict. If you
and I think that what is going on in our nation politically and in our
three branches of government is limited to the physical realm (e.g.,
politics) and not tied to the spiritual realm, we have already lost the
battle, experientially, on this side of eternity. If there was ever a time
that God's people needed to "suit up" and "rise up" with good angels
and Jesus in every area of government and politics, it is now! Yes, it's
going to get darker and darker in fulfillment of end-times prophecy

in anticipation of Christ's return, but let it never be said of us that Satan was able to step on the neck of this nation and proclaim victory in our lifetimes because we who possessed the spiritual weapons to defeat him in every area of life, including politics, let him!

Also, don't forget, as previously discussed in chapter 1, that we are also currently involved in a "dress rehearsal" that doesn't get canceled just because the "weather forecast" isn't "good." Remember, God designed this dress rehearsal we're currently in called "life" to prepare each of us for the "greatest show on earth" that will occur during our Millennial Reign with Christ. As discussed in the opening chapter, our assignments in the Millennial Reign will be based on how well we rule and reign now, regardless of the "forecast." Believers who are faithful to do what God has called them to do in every area of life, including government and politics, will be made rulers over many things in their Millennial Reign with Christ (Matthew 25:21).

Now you hopefully understand why the "polishing brass on a sinking ship" analogy is flawed. It assumes every believer is "going down" for the last time and staying down. No friend. We will one day, at Christ's coming, be resurrected from the dead (1 Corinthians 15:52), then following a seven-year period known as the Great Tribulation (Daniel 7; Revelation 13), we will rule and reign with Christ for 1,000 years based on our faithfulness in the here and now (Revelation 20:4.).

The fifth reason why many in the church believe Satan's "big lie" that Christians should not be involved in politics is because "It causes too much church division." This "smells" a bit like our earlier "big lie," the church believes; that is, that unity is more important than theology. The faulty church assumption here is that if it creates division, it has to be "bad." Says who? Since when is confronting "evil" wrong even when it causes division? I guess Jesus was wrong then when He confronted Pontius Pilate, knowing it could create some division among His followers who would have preferred that He remain quiet under the threat of crucifixion? I don't think so!

As I said earlier, unity is only worth fighting for when we don't have to compromise truth, holiness, righteousness, and justice to achieve it. If given a choice, I would rather be in a church that is "divided" on the issue of Christian involvement in politics than be in a church that is united on the belief that Christians shouldn't be involved in politics! I believe every church leader will give an account for how they utilized the influence God gave them to educate and encourage their congregations to confront the evils (political and nonpolitical) of the day to the greatest extent possible, whether those "evils" be inside their house, their "sheep's" house, God's house, the courthouse, both houses of Congress, or the White House. If we are more concerned with the division we could create in our churches through our involvement in government and politics than we are confronting the evils of our day, we really need to ask ourselves whose kingdom we're building.

The sixth reason why many in the church believe Satan's "big lie" that Christians should not be involved in politics is because church leaders say, "It could jeopardize our nonprofit, tax-exempt status." Wow, I wouldn't recommend this excuse on Judgment Day, Pastor!

Many people don't realize it, but from the birth of this nation until 1954, churches and other nonprofit organizations routinely endorsed or opposed candidates for political office.[229] In 1954, the Internal Revenue Code, not the Constitution, was amended when Lyndon Baines Johnson ran for United States Senate. After winning his election, Johnson, in response to opposition from nonprofits and churches who opposed his candidacy, proposed retaliatory legislation to amend the Internal Revenue Code, prohibiting nonprofits and churches from endorsing or opposing political candidates. The 1954 *Johnson Amendment* violates every pastor's rights to free speech under the First Amendment. This is why from 1954 to present, not one church has lost its tax-exempt status for endorsing or opposing a political candidate[230] contrary to what anti-Christian liberal front groups would have us believe.

Many who claim that endorsing or opposing a political candidate in the pulpit is prohibited activity wrongly cite the church at Pierce Creek in Binghamton, New York (hereafter referred to as "Pierce Creek") to support their position. In this *one* case, the IRS, in response to Pierce Creek taking out full-page ads in the *USA Today* and *The Washington Times* to oppose then-Governor Bill Clinton for President in 1992, merely revoked the church's tax-exempt "letter" ruling, which churches, unlike other nonprofits, don't even need. This letter from the IRS only informs churches that they meet the requirements for tax-exempt status. Most churches don't even receive one because it is already understood that they are tax-exempt.

Yet, even with the Constitution and case law in their favor and an IRS that dares not "pull the trigger" at the end of the day for fear of lawsuits based on unconstitutionality, many pastors will still not support or oppose political candidates out of fear they could lose their tax-exempt status. Meanwhile, the devil continues to unravel our nation one immoral law and one unconstitutional judicial decision at a time. Fortunately, some Christian organizations refuse to be silenced and are "stepping up" to encourage pastors all across America to exercise their right to uncensored free speech under the First Amendment.

One such group is the Alliance Defending Freedom (ADF) who, through its annual Pulpit Freedom Sunday, which began on September 28, 2008, has encouraged pastors to preach publicly about candidates in a challenge that has yet to be answered by the IRS. Pastoral participation, which began in 2008 with thirty-one pastors, has increased to over 4,100 pastors in 2016 from all fifty states.[231] Clearly, a movement has begun. ADF Senior Legal Counsel Erik Stanley said the following (*italics* used for emphasis):

> ADF is not trying to get politics into the pulpit. Churches can decide for themselves that they either do or do not want their pastors to speak about electoral candidates. *The point of the Pulpit Initiative is very simple: the IRS should not be the one making the decision by threatening to revoke a church's tax-exempt status. We need to get the government out of the pulpit.*[232]

To be clear, pastors and churches may not only successfully express endorsement of (or opposition to) political candidates, but they may also host voter registration drives. Churches may also be host sites for balloting and conduct forums where candidates have the opportunity to address congregants or answer questions from a moderator. Additionally, churches may distribute voter guides that highlight candidates' views, as well as assist members with voter registration and voter education.[233] Currently, some churches schedule registration drives at least three consecutive Sundays leading up to the month before an election. The Southern Baptist Convention relies on written and spoken engagement on political issues at the national level to inspire action among believers.[234] The Ethics and Religious Liberty Commission of the Southern Baptist Convention regularly publishes dispatches about debates happening in the public square.[235] Way to lead! Keep it up!

Finally, let me say that for a church to not do what we have the Constitutional right and, more importantly, biblical responsibility to do out of fear of politicizing the pulpit or losing our tax-exempt status, whether these fears are real or unfounded, is not only shameful and cowardly, but it is exactly what Satan wants us to do! Every pastor in America, who has truly been called by God to the office of Pastor, has the responsibility to confront evil and educate their congregations on any and all political, moral, and ethical issues of the day that run contrary to the Word of God, regardless of the consequences. If you can't, then you're in the wrong profession!

And we wonder why the culture is transforming us instead of the other way around. It is partly because we, the church, in many cases, have allowed fear, greed, ignorance, and cowardice to "call the shots" and rule the day. So, Pastor, will you stand up for Christ and confront the political evils of our day that run contrary to the Word of God regardless of the consequences? Or will you continue to allow yourself to be unconstitutionally censored for a tax break? It's time for every one of you to "play the man!" Our nation needs you like never before!

The sixth reason why many in the church believe the big lie that Christians should not be involved in politics is because we have this "holier than thou" belief that we should only be known for what we are "for" and not for what we are "against." This supposedly makes us appear more "loving." Oh, so when Jesus told the moneychangers that He was "against" them turning the Father's house into a den of thieves and drove them out of the Temple, He was wrong? Was He wrong for rebuking His disciples on different occasions for being "against" their lack of faith, pride, and unbelief? There are countless other examples in God's Word.

The truth is, we should be known for both what we are "for" *and* what we are "against." The problem is when the world only knows what we are "against" and not what we are also "for." As parents, our children know what we are "for" and "against." In healthy marriages, husbands and wives know what their spouses are "for" and "against." Employees, through corporate policy, know what the employers are "for" and "against." Similarly, Washington should know what we are "for" and "against," and we should know what they are "for" and "against" so we can adequately confront evil and educate where necessary.

The last reason why many in the church believe Satan's "big lie" that Christians should not be involved in politics is because they say, "Jesus is the hope of the world, not the government." The late Chuck Colson, who founded Prison Fellowship Ministries and BreakPoint Ministries, said, "The hope that each of us has, is not in who governs us, what laws are passed, or what great things we do as a nation. Our hope is in the power of God working through the hearts of people, and that's where our hope is in this country; that's where our hope is in this life."[236] While I wholeheartedly agree that Jesus is the hope of the world, guess who he works through to secure that hope? Colson tells us, "[t]hrough the hearts of people." That would be us!

Still, some in the Christian community say, "Our mission lies not in changing the nation through political activism but in changing hearts through the hope of Christ." To this, I say, okay, but why does it have to be one or the other? Why can't it be both? In other words, why can't we stand up for righteousness and justice (two attributes of Christ's character) through political processes while we're changing hearts (including those of our elected officials) through the hope of Christ? "Because you can't legislate morality," some say. "Real change has to come from the heart."

To this, I say, you're right. Real biblical change has to come from a heart that has been radically transformed by the love of Christ. However, since when is defending moral laws that keep us from killing one another, killing babies, or "killing" the traditional family not a kingdom pursuit while we're waiting for real change to take place in the hearts of man who, once saved, will double that effort? And what about the many who have (and will) come to faith in Christ while pursuing these endeavors?

Did you know that the Rule of Law that this country was founded on and adheres to and that uncivilized nations reject was first put in place by elected officials (some of who were Christians) for this very purpose—to keep us from killing one another? And guess what? It works. While I would concede that it is not nearly as good as a changed heart, you have to admit that it's kind of hard to change the heart of someone who has been murdered! Did you know that nearly 100 percent of all reported crime is committed by approximately 15 percent of the population?[237] So while you can't legislate morality in a person's heart, the fear of going to jail has the uncanny ability of making people behave morally on the outside while the Holy Spirit is trying to get to them on the inside!

God places a high value on righteousness and justice. His Word says, "Whoever says to the guilty, 'You are innocent,' will be cursed by peoples and denounced by nations, but there will be delight for those who convict the guilty and a pleasing blessing will come upon them" (Proverbs 24:24–25 GW). Sounds like the Lord's work to me. It's one of the reasons why I became a rank and file FBI agent!

Can you imagine what mayhem we would have all across America and around the world if law enforcement officers and military personnel left their posts tonight because they no longer viewed righteousness, justice, and national defense as worthy pursuits? Incidentally, do you know how many people have found Christ in jail? Many, including Chuck Colson. Did you know that sometimes God allows some of us to get locked up so He can set us "free?" That's how Colson's Prison Fellowship Ministries got started, resulting in countless numbers of prisoners coming to faith in Jesus Christ!

Any successful person, if asked, will tell you that they found hope from someone influential in their life. It was someone who said something like, "I believe in you" or "You matter!" or "I see incredible potential and worth in you." or "God is really going to use you." For me, that was my mother. While she is no longer alive, God used her to give me a hope and a future (Jeremiah 29:13). I have tried to instill that same hope in my children and trust they will do the same with their children.

In the same way a parent can bring hope to a child, God can bring hope to a nation through those He utilizes in elected positions. Look how God used former presidents Abraham Lincoln and Ronald Reagan to bring hope to millions of Americans and the world that slavery and the Cold War, respectively, would end. So, yes, Jesus is the hope of the world, but He wants to express that hope, represent that hope, seize that hope, and secure that hope through us! If we expect to be able to do this, we must be involved in politics!

So for those of you who still think Christians shouldn't be involved in politics after all that, let me ask you something. While there are certainly exceptions, how has the overall lack of involvement in politics by *real* Christians been working out for us so far? From what I can tell, it has gotten us abortion, gay marriage, a national debt above $22 trillion,[238] over $124 trillion in unfunded liabilities,[239] deep state corruption, and liberal judges who continue to rule on cases that undermine Christian morality, decency, and family values. Is this really how God expected us to rule our world under His hand (chapter 1)?

Many would argue that the consequences of a lack of Christian involvement in politics have been even more severe in other nations. I wouldn't disagree. In the twentieth century, atheistic and secular humanistic leaders gained control of governments all across Europe, Asia, and Africa as a result of a lack of Christian involvement. What was the result? Take a look at the following:

According to historian R. J. Rummel,
"Almost 170 million men, women and children
have been shot, beaten, tortured, knifed, burned,

> starved, frozen, crushed, or worked to death; buried alive, drowned, hung, bombed, or killed in any other of the myriad ways governments have inflicted death on unarmed, helpless citizens and foreigners."[240]

God is not only looking for us to get involved in politics, but He joins us when we give Him the right to do so. There are some things God will not intervene on unless we ask Him to because He wants to know we want Him, need Him, and have expectations of Him. In other words, He has given us the right to leave Him out.[241] And this is, sadly, exactly what many of us have done because Satan has convinced us that we shouldn't be involved in politics.

I can still hear some of you saying, "Well, God doesn't want us spending our energy, time, or money in governmental affairs."

Really? Then why do so many Christians send their children to government-subsidized schools and participate in the government census? You may also want to look at your pay stub the next time you get paid and see how much of your energy, time, and money went to Medicare/Medicaid, Social Security, and the IRS for governmental affairs. Some say, "Well, paying my fair share of taxes to the government is very different than getting involved in politics."

Aren't you glad Moses, Daniel, Joseph, Nehemiah, Paul, and Jesus didn't take that position with the political establishment of their day? For in doing so, they turned the hearts of the people toward God. Each of them understood what was at stake. Do you?

Still some will say, "Yeah, but when believers think the growth and influence of Christ can somehow be allied with governmental policy, they corrupt the mission of the church."

Says who? It depends on what you believe the mission of the church is and to whom it extends. If you believe, like Jesus, that the mission of the church (us) is to make disciples who will, in turn, "go" and make more disciples to demonstrate the comprehensive rule of God in every area of life, then why should that work stop at the Beltway or in the hallway of Congress? Who knows? Our involvement might even "wake up" some of the Christians already there who forgot why they are there and whose kingdom they represent. You know, those of you whose greatest loyalty has not been to Jesus Christ and His Word but to your political party and political future!

We're supposed to be one nation under God, right? A nation founded on Judeo-Christian values whose Lord and Savior is Jesus Christ, the Lord of Judeo-Christian values, right? Well, it's time for some of you that are in politics to get under God (i.e., under what His Word has to say) or get out of Congress!

Can you imagine if we had the opportunity, as voters, to put the elected officials and judges in place to overturn Roe v. Wade but didn't because we didn't want to appear to be allied with the government and corrupt the mission of the church? Give me a break! And guess what? We have that opportunity under the current administration, and many of you know it! Did you know that if the average Christian in America would take politics as seriously as we do our family vacations and church attendance, we could overturn Roe v. Wade in one or two election cycles?

Christians used to ask me all the time, "How can you be a G-man and a Christian? I could never do that."

I would just smile and say, "It's easy. God is only interested in love and grace. He's no longer interested in justice and righteousness." I usually got a chuckle by those who got my point and a puzzled look by those who didn't.

While Christians should be involved in politics for all the reasons I have outlined above, let me be clear and say I do not believe we should be involved in partisan politics. It amazes me how many Christians are more loyal to their political party and their party's "word" than to God and His Word. Contrary to what many Christians believe, God is not a Republican or a Democrat. Though Jesus entered Jerusalem to shouts of "Hosanna in the highest!" (Mark 11:10) on a donkey to symbolize peace, ordinariness, and humility, Jesus doesn't ride on the back of donkeys or elephants! Thus, every Christian should be supporting candidates that best represent the Christian values and ethics of Jesus in the areas of morality, decency, health, public safety, national security, defense, and fiscal and personal responsibility. We should be supporting candidates that reflect love of God, love of others, truth, honor, honesty, holiness, righteousness, and justice while opposing those who don't, regardless of party affiliation.

While Christians should be involved in politics, we should definitely be wise in how we do it as captured in the following:

> We must not seek to legislate even biblical moral teachings where the value of that teaching will only be recognized by Christians—in other words we don't want to prosecute blasphemers or adulterers, even though such things violate God's laws. We should strive to legislate socially moral teachings whose meaning can be meaningfully argued for in a pluralistic society—laws against abortion, laws protecting women, the handicapped, and the elderly; laws against pornography and child abuse; can all be argued for on the grounds of broad social appeal, even for the non-Christian.[242]

As many of you know, the Bible has much to say about how Christians should relate to their government and elected officials as seen here in the following (*italics* used for emphasis):

> Let every person be subject to the governing authorities. For there is no authority except from God, and those that exist have been instituted by God. Therefore whoever resists the authorities resists what God has appointed, and those who resist will incur judgment. *For rulers are not a terror to good, but too bad.* Would you have no fear of the one who is in authority? Then do what is good, and you will receive His approval, *for He is God's servant for your good.* But if you do wrong, be afraid, for He does not bear the sword in vain. For He is the servant of God, an avenger

who carries out God's wrath on the wrongdoer. (Romans 13:1–4 ESV)

> For because of this you also pay taxes, for the authorities are ministers of God, attending to this very thing. Pay to all what is owed to them: taxes to whom taxes are owed, revenue to whom revenue is owed, respect to whom respect is owed, honor to whom honor is owed. (Romans 13:6–7 ESV)

Romans 13 is a treatise by Paul and the Apostles on the institution of model government. As we rightly divide the word of truth and take the above passage in its proper context, we will discover six truths:[243]

1. Government is ordained by God.
2. Government officials are to be *good* ministers who represent God.
3. We the people must obey good and godly laws.
4. Good government is not to be feared.
5. We are to pay honor and custom and constitutional taxes to whom it is due (i.e., render unto Caesar what is Caesar's; Matthew 22:21).
6. The government is to protect the righteous and punish the wicked.

We see a similar theme expressed in 1 Peter 2 (*italics* used for emphasis):

> Be subject for the Lord's sake to every human institution, whether it be to the emperor as supreme, or to governors *as sent by Him to punish those who do evil and to praise those who do good. For this is the will of God, that by doing good you should put to silence the ignorance of fool-*

> *ish people.* Live as people who are free, not using
> your freedom as a cover-up for evil, but living
> as servants of God. Honor everyone. Love the
> brotherhood. Fear God. Honor the emperor. (1
> Peter 2:13–17 ESV)

Both passages of scripture above highlight the function and purpose of *godly,* not ungodly, governmental authority—to promote good, discourage evil, and to protect its citizenry. Governments that are not doing this are not acting on behalf of God. To not be involved in politics under these circumstances would be to deny the Lordship of Christ in these fundamental areas of human endeavor.

Much is said in Exodus 21–22 regarding the role of government in setting limits and boundaries against such "sins" as manslaughter, premeditated murder, assault, kidnapping, slavery, abortion, infanticide, property crimes, criminal negligence, assaulting parents, robbery and bestiality. Deuteronomy 17 and 22 address laws and justice surrounding violations of a court order, perjury, malicious accusation, building code enforcement, juvenile delinquency, and rape.[244] None of these laws and protections against such "sins," however, would have existed if God's people of that day did not get involved in politics!

A Christian who is truly living for Christ does not live their life to avoid political involvement but approaches it with the wisdom, courage, commitment, humility, and responsibility it requires. Besides obeying the laws of the land, confronting and educating others, and supporting and voting for candidates and legislation that best protect its citizens and uphold Christian values, there will also be times when Christians must disobey the laws of the land and its leaders. Here's where wisdom and courage are needed. God would never ask His people, for example, to demonstrate their allegiance and loyalty to the government by doing something immoral, unethical, or contrary to scripture. This is the dividing line for the Christian. It is the cost of true discipleship and worth every penny.

God left us plenty of examples of this in the Old and New Testaments to encourage us. Remember Shadrach, Meshach, and

Abednego, who refused to bow down to the golden statue that King Nebuchadnezzar had erected and Daniel who disobeyed King Darius' decree by continuing to pray to God and not King Darius? Then there were Moses' parents who hid Moses from Pharaoh, and Rahab, who lied to King Jericho's officials to protect the spies sent from Joshua's camp. Maybe you remember Paul and his followers, who, in Acts 17, did contrary to all of Caesar's decrees to proclaim Jesus Christ as King. Then, of course, there was Jesus Christ himself, who lived in direct opposition to the political leaders of His day to fulfill the Father's will.

Today, there are courageous men and women all around us who have served the Lord with distinction and honor in their chosen careers in the government who have unashamedly laid everything on the line for Christ in opposition to the government they serve. Some military chaplains, for example, have chosen to end their distinguished careers (even one year before retirement!) because they were unwilling to perform gay marriages for military members. On September 5, 2015, Kentucky Clerk, Kim Davis, a local government employee, went to jail for refusing to issue marriage licenses to same-sex couples in violation of her Christian beliefs and morals. All such Christians understand that when God's Word and the "kings" word conflict, God's Word has the final word. Why? Their love for Jesus Christ and desire to please Him above all else rule the day. You see, unlike most of us, they are living for a more magnificent day than today (i.e., their Judgment Day)!

Paul encouraged all followers to do the same thing in the Book of Acts (Acts 5:29), yet even when Paul was falsely accused and sentenced in Jerusalem, he exercised his Roman rights to appeal unto Caesar (Acts 25:11).

God involves himself in the affairs of the government every day. The Bible says that He not only appoints and institutes governing authorities, as we have already discussed, but that He rules over them (Psalm 22:28, 47:8; Daniel 4:17).

While most of us focus on the attributes of the virtuous women in Proverbs 31 and not on her husband, do you remember his profession? If Christians are not supposed to be involved in politics, he clearly didn't get the memo. He is "a well-known man *who sits in the council meeting with other civic leaders*" (Proverbs 31:23 NLT). Why? Because he was a civic leader himself (i.e., a politician)!

God's Word says that when the godly are in authority, the people rejoice. But when the wicked are in power, they grow (Proverbs 29:2). It's every Christian's job, to the best of our ability, to make sure that the godly are in positions of authority. This requires our involvement in politics!

Some say, "I get involved in politics by praying for our nation and its leaders."

Great. While prayer is one of the best ways each of us can get involved in politics, there is also a tremendous need for education and loving confrontation when it comes to the political issues of our day. God is looking for us to "walk" by faith (2 Corinthians. 5:7), not just pray by faith. This requires action within the boundaries and limitations of God's Word.

This brings us to a critical issue. We must know what the Word of God says on a particular political issue *before* we open our mouths. If what we, and others, have to say on a particular political issue is different than what God has to say on the same matter, God's right and we're wrong!

It is staggering to me, for example, how many Christians vote for candidates who endorse a "big" government agenda (i.e., socialism) when God, throughout the Old and New Testaments, is clearly for limited government. In the beginning, did God not give Adam and Eve maximum freedom with minimum limitations and great consequences for breaking those limitations in the garden (Genesis 2:16–17; Mark 12:17)? You bet. Don't believe me? Do your own research, especially *before* you educate and lovingly confront others to support a big government agenda!

Certainly, our forefathers felt the same way as we saw earlier when we discussed Jefferson's Danbury letter and the Webster Letter. However, President Abraham Lincoln may have given us the best glimpse into our forefather's desire for limited government on November 19, 1863, when he concluded *The Gettysburg Address* with these famous words that will never be forgotten:

[t]hat we here highly resolve that these dead shall not have died in vain—that this nation, *under God*, shall have a new birth of freedom—and that government *of the people, by the people, for the people*, shall not perish from the earth.[245]

Those who apply God's principles to government and politics pave the way for multigenerational blessings. Do not underestimate the ability of man to make a difference in politics. In 1768, a Christian minister named John Witherspoon became president of the College of New Jersey, now Princeton. While at Princeton, *he taught biblical principles of government*. Of the 478 men who graduated from Princeton during his tenure, 114 became ministers, thirteen became state governors, three became US Supreme Court judges, twenty became US Senators, thirty-three became US Congressmen, one became a vice-president, Aaron Burr, and one became the President of the United States, James Madison.[246] As a Christian, Witherspoon exerted an enormous amount of influence. While none of us are John Witherspoon, each of us can still make a tremendous impact wherever God has placed us and some of you, even greater than Witherspoon!

Since 1996, the number of Americans who believe that churches should *not* be involved in politics has increased from approximately 33 percent to 54 percent.[247] Is it any wonder why the culture is transforming us instead of the other way around?

In 2012, author and apologist Frank Turek had this to say about the topic at the First Baptist Church in Charlotte, North Carolina:

> You won't be able to preach the Gospel if you don't get involved in politics. Politics affects everything we do. The rules we set politically affect churches, finances, your children, what you can and can't do. What if you were to die tonight? If you want to evangelize, you have to be sure you have political freedom to evangelize. That means getting involved in politics. We're called to be salt and light; we're not called to be tax exempt.

The breakdown of the family is largely due to the fact that "the church hasn't been the church." If the church had been the church, and had been engaged in every area of life, we wouldn't have any of these problems.[248]

I couldn't agree more, brother! Thank you.

In his current position with the Faith and Freedom Coalition, RNC member and President of the Iowa Faith Ad Freedom Coalition, Steve Scheffler, says the following:

> I have witnessed, firsthand, the hesitation many church leaders feel to comment on political issues, whether out of compliance with IRS regulations or out of fear that political debates would lead to congregational conflict. Some churches refuse to hand out [the] organizations' voter guides, even though they've been carefully vetted for violations.[249]

Note what Gregory A. Boyd, in his book, *The Myth of a Christian Religion, Losing Your Religion for the Beauty of a Revolution,* says about Jesus's role in politics:

> Jesus kept the kingdom holy by how He lived, and we are called to do the same. At the same time, every aspect of Jesus' life—including His death, confronted some aspect of the polis (Greek for "society") and was in this sense political. In fact, while Jesus didn't utter a word about politics, He was a subversive political revolutionary. His life, ministry, teachings, death, and resurrection revolted against every unjust and oppressive aspect of the polis. This is why Jesus was a threat to the religious and political authorities—and ultimately why they felt they had to

crucify Him. We who have pledged our lives to
following Jesus are to be political revolutionaries
in this same way.[250]

We are living in a day when God has been kicked out of every
conceivable institution in America from our house to the White
House. If God's Word says, "Blessed is the nation whose God is the
Lord" (Psalm 33:12 ESV), then what shall become of a nation that
worships many gods, including "rock stars" in government and politics who elevate their word above God's Word? Better yet, what are
God's people willing to do about it?

Before coming to a close on this "big lie" that Satan has gotten
the church to believe—that is, that Christians shouldn't be involved
in politics—I would be cowardly and derelict in my duties if I did
not make this statement. Some of the same Christians who believe
that they should not be involved in politics are some of the same
Christians who do not hesitate to get involved in church politics to
either preserve or advance their own kingdoms.

Few things are more nauseating to me than watching the game
of politics being played out in God's house! Quid pro quo deals and
insider trading don't just occur on Wall Street and The Hill. Powerful,
influential church leaders are "buying" special treatment and favors
with other powerful, prominent church leaders to push a politically
correct agenda that is not God's agenda (e.g., gay marriage, women
pastors, homosexual ordinations, and prosperity theology). For those
of you who now see the importance of Godly Christian involvement
in politics, I hope you now see that your involvement may need to
begin with your own politically correct church!

As I turn the corner to the next "big lie," I believe each of us
must ask ourselves the following question. Am I doing everything I
can to exercise my rights and privileges as a citizen in the political
realm to demonstrate the comprehensive rule of God in every institution in America from my house to the White House according to
my means and ability?

I like what St. Augustine said, "Those who are citizens of God's
kingdom are best equipped to be citizens of the kingdom of man."[251]

Do we believe this? If so, it's about time we started acting like it, wouldn't you agree?

The next big lie that Satan has gotten many in the church to believe to destroy the foundations of our lives and every institution in America we comprise from our house to the White House is that Christians shouldn't fear God. This is a "biggie," and its repercussions have been enormous as you are about to see. Some would argue that the absence of the fear of God is the greatest cause for the moral, social, and spiritual decline we are facing in America, and I wouldn't disagree for a second.

The argument surrounding this "big lie," even from many mature Christians, goes like this, "God is love; therefore, why would we fear Him?"

"How could Jesus who desires to have a close and intimate relationship with us want us to fear Him?"

"What kind of gracious and loving God would want us to fear Him?"

"Do you think God is waiting to 'tase' us with a lightning bolt the second we mess up or something?"

I certainly don't believe this; otherwise, I would have been dead a long time ago. The common Christian belief that we should not fear God couldn't be any more unbiblical.

"Have you not read…" (Mark 12:26; Matthew 19:4)? There's our problem once again! One of the great tragedies in the church today is that many of us are experts on everything but have read nothing. God's Word says that the [reverent] fear of the Lord [that *is*, *worshipping Him and regarding* Him as truly awesome] is the beginning and the preeminent part of knowledge [its starting point and its presence]; but arrogant fools despise [skillful and godly] wisdom and instruction (Proverbs 1:7 AMP). Solomon, the wisest man who ever lived, told us, in essence, that it is impossible to obtain any wisdom without first possessing a healthy fear of the Lord.

To fear God means to take Him seriously. While Jesus is the Lover of my Soul (Psalm 23:3), my Abba Daddy (Romans 8:15), my Rock (Psalm 19:14), my Redeemer,[252] my Shield (Psalm 28:7), my Fortress and my Deliverer (Psalm 18:2), my Healer (Isaiah 53:5),my

Provider (Philippians 4:19), my Anchor (Hebrews 6:19), my Savior (Isaiah 43:11), my Lord (Romans 10:9), my King (Revelation 19:16), my friend (Proverbs 18:24), He is also my Master (John 13:13), Ruler (Psalm 22:28), High Priest (Hebrews 4:14), Lion of the Tribe of Judah (Revelation 5:5), Mighty One of Israel (Isaiah 1:24), King of kings (Revelation 19:16), Lord of lords,[253] Holy One (1 John 2:20), Strong Tower, Great I Am, and Righteous Judge who will one day judge the quick and the dead at His appearing (1 Timothy 4:1 KJV). That would be you and me! Oh, did I also mention "all-consuming fire" (Hebrews 12:29)?

God's Word says that Jesus is high and lifted up and seated at the right hand of God the Father (Isaiah 6:1). Because He sits "high" and we sit "low," those who take Him seriously (i.e., fear Him) allow Him to call the shots. At least that's the way it's supposed to work. In those few short sentences, the Holy Spirit had me cut to the heart of why I believe many Christians have conveniently bought the "big lie" that we shouldn't fear God. You see, as long as we don't have to fear God, we can keep Him on the same level as us and don't have to dethrone ourselves and allow His Word to have the final word. We can treat Him like a BFF whose advice we may or may not heed. This way, we can control the situation. At least, that's what Satan is hoping.

Other Christians don't believe we should fear God because they think it means that they need to be afraid of God. We take our human experience of fear that puts distance between us and those we fear and say, "This makes no sense with a God I love and a God who loves me. We want to be close to one another." And you're right, it makes no sense if the fear of man and the fear of God were the same, but they aren't.

Remember, God sits high in authority, and we sit low under His authority. When our relationship with God is proper, we willingly come under His authority as our priest, protector, and provider and benefit from the spiritual covering He provides. We give Him our highest praise, worship, honor, and respect. Because we know He loves us, we also know He will discipline us when we get out of line, which instills a healthy fear and respect for His position. No, the fear of man and the fear of God are not the same!

The closest human relationship we have to compare our relationship to God with, which is a far cry from this, might be the relationship some of us had with a loving but firm earthly father who was not afraid to discipline us when necessary in order to make us "holy." While I had a loving relationship with my father growing up whom I desired to be close with, there was also a healthy fear. I knew if I got out of line, there would be consequences. I came to learn and appreciate that the discipline I received as a child by my earthly father, and now, by my heavenly Father, is evidence that they both love me (Hebrews 12:6). And because they love me, they were/are invested in my "holiness" (Hebrews 12:10–11).

This is seldom true of the people we fear in the world. The fact that God disciplines me (as my earthly father did when I was a child) is evidence of my sonship; that is, that I "belong" to God (Hebrews 12:7–8). In fact, if God never "spanked" me, it would be evidence that I "belonged" to another father! Needless to say, the healthy fear we have of God is in no way similar to those we fear who are not similarly invested in our sonship. Those in the physical realm have not earned the same right to our submission, honor, respect, worship, and reverence.

Still, many Christians believe that the love of God has eliminated the need for the "fear of God." I like how this author addresses this argument:

> They believe God has revealed His love through Christ so that the fear of God is no longer needed. In fact, they would contend that holding to the fear of God somehow restricts God's child in knowing the full potential of His love. They would state that the love of God and the fear of God are mutually exclusive apprehensions of God. If one fears God, He does not really know the love of God. Or, if one really knows of God's love, then He does not fear God.

The problem with this thinking partly stems from interpreting the fear of God to mean "bully" instead of "awesome."

Additionally, their concept of the love of God is this over-patronizing image, which only affirms and never chastises. These people ignorantly suppose the God of the Old Testament to be wrathful and fearsome, while the image of the God of the New Testament is loving and all-accepting. Some of these people focus on God being like a warm Mom rather than a mean Dad. Usually these people have a problem with understanding and appreciating God's authority and also want to legitimize their own self-expression.[254]

For those of you who still have great difficulty believing that God wants us to have a healthy, reverential fear of Him so we'll take Him seriously, it may help you to see *why* He wants us to fear Him.

First, God knows that if we fear Him, He will be able to trust us to do His will. Remember the story of Abraham who, in obedience to God's instructions, laid His only son on the altar to be the sacrificed? Many, including me, forget what God said to Abraham just before Abraham, with knife raised, was about to take the life of His only son (*italics* used for emphasis):

> Do not lay your hand on the boy or do anything to Him, *for now I know that you fear God*, seeing you have not withheld your son, your only son, from me. (Genesis 22:12 ESV)

While most of us will never experience a test like this, thank God He uses the tests and trials of our lives to see where our greatest allegiance and loyalty lie. It's also the reason why many of us continue to face the same tests and trials! God wants to be able to trust us with a greater work but won't until He knows He can trust us in the current trial we are facing! No fear. No trust. No great work! Know fear. Know trust. Know great work!

Satan wants every Christian to believe that they don't have to fear God to gain God's trust for the "greater work." You have to admit, it's is a "charming lie" to minimize the amount of territory we can reclaim from Satan in the earth, don't you think? You see, Satan knows that when we fear God instead of him, we will obey God instead of him and crush Satan's power and influence in the earth! This begs the question of each of us, "Have we earned God's trust yet by proving that we fear Him?" While none of us like trials, I would encourage you to think about this the next time you face one.

Secondly, God knows that if we fear Him, we can be trusted to *justly* lead those He has given us to lead, whether it be a wife, children, a congregation, employees, military personnel, freshmen Senators, constituents, athletes, or (fill in the blank). Note the following (*italics* used for emphasis):

> The Spirit of the Lord spake by me, and His Word was in my tongue. The God of Israel said, the Rock of Israel spake to me, *He that ruleth over men must be just, ruling in the fear of God*. And He shall be as the light of the morning, when the sun riseth, even a morning without clouds; as the tender grass springing out of the earth by clear shining after rain. (2 Samuel 22:2–4 KJV)

Can you imagine how different our cities and nation would be if all of our elected officials were ruling justly in the fear of God? I know!

God also knows that if we fear Him, we, His children, will escape a life of vanity and find true meaning, fullness, and significance as declared here in the following (*italics* used for emphasis):

> Let not your mouth lead you into sin, and do not say before the messenger that it was a mistake. Why should God be angry at your voice

and destroy the works of your hands? *For when dreams increase and words grow many, there is vanity; but God is the one you must fear.* (Ecclesiastes 5:6–7 ESV)

I don't know about you, but I see a lot of vanity inside the Beltway that a healthy fear of God would eradicate overnight!

Fear of God also helps us deal with sin. Proverbs says that by mercy and truth, iniquity is purged, and *by the fear of the Lord,* men depart from evil (Proverbs 16:6).

The fear of God also protects us. God's Word says that God has given a banner to those who fear Him that we may display it because of the truth; we may be delivered, saved with His right hand (Psalm 60:4–5).

The Bible also says that those who fear the Lord are worthy of praise as seen in the description of a Proverbs 31 woman. "Charm is deceptive and beauty is vain, *but a woman who fears the Lord is to be praised*" (Proverbs 31:30 NIV).

King David, a man's after God's own heart (1 Samuel 13:14), said that anyone who fears the Lord is His friend (Psalm 119:63). Note, just sixteen verses later, David asks only to be reconciled *with those who fear the Lord* and know His decrees (Psalm 119:79 NLT). Many of us should be a lot more like King David when it comes to picking our friends and deciding whether or not we should "reconcile" with certain people who have no desire to live for God.

Remember Dave and Megan from chapter 2? Up until their marriage ended and beyond, Megan continued to believe that she was the spiritual leader of her children. While Dave forgave her, it was her unwillingness to confess her sin, repent, and operate under Dave's authority as the spiritual leader of her children that made it impossible for them to reconcile and operate as one under God's divine order for their family. Fear of the Lord with a proper understanding of God's spiritual hierarchy for the family would have caused Megan to renounce her idolatry (i.e., her divine order *over* God's divine order) and healed their marriage instantly! Incidentally, now is probably a good time to tell you that the reason why I am so familiar with Dave and Megan's story is because I am Dave.

Satan's greatest fear is that we will one day "wake up" and operate in the fear of the Lord in every area of life. Why? Because he'll be out of a job and he knows it! While we can't control things that are outside of our "gardens" (chapter 1), it should be every Christian's goal to make sure he's out of a job in our gardens! Having a healthy, reverential fear of the Lord and His Word makes this possible.

One of the most compelling verses of scripture dispelling the "big lie" that Christians are not supposed to fear God came from Jesus himself who was preparing the disciples for persecution. He told them not to fear those who could kill the body only but rather Him who had the power to destroy soul and body in hell (Matthew 10:28).

This brings us to the next reason why God wants us to fear Him. He wants us to recognize that He alone is the Righteous Judge (Psalm 7:11 NASB) who will judge us all. The Bible says that it is appointed unto man to die once, but after this, the judgment (Hebrews 9:27). I don't know about you, but knowing that I will one day face my Creator and give an account for every idle word spoken (Matthew 12:36) scares me to life. How about you?

The Book of Psalms is loaded with reasons why God wants us to fear Him. Psalm 15 says that those that fear Him are among those who get to dwell with God in His sanctuary and live on His holy hill (Psalm 15:1–4). How amazing is that? Psalm 25 says that the man who fears the Lord will be instructed in the way chosen for Him. "He will spend His days in prosperity, and His descendants will inherit the land. The Lord confides in those who fear Him; He makes His covenant known to them" (Psalm 25:12–14 NIV). Amazing, right?

In Psalm 128, the man who fears the Lord receives a blessing from His wife and children as seen here in the following (*italics* used for emphasis):

> *Blessed are all who fear the Lord*, who walk in obedience to Him. You will eat the fruit of your labor; blessings and prosperity will be yours. *Your*

wife will be like a fruitful vine within your house;
your children will be like olive shoots around your
table. Yes, this will be the blessing for the man who
fears the LORD. (Psalm 128:1–4 NIV)

Note these other powerful passages of scripture that apply to those who fear God:

1. But the love of the Lord remains forever with those who fear Him. (Psalm 103:17 NLT)
2. Reverent and worshipful fear of the Lord is a fountain of life, that one may avoid the snares of death. (Proverbs 14:27 AMP)
3. God has compassion on those who fear Him as a father has compassion on His children. (Psalm 103:13)
4. God extends mercy to those who fear Him from generation to generation. (Luke 1:50)
5. God provides food for those who fear Him; He remembers His covenant forever. (Psalm 111:5)
6. God delights in those who fear Him, who put their hope in His unfailing love. (Psalm 147:11)
7. Those that fear the Lord show that they hate what God hates—pride, arrogance, evil behavior and perverse speech. (Proverbs 8:13)
8. Those who fear the Lord understand that God alone is all-powerful and worthy of our sacrifice and praise. (John 1:15–16)
9. By humility and the fear of the Lord are riches, honor, and long life. (Proverbs 22:4)
10. Those that fear God will never turn away from Him. (Jeremiah 32:40)

I hope you now see that it is not only right to have a healthy, reverent, and worshipful fear the Lord but that it is foolish if we don't.

Ladies, while I'm sure your Christian husband loves you dearly, it is the fear of the Lord and the consequences that God will invoke on him that keeps him from committing adultery against you.

I believe the fear of the Lord will keep Christian men from placing their careers ahead of their families, women from usurping their husband's authority, men from abdicating their spiritual responsibilities at home (chapter 2), and women from elevating the parent-child relationship above the husband-wife relationship.

In the context of the local church, I believe the fear of the Lord will cause pastors to refuse to ordain homosexual ministers or perform gay marriages (Leviticus 18:22, 20:13; Romans 1:26–27; 1 Corinthians 6:9–10; 1 Timothy 1:9–10). It will cause churches to renounce prosperity theology, salvation without repentance, the appointment of women to "overseer" positions (e.g., pastor, co-pastor, and elder), tolerance above righteousness, and unity above theology. It will cause church leaders to operate as kingdom's court on kingdom matters using the King's Word and not to neglect, cower away from, or be too busy for loving confrontation and church discipline when needed.

The fear of the Lord will cause elected officials at every level of government to balance their budgets, cut wasteful spending, and to put an end to pay-to-play quid pro quo corrupt political practices. It will cause elected officials and politicians to overturn and abolish immoral laws, enact moral laws, enforce and correctly interpret present law, keep the government out of the affairs of the church (e.g., overturn the Johnson Amendment), and allow every American to enjoy their constitutional right to the free exercise of religious freedom and liberty in publicly funded institutions (e.g., prayer in public schools). The fear of the Lord will cause every American voter to vote "God's conscience" on election day and to replace every corrupt politician with someone who has God's back first instead of their own.

Fear of the Lord will keep men from trafficking humans and drugs, shedding innocent blood, and committing acts of domestic and international terrorism.

A healthy, holy, reverent, worshipful fear of the Lord will cause Christians all across America to acknowledge Him, listen to Him, and put away their "idols."

The consequences of not fearing God have been enormous from our house to the White House, wouldn't you agree? A home that does not fear the Lord becomes a church that does not fear the Lord, which ultimately becomes a city, state, and a nation that does not fear the Lord. Have you looked around lately?

So if the big lie the church believes is that Christians should not fear God, I now hope you now see that until we do, our homes, families, churches, cities, and nation don't stand a chance!

There's probably no better way to conclude our discussion on the importance of fearing God than by reflecting on the words of the wisest man who ever lived, King Solomon, who after laying out his case for the meaninglessness of life, said the following (*italics* used for emphasis):

> Here is my final conclusion: *Fear God* and
> obey His commands, for this is the duty of every
> person. God will judge us for everything we do,
> including every secret thing, whether good or
> bad. (Ecclesiastes 12:13–14 NLT)

The next big lie that Satan has gotten many in the church to believe to destroy the foundations of our lives and every institution in America we comprise from our house to the White House is that *prosperity theology* is biblical.

I've referred to it several times already. What exactly is prosperity theology? Prosperity theology (sometimes referred to as the prosperity Gospel, "the health and wealth Gospel," the Gospel of success, or "seed faith") is a religious belief held by many Christians, which says that financial blessings and physical well-being are the will of God for every individual. Faith, positive speech, and donations to religious causes will increase one's material wealth.[255]

In a nutshell, adherents to prosperity theology believe that God exists to make them "happy," healthy, and wealthy.[256] The following is a direct quote to the congregation of Lakewood Church in Houston, Texas, from Victoria Osteen, wife of Joel Osteen, and co-pastor of one the largest, most famous prosperity theology churches of our day. If you are true follower of Jesus Christ, this should make your spiritual skin crawl:

> I just want to encourage everyone of us that when we obey God, we're not doing it for God—I mean, that's one way to look at it—we're doing it for ourselves, because God takes pleasure when we are happy...that's the thing that gives Him the greatest joy.
>
> So I want you to know this morning—just do good for your own self. Do good because God wants you to be happy... When you come to church, when you worship Him, you're not doing it for God really. You're doing it for yourself, because that's what makes God happy. Amen?[257]

Prosperity theology is described as "an aberrant theology that teaches that God rewards faith, displayed through hefty tithing, with financial blessings."[258] Referred to as "transactionalism," those who embrace this false theology see the Bible as a contract between God and humans: If humans have faith in God, He will deliver security and prosperity.[259]

While prosperity theology first came to prominence in America in the 1950s, it gained its greatest traction in the 1980s when tel-evangelists Jimmy Swaggart and Jim and Tammy Bakker champi-oned it.[260] Today, its most famous faces include celebrities like Joel Osteen, Joyce Meyer, T. D. Jakes, Benny Hinn, Creflo Dollar, and Paula White.[261]

One prosperity theology figure, known for his mass-miracle ministry to millions, says, "God created the wealth of this planet and placed it here for the prosperity of His children."[262]

Really? I don't recommend telling that to Christian missionar-ies being martyred for the faith in places like North Korea, Yemen, and Saudi Arabia! Unlike the true Gospel that has the humiliation of its God (Jesus) as the centerpiece of its religion who is worthy of our highest praise, honor, sacrifice, and worship, prosperity theology offers adherents a God who primarily exists to advance man's kingdom. But not before adherents exercise enough faith through their "tithing," "financial gifts," "special offerings," "seed money," and "end-of-year donations."

One of the strongest undercurrents of the prosperity theology movement is the belief that if you have enough faith, things like poverty, material deprivation, lack, and insufficiency will no longer be a part of your life. Prosperity theologians focus on God's "immeasurable favor" poured out on all people. However, this favor is only available to those who correct their thinking.[263] Never mind the fact that God's Word says, "The Lord sends poverty and wealth; He humbles and He exalts" (1 Samuel 2:7 NIV).

Prosperity Gospel churches believe that wealth is always a sign of God's grace and favor. No wealth, no favor. Know wealth, know favor. So where does that leave poverty-stricken Christians suffering for the Gospel around the world? Somehow without God's grace and favor? Wow! To the persecuted Church in Smyrna, Jesus said, "I know about your suffering and your poverty—but you are rich" (Revelation 2:9 NLT)! Did Jesus somehow get it all wrong too, Preacher? In the same way that wealth doesn't necessarily mean someone has God's favor or approval, a lack of wealth doesn't necessarily mean someone doesn't have God's favor or disapproval. But don't bother telling any of this to the prosperity theology crowd. It doesn't pay. Literally. Suffering and wealth in the same sentence simply do not compute in the mind of anyone who is involved in prosperity theology.

Prosperity theology says "God is not glorified in poverty." So much for the Christians hiding in underground churches in China and Syria who are trusting God for their next meal, running water, medicine, or their lives! If our Gospel message cannot be preached with credibility in Syria, it should not be preached in Houston, Texas!

Today's American prosperity Gospel church says that Jesus came to make you "bigger and better." It says that the best churches in America are the biggest churches in America with the biggest budgets. Never mind the fact that the further Jesus got in His ministry, the smaller the crowds got. Never mind the fact that Jesus gave up His riches in heaven to become poor for our sake on earth so that we, by His poverty, might become rich in Him (2 Corinthians. 8:9).

For those of you who believe this prosperity theology garbage, what Bible are you reading? In the book of Luke, Jesus lifted up His eyes toward His disciples and said, "Blessed are you who are poor [in spirit], for yours is the kingdom of God" (Luke 6:20 ESV). In the book of James, where favoritism in the house of God is shown to the rich man in fine clothing over the poor man in filthy clothing, James says, "Listen, my beloved brethren: Has God not chosen the poor of this world to be rich in faith and heirs to the kingdom which He promised to those who love Him" (James 2:5 NKJV)?

Prosperity theology churches are polished sensualistic churches that think along the lines of what is pleasing to the masses versus what is pleasing to God. What productions will make the "biggest splash" versus what will increase our faith and allegiance to Christ. Generally, the bigger a prosperity Gospel church gets, the smaller their message gets.

Prosperity theology only allows God to give His people "good" things. God does not have the freedom to give His people "bad" things. But this latter message doesn't exactly fill empty seats on a Sunday morning or, more importantly, the offering plate. We have to go no further than the Book of Job (though there are certainly earlier examples) to expose this counterfeit teaching.

Do you recall what Job said to the messenger after the messenger told Job the bad news? That is, that while Job's sons and daughters were feasting at the oldest brother's house, a great wind swept in and destroyed his house and killed all of Job's children? After Job arose, tore his robe, shaved his head, and fell to the ground in worship, he said, "Naked I came from my mother's womb and naked shall I return; blessed be the name of the Lord" (Job 1:21 ESV). Then, just a few verses later, after God allowed Satan to afflict Job with sores from the soles of his feet to the top of his head, remember what Job said to his wife after she told him that he should "curse God and die?" He says, "You speak as one of the foolish women speaks.

Shall we indeed accept good from God and not accept adversity" (Job 2:10 NASB).

Solomon also said, "Enjoy prosperity while you can. But when hard times strike, realize that both come from God" (Ecclesiastes 7:14 NLT). However, don't tell this to adherents of prosperity theology. And whatever you do, don't tell them what the prophet Samuel said, "The Lord makes poor and makes rich; He brings low and lifts up" (1 Samuel 2:7 NKJV).

Because God primarily exists to meet their needs, prosperity theology churches are big into "name it and claim it" theology. Here, you "name" whatever you want and "claim" it as yours. If you want a big house, a nice car, and new clothes, just "name it and claim it." Born out of the Norman Vincent Peale *Power of Positive Thinking* era that heavily influenced an arm of the prosperity theology movement, what you say and confess, you will possess! What the prosperity theology crowd fails to see or intentionally ignores, however, is that God will only allow His people to "name and claim" things that He wants them to have. And what He wants us to have will always be in line with His will (as outlined in the Word), which will always benefit God and others, not just us! James cuts right to the heart of the matter when he says, "Ye ask, and receive not, because ye ask amiss, that ye may consume it upon your lusts" (James 4:3 KJV).

God knows when we are giving to "get" versus giving out of gratitude for all He's done for us, whether we "get" or not. But again, don't try telling this to the prosperity theology crowd. They'll have none of it. Don't bother sharing the words of Jesus himself who said, "If any man would come after me, let Him deny himself, and take up His cross, and follow me. For whosoever would save His life shall lose it, and whosoever shall lose His life for my sake shall find it" (Matthew 16:24–25 ASV). There's no room for personal denial inside the walls of any prosperity theology church!

Can you imagine telling Christian missionaries and martyrs of the faith around the world that "God primarily exists to meet their needs so they can live their best life now?" May God forgive us!

Prosperity theology adherents also believe that the Bible must live up to their standards versus us living up to God's standards. In so many words, they say, "I will judge the God of the Bible based on my morality rather than the God of the Bible judging me based on God's morality."[264]

It should, therefore, be no surprise that things like repentance, sin, judgment, righteous suffering, self-denial, and church discipline are nowhere to be found in prosperity Gospel churches.

When prosperity theologians say that Christians who give generously should expect financial rewards on this side of heaven, they take scriptures like the following one entirely out of context:

> Give, and it will be given unto you: good measure, pressed down, shaken together, and running over will be put into your bosom. For with the same measure that you use, it will be measured back to you. (Luke 6:38)

Nothing like a little manipulation from the pulpit to fill the church coffers. Instead of giving out of a heart of love and obedience to Christ to further the Gospel regardless of what we get in return, prosperity Gospel teachers make giving all about what "man" will receive if they exercise the proper faith and simply "obey." Instead of making Christ and His kingdom the center of our giving, prosperity theology preachers make "man" the center of giving.

You say, "Wait a minute, Spence, but Luke 6:38 above does say, 'Give, and it will be given unto you...'"

You're right; however, if you begin at Luke 6:36 (instead of verse 38) and end at Luke 6:42, you will see a totally different context and meaning to this scripture than the one being repackaged, resold, and redistributed to congregations all across America:

> "Be merciful, even as your Father is merciful. Judge not, and you will not be judged; condemn not, and you will not be condemned; forgive, and you will be forgiven; give, and it will be given to you. Good measure, pressed down, shaken together, running over, will be put into

your lap. For with the measure you use, it will be measured back to you." He also told them a parable: "Can a blind man lead a blind man? Will they not both fall into a pit? A disciple is not above His teacher, but everyone when He is fully trained will be like His teacher. Why do you see the speck that is in your brother's eye, but do not notice the log that is in your own eye? How can you say to your brother, 'Brother, let me take out the speck that is in your eye,' when you yourself do not see the log that is in your own eye? You hypocrite, first take the log out of your own eye, and then you will see clearly to take out the speck that is in your brother's eye.'" (Luke 6:36–42 ESV)

I hope you can now see that Jesus did not give us this passage of scripture to show us how we could guarantee ourselves a new house, a new car, a new wardrobe, and money in the bank. He gave it to us to teach us a critical biblical principle, which is whatever we give others, good or bad, will be given unto us. In other words, if we "give" mercy and forgiveness to others in the same way that it has been given to us by Christ, for example, mercy and forgiveness will be given to us. If we dispense judgment and condemnation to others, expect others to dish out judgment and condemnation to us. If we are generous, gracious, and compassionate with our money and time, for example, others will be generous, gracious, and compassionate with their money and time to us.[265]

In other words, whatever we give, whether it be hope, judgment, or peace, we will get back in good measure, pressed down, shaken together, and running over. But don't waste your time telling this to the prosperity theology crowd; again, it doesn't "pay." It is much more lucrative for them to make Luke 6:38 about what "financial blessings" congregants will receive if they will only exercise the proper faith and give accordingly.

But why would they change their tactics now? It's been "paying off," literally, for decades? I'll tell you why. Because God's sitting on His throne and He will not be mocked (Galatians 6:7), and you and I will have to answer for it all on Judgment Day. That's why. For nothing is hidden that will not be made manifest nor anything made secret that will not be known and come to light (Luke 8:17 ESV).

Prosperity Gospel churches are all man-centered institutions, not Christ-centered institutions. Jesus is reduced to a Santa Claus of sorts where physical blessings get elevated above spiritual blessings.

One of the quickest ways to determine if prosperity theology exists in your church is to look at what is being emphasized or conveniently omitted. Is the *emphasis* on Christ and the expansion of His kingdom through the fulfillment of the Great Commission by every member? Or is the *emphasis* on man and the expansion of His kingdom through the giving of every member? Is the *emphasis* placed on giving for Christ's benefit or our benefit? The operative word is *emphasis*. Does the unspoken message coming from the pulpit, in substance or in part, say that God can only "bless" you with happiness, health, wealth, and prosperity when you give? If so, you have unwittingly placed yourself underneath the leadership, manipulation, and control of prosperity theology. If this is you, I urge you to get out now while you still can!

So if prosperity theology is counterfeit theology, what then is true biblical prosperity? Let's take a look. The root word *prosper* or some form of the word appears over eighty times in the Old and New Testaments. The most common Hebrew word for "prosper" is *tsalach*, which means "to advance, make progress, succeed, or be profitable" (Old Testament Hebrew Lexicon—King James Version).

Another Hebrew word for prosperity is *shalom*, which we often associate with "peace," but the peace that Christ went to war for on the cross is a more complete peace.[266] According to Strong's concordance, "shalom" is completeness, soundness, welfare, and peace.[267] It represents completeness in number and safety and soundness in your physical body.[268] "Shalom" also covers relationships with God and people.[269] We see this meaning of "peace" for prosperity in the often quoted Jeremiah 29:11. While the New International Version of this same scripture says, "For I know the plans I have for you," declares the Lord, "plans to *prosper* you and not to harm you, plans to give you a hope and a future;" the King James Version says, "For I know the thoughts that I think toward you, saith the Lord, thoughts of *peace* and not of evil." Thus, peace and prosperity are related.

"Prosper," in Hebrew, is also the word *sakal* (pronounced 'saw-kal'). It is the same word for "success," which means to be prudent, to consider, be circumspect, good stewards of what God has given us (*Strong's Greek and Hebrew Lexicon*).

Prosperity, in the Greek, means ease, quietness, salvation, righteousness, spiritual wellness, everything good that comes from God's hand.[270]

Biblical prosperity is also used in the context of war. In 1 Kings 22, King Ahab of Israel, at the request of King Jehoshaphat, agreed to summon the prophets to see if he (King Ahab) should go to war against the city Ramoth-Gilead still occupied by the Arameans. All of the prophets agreed that they should go up to Ramoth-Gilead and *prosper,* for the Lord will deliver it [Ramoth-Gilead] into the king's hand (1 Kings 22:12 NKJV). Other translations for the word *prosper* in this same verse say "do well" (1 Kings 22:12 NLV), "be victorious" (1 Kings 22:12 NLT) "win" (1 Kings 22:12 NCV), "succeed" (1 Kings 22:12 NET), or "triumph" 1 Kings 22:12 ESV).

In 3 John, John says, "Beloved, I pray that you may *prosper* in all things and be in health, just as your soul *prospers*." The Greek word "prosper" here, *euodoo* (pronounced 'yoo-od-o'-o'), means "to have a successful journey through life" (*Strong's Greek and Hebrew Lexicon*).

But how do we become "prosperous" according to God's Word, now that we've defined it? Joshua says we become prosperous by continually abiding with and obeying the Word of God as seen here in the following (*italics* used for emphasis):

> This Book of the Law shall not depart from
> your mouth, but you shall meditate in it day and
> night, that you may observe to do according to
> all that is written in it. *For then you will make*

> *your way prosperous* and then you will have good
> success. (Joshua 1:8 NKJV)

My point in taking the time to define what prosperity is and to show us how one becomes prosperous from God's Word is to highlight how far prosperity theology churches are from a true and accurate understanding of biblical prosperity! It is my hope and trust that you now see that biblical prosperity has little to do with health and wealth and much more to do with obedience to God's Word and the condition of our hearts.

While earthly riches are certainly among the gifts that God gives to some to expand His kingdom, it is abundantly clear throughout scripture that God values spiritual riches above earthly riches.

Jesus often warns us of the dangers of pursuing earthly riches over spiritual riches. One of the most famous passages in the Bible that highlights this comes right after Jesus confronts the rich young ruler who, when asked what he must do to inherit eternal life (Mark 10:17), was unwilling to forsake his riches to inherit "treasures in heaven" (Mark 10:21). Three verses later, when the man went away, sad because he was unwilling to forsake his great wealth, Jesus turns to His disciples and says the following: "It is easier for a camel to go through the eye of a needle, than for a rich man to enter into the kingdom of God" (Mark 10:25 KJV). Good luck hearing this at any prosperity theology church.

Recall, when Jesus sent His disciples in Luke 9 to preach the kingdom of God and to heal the sick, He told them to take nothing for the journey, not even a staff, bag, *money*, or more than one tunic each (Luke 9:1–3). Did you catch it? In a day when prosperity theology pastors are telling their congregations that it takes money for the church (i.e., the senior pastor) to proclaim a watered-down Gospel message that doesn't require repentance at their "many campuses," Jesus tells *all* of His disciples to get out of the "pews" and go into all the world and proclaim *the* true Gospel that does require repentance (Matthew 3:2, 4:17; Mark 1:15; Luke 24:47) to all creation (Mark 16:15) and leave your money behind!

I love what James has to say on the topic:

> Christians who are poor should be glad, for
> God has honored them. And those who are rich
> should be glad, for God has humbled them. They
> will fade away like a flower in the field. The hot
> sun rises and dried up the grass; the flower with-
> ers, and its beauty fades away. So also, wealthy
> people will fade away with all of their achieve-
> ments. (James 1:9 NLT)

Before ending the "big lie" that Satan has gotten many of us to believe, that is, that prosperity theology is biblical theology, please allow me to make a few other points many of you already know regarding earthly riches lest some hear what I am not saying. First, God is not against material wealth as long as we acknowledge Him as the source, keep an "open" hand to others, use it to build His kingdom, and recognize that we are mere stewards over what He has given us since it ultimately belongs to Him.

Second, throughout scripture, we are admonished to live within our means and be content with what we've been given. Paul tells us that true godliness with contentment is great wealth (1 Timothy 6:6). *Content* is a word that doesn't exist in any prosperity theology church. The day their leaders and congregations become content with what they have is the day the prosperity theology movement "dies." No prosperity theology church is going to let that happen; hence, the ongoing "dance" to manipulate their sheep into future giving with the promise that if they do, they will receive good health, wealth, and prosperity and "reach their destinies." Never mind the fact that sister Joan, a faithful tither in the church for years, died an early death to cancer, leaving three grieving children behind.

Maybe some of you are saying, "Fine, but what's the big deal with prosperity theology at the end of the day? So what if a few megachurches are 'off the rails?'"

So glad you asked. First, and foremost, we're not talking about a few megachurches as captured in this article from *Christianity Today*, titled "The Prosperity Gospel is Surprisingly Mainstream":

As the size and number of their congregations, TV ministries, and best-selling books confirms, the contemporary footprint of the American Prosperity Gospel is large, indeed. This buttresses Bowler's [Kate Bowler, author of *Blessed*] larger argument that the Prosperity movement is no religious sideshow. Citing studies, Bowler shows that 17 percent of all Christians in America openly identify with the movement; that every Sunday, over a million people attend Prosperity-oriented megachurches—43 percent of which boast multiethnic or multicultural congregations; and that two-thirds of all Christian believers are convinced that God, ultimately, wants them to prosper. In effect, she argues that if a substantial number of people identify with the Prosperity Gospel and accept its common teachings, then it must be closer to the mainstream than one might imagine.[271]

Thus, given the enormity of this movement that has grown even bigger since the writing of this 2013 article cited above, it's a very big deal. Instead of being one unified Church that is focused on Jesus, making disciples, and building His kingdom, whether we're "happy," healthy, wealthy, or not, a large segment of the church, under satanic control, is focused on how to live their best lives now so they can reach their destinies. Said another way, if seeking our best lives now and destinies aren't tied to His kingdom and glory, then we're working for the "other" kingdom! That's why it's a "big deal," friend. I firmly believe the prosperity theology movement, which is now nearly five decades old, is directly responsible, in part, for why 95 percent of all believers have never won a soul to Christ.[272] Living a life that is primarily focused on us and what we want makes it impossible to live a life that is primarily focused on Jesus and what He wants! While I'm for smiles and positive thinking (though I prefer positive believing!), if our smiles and positive thinking don't translate into kingdom expansion for God's glory, we'll be the positive thinking fools answering for it on Judgment Day!

Prosperity theology causes our hearts and loyalties to be divided between the kingdom of self and the kingdom of God. Jesus will not compete with our idols, beloved, even when that idol is us! The Bible says that we cannot serve both God and mammon because we'll hate one and love the other or be devoted to one and despise the other (Matthew 6:24). As we learned in chapter 1, if we are not willing to deny ourselves, take up our crosses, and follow Jesus, then we're following another leader, remember?

One of the devil's greatest schemes and strategies is to get churches to compete with one another on size (number of buildings, campuses, budget size, and weekly attendance) and influence. He knows that if he can get us to compete with one another, we'll never become "one," and thus, able to reclaim significant amounts of territory that Adam and Eve gave him (chapter 1)!

Please understand that I do not believe the issue is "big churches." There are "big churches" in America that are truly doing the work of God. My problem, as it was for Paul and for many of you, is false theology that causes us to major on the minor (us and our kingdoms) and minor on the major (Christ and His kingdom). It just so happens that prosperity theology has "hit" an overwhelming number of megachurches that have enormous influence over millions of believers.

The Bible says that there are many who walk along the Christian road who are really enemies of the cross of Christ. Their future is eternal loss, for their god is their appetite: they are proud of what they should be ashamed of, and all they think about is this life here on earth (Philippians 3:18–19 TLB). Sadly and tragically, this describes the prosperity theology movement in America to a T.

While the devil would love to convince us that the prosperity theology could never infiltrate our church, its "tentacles" are now in and around most, if not all, major metropolitan cities in America. Thus, it is highly likely that it is already in your church or located at a "theater near you." Beware.

The prosperity theology movement is right at the epicenter of the angelic conflict we're in the middle of as described in chapter 1! Those who have been ensnared by prosperity theology have no idea that Satan is using them to advance his kingdom and glory. Remember, to be primarily focused on our kingdoms (i.e., *our* best lives now and *our* destinies) is to be primarily focused on Satan's kingdom. It's the same "hat trick" that Satan played on Adam and Eve. What Satan, in essence, told Eve is no different than what every good prosperity theology preacher tells their "victims" today, which is, "If you just fix your thinking, you can live *your* best life now and reach *your* destiny!"

Notice obedience to the Word of God and the need to live holy lives that are pleasing to God are rarely, if ever, part of the "mantra." Another slick tactic of the enemy to keep us in chains! Said another way, we will never be able to live our best lives now to advance God's kingdom and bring Him glory when obedience to God's Word and the pursuit of holy living aren't a top priority!

Thus, if you have been ensnared by the "big lie" that Satan has gotten many in the church to believe, which is that prosperity theology is biblical theology. I pray you now see it is straight from the pit of hell! I also pray that you take whatever actions are necessary to break its power and influence over your life and the life of your family. If you decided to do this, let me be the first to congratulate you! Now give someone else a copy of this book so they'll do the same thing!

If you need to leave your current church based on what you've read, please know that while the numbers are rapidly dwindling, there are still many good Bible-believing churches in America. Find one as soon as you can, enjoy your newfound freedom in Christ, and don't ever look back!

For those pastors who know they are caught up in prosperity theology under the conviction of the Holy Spirit and don't know what to do, you know exactly what to do. Repent privately, then publicly (like some of you have) for the damage you have caused to the body of Christ, receive Christ's forgiveness, let your kingdoms "fall," and "go and sin no more" (John 8:11). If you choose not to, let this day be recorded against you (Deuteronomy 30:19) that your greatest problem is not me, anyone else, or any other issue you're facing. Your greatest problem is the Lord Jesus Christ! Consider this warning a blessing and play the man!

We will never be able to transform our nation until we corporately deal with this "cancer" that continues to ravage the body of Christ and every institution in America from our house to the White House. Individuals who think life is first about their happiness, health, wealth, and prosperity become individuals, families, churches, cities, and a nation who think life is first about their happiness, health, wealth, and prosperity. Have you been on social media lately? If we expect to build His kingdom, it's time we stopped being preoccupied with ours! Said another way, if life is truly "all about Him" and not about us, isn't it time we started acting like it?

The next big lie that Satan has gotten many in the church to believe to destroy the foundations of our lives and every institution in America we comprise from our house to the White House is that the *primary* mission of the church is something other than the Great Commission. Think about this for a second. Jesus could have said anything He wanted to say right before He left the earth. Yet, the last thing He said to His disciples (us), and arguably the most important thing, was this: "Stay ye, therefore, and invite someone to church so 'Pastor X' can preach a Gospel message that might require repentance while the rest of us run the church's food bank, start a Zumba class, sing in the choir, serve in the nursery, help out in children's church, assist the youth pastor, become an 'official' church member, start a new campus, become an elder, teach Sunday school, join a small group, head-up women's ministries, organize a quarterly men's prayer breakfast, be an usher, or try out for the worship team." Oh, this wasn't what Jesus told us to do before He left the earth? Could have fooled me!

Did you know that it is possible to do "good things" without ever getting around to the "Great Thing?" Many of us have forgotten, or if we were honest with ourselves, have conveniently ignored what Jesus said before His ascension.

> Go therefore and make disciples of all
> nations, baptizing them in the name of the Father
> and of the Son and of the Holy Spirit teaching
> them to observe all that I have commanded you.
> And behold, I am with you always, to the end of
> the age. (Matthew 28:19 ESV)

You'd think it was called the Great Suggestion or something?

Mark's account of the Great Commission is slightly different and says, "Go into all the world and preach the Gospel to every creature. He who believes and is baptized will be saved; but He who does not believe will be condemned" (Mark 16:15–16 NKJV).

As I use the term Great Commission going forward, it will include the combined accounts of Jesus's words in Matthew (People Group Perspective) and Mark (Individual Perspective); that is, "Go into all the world and preach the Gospel to every creature, make disciples of all nations, baptizing them in the name of the Father, Son, and Holy Spirit, teaching them to observe all that I have commanded you..." The reason why I use this combined account is that Jesus makes it clear that He not only wants us to "preach the Gospel" but also to "make disciples" since it is very possible to do the former without, tragically, ever getting around to the latter!

While I am not the first to say this, it cannot be emphasized enough, given the current level of chaos we are experiencing in our nation. What, you ask? It's this. The single greatest tragedy in the church today is that the overwhelming majority of God's people refuse to fulfill the *primary* mission of the church. Instead of "going" and preaching the uncompromised Word of God and making disciples of all men, we're "staying" and doing everything we can to keep people comfortable while they "die." Contrary to the belief of many, Jesus directed the Great Commission to all of His followers (us). While I am grateful for the many pastors who faithfully preach the true Gospel (because many don't!) and provide an opportunity for unbelievers to repent and have their sins forgiven by Christ, this is a "far cry" from what Jesus commanded.

So why aren't the overwhelming majority of Christians fulfilling the Great Commission? While the reasons are many, I believe one of the biggest reasons is because most of us have not become true disciples ourselves. You see, it's hard to get excited about making "fishers of men" when we ourselves are not "fishers of men." In fact, it's impossible to make fishers of men when we ourselves are not fishers of men. So instead of becoming true disciples who consistently deny our wills for His will, take up our crosses (i.e. the instruments of our death where we are willing to spiritually "die" to self), and follow Him (i.e. allow His Word to have the final word), many of us in the church today deny ourselves little, die to nothing, and follow another leader.

Remember, 95 percent of all Christians have never won a soul to Christ.[273] Think about the far-reaching ramifications of what I just said. This means that the best-case scenario, where the leadership of the church understands and seeks to "live out" the Great Commission as the *primary* mission of the church, pastors, and ministers of the Gospel are virtually alone in their efforts to transform their surrounding communities with the Gospel! Forget "making disciples." Thus, it begs a tough question for all of us. How can we say we're disciples of Jesus if we're unwilling to do what He told us to do? Far too many of us are forsaking the "Great Thing" for "good things" and calling it discipleship. No dice. This must absolutely break God's heart.

Now consider this most sobering question in light of what I just said. What *eternal* value is there in having all these wonderful discipleship platforms (i.e., small groups, men's and women's ministries, Christian conferences, Christian cruises, prayer breakfasts, and guest speakers) if, in the end, we are not going to do what Jesus told us to do to build His kingdom and magnify His glory worldwide? Obviously, they have value. But that's not what I asked you. I said, "What *eternal* value do they have?"

In other words, what good is information if it's not going to result in a transformation of the culture? It's like me going to the FBI Academy for new agent training where you learn all this "cool stuff" and then never using it to collect evidence that puts criminals in jail.

Many pastors are asking themselves the same question regarding the mission of the church, and my heart goes out to all of them for the tremendous burden they must carry in many cases alone! Remember, this is the "best-case scenario" in the most biblically-based churches in America whose leadership actually understand what the *primary* mission of the church is and seek to fulfill it.

To highlight the magnitude of this crisis in the church today, take a look at the following sample of thirteen mission statements (as of April 24, 2020) taken from the websites of top-ranked, well-known churches in America to see how they compare with the *primary* mission of the church as outlined by Jesus:

1. Westover Hills (San Antonio, Texas): "Making New, Making Great" by knowing and accepting Christ and placing Him at the center of our lives and seeking a strong relationship with Him.[274]

2. The City Church (Kirkland, Washington), now called Churchome—Kirkland: No mission statement, however, their "Our Call" statement says, "We want to create an environment where people can experience God's love no matter who they are, what they are going through, or what they believe."[275]

3. Fellowship Church (Grapevine, Texas): "To Reach up, Reach out, and Reach in."[276]

4. Elevation Church (Matthews, North Carolina): "Elevation Church exists so that people far from God will be raised to life in Christ."[277]

5. Hillsong Church (Sydney, Australia): "To reach and influence the world by building a large Christ-centered, Bible-based church, changing mindsets and empowering people to lead and impact in every sphere of life."[278]

6. City of Grace (Phoenix, Arizona)—now known as Hillsong, Phoenix: Same mission statement as #5.[279]

7. Gateway Church (Southlake, Texas): "To help each person at Gateway believe in Jesus, belong to family, become a follower, and build God's kingdom."[280]

8. National Community Church (Washington DC): "We exist to worship and follow Jesus. Our mission is to do as Jesus did, together, wherever we are. Every church has the same mission: to make disciples. But different churches accomplish this in different ways."[281]

9. Community Christian Church (Naperville, Illinois): "Helping people find their way back to God."[282]

10. Granger Community Church (Granger, Indiana): "Helping people take their next step toward Christ...together."[283]

11. Coral Ridge Presbyterian Church (Ft. Lauderdale, Florida): "We equip our people to develop a biblical worldview, share the Gospel, build healthy relationships, transform communities, and renew culture."[284]

12. The Potter's House (Dallas, Texas): "To become a global voice, along a lifelong journey of spiritual and economic hope, encouragement and empowerment to people locally, nationally and around the world."[285]

While some of these mission statements may sound good, feel good, and have wonderful, Christ-honoring goals and intentions, I trust you now see how different they are than the *mission statement* given to us by Jesus himself known as the Great Commission. For those of you who read them and say, "Well, that's what they mean—to fulfill the Great Commission"—really? Then, why not just use the words Jesus used? Why reinvent the wheel and create unnecessary confusion with a "feel-good" statement that just makes it seem like you're trying to "one-up" Jesus or compete with other churches to see who can have the "coolest" or most "compassionate," "loving," "holy," "seeker-sensitive" mission? Whatever the reason you have, it's a sin to portray the primary mission of the church as anything other than what Jesus says it is—period. If you don't like this, take it up with the Holy Spirit! He wrote the book. I just try to follow it.

Of the fifty top-ranked megachurches in America I examined, [286] only two had Jesus's Mission Statement as their mission statement. The first church was Second Baptist Church in Houston, Texas,[287] the largest Baptist Church in America. Now, for all the other churches that don't have the Great Commission as your *primary* mission statement, does the Second Baptist Church in Houston have it all wrong? If they did, so did Jesus. "No," you say. "We both have it right. We just have a different way of saying the same thing."

Oh really? I'm not even sure what some of you are trying to say. I don't see the Great Commission at all in some of your mission statements. Incidentally, Second Baptist, how many hours in leadership meetings did you spend thinking up your mission statement? Oh, none, because Jesus already did it for you so you could use your time more effectively elsewhere? Kudos, Second Baptist! Way to be good stewards of God's time!

By the way, while I'm sure you get this often from all your First Baptist friends, it's great to know where the *Second* Baptist is finally located.

The only other church to have the Great Commission as their mission statement was Hopewell Missionary Baptist in Norcross, Georgia.[288]

The next closest church in the list of fifty top-ranked megachurches in America to have the correct mission statement is Christ Church of the Valley in Peoria, Arizona. Their mission statement is "to win people to Jesus Christ, train believers to become disciples, and send disciples out to impact the world."[289]

New Hope Fellowship in Honolulu, Hawaii, similarly, says their mission is "To present the Gospel of Jesus Christ in such a way that turns non-Christians into converts, converts into disciples, and disciples into mature fruitful leaders who will in turn go into the world and reach others for Christ."[290]

Christ Fellowship (Miami, Florida) and Biltmore Baptist (Arden, NC) simply say their mission statements are "Helping you follow Jesus"[291] and "To glorify God by making disciples of Jesus who reach up, reach in, and reach out"[292] respectively.

Calvary Chapel in Ft. Lauderdale, Florida, had the shortest mission statement—"To make disciples by connecting people to God, connecting people to people, and connecting people to outreach."[293]

Spanish River Church in Boca Raton, Florida, says their mission is "To practice Gospel living to help the casually connected deeply engage with Jesus."[294]

While Gateway Church's mission statement is not the Great Commission (and should be!), the mission of *Gateway Outreach* is "to equip, empower, and mobilize people to make a kingdom impact outside the walls of Gateway Church. At Gateway, outreach is about building God's kingdom through Christ-centered, church-led community transformation where we live and around the world."[295]

While the church is very active in Global Missions, no mission statement nor anything resembling a mission statement could be located on the website of the largest church in America, Lakewood Church,[296] in Houston, Texas, home to Joel Osteen with over 52,000 weekly attendees.[297]

Even Saddleback Church (Lake Forest, CA), home to Pastor Rick Warren, author of the second best-selling nonfiction book of all time after the Bible, *The Purpose Driven Life*, whose church was ranked #1 in Newsmax's 2013 list of "Top 50 Megachurches in America" says its mission is "to provide a place where the depressed, the hurting, and hopeless can come and find help. To be a place of family, community, and hope."[298]

So as you can see, while some churches in America understand what the primary mission of the church is according to the teachings of Jesus himself, most do not, or if they do, are not accurately reflecting it in their mission statements for the world to see. And as you can see, these include some of the most influential, "successful" churches in America.

Please don't misunderstand me. Many of these churches are doing wonderful works in the name of Jesus Christ that should be commended and applauded. Still, far too often, churches are forsaking the "best work" for "good works" because "that's the pastor's job" or what missionaries do. No, beloved. It's our job—every person reading this book who claims to be a follower of Jesus Christ. Remember, 95 percent of all Christians, including those doing "good works" in these "successful" churches, have never won one soul to

Christ![299] This is the "sin," brothers and sisters, and what Satan has so cleverly orchestrated and disguised to keep Christians "off mission."

Is it any wonder why so many Christians in America don't know what the *primary* mission of the church is when the most "successful" churches don't know what it is? Or if they do, can't communicate it or get their flock to execute it? Think I'm kidding? Ask three Christians in your church this Sunday what the *primary mission* of the church is according to Jesus? You'll be shocked! And if you think we're confused, ask an unbeliever. You'll be even more shocked! If nothing else, I guarantee it will open the door for you to share the Gospel with them!

While it should not be surprising given the schemes and strategies of the devil, it still amazes me how many Christians believe that it is not their responsibility to share the Gospel and make disciples. Whether we truly believe this or use it as a convenient excuse to justify our disobedience, only God knows. Either way, it's time to set the record straight. While all of us do not hold the office of an evangelist (Ephesians 4:11), we are all called to evangelize in fulfillment of the Great Commission (1 Peter 2:9, 3:15; Acts 8:4), not just pastors!

If this is not our top priority as a "follower" of Jesus Christ and the primary mission of our churches, then our churches are "out of order" (chapter 2). If your priorities are in order, but your church is "out of order" and your loving attempts to encourage your church leaders are met with "deaf ears" or empty promises over a reasonable waiting period (three to six months), I strongly encourage you to find a new church that not only has the Great Commission as its *primary* mission over the marquee but where its members (and not just the pastor) are executing it! There's way too much at stake and way too little time for us to be playing any more church games while our nation is on the brink of spiritual collapse brothers and sisters!

Let it be a standing rebuke to all of us that approximately 2.16 billion people worldwide in over 7,368 people groups out of 17,298 (or 42.6 percent) have still yet to be evangelized[300] while we go to our comfortable churches week after week and consume all we can to learn how to live our best lives now and reach our destinies! May God help us! We will all (especially those in leadership) give an answer on that day (i.e. Judgment Day) for not only what we do but what we fail to do with the knowledge we've been given (James 4:17). You're welcome.

For pastors who are rightly interested in unity among the church of Jesus Christ in America, can you imagine how unified we would be overnight if all of us had the same mission statement as Jesus and faithfully executed it daily? Did you just hear what I heard in the spirit? It was demons screeching in terror! What up to now has been cleverly concealed under a thin veil of deception is now exposed!

And for the many churches who claim to be fulfilling the *primary* mission of the church regardless of what your mission statements say, explain why 95 percent of all Christians (you know, the ones sitting in the pews of "your" churches all across America) have never won a soul to Christ,[301] much less make a disciple? Don't believe me? I challenge you to take a "with every head bowed and every eye closed" show of hands poll next Sunday. Can't do it? Or won't do it? Afraid of what you might see? Or afraid of how it could impact tithing? Whose kingdom did you say you were building? Incidentally, what do you find more offensive? My choice of words or the excuses some of you continually make that prevent you from lovingly challenging your congregants to fulfill the Great Commission?

You and I will answer. Nearly every week, my pastor shares a testimony on how he shared the Gospel in our community the previous week. He lovingly challenges *every person* in the pews to do the same thing. That, beloved brothers and sisters, is leadership consistent with the *primary* mission of the church! Is that what you do, Pastor? It should be!

An October 2017 Barna study revealed that over one-half (51 percent) of churchgoing Christians in the US are not even familiar with the term *"Great Commission."*[302] You and I can say our churches are making disciples who "go" and preach the Gospel and make other disciples all we want, but the statistics show otherwise. The sooner we stop kidding ourselves, the sooner we can begin transforming the world around us instead of the other way around. While inviting people to church to hear the Gospel (assuming it is the true Gospel that requires repentance and not a watered-down version of the Gospel that doesn't) and respond to it is essential, necessary, and should continue, it's a far cry from what Jesus commanded.

As for all the "good works" that we, the church, need to continue doing in our communities, many of us need to change how we do it if we want to be "on mission." For example, all of us should have a place "on-site" where those who receive food, clothing, tutoring, car repairs, home repairs, moving assistance, or (fill in the blank) have an opportunity to hear the Gospel and respond to it! The answer is not "just invite them to church." Yes, invite them to church, but what does that do for the many who will never come? Secondly, how does this "fix" the larger problem of "pushing off" on the few what all of us should be doing? Meanwhile, we've just missed out on the only opportunity we may ever have to share the Gospel message with them and the only opportunity they may ever have to respond to it!

So many pray for God to open up doors with others to share the Gospel, and when He does, we slam the door in His face! It's mind-blowing to me (though not surprising given the schemes and strategies of the enemy) how we go into communities week after week, month after month, and year after year to give those in need "bread and water" but never give them the Bread of Life and Living Water! Instead, we take the golden opportunity God has given us and leave people in the same lame spiritual condition we found them in—"lost." What kind of ministry is that? How are we demonstrating love to those around us when we're willing to let them go to hell so we can feel good about ourselves?

Said another way, we gave them everything but what they really needed! Is this really what Jesus died for on the cross? How are we any different than any other secular charitable organization doing "good works?" We're not! We might as well join the Peace Corps where its volunteers are prohibited from sharing the Gospel. In this way, we can just blame our negligence on their policies and procedures of the organization to alleviate any guilt we may have for not doing what Jesus told us to do! Selah.

Throughout the ages, the church has never struggled doing "good works." We got that down! We understand that faith without works is dead (James 2:26) and that this has nothing to do with earning our salvation. It is a byproduct of our salvation. Got it long ago. However, works that do not result in others placing their faith in the finished works of Jesus Christ alone for the forgiveness of their sins are also "dead." Not "dead" in the physical sense, but "dead" in the spiritual sense. While "good works" will always have tremendous societal value, they have no kingdom value unless we can tie them to the King and the expansion of His kingdom through the preaching of the Gospel and "making disciples." This is majoring on the "major!"

The Bible says that on Judgment Day, all of our works built on the foundation of Christ will be tried in the fire, and the fire will reveal what kind of work each builder has done (1 Corinthians 3:13). What kind of *eternal* value do you think "good works" not tied to the Great Commission will have? I'll tell you—none. While Jesus did many "good works" in the name of love and compassion, His primary motive and ultimate objective for doing so was the transformation of the human heart; that is, to see people repent, become disciples, and then "go" and make more disciples. Is this the goal behind our "good works" and the "good works" in our churches? Would there be enough evidence of this to convict you?

As the cliché goes, success is not teaching someone how to fish. It is teaching someone how to fish who will, in turn, "go" and teach someone else how to fish. This is the heart of the Great Commission. But how can we teach others to be "fishers of men" when we're not willing to become "fishers of men" ourselves? We're back to the heart of the problem and why so many pastors are understandably frustrated.

Few things are more rewarding to a parent than when they hear their child give someone else the same advice they gave them (their child) many years earlier. A similar feeling must come over a teacher when one of their former students returns many years later and says, "Ms. Wilson, I just wanted you to know that the reason I love math so much and have given my life to teaching it to others was because of you! Thank you for your investment in me so I can now invest in others!"

I had this experience. While in grade school, I had an amazing band teacher who greatly influenced my love and appreciation for woodwind instruments, primarily the clarinet and saxophone. His name was Mr. Reed. How appropriate, right? For those of you who saw *Mr. Holland's Opus*, he was my Mr. Holland. He believed in me when I didn't believe in myself. Many years ago, after graduating from high school, I went back to see if I could find him so I could tell him what an impact he had on my life and thank him for not only what he taught me but how he taught me.

I found him. He remembered me. I told him what a profound influence he had had on me and that my love for music and desire to continue playing all these years was in large part due to him! His now older eyes began to fill with tears. God allowed me to give Mr. Reed a precious gift that day because he had given me a precious gift many years before that continues to bear fruit in my life and the lives of others for the kingdom. At random moments in my life, I have found myself reflecting on my days with Mr. Reed, thinking, *Mr. Reed, while I was just a little boy who thought little of God when you were teaching me how to play the clarinet, I feel confident that you must have been a Christian man by way you taught me and passed on your love of music to me. Thank you. I'll be looking for you in heaven!*

Without knowing it, Mr. Reed was making a music "disciple" who would, in turn, "go" and make more "music disciples." As wonderful as this is, however, infinitely more important than this is making disciples for Jesus Christ who will "go" and make more disciples for Jesus. As a Christian, there is nothing more significant we can do on this side of eternity than become a disciple who makes disciples for God's kingdom and glory.

Because we're "off mission," our nation is filled with undisciplined Christians who are unwilling to "pay" the high cost of discipleship. And make no mistake, there's a high cost. However, I would argue that the cost of irresponsibility and disobedience has also been great in light of our present-day chaos, wouldn't you agree?

This brings us to how this "big lie," which is that the *primary* mission of the church is something other than the Great Commission causes us to destroy the foundations of our lives and every institution in America we comprise from our house to the White House. Ready? Here it is. Jesus only shares His power with true disciples; that is, those He can trust to follow Him and do what He commanded.[303] Jesus does not share His power with mere converts who can't be trusted to follow Him. Satan knows this. Therefore, if Satan can keep us from becoming disciples who never get around to making disciples in fulfillment of the Great Commission, He can block the flow of God's power that is needed to the church (us) to transform the world around us!

You see, the reason why God only shares His power with disciples is because He doesn't want His power falling into the wrong hands so we advance the wrong kingdom by doing what we, not He (God), think is right! God is looking for us to advance His kingdom, not Satan's kingdom, remember? Only true disciples can be trusted to do this. This means that until we are ready to submit to God's authority and follow Him as true disciples who understand what our primary mission is and seek to do it, we will never experience God's power and be able to transform the world around us. Now you understand why, with rare exceptions, the church in America today is so spiritually impotent and why the world is transforming us instead of the other way around!

While mere converts alone will go to heaven when they die, they are of no kingdom use to God in the here and now! Read that again, beloved. I know it's a strong statement, but it's the truth and why, I firmly believe, we are living in a post-Christian era in America. No disciples, no power. No power, no transformation. No transformation, no territory (chapter 1). Know disciples, know power. Know power, know transformation. Know transformation, know territory!

While we discussed this concept of "territory" extensively in chapter 1, if you recall, I'd like to touch on it again here since it is incredibly applicable to our discussion. The goal of any *successful* mission, whether secular or spiritual, involves the acquisition and transformation of territory. Take a quick look at the primary missions of the four branches of our military. In a nutshell, the primary mission of the Army is to *transform* "land" through sustained land dominance. The primary mission of the Navy is to *transform* the "sea lanes" to maintain the freedom of the seas. The primary mission of the Marine Corps is to *transform* "beachheads" for amphibious operations. And, finally, the primary mission of the Air Force is to *transform* airspace for aerial warfare. Gotta love it, right?

Every CEO wants to know the same thing. Who's going to seize, occupy, and transform the most territory for their kingdom? Will it be McDonald's or Burger King? Coke or Pepsi? Google or Amazon? Oracle or IBM? the LA Rams or the New Orleans Saints? China or the United States? The Republicans or the Democrats? For purposes of our discussion, will it be the kingdom of darkness or the kingdom of light? Satan wants to know! And make no mistake about it, if you and I are not advancing the kingdom of God through the fulfillment of the Great Commission, we are being used to advance the other kingdom, even when it seems like the "other" kingdom is a "nice" kingdom! Another "slick trick" of the devil.

While "nice" is nice, a "nice" church is no threat to hell if it never spiritually seizes, occupies, and transforms the territory around it for the kingdom of God through fulfillment of the Great Commission! You see, Satan is not opposed to "good works" as long as those good works don't lead to the "great works" of salvation, discipleship, transformation, reclaimed territory, and glory for God! This is what Satan's cares about. His greatest fear is that we will one day "wake up" and realize this! Ha ha, devil. Too late for that. Talk to Jesus if you don't like it! We're with Him!

For those of you who think the church of Jesus Christ has been successful in fulfilling the Great Commission in America over the last number of decades, where's the evidence of the spiritual transformation in our culture? I didn't ask where the evidence of spiritual transformation was inside your church. I asked where the evidence of spiritual transformation was in our culture as a result of the spiritual transformation that is supposedly taking place inside our churches? This is the "sin," brothers and sisters! We are not transforming the culture, but the culture is transforming us!

"Every empty seat in our church is a sin," says one pastor.

To this, I would respond, "Well, maybe, but maybe not." Certainly, it is a sin if you want that seat filled because you're more interested in building your kingdom than God's kingdom. Yes, it is a sin if you have a "gather and count" mentality so you can "feel good" about the size of your "kingdom" when compared to another pastor's kingdom. But it's not a sin if you want to see that empty seat filled with someone who will become a disciple who will "go" and make more disciples.

I don't know about you, but I'd rather be in a church with ten disciples and another ten in training that has 100 empty seats than be in a consumer-based, spiritually anemic church with 50,000 people who never become disciples that "go" and make more disciples with no empty seats! Do you feel the same way? You should if you understand the primary mission of the church! Sadly, most Christians in America, including many pastors, would rather "ooh and aah" over the 50,000-member church in Houston, Texas, than fix the problem.

Satan has done a wonderful job at getting pastors to compete with one another instead of unifying with one another on how to best help one another fulfill the primary mission of the church. "How big is 'your' church?;" "How big is 'your' budget?;" "How much money did you bring in this year?; "How many locations do you have?;" "How many services?;" "In how many different countries?;" "How many people attend each service;" and "How big is your e-Fam?" These are just a sample of some of the nauseating questions pastors routinely ask one another when they assemble for retreats, conferences, and conventions. It's no different than a Wall Street cocktail party. Where's the emphasis on the Great Commission? Jesus wants to know.

In case you haven't noticed, we are not pushing back the forces of darkness with the transformational power of the Gospel of Jesus Christ in the world today saints; the world, Satan, and his demons are pushing us back and daring us to stand up and challenge them. Jesus Himself said, "I must preach the good news of the kingdom of God to the other towns as well; for *I was sent for this purpose*" (Luke 4:43 ESV). Is this how you feel? We say we want to be like Jesus. Do we really mean it? Or is it just self-righteous "Christian-ese?" Satan wants to know! Jesus already does!

This "cuts" to the heart of the problem and the reason why I believe most Christians in America do not fulfill the Great Commission besides the sad fact that we are unable to export what we ourselves have not first "imported"—fear. In my first book, *Do You Want to Get Well?*, I dedicated a whole chapter to man's greatest fear—the fear of rejection. Instead of remembering that it is Christ who is ultimately rejected whenever we share the Gospel and people don't respond, we make our Gospel-sharing experiences about us, which is what Satan wants us to do. You see, Satan knows that if he can get us to take others' rejection personally, we won't do what poses the greatest threat to the preservation and expansion of his earthly kingdom. If the fear of being rejected keeps you from fulfilling the Great Commission, I would highly recommend that you get a copy of my first book and devour this chapter!

While there are many things I don't know, one thing I do know is that the 500+ people who responded to the Gospel message, by God's grace, over the last three years would still be dead in their trespasses and sins if I had not been willing to get out of my comfort zone to "go" and do what Jesus commanded. Remember, many of these individuals were already attending Bible-believing churches when I met them but could not explain the basis of their Christian faith to me. This highlights another huge problem in the church, proving that the Great Commission, contrary to all the assertions otherwise, has not been the primary mission of most churches in America. What problem is it? Our churches are filled with people who think they are "saved" but are not. It's a little difficult to fulfill the Great Commission under these circumstances, wouldn't you agree?

While all the "big lies" I covered before this one have had a devastating impact on our homes, society, churches, and nation, none, in my opinion, has had a greater impact than this one. Can you imagine what every institution from our house to the White House would look like if God had true disciples fulfilling the Great Commission in every institution from our house to the White House? Things like fatherlessness, domestic violence, school shootings, suicide, drug overdose, teen pregnancy, abortions, sexual assaults, gang violence, and "deep state" corruption would decrease overnight. The Supreme Court would overturn Roe v. Wade, gay marriage would no longer be the law of the land, and our nation would no longer be a "tinderbox" of division spiritually, morally, socially, and politically.

Can you imagine where we would be as a nation today if our military personnel and law enforcement officers neglected or refused to execute their primary missions? Yet, this is exactly what we've done as the body of Christ in America and wonder why things continue to unravel around us exponentially.

We are not seeking Him first when His primary mission for us is second, last, or not even on the radar! What many of us don't realize is that when we forsake Jesus's primary mission for another mission; either intentionally or unintentionally, we are forsaking Him. Don't agree? If you were the commanding officer of the military personnel I referred to above who abandoned the primary mission of your unit, would they not also be abandoning you? Would it not have grave consequences on the "battlefield?" You bet. The same is true on our "battlefield." Unrestrained evil. Sexual deviancy. Unimaginable acts of senseless violence. Who's opposing Satan and his demons? Not us, by the look of things!

Precious brothers and sisters, we are the only ones, through Christ, who have the power to change the trajectory this nation is on. Only one question remains. Will we?

To the Christians and churches who know what their *primary* mission is and have been faithfully discharging their duties, you have my greatest respect! Why? Because you hold the key to ushering in the greatest revival our nation has ever seen to advance God's kingdom and magnify His glory in the earth! In the words of Paul, continue to fight the good fight, keep the faith, and finish your course, for in the future, there is laid up for you the crown of righteousness which the Lord, the righteous judge, will award to you on that day; and not only to you, but to all those who long for His appearing (2 Timothy 4:7–8).

For those who believed the "big lie" that the *primary mission* of the church is something other than the Great Commission, now you know the truth. While we continue to do "good works," may each of us be fully committed to the "Great Work" from this day forward from our house to the White House to transform the world for His glory!

The next big lie that Satan has gotten many in the church to believe to destroy the foundations of our lives and every institution in America we comprise from our house to the White House is that there are no perfect churches. While this statement is technically true because churches have imperfect people, and the church is not a building but the people in it, I find it to be extremely misleading. In many ways, I believe it is a gross mischaracterization of the true state of the church. You see, the statement that there are no perfect churches is as true for the most unbiblically-based church in America as it is for the most biblically-based church in America.

Please allow me to let you in on a little secret. Many of you know it already. All of our churches, like all of us, are *far* from perfect. I don't know about you, but I've never walked on water or had even one perfect day since I was born! Do you know what this means? We, the church, are a lot further from perfect than many of us would like to admit. The lone fact that 95 percent of all Christians have never won a soul to Christ[304] is evidence of this alone, wouldn't you agree? God knows it. The question is, do we know it? Or are we too proud to admit it?

It has been my experience that when Christians say, "Well, you know, no church is perfect," it is usually in response to some sort of justification for why they are attending a particular Church. It is also sometimes said to justify why they, or another, should not leave a particular church or why every Christian should be a part of "the local church." While God's Word is clear on this last point (Hebrews 10:25), it is also clear that when we do assemble, we should be worshipping God in spirit and in truth (John 4:24). In other words, we not only need to assemble with other believers, but we need to assemble in ways that bring honor and glory to God. This last point underscores the modern-day crisis in the church today that is big on assembling but small on spirit *and* truth.

In my experience, the phrase "No church is perfect" is "code" for "You might as well just stay here anyway, friend, because the church down the road has its own set of 'issues.'" What I believe these well-intentioned Christians don't realize, however, is that all issues are not created equal. For example, church leaders who can't agree on how to spend their annual budgets are very different than church leaders who subscribe to "prosperity theology."

A church that is divided over whether or not they should fund a building project is very different than a church denomination who has changed their bylaws to allow women to occupy the office of pastor, associate pastor, or elder in violation to scripture (1 Timothy 2:12–14, 3:1–13; Titus 1:5–9; Acts 6:1–6). Leaving a church that no longer "entertains" us (which is never a good reason to go!) is very different than leaving a church that has become "gay-affirming" versus "gay-accepting." A church that is quibbling over what color the carpet and walls should be (as annoying as this is!) is very different than a church that has elevated tolerance above righteousness to appear more "seeker-sensitive." You get the idea.

As stated above, while no church is perfect, some churches are a lot "sicker" spiritually than others because their "issues" are very significant issues that violate scripture. Too often, we use the phrase, "Well, you know, brother, no church is perfect" as a convenient excuse to spit in the face of God by tolerating things Jesus would never tolerate. That's the issue, friend, and why this "big lie" has been a very useful tool in the hands of Satan to render much of the church in America powerless and ineffective for Christ!

The bottom line is this: Does the church I am attending seek to obey (not perfectly, but faithfully) *all* of God's Word or just the parts they like or agree with? Worse yet, do they invent their own version of Christianity to build their kingdom instead of God's kingdom (e.g., prosperity theology)?

Question: If you are currently in a church that you believe is "not perfect" but "pretty darn good," what incentive is there to sin *less* and glorify God *more*? Remember, if the devil can't neutralize us with false teaching and idolatry, he's happy to neutralize our impact for the kingdom with pride!

Now ask yourself this question: If the best churches in America that seek to obey all of God's Word are far from perfect (as stated above), what does that say about churches that are *farther* than far from perfect? You know, the overwhelming majority of churches in America who either subscribe to an à la carte Christian model (i.e., take what they like and leave the rest) or invent their own version of Christianity (e.g., salvation without repentance)? Now take your answer to that question and answer this question. If the best churches in America are far from perfect and represent the minority of all churches in America, and the rest of our churches are farther than far from perfect and represent most churches in America, how can we possibly transform our culture when all or most of us arrogantly believe our churches aren't perfect but "pretty darn good?" The last time I looked, God opposes the proud. Without His assistance, I can, however, guarantee one thing. The culture will continue to transform us!

In case you haven't noticed, the way we've been doing church is not reaching the culture folks! But the culture is reaching us! This means that it is time for all of us to change! You're familiar with the definition of insanity—doing the same thing expecting different results.

Most, if not all of us under the conviction of the Holy Spirit, know where we need to change. Believe me. I can't even read my own blasted book without seeing where I need to change! The important thing is that we take decisive action based on the Word of God and never look back!

So now who, in the church, would be arrogant or irresponsible enough to say the same thing about our nation; that is, "You know, America is not a perfect nation, but we're pretty darn good"?

Only when God's people, who are far from perfect, humbly seek to do the will of God in every area of life will we, in Christ, have the capacity and ability to transform society from our house to the White House.

Beloved, don't ever forget that God's barometer is a lot different than our barometers when it comes to the spiritual health of our churches. The power and strength needed to reclaim what has been stolen from us to advance God's kingdom and magnify His glory is perfected in weakness (2 Corinthians. 12:9), not pride. Paul said, "Therefore, most gladly I will rather boast in my infirmities, *that*

the power of Christ may rest upon me" (2 Corinthians. 12:9 NKJV).
If there was ever a time that we needed the power of God resting
on us to repair the foundations of our lives and every institution in
America we comprise from our house to the White House, it is now!
May it begin with us!

The next big lie that Satan has gotten many in the church to
believe to destroy the foundations of our lives and every institution
in America we comprise from our house to the White House is that
prayer is never a waste of time. What? Did you just hear more plates
crashing?

When was the last time you heard a Christian say that prayer
can be a total waste of time? Heresy, right? If you've been around the
local church for a while, it is highly likely you have heard some, if not
all, of the following powerful little prayer "ditties:"

"Prayer is heaven's secret weapon."[305]

"If you only pray when you're in trouble…you're in trouble."[306]

"When man prays, God works."[307]

"Prayer is putting oneself in the hands of God."[308]

"Prayer is the key that unlocks all the storehouses of God's
infinite grace and power."[309]

"Prayer changes things…starting with the one who prays."[310]

"Prayer is the engine room of the church."[311]

"Prayer is man's greatest power."[312]

"Prayer is a declaration of war."[313]

"Prayer is speaking truth to truth."[314]

"Prayer is earthly permission for heavenly intervention."[315]

Personally, I love them all. However, the assumption in them
all is that God hears every prayer and that all prayer is created equal.
But is this really what scripture teaches? Some of you are about to be
shocked!

It should come as no big surprise that the Bible has much to
say on the subject of prayer. For example, the effectual fervent prayer
of a righteous man (or woman) avails much (James 5:16). When
the righteous cry out, the Lord listens; He delivers them from all
their troubles (Psalm 34:17 NLT). Great promise, right? But what
happens when fervent prayer is offered up by someone who has no

intention of living a righteous life; that is, by someone who turns his ear from hearing the law or by someone who refuses to obey what they have been taught (2 Thessalonians 3:14)? The Word of God says that the prayers of this man or woman will not only not be heard but are an abomination (Proverbs 28:9). What? That's right. Another translation of the same verse says that God has no use for the prayers of the people who won't listen to Him (Proverbs 8:9 MSG). Really? Really.

The implications of what I just said in our everyday life as you might guess are staggering since what happens in the physical realm (where we live) is tied to what happens in the spiritual realm where prayer operates. For example, a Christian husband praying for work after losing his job is wasting his time (and others' time) if he refuses to update his resume, submit job applications, follow-up with prospective employers, and go on interviews.

Similarly, a Christian wife praying for relief from excessive anxiety in the workplace is wasting her time if she is consistently putting her career ahead of her family to climb the corporate ladder. Additionally, husbands and wives are totaling wasting their time praying for God to heal their marriage if they have no desire to operate within the framework of their God-ordained roles (chapter 2). Why? Because in all three examples and others like them, God will not act contrary to His character and Word, even when we're "sad" or "desperate."

It's like praying to lose weight or get out of debt without diet, exercise, or putting limits on our spending. It's a total waste of time! Instead, what I usually recommend to someone who is not willing to do their part in such areas is to buy a box of "really good" overpriced chocolates without telling their spouse and eat them in their car alone in one sitting. Oh, and don't forget to pray and give thanks first! While this may have made some of you angry and others laugh, is this not the way many of us act before getting "uppity" at God when He doesn't answer our prayers? Satan must get a real kick out of these types of prayers that we immediately nullify with our irresponsibility, disobedience, and outright rebellion to God's Word!

There are similar applications of this "big lie" inside the church. For example, church leaders who continually pray for a mighty move of the Holy Spirit in their church can "forget it" if they consistently, for example, elevate unity above theology and tolerance above righteousness. Pastor, you might as well charter a boat and take their entire church staff fishing in the Keys! Or, if you don't like fishing, I would recommend a day on the beach or some sightseeing! May I go?

This lie also impacts Washington. For example, Christians in Congress are wasting their time praying for our safety and security on the southern border if they are unwilling to put their petty politics aside and appropriate funds to build a "wall" that will decrease the flow of human trafficking, violence, drugs, and terrorism. Christians in Washington can attend weekly prayer breakfasts, offer up "nice" prayers at the National Day of Prayer, and say "God bless America" after every political speech all they want. However, it's a total waste of time if they are going to turn around and support, defend, enact, pass, interpret, enforce, or "turn a blind eye" to immoral laws and legislation that run contrary to the Word of God. Such assemblies are a stench to God (Amos 5:21 NIV).

You say, "Wait a minute, Spence, are you saying that God doesn't answer prayers when we 'turn our ear from His law and refuse to obey Him?'"

Yes, that's precisely what I'm saying, except God, as always, said it first. Proverbs says, "The Lord is far from the wicked [and distances himself from them], but He hears the prayer of the [consistently] righteous [that is, those with spiritual integrity and moral courage]" (Proverbs 15:29 AMP).

Another similar passage in Proverbs says the following (*italics* used for emphasis):

> When terror strikes you like a storm and your calamity comes like a whirlwind, when distress and anguish come upon you. *Then they will call upon me, but I will not answer; they will seek me diligently but will not find me. Because they hated knowledge and did not choose the fear of the*

*Lord, would have none of my counsel, and despised
all my reproof, therefore they shall eat the fruit of
their way, and have their fill of their own devices.*
(Proverbs 1:27–31 ESV)

Isaiah 59:2 says, "But your iniquities have separated you from
your God; And your sins have hidden His face from you, *So that He
will not hear*" (Isaiah 59:2 NKJV).

Prayer is a total waste of time when we entertain a desire or
intention to sin in our hearts. Psalm 66 says, "If I had cherished
iniquity in my heart, *the Lord would not have listened*" (Psalm 66:18
ESV). The meaning is not literally "[i]f I have 'seen' any iniquity in
my heart—for no one can look into His heart and see that it is not
defiled by sin; but instead, if I have *cherished* it in my soul; if I have
gloated over past sins; if I am purposing to commit sin again; if I am
not willing to abandon all sin, and to be holy."[316] This can also mean
forming wicked schemes in our hearts or having a complacent view
of wickedness in others.[317] The end result is the same—God does not
hear our prayers.

Psalm 145:18 says, "The Lord is near to all who call on Him, to
all who call on Him *in truth*." So what does that mean for the man or
woman of who calls on God in prayer *without truth*? You guessed it.

James says that God will also not answer our prayers when we
pray with a selfish motive, as seen here in the following:

> You want something you don't have, and
> you will do anything to get it. You will even kill!
> But you still cannot get what you want and you
> won't get it by fighting and arguing. You should
> pray for it. *Yet even when you do pray, your prayers
> are not answered, because you pray just for selfish
> reasons.* (James 4:2–3 CEV)

Pretty clear, right? Incidentally, this is why "name it and claim
it" praying is a total insult to God as discussed earlier. If the primary motivation of our prayers is to advance our kingdoms instead

of God's kingdom by using what He gives us only to benefit ourselves and not others, God is not interested in answering our prayers. I firmly believe this is the reason why so many of our prayers never get answered. If God can't bless us to be a blessing to others, why should He bless us?

For example, praying for a bigger home to accomplish more Christian hospitality, discipleship, teaching, training, and evangelism is very different than praying for a bigger home to keep up with the Joneses or to impress our coworkers, friends, and extended family. Praying that our child would be the next Olympic gymnastics champion to make a name for ourselves and "wow the world" is very different that praying that our child would be the next Olympic gymnastics champion so more people would come to know Jesus Christ through their humble witness for Christ.

For you singles, praying for a mate that will help you improve your self-image and advance your own kingdom agenda is very different than praying for a mate who will reflect His image and partner with you in advancing God's kingdom agenda! Trust me, God is very interested in answering our prayers, but they must be in line with His character and will as outlined in His Word; otherwise, we're wasting our time!

The Lord does not see as man sees, for man looks at the outward appearance, but the Lord looks at the heart (1 Samuel 16:7). Motive is everything when it comes to prayer, beloved, just as it is in every other area of the Christian life. God knows the motive of our hearts before we even open our mouths. He knows when we are praying to impress others with our religious zeal, vocabulary, or knowledge of the scriptures, and He knows when we are praying to merely "be blessed" rather than to "be a blessing." All of these motives are detestable to God and will not only not cause God to not move toward us but to oppose us (James 4:6).

This is why it is so critical for parents to transition their children beyond prayers of "bless our cat," "bless our lizard," "bless this food," "bless our family," "bless our sleep," "bless our day," to prayers that bring heaven to earth to advance God's kingdom and bring Him glory. Besides being prayers that are guaranteed to be heard by God, if we don't do this, we run the risk of teaching our children, who will most likely be parents themselves one day, that prayer is all about "being blessed" instead of "being a blessing."

Many Christians today are not getting their prayers answered because they are praying contrary to God's will. God's Word says that if we ask anything according to His will (that is, consistent with His plan and purpose), He hears us. And if we know (for a fact, as indeed we do) that He hears and listens to us in whatever we ask, we (also) know (with settled and absolute knowledge) that we have (granted to us) the requests which we have asked from Him (1 John 5:14–15 AMP).

John 16:24 says, "Until now you have asked nothing in my name. Ask, and you will receive, that your joy may be full" (John 16:24 NKJV). To ask in Jesus's name is to ask according to His will found in His Word. While it's good to pray "in Jesus' name," tacking His name onto a prayer that is contrary to His will is wasted breath.

E. Stanley Jones, a twentieth-century missionary and theologian, said the following about prayer and the will of God:

> Prayer is surrender to the will of God and cooperation with that will. If I throw out a boat-hook from the boat and catch hold of the shore and pull, do I pull the shore to me, or do I pull myself to the shore. Prayer is not pulling God to my will, but the aligning of my will to the will of God.[318]

Martin Luther King said, "Prayer is not overcoming God's reluctance but laying hold of His willingness."[319]

God's Word says that for our prayers to be effective, we must be abiding in Christ, and His Word must be abiding in us. Specifically, Jesus said, "If you abide in me *and* my words abide in you, *ask whatever you wish, and it will be done for you*" (John 15:7 ESV). We should, therefore, not expect to have our prayers answered *if* we are not abiding in Him *and* His Word is not abiding in us.

Note that abiding in Jesus alone is not sufficient to have our prayers answered. We also have to have God's Word, the Bible, abiding in us. Why? Because if His Word is not abiding in us, we can't possibly know His will, and if we're not praying His will, He will not answer our prayers. We have just wasted another opportunity to reclaim territory in the earth that Adam and Eve turned over to the devil. That's the real issue, remember (chapter 1)?

According to John 1:1, Jesus and His Word are inseparable. Revelation 19:13 says, "[H]is name is the Word of God." Therefore, it is impossible to say that we are abiding in Christ if we part from His Word. To reject one is to reject the other, resulting in unanswered prayer.

Prayer is also a waste of time where doubt and "double-mindedness" are present as seen here in the book of James:

> But let Him ask in faith, with no doubting,
> for the one who doubts is like a wave of the sea
> that is driven and tossed by the wind. *For that
> person must not suppose that He will receive any-
> thing from the Lord*; He is a double-minded man,
> unstable in all His ways. (James 1:6–7 ESV)

Doubt communicates a lack of trust in God. If God can't trust us to trust Him, He can't trust that we will follow Him and use what He gives us through answered prayer to advance His kingdom. So He doesn't answer our prayers. Can you blame Him? All of us experience doubt from time to time. This is not the person being referred to in the above passage of scripture. The above scripture refers to the man or woman who doubts as a way of life a double-minded person.

Pride also causes our prayers to be a total waste of time. "God resists the proud but gives grace to the humble" (James 4:6 NKJV). Need I say more?

While many Americans are against prayer, there is a large "unsaved" segment of our society that thinks its "cool," "all good," and even "sexy" as long as you don't get too "cra-cra" about it or, God forbid, offend anyone. Needless to say, God is not impressed. Satan, however, must find it amusing!

As alluded to earlier in our discussion about motive, prayer is also a total waste of time if the primary reason we are praying is so that others will see us. Jesus said, "When you pray, don't be like the hypocrites who love to pray publicly on street corners and in the synagogues where everyone can see them. I tell you the truth, *that is all the reward they will ever get*" (Matthew 6:5 NLT).

Prayer is also a total waste of time when we are harboring unforgiveness in our hearts. Jesus said that if we don't forgive others, He will not forgive us (Mark 11:26). If Jesus has not forgiven us because we refuse to forgive others, how likely do you think it is that He will answer our prayers?

Prayer can also be a total waste of time when we refuse to tithe. In Malachi 3, God is having a one-way conversation with the descendants of Jacob who scorned God's decrees and failed to obey Him. God asserts that they are in denial that they have ever departed from Him by cheating Him out of tithes and offering due Him, saying the following (*italics* used for emphasis):

> You are under a curse, for your whole nation has been cheating me. Bring all the tithes into the storehouse so there will be enough food in my Temple. *If you do, says the Lord of Heaven's Armies, I will open the windows of heaven for you.* I will pour out a blessing so great you won't have enough room to take it in! Try it! Put me to the test! (Malachi 3:9–10 NLT)

The implication in the italicized statement above is that if we don't bring our tithes into the storehouse, God will not open the windows of heaven for us and dispense spiritual blessing. God's home is in heaven. His "windows," like His "doors," are points of entry to/from Him from/to us. No tithe, no access, no spiritual blessing. Know tithe, know access, know spiritual blessing.

Covetousness also blocks prayer. Why? Because God is not going to waste time answering the prayers of a man or woman who falls into temptation and is trapped by many foolish and harmful desires that plunge them into ruin and destruction (1 Timothy 6:9). Said another way, because the love of money is the root of all evil, God is not going to waste time answering the prayers of those who, out of greed and envy, will wander from the true faith and pierce themselves with many sorrows (1 Timothy 6:10).

Finally, our prayers are a waste of time if we know we have offended a brother or sister in Christ and do not attempt to reconcile with that person before offering up prayer. While Matthew 5:24 deals specifically with gifts and offerings, this biblical principle applies equally to prayer "offerings." Here's the verse:

> Leave your offering there before the altar,
> go first and be reconciled with your brother, and
> then come and present your offering. (Matthew 5:24 NASB)

Maybe you're saying, "Okay, but how do you explain the fact that God answered my prayers when I was rebelling against Him, praying contrary to His will, and doubting His Word?"

Before I answer this, allow me to ask you a question. How do you know it was God who answered your prayer?

"What?" you say.

You see, God is not the only one who answers prayer. Yes, that's right. While God is more than able to do whatever He wants to do, regardless of what we do, it is totally contrary to His character to answer prayers from those who willfully and persistently walk in rebellion to Him. But guess who's more than happy to, especially if it will cause us to follow him so he can use us to advance his kingdom and bring him glory in the earth? That's right. Satan. Where do I get this? Matthew 4 and Luke 4.

Remember in Matthew 4 and Luke 4 when the devil took Jesus to a very high mountain and showed Him all the kingdoms of the world? Satan, at that moment, was prepared to give Jesus anything

He wanted in connection with any of kingdoms of the world that Adam and Eve turned over to Him (Satan) when they "fell" if Jesus would just bow down and worship him. Let's take a look at Luke 4 together (*italics* used for emphasis):

> Then the devil took Him up to a high mountain and showed Him all the kingdoms of the habitable world in a moment in time [in the twinkling of an eye]. And He said to Him, "*To you I will give all this power and authority and their glory* (all their magnificence, excellence, preeminence, dignity, and grace), *for it has been turned over to me, and I will give it to whomever I will.* Therefore, if you will do homage to and worship me [just once], *it shall all be yours.*" (Luke 4:5–7 AMPC)

Think about that. The devil is showing us that if we will "bow down and worship him" (i.e., allow His Word to have the final word). He, as the "ruler of the earth" (1 John 5:19), has the power and ability to answer any "prayer request" we have involving earthly kingdoms. You see, Satan knows that if he can deceive us into believing that it is God answering our prayers when it's really him, it is highly unlikely that we will follow and worship God—especially when we're getting what we want! You have to admit it's a "slick trick," though easily avoided when we, and our prayer lives, are submitted to the will of God. Needless to say, Satan is furious that you now know this or just needed a "friendly reminder." Ha ha, devil! See Jesus if you don't like it! You know, the one that defeated you at Calvary! We're with Him, remember?

The consequences of unbiblical prayer have been enormous. Besides the fact that God's people in America have wasted a lot of time, it has resulted in little heavenly intervention in America's affairs. And because there has been little heavenly (supernatural) intervention in America's affairs, there has been little divine assistance from God and good angels to address the chaos around us. And because there has been little divine assistance from God and good angels to address the chaos around us, Satan and his well-organized legion of demons have been successfully advancing their kingdom agenda virtually unopposed by us and good angels in every institution in America from our house to the White House (chapter 1). I know!

Have you been unknowingly aiding and abetting the enemy by allowing him to unknowingly "aid and abet" you? Operating underneath God's authority, which never runs contrary to His Word, is the key to victory in every area of the Christian life, including prayer beloved!

While prayer is heaven's secret weapon, up to now, it has not been many of our secret weapons, having grave consequences. Please don't ever forget what I am about to say. Ready? Without us, heaven will not (chapter 1). Without heaven, the earth cannot![320] Biblical prayer opens the floodgates of heaven. No biblical prayer. No heavenly intervention in earth's affairs. Satan is free to rule and reign, virtually unopposed, within God's sovereign boundaries. Know biblical prayer, know heavenly intervention in earth's affairs. Satan and demons must flee!

One of Satan's greatest fears is that God's people all across America would begin praying biblically. If there was ever a time that heaven needed us to give it license to impact earth,[321] it is now!

As we near the end of our discussion on this big lie that prayer is never a waste of time, maybe you are asking yourself, like me, the following difficult but necessary question: "I wonder how much of my prayer life up to now has been in vain and a stench in the nostrils of God?" The good news is that we've exposed this lie, and we now know how to pray right going forward to bring heaven to earth!

Our ability to experience closeness and intimacy with God, live a victorious life in Christ, help others, and fulfill the reason for which we were created (chapter 1) is contingent upon our ability to pray as Jesus taught us to pray (Matthew 6:9–13).

Now we know the truth. Not all prayer is created equal. Given the seriousness of this issue, it is only fitting that I end with a prayer. This prayer is for all who are willing to admit, at least at some level, how ignorant or arrogant we've been on this issue of prayer, how often we have offended a holy God, and finally, how strongly we desire to pray biblically going forward given what's at stake. If you sense the conviction of the Holy Spirit, please join me in the following prayer:

> Lord Jesus, thank you for loving me enough to expose this sin in my life so that I could stop grieving your heart and begin using my prayer life to advance your kingdom and bring you glory. I have been prideful to think that you would hear and respond to my prayers while walking in disobedience to your will as outlined in your word to fulfill my selfish and often lustful desires. I confess that many of my prayers have been self-centered to advance my kingdom instead of yours. I now recognize that I have hurt you deeply.
>
> I ask you to please forgive me and help me to pray the way you taught me how to pray so that your kingdom would come, and your will would be done on earth as it is in heaven (Matthew 6:9). Thank you for being faithful and just to forgive [me] and cleanse [me] from all unrighteousness (1 John 1:9). I receive your forgiveness now.
>
> Finally, help me to abide so closely with you and your word that I would immediately recognize when I am praying outside of your will.
>
> May the words of my mouth and the meditation of my heart be pleasing to you (Psalm 19:14) from this day forward as I seek to pray in a way that unleashes the power of heaven into earth's affairs for your glory! In Jesus's name, Amen!

If we want to advance God's kingdom and bring Him glory in every institution in America from our house to the White House through the power of prayer, our prayers *must* emanate from unselfish, obedient hearts that are fully surrendered to the will of God found in the Word of God. A heart like this, God will not despise (Psalm 51:17).

The next big lie that Satan has gotten many in the church to believe to destroy the foundations of our lives and every institution in America we comprise from our house to the White House is that Christians should always be silent before their accusers or enemies (i.e. those who mistreat or abuse them) like Jesus.

Some of the more popular scriptures quoted by some to support this "big lie" are as follows:

> He was oppressed and afflicted *yet He opened not His mouth*. Like a lamb that is led to the slaughter, and like a sheep that is silent before her shearers, *so He did not open His mouth.* (Isaiah 53:7 NASB)

> When they heaped abuse on Him, *He did not retaliate; when He suffered He made no threats,* but entrusted himself to Him who judges justly. (1 Peter 2:23 BSB)

> Now Jesus stood before the governor, and the governor asked Him, "Are you the King of the Jews?" Jesus said, "You have said so." But when He was accused by the chief priests and elders, *He gave no answer.* Then Pilate said to Him, "Do you not hear how many things they testify against you?" *But Jesus gave no answer, not even to a single charge,* so that the governor was greatly amazed. (Matthew 27:13–14 ESV)

> When Herod saw Jesus, He was very glad, for He had long desired to see Him, because He had heard about Him, and He was hoping to see some sign done by Him. So He questioned Him

at some length, *but He made no answer.* (Luke 23:8–9 ESV)

What many forget is that the same Jesus that was "silent" before His "accusers" above is the same Jesus that denounced the Pharisees in Matthew 23 and the same Jesus that objected when He was struck by one of the officers of the high priest before being sent to see Pilate in John 18 (John 18:23). It is the same Jesus who spoke openly against the hypocrisy of the religious and political leaders of the day who were, in Jesus's words, more interested in the outside of the cup than the inside of the cup (Matthew 23:25–26). It is also the same Jesus who, after telling His disciples that He is sending them out as sheep among wolves, tells them they will be dragged before governors and kings (i.e. their enemies) where they will not be silent but *bear witness for His namesake* (Matthew 10:16–18). Certainly, if Jesus wanted them to be silent before their accusers, He would not have told them to not be anxious about *what they would say,* "*For it is not you who speak, but the Spirit of your Father speaking through you*" (Matthew 10:20).

If Jesus wanted His disciples to be peaceful pacifists, He would not have advised them in Luke 22 to defend themselves against their accusers when necessary. As you may recall, Jesus told His disciples that the scripture must be fulfilled concerning Him and to not only bring their moneybags and knapsacks with them this time but to exchange their cloaks for a sword (Luke 22:36–38).

And who can forget the time Jesus drove the money changers (i.e., "enemies" of the temple) out of the temple, *declaring,* "My temple will be called a house of prayer, but you have made it a den of thieves" (Luke 19:46 NLT). I guess silence wasn't golden here either.

The Apostle Paul also bore witness to the necessity of "speaking up" at certain times before his accusers and enemies. He made it abundantly clear to the tribune when they ordered him to be brought into the barracks for examination by way of flogging that he was a Roman citizen and that there could be severe consequences if he were unlawfully harmed (Act. 22:24–29).

But it does beg the following question, doesn't it? Why was Jesus silent before His accusers and enemies in certain circumstances and not in others? While the Bible doesn't say, I believe it was—at least in part—to teach us a very valuable lesson about Jesus; that is, that when we try to "paint" an infinite God into a finite "box," we display how little we know about Him. If the Apostle Paul declared how impossible it is for us to understand Jesus's decisions and His ways (Romans 11:33 NLT), why would you and I think we can?

What is critical to highlight, however, is that even in those cases when Jesus spoke before His accusers, He never repaid evil for evil (Romans 12:17) or a railing for railing with the same powerful, lying, reproachful language as His accusers, becoming like them. Jesus's message was far above the "eye for an eye, tooth for a tooth" teaching that existed under Mosaic Law. Even under Mosaic Law, if someone gouged your eye out, that wasn't a license to go out and murder them. You could only take their eye. Jesus not only called for more limitations on vengeance but the forfeiting of personal revenge altogether.

Jesus, unlike so many in the church today, understands that there is a huge difference between confronting evil versus seeking vengeance or personal revenge. In other words, Jesus understands that it is possible to confront evil while desiring to see redemption for the perpetrator.[322]

While Jesus was "silent" before His accusers when it came to revenge and personal vengeance, He was not always silent before His accusers, as seen above, when it came time to fulfill the will of the Father in the earth. This last statement is very significant. In other words, Jesus knows when silence or speech is necessary to best serve the Father's will in any given situation. However, even in those instances before His crucifixion when Jesus broke silence, it was never motivated by personal revenge or vengeance but by righteousness, holiness, love, justice, and an unwavering commitment to the Father's will. This is what Jesus's call to "turn the other cheek" (Matthew 5:39), "love your enemies" (Matthew 5:44, and "bless those who curse you" (Matthew 5:44) is all about—even when opposing their actions.[323]

The wisest man that ever lived, Solomon, also recognized the need to speak at times and the need to be silent at times, for example, when responding to a fool. Certainly, we could argue that Jesus's accusers and enemies were "foolish," wouldn't you say? Maybe you're familiar with these back-to-back passages in Proverbs where, in one breath, Solomon says, "Do not answer a fool according to His folly, or you yourself will be like Him (Proverbs 26:4 NIV);" and in His next breath, says, "Answer a fool according to His folly or He will be wise in His own eyes" (Proverbs 26:5 NIV).

So which is it, Solomon? Should we be quiet or say something when responding to a fool? Why the apparent contradiction? I believe it's to illustrate that two seemingly similar situations are seldom the same to a man or woman of God who can correctly "discern" the intentions of a fool (Hebrews 4:12). In other words, while all fools may be foolish, not all fools are created equal. For example, some fools may want others to become like them while others may just want to appear "wise in their own eyes." Solomon is saying fool #1, for example, may need no response, but fool #2 may need one. Let godly wisdom and discernment guide you.

In the famous "A Time for Everything" chapter in the Book of Ecclesiastes, Solomon couldn't have been any clearer on this issue when he said, "There is a time to keep silent and a time to speak" (Ecclesiastes 3:7 NCV).

I like what one anonymous person said when he declared, "Wise men are not always silent, but they know when to be."[324]

We would also do well to remember that while silence might be the appropriate response before our "accusers" and "enemies" as Jesus often demonstrated, none of us were sent by God to be crucified on a cross for the sins of the world, buried, and then resurrected. Thus, to justify our silence based on Jesus's justification for silence, which was to carry out the will of the Father on the cross, is not equal justification. However, the principle we can take from Jesus's life and apply to ours is invaluable!

You see, Jesus seldom passed up the opportunity to tell us who He was "working for" (the Father) and why He came to earth (i.e., to bring honor and glory to the Father by fulfilling His will in the earth). Thus, it would stand to reason that Jesus's decision to be silent or to speak to His accusers and enemies hinged on which option He believed would help Him achieve these goals most effectively. Therefore, when you and I find ourselves standing before our "accusers" and "enemies," we should be asking ourselves the same question: Which action—silence or speech—will best bring honor and glory to the Father by fulfilling His will at that moment (chapter 1)? Then do it!

"But what if I'm unsure if God wants me to speak up or be silent at that moment?" you ask.

Great question. That's why God gave us the Holy Spirit. If you're a Christian, ask the Holy Spirit living on the inside of you what you should do at that moment. Many times, you don't even need to ask. He lovingly volunteers it! Then when He tells you what to do. Do it!

"Okay, but how do I know if it's the Holy Spirit leading me and not my flesh?" you ask.

Another great question. The Holy Spirit will never lead you to do something that violates scripture. For example, if you're a wife, He would never ask you to be the leader of the family, even if your husband is "happy" to follow (chapter 2)!

To this end, Jesus gives us two examples where silence is necessary if we want to carry out the Father's will in the earth with those who have no interest in biblical truth. Jesus counseled His disciples to not waste "nuggets of truth" on those who would not appreciate them, saying, "Do not give what is holy to the dogs; nor cast your pearls before swine, lest they trample them under their feet, and turn and tear you in pieces" (Matthew 7:6 NKJV). Secondly and similarly, Jesus told His disciples that if anyone would not welcome them or listen to their words (certainly this would include our "enemies" and "accusers"), leave their home or town and shake the dust off their feet (Matthew 10:14 ESV).

But maybe you're asking, "What do I do when those 'accusers' or 'enemies' live in my home?"

Great question. The same rules apply. If they are opposing you due to willful, persistent "sin" in your life, repent. If, however, they are behaving like an "enemy" because you have taken a firm, uncompromising stand for Jesus Christ in your home that they don't "like" or even "hate," then do what I suggested above for the same reasons given above. Sometimes it will involve silence, other times it will require speech. Remember to ask yourself, "What will advance God's kingdom the most at that moment?" Then ask God to give you the courage to do it.

While Jesus wasn't promoting violence when He said He didn't come to bring peace, but a sword that would separate even members of our own households (Matthew 10:34–35), He definitely embraces the conflict that comes with the incursion of truth.[325]

Two excellent examples from God's Word of individuals who had to deal with enemies from their own households with the "incursion of truth" were Job and Jesus himself. I discussed both of them earlier when we covered the "big lie" that "tolerance is more important than righteousness." Both of these examples come in again nicely here. While Job's wife and Peter were "family" to Job and Jesus, respectively, and certainly not Job and Jesus's "enemies," they were absolutely doing the work of the enemy when Job and Jesus rebuked them, respectively. Can you imagine what a victory it would have been for Satan if Job and Jesus had listened to their "family members" instead of "stepping up?" Job would have cursed God and possibly died sooner, and Jesus wouldn't have gone to the cross! I'm sure glad they both said something. How about you?

The point in sharing all of this is that the devil, our enemy, will use whoever he can, including family members, to thwart the purposes of God in our lives if we allow it. Silence is not how we should be responding to these types of attacks from them as "compassionate" as others may appear as in the case of Peter. Remember, Adam was silent when Satan convinced his wife to disobey God and eat the fruit from the forbidden tree in the middle of the garden. God is not looking for a repeat performance from us under similar circumstances. He's looking for us to respond to these attacks with the Word of God, which, because it is quick and powerful and sharper than any two-edged sword (Hebrews 4:12) may even "cut" family members who are "out of line" (e.g., Job's wife and Peter). While this is certainly no license to be abusive in any way, we must be prepared to take a righteous stand when necessary (even with those closest to us) if we expect to fulfill the Father's will in the earth. And if we happen to be the one acting like Peter or Job's wife, we should "welcome" (not like!) the same rebuke from others. Yes, I know this is hard!

We are not advancing God's kingdom and glory when our silence is being used to "keep the peace," allow evil to flourish, "punish" or "avoid" others, or as a means of abdicating responsibility as stated earlier. Again, it was Adam's silence that allowed the devil (our enemy and "accuser") to orchestrate the greatest coup d'état the world has ever known that we're still paying for today!

Maybe you're wondering, "Okay. So what? What's the big deal if the church believes the lie that Jesus was always 'silent' before His accusers and enemies?"

Glad you asked. It's no big deal at all if, for example, you're happy that prayer has been taken out of public schools and your tax dollars are being used to fund LGBTQ education. It's not a big deal at all if you're "for" gay marriage, homosexual ordinations, women pastors, salvation without repentance, prosperity theology, and abortion. You see, while those of us who still understand that these are "sins" have been virtually "silent" on these and other issues because we believe "that's what Jesus would do," the devil has been sifting our homes, churches, cities, and nation like wheat!

Said another way, our decades of silence have been our consent for the culture, under the rulership of Satan, to advance its secular, immoral agenda. And that's exactly what they've done! That's the issue! However, it's much worse than that. Not only is society—who used to look to the church for guidance on the moral and social issues of the day—no longer following our lead, but we're following theirs! And why? So we can gain their acceptance! How messed up are we?

Satan must be having an absolute "field day" watching God's people not only "kowtow" to the culture but advance the culture's agenda for him!

While there are notable exceptions in the Christian community of pastors with local, regional, national, and international influence who have been willing to "call out" this "cancer" of silent passivity, there are not nearly enough when compared to the "opposition movement" being run by Satan and his well-ordered legions of demons who, unlike us, are totally unified!

Imagine where we would be if our foreign policy with countries like Iran and North Korea consisted of nothing more than "silence?"

You've heard the famous quote, "The only thing necessary for the triumph of evil is for good men to do nothing."[326] It's also true when we say nothing.

As we come to the close of this chapter, I trust you see and "feel" what an enormous impact all of these "big lies" have had, not only on our individual lives but in every institution in America we comprise from our house to the White House. The good news is that we not only know what has caused the foundations underneath them to "shift" but how to stop them from shifting once and for all. Our victory, however, is not going to come without a fight as you're about to see! I hope your harness is still locked!

Prayer of Repentance (if applicable)

Dear Jesus, I am overwhelmed by your deep and abiding love for me. I recognize that it is only by your grace that these "lies" have been exposed. Only you know the extent of the chaos, confusion, and devastation they have caused from my house to the White House. I am overwhelmed with gratitude that you have made a way for me to reverse the curse that I brought upon myself and others through my belief in these lies.

You told us from the beginning that if we wanted to have a relationship with you and experience the benefits of that relationship that we had to do things your way. I confess that I have not only not done things your way by rejecting your truth for Satan's lies, but that I have pridefully and self-righteously expected you to heal my home, church, city, and nation while I continued to operate under these lies. I am broken beyond words over what my sin has done to you and ask for your forgiveness.

I specifically repent for believing the "big lie(s)" that [state the specific big lie(s) you believed] and exchange it [or them] right now for the truth found in your word. You said that if I continue in your word, then I am your disciple; and I shall know the truth and the truth shall set me free (John 8:31–32). I want to be a true disciple and I want to be free! Please, right now, tear down and demolish every demonic stronghold that has been formed against me and every institution in America from my house to the White House through belief in these "big lies" and help me and others never to become ensnared by them again.

I recognize that I have not only hurt you by living these lies but that I have also hurt others. Please help me, by your Spirit, to identify those I need to seek forgiveness with and the grace and courage to do it. Help me to release all expectations that others would do the same with me.

Now that I am walking in truth and underneath the authority of your word in the areas I identified above, I, by faith, ask you for divine assistance from good angels so that, I, with you, them, and other believers can reclaim territory from Satan in the earth for your glory!

Thank you for your steadfast love and mercies toward me that never cease and are new every morning (Lamentations 3:22), and for standing more prepared to forgive my sins than I am to commit them, more willing to supply my needs than I am to confess them. A love like this compels me to allow the truth of your word to have the final word in every area of my life from this day forward so that Satan will never again be able to exercise His power over me as I advance your kingdom in the earth and bring glory to your name! Amen!

Verses to Remember

1. And the great dragon was thrown down, that ancient serpent, who is called the devil and Satan, the deceiver of the whole world—he was thrown down to the earth, and his angels were thrown down with him. (Revelation 12:9 ESV)

2. For we wrestle not against flesh and blood, but against principalities, against powers, against the rulers of the darkness of this world, against spiritual wickedness in high places. (Ephesians 6:12 KJ21)

3. He was a murderer from the beginning and does not stand in the truth because there is no truth in him. Whenever he speaks a lie, he speaks from his own nature, for he is a liar and the father of lies. (John 8:44 NASB)

4. They traded the truth about God for a lie. So they worshipped and served the things God created instead of the Creator Himself, who is worthy of eternal praise! Amen. (Romans 1:25 NLT)

5. [f]or we are not ignorant of his devices. (2 Corinthians. 2:11 KJV)

6. If ye continue in my word, then are ye my disciples indeed; And ye shall know the truth, and the truth shall make you free. (John 8:31–32 KJV)

7. Let God be true but every man a liar. (Romans 3:4 NKJV)

8. The God of peace will soon crush Satan under your feet. (Romans 16:20 ESV)

9. And the devil that deceived them was cast into the lake of fire where the beast and the false prophet are, and shall be tormented day and night forever and ever. (Revelation 20:10 KJV)

CHAPTER 7

✦✦✦

General Quarters!

"This is *not* a drill. This is *not* a drill. General Quarters! General Quarters! All hands, man your battle stations! Set Condition Zebra throughout the ship!"[327]

General Quarters, or "GQ" for short, is a readiness condition set by naval commanders aboard ships and submarines whenever naval action against the "enemy" is imminent. All battle stations are quickly and fully manned and alert; ammunition is ready for instant loading, and guns and guided missile launchers may be loaded.[328] Condition Zebra, or "Zebra" for short, ensures that all hatches (i.e., internal doors and openings) and fittings are properly secured aboard ship to sustain damage from fire or flood.[329] When crewmembers set Zebra, they get dressed for battle and move "smartly" (quickly and carefully) through the ship to their battle stations.

Fellow believers, the GQ alarm is sounding in America. Its sound is loud, clear, and strong. While many in the church can hear it, others have tragically chosen to ignore it or are MIA (missing-in-action), despite their regular church attendance. Most alarming, however, are the multitudes of Christians all across America who hear nothing, or worse yet, "angels singing" because more and more churches are aligning themselves with the culture.

Meanwhile, our ship, *America*, has been "hit," and all of its compartments have taken on water. Satan, our enemy, is the one

483

who has "hit" us. He's "hit" us in the "Main Compartment" called "The Family," and because we have not been able to stop the flooding there, the "Church Compartment" has now been flooded. And because we have not been able to stop the flooding there, our "local, city, state, and national compartments" have now been "flooded" along with their respective academic, governmental, media, military, and economic "sub-compartments." *America* is now "listing" (leaning to one side) under the weight of all this floodwater. If "watertight integrity" is not restored to "her" soon, she will sink!

While many Christians are waiting to see what God's going to do, God is waiting to see what we're going to do when He declared, "Let them rule" (Genesis 1:26), remember (chapter 1)?

Do you know how we can tell we're in the middle of a war? Easy. There are spiritual casualties and prisoners of war (POWs) all around us. Christian men and women of all ages are being held hostage by the enemy through various strongholds (2 Corinthians. 10:4), including but not limited to drugs (illegal and prescription), alcohol, eating, gambling, gaming, sex, porn, social media, and work "addictions." Now add to this staggering number the countless Christians being held hostage by greed, anger, envy, lust, pride, idolatry, fear, depression, anxiety, unforgiveness, bitterness, discrimination, class warfare, racism, feminism, chauvinism, hedonism, liberalism, materialism, and elitism. It's quite a "prison population," wouldn't you agree? Instead of ruling our worlds under God's hand to advance His kingdom, many of our worlds are ruling us under Satan's hand to advance his kingdom!

While it would be nice if we could just close the "hatches" of our "Family Compartments" to keep our family floodwaters from flooding our churches, cities, states, and nation, no such damage control system, like Zebra, exists for the family. I believe God designed it this way. What? Why? To show us that the key to having "watertight integrity" in every compartment "downstream" of the family is having watertight integrity at home. Said another way, if we want any hope of restoring our nation, we must first restore the family.

While I believe most of us in America have been totally oblivious to the "angelic war" we have been placed in the middle of (chapter 1), it has also been my experience that many in the church are equally oblivious to it. Or, if aware, they have little to no idea what a "key player" they are in it as communicated in the opening chapter of this book. Most Christians (including myself for many years) do not realize, for example, that at conversion, they signed an "enlistment contract" with God to be in the army of God (2 Timothy 2:4). Few of us understand that, under this enlistment contract, God expects us to carry out our duties by reclaiming territory in the earth from Satan to advance God's kingdom. The widespread ignorance of our mission has not only been the devil's bliss but his "ticket" to usurp God's power and authority in the earth through us, and in the case of America, to destroy every institution in America from our house to the White House! I'd say he's done a pretty good job up to now, wouldn't you agree?

Isn't it time we got *more interested* in building God's kingdom than in building our kingdoms? Isn't it time we got *more interested* in "fixing" His house that lay in ruins (Haggai 1:4) than in remodeling our houses? And isn't it time we got *more interested* in following Jesus than in who's *following* us on social media?

While this angelic war we're in the middle of began the minute Adam and Eve showed up in the earth, it didn't start in the United States of America until 1776, the year America "showed up" as a nation. From then until now, this angelic war has and will continue to be (until Jesus returns) waged for the "territory" of our lives, homes, churches, communities, cities, states, and nation with increasing fierceness (chapter 1). Until Christ returns or we experience physical death, whichever occurs first, God expects each of us to reclaim as much territory as possible, remember?

God's Word says, "No man that warreth entangles himself with the affairs of this life; that He may please Him who has chosen Him to be a soldier" (2 Timothy 2:4). Does this describe us? Or are we so entangled with the affairs of this life that we're unable to please Him who chose us to be soldiers? Some of you didn't even know you were chosen by God to be a soldier when you accepted Christ, did you?

It should be no surprise to anyone by now that this chapter is a "call to arms." However, earthly weapons won't do. This is a spiritual battle, and spiritual battles can only be fought and won with spiritual weapons! If you and I are waiting for the current or next administration to fix the social, moral, and spiritual mess we're in, we're the fools!

In military warfare, it is critical to know your enemy. I wish more Christians felt the same way. Can you imagine Seal Team 6, who was responsible for killing Osama Bin Laden, saying, "No need to study the weaponry, tactics, and strategies of al-Qaeda? Let's roll!"

Yet, this is exactly what many of us Christians do when it comes to spiritual warfare. And we wonder why there are so many spiritual casualties and POWs in the church today.

In the game of football, coaches routinely have their players watch "game film" to learn the opposing team's strengths, weaknesses, tactics, and strategies. Every good coach understands that watching their "enemy's" game film is critical if they expect to be victorious on the 100-yard "battlefield" called football. Did you know that Satan has seen all of our "game film," covering the entirety of our lives? He knows all of our strengths and weaknesses and knows where you and I are most vulnerable. He knows which tactics and strategies work against us and which ones don't. He knows when we're "walking" in the truth and when we're not. He knows where our convictions are weak and malleable, when they are rooted in partial truth, and when they are rooted in no truth at all. In other words, he knows where we rightly and wrongly divide the word of truth (2 Timothy 2:15).

How does he know this? Because he knows the Word of God better than most of us do! Have you forgotten how he quoted it to Jesus in Matthew 4 (Matthew 4:6)? What do you know about him?

Still don't think it's necessary to study Satan's "game film?" In 2 Corinthians 2, Paul is discussing "a man" who brought trouble to the Corinthian church. Initially, many in the church opposed the man. Paul, however, is now encouraging them to forgive the man so he (the man) does not get overcome by discouragement. In verses 10–11, Paul says the following (*italics* used for emphasis):

> Anyone you forgive, I also forgive. And
> what I have forgiven—if there was anything to

forgive—I have forgiven in the sight of Christ for your sake in order that Satan may not out-wit us. *For we are not unaware of His schemes.* (2 Corinthians. 2:10–11 NIV)

Another translation of this last sentence says, "*[f]or we are not ignorant of His wiles and intentions*" (2 Corinthians 2:11 AMPC).

J. B. New Testament says, "*[a]nd well we know his methods*" (2 Corinthians. 2:11 PHIL).

The King James Version says, "*[f]or we are not ignorant of His devices.*" Paul could not have made such an emphatic statement unless he was familiar with Satan's "wiles," "intentions," "methods," and "devices" (i.e., had studied his "game film").

God also knows Satan very well. Recall, it was God who gave Satan his name when Lucifer, who became Satan, was cast out of heaven (Luke 10:18). Before this, we know Lucifer was one of God's archangels established by God to be the angel of worship whose ministry surrounded the heart of heaven.[330] God witnessed his rebellion, observed his pride, watched him recruit one-third of the angels to join him in his rebellion (Luke 10:18; Revelation 12:4), and saw him employ the same "weapons," "countermeasures," "tactics," and "strategies" with Adam and Eve in the garden that he employed with God in heaven.

In Genesis 3, God (and we) observed Satan's game film. God (and we) saw how Satan circumvented God's chain of command by going to the woman instead of the man (chapter 1) and saw how Satan revealed his "weapon of choice," which are always lies about what God "really said." God (and we) observed Satan employ "countermeasures" (more lies) against Eve to counter what she told Satan that God told her. Then God (and we) saw Satan deliver the "death blow" to man by appealing to Eve's pride (your eyes will be opened, and you will be like God; Genesis 3:5).

Finally, God (and we) observed Satan convince Eve that acting independently of God was how she could live her "best life now." The question is, did you and I learn anything?" If so, then why is the same "play" still working against us thousands of years later? The truth is, most of us *haven't* studied Satan's "game film"; otherwise, our homes, churches, cities, states, government, and nation would reflect it!

Lest you hear what I'm not saying, I said it is critical to know your enemy, not "obsess" about the enemy. But while we're here, I wish I had a loaf of bread and a bottle of water for every time a Christian told me that all you need to be successful in spiritual warfare is Jesus. You and I could feed the multitudes and forget about the armor of God that God told us to wear in the angelic conflict He placed us in the middle of to advance His kingdom. Well, at least the first part of the prior statement is correct. We could feed the multitudes. I trust you get my point.

While God is with us and made us legally victorious through Christ, He's waiting for us to go get it so we can "experience" it in the here and now with the help of Jesus and good angels (chapter 1)! This requires knowing God, knowing your enemy, suiting up, and "walking" by faith, just like Abraham, Moses, Joshua, Esther, Rahab, Samson, Daniel, David, Peter, Timothy, Paul, Silas, and other heroes of the faith did. Aren't we glad they did?

Thus, the devil's goal, since the beginning of time, has never changed. In the case of America, as described at the beginning of the chapter, he wants to "flood" every institution America from our house to the White House with his lies so he can "call the shots," set the agenda, and control the outcome. Now you know why I dedicated an entire chapter to exposing the "big lies" that Satan gets us to believe. No lies. Know victory!

So if we're in a battle that demands we go to GQ in the spirit realm, what does it look like? Great question. Let's go back to our ship illustration. While it is very different in many aspects, I believe there are some striking similarities between the Navy's version of GQ and what our version of GQ should look like as the army of God. Let's take a look at some of them.

The first similarity between the Navy's version of GQ and the army of God's version of GQ is that they both require us to "dress for battle" before we man our "battle stations!" Aboard ship, the moment the GQ alarm sounds, navy personnel may be seen rushing to their "battle stations." Modifications to their uniforms begin en route and are often completed within seconds to offer protection against fire and flood.

In boot camp, one of the many "motivational training exercises" I was required to participate in included unannounced "uniform races." When our drill instructor blew his whistle, we had to change from whatever uniform we were currently in to one of five or six different uniforms issued to us. While the slowest person always got singled out (yes, it happened to me!), if the entire unit was not successful in going from uniform to uniform in the allotted time, we would have to "try again." Without realizing it at the time, our drill sergeants and upperclassmen were preparing us for GQ.

Now compare this to how we operate in the army of God. Many of us are "lucky" if we even remember we have a uniform to wear (i.e., the armor of God) much less remember what the name of each piece of armor is, the purpose each piece serves, and how to put each piece on correctly as if our life depended on it. Some of us, however, are good at taking it off. How do I know? Because we keep putting it back "on" each day during our prayer and devotion time! During GQ in the Navy, your "battle dress" never comes off! It should be no different in God's army since we are in a continuous "battle" with Satan and His demons who tirelessly desire to seek, kill, and destroy us (Ephesians 6:10; John 10:10)! Can you imagine how many fewer casualties and POWs there would be in the army of God if we would dress for battle like the Navy does?

If you've been around the local church, you've likely heard many teachings on the armor of God. This will not be another one of them. You're welcome. However, there are a few key points that may or may not be new to some of you that are worth a few moments. First, we must put on the *full* armor of God if we want to stand against the devil's schemes (Ephesians 6:11). No missing pieces that leave us exposed to the enemy. *Every* piece of armor in the Ephesians 6 arsenal is essential if we expect to be victorious in the angelic battle we've been placed in the middle of.

The six pieces of armor are divided into two categories of three each. The first three we are supposed to have "on" at all times (i.e., the belt of truth, the breastplate of righteousness, and the shoes of peace). The last three (i.e., shield of faith, helmet of salvation, and sword of the Spirit) we are to "take" or "take up" and use as needed.

Secondly, each piece of armor must be on *correctly*. For example, it does no good to put the "breastplate of righteousness" (Ephesians 6:14) on backward (i.e., rely on our righteousness instead of Christ's righteousness), leaving our hearts exposed to the lies and deceptions of the enemy. Similarly, it does no good to put on the belt of truth if we're not going to fasten it securely (i.e., hold fast to the truth of God's Word), especially when the other pieces of armor depend on it to keep them secure). Additionally, what good is it to take the helmet of salvation that protects the head, the mind, and the control center of the body if we're not going to pull it down completely over our heads to allow our spiritual standing in Christ (i.e., justification through salvation) to fully protect our thinking? And so on.

You get the idea. The Navy also recognizes this. In the "uniform races" I described above, if we forgot one article of clothing or put it on incorrectly, we had to change back into our previous uniform and then back into the new uniform with no extra time! And one guess what happened if we didn't do it fast enough?

You see, every commanding Officer knows that their crewmembers receive the most protection against their enemy when they are wearing *all* of their required gear *correctly*! Our Commanding Officer, Jesus Christ, also understands this. He understands it's the difference between spiritual "life" and "death." How about you, soldier? Do you understand that there is no safer place we can be than fully armed with our identity in Christ? You realize that's what the armor of God is all about, right? Every piece is a reminder of who we are in Christ and what we've been given! Excellent! Then what lengths are you willing to go to in order to "dress for success" going forward?

Another similarity between God's army and the Navy when it comes to GQ is that both groups have "battle stations." Maybe you're wondering where your "battle station" is in God's army. Easy. It's in your "garden" (chapter 1). Just imagine how differently our homes, churches, cities, and nation would be if all of God's people were "suited up" correctly in their "gardens" prepared to reclaim territory for the kingdom of God.

Another similarity between the army of God and the Navy when it comes to GQ is that they both require their "battle stations" to be "fully manned." In other words, participation by all personnel is mandatory. At least that's the way it's supposed to work. Sadly, our homes, churches, and nation tell a different story, don't they?

In the Navy, if you do not report to your "battle station" during "GQ" (or to your normal duty station for that matter) in the correct uniform at the proper time to assume your duties, you will face disciplinary action. If you do it again, chances are high you will be "relieved of duty" permanently! Did you forget what happened to Adam after his "Commanding Officer" (The Lord God) found him "guilty" of "dereliction of duty" offenses for not properly assuming his post in the Garden of Eden? He and his lovely bride were "driven" from the garden...forever!

Do we somehow think we're exempt from similar consequences when we commit similar "dereliction of duty" offenses in this war God has placed us in the middle of because we cannot be trusted to do the right thing? Could it be that some of our individual Christian lives, marriages, homes, and churches are operating in the environment of a "curse" because we're not "reporting for duty" at our "battle stations" in the correct uniform to wage war on God's behalf? While I recognize chaos came into the world as a consequence of the fall, the chaos in the world should not be ruling *our* worlds![331] "General Quarters! General Quarters!"

Another similarity between the army of God and the Navy when it comes to "GQ" is that they both require "ammunition at-the-ready" for instant loading. Truth is our ammunition, precious ones. We saw this in the last chapter. Jesus understands this; do we? If you recall in Matthew 4, Jesus was "packing truth" when He "returned fire" on the devil. He wasn't "packing" logic, intellect, majority, or expert opinion. He didn't ask the devil to give Him a minute so He (Jesus) could consult with a priest, pollster, religious scholar, scribe, psychic, family member, coworker, or any of His disciples. "Truth" was at the ready. Jesus, fully God and fully man, "hit" the devil hard with three "rounds of truth," "center mass," straight from God's Word without one malfunction or the slightest hesitation until the threat was eliminated (i.e., the devil fled).

Is this how we operate? It should be. Do we have "truth" at "the ready?" Sadly, not only do many of us who have been "walking" with Jesus for many years not have truth at "the ready," but we proudly get advice from family members, coworkers, and friends who do not have truth at the ready. Did you forget that 65 percent of all church-goers rarely read their Bibles?[332] It's a little tough to "pack truth" with a track record like this, wouldn't you agree? Do you realize that if the Navy and the other armed services handled their ammunition as infrequently as most Christians do in America, we would all be speaking another language? Many of us already do. It's called "spiritual gibberish" that has no power because we refuse to allow God's Word to have the final word in every area of life!

God's Word says that wisdom [the correct application of biblical truth] is better than weapons of war (Ecclesiastes 9:18). Do we believe this? Really? Where's the evidence in our culture? We should be packing truth at our sides from God's Word at all times. Incidentally, could this be why the sword of the Spirit, which is the Word of God (Ephesians 6:17), is at our side, that is, for rapid deployment? You bet soldier!

Another similarity between the *real* army of God and the Navy when it comes to GQ is that both groups train extensively for the "real thing." While those of us in God's army are always, technically, in the real thing, we should always be looking for ways to improve. The Navy conducts so many GQ exercises from the moment the ship leaves the pier that crewmembers not only know where their battle stations are but how long it will take them to get there in uniform with "ammunition at the ready" in total darkness! In total darkness? Yes, to simulate a complete electrical failure, which is a distinct possibility when you've been "hit" by the enemy at sea, these "drills" are frequent and relentless to ensure the commanding officer that each member of his crew is ready for battle at all times!

So how well does your training compare? Has the devil ever hit you so hard that it caused a total "blackout" in your life where you were unable to get your bearings? Were you able to get your "battle dress" on in the dark and make it to your battle station? I hope you're beginning to see, like me, how far we, the church, are from God's standard and why every institution in America from our house to the White House is in an utter state of chaos and confusion!

While there are many illustrations of GQ throughout the Bible, my all-time favorite next to the one we looked at in Matthew 4 may be found in the book of Nehemiah. If you recall the story, Nehemiah, who was cupbearer to King Artaxerxes, King of Persia, has just learned that the walls of Jerusalem still lay in ruins seventy years after the rebuilding of Solomon's Temple in BC 515. By way of historical context, it was Nehemiah who led the third group of Jewish exiles out of Babylon, in, or about BC 445.

To the Jewish people, the walls surrounding the city of Jerusalem represented power, strength, protection, peace, Jewish national identity, and beauty. The walls protected the temple where God's presence resided against attack and ensured the continuity of worship.[333] Nehemiah desired to reunite the Jews, remove the shame that came with the broken-down walls, and bring political, social, and economic stability back to Jerusalem. In doing so, he would bring glory to God and restore the reality and power of God's presence among his people.[334] Nehemiah understood that this was not just a battle that he had to fight but a battle that he had to win! In modern-day language, he was in it to win it!

Note the sequence of events that transpires immediately after Nehemiah hears the report from Hanani, one of his brothers, along with others from Judah that the walls and gates of Jerusalem still lay in ruins (*italics* used for emphasis):

> When I heard this, *I sat down and wept.* In fact, *for days I mourned, fasted, and prayed* to the God of heaven. Then I said, "O Lord, God of heaven, the great and awesome God who keeps His covenant of unfailing love with those who love Him and obey His commands, listen to my prayer! Look down and see me praying night and

day for your people Israel. *I confess that we have sinned against you. Yes, even my own family and I have sinned! We have sinned terribly by not obeying the commands, laws, and regulations that you gave us through your servant Moses.* Please remember what you told your servant Moses: 'If you sin, I will scatter you among the nations. *But if you return to me and obey my commands, even if you are exiled to the ends of the earth, I will bring you back to the place I have chosen for my name to be honored.'* We are your servants, the people you rescued by your great power and might. O Lord, please hear my prayer! Listen to the prayers *of those of us who delight in honoring you. Please grant me success now as I go to ask the king for a great favor. Put it into His heart to be kind to me."* (Nehemiah 1:4–11 NLT)

Awesome, right? I like to call this Nehemiah's "pre-GQ posture." It is not only marked with mourning, fasting, and biblical prayer but confession, repentance, humility, and petition. Nehemiah understood at least five things were needed if he was going to be victorious in the battle God wanted him to fight. First, he needed to be emptied of himself to be filled with God's life-giving power and presence (the purpose of fasting). Secondly, he needed to pray to get heavenly intervention in earth's affairs. Thirdly, he needed to be broken of any desire to act independently of God. Fourthly, he needed God's forgiveness and God's favor, which included permission, protection, and provision by a secular government (the king). Finally, he needed to act!

Nehemiah and the Jewish people, along with the priests, nobles, officials, and others in Nehemiah's "working party" represented the first legitimate threat to the authority and security of the enemy in the region (Jerusalem). Nehemiah's enemies, the Samaritan officials, understood that to relinquish the land to Nehemiah was to seal their fate! They had no interest in doing that! Sound familiar?

Satan must have felt the same way when he realized Adam and Eve had moved into HIS territory! In Nehemiah 2, Nehemiah is getting ready to wage war against an enemy that has been "happy" to occupy Jerusalem since the Babylonian captivity began in BC 586.

In Nehemiah 2 and Nehemiah 4, we are introduced to Nehemiah's enemies by name: "When Sanballat the Horonite and Tobiah the Ammonite official heard of my arrival, they were very displeased that someone had come to help the people of Israel" (Nehemiah 2:10 NLT). While Nehemiah had other enemies in the area, we learn that Sanballat and Tobiah were the chief instigators serving under the king of Persia as regional governors. Sanballat is described as "the Horonite." Bible scholars believe this gives reference to the Moabite city of Horonaim (Isaiah 15:5; Jeremiah 48:5,34), which suggests that Sanballat was in all likelihood, a Moabite.

The Moabites, who worshiped the god Chemosh, were in fierce opposition to the Israelites. Sanballat was the governor of Samaria. Samaria was located some thirty miles north of Jerusalem. Tobiah, an Ammonite, was the governor of Ammon (temple and palace located in modern-day Jordan to the East) and possibly Sanballat's servant.[335] Another enemy, and regional governor, Gesham, the Arab, mentioned in Nehemiah 2:19, was most likely from the region south of Judah.[336] Then finally, to the west of Jerusalem, the men of Ashdod, who appear in Nehemiah 4:7. In summary, Nehemiah had enemies to the north (Sanballat & Co.), south (Gesham & Co.), east (Tobiah & Co.), and west (the men of Ashdod)! Ever felt that way? "General Quarters! General Quarters!"

One of the many things I love about Nehemiah, besides the fact that he knew God was with him and that God had already given him the victory, was the fact that he understood, from day one, that his battle was ultimately about reclaiming territory from the enemy (chapter 1)! Nehemiah understood that the one who owns the territory is the one who gets to occupy it, and the one who gets to occupy it is the one who gets to approve "renovations." And the one who gets to approve renovations is the one who gets to decide how the renovation will be used. And the one who gets to decide how the renovation will be used is the one who gets to decide if it will be used to advance the kingdom of God or the kingdom of darkness! Did you know that the same thing is true of the territory you currently have and of the territory you will reclaim from Satan in the future? Now you do!

By Nehemiah 2:17, Nehemiah has confirmed that the walls and gates of Jerusalem were damaged. Additionally, he has confirmed that the enemy is in the region. It's now time for him to sound "General Quarters." If Nehemiah could have adapted the Navy's GQ announcement to his day, it might have sounded something like this:

> This is *not* a drill. This is *not* a drill. General Quarters! General Quarters! Men and women of Jerusalem, man your battle stations! Set Condition Zebra throughout the city of Jerusalem. God is with us! Repair and rebuild the walls of Jerusalem that we may no longer suffer derision! Rise up and build! Cheers!

Note the similarities between the above GQ announcement and Nehemiah's actual "GQ announcement" below (*italics* used for emphasis):

> You see the trouble we are in, how Jerusalem lies in ruins with its gates burned. *Come, let us build the wall of Jerusalem, that we may no longer suffer derision.* And I told them of the hand of my God that had been upon me for good, and also of the words that the king had spoken to me. And they said, *"Let us rise up and build."* (Nehemiah 2:17–18 ESV)

Needless to say, Nehemiah and his Jewish working party were "all-in." With the enemy circling them like sharks, Nehemiah and his fellow Jews began repairing and rebuilding different sections of the wall—the Sheep Gate and areas next to it, the Fish Gate, the Gate of Yeshanah, the Valley Gate, the Dung Gate, the Fountain Gate, and all areas in-between to points opposite of the Water Gate,

Muster Gate, and areas above the Horse Gate. Repairing each gate was of paramount importance as each gate served a critical function according to its name. I highly recommend a personal study on each of these gates sometime!

Note, everyone is "prayed up," "suited up" (in their "full battle dress"), and has shown up to their battle stations (i.e., their assigned sections on the wall) on time. Work is underway. "Ammunition" is at the ready for instant loading (i.e., Nehemiah and his workers are armed with truth to respond to the taunts of the enemy), and spears, bows, and swords are at the ready for deployment, if necessary. Let's now examine each of Nehemiah's "wartime preparations" a little more closely.

As you read through the book of Nehemiah, it doesn't take long to realize how important prayer is to Nehemiah. We find him praying at every critical juncture in his mission until he completes the wall, which incidentally only took fifty-two days (Nehemiah 2:17–18 ESV)! After his opening prayer to God that we looked at above, he goes before the king. The king asks him, "What are you requesting [Nehemiah]?"

Nehemiah says, "So I prayed to the God of heaven. And I said to the king, 'If it pleases the king'" (Nehemiah 2:4–5 ESV).

Wait. Don't miss what just happened! Nehemiah is asked a question by the king, his "boss," the most powerful man in the region, and then Nehemiah *stops to pray before* answering the king. Would you do that? Not me! I'd answer the king right away. Gotta love Nehemiah! After Nehemiah offers up an honorable and humble prayer, the king "showers" Nehemiah with the protection, provision, favor, and blessing Nehemiah needs to be victorious!

Life Application: When we are operating by God's will for our lives, He will use whoever He wants, including a secular government and king, to help us achieve His purposes and plans in the earth. Nehemiah understood this. Do we?

The next time we see Nehemiah praying is in Nehemiah 4 after Sanballat fires a series of taunting lies at Nehemiah in the presence of Sanballat's friends and the army of Samaria captured here in the following (*italics* used for emphasis):

What does this bunch of poor, feeble Jews think they are doing? Do they think they can build the wall in a single day by just offering a few sacrifices? Do they actually think they can make something of stones from a rubbish heap—and charred ones at that? (Nehemiah 4:2 NLT)

Tobiah the Ammonite, who was standing beside Him, remarked, "That stone wall would collapse if even a fox walked along the top of it!" *Then I prayed, "Hear us, our God, for we are being mocked. May their scoffing fall back on their own heads, and may they themselves become captives in a foreign land! Do not ignore their guilt. Do not blot out their sins, for they have provoked you to anger here in front of the builders."* (Nehemiah 4:3–5 NLT)

Love it! Nehemiah reminds God that what Nehemiah's enemies are doing to Nehemiah and his builders is not nearly as bad as what they are doing to God by provoking God to anger in front of them. Talk about prayer that moves the heart of God! When was the last time you prayed about what your enemies were doing to God versus what they were doing to you? Don't worry, I got my toes too.

The next time we see Nehemiah praying is when Sanballat and Tobiah and the Arabs and the Ammonites and the Ashdodites heard that the repairs to the wall were going forward and the breaches were closing (Nehemiah 4:7–8). We learn that they became furious and plotted to fight against Jerusalem and to cause confusion. This came as no surprise to Nehemiah who had already familiarized himself with the enemy's game film. In response to this, Nehemiah said, "*And we prayed to our God* and set a guard as a protection against them day and night" (Nehemiah 4:9 ESV).

Notice action always followed Nehemiah's prayers. Is this true of you?

The last time Nehemiah strategically offers up a prayer before the wall is complete is after he learns about several lies his enemies had put in a letter addressed to him. The letter falsely accused Nehemiah and his "crew" of rebuilding the wall because he (Nehemiah) and the Jews were intending to rebel. The note read, "According to these reports, you [Nehemiah] wish to become their king" (Nehemiah 6:6 ESV). After reading this, Nehemiah *prays* for strength to continue the work (Nehemiah 6:9 NLT). Nehemiah understood that prayer would give him the strength he needed to overcome his opposition and complete his mission.

Now let's take a look at Nehemiah's battle dress, battle stations, and weaponry while at "GQ." In the following passage below, we see that Nehemiah and his working party all have their "battle dress" on and are at their "battle stations" with weapons in hand completing their work (*italics* and brackets [] used for emphasis):

> At that time the Jews who lived near them came from all directions and said to us ten times, "You must return to us." *So in the lowest parts of the space behind the wall, I stationed the people by their clans* [battle station], *with their swords, their spears, and their bows.* And I looked and arose and said to the nobles and to the officials and to the rest of the people, "Do not be afraid of them. Remember the Lord, who is great and awesome, and fight for your brothers, your sons, your daughters, your wives, and your homes." When our enemies heard that it was known to us and that God had frustrated their plan, we all *returned to the wall* [battle stations], each to His work. (Nehemiah 4:12–15 ESV)
>
> So it was, from that time on, that half of my servants worked at construction, *while the other half held the spears, the shields, the bows, and wore armor* [battle dress]; and the leaders were behind

all the house of Judah. Those who built on the wall, and those who carried burdens, loaded themselves so that with one hand they worked at construction, *and with the other held a weapon. Every one of the builders had His sword girded at His side as He built.* (Nehemiah 4:16–18 NKJV)

And the one who sounded the trumpet *was beside me* [battle station]. Then I said to the nobles, the rulers, and the rest of the people, "The work is great and extensive, and we are separated far from one another on the wall. Wherever you hear the sound of the trumpet, rally to us *there* [battle station]. Our God will fight for us." (Nehemiah 4:18–20 NKJV)

So we labored in the work, *and half of the men held the spears* from daybreak until the stars appeared. At the same time I also said to the people, "Let each man and His servant stay at night in Jerusalem, that they may be our guard by night and a working party by day." So neither I, my brethren, my servants, nor the men of the guard who followed me took off our clothes [battle dress], except that everyone took them off for washing. (Nehemiah 4:21–23 NKJV)

Did you catch that last sentence? They only took their battle dress off for washing!

Ammunition at the ready? While I'm sure Nehemiah and his "working party" were fully prepared to defend the homeland with the physical weapons they had on them, the Book of Nehemiah never mentions Nehemiah using anything other than spiritual weapons. Every time, Nehemiah used the "ammunition of truth" (i.e., the Word of God) to counter the lies of the enemy. And one guess how many times he "fired?" Three! Sound familiar? Remember Jesus in Matthew 4? I know, God's Word is so amazing and prophetic!

The first time Nehemiah pulled out his "truth ammo," if you recall, was after he had secretly assessed and confirmed the damage to the walls and gates of Jerusalem, "rallied the troops," and charged them to strengthen their hands for the good work. God's Word says, "But when Sanballat the Horonite and Tobiah the Ammonite servant and Geshem the Arab heard of it, they jeered at us and despised us and said, 'What is this thing that you are doing? Are you rebelling against the king'" (Nehemiah 2:19 NASB)? Little did they know that the King of kings had already given Nehemiah the favor of the king! In response to this "fiery dart," Nehemiah takes up his shield of faith that he knows will quench every "fiery dart" of the enemy (Ephesians 6:16), "draws," and "fires" the following first round of "truth ammo" (*italics* used for emphasis):

> *The God of heaven will make us prosper and we His servants will arise and build, but you have no portion or right or claim in Jerusalem.* (Nehemiah 2:19–20 ESV)

Remember, Nehemiah already knew God had given him the city. Did you know that others cannot lay a right or claim to what God has already given you? The courage Nehemiah displays came from this conviction. Does ours?

The second time Nehemiah "draws" and "fires" the "ammo of truth" at his enemy is in response to a five-round "salvo," consisting of five separate messages from the enemy requesting Nehemiah's presence at one of the nearby villages. Nehemiah, realizing that this was merely a plot to harm Him, "draws" and "fires" four of the five rounds of "truth," which are identical, on Sanballat and Geshem in response to the first four messages (one round per message). Note Nehemiah's response below on these four occasions (*italics* used for emphasis):

"I'm doing a great work; I can't come down.
Why should the work come to a standstill just so I
can come down to see you?" (Nehemiah 6:3 MSG)

The fifth round of "truth" comes in response to Sanballat send-ing his servant to Nehemiah the fifth time with an open letter that read, "It is reported that you [Nehemiah] and the Jews intend to rebel; that is why you are building the wall" (Nehemiah 6:6). Upon receiving this information, Nehemiah "draws" and "fires" the follow-ing fifth round of "truth" on Sanballat (*italics* used for emphasis):

You know you are lying. There is no truth in
any part of your story. (Nehemiah 6:8 NLT)

Nehemiah, unlike so many of us, understood that the lies of his enemies were nothing more than fear and intimidation tactics to break Nehemiah's resolve and stop the work (Nehemiah 6:8–9 ESV). Again, right out of Satan's "playbook." While the devil's efforts to stop the work of God through Nehemiah were relentless, Nehemiah's resolve to complete the task God had called him to was greater! Is this our story? If not, it can be!

The last time Nehemiah "draws" and "returns fire" on his ene-mies with the "ammo of truth" occurs immediately after the previ-ous "exchange of fire" as seen here in the following *(italics* used for emphasis*)*:

Later I went to visit Shemaiah son of Delaiah
and grandson of Mehetabel who was confined to
His home. He said, "Let us meet together inside
the Temple of God and bolt the doors shut.
Your enemies are coming to kill you tonight."
But I replied, *"Should someone in my position run*
from danger? Should someone in my position enter
the Temple to save His life? No, I won't do it!" I
[Nehemiah] realized that God had not spoken to
Him [Shemaiah], but that He [Shemaiah] had

uttered this prophecy against me because Tobiah and Sanballat had hired Him. They were hoping to intimidate me and make me sin. Then they would be able to accuse and discredit me. (Nehemiah 6:10–13 NLT)

Did you know that Satan's scheme to "derail" us can even come through those we are serving (i.e. those we least expect)? Remember how Satan used Peter, one of Jesus's own disciples, to try and keep Jesus from going to the cross in Matthew 16:21–23? It's the same "power play." Once again, had Nehemiah not been familiar with the enemy's "game film," the victory that God had for Nehemiah would have never been realized!

Nehemiah understood that derision (Nehemiah 2:19), defiance (Nehemiah 4:8), distraction (Nehemiah 6:1–4), defamation (Nehemiah 6:5–9), deception (Nehemiah 6:10–14), and dissension (Nehemiah 6:16–19) all come straight out of the devil's "playbook" to stop God's work. Nevertheless, he continued to trust God and work with all his might until he completed the wall.

Nehemiah was successful in "battle" because he knew his God, knew his purpose, knew how to obtain the favor of God and "secular kings," knew his enemy, knew how to dress for battle, knew the location of his "battle station," knew how to pray, knew how to use the "ammo of truth," and he knew that his mission involved seizing, occupying, and reclaiming "territory" for the kingdom of God!

I hope you see the striking similarities between Nehemiah and Jesus (in Matthew 4) in the preparation and execution of their battle plans. Why? Because it's ours! I'm going somewhere!

Did you know that because we have accepted Jesus Christ as our Lord and Savior, we, like Nehemiah, have been given God's protection, provision, favor, and blessing? Did you know that we represent a legitimate threat to the "enemy" in our region that, up to now, has been content to occupy every institution in America from our house to the White House? Most importantly, did you know that God has already given us everything we need to reclaim these institutions if we, like Nehemiah, will simply "walk by faith?"

Nehemiah understood that his victory hinged on his ability to abide in God and His Word. Did you know that after all the repairs to the city walls and gates were complete, the Jewish people recognized that the root of all their problems had been the absence of God's Word in their lives? However, it didn't stop with merely identifying the problem (i.e., "talk") like it does with so many of us. They actually did something about it.

To demonstrate their commitment to God's Word going forward, Ezra, the priest, Nehemiah's contemporary, came and read the Word of God to the Jews for several hours (Nehemiah 8). What is striking about this account is not only that he did it, and no one left or fell asleep, but *where* he did it. He intentionally re-centered the Word of God "downtown" in the center of Jerusalem. He faced the square just inside the Water Gate (water in scripture denotes "life"—intentional choice of location by Ezra] from early morning until noon and read aloud to everyone who could understand. All the people paid close attention to the Book of the Law (Nehemiah 8:3 NLT). You see, Ezra and Nehemiah recognized something that very few of us do. Revival occurs when God's people return to Him (i.e., "repent") by responding to His Word. Ezra and Nehemiah understood that when the Word of God gets "sidelined," the God of the word gets "sidelined."[337] Neither one of them wanted that to ever happen again.

Why do I share this? It should now be obvious. Before we can focus on rebuilding the "walls and gates" of America that lay in spiritual ruins, we have to focus on rebuilding the "walls and gates" of our individual lives, homes, churches, and cities that lay in ruins due to the absence of God and His Word in our lives.

If God could reverse years of deterioration in Jerusalem through one man who was willing to "empty" himself, pray, submit to God, plea for God's forgiveness, seek God's favor from a secular government, and "walk by faith," He can reverse years of moral and spiritual deterioration in America through those of us who are willing to do the same! I hope you're willing because we're about to do it in Jesus's name!

Now, in preparation for the spiritual battle about to be waged by God's people all across America, hear and heed the sound of General Quarters!

> This is *not* a drill. This is *not* a drill. General Quarters! General Quarters! Men and women of God in America, man your battle stations! God is with us! The time has come to repair and rebuild the walls of our lives and every institution in America we comprise from our house to the White House for God's kingdom and glory! Remember the Lord, who is great and awesome, and fight for your brothers, your sons, your daughters, your wives, your homes, your churches, your cities, and this nation! Rise up and build! Cheers!

Prayer of Repentance (if applicable):

> Heavenly Father, as in the days of Nehemiah, I weep and mourn at the sight of our spiritual "walls and gates" which once stood high around every institution in America from our house to the White House, but now lie in ruins due, in part, to my sin. Not only have I passively stood by and watched Satan tear-down and demolish these walls and gates, but I have, unlike Nehemiah, refused to get up, suit up, and show up to my battle station with other believers to begin the process of repairing and rebuilding them. In the words of Nehemiah, "Yes, even my own family and I have sinned" (Nehemiah 1:6)!
> Instead of fighting your battles to advance your kingdom and bring you glory, I have been fighting my battles to advance my kingdom and

bring myself glory. In doing so, I have shamefully "sidelined" you, the truth of your word, and the purpose for which I was created, allowing the enemy to inflict great damage to my home, church, city, and this nation. However, greater than all of this is what I have to done to you. Will you please forgive me?

I choose to turn from this shallow, self-centered, lukewarm existence I've been living to take my place on the 'walls of America' that lie in moral and spiritual ruins. I recognize I will be joining other 'armed and dangerous' saints who are not afraid to use their spiritual weapons against Satan and His demons in their respective regions of the US to reclaim what has been stolen from us from our house to the White House.

Thank you for your steadfast love and mercies toward me that are new every morning (Lamentations 3:22) and for standing more prepared to forgive my sins than I am to commit them, more willing to supply my needs than I am to confess them. A love like this compels me to want to faithfully and courageously discharge my duties until our work is complete so that your kingdom would come and your will would be done on earth as it is in heaven (Matthew 6:9) for your glory. Amen."

Verses to Remember:

1. Why are you living in luxurious houses while my house lays in ruins? (Haggai 1:4 NLT)
2. No one engaged in warfare entangles himself with the affairs of this life, that he may please Him who enlisted him as a soldier. (2 Timothy 2:4 NKJV)

3. For though we walk in the flesh, we do not war after the flesh: (For the weapons of our warfare are not carnal, but mighty through God to the pulling down of strong holds;) casting down imaginations, and every high thing that exalteth itself against the knowledge of God, and bringing into captivity every thought to the obedience of Christ; (2 Corinthians. 10:3–5 KJV)

4. So I prayed to the God of heaven. And I said to the king, "If it pleases the king, and if your servant has found favor in your sight, that you send me to Judah, to the city of my fathers' graves that I may rebuild it." (Nehemiah 2:4–5 ESV)

5. Then I said to them, "You see the trouble we are in, how Jerusalem lies in ruins with its gates burned. Come, let us build the wall of Jerusalem, that we may no longer suffer derision." And I told them of the hand of my God that had been upon me for good, and also of the words that the king had spoken to me. And they said, "Let us rise up and build." (Nehemiah 2:17–18 ESV)

6. Lest Satan should get an advantage of us: for we are not ignorant of His devices. (2 Corinthians. 2:11 KJV)

7. Finally, be strong in the Lord and in the strength of His might. Put on the whole armor of God, that you may be able to stand against the schemes of the devil. (Ephesians 6:10–11 ESV)

8. When our enemies heard that it was known to us and that God had frustrated their plan, we all returned to the wall, each to his work. (Nehemiah 4:15 ESV)

9. Wherever you hear the sound of the trumpet, join us there. Our God will fight for us! (Nehemiah 4:20 NIV)

10. I shot back, "The God-of-Heaven will make sure we succeed. We're His servants and we're going to work, rebuilding. You can keep your nose out of it. You get no say in this—Jerusalem's none of your business!" (Nehemiah 2:20 MSG)

11. It is written… (Matthew 4:4 ESV)

12. For we walk by faith, not by sight. (2 Corinthians. 5:7 KJV)
13. No weapon that is formed against you shall prosper and every tongue which rises against you in judgment you shall condemn. This is the heritage of the servants of the Lord. (Isaiah 54:17 AMP)
14. Do not be afraid of them. Remember the Lord, who is great and awesome, and fight for your brothers, your sons, your daughters, your wives, and your homes. (Nehemiah 4:14 ESV)

CHAPTER 8

❖❖❖❖

Operation Heal America

Welcome to the title chapter of this book and the reason for which this entire book was written. Unless you've been living in a mine shaft or on a remote island without an Internet connection for the last several years, you have likely come to the same conclusion as me and many others in the Christian community. Our homes, churches, cities, and nation are in trouble. While this is probably no surprise to you at this point, it may be a surprise to learn whom God is holding responsible.

Contrary to what many Christians believe, God is not holding Satan, demons, unbelievers, past and present administrations, Congress, Republicans, Democrats, Progressives, Liberals, Conservatives, academia, fake news, special interest groups, lobbyists, "underground" operatives, the "deep state," or Hollywood responsible for the chaos in the world today. He is holding "His people" responsible. Darkness is just doing what it knows to do. In other words, the reason why darkness has invaded every institution in America from our house to the White House is because we, the light of Christ, have not invaded every institution in America from our house to the White House! Have we forgotten, beloved brothers and sisters, that we are the light of the world (Matthew 5:14–15) and darkness is subject unto us through His name (Luke 10:17)?

What many of us would never do at home to avoid "bumping" into furniture, tripping, falling, stubbing our toes, or breaking a hip, we routinely do as "believers." What is it we're doing? It's more about what we're not doing. We're not, collectively, letting our lights shine for Christ in society. While everyone else is "coming out of the closet" to transform the culture around them, the overwhelming majority of Christians in America are staying "in the closet" and transforming no one for Christ in the culture around them.

Beloved brothers and sisters, our problem is not numbers. Christians abound in every conceivable institution in America. God has Christians on Wall Street, "Main Street," and most likely on your street. Our problem is "sin," and more specifically, our unwillingness to "turn" from it so we can "burn brightly" for Christ in our homes, churches, cities, states, and nation. Instead of telling the world, the flesh, and the devil what to do in Jesus's name, we're allowing them to tell us what to do! Instead of allowing God's Word to have the final word from our house to the White House, too many of us have allowed our political preferences, the latest polling data, or the "court of popular opinion" to have the final word. Instead of "tearing our hearts" over offending a holy God with our disobedience, rebellion, and idolatry, many in the church today are "beating their chests" and "wringing their hands" over how they can keep from offending people.

Sadly, it is my conviction that many of us in America have counted the cost of true discipleship and decided it's way too expensive. Like those in Jesus's day, many of us have decided it's too much work, time, sacrifice, rejection, persecution, pain, loss, suffering, and way too risky in a nation that is becoming increasingly intolerant and hostile toward Christianity. In other words, "It's way too much like being Jesus." For others, following Christ is just too much of a "cosmic killjoy." How this must break the Father's heart after all He's done for us!

Thus, the days of blaming the "world" for the mess we're in while we neglect to become true disciples are over; assuming, that is, we want God to repair the walls and gates of America from our house to the White House that lie in moral and spiritual ruins.

With the proper foundation now laid from previous chapters and the deafening sound of GQ in our ears, there is no clearer, more concise "battle plan" to bring spiritual healing and revival to a nation like this from our house to the White House than the one found in 2 Chronicles 7:14:

> If my people, which are called by my name,
> shall humble themselves, and pray, and seek my
> face, and turn from their wicked ways; then I will
> hear from heaven, and will forgive their sin, and
> will heal their land. (KJV)

In this powerful and familiar verse, God makes it abundantly clear whom the problem and the solution lie with—us!

However, before we go any further, please allow me to quickly deal with another lie from Satan that he will deploy to try and stop some of you before we even get started! Contrary to the views of many who believe that this Old Testament scripture has no relevance in our New Testament lives, that couldn't be further from the truth. While we have been redeemed from the curse of the law of the Old Testament unto salvation through Christ, principles from the Old Testament may still be applied to our New Testament lives. It's one of the many reasons why God gave us the Old Testament and why most of you have taken principles from the Old Testament lives of Abraham, Sarah, Moses, Joseph, David, Abigail, Ruth, and Esther and rightly applied them to your lives. The same is true of 2 Chronicles 7:14. Now is no time for any of us to be "cherry-picking" which Old Testament principles apply to our lives and which ones don't.

The common theme that runs from Genesis to Revelation and ties the Old Testament to the New Testament is the theme of the kingdom of God.[338] Is 2 Chronicles 7:14 somehow inconsistent with this theme? Hardly! Quite the opposite. Still some of you again say, "Yes, but we are no longer under the 'law' of the Old Testament, but under 'grace' in the New Testament."

To this I respond, "Agreed." However, number one, 2 Chronicles 7:14 is not addressing how an unbeliever obtains salvation (i.e., becomes "justified") but how a nation returns to God to experience spiritual healing. In light of this, are you going to tell me that our need to humble ourselves, pray, seek His face, and "turn from our wicked ways" to receive spiritual healing are spiritual principles confined to the Old Testament only?

Still some of you say, "Yes, but the promises contained in 2 Chronicles 7:14 *only* apply to the nation of Israel."

Says who? The last time I looked, the principles found in 2 Chronicles 7:14 applied to God's covenant people, right? In the Old Testament, God's covenant people were the Jews. In the New Testament, God's covenant people are the body of believers known as the church of Jesus Christ, who have accepted Jesus's sacrificial death on the cross as the *only* acceptable form of payment for their sins. That would include, in all likelihood, the vast majority of you reading this book—His people! Please tell me you're done believing this lie so we can get to the good part? We need you!

In America today, we, His covenant people, number somewhere between 25.4 percent (the approximate number of Evangelical Christians in America)[339] and 70.6 percent (the number of Americans who identify themselves as Christians)[340] of all Americans. As of April 26, 2020, the US population was approximately 330,653,000 Americans.[341] This means that the solution to the chaos in America today rests with somewhere between approximately 84 to 233 million Americans.

Now imagine what would happen if this many people in America would humble themselves and pray and seek His face and turn from their wicked ways? We don't have to imagine. The verse tells us. God would hear from heaven, forgive our sin, and heal our land!

In 2 Chronicles 6, King Solomon has just finished building God's temple in Jerusalem and has offered up a prayer of dedication. In this prayer, Solomon affirms that He wants to lead God's people God's way. After Solomon's prayer at the beginning of 2 Chronicles 7, the glory of God fills the temple (2 Chronicles 7:1–4). His people offer sacrifices and then hold a seven-day feast that culminates into a celebration on the eighth day. In the night, God appears to Solomon and tells him that if his people ever reject God's ways and turn away from him, but repent (i.e. "turn back to Him"), He will hear their prayers, forgive their sins, and heal their land (2 Chronicles 7:14).

In the business world, investment bankers, brokers, borrowers, lenders, collateral agents, and third-parties frequently enter into what is commonly referred to as "Term Sheets." Term sheets outline the "terms and conditions" wherein one party (Party A) is willing to enter into a transaction with another party (Party B) when that party (Party B) agrees to the terms and conditions set forth by Party A. Second Chronicles 7:14 is God's "Term Sheet" with "His people" for healing our land, in this case, America. In this verse, God tells us that if we want Him to fix the mess we've made (i.e., heal our land), we have to first be willing to fulfill the terms of His Term Sheet, which are, incidentally, nonnegotiable!

What I have just described above should already sound familiar to you from our discussion on conditional and unconditional covenants in chapter 2. Second Chronicles 7:14 is a conditional covenant, that is, if we agree to do "a," "b," "c," and "d;" God will agree to do "e," "f," and "g." If we don't... He won't. Up to now, we haven't; so He hasn't. Read that again, mighty warrior, and let it sink in.

In case you haven't figured it out yet, beloved, God doesn't operate on our terms even when they're nice, religious, fair, nonpartisan, tolerant, or good; unless, of course, they line up with His terms! It's really simple with God. We either play by His rules or He doesn't play. However, as you may have noticed, He won't stop us from playing. It's why we're in this mess!

Our ability to fulfill each term found in 2 Chronicles 7:14 is the key to receiving the healing that God has for us in every institution in America from our house to the White House so we can expand His kingdom and magnify His glory worldwide!

While my focus is on America, these terms and conditions obviously apply to any nation. In the last chapter, for example, we saw how Israel abided by each of them under the leadership of Nehemiah. It not only resulted in them being able to rebuild the walls and gates of Jerusalem but in them being able to rebuild the lives of the Jews who had rejected God's ways for their ways. God wants to help us do the same thing if we, like Nehemiah, will agree to do it God's way!

But what does the application of 2 Chronicles 7:14 look like for "His people" in America today? You know more than you think after following Nehemiah in the last chapter. It looks like what Nehemiah did yesterday, today. Will God not do for us in America what God did for Nehemiah in the city of Jerusalem if we do what Nehemiah did yesterday, today? You bet He will. How can I be so sure? Because He's the same God yesterday, today, and forever (Hebrews 13:8)!

While I am certainly not the first person to urge Christians all across America to fulfill the terms of 2 Chronicles 7:14 so God would fulfill His terms to us, I may be the first, by God's grace, to devise a national plan to achieve it! However, if we expect to make this dream a reality, we must have a complete and accurate understanding of each term contained in 2 Chronicles 7:14. If we don't, Satan will be able to easily "scramble-up" the Word of God in our lives as He did with Adam and Eve and stop what He knows poses a direct threat to Him! Again, while many of you are familiar with the teaching of 2 Chronicles 7:14, I guarantee you are about to learn something new! Before we get started, now is a great time to hit the "pause button" and get your favorite drink or use the restroom if you need to. Ready?

First, the word *if*. God's promise to heal America today, as it was with the nation of Israel yesterday, comes with a condition—*if*. As I said above, 2 Chronicles 7:14 is a conditional covenant. God only obligates himself to abide by the terms of 2 Chronicles 7:14 (hereafter referred to as "God's Term Sheet for Healing America"), *if* we abide by *His* terms first. While God is certainly capable of healing America anyway and any time He wants, He says He will only do it *if* we do what He says first. I'm not aware of Him changing His mind, are you? Did you hear me precious ones? He said He only is going to hear our prayers, forgive our sin, and heal our land *if* we do what He requires first. *If* we refuse, then guess what? We get what we deserve. While this is clearly not what God or we want, we don't get to choose the consequences, remember?

This means that the "ball" is in our court. Without ever talking about our responsibility to satisfy God's terms *first,* many Christians say things like, "Why doesn't God do something?" or "How did things get so 'messed up?'" or "How did we become such an immoral nation?" or "How did gay marriage become the law of the land?" So many Christians I meet today are waiting for God to act when God is saying, "I'm waiting for you to act [chapter 1]." So many Christians expect God to fulfill His end of the agreement while we continue to neglect ours. Conditional covenants don't work that way, beloved. Really? Really. And notice, God said, "*If* my people," not "When my people," which suggests that God knew some of His people would refuse to abide by His terms. May it never be said of us!

You see, God knows something about us that many of us don't know about ourselves. What is it, you ask? He knows that many of us are happy to do what He wants as long as it meets *our terms,* but when it doesn't, and we go our own way, that we still expect Him to fulfill His terms to us. In other words, once we, not God, are done calling all the shots, we want to be able to tell God, "Okay, God, now heal my marriage, heal my home, heal my finances, heal my career, heal my church, heal my city, and heal my country."

No dice. God doesn't play second fiddle to anyone, including you or me! He, not we, sets the terms for spiritual healing and revival! It's His covenant, remember?

Do we, as believers, really believe that our lives are not our own and that we were bought with a price (1 Corinthians 6:19–20)? Then why do so many of us insist on dictating the *terms* of our healing? This arrogant posture is precisely why I believe our nation has not experienced spiritual healing and revival to date despite all of our praying, fasting, church attendance, "good works," and Bible studies.

While God will never force us to do things His way, He will not heal our land until we do. While some of you may be surprised to see how quickly our society and nation are unraveling due to our neglect, irresponsibility, disobedience, and outright rebellion, none of it is a surprise to God! He knew His people would reject His ways for their ways. You would have thought we would have learned something from Israel. I'm thinking God did too! Thank God it's not too late! This concludes the word *if*.

The next two words in 2 Chronicles 7:14 are "my people." God, again, is looking for "His people" to right this mess. "If *my people*..." Again, God didn't say, "If *Washington*;" "If *the LGBTQ community*;" "If *Planned Parenthood*;" "If *the media*;" "If *Wall Street*;" "If *Hollywood*;" "If *President Trump*;" "If *Congress*;" "If *The Department of Justice or the FBI*;" "If *The Supreme Court*;" "If *lobbyists*;" "If *special interest groups*;" "If *the darkness*;" "If *Satan*;" He said, "If *my people*..."

If you have repented of your sin and accepted the free gift of salvation offered through Christ's death on the cross for the forgiveness of your sins, then you are one of His people. If you haven't, then you are not. Again, these are His terms, not mine. I didn't write the book. I just try to follow it.

However, the good news is that you can be one of *His people* right now if you are willing to do what I just said. Go ahead. I'll wait. Did you know that this could have been the very reason why you read this book? Praise God! If you just did this, congratulations, and welcome to the family! You are now one of His people! Tell at least three people, find a good Bible-believing church, get baptized, study God's Word, begin the process of becoming a disciple, and pay very close attention to the rest of this book because it now involves you! Aren't you glad you read this book? I am!

The reason the spiritual healing of America is in the hands of His people and not "unbelievers" is because the root problems plaguing our homes, churches, cities, and nation are inherently spiritual as I have discussed extensively throughout this book. Since we know spiritual battles can only be fought (and won!) with spiritual weapons, God can only use those who possess and utilize spiritual weapons to win these battles. That would be us! What a calling! What a God! Is this exciting or what? That covers the phrase *"my people."*

The next phrase in 2 Chronicles 7:14 says, *"[w]ho are called by my name."* To name something is to "own it" as we saw back in Genesis. When my parents gave me the last name Spence, they were telling the rest of the world that I "belonged" to them. People instinctively want to know who they are, who others are, and where they and others belong. Parents solve this dilemma for us when they name us. Did you know that God also solved this problem for us when He named us sons and daughters at conversion? He declared to the world and the devil that we belong to Him! It still makes me weep with joy every time I think about it!

What I find interesting about this first phrase in 2 Chronicles 7:14, "*If my people who are called by my name*" is that at first glance, it seemed to be redundant. *Of course, your people are called by your name*, I thought. Then it hit me. There's a big difference between a believer who understands that they belong to Jesus Christ and will, therefore, identify and associate themselves with Jesus versus someone who "belongs" to a generic "God" who is not Jesus. I hope you're in the first camp; otherwise, you're not one of His people. These are His terms, not mine, remember?

To drive this point home even further, the Complete Jewish Bible (CJB) translation of this phrase "[w]ho are called by my name," is "*who bear my name*." When we are "saved," God's Word says that He inscribes *us* on the palms of His hands and that our "city walls are continually before [Him]" (Isaiah 49:16). This is a beautiful picture of God's constant love, care, and concern for us as His children. In the same way that owners of certain livestock "brand" their animals to tell others who their animals belong to, God spiritually "brands" His name on our hearts at the time of our conversion to declare to the world that we belong to Him!

The final point I'd like to make regarding this first phrase, "*If my people who are called by my name*" is that it's going to take the majority of God's people fulfilling *God's Term Sheet for Healing America* if we expect God to heal America. We saw this in the Old Testament with the nation of Israel, right? It wasn't just a small group of Israelites that repented. It was the entire nation—over and over again. While personal spiritual healing and revival can come to those who fulfill God's terms individually, it will only come to a nation (e.g., America) when *His people* of that nation meet His terms first.

The next part of God's *Term Sheet for Healing America* is the phrase "*will humble themselves*." God says that He will not heal our land spiritually until His people humble themselves. I love what this author has to say about humility here in the following (*italics* used for emphasis):

> Humility comes from the Latin word "humus," which means ground. The humble person is one who lives, so to speak, on the ground floor. They are not self-important, nor self-assertive; they do not insist on their own rights or their own way; and they do not put on a show of false modesty in order to impress people. The Greek word for humility is *Tapeinos*. It means to have an accurate estimate of oneself in relation to God and others. The humble acknowledge that all they have and all they are, they owe to God; and they submit to Him.
>
> There are two ways to be humbled: (1) God can humble us through experiences and chastening; and (2) we can humble ourselves freely and willingly. The last option results in forgiveness and healing. *But if the humility is collective and involves many of God's people, the forgiveness and healing can be all-encompassing. Let us all humble ourselves so that God may heal our land.*[342]

Please note, in 2 Chronicles 7:14, God tells us to humble ourselves even before we pray! Interesting, right? Since when do Christians do anything before they pray? God's Word offers a possible clue. It says that God resists the proud but gives grace to the humble (James 4:6; 1 Peter 5:5). As we previously discussed in chapter 6, pride is one of the things that keeps our prayers from reaching God's ears. It's a barrier to intimacy. Since prayer is the most intimate exchange we can have with God, it may explain why God wants us to *humble ourselves* before we pray. After all, how intimate do you think God wants to be with us when we are "full of ourselves?" How intimately do you like to be with those you love when they are "full of themselves?"

We also need to consider this: God would not be directing us to humble ourselves unless He thought we had a problem with pride. Did you hear me? God believes *His* people (we, fellow Christians) have a problem with pride. Remember what I said earlier about pride? At its root, it's self-worship. So think about it. Why would God heal our nation if we're just going to turn around and use what He gives us to worship ourselves (i.e., to build our kingdoms and bring ourselves glory)? I wouldn't heal our land either, would you? On the other hand, when we humble ourselves, God can trust we will use our "healed America" to expand His kingdom and glory worldwide!

I don't know about you, but I'm personally disgusted at how arrogant and prideful I can be with family, friends, fellow believers, and coworkers even after all these years. How about you? Do you inwardly gloat when you're right or take great pleasure proving others wrong? Are you *proud* of the material possessions you've been able to amass for yourself and your family? Or are you thankful to God for what He's given you and hold it all with an open hand? When things go well for you, are you proud or grateful? When things don't go well for you, do you complain? Or are you worshipful and dependent on God? Do you praise yourself when success comes your way? Or do you let another praise you and not your own mouth (Proverbs 27:2)? Do you expect others to serve you because of who you are and what you've done? Or do you seek to serve others because of who He is and what He's done? Are you proud to be an American because deep down, you believe Americans are superior to those of another nation? Or are you blessed to be an American so you can be a blessing to others around the world who also made in the image and likeness of God?

In case some of you thought that the last statement was a "commercial" or an endorsement for illegal immigration, I assure you it was not. I am very much "for" *legal* immigration and obeying the laws of the land (i.e., federal immigration laws) as we continue to demonstrate "compassion" to those around the globe who need it... in their respective countries!

If we were truly honest with ourselves, many of us would admit that pride is a large part of our everyday lives. God knows it. The question is, do we know it? Or are we too proud to admit it? Sadly, many of us are just too "cute," sophisticated, talented, wealthy, or famous for God to help! If we want God to heal our land from our house to the White House and not continue to oppose us (James 4:6), we'd better deal with our pride from our house to the White House!

God's Word says that those who exalt themselves will be humbled and those who humble themselves will be exalted (Matthew 23:12). The same is true of a nation and society. A nation and society that exalt itself will be humbled, and a nation and society that humbles itself will be exalted. In light of this, we Christians, who number somewhere between 83 and 231 million Americans, if you recall, and who are positioned at every level of society should, therefore, consider asking ourselves the following question: How much humility is on display in our house, the church house, the schoolhouse, the courthouse, both houses of Congress, and the White House? What would Jesus say about our social media accounts? Do they say, "Look at me, look at me, look at me?" Or "Look at Him, look at Him, look at Him?"

God's Word also says that pride goes before destruction and a haughty spirit before a fall (Proverbs 16:18 KJV). No "wiggle room" here. Said another way, pride always comes before the destruction and fall of an individual life, marriage, home, church, city, and nation. Many of you, like me, have already experienced the consequences of pride in your lives. What other consequences will we have to face before we finally deal with this "cancer" that is eating us from the inside out?

If God opposes the proud but gives grace to the humble (James 4:6) and God thinks *His people* in America are collectively proud, then guess what? He's opposing us. Could this be part of the reason why we're witnessing unprecedented levels of chaos and evil in our nation today despite all of our religious activity? Could God be waiting for us to humble ourselves? Yes!

The next term is "and *pray*." The next requirement in God's *Term Sheet for Healing America* that He expects us to abide by if we want Him to hear our prayers, forgive our sins, and heal our land, is *pray*. It has been said, "Only when we have God's heart will we invoke His hand."[343] Prayer gives us access to God's heart.

It's probably no secret to many of you (given the earlier statistics I shared) that the average Christian spends little to no time in prayer each day.[344] One study revealed that the average Christian conservative in America spends about six hours in prayer per year, but nearly 400 hours on politics, 150 hours on entertainment, 120 hours on vacation, 100 hours on sports, 90 hours on hobbies and at shopping malls, 50 hours on pornographic websites, and around 45 hours drinking coffee like Starbucks![345] Is it any wonder why we're facing a moral and spiritual crisis in America?

Recall, however, it is not just prayer that God is looking for, but biblical prayer. Again, in chapter 6, we discussed many things that block prayer and make it a total waste of time. Now you know why I did this. Since prayer is a requirement for God to heal our land, it is critical that we do not forget what we read in chapter 6 to ensure that we are engaging in biblical prayer. Remember the critical role prayer played in the life of Nehemiah? There wasn't one prayer of Nehemiah's that God didn't hear. Why? Because Nehemiah understood that *not* all prayer is created equal. It's critical we do too; that is, if we want God to hear our prayers, forgive our sin, and heal our land.

The next term in *God's Term Sheet for Healing America* that He expects us to comply with before He heals our land is "*seek His face.*" Notice, it doesn't say "seek His hands." While I, like you, are grateful for the hands that provide comfort, healing, assistance, and care in time of need, far too many of us are looking for a handout (from God) rather than a face-off.[346] One of the quickest ways we can "derail" this mission and miss an incredible opportunity to love God and be loved by Him and others along the way is to seek His hands before we seek His face.

Love, closeness, intimacy, deception, truth, guilt, kindness, shame, sadness, joy, pride, peace, anger, acceptance, manipulation, and fear, for example, can all be seen in the face. It's why parents want to see their children's eyes when they are talking to them and why dads want to look in the eyes of the young man who comes to take his "little girl" out for the evening. It's why brides and grooms look into each other's eyes when they recite their wedding vowels, why hiring managers look for good eye contact from applicants during job interviews, and why criminal investigators like to see the eyes of the ones they are interrogating.

Jesus desires an intimate relationship with us. In His presence, everything changes. As we worship and adore Him, God transforms us by His presence and power. Not only do blind eyes see, deaf ears hear, and the lame walk, but those who have been "spiritually sick" for years receive spiritual healing in an instant (John 5). If there was ever anything we, in the United States of America, need, it is spiritual healing in an instant. However, none of this is possible when we are more interested in a handout than a face-off.

Jesus not only wants us to *seek Him,* but He wants us to seek Him *first.* He tells us in Matthew 6:33 that if we seek *first* the kingdom of God and His righteousness, all these other things we seek will be added unto us (Matthew 6:33). The kingdom of God has a King. His name is Jesus! In the verses leading up to Matthew 6:33, Jesus is addressing the worry and anxiety Jewish Christians had for their lives. While Jesus limits this discussion to food, drink, and clothing, the cure found in Matthew 6:33 is the same cure for all anxiety. What is important to note here is that the New Testament teaching of Jesus in Matthew 6:33 is consistent with the Old Testament teaching of the Lord through Solomon in 2 Chronicles 7:14, which is that God will not act on our behalf until we seek Him *first.*

But why is He so interested in having us seek Him *first?* Because He only shares His authority with those who "have His back" first. This is one of the reasons why suffering for Christ is our "friend." It tells us, and Him, who's first. If we "fold" in the face of what we may lose for following Him first, He's not first. Thus, we should not expect Him to hear our prayers, forgive our sin, and heal our land.

We love the part of the verse that says, "That I may know Him and the power of His resurrection" (Philippians 3:10) but don't care much for the part that says "and the fellowship of His suffering being made conformable even unto death" (Philippians 3:10). However, we will never really know Him until we are willing to identify with *both* parts of Him. The one who *seeks His face* is willing to know both parts of Him. I believe this is what He's after before He will agree to heal our homes, churches, cities, and nation.

Seeking Jesus first also means that we seek His Word first since He and His Word are one (John 1:1). We must understand that it is impossible to seek God *first* if His Word is *second*, last, or not even in the arena. Satan has tragically convinced many Christians that God can be "first" in our lives while what God has to say about a matter can be second, last, or worse yet, completely rejected. No dice. True disciples seek to allow God's Word to have the final word in every area of life even when it runs in conflict with the world around them and those closest to them. It is here where you and I will discover who we truly serve despite our Sunday morning declarations and testimonies of God's "goodness" and "faithfulness."

Said another way, the test of our true allegiance and loyalty to Christ is when we know seeking Jesus and His Word *first* could cost us something or everything. Maybe it's a marriage, a friendship, a son or daughter, a promotion, popularity, reelection, present or future business, or even our lives. Yet, we choose to seek Him and His Word *first* anyway. This is the mark of Christian excellence! What I want you to see is that it is also the reason why God has not healed our nation. What? That's right. While God will never stop loving us, until He knows that He and His Word have first place in the lives of "His people" in America, He knows He cannot trust "His people" to rule America His way. In other words, why would He heal our nation when He knows we're just going to turn around and rule it our way, which is really Satan's way?

All of us have people in our lives that we love but don't trust, right? It's why some relationships end or never become what they were intended to be, even when forgiveness is extended and accepted. No trust, no *real* connection. Just survival. For those "surviving" instead of "thriving" in marriage due to lack of trust, you know exactly what I'm saying. This is not marriage as God intended.

Conversely, some of us may also have people in our lives who love us but don't trust us. God is no different. He not only wants us to trust Him, but He wants to know He can trust us. You see, before

God will heal our land, He wants to know He can trust us to rule it His way. Individuals and nations who consistently seek Him and His Word *first,* regardless of the cost, have earned His trust! Does this describe you?

Before we leave this phrase, "*seek my face,*" and go to the final term in 2 Chronicles 7:14 that we must fulfill if we expect God to fulfill His terms with us, please allow me to make one last point regarding this word *seek.* To "seek" is to go actively "in search or quest of," "to look for," "to search for by going from place to place," or "to endeavor to find or gain *by any means*" (Webster's Dictionary 1828—Online Edition).

As a former Navy pilot, these definitions have significant meaning to me. One of the missile systems I was required to become familiar with was the AIM-9 Sidewinder short-range air-to-air antiaircraft heat-seeking missile system developed by the Navy (U). Without getting too technical or in trouble for sharing too much information, all objects with a temperature greater than absolute zero (minus 460 degrees F) emit infrared energy or heat (U). The AIM-9 heat-seeking missile was designed to shoot down enemy aircraft by "locking-on" to the heat from the enemy aircraft's exhaust. A great advantage of this missile system is that it is unaffected by daylight, darkness, or bad weather. Additionally, its "fire-and-forget" technology allows the pilot to fire the missile without having to wonder if it will acquire the target and destroy it. The "kill probability" of the AIM-9L used by RAAF F/A-18 aircraft in the Falklands War was 80 percent.[347] This means that when the missile was fired, it was successful in "seeking," "acquiring," "locking on," and destroying its intended target eight out of ten times.

While Jesus is certainly not the target of our destruction but the target of our intimacy, I wonder how successful we are in locating and acquiring Jesus when we search for Him? Is our search for Him unaffected by daylight, darkness, or the "bad weather" around us? Or do we consistently allow outside influences to keep us from acquiring Him?

God's Word says that if we seek Him, *we will find Him* when we search for Him *with all of our hearts* (Jeremiah 29:13). This brings me to the main reason why so many of us don't find Him when we search for Him. We don't do it with *all* of our hearts. We do it with divided hearts that are loyal to our kingdom and His kingdom (chapter 4). No dice.

May we be like King David who, after the Lord said, "Seek my face [in prayer require my presence as your greatest need]," declared, "Your face, Lord, I will seek [on the authority of your word]. Do not hide your face from me" (Psalm 27:8–9 AMP).

What's truly amazing about our Lord for those who, like me, have been "guilty" of being more focused on a handout than a face-off from God is the moment we discover that when we do get it right, His hands were already extended! That's our Jesus!

The final term in *God's Term Sheet for Healing America* that His people must satisfy before God will agree to hear our prayers, forgive our sin, and heal our land involves "*turn[ing] from [our] wicked ways.*" Something tells me that God saved this term for last because He knew we would not be able to do it or even want to until we were first willing to *humble ourselves* and admit that there are, in fact, "wicked ways" that we need to "turn from." I also believe God knew that we would not be able to do it or even want to until He could reveal to us, in *prayer*, an unconditional love so great amid our sin that it would motivate and empower us to want to *turn from our wicked ways*. And finally, I believe He knew that we would not be able to *turn from our wicked ways* or even want to until we could see Him in a way that we've never seen Him before, which occurs when we *seek His face* before we seek His hands. Turning from our wicked ways is probably last because God knew that what we would not be able to do or want to do first, we would joyfully and willingly do last!

Notice, the phrase says *turn* from our wicked ways. It does not say *confess* our wicked ways. Why do I say this? Here's why. Did you know that it is possible to *confess* our wicked ways and never turn from them? That's right. While it is impossible to repent without confessing, it is possible to confess without repenting. Allow me to explain with this example. If you and your spouse are driving down the highway together and your spouse discovers they have taken a wrong turn (I know!), it's good for them to *confess* it as early as possible, wouldn't you agree? Especially if you were not paying attention either! However, what if they confessed it but didn't get off at the next exit and kept going in the wrong direction? Ridiculous right? Yet, isn't this precisely what many of us do with our diet programs ("Aw, man, I'm eating way too much!"), our family budgets ("We need to stop spending so much!"), and addictions ("I really need to get some help for my porn addiction.")?

We confess our "sin," which is good, but we never "turn" from it! We just keep eating, spending, and "feeding" our addictions (i.e., going in the "wrong" direction). Repentance, however, is when we not only confess that we are going in the wrong direction (i.e., are engaged in "sin") but get off at the next exit, take the exit ramp to the overpass, turn onto the overpass, exit off of the overpass to the on-ramp that takes us in the right direction, and then "go" in the proper direction. Anything short of what I have just described is not true biblical repentance. Satan understands this. Do we?

Thus, confession alone, without repentance, is no threat to Satan. It must be funny to him to hear a person confess his "sin" repeatedly but then watch him continue to go in the wrong direction! Repentance, on the other hand, is anything but funny to him. It is a direct threat to the preservation and expansion of his kingdom and glory. You see, when we repent, as I described above, we reposition ourselves under God where His power is now free to flow to us and where we are now able to receive angelic assistance to reclaim territory from Satan. Thus, Satan's goal, whenever we do confess our sins, is to make sure our confession never "graduates" into repentance. This means that if he *can't* keep us from getting off at the next exit to "turn around," he will try to keep us from finding the overpass. And if he can't keep us from finding the overpass, he will try to keep us from finding the on-ramp that leads to the "new" direction. And if he can't keep us from finding the on-ramp that leads to the "new" direction, he will make it difficult for us to "merge" with oncoming traffic to go in a "new" direction. And finally, if he can't keep us from successfully merging with the oncoming traffic to go in a "new" direction, he will try to get us to take another "wrong turn," so we never make it to our intended destination.

Thus, it is critical that when we do *turn* from our wicked ways, we do so quickly and completely so we only have to "backtrack" a mile or two instead of hundreds of miles! In this way, we don't waste a bunch of God's time and are able reach our intended destination with God more quickly. I pray this has helped you to understand what true repentance means! The devil is furious that you now know this!

One trick Satan uses to keep us from *turning from our wicked ways* is to try to get us to see our sin as something other than what it really is—sin. We talked about this earlier. However, in this context, Satan knows that God will not be able to fulfill His promise to us in 2 Chronicles 7:14 if we, as the body of Christ, don't see our ways as "wicked," or worse yet, see our "wicked ways" as "good." For example, if you are a pastor who believes that you and your congregation should endorse homosexuality as an alternative lifestyle in the name of diversity, tolerance, and compassion, and ordain and marry homosexuals, you cannot *turn from your wicked ways.*

Husbands and wives, if you don't know your roles and won't stay in your "lanes," you can't *turn from your wicked ways.* If you think it's okay for God to "marry" you and man to divorce you for reasons God does not allow, you can't *turn from your wicked ways.* If we, as individuals, think it's okay to build our kingdom while we neglect or ignore God's kingdom, we cannot *turn from our wicked ways.* In other words, if our word, and not God's Word, gets to have the final word, we cannot *turn from our wicked ways!*

We can only *turn from our wicked ways* when we are willing to acknowledge that our ways are, in fact, wicked, according to the Word of God, which brings me to the first reason why we don't *turn from our wicked ways.* As just stated, we don't know they're *wicked* because we don't know the Word of God! If friends, family, coworkers, Hollywood, talk show personalities, pollsters, society, and social media are allowed to define what is *wicked* for us and what isn't, then what do you and I need to turn from, right? Sadly and tragically, these are the days in which we live. Yes, even in the church!

When we are unable to see our wicked ways as wicked, we are spiritually blind. Spiritual blindness is such a powerful and effective strategy of the enemy because it not only masks "wicked ways" that we need to "turn from," but it can cause us to *turn from our wicked ways* in the wrong direction. What? To use another driving illustration, have you ever been driving down the road only to discover that you were going the wrong way, then, after making what you thought was the proper course correction, discovered you were still going the wrong way? Well, at least you realized it! Sadly and tragically, there are many Christians who take one "wrong turn" after another and never realize they are still going the wrong way. A common example of this might be a Christian wife who divorces her husband because she believes she has a right to be happy (wrong turn #1) and then marries another man (wrong turn #2), committing adultery because she did not have biblical grounds for divorce (chapter 2). She spends the rest of her life believing it was "God's will" for her to get the divorce and "helps" other "unhappy" Christian wives to do the same thing. Spiritual blindness. Satan doesn't even need to show up! Easy day.

Spiritual blindness, like the one who manufactures it, Satan, has many "heads." If Satan can't "blind" us to our "wicked ways," He will try to trick us into calling our "wicked ways" something other than what God calls them…sin. Remember what I said in our opening chapter? Jesus didn't die on the cross for mistakes, hurts, habits, hang-ups, accidents, or poor judgment. He died for "sin." Satan knows that if he can get us to relabel or recategorize our sin and call it something other than what God calls it, we will be less likely to repent of it, and thus, remain enslaved to him.

You see, if we, as the body of Christ, think we are *turning from our wicked ways* when we really haven't, we haven't met the terms God requires for Him to hear our prayers, forgive our sin, and heal our land. That's the issue, friend! We have unknowingly made impossible that which was possible through Christ! Why? Because *we* want to be able to define "wickedness" on our terms, not His, and turn in the direction we think is right versus the way His Word says is right.

Remember, men, we haven't reached biblical manhood until Jesus can tell us what to do. Until Jesus's Word can have the final word in every area of our lives, we're just males. The same is true of you, ladies. Until Jesus can have the final word in every area of your lives, you're just females. God is not looking for males and females, He's looking for kingdom men and kingdom women to reclaim this "thing" on earth as it is in heaven in preparation for His return and our Millennial Reign with Him, remember (chapter 1)?

Another reason why we don't *turn from our wicked ways* is because we're unwilling to "dethrone" ourselves. You see, we, like Satan, love to sit on the throne of our lives and "call the shots." What many of us don't realize, however, is that this wasn't originally our idea. It was Satan's! Getting us to stay on the throne is very easy because he knows we're inherently proud, selfish, and rebellious as a consequence of the fall and want to control every aspect of our lives and others' lives (in many cases) if we were truly honest!

It's also hard for us to *turn from our wicked ways* when Satan can convince us that everyone else is the problem. Back to the pride issue, which again is evidence of our need to humble ourselves. If you and I are becoming more aware of and grieved by our "sin" as time goes on, it is a sign that we are growing in our relationship with Christ. If, however, we are becoming less aware and less grieved by our "sin" as time goes on, the opposite is true. I have found that it is usually those of us in the second group who think that everyone else is the problem.

Another obstacle that keeps us from *turning from our wicked ways*—or to use the biblical term, *repenting*—is rejecting the power of Christ that could make us holy (2 Timothy 3:5). We forget that when we were "born again," the Holy Spirit came to live on the inside of us. And because of this, we have been given an appetite for holiness that is greater than any other desire.[348] The Holy Spirit is our Helper who wants to help us become holy (John 14:26), but only if we'll let Him by doing things His way; that is, by following His Word. So instead of releasing what's on the inside of us (i.e., the power of the Holy Spirit) through brokenness (i.e., realizing this world is not our home), many of us spend the majority of our lives trying "to do what's right" or "fix what's wrong." While this has some value, we're back to an "outside-in" approach, which over time fails to get to the heart, not to mention that it often involves "worldly advice" from others that runs contrary to the Word of God. We're back to digging cisterns, broken cisterns that can't hold any water (Jeremiah 2:13). We can never truly repent until we're willing to deal with our "sin" from the inside-out as discussed earlier since true repentance occurs at the heart level where the Holy Spirit resides.

I mentioned the word *brokenness*. Let's unwrap this word a bit more to examine its relationship to the Holy Spirit so we can fully deal with this obstacle to repentance. The Bible talks about three different types of soil in the Parable of the Sower found in Matthew 13. Brokenness is a key "ingredient" found in all "good soil." God's Word tells us that a broken and contrite heart He [God] will not despise (Psalm 51:17). Said another way, the Holy Spirit inhabits brokenness. Why? Because it gives Him the ability to change us into what He wants us to be since our self-sufficiency is no longer getting in His way.

In the same way that a horse trainer knows that he cannot get a wild horse to go in the direction he wants it to go until it is "broken," the Holy Spirit knows that He cannot get us to go in the direction He wants us to go until we are broken. When we refuse to be broken, we reject or "disinvite" the power of the Holy Spirit needed to "turn from our wicked ways" or "tame" our waywardness. This is how people stay stuck in patterns of habitual sin their entire lives and never get free.

This is, incidentally, one of the main reasons God allows trials into our lives. He is trying to break us of our self-sufficiency so that the Holy Spirit will be able to lead us in the direction He wants us to go! You'll know you have the spirit of brokenness operating in your life when you desire to know Jesus and His Word more than you desire to see the circumstances of your life improve.[349] Meditate on that for the rest of your life! I know!

Bearing a very close resemblance to brokenness that is equally essential for accessing the power of the Holy Spirit needed to *turn from our wicked ways* is a term called *surrender*. While many books have been written on the topic of *surrender*, I find it best defined in two simple sentences. "Jesus, I can't, but I know you can. Do in me what I am unable to do for myself."

When we say this and mean it by giving Him the right to rule over every area of our lives, the Holy Spirit is finally able to move us in the direction of His will because we're no longer opposing Him. But notice, I said His will, not our will. Some of us surrender so *our* wills can be done. This is not biblical surrender. True surrender is laying down our will for His will. It's giving God the power to "over-rule" us in every situation according to His Word.

Surrender is what we do after we invite the power of the Holy Spirit into our situation through brokenness. Said another way, surrender is a by-product of brokenness. Maybe this illustration will help. During arrests, law enforcement officers routinely ask their subjects to "get their hands up." We don't want to see just one hand up. We want to see both hands straight up over their heads, signifying a complete surrender so that we can place them into custody. Not until they have fully surrendered into our custody can we lead them in the direction that we want them to go. None of this, however, is possible until the arrestee has been "broken" on the inside. Once broken on the inside, they are willing to surrender.

While the Holy Spirit isn't looking to deprive us of freedom, He is looking for us to fully surrender to His will and place ourselves into His "custody" so He can lead us in the direction He wants us to go without wondering if we're going to "break bad." Complete surrender gives Him this assurance. Thus, repentance can only occur where this is brokenness and surrender.

Did you know that *turning from [our] wicked ways* sometimes requires us to worship with a knife? That's right. Tambourines are nice, but sometimes it is necessary to "cut" things out of our lives that have been hindering us from following God. The author of Hebrews says it this way, "*[l]et us lay aside every weight, and the sin which so easily ensnares us, and let us run with endurance the race that is set before us*" (Hebrews 12:1 NKJV). You see, God knows we will not be able to successfully run the race He has for us when we're being "weighed down" by people and circumstances that hinder His plans and purposes for us.

If you're single or engaged, for example, it might mean that God is calling you to "cut off" a relationship or a friendship that you know is not of God. For someone else, it may mean "cutting away" an obsession with a career, hobby, ministry, addiction, or interest that leaves little or no time for God and others. All of us, if we were honest with ourselves, know what we need to "cut." However, if you're not sure, all you have to do is ask the Holy Spirit to reveal it to you. He will, either directly or indirectly, through a trusted mature Christian friend, if you and I will have the courage to ask them. Once God reveals what you need to "cut," do it immediately and never look back.

I don't know about you, but I feel lighter already. I just went through a season of "cutting" things and people out of my life that were hindering the plans and purposes of God. While it was extremely difficult, it feels great to be free and in the center of God's will again!

We see a nice "call to repentance" in the book of Joel where the people of Judah in the Southern kingdom had become prosperous and complacent, turning to lives of self-centeredness, idolatry, and other sins. Joel, who prophesied from approximately BC 835–796, is used by God to warn Judah of God's impending judgment for their sins and to urge them to *turn from their wicked ways* back to God. Hear his prophetic cry:

> Turn to me now, while there is time! Give me your hearts. Come with fasting, weeping, and mourning. Don't tear your clothing in your grief; instead tear your hearts. Return to the Lord your God, for He is gracious and merciful. He is not easily angered. He is filled with kindness and is eager to not punish you. (Joel 2:12–13 NLT)

> Blow the trumpet in Jerusalem! Announce a time of fasting; call the people together for a solemn meeting. Bring everyone—the elders, the children, and even the babies. Call the bridegroom from His quarters and the bride from her private room. The priests, who minister in the Lord's presence, will stand between the people

and the altar, weeping. Let them pray, "Spare your people, Lord! They belong to you, so don't let them become an object of mockery. Don't let their name become a proverb of unbelieving foreigners who say, 'Where is the God of Israel? He must be helpless!'" (Joel 2:15–17 NLT)

Joel's cry of yesterday is the cry of modern-day prophets in America today who, like Joel, are warning of God's impending judgment for sin while urging God's people in America to turn back to God. I join them in this desperate hour not as a self-proclaimed prophet but as one who firmly believes that if there is one central message that we need to hear and heed if we expect God to respond to the cry of His people and heal our land, it is "Repent!"

The need for God's people to repent is certainly not confined to the Old Testament. While there were notable and praiseworthy things that Jesus acknowledged to the angels of the churches of Ephesus, Pergamum, Thyatira, Sardis, and Laodicea in Revelation 2 and Revelation 3, His central message to each of them was the same—"Repent."

Incidentally, while I'm here, to church leaders with national influence, while I "get it," please stop telling the rest of us to pray for unity and begin urging us to "repent" for not allowing God's Word to have the final word in every area of life. Can you imagine how unified we would be if we did this and then sought to align ourselves underneath it?

God is calling us to return to Him (i.e., repent) now while there is time. Remember, while He leaves the choice with us, we do not get to choose the consequences if we don't. The ball is in our court. Will we give our hearts to God? Or will we continue to give our hearts to the idols of this "world" that will never fully satisfy us? Will we come with fasting, weeping, and mourning like Nehemiah or have no heart for it? Will we simply tear our clothing as an outward expression of our grief and shame? Or will we "tear our hearts" because of what we've done to the name and reputation of Jesus Christ?

Finally, to be crystal clear for the many of you who, like me, have been praying for revival to come to America, revival cannot nor will not ever come to America, based on the authority of God's Word, until God's people in America repent! Let God be true and every man a liar (Romans 3:4), including me! Make no mistake. The reason why revival has not come to America despite all of our praying, hand-wringing, and chest-beating is because God's people all across America have refused to repent. That is, up to now! By *turning from our wicked ways*, we will have fulfilled our requirement for revival that not even the Holy Spirit, based upon the promises of God's Word, will deny! No? When was the last time you saw God renege on a promise He made to His people when they did what He required?

While revival in America will impact countless numbers of unbelievers all across America who will receive Jesus Christ as their personal Lord and Savior, we mustn't forget that true revival is not for the "unsaved." It's for the "saved." The "saved" need "reviving" because they have fallen asleep spiritually. However, the two are most definitely intertwined. You see, when the "saved" get "revived," they begin sharing the Gospel again, and the "lost" get "saved."

But the fruits of revival for the "saved" go well beyond this. In the case of our nation, God's people of this nation return to allowing God's Word to have the final word in every institution in America from our house to the White House as the Holy Spirit empowers us to advance God's kingdom and magnify His glory worldwide!

Now that we have addressed all of the terms in *God's Term Sheet for Healing America* found in 2 Chronicles 7:14, there's only one thing left for us to do—fulfill them so God will hear the collective "cry" of His people, forgive our sin, and heal our land!

Before we go any further, please allow me to share a couple of things I believe are essential for you to know about me and this exciting mission we are about to embark on together. First, I was hoping someone else would do it! I prayed for many years that God would use someone more qualified than me with church influence at the national level to step up and do what God asked me to do. After years of unanswered prayer and silence from heaven, it became clear that God wanted me to do it!

I'll never forget the day I got my "orders." "Wait! What? What do you want me to do? Please, find somebody else. This is not my area of expertise."

Then, slowly, over the days, weeks, months, and years that followed, my shock and disbelief turned to great joy as I came to realize that God really did want to use someone as sinful and small as me to do this great work with you for Him. Then it occurred to me. This is exactly what He does! He qualifies the unqualified when the unqualified are willing to step up with the gifts, talents, and abilities He gave them to align their wills with His will to advance His kingdom and magnify His glory! And make no mistake, this is what 2 Chronicles 7:14 is all about—putting God on display!

You see, the only proper response there will be after knowing God has heard our prayers, forgiven our sin, and healed our land will be all-out praise and worship to the only true God, our Lord, and Savior Jesus Christ who alone is worthy!

The Holy Spirit spoke these words to me that I would now like to share with you:

> Jim, while you were waiting for someone else to act, I've been waiting for you to act. Stop ignoring me. Do you realize that I allowed you to become a Special Agent with the FBI so you would know how to be my "Special Agent" in the earth for such a time as this? While the FBI credentials I allowed you to carry for over twenty years gave you legal power and authority to act on behalf of the United States, they weren't your first set of credentials. You received your first set when you accepted Jesus as your personal Lord and Savior. All of my children have them, but not all of them know it. Like your FBI credentials, your spiritual credentials, however, give you legal power and authority to act on my behalf in

the earth to advance my kingdom and bring me glory. You remember when I showed you this on the job, right?

I'm giving you these orders because I need someone from the "outside" with your background and experience, who is not immersed in church politics or afraid to "buck" the religious "establishment" that only exists to advance (or preserve) its kingdoms and glory. I need someone who not only sees the enormity of the problem, but feels the enormity of the problem with the vision, skills, courage, commitment, and conviction that I gave him to act.

Furthermore, I need someone undistracted with the affairs of this life who can fully dedicate themselves to the successful completion of this mission. I need someone who understands and will respect my chain of command and not go rogue on me. Finally, I need someone who, because of their training and experience, cannot be "bought," co-opted, bribed, or recruited to complete any other mission than the one I give him.

I want you to take your thirty-six years of operational experience from the Navy and FBI and write an Operation Order (OPORD) for my people in America centered on 2 Chronicles 7:14 that, if followed, would obligate me to fulfill my terms to them. And remember this. While I will do what I said I would do if my people do what I told them to do, it will, first and foremost, be about my kingdom and glory in preparation for my return! Call it *Operation Heal America*.

Now, go in my name with my favor and do what I've asked you to do. I will provide every resource you need as you walk by faith and not

by sight (2 Corinthians. 5:7). Do not be moved
by what you see or hear. No weapon formed
against you will prosper and every tongue that
rises up against you in judgment you shall condemn (Isaiah 54:17 NKJV).

Finally, and most importantly, remember,
I'll be with you even until the end of the age
(Matthew 28:20).

We have now arrived at the most important part of the book.
Imagine now, if you will, two piercing sounds that no man can
silence. The first one is the sound of a GQ alarm in the spirit coming
through every smart device, streaming platform, satellite and digital
channel, and media outlet all across America. It's not a "test" of the
Emergency Broadcast System. This alarm is real! The second sound is a
series of powerful blasts coming from a shofar (ram's horn) to signify
our call to "spiritual awakening," "battle," and "repentance."[350] Both
of these sounds quickly become the number one trending story on
social media. Every news network in America is covering them. We
are the only ones who understand what's going on. It demands a
response. Though we've never heard anything like this before, it's as if
we've been waiting for this moment our entire lives. God's people are
getting dressed for "battle" and moving smartly toward their "battle
stations." The stage is now set.

With the past behind us and the cross before us, it is now time
to give you, fellow Special Agents-in-Christ, the OPORD God gave
me that, if followed, will lead to the greatest spiritual healing and
revival America and the world have ever known for His glory!

If you were never in the military or worked in law enforcement
before, not to worry. You just entered the demilitarized zone. Please
know I made every effort to make this OPORD as easy to follow as
possible! The concept of an OPORD, however, is more familiar to
you than you may think. While I didn't call it an OPORD in chapter
2, flight plans are a type of OPORD. As you note the broader application of this 2 Chronicles 7:14 OPORD, you will undoubtedly see
similarities between the two. That leaves one final question. Are you

ready to step on the neck of the enemy and proclaim victory in Jesus's name? Excellent! Let's begin!

Operation Heal America, like every OPORD, consists of the following five sections: 1) Situation, 2) Mission, 3) Execution, 4) Service Support, and 5) Command and Signal.

The *Situation*, as I have described throughout this book, is dire. The "walls" and "gates" of every institution in America from our House to the White House have fallen spiritually. While the "enemy" is all around us, as he was in the day of Nehemiah, we are no longer ignorant of his devices. Furthermore, the victory is ours in Christ. All we have to do is go out and get it by faith like Nehemiah and the Israelites did!

Our *Mission* will be to execute *God's Term Sheet for Healing America* as outlined in 2 Chronicles 7:14, beginning January 1, 2022, for forty days, and every January 1 after that, for forty days, through January 1, 2028. Maybe some of you are thinking, "Did he just say that we will be doing this every January 1 for forty days over the next seven years?"

I did. I know that seems like a long time, and Jesus could return before then or heal our land sooner according to His sovereign plan, but He may not. And we didn't get here overnight! I firmly believe it's going to take some time for this "sleeping giant" called the church that has "lost its way" to "wake up," "rise up," "suit up," and "team up" all across America to satisfy God's terms. Recall the spiritual healing of a *nation* requires *His people* to be engaged, *nationally*, not just locally or regionally.

I'm asking pastors from churches all across America who profess salvation through Jesus Christ alone (i.e., "His people") to conduct a "Pre-Op brief" at their respective churches at least thirty days before the January 1, 2022, start date (Year One). Do the same thing before each subsequent January 1 start date (Years Two to Seven). The purpose of this "Pre-Op brief" is to outline how your church will implement *Operation Heal America* (i.e., what I'm about to cover with you).

Before I discuss the *Execution* of *Operation Heal America*, I would like you to know why I chose the above two time periods of forty days and seven years, respectively. Some of you already know. Bear with me. I guarantee you will learn something new.

The first period of forty days has been a popular time utilized by many church leaders, Christian authors, and Bible teachers over the years to achieve various objectives and for a good reason.[351] God generally uses the number forty in scripture to signify a period of testing, trial, or probation.[352] Here are a few examples:[353]

1. It rained for forty days and forty nights when God wanted to cleanse the world and start over (Genesis 7:12).
2. Noah waited another forty days after it rained before he opened a window in the Ark (Genesis 8:6).
3. Embalming required forty days. Though this was an Egyptian custom, the Egyptians recognized forty days for the preparation of going into a "new life," what they called the afterlife (Genesis 50:3).
4. Moses was on the mountain with God for forty days where he did not eat bread nor drink water...twice (Exodus 24:18, 34:28–29; Deuteronomy 10:10)!
5. It took the spies forty days to search out the Promised Land and bring back fruit (Numbers 13:23–26).
6. The Israelites spent forty years in the wilderness, one year for each day they explored the Promised Land (Exodus 16:35; Numbers 14:33–34).
7. Goliath came for forty days (twice a day, morning and evening) before being killed by David (1 Samuel 17:16).
8. Elijah, strengthened by one angelic meal, went forty days to Mount Horeb, where the Lord passed by, and he heard the voice of God (1 Kings 19:8).
9. Jonah warned the city of Nineveh that they had forty days until God would overthrow Nineveh if they didn't repent. The people repented in those forty days, and God spared the city (John 3:4,10).
10. Jesus fasted for forty days in the wilderness (Matthew 4:1–2).

11. Jesus was on the earth for forty days between His resurrection and ascension (Acts 1:3).

We, too, as God's people in this nation, are about to go through a period of testing, trial, and probation like never before in our lifetime as we execute *Operation Heal America*. Thus, it is only fitting that we use the number God uses in such circumstances—forty.

Now the number seven. I chose seven years for a few reasons. First, as most of you know, the number seven represents completeness and perfection in scripture. Secondly, for practical reasons. Seven years, as I previously stated, allows adequate time for "His people," nationally, to discover what's going on and "step up." Lastly, something known as the *Year of Jubilee* followed a multiple of seven years. What? You'll find out shortly. No peeking. Yes, this is very exciting!

The next section of our *Operation Heal America* OPORD is the *Execution* phase. Each forty-day execution period will involve forty days of prayer and fasting while we, individually and corporately, complete every term God requires of us in *God's Term Sheet for Healing America*. During our forty-day execution period, we will "empty" ourselves of pride (i.e., "humble ourselves"), offer up biblical prayer (i.e., "pray"), seek God's presence (i.e., "His face"), and repent (i.e., turn from our wicked ways) individually and corporately.

While some of you will choose to pursue traditional fasting—that is, a partial or full fast from food—please make sure whichever one you do "hits you in the gizzard" without posing any health risks. For example, just the thought of giving up all caffeine products for forty days causes me to "wig." Whatever item(s) you deny yourself should genuinely be a sacrifice that causes you to hunger and thirst for more of Jesus. Denying myself olives, for example, is not a sacrifice at all because I detest them.

Some of you, for example, may want to consider fasting chocolate or red meat. Others may decide to do both. Some may want to "fast" certain meals, for example, like lunch every day. Yet others of you may want to consider a forty-day fast from all forms of social media, computer games, and yes, even your smartphones (emergency only)! Singles, it may be a forty-day fast from all dating, assuming you are dating. Again, not a huge sacrifice if you aren't dating or have no interest in it. For others, it may be a forty-day fast from some or all forms of streamed content or sports. I bet if some of you would do a forty-day fast from digital, cable, or streamed TV, a large percentage of you wouldn't even renew your contracts after discovering how much "junk" you were watching, how much extra time you have, and how much money you're saving. Maybe it's a forty-day fast from fishing, hunting, or shopping! I should have hit just about most, if not all, of us in the "gizzard" by now. You're welcome.

Church leaders, you'll want to periodically remind those in your congregations why you, and they, are fasting. In other words, this is not merely a "religious" exercise or a competition to see who can sacrifice the most or "go the distance." It's "emptying" ourselves physically to be "filled" with more of Him spiritually for the task ahead. If we fast in the flesh, the only one that will win is Satan! Consider going back and rereading the story of Nehemiah to set the proper tone for a biblical fast. Daniel is another excellent example.

Regarding prayer, I'm asking every church leader from every Bible-believing church in America to organize prayer in their respective "Temples" for forty days to coincide with our forty-day fast. Have online sign-up sheets available at least two months in advance of the January 1 start date to cover each of the forty days. Ask each church member to commit to at least a one-hour block of prayer in the "Temple" during the forty days. Ensure there is at least one person scheduled to pray in the "Temple" on each of the forty days. If those in larger churches want to sign up for more "blocks" of time or want to pray "around the clock," fine, but establish the former as the minimum requirement.

When we open the doors of our churches all across America during these forty-day periods, there should be so much of God's presence, power, and glory flowing out of them that it "spills" out into our homes, communities, cities, and nation. If we do it right, the "current" will be so strong that it will begin to "push back" the floodwaters of the culture that, up to now, have been pushing us back.

Because this too is not a competition, ask those who participate in "Temple" prayer to please keep their fasting and prayer commitments to themselves. The devil will be looking to turn this into a local and national competition, even among church attendees and churches, so we will begin comparing ourselves and our churches to what others and other churches are doing and lose sight of our goal. Do not give the enemy this satisfaction!

As God's Word says, don't let your left hand know what your right hand is doing (Matthew 6:3)! Maintain a spirit of brokenness and humility at every turn. The minute we turn this into a competition amongst ourselves is the minute our mission is "grounded" as the Holy Spirit and God's glory depart. Be keenly aware of this, beloved! There is way too much at stake!

Keep in mind, during each of our seven forty-day periods, there will be those in your congregations who do "shift work" and may need access to the church after-hours to pray. This will likely require the need for safety/security volunteers. Even during regular working hours, church leaders should plan to have volunteers on-site to ensure the safety and security of their people and facilities. Many of you already have security volunteers, so this should not be a "heavy lift." If you don't, you know what you need.

"Temple" prayer should be conducted in the main sanctuary of the church. Besides creating the atmosphere of expectancy, which is the breeding ground for a miracle at the spiritual epicenter of our churches "as one," nationally, this will minimize the number of safety/security/facilities management personnel and services needed in other parts of the building.

Those who are part of small groups or Bible studies that will continue to meet over the forty days should consider using this time for additional prayer.

All those participating in "Temple" prayer should maintain a solemn assembly on the church grounds at all times. To the greatest extent possible, there should be no other groups, functions, meetings, or ministries convening at your church during this forty-day period that could disrupt, compete with, or distract from prayer in the "Temple." Not only will this be a holy and historic moment in the lives of our churches but our nation. Thus, we should treat "Temple" prayer with the greatest sense of awe, reverence, sensitivity, sobriety, and seriousness.

Now that we've discussed the operational side of our forty days of prayer, it's time to cover what we will be praying about "as one" in our respective "Temples" all across the nation. No surprise here—2 Chronicles 7:14.

However, before we get to this, in the weeks leading up to each January 1 start date, senior pastors and congregations all across America shall pray the following with one voice that:

1. The power of the Holy Spirit would "rain down" upon us to enable us to do what we will not otherwise be able to do.
2. Jesus would expose and tear down every stronghold, imagination, "high thing," hindrance, and blind spot to biblical prayer (chapter 6) so God would act on our behalf.
3. Every assignment and strategy of the Enemy over us, our families, our churches, our cities, and our nation would be rendered powerless and ineffective, in Jesus's name.
4. God would give us, like Nehemiah, the protection, provision, favor, and resources of secular "kings" at the local, state, and national levels.
5. God's people would fulfill the Great Commission and reclaim "territory" from Satan in the earth like never before.
6. None of God's people, under the power and conviction of the Holy Spirit, would be content, or able, to sit on the "sidelines" any longer.
7. God would show us that Jesus has already given us the victory.
8. This national move of God would spark the greatest revival the world has ever seen.
9. God would receive all the glory, and man would receive none.

Beginning on day one of each forty-day execution period, and every day after that until the forty days are complete, all of God's people will pray the following in accordance with 2 Chronicles 7:14:

1. God would show His people, individually, and corporately, where there is evidence of pride and what it has "cost us" in our relationships to Christ and one another in our homes, churches, cities, and nation.

2. The Holy Spirit would give us the passion, courage, vision, willingness, and ability to begin the process of *humbling ourselves* under the mighty hand of God (1 Peter 5:6) in every institution in America from our house to the White House.

3. God's people would make biblical prayer a daily priority.

4. We would seek the face of God, individually, and corporately as a nation of "believers" to transform every institution from our house to the White House.

5. The Holy Spirit would expose our individual, corporate, and national "sins" in such a way that it would cause our national leaders (like the king of Nineveh) to cover themselves in "sackcloth and ashes," issue a proclamation requiring every American to do the same thing, and decree that the time has come for every American citizen to call out to God and turn from our evil ways (Jonah 3:6–8).

6. God's people would start such an enormous "tidal wave" of repentance across this nation that the rest of the world would not be able to ignore it, deny it, escape it, stop it, or refuse it.

The demonic opposition to this national move of God will be unprecedented. How do I know? Because we, like Nehemiah, are about to move into the enemy's territory. He's not going to hand it over easily! What's different is that we, God's people, now know it belongs to us and are prepared to do something about it all across America! Therefore, we don't need to fear demonic opposition. But we do need to be aware of it, stay close to Jesus, fight our spiritual battles with spiritual weapons as Nehemiah did, and remember if God is for us, no one can be against us (Romans 8:31 NKJV)!

As God's people in churches all across America begin to realize what God is doing and "step up," it's only a matter of time before we attract local, regional, and national media attention. If any member of the media approaches you, you should direct them to a preselected media representative at your church to ensure that churches all across America are communicating one central message to the press about what this is about! Wherever possible, the "media rep" for your church should be you, Pastor. What will you tell them? This: "What you are witnessing, not only here, but all across America are God's people returning to Him and His Word so God would hear the collective cry of His people, forgive our sin, and heal our land." It's that simple.

There will undoubtedly be additional questions from the press. All of the collective responses should stay centered on 2 Chronicles 7:14, God's Term Sheet for Healing America. Many will not understand. Expect it. That's okay. That's the Holy Spirit's job. Be professional and respectful. Don't be distracted or derailed by excessive media attention (positive or negative!), which is right out of Satan's playbook, remember? Stay focused on Jesus and the mission!

OPORD Execution wouldn't be complete without a discussion on contingency plans. Contingency plans address how personnel will handle potential obstacles and hindrances to mission accomplishment that could arise. For example, I recognize that some of you, due to health, work, travel, and other commitments may not be able to participate in "Temple" prayer with the rest of your church. No worries, no guilt. Pray wherever you can. God knows your heart. However, if you are otherwise able to pray at your church, but don't because you don't have a means of transportation, that's workable. I'm sure there are those in your congregation who would be happy to assist. Church leaders should plan accordingly for this contingency.

For some of you, depending on where you live, winter weather (i.e. snow and ice) may also prevent you from getting to church to pray during your designated time. After all, we are talking about January! Additionally, depending on the severity of the weather, your church may be closed. Again, God knows our hearts. The safety, security, and welfare of all of God's people is of utmost importance. Be safe. No guilt.

While these forty days will be a very exciting time in your life and the life of the church, locally and nationally, it will also be a very demanding and draining time, especially for those in leadership and their families. Please make sure you are making this whole process as easy as possible for them through your love, support, prayers, commitments, and service.

As your church commits to forty days of prayer and fasting, beginning January 1, 2022, and every January 1, thereafter, through January 1, 2028, each forty-day period of execution will contain six Sundays, except for the year 2024, which has five Sundays. The sermon guidance I provided below is for the years where there are six Sundays since this will be the "norm." Make whatever modifications are necessary for 2024. I hope you're beginning to see that I tried to make this as easy as possible for us to do what we need to do, so God will do what He said He would do!

Every senior pastor shall dedicate the six Sunday services during the forty days of fasting and prayer to, yes, the teaching and preaching of 2 Chronicles 7:14. While you may want to create your own six-week sermon outline, feel free to use the material in this chapter and other sections of this book as necessary. No need to "reinvent the wheel" unless there are other things that you would like to include. By all means. However, please cover every term in *God's Term Sheet for Healing America* and provide enough time at the end of each Sunday service for a congregational response, so people have an opportunity to "do business" with God before they leave.

Dedicate the first Sunday sermon to the first term in God's Term Sheet for Healing America, that is, who God considers to be a "relevant party" in this Term Sheet (i.e., "His people"). This is a great Sunday for an "altar call," so those who are not "relevant parties" have an opportunity to become relevant parties. Don't miss this incredible opportunity to share the Gospel! Invite your "unsaved" friends and family members.

Dedicate the second Sunday sermon shall to the second term in God's Term Sheet for Healing America; that is, what it means to humble ourselves from a biblical perspective as previously discussed.

Dedicate the third Sunday sermon to the third term in God's Term Sheet for Healing America; that is, "and pray." Make sure you cover all the hindrances to biblical prayer that I discussed in chapter 6 so we, all across America, are praying prayers that will reach God's ears and not hit a glass ceiling.

Dedicate the fourth Sunday sermon to the fourth term in God's Term Sheet for Healing America; that is, what it means to "seek His face." Again, feel free to use the information I provided in this chapter.

This brings us to the fifth Sunday service, which marks the beginning of our National Call to Repentance! Remember the Prophet Joel? Now's the time to sound the ram's horn! If you don't have one, get one, and figure out who's going to "blow it." Blow it in your city! Call the people together for a solemn meeting. Bring everyone—the elders, the children, and even the babies. Call the men, women, husbands and wives, fathers and mothers, sons and daughters, sisters and brothers from our house to the White House to come into the house of the Lord. Let us return to the God of Abraham, Isaac, and Jacob, to the one true God that is, our Lord and Savior Jesus Christ, who for the joy set before Him endured the cross, despising the shame (Hebrews 12:2).

The first several chapters of this book were written largely in part for this fifth Sunday service. Why? So that we would have little problem identifying individual and corporate "sins" that we need to repent of.

For those having difficulty identifying any "sin" in their lives or in the lives of their church that they or the corporate body need to "repent" of, may we remember the words of Paul: "If we say we have no sin, we deceive ourselves, and the truth is not in us" (1 John 1:8). Here's the issue: If we want God to heal our land for His glory, we all must repent. Again, to make it easier for us, where applicable, I included a Prayer of Repentance at the end of the first seven chapters. May we each be like David, who not only repented of known sins but also of unknown sins saying, "How can I know all the sins lurking in my heart. Cleanse me from these hidden faults" (Psalm 19:12 NLT).

Men, as the spiritual leaders of your families, your family should see you taking the lead on this. In preparation for this fifth Sunday service, if there is any sin that you need to confess and repent of before your wife or children, for example, do it! If there was ever a time that Christian men everywhere need to "play the man," it is now! Same advice to you ladies. Play the woman, even if you're husband doesn't play the man. You too, teenagers. Some of you have made life a "living hell" for your parents through your open rebellion to God's Word despite your parents' best attempts to raise you in the nurture and admonition of the Lord (Ephesians 6:4).

By the time the National Call to Repentance occurs during the fifth Sunday service at churches all across America, you will have established the proper environment for individual and corporate repentance in your house of worship. Furthermore, much of the fear and anxiety surrounding this fifth Sunday service that Satan will try to use to keep us from turning from our wicked ways, individually and corporately all across the nation, will have been eliminated or significantly reduced.

Some family members may choose not to "repent" of offenses that they have committed against other family members in preparation for the National Call to Repentance during the fifth Sunday service. That's okay. Let the Holy Spirit deal with them while the Holy Spirit deals with you and me. Remember, you and your church will be executing *Operation Heal America*, unless God chooses to bring spiritual healing and revival to our land sooner over a seven year period. Thus, there is plenty of time for the Holy Spirit to move on rebellious hearts and to exercise church discipline according to Matthew 18:15–18 and 1 Corinthians 5–6 (chapter 2) where necessary.

While it would be wonderful if everyone of us turned from our wicked ways before or during this first National Call to Repentance, God the Father, Jesus, and the Holy Spirit are more than able to deal with those who don't. No worries. Stay focused on "your side of the street" and let God deal with them. If the Father, Son, and the Holy Spirit can't handle our problems, we're all sunk! While I am not trying to minimize the pain of "sins" committed against you or by you, we should not allow what others do or don't do to "rob" us of the opportunity to repent of our "sins." Additionally, we mustn't forget that the same "sins" that have kept God from healing this land because we refuse to "turn" from them are the same "sins" grieving His heart. Does that matter to you?

We may also need to repent of sins that we have committed against others outside of our immediate families. Please use wisdom and discretion and allow the Holy Spirit to lead you to those He identifies in preparation for this fifth Sunday. If you need help in this area, do not be afraid to ask for it!

It is critical to remember that each of us can turn from our wicked ways, whether others believe we have done so or not. While it would be nice, we don't need others' forgiveness or "blessing" to turn from our wicked ways. Repentance is, first and foremost, about God and us. It's not first about us and others. When we "turn from our wicked ways," we are turning back toward God, regardless of what others do or don't do.

Please understand, however, to the extent you and I are unwilling to confess our sins to God and one another and turn from our wicked ways, we remain spiritually "sick." In doing so, we delay God's healing from our house to the White House (James 5:16). No confession, no repentance, no spiritual healing. Know confession, know repentance, know spiritual healing—individually, corporately, and nationally.

In preparation for the National Call to Repentance during the fifth Sunday service, every pastor shall purchase (or construct) a wooden cross, minimum height four to six feet. Stand it securely at the front of the sanctuary before the first forty-day start date, January 1, 2022. The cross should be easily accessible to each person in your congregation. No one should have to walk up any steps or over any ropes or wires to reach it. Consider placing the base of the cross into a block of cement. With the cross now in place, you have at least two options. First, you can stage one or more light hammers, along with a bucket of nails, at the foot of the cross. Option two is to use thumbtacks with no hammer if it's "soft" wood.

After the *National Call to Repentance* is sounded on the ram's horn, instruct your ushers to hand out one small piece of paper (at least two-by-two inches) to each person in attendance. Small index cards work nicely. Tell those in your congregations to place the individual "sins" that they wish to *turn from* on one side of the card and the corporate "sins" they believe they, as a church, need to *turn from* on the other side of the card.

Pastors, this is no time to be defensive. All of us, including you, should want to change. Just to be clear, our corporate sins would be the sins that we have committed as a corporate body. For example, if Jesus were to visit your church and mine as He did the seven churches in Revelation 2–3, would Jesus say as He did about the church of Ephesus that your church has forsaken its first love (Revelation 2:4)? Would He say as He did about the church of Pergamum that there are some at your church who hold to the teaching of Balaam who taught Balak to put a stumbling block before the sons of Israel so that they might eat food sacrificed to idols and practice sexual immorality (1 Corinthians 8:1)?

Modern-day translation: Would Jesus say that your church is allowing the culture to infiltrate your church, wherein, what you are allowing inside the church is not much different than what is going on outside your church?

Would He say some of you are holding to the teaching of the Nicolaitans (Revelation 2:6,14–15)?

Modern-day translation: Would Jesus find your church "guilty" of teaching doctrine that encouraged worldliness by lowering God's standards of holiness (e.g., salvation without repentance and homosexual ordinations)? Would Jesus say to your church and mine what He said to the church in Sardis, "I know your works. You have the reputation of being alive, but you are dead. Wake up, and strengthen what remains and is about to die, for I have not found your works complete in the sight of my God" (Revelation 3:1–2 ESV). Would Jesus say to your church and mine as He did to the angel of the church in Laodicea:

I know your works: you are neither cold nor hot. Would that you were either cold or hot! So, because you are lukewarm, and neither hot nor cold, I will spit you out of my mouth. For you say, I am rich, I have prospered, and I need nothing, not realizing that you are wretched, pitiable, poor, blind, and naked. (Revelation 3:15–17 ESV)

Maybe you're in a church that has allowed women to teach and occupy "overseer" positions and "offices" over men in direct violation to 1 Timothy 2:11–14, 3:1–13; Titus 1:5–9; and Acts 6:1–6. Perhaps you're in a church that doesn't execute the primary mission of the church (i.e., the Great Commission). Maybe your church elevates tolerance above righteousness or unity above theology. Perhaps you're in a church with leaders who do not believe Christians should be involved in politics or an LGBTQ-affirming church.

Give sufficient time for everyone to complete both sides of the card (ten to fifteen minutes minimum). While this amount of time will seem like an eternity, trust me when I say the Holy Spirit will use every second. This is also an excellent place for some quiet worship music with some brief words from the senior pastor on the meaning and significance of what will transpire after these ten to fifteen minutes (see below).

Next comes the invitation. As if you were serving communion at the front of the church, invite section by section (one row at a time) to come down and "nail" their "sin" (the piece of paper or index card containing their individual and corporate sins) to the cross. The male leadership of the church (pastors, associate pastors, elders, and deacons) should be "ready" to assist anyone who looks like they need it to ensure the safety of all. Larger churches should allocate additional time for this procession. Expect it to take the entire church service to complete.

You may even want to have two crosses (one on the left side of the sanctuary and one on the right side) or three crosses (left, center, and right). An adequate number of crosses will ensure that there is sufficient time for everyone to "nail" their "sins" to the cross before service is over. Churches with multiple services may want to consider combining services into one large service if possible. While you want to "move things along," you do not want to rush this extremely holy moment in the life of the church and our nation if people need extra time beyond the regular service time. Do what works for you, but make sure you do it in a way that ensures everyone has the opportunity to "nail" their individual and corporate sins to the cross.

Another option, to save time, is to have church members deposit their index cards into a large basket located at the foot of the cross.

I like the first option better for a couple of reasons. Jesus dealt with our sin "on" the cross, not at the foot of the cross. While the foot of the cross has its place in the Christian life, our sin was "nailed" to the cross because Jesus, our sin-bearer, was nailed to the cross! Physically nailing our sin to the cross is a reminder that Jesus defeated all of our sin and the power it had over us when He was nailed to the cross. Colossians says that when God made us alive together with Christ, having freely forgiven us all our sins, He canceled out the certificate of debt and completely removed it by nailing it to the cross (Colossians 2:13–14). While the devil wants us to forget this, physically nailing our sins to the cross makes it easier for us to "experience" in our hearts what some of us have only been able to "get" in our heads.

The impact of visibly nailing our sins to the cross will be "felt" as we "rise up" from where we're seated and symbolically move in a "new" direction. It will we "experienced" as we approach the symbolic instrument of Jesus's death where Jesus dealt with our sin once and for all. We will feel the impact when we pick up the hammer and nail to remind us that it was our sin that put Him on the cross. And we will "experience" His forgiveness when we physically nail our individual and corporate sins to the cross to demonstrate that we believe Jesus defeated them. Now add to this what we will "experience" knowing "believers" all across the nation are doing the same thing, and you have a breeding ground for a miracle! Talk about church unity and putting God's power and glory on display!

That brings us to the sixth and final Sunday service that coincides with the completion of our forty-days of fasting and prayer. The sixth Sunday will be reserved for a sermon on what God said He would do now that we've done what He told us to do, that is, "[h] ear from heaven, forgive [our] sin, and heal [our] land." Hear the Prophet Joel again:

> Then the Lord will pity His people and jealously guard the honor of His land! He will reply, "Look! I am sending you grain and wine and olive oil enough to satisfy your needs. You will no longer be an object of mockery among the surrounding nations. I will remove these armies from the north and send them far away. I will drive them back into the parched wastelands, where they will die. Those in the rear will go into the Dead Sea; those at the front will go into the Mediterranean. The stench of their rotting bodies will rise over the land." (Joel 2:18–20 NLT)

Pastors, explain how God has heard our prayers and forgiven our sin because we have aligned our wills with His will. Explain that a "healed America" is an America that experiences the spiritual benefits and blessings of God because it has re-centered itself on the Word of God. As it was for the nation of Israel when they re-centered their lives back on the Word of God (Nehemiah 8), so shall it be for the United States of America. Again, hear the Prophet Joel saying:

> Don't be afraid, O land! Be glad now and rejoice, because the Lord has done great things. Don't be afraid, you animals of the field, for the wilderness pastures will soon be green. The trees will again be filled with fruit; fig trees and grapevines will be loaded down once more. Rejoice, you people of Jerusalem! Rejoice in the Lord your God! For the rains He sends demonstrates His

faithfulness. Once more the autumn rains will come, as well as the rains of spring. The threshing floors will again be piled high with grain, and the presses will overflow with wine and olive oil.

The Lord says, "I will give you back what you lost to the swarming locusts, the hopping locusts, the stripping locusts, and the cutting locusts. It was I who sent this great destroying army against you. Once again you will have all the food you want, and you will praise the Lord your God, who does these miracles for you. Never again will my people be disgraced. Then you will know that I am among my people Israel, that I am the Lord your God and there is no other. Never again will my people be disgraced." (Joel 2:21–27 NLT)

Lest there be any confusion, 2 Chronicles 7:14 is not God's promise to heal our nation economically, politically, or geopolitically. It's is a promise to heal our land spiritually. However, that being said, when God's people of any nation re-center their lives back on God and His Word and put away their "idols," it is only a matter of time before what's happening on the "inside" of us transforms the world around us in other ways. This is especially true when 83 to 231 million people are doing it!

For example, nobody will have to tell our elected officials to balance our budget, reduce government spending and onerous taxes and regulations on citizens and corporations, outlaw abortion, enact and enforce marriage laws that only make marriage legal between one man and one woman, withdraw taxpayer funding from public educational institutions that promote LGBTQ education, fix the VA, and prosecute deep state corruption at the highest levels of the FBI, Department of Justice, and State Department.

A nation like the United States of America, who has re-centered itself on God and His Word and put away its idols, will automatically negotiate fair trade deals for the US with its foreign trading partners, combat terrorism and nuclear proliferation around the world, and have, as a top priority, a strong military for national defense.

Second Chronicles 7:14 is also not a promise to heal our physical bodies of sickness and disease on this side of heaven. While there are certainly exceptions (John 5:14), the Bible does not link physical healing, in all cases, to spiritual healing. In other words, there are many cases where those who are spiritually healed on this side of heaven do not receive physical healing on this side of heaven. While God has the power and ability to heal anyone He wants on this side of heaven physically and sometimes does, He sometimes chooses to wait until the "believer" gets to the other side of heaven to receive their physical healing.

Finally, 2 Chronicles 7:14 is not a promise that a healed America will no longer experience the consequences of living in a fallen world. Within God's sovereign powers, Satan will continue to be the ruler of this world (John 12:31, 14:30; 2 Corinthians. 4:4; 1 John 5:19) until Jesus returns to fully reclaim what we have left unclaimed. This means, until then, we will continue to be in the middle of this angelic conflict I have described throughout this book and experience the consequences of living in a fallen world. However, Satan will no longer be ruling our worlds!

So then, what would a spiritually healed America look like if we're still going to be experiencing the consequences of living in a fallen world? While there is much that could be said in response to this question, it would require another book to do it. Thus, I will simply share a few amazing thoughts that the Spirit revealed to me through the Word.

In a spiritually healed America, God and His Word get re-centered in the home, and we put away our idols. Husbands, wives, fathers, mothers, and children return to their proper places in "formation" behind Christ (chapter 2) to fulfill Christ's mission first, not theirs. God's priorities become our priorities. Everything and everyone else takes a backseat to Jesus Christ and His kingdom agenda.

In a spiritually healed America, God, and His Word get re-centered in God's house, the church, and we put away our idols of tolerance, appeasement, and compromise. "Cheap grace" ends, and holy living becomes a priority once again. Watered-down Gospel messages that don't require repentance become a thing of the past. God's Word is proclaimed without compromise, and His people worship Him in Spirit and truth. His power, presence, and glory transform the surrounding community, city, and nation. The Gospel goes forth in power, and the Great Commission becomes the primary mission of every church in word and deed. Christians experience deliverance from various strongholds, and territory that was stolen gets reclaimed for the kingdom of God. False prophets and teachers are exposed and abandoned, and the church returns to its first love—Jesus Christ. Signs and wonders follow those who believe (Mark 16:17–18), and God receives all the glory!

In a spiritually healed America, the Word of God gets re-centered in the public square. Unconstitutional separation between church and state lawsuits get dismissed in local, state, and federal courts, and the church is once again able to exercise religious freedom and liberty in the public square without fear of governmental interference or reprisal. Prayer returns to our classrooms and sporting events, and things like the Ten Commandments and other religious symbols are proudly displayed in and on our government buildings and monuments once again. American history books are rewritten to once again contain accounts of America's rich Judeo-Christian heritage. Our public schools go back to being places of education instead of places of indoctrination for the advancement of radical moral, social, and political agendas.

In a spiritually healed America, modesty, morality, and decency return to the culture. Love of God and love of our neighbor as ourselves flow like oil on Aaron's beard (Psalm 133:2) from the highest office of the land to the poorest and most needy among us.

In a spiritually healed America, family, church, and government (God's three divine institutions) operate underneath the authority of God and His Word. America becomes one nation under God again. God's people vow their *greatest* allegiance and loyalty to their Creator and King Jesus Christ, the cross, and His founding document (i.e., the Holy Bible), not to earthly kings, the American flag, and its founding documents (e.g., the Constitution and the Declaration of

Independence). Yes, I love our country and its founding documents, but not more than Jesus and His founding document!

In a spiritually healed America, local, state, and federal judges understand that where the nation's founding document (i.e., the Constitution) contradicts God's founding document (i.e., the Holy Bible), God's Word has the final word. Farewell to gay marriage and abortion.

In a spiritually healed America, Satan and demons tremble. Angels routinely ascend and descend upon the Son the Man (John 1:51),bringing heavenly intervention into earth's affairs. The Holy Spirit is active and "alive" in the lives of His people. God's people walk by faith, not by sight (2 Corinthians. 5:7). False prophets and teachers are exposed as the world watches their kingdoms fall.

Pastors, there are two options during this sixth Sunday service, depending on how long your sermon lasts. Option 1: If your message is shorter than usual, spend the rest of the service on testimonies to highlight all the great things God has done over the last forty days.

Option 2: If your message is a normal length, schedule testimonies for the following Sunday.

When we obey God, amazing things begin to happen. Heaven comes to meet us. Many in your congregations will want to share what God has done or is currently doing in their lives. Give them this opportunity. It will not only "bless" them, but it will be a huge source of hope, encouragement, and blessing to others as you prepare for your next forty-day execution period the following January. Most importantly, however, it's an opportunity for us to put Jesus Christ on display!

Also, be ready to testify outside of the walls of your church when those whom you least expect, approach you and say, "What's going on? Why are all these churches in the news?" For those of you praying for an "open door" to share the Gospel, you just got one!

Testimonies are also an excellent barometer to see where the church is making progress or where it may be "stuck." If you're a pastor, you should want to know both. For example, if nobody has a testimony to share, that's an indicator something's wrong. If there are a bunch of testimonies on "seeking God's face," but very few testimonies on how God is dealing with people's pride, it may be an indication where you need to spend some extra time.

Maybe you're saying, "Wait a minute, there's no way to cover all the testimonies we are going to have in just one Sunday service."

You're right! This is why I highly recommend having "Testimonial Sunday" on at least the first Sunday of each month until the next forty-day cycle begins on January 1. This accomplishes many things. First, it keeps what has just transpired fresh on the minds and hearts of God's people locally, regionally, and nationally in anticipation of what will happen the following year. Secondly, it's an ongoing barometer to assess progress and to make whatever modifications are necessary as just mentioned. Finally, it allows God's people all across this great nation to continually boast in the Lord about all the great things He has done!

The last two remaining sections of our OPORD in *Operation Heal America* are *Service Support* and *Command and Signal*.

In an actual military OPORD, Service Support includes things like supplies, transportation, medical evacuation protocols, personnel needs, and how a particular military unit will handle prisoners of war (POWs). We have already discussed some of these concepts in earlier chapters. Thus, it shouldn't be too difficult.

Supplies, in a military OPORD, generally include things like rations, uniforms and equipment, arms and ammunition, and procedures on how captured material (i.e. the "spoils" of war) will be handled. As you recall from chapter 1, God has placed us in the middle of a war, an angelic conflict, to reclaim territory in the earth, through Christ, that Adam and Eve turned over to Satan, for the advancement of God's kingdom and glory. This means that our mission is guaranteed to be met with fierce opposition from the Enemy as previously discussed.

Supplies like food, water, and fuel are typically "rationed" in times of war, so troops have enough provisions to last the duration of the conflict. In a spiritual war, however, we don't have to worry about such things. God, our Provider, has promised to supply all of our needs (i.e., provisions) according to His riches and glory in Christ Jesus (Philippians 4:19). In Him, we have all the spiritual "rations" (spiritual food, spiritual armor, and spiritual weapons) we will ever need!

Rest assured, however, as we saw with Nehemiah, that the enemy and his minions are going to be right on the front line, taunting and telling us that we're wasting our time. He's going to tell us lies like even if we do what God told us to do, God is not going to do what He said He would do. The devil will surely tell us that this is an Old Testament promise that doesn't apply to us today, and that if God really loved us, He wouldn't require us to do anything. He would just heal our land. Expect fiery darts of deception, doubt, discouragement, and distraction. Nothing new for those of us who know Satan's "game film." Plus, we have Jesus and the truth of His Word! When the devil reminds us of our past, we can remind him of his future! It is written. Remember?

One new area, however, we have not previously discussed is how "spoils of war" will be handled. In the earthly realm, spoils of war are "enemy movable property lawfully captured, seized, confiscated, or found, which has become United States property in accordance with the laws of war."[354]

Similarly, in the spiritual realm, "spoils of war" are enemy movable property that has been lawfully captured, seized, confiscated, or found, which has become property for the kingdom of God according to the Word of God! As we complete our mission, we will take back everything that the enemy has stolen from us from our house to the White House for God's kingdom and glory. Remember, Special Agents-in-Christ, as God's agents, we have each been given "spiritual credentials" by God to exercise legal authority on behalf of Him in the earth. It's now time to use them for kingdom business! Don't be afraid to tell the enemy and his minions who you are and why you're here in Jesus's name!

Maybe you're wondering what we'll do with the spoils of war? Equally easy given what you now know. We'll handle the spoils of war like everything else God's given us to rule. After we return to God, re-center our lives on His Word and put away our idols, whatever we take back from the enemy that belongs to us (e.g., relationships, peace, joy, and other spiritual blessings) will be placed under the authority of Jesus Christ and His Word.

I love talking about the "spoils of war." You know why? Because it assumes we've already won! And we have! Jesus has already given us the victory! All we have to do is go get it with the authority we have in Christ! I love being God's Special Agent; don't you?

The final items under *Service Support* include transportation, medical evacuation protocols, personnel needs, and how we will handle prisoners of war (POWs). I love this part!

We've already discussed some transportation contingencies. Regarding "medical evacuation protocols," as a former Navy helicopter pilot whose last active duty assignment was onboard the hospital ship, *USNS Comfort (T-AH-20)*, now being used in the coronavirus pandemic, I am somewhat familiar with medical evacuation protocols. While we are completing our mission, we will undoubtedly have some "casualties;" that is, believers who will either refuse to put their spiritual armor on or who will refuse to put their "armor" on correctly.

As a result, Satan's fiery darts will hit them. There will also be those who will not have sufficient (or any) ammunition (i.e., truth) with them to respond to the taunts, temptations, and lies of the enemy. Instead, they will rely on human intellect, expert opinion, polling data, social media, and what news networks, friends, coworkers, and family members have to say. Sadly, some of these "casualties" will even refuse our help and "die" on the spiritual battlefield oblivious to what just hit them.

For those who want to be helped, it will be our responsibility to help them get the "medical attention" they need (i.e. love, truth, support, encouragement, prayer, accountability, discipline where appropriate, reproof, correction, and training in righteousness) at the nearest medical treatment facility (i.e. their local church) so that they can be healed and redeployed to the battlefield as quickly as possible to help us successfully complete our mission. This, by the way, is one of the huge benefits of having significant time built in between successive years for those who *do* want to get well.

Warning: Besides praying for them, do not allow Satan to get you to waste valuable time and effort on those who have no desire to be healed and "redeployed." Shake off the dust from your feet (Acts 13:51) and move on to help those who do.

We already addressed personnel needs in the Execution section of our OPORD. Remember, God needs "all hands on deck." No MIAs!

Concerning POWs, this too should come as no surprise given what you now know. When Jesus died on the cross, God's Word says that Jesus disarmed the powers and authorities triumphing over them by the cross (Colossians 2:15). It also says that God placed all things under His feet (Ephesians 1:22; 1 Corinthians 15:27). Guess what that means for those of us who are in union with Christ (Ephesians 2:10; Galatians 2:20; Colossians 2:12)? It means that Satan and His demons are also underneath our feet! We have been given power to tread upon serpents and scorpions and over all the power of the enemy (Luke 10:19). Furthermore, God's Word says that Satan will receive a 1,000-year "jail sentence" during our Millennial Reign with Christ on the earth before being released from prison "for a little while" (Revelation 20:2). Then, God will throw Satan into the lake of fire and sulfur where the beast and the false prophet are to be tormented day and night forever and ever (i.e., Satan will receive his permanent "jail sentence"; Revelation 20:10).

In light of this, you may be wondering, "Then why all the 'fuss' about POWs?" Because while many in the church understand that Satan is under our feet, legally, few of us understand that Satan is under our feet experientially. You see, like Joshua and his army commanders, God wants us to "experience" what it feels like to step on the neck of our enemies! And trust me, it's going to feel good! Some of you already know what I'm talking about!

I love what Joshua said to his men after he summoned them and they came forward and stepped on the necks of the five Amorite kings at Joshua's direction. Why? Because it is the same thing the Holy Spirit is saying to us (*italics* used for emphasis):

> So they came forward and placed their feet
> on their necks. Joshua said to them, "*Do not be
> afraid; do not be discouraged. Be strong and cou-
> rageous. This is what the Lord will do to all the
> enemies you are going to fight.*" (Joshua 10:24–25)

Thus, contrary to what the enemy would have us believe, the issue of dealing with POWs is quite simple! We, in Christ, will step on the necks of all the spiritual enemies that oppose us and take no prisoners since Jesus has already sentenced Satan and demons to "death row" to await "execution!"

As for those who will oppose us in the physical realm (men), they are not our real enemy. Remember, we do not wrestle against flesh and blood but against principalities, against powers, against the rulers of the darkness of this world, against spiritual wickedness in high places (Ephesians 6:12). Therefore, we should not be "wres-tling" with "men" who oppose us. There will be a time, however, to speak and a time to be silent. Be respectful, not confrontational, and do whichever one at that moment will best serve the Father's will, remember?

The final section of *Operation Heal America* is *Command and Signal.* In a military OPORD, the *Command* portion would not only include who our Command Leader is and what our chain of com-mand is, but where both will be located, before, during, and after the mission is complete. The *Command* portion would additionally include the location of the command post (i.e., where the operation will be coordinated from), and a brief discussion on succession of command (i.e. who will take the on-scene commander's place if he is no longer able to perform his duties). Again, much of this should be fairly obvious to you at this point.

As followers of Jesus Christ, our "chain of command" never changes. Jesus Christ is at the top of the "chain," followed by the leadership of the local church (under Christ's authority), then us, underneath the leadership and authority of our local churches. I will assume the duties and responsibilities as national "on-scene commander" (OSC). In this capacity, I will serve and assist "Team

Leaders" (i.e., biblically-based pastors and church leaders), as needed, all across America with the successful implementation of *Operation Heal America*.

Our Command Leader, Jesus Christ, is everywhere His people are working through the power of the Holy Spirit that resides in each one of us. I, and my team, will also be wherever you are thanks to the age of connectivity. Regarding succession of command, it's a nonevent. Jesus will always be in charge. If I, on the other hand, for whatever reason, am unable to complete my duties and responsibilities as OSC of *Operation Heal America*, a suitable replacement will be named immediately. Monitor the ministry website for all relevant details.

Our Command Post (CP) or "hub of operations" will be the ministry website located at www.operationhealamerica.com. Here, senior pastors, and you, my beloved brothers and sisters in Christ, will receive everything you need to complete the mission through your local church successfully. You will find information on registration, promotional materials, a yearly calendar, FAQs, speaking requests, testimonials, online resources, donation, and volunteer opportunities and a weekly blog.

At the center of our homepage, you also will see a map of the US, depicting how many Bible-believing churches (by state) have said "yes" to *Operation Heal America* and registered for the upcoming year. For example, if you are from the state of Iowa, rejoice, and again I say rejoice because you're not a Cornhusker. Sorry, couldn't resist! Now that I've lost all of you from Nebraska, on a more serious note, if you're from Pennsylvania and you see the number 1,156 on the state of Pennsylvania, this means that 1,156 Bible-believing churches have registered to complete *Operation Heal America* so far in Pennsylvania in the upcoming year. There will also be a "countdown clock" showing how many days remain until our next January 1 start date. Thus, at any time, anyone will be able to go to the ministry website to see how registration is progressing nationwide before the next start date. It will also help us to see which states may need some additional "encouragement" and "motivation" to get their

Bible-believing pastors to "step up" and register. Please allow me to spend a few moments on this last point.

All of us have contacts with "believers" (family, friends, and relatives) from Bible-believing churches in other states around the nation. Please, I urge you to contact them by all means available and ask them to "spread the word" to every Bible-believing church they can—locally, regionally, and nationally—about what God is doing. Encourage those you speak with to do the same thing. With God behind us, there is no reason why this shouldn't be the number one trending story in America—to God be all the glory!

Pastors, this is also an excellent opportunity for you to use your influence locally, regionally, and nationally to encourage as many Bible-believing pastors you know (who profess salvation through Jesus Christ alone) to "step up" and join *Operation Heal America*. Our nation needs you like never before! With your full participation, we will be successful, in Christ, and see, by faith, the greatest revival our nation has ever experienced as we return our individual lives, homes, churches, cities, and nation back to God. Without you, this will be nothing more than an exercise in futility as our nation sinks further and further into evil, immorality, wickedness, and idolatry.

For the many pastors who will "step up," thank you in advance! I love and appreciate all you do for the body of Christ more than you will ever know! We got your back! No one I know has a tougher job than you! Now be strong and courageous, do not be afraid nor be dismayed, for the Lord your God is with you wherever you go (Joshua 1:9 NKJV)!

Whether church leaders register their churches on the first day of registration, which will begin on May 6, 2021, or later in the year, I am urging those who register to please see the mission through to completion. This first day of registration, May 6, 2021, will coincide with the National Day of Prayer. On this day and the first Thursday in every May after that (i.e., May 5, 2022, May 4, 2023, etc.), Bible-believing churches all across America will be able to register (through December 1) for each respective January 1 start date. Please do not wait until the last minute to register. We're at GQ, remember?

While registration will be free, *Operation Heal America* will depend on God's faithfulness through donations, gifts, and book sales to meet its monthly operating costs. Additionally, and at no cost, I would be honored to speak with pastors, church leaders, and congregations regarding the implementation of *Operation Heal America*. Please keep in mind, the closer we get to a January 1 start date, the less available I will be. Click on the "Speaking Requests" button at our ministry website for more details.

Maybe God is calling you to become a larger part of *Operation Heal America* by volunteering your time or resources. If so, please go to our website for more information.

Operation Heal America LLC is a kingdom company dedicated to unleashing spiritual healing and revival in every institution in America from our house to the White House through obedience to 2 Chronicles 7:14 for the advancement of God's kingdom and magnification of His glory worldwide.

This brings us to the *Signal* portion of the *Command and Signal* section of *Operation Heal America*. The *Signal* portion of *Operation Heal America*, as in any military OPORD, includes how we will communicate key events throughout the operation. As discussed above, we will utilize the *Operation Heal America* website as our primary means of communicating all information, including key events, to the "field." Such key events will include, but not be limited to, upcoming speaking events, media events, and an annual *Operation Heal America State of the Union address* that will occur every February, beginning February 2022, and every February thereafter through February 2028.

The ministry website will provide you with the most relevant and timely information available as well as provide answers to additional questions you may have not listed among our FAQs. Please keep all questions as brief as possible so we can answer as many as possible in a timely fashion.

I mentioned the "Testimonies" button on our website earlier. Please consider sharing a testimony on what God is doing in your life as we take this glorious seven-year journey together. In many ways, and on many days, it will "feel" as if we're running a marathon. Your testimonies will be like fruit and water stations to weary runners. May each of us take every opportunity to "refresh" and encourage one another along the way by sharing all the great things God is doing!

The *Signal* section of *Operation Heal America*, as in any military OPORD, also includes how we will signal one another for "backup" and reinforcements when encountering the enemy. As stated above, it is certain we will face demonic opposition in this epic spiritual battle to bring spiritual healing and revival to America. However, there is no reason in this age of connectivity that any church should be "going it alone." To this end, it is critical that we operate as one body and watch one another's backs so the enemy cannot divide and conquer us. Practically speaking, this means that if you are getting "attacked" by the enemy and need help, don't be afraid to pick up your ram's horn and blow it online for "backup." Trust me when I say that other churches will need you to do the same thing for them before all is said and done! We're in this together, remember?

If you recall, one of the main reasons why Nehemiah was successful in achieving the victory that God had for Him was because there were no "family gaps" along the city wall; thus, no place for the enemy to penetrate. Each family reported to their "battle stations" and positioned themselves next to one another. Everyone had one another's backs with a spear in one hand for the enemy and a trough in the other hand for working. Similarly, God is looking for each one of His churches in America to report to their "battle stations" and position themselves as "family units" on the spiritual wall of our nation in their respective geographic regions, if you will, with no gaps on the wall. In this way, we, as one, can rebuild the spiritual walls and gates of America from our house to the White House that lie in spiritual ruin without any intrusion from the enemy. Can you picture it?

Operation Heal America is how we will accomplish this by God's grace! And, oh, by the way, if you want to do it in fifty-two days, like Nehemiah, instead of seven years, I'm all in!

As advertised, I have attempted to make *Operation Heal America* as simple, streamlined, and user-friendly as possible without compromising *God's Term Sheet for Healing America* in accordance with 2 Chronicles 7:14. For years, Christians (and even many non-Christians) have been praying that God would heal our nation spiritually. Here's our opportunity! Let's not blow it; unless, of course, it's the ram's horn!

If you're looking for more specifics other than what I have covered here, please know that I specifically didn't include any to give pastors and leaders freedom to "tweak" what I have outlined above for their particular churches. Warning: As you are making whatever modifications are necessary, make sure you do what God told us to do so He will do what He said He would do!

If you think this is radical, you're right! It's radical. But I would argue that we needed something radical. We didn't get into this "mess" overnight, and we're not going to get out of it without a radical commitment to 2 Chronicles 7:14.

How amazing would it be if God used His people all across America to lead the way for the nations of the world to repent resulting in the greatest revival the world has ever known? Is that not the heart and will of God? The world already looks to the United States for leadership in so many areas. Do you think this area would be any different? Could this be the underlying reason why God even allowed us to become a nation in the first place?

In the words of Winston Churchill, could this be our finest hour? Who but God would be able to stop such a giant "tidal wave" of repentance from our shore to every shore around the globe from sea to shining sea? A watching world would be forced to stand in awe of the one true God who is worthy of all worship, honor, praise, and glory forever!

This brings us to the very exciting, long-awaited *Year of Jubilee* I briefly mentioned earlier. By faith, we will experience the *Year of Jubilee* in 2029, following our seven-year commitment to *Operation Heal America* (2022–2028). Unless, that is, God decides to fulfill His promise to us in 2 Chronicles 7:14 sooner or the rapture occurs as stated earlier. But what exactly is the *Year of Jubilee*?

The first reference to the *Year of Jubilee* in the Bible appears in Leviticus 25. God tells Moses to explain to the people of Israel that there shall be a Sabbath rest *for the land* every seven years (referred to as a "Sabbath Year"). Then God provides Moses with the following instructions (*italics* used for emphasis):

> And thou shalt number seven Sabbaths of years unto thee, seven times seven years; and the space of the seven Sabbaths of years shall be unto thee forty and nine years.
>
> Then shalt thou cause the trumpet of the *jubilee* to sound on the tenth day of the seventh month, in the day of atonement shall ye make the trumpet sound throughout all your land.
>
> And ye shall hallow the fiftieth year, and proclaim liberty throughout all the land unto all the inhabitants thereof: it shall be a *jubilee* unto you; and ye shall return every man unto His possession, and ye shall return every man unto His family.
>
> A *jubilee* shall that fiftieth year be unto you: ye shall not sow, neither reap that which groweth of itself in it, nor gather the grapes in it of thy vine undressed.
>
> For it is the *jubilee*; it shall be holy unto you: ye shall eat the increase thereof out of the field. (Leviticus 25:8–12 KJV)

If you do a short study on the *Year of Jubilee* in the Old Testament, you will find that it involved a year of release from all indebtedness and all types of bondage or servitude. Those who sold themselves as hired servants to fight off poverty were released. Property that was forfeited or sold for money was returned to its original owner, and all debts were forgiven. It was also a year of rest for the land where no one could "sow" or "reap" a harvest. The people of Israel would rely on an earlier increase of crop (before the *Year of Jubilee*) that God commanded His blessing upon that would not only get them through the *Year of Jubilee* but be sufficient for three years. (Leviticus 25:21)

If there is one word that defines what the *Year of Jubilee* represented to the nation of Israel in the Old Testament, it is the word *liberty*. Inscribed on The Liberty Bell, located in Philadelphia, are these words "plucked" straight out of Leviticus 25:10—"*Proclaim Liberty Throughout All the Land unto All the Inhabitants Thereof Lev XXV VS X*" (Leviticus 25:10 KJV). While the Liberty Bell was originally constructed in 1751 to commemorate the fiftieth anniversary of William Penn's 1701 Charter of Privileges, which served as Pennsylvania's original Constitution, the Liberty Bell has become known as an iconic symbol of America's independence from oppression and tyranny. Interestingly, the Liberty Bell was formerly known as the State House Bell. It acquired the name Liberty Bell when, in the late 1830s, it became a symbol of the anti-slavery movement.[355]

Are you starting to pick up on a common theme? Not only did the *Year of Jubilee* and the Liberty Bell hallow the fiftieth year to mark their respective occasions in time and history, but both became symbols of *liberty*. If you're like me, you'll never look at the Liberty Bell the same way again. Please remember this critically important word—*liberty*. I'll return to it shortly.

The next reference to the *Year of Jubilee* in scripture comes by way of the prophet Isaiah who refers to it as *the acceptable year of the Lord*. Isaiah prophetically announces to the world an even greater *Jubilee* for Jew and Gentile alike that involves God's full plan of redemption through Jesus Christ. What Isaiah declares years before the coming of Christ is later handed to Christ in a scroll by a synagogue assistant at the start of Jesus's public ministry. In Luke 4, Jesus unrolls the scroll, goes to the place of Isaiah's prophecy and reads it aloud for all to hear. Note the slight variation of Jesus's reading (second paragraph below) from Isaiah's prophetic reading (first paragraph below) in the following King James translations (*italics* used for emphasis):

> The Spirit of the Lord is upon me; because
> the Lord hath anointed me to preach good tid-

ings unto the meek; He hath sent me to bind up the brokenhearted, to proclaim *liberty* to the captives, and the opening of the prison to those who are bound; to proclaim *the acceptable year of the Lord.* (Isaiah 61:1–2 KJV)

The Spirit of the Lord is upon me, because He hath anointed me to preach the Gospel to the poor; He hath sent me to heal the brokenhearted, to preach deliverance to the captives, and recovering of sight to the blind, to set at *liberty* them that are bruised, to preach *the acceptable year of the Lord.* (Luke 4:18–19 KJV)

There's our word *liberty* again. The "spiritual liberty" that the prophet Isaiah spoke of was now here, in Christ, to all who were/are spiritually "dead," spiritually broken, spiritually captive, and spiritually blind. Jesus wanted His people to know, then and now, that the kind of liberty He offers goes far beyond mere liberty from debt, servitude, and having to work the land in the fiftieth year. That's right. Jesus, then and now, wants His people to know that He is the fulfillment of the *Year of Jubilee* (Luke 4:21). In Christ, we are free from the debt of sin, slaves to no one and nothing but Christ, and able to find rest in Him every day because we no longer have to labor to make ourselves acceptable to God through good works! A much greater Jubilee, wouldn't you say? Thank you, Jesus! There are no words to express how grateful we are to you!

The *acceptable year of the Lord* is acceptable because it is the year when God's will was and is being fulfilled through Jesus Christ. Thus, it is right now and almost two thousand years in its unfolding.[356] However, this is the critical point we must understand. While the *Year of Jubilee* is available to us because Christ has come, it has not been our individual and collective "experience" because most of His people (us!) are still entangled with the yoke of slavery (Galatians 5:1). In other words, while Jesus secured liberty for us "legally" on the cross once and for all, it has not been our "reality" due to unaddressed sin.

Try this illustration. Before we can "experience" the abundant supply of electricity that our power companies make available to us to light, cool, and heat our homes, we have to "complete the circuit" to our lights, air conditioners, and heating units by turning them "on," right? Similarly, before we can experience the abundant supply of power (i.e., "liberty" and "spiritual healing") that Christ has made available to us, we have to "complete the circuit" with Christ. We do this when we stand fast in the liberty wherewith Christ has made us free and no longer allow ourselves to be entangled with the yoke of slavery (Galatians 5:1).

That's what's so exciting about this OPORD! Fulfilling the terms of 2 Chronicles 7:14 "completes the circuit" for God's people to "experience" the endless supply of spiritual liberty and healing that Christ has made available to us through Him. Said another way, we will finally be able to experience Jesus as the "spiritual fulfillment" of the *Year of Jubilee* because we will have satisfactorily dealt with our sin once we "turn from our wicked ways." In other words, we can only experience the *Year of Jubilee* after the Day of Atonement (i.e. confession and repentance)! You see, most Christians in our consumer-based churches in America want to be able to skip the Day of Atonement but still experience the Year of Jubilee. No dice! Jesus will deal our arrogance, spiritual blindness, and immaturity head-on as we execute this 2 Chronicles 7:14 OPORD!

Thus, spiritual healing and spiritual liberty go hand in hand; that is, where there is spiritual healing, there is spiritual liberty, and where there is spiritual liberty, there is spiritual healing. However, none of this should be a surprise since both roads lead back to our Liberator and Healer, Jesus Christ!

Therefore, since Jesus fulfills the spiritual intent of the *Year of Jubilee* today, and every day is the acceptable day of the Lord with Him, there is, technically, no need to wait seven years (2022–2028), much less fifty years! So then again, you may be wondering, "Why declare 2029 as our *Year of Jubilee*?" Because, as previously stated, I believe it will take every bit of seven years for God's people to "wake up," "rise up," "step up," "suit up," and "show up" at their battle stations to complete *Operation Heal America* before we will "experience" the *Year of Jubilee.*

While God could make all of this happen much sooner than 2029 as I have repeatedly said, we are much less likely to experience a "power interruption" in the eighth year (after meeting His terms for seven years) than we are in the early years when some of us are still trying to "wake up" and "step up!" Based upon the promises of God found in the Word of God, if we complete what God told us to do in this Sabbath of years (2022–2028), we will *experience* the *Year of Jubilee* in 2029!

While some of you may have difficulty believing what I am about to tell you or think this is nothing more than a mere coincidence, trust me, with God as my witness, it's true. I hope your harness is still locked!

You see, not before, but *after* telling you everything I just told you above, I discovered the following (*italics* used for emphasis):

> The last time a jubilee year was officially celebrated [by the Jewish people] may have been as late as about the year 122 B.C.—and no later. From this premise, a jubilee year may have been celebrated in Judea about the year 172 B.C. (+ or - 1 year).
>
> *If a jubilee year was celebrated in this modern era, as a projection of jubilees celebrated in the Temple era—it is probable that the next jubilee year would correspond to about the year A.D. 2029 (+ or - 1 year)."*[357]

I know! I love you, Holy Spirit! You see, approximately eighteen months *before* I ever wrote the majority of this chapter and discovered the above, the Holy Spirit directed me to select December 31, 2019, as my FBI retirement date. Shortly after, and again before writing this chapter, I was prompted by the Spirit to publish this book in 2020 following retirement. With an estimated release date in the fall/

winter of 2020 and a marketing and advertising campaign that would begin before this and extend through publishing release and registration, I selected January 1, 2022, as the start of the seven-year period in which we would fulfill God's Term Sheet for Healing America (2022–2028). In other words, before I ever discovered the above projection, I believed that we could experience the *Year of Jubilee* as a nation in 2029! I still smile every time I think about it! Why do I feel like God does too?

On the Jewish calendar, the Year of Jubilee begins on the Day of Atonement (how appropriate, right?), which Jews observe on the tenth day of the seventh month (Yom Kippur). Yom Kippur on the Jewish calendar, in 2029, begins on Tuesday, September 18, 2029 (at sunset), and goes through Wednesday, September 19, 2029 (until nightfall), on the Christian calendar.[358] Given the fact that Jesus already atoned for the sins we will have repented of during *Operation Heal America*, it's only appropriate that we celebrate the year that the acceptable day of the Lord (the Year of Jubilee) became our collective "experience" during these twenty-four hours. If God moves more quickly than 2029, we'll joyfully adjust our celebration timetable to Him. While I recognize that many Christians already honor the high holy day (Yom Kippur) in their unique way, the central theme of our celebration will be one of thanksgiving, honor, and praise for what God has done!

What many have only seen in their visions, dreams, and "prayer closets" is about to become a reality! There will be only one suitable response—all-out worship and praise to the one true God, Jesus Christ! Use your imagination and be creative. It should be a celebration like no other. God knows we've been waiting for it long enough! Give Him all the glory!

Pastors, keep in mind, this celebration period is also an excellent time for testimonies on how the *Year of Jubilee* is manifesting itself in the lives of God's people in the church God gave you.

The bonds of friendship and peace formed in our churches and across the nation as we complete *Operation Heal America* together and celebrate the *Year of Jubilee* will be like none other in history and will extend into eternity! The testimonies of God's faithfulness will only be surpassed by His manifest presence! Some of you who have been praying for Jeremiah 29:11 to become a present-day reality for you will receive God's plan to prosper you and give you hope and a future (Jeremiah 29:11). God will pour out His Spirit on all people. Our sons and daughters will prophesy, our young men will see visions, and old men will dream dreams (Joel 2:28; Acts 2:17). We will praise God for victories past, present, and future. It will truly be a taste of heaven on earth!

At one time in history, all who proclaim salvation through the finished works of Jesus Christ on the cross alone will stand fast in the liberty wherewith Christ has made them free and with God's help, never be entangled again with the yoke of slavery (Galatians 5:1).

In the same way that the *acceptable year of the Lord* is not a literal year but a declaration that Jesus came to fulfill the will of the Father, our *Year of Jubilee* will not be a literal year but a declaration that we, in Christ, as one, intend to fulfill the will of the Father on earth as it is in heaven. You wanted revival, you got it!

I can think of no better way to end this chapter than with the words of Hosea:

> Come, let us return to the Lord; for He has torn us, that He may heal us; He has struck us down, and He will bind us up. After two days He will revive us; on the third day He will raise us up, that we may live before Him. Let us know; let us press on to know the Lord; His going out is sure as the dawn; He will come to us as the showers, as the spring rains that water the earth.
> (Hosea 6:1–3 ESV)

Verses to Remember

1. If my people who are called by my name will humble themselves, and pray and seek my face, and turn from their

wicked ways, then I will hear from heaven, and will forgive their sin and heal their land. (2 Chronicles 7:14 NKJV)

2. You are the light of the world. A city that is set on a hill cannot be hidden... Let your light so shine before men, that they may see your good works and glorify your Father in heaven. (Matthew 5:14,16 NKJV)

3. Look, I have inscribed your name on my palms; your walls are constantly before me. (Isaiah 49:16 NET)

4. And whoever exalts himself will be humbled, and He who humbles himself will be exalted. (Matthew 23:12 NKJV)

5. First pride, then the crash—the bigger the ego, the harder the fall. (Proverbs 16:18, MSG)

6. Pray without ceasing. (1 Thessalonians 5:17 KJV)

7. I have sought your face with all my heart; be gracious to me according to your promise. (Psalm 119:58 NIV)

8. If we say we have no sin, we deceive ourselves, and the truth is not in us. If we confess our sins, He is faithful and just to forgive us our sins and to cleanse us from all unrighteousness. (1 John 1:8–9 NKJV)

9. Sanctify a fast, call a solemn assembly, gather the old men and all the inhabitants of the land unto the house of Jehovah your God, and cry unto Jehovah. (Joel 1:14 ASV)

10. Who can understand His errors? Cleanse thou me from secret faults. (Psalm 19:12 KJV)

11. And ye shall hallow the fiftieth year, and proclaim liberty throughout the land unto all the inhabitants thereof: it shall be a jubilee unto you; and ye shall return every man unto His possession, and ye shall return every man unto His family. (Leviticus 25:10 ASV)

12. He has sent Me to heal the brokenhearted, To proclaim liberty to the captives And recovery of sight to the blind, To set at liberty those who are oppressed. (Luke 4:18 NKJV)

13. Stand fast therefore in the liberty by which Christ has made us free, and do not be entangled again with the yoke of bondage. (Galatians 5:1 NKJV)

14. "In the last days," God says, "I will pour out my Spirit upon all people. Your sons and daughters will prophesy. Your young men will see visions, and your old men will dream dreams." (Acts 2:17 NLT)

15. Will you not revive us again that your people may rejoice in you? (Psalm 85:6 ESV)

CHAPTER 9

❖❖❖❖❖

Even If He Doesn't

The world's greatest leaders, athletes, musicians, singers, songwriters, superheroes, politicians, movie producers, Hollywood celebrities, and corporate executives have nothing on these guys. I don't know about you, but one of my all-time favorite stories in the Bible is the story of Shadrach, Meshach, and Abednego found in the book of Daniel.

Maybe you remember. In approximately BC 600, King Nebuchadnezzar has just besieged Jerusalem and has taken the Israelites into captivity in Babylon. Among those in captivity are three Hebrew youths—Shadrach, Meshach, and Abednego—who along with Daniel have found great favor with King Nebuchadnezzar because of their wisdom, knowledge, character, and in the case of Daniel, his ability to interpret the king's dreams.

Now, if you're going to be held captive by the enemy, you want to be Daniel, Shadrach, Meshach, and Abednego. King Nebuchadnezzar, up to this point in time, has been highly impressed with their training and desirous to see them occupy key positions in Babylon. He has just appointed Daniel to be ruler over the whole province of Babylon and chief administrator over all the wise men of Babylon (Daniel 2:48). Similarly, the king appoints Shadrach, Meshach, and Abednego to serve over the king's administrative affairs under Daniel.

However, all this changes one day when rumors begin to swirl around the province that Shadrach, Meshach, and Abednego will not bow down to the golden image that King Nebuchadnezzar has erected (approximately ninety-feet high, nine-feet wide) on the plain of Dura. In violation of the king's decree and now subject to death by incineration (i.e., the fiery furnace), the king asks Shadrach, Meshach, and Abednego, which god will be able to deliver them out of his hands?

If you're a regular church attendee, you've likely heard the story of Shadrach, Meshach, and Abednego many times. However, if you're like me, you're more familiar with what happens after Shadrach, Meshach, and Abednego get thrown into the fiery furnace than you are with what happens to them before they get thrown into the fiery furnace.

You know, the fact that after Shadrach, Meshach, and Abednego get thrown into the fiery furnace that is seven times hotter than normal, the king observed, not three but four men walking around in the fire, all unbound and unharmed. And the fourth person appeared like "the Son of God" (Daniel 3:25). While this is no doubt "shout-it from the rooftop" material, I'd like to spend the rest of the chapter looking at what happened to the three Hebrew youths before King "Nebby" threw them into the fiery furnace. Specifically, I'd like to focus on what they *said* to the king before they were bound and thrown into the fiery flames.

When the king asks them who will be able to deliver them out of his hands, their response to him, I believe, are some of the most powerful words ever spoken by anyone at any time in history. They serve as a model to anyone who claims to be a true follower of Jesus Christ. Hear them now and let them permeate every fiber of your being before I use them to make a few critical points regarding *Operation Heal America* (*italics* used for emphasis):

> King Nebuchadnezzar, we do not need to defend ourselves before you in this matter. If we are thrown into the blazing furnace, the God we serve is able to deliver us from it, and He will

deliver us from your Majesty's hand. *But even if He doesn't*, we want you to know, Your Majesty, that we will not serve your gods or worship the image of gold you have set up. (Daniel 3:16–18 NIV)

There it is. By far, one of the greatest quotes of all time. While I find their entire response to King Nebby to be absolutely "jaw-dropping" in light of the consequences they faced, the last sentence for me, in particular, takes the cake. Please stop here for a moment and consider this. Can you imagine how different America would be if we, the church of Jesus Christ in America, exercised the kind of faith, courage, commitment, conviction, and love for God displayed here by these three Hebrew youths? Incidentally, did you know that religious scholars put them between the ages of eleven and thirteen? I know! Can you imagine how different things would be from our house to the White House if we, like Shadrach, Meshach, and Abednego, refused to bow down to the idols of the culture *even if God doesn't rescue us* from the chaos and "hell" around us?

Now take this and apply it to the last chapter. Can you imagine the personal revival and kingdom impact we would have from our house to the White House if we would live our lives like Shadrach, Meshach, and Abednego, *even if God doesn't* heal our land? Read that again beloved.

Thus, it begs the question. In light of all the preceding chapters and the reason for which this book was written (chapter 8), do we believe, like Shadrach, Meshach, and Abednego, that God is more than able to deliver us from the fiery furnace of evil and immorality that seeks to destroy us and every institution in America from our house to the White House? Secondly, are you and I willing, like them, to sincerely and boldly declare to every evil and corrupt earthly king in America being controlled by Satan and his demons that our God *will* deliver us from their hands? Okay. Now comes the real test. Are you and I, like Shadrach, Meshach, and Abednego, willing to look the evil and corrupt "kings" of our day squarely in the eyes and say, "But even if our God doesn't [rescue us] from the fiery furnace of evil and immorality around us, we will still not bow down and serve your gods or worship the images of gold you have set up"?

While some have already looked "hell" in the face and made such a declaration, many have not after counting the cost. How do I know? Have you looked around lately and observed all the idol worship going on in American churches today? We have some of the "nicest," "coolest," most "compassionate" and "loving" churches embracing prosperity theology, gay marriage, homosexual ordinations, female pastors, tolerance above righteousness, unity above theology, and every mission but the primary mission of the church! And why? Because many of us in those "nice," "cool," "compassionate," "loving" churches, unlike Shadrach, Meshach, and Abednego, are more interested in our kingdoms than His kingdom, more interested in being politically correct than biblically correct.

The good news is that even if God does not heal our land, you and I, like Shadrach, Meshach, and Abednego, do not have to bow down to the idols of our day. And in refusing to do so, we can still experience personal healing and revival to advance God's kingdom and magnify His glory (chapter 1)! Yes, this will require some of you to find a new church immediately!

While I believe with all my heart that God will heal our land when we complete *Operation Heal America*, we must ask ourselves the hard question, which is, "What if He doesn't?" What if He doesn't because we refuse to fulfill His terms? And make no mistake, this will be the only reason why He doesn't because He's a Promise Keeper! But the real question to each of us is this. Even if He doesn't heal our land, will we shrink back and never experience the personal spiritual healing and revival that God has for each of us by doing what is required to build His kingdom and have to answer for it on Judgment Day? Or will we obey 2 Chronicles 7:14 regardless of what anyone else does and declare to the enemy, in Jesus's name, that we will not worship the "gods" our culture has erected but instead build God's kingdom regardless of the consequences? Believe me. Satan wants to know!

While some of you will not enjoy hearing this, and it certainly is no attempt to manipulate anyone into doing what only the Holy

Spirit can make each of us do, we have all "graduated" to a new level of accountability. Jesus said it this way: "For unto whomsoever much is given, of Him shall much be required" (Luke 12:48 KJV).

In the hymn "I Have Decided to Follow Jesus," there is a popular stanza that goes, "Though none go with me, still I will follow."[359] Is this how you feel regardless of what others do *even if He doesn't* heal our land?

If we could somehow interview Shadrach, Meshach, and Abednego today and have them explain to us *why* they said what they said to King "Nebby," I believe they would say something like the following:

1. We will not be ruled by fear, but by faith in the One who has the keys of death and hell (Revelation 1:18 GW).
2. We trust God in every situation; therefore, we don't have to understand what God is doing or not doing to obey Him.
3. We decided a long time ago to obey God and leave the consequences to Him.[360]
4. We would rather die than grieve the Holy Spirit whereby we are sealed unto the day of redemption (Ephesians 4:30).
5. To live is Christ and to die is gain (Philippians 1:21).
6. God's will for us is far more important than our comfort and security.
7. The sufferings of this present time are not worthy to be compared with the glory which shall be revealed in us (Romans 8:18 KJV).
8. Jesus Christ paid the ultimate price for us; how could we not do the same for Him?
9. We would rather die physically than die spiritually by forsaking our Lord and Savior Jesus Christ to worship an idol.

You see, Shadrach, Meshach, and Abednego believed what the sixteenth-century German Reformer, Martin Luther, believed when he said, "There are two days in my calendar: This day (today) and that day (Judgment Day)." How does your calendar compare?

While I believe with all my heart, as previously stated, that God will heal America when we do what He requires because He said He would, this will not even be the "real prize" as Shadrach, Meshach, and Abednego understood. The real prize will be in knowing that you and I were willing to follow Jesus to the ends of the earth no matter what—*even if He doesn't!*

Verses to Remember

1. King Nebuchadnezzar, we do not need to defend ourselves before you in this matter. If we are thrown into the blazing furnace, the God we serve is able to deliver us from it, and He will deliver us from your Majesty's hand. But even if He doesn't, we want you to know, Your Majesty, that we will not serve your gods or worship the image of gold you have set up. (Daniel 3:16–18 NIV)

2. [B]ut as for me and my house, we will serve the Lord. (Joshua 24:15 AMP)

3. And grieve not the Holy Spirit of God, whereby ye are sealed unto the day of redemption. (Ephesians 4:30 KJV)

4. For to me, to live is Christ and to die is gain. (Philippians 1:21 NIV)

5. For I consider that the sufferings of this present time are not worth comparing with the glory that is to be revealed in us. (Romans 8:18 ESV)

CHAPTER 10

❖❖❖❖❖

What Now?

In the last chapter, we covered the greatest contingency you and I could face in *Operation Heal America*; that is, what each of us will do if God does not bring spiritual healing and revival to our land. While it was worth every ounce of time and attention, please understand that God has already given us the victory! Like Nehemiah, all we have to do is go get it by doing what God requires. Only one final question remains. Are you ready to make "His story" with me?

As we begin making our final preparations to run the race with endurance that is set before us (Hebrews 12:1–2), maybe you're feeling a bit overwhelmed, disoriented, and confused about what we need to do next. Perhaps you're thinking, "I want to be a part of *Operation Heal America*, but what now?" This chapter was written for you. Whether you came late to the party or arrived right on time (before the January 1, 2022, start date), no worries. Come just as you are, bring someone with you, and complete the following steps before the next January 1 start date:

1. Begin praying.
2. Visit the ministry website at www.operationhealamerica. com, where you will find relevant resources and information on registration, schedule of events, testimonials,

volunteer and donation opportunities, and other useful information.

3. Tell as many people as possible (locally, regionally, and nationally), especially your pastors and church leaders, about *Operation Heal America* through every communication platform available and urge them to visit the ministry website for more information.

4. Obtain multiple copies of *Operation Heal America* to give to others. Ensure that your pastor and church leaders have a copy. If they don't, put a copy in their hands and ask them to read it as soon as possible. Pastors: It is critical, for obvious reasons, that you and your church get out in front of this "tidal wave" that is about to "hit" you and other churches across America.

5. Begin establishing a pre-GQ posture individually and corporately (chapter 7).

6. Pastors: Register your church for *Operation Heal America* at www.operationhealamerica.com, beginning May 6, 2021, the National Day of Prayer, and encourage as many other Bible-believing pastors and church leaders you know locally, regionally, and nationally to do the same.

7. Complete all preparations at your church before the first January start date (January 1, 2022) and, again, before every subsequent January 1 start date up to and including the last January 1 start date, which will be January 1, 2028. Preparations shall include, but not be limited to the following (see chapter 8 for more details):

   a) Constructing, or procuring, one or more crosses (four to six feet), as appropriate, for your sanctuary. Safely secure them at the front of the sanctuary.

   b) Appointing key personnel for marketing, advertising, facilities management, security, transportation, public affairs (media rep), and communications.

   c) Scheduling planning and progress meetings at your church with key personnel as frequently as necessary and applicable to identify and correct all deficiencies early.

d) Having "family meetings" at home to discuss relevance, impact, and preparations to ensure participation by every age-appropriate member of the family to the greatest extent possible.

8. Monitor the ministry website for relevant details.

9. Hold one other accountable to see this mission through to the end.

Now a tough but necessary admonishment for us all. To those who are part of a local church whose leadership has no interest in participating in *Operation Heal America* in light of the spiritual crisis we are facing in our nation, I would strongly consider whether God wants you to stay at that church. If this were my pastor's position, I'm outta there! We have no more time for "church games." I don't care how big "your" church is, Pastor! It's time for all of us to lay aside our egos and agendas and do what God told us to do so He will do what He said He would do for His glory! That means no gaps on the "wall," remember?

God's church includes all of His church. The days of "going it alone" with only the churches in our denomination need to "die." If the people of that church denomination recognize the finished works of Jesus Christ on the cross as the only legitimate payment to satisfy the penalty of our sins, then the people of that church denomination are our brothers and sisters in Christ! It's a waste of breath to ask God to "warranty" His church (i.e., to "fix" us so we can impact the culture) while we continue to be divided over non-substantive denomination differences. Our future and, more importantly, God's kingdom and glory, which, incidentally, have no denominational "walls," are at stake!

May our primary allegiance and loyalty be to our Lord and Savior Jesus Christ, not to any denomination, including our own! It is shameful even to have to suggest that some pastors and Christians would not participate in *Operation Heal America* because they might have to be on the "wall" next to someone from another denomination who is, otherwise, a brother or sister in Christ. Now is the time to show who and what we are unified around—Jesus Christ, the cross, and His mission! May God have mercy on us all if we allow our denominational differences to keep us from completing this mission!

Our impact for Jesus Christ in the culture as we execute *Operation Heal America* will be totally marginalized if the rest of the world continues to see us as a "house divided." Hasn't this "sad song" been playing long enough? Here's a beautiful opportunity to show the rest of the world how unified we are as we bring desperately needed hope to many! Who knows? The new "us" might even cause the rest of the world to want to know about our Jesus!

One thing is for sure. If we, the church of Jesus Christ in America, continue to act independently of one another and do not join forces with one another under Christ, our nation will continue to unravel morally, socially, and spiritually with no one to blame but us! That's right. God is going to come looking for us first, just like He did with Adam and Eve. And what will your excuse be then, Pastor, for why you couldn't join the rest of us on the wall? Baptists don't fellowship with "AG" churches or, God forbid, nondenominational churches? Really? Wow! Good luck with that one on Judgment Day!

If God's people do not "step up" and fulfill His "terms," the opposite of 2 Chronicles 7:14 will continue to be our reality. God will not hear our prayers, not forgive our sins, and not heal our land. He will continue to oppose our nation, passively judge our nation, give us over to our own devices, and allow our country to experience greater and greater consequences until one of two things happens (excluding the rapture). We either repent as a nation or cease to exist as a nation. In the meantime, barring repentance, we will never fulfill the reason why we were created and "push off" on the next generation what God made possible through us in this generation!

If you're a pastor, maybe you're thinking, "Look, we're not going to participate because we're already doing this in our church. We make it a practice to humble ourselves, pray, seek His face, and turn from our wicked ways and will continue to do so."

To this, I would respond, "Great, all the more reason why we need you to join us." We need your example and leadership to help other churches around the nation do the same thing. We are all members of one body in the body of Christ, right? Will you leave us without a hand? Pretty self-centered, Pastor. And who is going to fill the gap that your church leaves on the wall?

We think we've cried some tears over some of the decisions our children have made. Imagine how God must feel about us when He looks at how the world has transformed us? Will we continue to spurn His loving plea for us to repent with this tremendous opportunity we've been given to see Him heal our land? God, I hope not!

Do not allow Satan, through the willing hearts of men, and possibly even those closest to you, to steal, kill, and destroy this epic opportunity God has given us. Join me, and countless others, in making a firm commitment to *Operation Heal America!* Trust me, this is not a man thing. It's a God thing all based on His Word! If you've already done this, allow me to be the first say, "Welcome, and thank you!"

Finally, let me repeat it for those who didn't hear me before. I have no ulterior motives or hidden agenda but to see God bring spiritual healing and revival to every institution in America from our house to the White House for the advancement of God's kingdom and magnification of His glory.

For those of you who think that I'm just trying to "whip up" the church into a frenzy to make a name for myself or "hawk a book," you have wrongly and unfairly judged me and do not know my heart. Furthermore, you have allowed yourself to be used as an instrument of the devil. Please understand, I have already forgiven you whether you seek it or not. Send me a message via our ministry website, and I will gladly send you a free copy of the book that you think I'm "hawking" to try and make a name for myself. For those of you who know my heart but simply can't afford a copy because of your financial situation, please let me know, and I will send you a free copy as well.

As we come to the end of our time together, depending on how long it has taken you to get to this point, you and I have spent anywhere between several hours (if you're a speed reader!) to several days, weeks, or even months together. Please know that I am

587

eternally grateful for the time you have allowed me to spend with you! You now know my heart, and if you've agreed to participate in *Operation Heal America*, I now know yours! How good and how pleasant it is for brothers and sisters to dwell together in unity (Psalm 133:1 NKJV).

While the encouragement I have received on this journey thus far has been nothing less than amazing and humbling, please understand that I did not author this manuscript alone. The Holy Spirit directed my every step and penned everything on my heart before I could give it to you! Thus, all glory and honor go to my Lord and Savior, Jesus Christ! Please, therefore, do not make *Operation Heal America* about me or this ministry. Give all the glory to the One in whom it is due—Jesus Christ, our Lord, Savior, and King, who makes all things possible!

Now are you ready to step on the neck of the devil and proclaim victory in Jesus's name? What did you say? Your feet have been on his neck this entire time? Outstanding!

Did you know that God's Word says that we are not only conquerors but that we are more than conquerors through Him who loved us (Romans 8:37)? Good thing because we have a lot to conquer! However, I hope you caught the key to conquering—through Him who loved us. May His love be our fuel!

So what are we waiting for? In the words of Nehemiah, "The God of heaven will make sure we succeed (Nehemiah 2:20 MSG)!"

OMG. Stop. Did you hear that? Listen. Shh. There it is. Hear it? If I didn't know better, I think I just heard the sound of a shofar (ram's horn)!

Verses to Remember

1. Therefore we also, since we are surrounded by so great a cloud of witnesses, let us lay aside every weight, and the sin which so easily ensnares us, and let us run with endurance the race that is set before us, looking unto Jesus, the author and finisher of our faith, who for the joy that was set before

Him endured the cross, despising the shame, and has sat down at the right hand of the throne of God. (Hebrews 12:1–2 NKJV)

2. For the time has come that judgment must begin at the house of God: and if it first begin at us, what shall the end be of them that obey not the Gospel of God? (1 Peter 4:17 KJV)

3. Behold, how good and how pleasant it is for Brethren to dwell together in unity! (Psalm 133:1 ASV)

4. He must increase, but I must decrease. (John 3:30 ESV)

5. No, in all these things we are *more* than conquerors through Him who loved us. (Romans 8:37 NIV)

6. "The glory of this latter temple shall be greater than the former," says the LORD of hosts. "And in this place, I will give peace," says the LORD of hosts. (Haggai 2:9 NKJV)

7. The God of heaven will make sure we succeed. (Nehemiah 2:20 MSG)

ENDNOTES

————— ◆◆◆◆◆ —————

Introduction

1 "Evangelism Statistics," Bible.org, Feb. 2, 2009, www.Bible.org/ illustration/ evangelism-statistics.

2 Tony Evans, "How to Save a Nation in Trouble," Tony Evans: The Urban Alternative, accessed May 5, 2018, www.tonyevans.org/ how-to-save-a-nation-in-trouble.

Chapter 1

3 Dr. Tony Evans.

4 Federal Bureau of Investigation, "Contact Us," accessed Nov. 26, 2017, www. fbi.gov/contact-us.

5 Ibid.

6 Ibid.

7 Bruce Wilkinson, The Prayer of Jabez (Colorado Springs: Multnomah Press, 2000).

8 Tony Evans, "The Secret of the Seed," Radio—The Alternative (May 2017), Tony Evans Audio.

9 Bible Study Tools, accessed Jan. 5, 2018, www.biblestudytools.com/commen- taries/gills-exposition-of-the-Bible/1-peter-1-23.html.

Chapter 2

10 Dr. Charles Stanley.

11 Terence P. Jeffrey, "Obama Was First President to Spend More on Welfare than Defense," CNS News (Jan. 20, 2017), www.cnsnews.com/news/article/ terence-p-jeffrey/obama-was-first-president-spend-more-welfare-defense.

12 Paul David Tripp, What Did You Expect?? Redeeming the Realities of Marriage (Wheaton: Crossway, 2010).

13 James Spence, Do You Want to Get Well? (Enumclaw: WinePress Publishing, 2008), 4.

14 Green, Tierce. "A Clear Vision for Authentic Manhood," Authentic Manhood (Aug. 20, 2015), www.authenticmanhood.com/blog/a-clear-vision-for-authentic-manhood.

15 Life Application Study Bible (New Living Translation), Explanatory note, Ephesians 5:21–22 (Wheaton: Tyndale House Publishers), 1996.

16 Ibid.

17 Ibid.

18 Ibid.

19 Dr. Tony Evans.

20 Mike Mount, "US Triples Foreign Arms Sales in 2011," Security Clearance CNN (Aug. 27, 2012), security.blogs.cnn.com/2012/08/27/u-s-triples-foreign-arms-sales-in-2011.

21 "Jezebel, in Our Society—What is the Jezebel Spirit—Explication," Just Steps In (Apr. 28, 2017), juststepsin.wordpress.com/2017/04/28/jezebel-in-our-society-what-is-the-jezebel-spirit-explication.

22 Dave McKenzie, "Discerning the Jezebel Spirit," The Glory Gathering (Apr. 26, 2014), glorygathering.wordpress.com/tag/the-jezebel-spirit.

23 Francis Frangipane, "Discerning the Jezebel Spirit," Francis Frangipane Messages (Feb. 2003), francisfrangipanemessages.blogspot.com/2003/02/discerning-jezebel-spirit.html.

24 "The Curse of Jezebel," Hegewisch Baptist Church, Oct. 13, 2011, hbcdelivers.org/the-curse-of-jezebel.

25 Ibid.

26 Ibid.

27 Dispatch Staff, "OC Air Show Headlined by Blue Angels, Snowbirds," The Dispatch (Jun. 12, 2019), mdcoastdispatch.com/2019/06/12/oc-air-show-headlined-by-blue-angels-snowbirds.

28 Horatio Spafford, hymnist.

29 J01 Cathy Konn, The Blue Angels Creed, 1991–1993.

30 International Technology Education Association, "How to Put a Precision-Flying Test Pilot into a Space-Faring Robot," The Technology Center, October 1999, p. 2.

31 Peter Mersky, "The Blues—An Inside Look," Naval Aviation News (Sept.–Oct. 1988).

32 Ibid.

33 "Blue Angel How It Works (HIW) Interview Blue 5 Pilot Mark Tedrow," How It Works Daily (Jul. 30, 2015), www.howitworksdaily.com/blue-angels-hiw-interview-blue-5-pilot-mark-tedrow.

34 "How Do Aerobatic Display Teams Like the Blue Angels or Thunderbirds Fly Headlong Into Each Other Without Colliding." Quora, Apr. 5, 2015, www.quora.com/How-do-aerobatic-display-teams-like-the-Blue-Angels-or-Thunderbirds-fly-headlong-into-each-other-without-colliding-1.

[35] Unknown.

[36] Tony Evans, Kingdom Man Carol Stream: Tyndale House Publishers, 2012), 13.

[37] Suzanne Venker, "Mother's Day is Your Husband Your Child or Your Partner," Fox News Opinion (May12, 2017), www.foxnews.com/opinion/mothers-day-is-your-husband-your-child-or-your-partner.

[38] Yulia Vangorodska, Marriage and Divorce by the Numbers, Vangorodska Law Firm, blog post, Divorce, 2019.

[39] Tony Evans, "Spiritual Covering and Spiritual Authority," The Urban Alternative (Mar. 12, 2019), TonyEvans.org.

[40] Dr. Charles Stanley.

[41] Dr. Tony Evans.

[42] Ibid.

[43] Tony Evans, "Spiritual Covering and Spiritual Authority," The Urban Alternative (Mar. 12, 2019), TonyEvans.org.

Chapter 3

[44] Dr. Tony Evans.

[45] Tony Evans, Kingdom Man (Carol Stream: Tyndale House Publishers, 2012),165–166.

[46] Calvin Park, "Cutting a Covenant," Bible Study (Sep. 19, 2017), www.biblestudy-magazine.com/Bible-study-magazine-blog/2017/9/19/cutting-a-covenant.

[47] Dr. Tony Evans.

[48] Dr. Tony Evans.

[49] Dr. Tony Evans.

[50] Tony Evans, "Taking Marriage Seriously," The Urban Alternative (Sep. 1, 2016), TonyEvans.org.

[51] Charles Stanley, "The Ruin of Rebellion," a sermon by Charles F. Stanley, In Touch Ministries, Sep. 23, 2010.

[52] "The Dangers of Rebellion," Great Bible Study, accessed Nov. 6, 2018, www.greatbiblestudy.com/spiritual-warfare/the-dangers-of-rebellion.

[53] Quentin Fotrell, "Millions of Americans Keep This Dirty Secret from Their Partner," MarketWatch, Jul. 31, 2019, www.marketwatch.com/story/millions-of-americans-keep-this-dirty-secret-from-their-partner-2019-01-24.

[54] Dr. Tony Evans.

[55] Ibid.

[56] Ibid.

[57] Claude R. Bailey II, "Short Term Missions: Adult," OCBF Church (Sep. 7, 2014), p. 27, www.ocbfchurch.org/wp-content/uploads/2018/04/MissionApp-Adult.pdf.

[58] Tony Evans, "OCBF Ministry Volunteer Handbook," OCBF Church (Oct. 2011), p. 20, www.ocbfchurch.org/wp-content/uploads/2017/12/OCBF_Volunteer_Handbookwithcover_10-11.pdf.

59 James Spence, Do You Want to Get Well? (Enumclaw: WinePress Publishing, 2008), 1.

Chapter 4

60 United States Department of Justice, A Review of FBI Security Programs (Webster Report), Commission for Review of FBI Security Programs, 2002, 1.

61 FBI National Press Office. "Robert Hanssen," FBI, 20 Feb. 2001, www.fbi.gov/history/famous-cases/robert-hanssen.

62 United States Department of Justice, US v. Robert Philip Hanssen, Indictment, Federation of American Scientists, May 17, 2001, fas.org/irp/ops/ci/ hanssen_indict.html.

63 United States Department of Justice, "Affidavit in Robert Hanssen Spy Case," FBI, Feb. 20, 2001, www.fbi.gov/file-repository/hanssen-affidavit.pdf/view.

64 Elizabeth Nix, "Robert Hanssen American Traitor: On May 10, 2002, former FBI Agent Robert Hanssen was Sentenced to Life in Prison for Selling US Secrets to Moscow," History (Apr. 10, 2019), www.history.com/news/robert-hanssen-american-traitor.

65 FBI National Press Office, "Robert Hanssen," FBI, Feb. 20, 2001, www.fbi.gov/history/famous-cases/robert-hanssen.

66 Eli Hager, "My Life in the Supermax," The Marshall Project, Jan. 8, 2016, www.themarshallproject.org/2016/01/08/my-life-in-the-supermax.

67 Adrian Havill, The Spy who Stayed out in The Cold—The Secret Life of FBI Double Agent Robert Hanssen (New York: St. Martin's Press, 2001).

68 Ibid.

69 Ibid.

70 Ibid.

71 Monica Davey, "Secret Passage," The Chicago Tribune (Apr. 21, 2002), www.chicagotribune.com/news/ct-xpm-2002-04-21-0204210451-story.html.

72 United States Department of Justice, "Affidavit in Robert Hanssen Spy Case," FBI (Feb. 20, 2001), www.fbi.gov/file-repository/hanssen-affidavit.pdf/view.

73 Ibid.

74 United States Department of Justice, Office of the Inspector General, Unclassified Executie Summary: A Review of the FBI's Performance in Deterring, Detecting, and Investigating the Espionage Activities of Robert Philip Hanssen, 2003, 5.

75 Charlot1, "Robert Hanssen." Charlotte Investigations (July 11, 2018), charlotteinvestigations.net/robert-hanssen/2018/surveillance/.

76 Ibid.

77 James Risen, "Spy's Wife Speaks, After Taking a Lie Test," The New York Times (May 16, 2002), www.nytimes.com/2002/05/16/us/spy-s-wife-speaks-after-taking-a-lie-test.html.

[78] "Some American Opus Dei 'Works'—And a Few Prominent American Members," Are You Aware? Deception Is Everywhere (Oct. 31, 2008), areyouaware.wordpress.com/2008/10/31/some-american-opus-dei-works—-and-a-few-prominent-american-members.

[79] Ibid.

[80] David van Biema, "The Ways of Opus Dei," Time (Apr. 16, 2006), www.opuslibros.org/html/TIME_Opus_Dei_story.htm.

[81] United States Department of Justice, Office of the Inspector General, Unclassified Executive Summary: A Review of the FBI's Performance in Deterring, Detecting, and Investigating the Espionage Activities of Robert Philip Hanssen, 2003.

[82] Ibid.

[83] Ibid.

[84] Ibid.

[85] Ibid.

[86] Ibid.

[87] Paul Davis. "A Look Back at FBI Agent and Russian Spy Robert Hanssen," Paul Davis on Crime (Feb. 19, 2018), www.pauldavisoncrime.com/2018/02/a-look-back-at-fbi-agent-and-russian.html.

[88] United States Department of Justice, Office of the Inspector General, Unclassified Executive Summary: A Review of the FBI's Performance in Deterring, Detecting, and Investigating the Espionage Activities of Robert Philip Hanssen, 2003.

[89] Eric O'Neill. "Robert Hanssen Spy Case," C-SPAN, Feb. 20, 2007, www.c-span.org/video/?196420-4/robert-hanssen-spy-case.

[90] United States Department of Justice, Office of the Inspector General, Unclassified Executive Summary: A Review of the FBI's Performance in Deterring, Detecting, and Investigating the Espionage Activities of Robert Philip Hanssen, 2003.

[91] Ibid.

[92] "Ex-stripper Describes Her Time with Accused Spy," CNN (May 22, 2001), www.cnn.com/2001/US/05/22/hanssen.stripper/

[93] 28 CFR 0.85.

[94] United States Department of Justice, Office of the Inspector General, A Review of Various Actions by the Federal Bureau of Investigation and Department of Justice in Advance of the 2016 Election, 2018, 173.

[95] Guttmacher Institute, 2014.

[96] United States Court of Appeals for the Third Circuit, No. 09-2628, US v. Rafael Romero, a.k.a. Ralph Romero, Opinion of the Court, Jordan, Hardiman, and Van Antwerpen, on Appeal from the United States District Court for the District of New Jersey (DC No. 07-cr-00910-001) District Judge: Hon. Joseph A. Greenaway, Jr., 2010.

[97] Ibid.

[98] Ibid.

[99] The United States Attorney's Office, District of New Jersey, Press Release, "California CPA Sentenced to 57 Months in Prison for Defrauding New Jersey Religious Center, California Non-Profit Out of More Than $4 Million," 2016.

[100] Ibid.

[101] Tim Darragh, "CPA Who Gambled Away Church's Millions Sent to Prison." NJ.com (Apr. 5, 2016), www.nj.com/union/2016/04/cpa_who_gambled_away_churchs_millions_sent_to_pris.html.

[102] Ibid.

[103] Dr. Tony Evans.

[104] Dr. Tony Evans.

Chapter 5

[105] Alfonso Serrano, "Evangelical Quits After Gay Sex Scandal," CBS News (Nov. 4, 2006), www.cbsnews.com/news/evangelical-quits-after-gay-sex-scandal/.

[106] Daniel Blake, "Evangelical Head Resigns as Church Votes Haggard Guilty of 'Sexually Immoral Conduct,'" Christian Today, (Nov. 5, 2006), www.christiantoday.com/article/evangelical.head.resigns.as.church.votes.haggard.guilty.of.sexually.immoral.conduct/8214.htm.

[107] Steve Fullhart, "Former Minister Gets Seven Years for Solicitation," KBTX-TV (Sep. 29, 2009), www.kbtx.com/home/headlines/62582292.html.

[108] Robert Wilonsky, "It's Never Good When You're Arrested," Dallas Observer (May 16, 2008), www.dallasobserver.com/news/its-never-good-when-youre-arrested-with-a-webcam-and-condoms-7123939.

[109] Associated Press, "Evangelist Alamo Sentenced to 175 Years for Sex Crimes," San Gabriel Valley Tribune (Nov. 13, 2009), www.sgvtribune.com/2009/11/13/evangelist-alamo-sentenced-to-175-years-for-sex-crimes.

[110] Ibid.

[111] "Dr. Boyce: TD Jakes Should Stop Defending Bishop Eddie Long," News One (Jun. 22, 2011), newsone.com/1328755/td-jakes-defending-eddie-long.

[112] "Disgraced Hammond Pastor Gets 12 Years for Sex with Teen," CBS Chicago (Mar. 20, 2013), chicago.cbslocal.com/2013/03/20/disgraced-hammond-pastor-gets-12-years-for-sex-with-teen.

[113] Ibid.

[114] Anugrah Kumar, "Jury Indicts Ex-ROC Pastor for Child Sex Crime Gives Graphic Account of Abuse," The Christian Post (Sept. 21, 2013), www.christianpost.com/news/jury-indicts-ex-roc-pastor-for-child-sex-crime-gives-graphic-account-of-abuse.html.

[115] Melissa Hipolit, "Geronimo Aguilar, Former Mega-Church Pastor, Found Guilty of All Sex Crimes," CBS 6 News (Jun. 25, 2015), localtvwtvr.wordpress.com/2015/06/24/geronimo-aguilar-former-mega-church-pastor-found-guilty-on-all-counts-of-sexual-assault.

[116] Ibid.

ENDNOTES

117 Sandra Jones, "Former Richmond Pastor Geronimo Aguilar Sentenced to 40 Years in Prison for Sexually Abusing Children," CBS 6 News (Oct. 13, 2015), localtvwtvr.wordpress.com/2015/10/13/ former-richmond-pastor-geronimo-aguilar-sentenced-to-40-years-in-prison-for-sexually-abusing-children.

118 Morgan Lee, "Colorado Church Leaders Accused of Covering up Youth Pastor Sex Abuse Scandal," BishopAccountability.org, Nov. 10, 2013, bishop-accountability.org/news2013/ 11_12/2013_11_10_Lee_ColoradoChurch.htm.

119 Alex Burness, "This Cannot Happen:' Boulder Judge Sentences VineLife Church Leaders for Not Reporting Sex Assault," Daily Camera Boulder News (July 23, 2015), www.dailycamera.com/ 2015/07/23/ this-cannot-happen-boulder-judge-sentences-vinelife-church-leaders-for-not-reporting-sex-assault.

120 Ibid.

121 Ibid.

122 "The Ashley Madison Hack…In Two Minutes," CNN Business (Sep. 11, 2015), money.cnn.com/2015/08/24/technology/ashley-madison-hack-in-2-minutes/index.html.

123 Ibid.

124 Ed Stetzer, "My Pastor Is on the Ashley Madison List," Christianity Today, (Aug. 27, 2015), www.christianitytoday.com/edstetzer/2015/august/my-pastor-is-on-ashley-madison-list.html.

125 Cathy Lynn Grossman, "Clergy Sex Abuse Settlements Top $2.5 Billion Nationwide," USA Today (Mar. 13, 2013), www.usatoday.com/story/news/nation/2013/03/13/sex-abuse-settlement-cardinal-roger-mahony/1984217.

126 Ibid.

127 Daniel Burke and Susanna Cullinane, "Report Details Sexual Abuse by More than 300 Priests in Pennsylvania's Catholic Church," CNN Philippines (Aug. 15, 2018), cnnphilippines.com/world/ 2018/08/15/Pennsylvania-Catholic-Church-sexual-abuse-minors.html.

128 Ibid.

129 Ibid.

130 Ibid.

131 Richard Gonzales, "Pope Francis Acknowledges for First Time, Sexual Abuse of Nuns by Priests," National Public Radio (Feb. 5, 2019), www.npr.org/2019/02/05/691843161/pope-francis-acknowledges-for-first-time-sexual-abuse-of-nuns-by-priests.

132 Ibid.

133 Kate Shellnut, "Willow Creek Investigation: Allegations Against Bill Hybels Are Credible," Christianity Today (Feb. 28, 2019), www.christianitytoday.com/news/2019/february/willow-creek-bill-hybels-investigation-iag-report.html.

134 Ibid.

135 Ibid.

136 "40 percent of Pastors Admit to Having an Extramarital Affair," Standing Stone Shepherding Shepherds (2018), www.standingstoneministry. org/40-of-pastors-admit-to-having-extramarital-affair/.

137 Mark Denison, "Porn in the Pulpit: Facing it Head On," Covenant Eyes (Oct. 11, 2018), www.covenanteyes.com/2018/10/11/porn-in-the-pulpit/.

138 "The Leadership survey on Pastors and Internet Pornography." Christianity Today, accessed Mar. 14, 2018, www.christianitytoday.com/pastors/2001/winter/12.89.html.

139 Masci, David and Lipka, Michael, "Where Christian Churches, Other Religions Stand on Gay Marriage," Pew Research, Dec. 21, 2015, www.pewresearch.org/fact-tank/2015/12/21/where-christian-churches-stand-on-gay-marriage.

140 "Affirming Denominations," Gay Church, accessed Jul. 19, 2019, www.gaychurch.org/affirming-denominations.

141 "Poll: Christians Just Love Their Porn." Dvorak Uncensored (Aug. 8, 2006), www.dvorak.org/blog/2006/08/08/poll-christians-just-love-their-porn/.

142 Ibid.

143 "Morality Continues to Decay," Barna (Nov. 3, 2003), www.barna.com/research/morality-continues-to-decay/.

144 Holly Hein, Sexual Detours, The Startling Truth Behind Love, Lust, and Infidelity (New York: St. Martin's Press, 2000), 77.

145 CovenantEyes, Porn Stats, 250+ Facts, Quotes, and Statistics About Pornography Use (2018 edition), 28.

146 Ibid.

147 "Teenage Sexting Statistics." GuardChild, accessed Sep. 13, 2019, www.guardchild.com/teenage-sexting-statistics/.

148 CovenantEyes, Porn Statistics, 250+ Facts, Quotes, and Statistics About Pornography Use (2015 edition), 15.

149 Ibid.

150 Ibid.

151 Ibid.

152 CovenantEyes, Porn Stats, 250+ Facts, Quotes, and Statistics About Pornography Use (2018 edition), 5.

153 "The Internet Porn 'Epidemic:' By the numbers." The Week (Jun. 17, 2010), theweek.com/articles/ 493433/internet-porn-epidemic-by-numbers.

154 "Top Websites Ranking." SimilarWeb (Jul. 1, 2019), www.similarweb.com/top-websites.

155 CovenantEyes, Porn Stats, 250+ Facts, Quotes, and Statistics About Pornography Use (2015 edition), 10.

156 Christian and Sex Leadership Journal Survey, March 2005.

157 "Pornography and Media Addiction: The New Epidemic." TechMission Safe Families Keeping Children Safe Online, accessed May 19, 2019, safefamilies. org/pastorpage.php.

158 American Culture and Faith Institute, March 2018.

159 CovenantEyes, Porn Stats, 250+ Facts, Quotes, and Statistics About Pornography Use (2018 edition).

160 Manny Alvarez. "Porn Addiction, Why Americans are in More Danger Than Ever," Fox News (Jan. 17, 2019), www.foxnews.com/health/porn-addiction-why-americans-are-in-more-danger-than-ever.

161 Ibid.

162 Amanda Hess, "Do Christians Have Better Sex?" The XX Factor (Jul. 9, 2013), slate.com/human-interest/2013/07/the-family-research-council-argues-that-christians-have-more-orgasmic-frequent-sex.html.

Chapter 6

163 Michael Savage, The Savage Nation, radio broadcast, 2015.

164 "Most American Christians Do Not Believe that Satan or the Holy Spirit Exist," The Barna Group Ltd., Apr. 13, 2009, www.barna.com/research/most-american-christians-do-not-believe-that-satan-or-the-holy-spirit-exist/.

165 Ibid.

166 ABC News Poll, Most Americans Say They're Christian (July 18, 2014).

167 US Census Bureau, 2017.

168 James P. Shelly, "Was Jesus a Friend of Sinners?" Truth According to Scripture, accessed Jun. 13, 2019, www.truthaccordingtoscripture.com/documents/christian-life/was-jesus-a-friend-of-sinners.php#.Xpoxgm5FxPY.

169 Deitrich Bonhoeffer, The Cost of Discipleship Revised and Unabridged Edition Containing Material Not Previously Translated (New York: Macmillan Publishing Co. Inc., 1963), 45–47.

170 John Duncan, "Judge Not Lest Ye Be Judged," John and Ellen Duncom.com, accessed 12 Mar 2019, www.johnandellenduncan.com/jd_judgenot.htm.

171 McCarthy, Justin. "US Support for Gay Marriage Edges to New High," Gallop (May 15, 2017), news.gallup.com/poll/210566/support-gay-marriage-edges-new-high.aspx.

172 Ibid.

173 "Public Opinion on Abortion, Views on Abortion, 1995–2018," Pew Research Center, Religion & Public Life, Aug. 29, 2019, www.pewforum.org/fact-sheet/public-opinion-on-abortion/.

174 Unknown.

175 Walter A. Elwell, The Concise Evangelical Dictionary of Theology (Grand Rapids: BakerBooks), 2001.

176 Claude R. Bailey II, "Short-Term Missions," Adult, Oak Cliff Bible Fellowship, September 17, 2014, 21.

177 Ronald Arthur Hopwood, Rear Admiral, Laws of the Navy (fifth), Royal Navy, 1896.

178 St. Francis of Assisi.

179 Emily Stimpson, "Pope Francis and St. Francis: Preach the Gospel Always. And for the Love of God, Use Words." Catholicvote (Mar. 14, 2013), catholicvote. org/pope-francis-and-st-francis-preach-the-Gospel-always-and-for-the-love-of-god-use-words/.

180 "Evangelism Statistics," Bible.org, Feb. 2, 2009, www.Bible.org/illustration/ evangelism-statistics.

181 Attributed to St. Francis of Assisi.

182 Mark Batterson, Primal, A Quest for the Lost Soul of Christianity (Colorado Springs: Multnomah Books, 2010), 121.

183 Paul David Tripp, What Did You Expect? Redeeming the Realities of Marriage (Wheaton: Crossway, 2010).

184 Ibid.

185 Matthew Harmon, "What Does 'Saint' Mean?" Christianity.com (Oct. 16, 2013), www.christianity.com/jesus/following-jesus/repentance-faith-and-salvation/what-does-saint-mean.html.

186 Author Unknown.

187 Michael J. Kruger. "Saint or Sinner? Rethinking the Language of Our Christian Identity," Cannon Fodder (Jul. 15, 2013), www.michaeljkruger.com/ saint-or-sinner-rethinking-the-language-of-our-christian-identity/.

188 Dir. Roger Allers and Rob Minkoff, The Lion King, film (Walt Disney Pictures, 1994).

189 Ibid.

190 Ibid.

191 Ibid.

192 Ibid.

193 Ibid.

194 Ibid.

195 Ibid.

196 Ibid.

197 Ibid.

198 Ibid.

199 Neil T. Anderson, Victory Over the Darkness (Ventura: Regal Books, 1990), 45.

200 Dir. Roger Allers and Rob Minkoff, The Lion King, film (Walt Disney Pictures, 1994).

201 Jack Wellman, "What Is Apostasy? A Biblical Definition of Apostasy," Christian Crier (May 21, 2015), www.patheos.com/blogs/christiancrier/2015/05/21/ what-is-apostasy-a-biblical-definition-of-apostasy/.

202 Ibid.

203 Dr. Billy Graham, "Answers by Billy Graham." Billy Graham Evangelistic Association (Aug. 24, 2006), billygraham.org/answer/why-does-jesus-says-god-has-forsaken-Him-on-the-cross-how-could-god-have-abandoned-Him-right-when-He-needed-god-the-most-will-god-ever-forsake-us/.

[204] Ellicott's Commentary, Matthew Poole's Commentary; Cambridge Bible for Schools and Colleges.

[205] Barnes' Notes on the Bible; Meyer's NT Commentary.

[206] Kerby Anderson, "When Nations Die," Probe (May 27, 2002), probe.org/when-nations-die/.

[207] Kirk Cameron, 27 Kirk Cameron (Jan. 10, 2013), kirkcameron.com/articles/why-do-80-of-youth-leave-church-after-high-school/.

[208] "Evangelism Statistics," Bible.org, Feb. 2, 2009, www.Bible.org/ illustration/evangelism-statistics.

[209] World Health Organization, Centers for Disease Control and Prevention, European Centre for Disease Prevention and Control, and National Healthcare Corporation, April 19, 2020.

[210] Ibid.

[211] Thomas Jefferson, Letter to the Danbury Baptists, January 1, 1802.

[212] Ibid.

[213] Ibid.

[214] Rob Boston, "The Most Important Church-State Decision You Never Heard Of," AlterNet (Feb. 3 2007), www.alternet.org/2007/02/the_most_important_church-state_decision_you_never_heard_of/.

[215] United States Constitution, Amendment 14, Section 1.

[216] Hugo Black, Everson v. Board of Education of the Township of Ewing, 330 US 1, 1947.

[217] Jeff Myers, "Politics, Should Christians Get Involved?" Crosswalk.com, (Mar. 7, 2002), www.crosswalk.com/family/homeschool/politics-should-christians-get-involved-1128040.html.

[218] Dr. Wayne Grudem, Should Christians Be Involved in Politics & Government, Q&A video segment, April 5, 2013.

[219] Steven J. Cole, "Lesson 89: Christ: Lord of our Politics (Rom 13:1–7 and other Scriptures," Bible.org, Jul. 18, 2013, Bible.org/seriespage/lesson-89-christ-lord-our-politics-rom-131-7-and-other-scriptures.

[220] "Notional Christians: The Big Election Story in 2016." Barna (Dec. 1, 2016), www.barna.com/research/notional-christians-big-election-story-2016/.

[221] Pew Research Center, "How the Faithful Voted," November 7, 2012, Preliminary Analysis, www.pewforum.org/2012/11/07/how-the-faithful-voted-2012-preliminary-exit-poll-analysis/

[222] Ibid.

[223] Jim Hoft, "It's Official—Obama's Deficits in 6 Years more than all Prior US Presidents Combined," The Gateway Pundit (Mar. 15, 2015), www.thegatewaypundit.com/2015/03/its-official-obamas-deficits-in-6-years-more-than-all-prior-us-presidents-combined/.

[224] Alex Newman, "Welfare Hits Record Levels After 50 Years of War on Poverty," The New American (Jan. 10, 2014), www.thenewamerican.com/economy/economics/item/17367-welfare-hits.

225 "National exit polls 2012 data from NBCNews.com," NBC News (2012), accessed Oct. 12, 2019.

226 Edmund Burke.

227 Jeff Myers, "Politics: Should Christians Get Involved?" Christianity (2002), www.christianity.com/print/1128040/.

228 J. Vernon McGee.

229 Matthew Staver, "Pastors, Churches and Politics What May Pastors and Churches Do?" Liberty Counsel (2008), www.lc.org/Uploads/files/pdf/pastors_churches_politics_trifold_2008.pdf.

230 Ibid.

231 "Pulpit Freedom Sunday: Pastors Say Enough Is Enough," CBN News (Oct. 2, 2016), www1.cbn.com/cbnnews/politics/2016/october/pulpit-freedom-sunday-pastors-say-enough-is-enough.

232 "Pulpit Freedom Sunday," Alliance Defending Freedom (Sep. 25, 2008), www.adfmedia.org/ News/PRDetail/1977.

233 "Voter Guides and Churches." Alliance Defending Freedom (Oct. 20, 2010, www.adflegal.org /detailspages/blog-details/allianceedge/2017/10/18/voter-guides-and-churches.

234 Kelsey Dallas. "Churches proceed carefully when encouraging members to get politically involved," Deseret News (Oct. 28, 2014), www.deseret.com/2014/10/28/20551252/churches-proceed-carefully.

235 Ibid.

236 Charles Colson.

237 W. Gardener Selby, "Dan Patrick says all crime, in estimate, committed by about 15 percent of population, Politifact (Oct. 6, 2015), www.politifact.com/factchecks/2015/oct/06/dan-patrick/dan-patrick-says-all-crime-estimate-committed-15-p/.

238 US Treasury Department, June 15, 2019.

239 US National Debt Clock: Real Time, June 15, 2019.

240 Meyers, Jeff. "Politics: Should Christians Get Involved?" Crosswalk.com, Mar. 7, 2002. www.crosswalk.com/family/homeschool/politics-should-christians-get-involved

241 Dr. Tony Evans.

242 Steven J. Cole, "Lesson 89: Christ: Lord of our Politics (Rom 13:1-7 and other Scriptures." Bible.org, Jul. 18 2013, Bible.org/seriespage/lesson-89-christ-lord-our-politics-rom-131-7-and-other-scriptures.

243 Greg A. Dixon, "Rethinking Romans 13," Free Republic (Apr. 14, 2001), www.freerepublic.com/focus/f-religion/2366982/posts.

244 Ellen Craswell, "The Biblical Basis for Christians in Politics and Government," accessed 18 Jun 2016, www.poetpatriot.com/polchristians.

245 Abraham Lincoln, Gettysburg Address, November 19, 1863.

246 John Eidesoe.

247 "Majority of Americans Think Churches Should Stay Out of Politics," Pew Research Center, Politics and Religion, accessed 11 Jun 2017.

248 "Christians Must Get Involved in Politics, Says Renowned Apologist." The Christian Post (Apr. 6, 2012), www.christianpost.com/news/christians-must-get-involved-in-politics-says-renowned-apologist-72498/.

249 Ibid.

250 Gregory A. Boyd, The Myth of a Christian Religion, Losing Your Religion for the Beauty of a Revolution (Grand Rapids: Zondervan, 2009).

251 St. Augustine.

252 Ibid.

253 Ibid.

254 Bucknell, Paul J. "Misunderstandings of the Fear of God." Foundations for Freedom, accessed Apr. 21, 2020, www.foundationsforfreedom.net/Topics/FearGodMan/FearGod010.html.

255 J. Matthew Wilson, From Pews to Polling Places: Faith and Politics in the American Religious Mosaic (Washington: Georgetown University Press, 2007).

256 Cox, Daniel "Health Wealth and Happiness: A Review." Midwest Christian Outreach, 23 Mar. 2012, midwestoutreach.org/2012/03/23/health-wealth-and-happiness-a-review/.

257 Albert Mohler, "The Osteen Predicament—Mere Happiness Cannot Bear the Weight of the Gospel," Charisma News (Sep. 4, 2014), www.charismanews.com/ opinion/45267-the-osteen-predicament-mere-happiness-cannot-bear-the-weight-of-the-Gospel/.

258 "Prosperity Gospel," Christianity Today International, accessed Apr. 23 2020, www.christianitytoday.com/ct/topics/p/prosperity-Gospel/.

259 Jonathan L. Walton, Watch This! The Ethics and Aesthetics of Black Televangelism (New York: NYU Press, 2009), 94.

260 Martyn Wendell Jones, "Jim and Tammy Faye Bakker: A Scandal of the Self," The Weekly Standard (March 2, 2018).

261 Kate Bowler, Blessed: A History of the American Prosperity Gospel (Oxford: Oxford University Press, 2013).

262 T. L. Osborne.

263 Albert Mohler, "The Osteen Predicament—Mere Happiness Cannot Bear the Weight of the Gospel," Sep. 3, 2014, albertmohler.com/2014/09/03/ the-osteen-predicament-mere-happiness-cannot-bear-the-weight-of-the-Gospel/.

264 Steve Hill, Spiritual Avalanche, (Lake Mary: Charisma House, 2013).

265 Life Application Study Bible, New Living Translation, Explanatory note, Luke 6:37–38 (Wheaton: Tyndale House Publishers, 1996).

266 Eckardt, John. "The Real Meaning of Blessing and Prosperity." Charisma Magazine (Dec 26, 2012), www.charismamag.com/spirit/spiritual-growth/14838-the-real-meaning-of-blessing-and-prosperity.

267 Ibid.

268 Ibid.

269 Ibid.

270 Ibid.

271 Eskridge, Larry. "The Prosperity Gospel is Surprisingly Mainstream." Christianity Today, Aug. 22, 2013, www.christianitytoday.com/ct/2013/august-web-only/prosperity-Gospel-is-surprisingly-mainstream.html.

272 "Evangelism Statistics." Bible.org, Feb. 2, 2009, www.Bible.org/illustration/evangelism-statistics.

273 "Evangelism Statistics." Bible.org, 2 Feb. 2009, www.Bible.org/illustration/evangelism-statistics.

274 "It's All About Jesus," Westover Hills, accessed Apr. 24, 2020, www.westover-hills.church/about.

275 "Our Call," accessed Apr. 24, 2020, Churchome, accessed Apr. 24, 2020, churchome.org/about.

276 "Purpose and Beliefs: Why We Believe What We Believe." Fellowship Church, fellowshipchurch.com/purpose-beliefs/.

277 "More About Elevation Church," Elevation Church, accessed Apr. 24, 2020, elevationchurch.org/values/.

278 "About Hillsong." Hillsong Church, accessed Apr. 24, 2020, hillsong.com/sv/about.

279 "Join us Online." Hillsong Phoenix, accessed Apr. 24, 2020, hillsong.com/sv/phoenix/.

280 "Vision and Mission." Gateway Church, accessed Apr. 24, 2020, gatewaypeople.com/about/mission.

281 "About." National Community Church, accessed Apr. 24, 2020, national.cc/about.

282 "Naperville." Community Christian Church, accessed Apr. 24, 2020, communitychristian.org/naperville/.

283 "Mission and Values." Granger Community Church, accessed Apr. 24, 2020, grangerchurch.com/ mission-and-values/.

284 "Coral Ridge Presbyterian Church." ECFA, accessed Apr. 24, 2020, www.ecfa.org/ MemberProfile.aspx?ID=4475.

285 "About Us. Connecting the Hearts of People to the Heart of God." The Potter's House of North Dallas, accessed Apr. 24, 2020, tphnd.org/about-us/.

286 Moore, Johnnie. "Newsmax's Top 50 Megachurches in America," Newsmax (Nov. 11, 2015), www.newsmax.com/TheWire/megachurches-top-united-states-newsmax/ 2015/11/11/id/701661/.

287 "Our Mission Statement: The Great Commission," Second Baptist Church, accessed Apr. 24, 2020, www.second.org/who-we-are/our-mission/.

288 "Mission and Vision." Hopewell Missionary Baptist Church, accessed 24 Apr. 2020, www.hmbchurch.net/mission-vision/.

289 "About Us." Christ's Church of the Valley, accessed Apr. 24, 2020, ccv.church/about-us/.

290 "Core Values." New Hope O'AHU, accessed Apr. 24, 2020, enewhope.org/start-here/about/core-values/.

291 "Who We Are." Christ Fellowship, accessed Apr. 24, 2020, www.cfmiami.org/whoweare.

292 "About Us." Biltmore Church, accessed Apr. 24, 2020, www.biltmorechurch.com/about/.

293 "Welcome to Calvary." Calvary Chapel Ft. Lauderdale, accessed Apr. 24, 2020, calvaryftl.org/visit.

294 "Who We Are," Spanish River Church, accessed Apr. 24, 2020, www.spanish-river.com/about-us-1/.

295 "Outreach," Gateway Church, accessed Apr. 24, 2020, gatewaypeople.com/ministries/outreach.

296 Lakewood Church, accessed 24 Apr. 2020, www.lakewoodchurch.com/.

297 "Joel Osteen's Lakewood Church Ranked America's Largest Megachurch with 52,000 Weekly Attendance." Christian Post 8 (Sep. 2016), www.christian-post.com/ news/joel-osteens-lakewood-church-ranked-americas-largest-mega-church-with-52k-in-attendance-169279/.

298 "I'm New Here," Saddleback Church, accessed Apr. 24, 2020, saddleback.com/visit/about/new-here.

299 "Evangelism Statistics." Bible.org, Feb. 2, 2009, www.Bible.org/ illustration/evangelism-statistics.

300 "Status of World Evangelization 2020," Joshua Project, accessed Apr. 25, 2020, joshuaproject.net/assets/ media/handouts/status-of-world-evangelization.pdf.

301 "Evangelism Statistics." Bible.org, Feb. 2, 2009, www.Bible.org/illustration/evangelism-statistics.

302 "51 percent of Churchgoers Don't Know of the Great Commission," Barna (Mar. 27, 2018), www.barna.com/research/half-churchgoers-not-heard-great-commission/.

303 Dr. Tony Evans.

304 "Evangelism Statistics." Bible.org, Feb. 2, 2009, www.Bible.org/illustration/evangelism-statistics.

305 Unknown.

306 Unknown.

307 Angus Buchan.

308 Mother Teresa.

309 R. A. Torrey.

310 Chris Gibbs.

311 Charles Spurgeon.

312 W. Clement Stone.

313 Anonymous.

314 Anonymous.

315 Dr. Tony Evans.

316 Barnes' notes on the Bible, Bible Hub Commentary on Psalm 66:18.

[317] Ellicott's Commentary for English Readers, Bible Hub Commentary on Psalm 66:18.

[318] E. Stanley Jones.

[319] Martin Luther King.

[320] Samuel Anand, "Prayer—Giving License to Heaven," From the Heart of Samuel Anand, Nov. 8, 2010, samuelanand.wordpress.com/2010/11/08/prayer-giving-license-to-heaven-2/.

[321] Ibid.

[322] "Questions.org Answers to Tough Questions About God and Life." Questions.org, accessed Apr. 25, 2020, questions.org/attq/what-did-jesus-mean-when-He-said-to-turn-the-other-cheek-matthew-539 percentc2 percenta0/.

[323] Ibid.

[324] Anonymous.

[325] "Was Jesus a Pacifist?" Got Questions, accessed Apr. 25, 2020, www.gotquestions.org/Jesus-pacifist.html.

[326] Edmund Burke.

Chapter 7

[327] US Navy.

[328] US Department of Defense.

[329] Ibid.

[330] "Lucifer," Biblical People, Jun. 22, 2020, biblicalpeople.wordpress.com/2013/06/22/lucifer/.

[331] Dr. Tony Evans.

[332] National Opinion Research Center, University of Chicago; General Social Surveys, 1972–2008.

[333] Life Application Study Bible, New Living Translation, Book of Nehemiah: Megathemes: Vision, Wheaton: Tyndale House Publishers, 1996.

[334] Life Application Study Bible, New Living Translation, Explanatory Note, Nehemiah 1:2-4, Wheaton: Tyndale House Publishers, 1996.

[335] "International Standard Bible Encyclopedia, Tobiah." Bible Study Tools, accessed Apr. 25, 2020 www.biblestudytools.com/encyclopedias/isbe/tobiah.html.

[336] "Who Were Sanballat, Tobiah, and Gesham," Got Questions, accessed Apr. 25, 2020 www.gotquestions.org/Sanballat-Tobiah-Geshem.html.

[337] Tony Evans, "The Key to Your Solemn Assembly," Turning a Nation to God, Vol 2 CD series, 2014.

Chapter 8

[338] Dr. Tony Evans.

[339] "Religious Landscape Study," Pew Research Center Religion and Public Life, accessed May 4, 2019, www.pewforum.org/religious-landscape-study/#religions.

[340] Ibid.

341 "US Population (Live)," Worldometer, Apr. 26, 2020, www.worldometers.info/world-population/us-population/.

342 Rev. Dr. Darryl B. Starnes Sr., Heal Our Land, Bureau of Evangelism African Methodist Episcopal Zion Church, 2005.

343 Dr. Tony Evans.

344 Gary Linton, "Why Christians Don't Pray," Ministrymaker, Jan. 10, 2020, www.ministrymaker.com/why-christians-dont-pray.

345 "2009 Statistics for the Average American Christian Conservative: Compiled by The James Hartline Report," The James Hartline Report, March 21, 2010, jameshartlinereport.blogspot.com/2010/03/2009-statistics-for-average-american.html.

346 Jentezen Franklin.

347 Carlo Kopp, "The Sidewinder Story, The Evolution of the AIM-9 Missile," Air Power Australia, Jan. 27, 2014, ausairpower.net/TE-Sidewinder-94.html.

348 Dr. Larry Crabb.

349 Dr. Larry Crabb.

350 Berman, Rivkah. "Rosh Hashanah Shofar Blowing," Mazornet, accessed Apr. 26, 2020, mazornet.com/ holidays/RoshHashanah/shofar.htm.

351 "Meaning of Numbers in the Bible: The Number 40." Bible Study, accessed Nov. 26, 2019, www.biblestudy.org/bibleref/meaning-of-numbers-in-Bible/40.html.

352 Ibid.

353 "Instances in the Bible Where God Made Major Changes and Transformations After the Period of 40," The 40-Day Miracle, accessed Jul. 13, 2018, www.40day.com/ 40_in_the_Bible.html.

354 50 USC. Section 2204.

355 NCC Staff. "10 fascinating facts about the Liberty Bell." Constitution Daily, Jul. 8, 2019, constitutioncenter.org/blog/10-fascinating-facts-about-the-liberty-bell/.

356 DePra, David A., "The Acceptable Year of the Lord," The Good News, accessed Feb.5, 2018, www.goodnewsarticles.com/Jul04-1.htm.

357 "Chronology of Jubilees." The Design of Time, accessed Nov. 12, 2019.design-of-time.com/chronoj.htm.

358 "Jewish Holiday Calendars & Hebrew Date Converter." Hebcal, accessed Nov. 12, 2019, www.hebcal.com/.

Chapter 9

359 Anonymous.

360 Charles Stanley.

To contact the author and receive additional information regarding *Operation Heal America*, please visit www.operationheal-america.com.

ABOUT THE AUTHOR

James H. Spence is the founder and president of Operation Heal America LLC (www.operationhealamerica.com), a kingdom company dedicated to unleashing spiritual healing and revival from our house to the White House for the advancement of God's kingdom and magnification of His glory worldwide.

Now retired FBI Agent and retired lieutenant commander in the US Naval Reserve, this former white-collar crime investigator and Navy pilot is a graduate of the US Naval Academy who possesses a master's degree from the University of West Florida. Author of the book, *Do You Want to Get Well?*, James is an experienced speaker, teacher, mentor, worship leader, and evangelist.